FUNCTIONAL APPROACHES TO LANGUAGE, CULTURE AND COGNITION

Volume 163

David G. Lockwood, Peter H. Fries and James E. Copeland (eds)

Functional Approaches to Language, Culture and Cognition

FUNCTIONAL APPROACHES TO LANGUAGE, CULTURE AND COGNITION

PAPERS IN HONOR OF SYDNEY M. LAMB

DAVID G. LOCKWOOD
Michigan State University

PETER H. FRIES
Central Michigan University

JAMES E. COPELAND
Rice University

JOHN BENJAMINS PUBLISHING COMPANY
AMSTERDAM/PHILADELPHIA

The paper used in this publication meets the minimum requirements of American National Standard for Information Sciences — Permanence of Paper for Printed Library Materials, ANSI Z39.48-1984.

Library of Congress Cataloging-in-Publication Data

Lockwood, David G.

    Functional approaches to language, culture and cognition / edited by David G. Lockwood,   Peter H. Fries, James E. Copeland.

    p.   cm. -- (Amsterdam studies in the theory and history of linguistic science. Series IV, Current issues in linguistic theory, ISSN 0304-0763 ; v. 163)

    Includes bibliographical references and index.

    1. Functionalism (Lnguistics) 2. Cognitive grammar. 3. Historical linguistics. 4. Language and culture. I. Fries, Peter Howard. II. Copeland, James E. III. Title. IV. Series.

P147.L63   2000

415--dc21   98-46184

ISBN 90 272 3668 2 (Eur.) / 1 55619 879 5 (US) (Hb; alk. paper)   CIP

John Benjamins Publishing Co. • P.O.Box 36224 • 1020 ME Amsterdam • The Netherlands

John Benjamins North America • P.O.Box 27519 • Philadelphia PA 19118-0519 • USA

Sidney M. Lamb at home

Acknowledgments

Every work that is as large as this requires the active participation of many people in addition to those whose names appear on the cover. We would like to acknowledge in particular the help of two people who contributed a great deal to this work. Earl Herrick drew the artwork for the figures. In addition, Nan Fries contributed greatly on many different tasks, including organizational and formatting issues. We must also credit Adam Makkai, author of Chapter 5, with originating the idea for this volume and conducting the preliminary correspondence leading to it. He had originally intended to be its editor-in-chief, but due to illness, other commitments, and a prolonged absence on overseas appointment in Hong Kong, he eventually turned the project over to the present editors.

Table of Contents

PART II
Functional Approaches to the History of Language and Linguistics

A. Language Change: General Studies

Introduction

James E. Copeland
Rice University

This book is organized in two sections: Functional Approaches to the Structure of Language: Theory and Practice, and Functional Approaches to the History of Language and Linguistics. Each section is itself divided into three parts. In Section I, papers fall into three groups depending on whether they (a) develop a stratificational model, (b) focus on some related functional model of language, or (c) focus on the description of some particular set of language phenomena. Section II also falls into three parts: (a) Language Change: General Studies, (b) Language Change: Lexicon and Culture, and (c) History of Linguistics and Culture. The ordering of the parts of each section, and the ordering of chapters within each part reflects a general progression from papers which focus on more general and theoretical issues to papers which focus on more detailed issues of description. The linguists who were invited to contribute papers to this volume honoring Sydney Lamb have taken into account Lamb's lifelong interests in essentially these areas of language study, contributing articles representing their own work. A number of the authors, particularly in the first part, cast their discussions in the terms of Lamb's theoretical orientation (see below).

During the Rice University Symposium celebrating the 200th anniversary of Sir William Jones's statement about the genetic source of Sanskrit (cf. Lamb/Mitchell 1991), Robert Austerlitz of Columbia University prefaced his symposium paper with an anecdote and a laudatory comment on Lamb's early work. In remarks that were directed primarily to Lamb's graduate students at Rice, he commented particularly on the reception of Lamb's innovative dissertation on Mono/Monachi and its impact on the descriptive and theoretical thinking of the time. (In the 1950s the Berkeley faculty gave each of their graduate students a language to work on, and in Syd Lamb's case Mary Haas had assigned Mono, a California Uto-Aztecan language of the Numic branch.)

Although the Monachi grammar was never published as an independent volume, it stood as an exemplary descriptive grammar. This early work substantially advanced the boundaries of linguistic theory and formed the basis for Lamb's subsequent theoretical work on language — an orientation that he called stratificational linguistics for the first two decades. This theoretical orientation slowly moved toward becoming the first American cognitive theory of language, beginning in the early seventies. Lamb's work continues, and his latest book manuscript, *Towards a Cognitive Theory of Language*, fits appropriately under the now-current rubric of Functional Linguistics, reflecting Lamb's constant insistence on the interdependence of language form and function, and his rejection of autonomous formal linguistic structures of any kind. Networks of linguistic relations are instead viewed as ultimately interconnected with and determined by the modalities and processes of human cognition.

Austerlitz's comments were all the more appropriate, since Sydney Lamb, along with his Rice colleague Douglas Mitchell, had conceived and organized the Sir William Jones symposium with its historical focus. And while Lamb is not primarily known for his work in historical linguistics, he made major contributions in that field even as a graduate student. His pioneering article on a system for genetic taxonomy (Lamb 1959), had its beginnings as a graduate student project. The terminology developed there and in subsequent papers (Lamb 1958, 1964a) still furnishes the basis for historical work today. His recent work on historical linguistics is well known (cf. Lamb/Mitchell 1991; and Lamb [forthcoming]).

The notion of Functional Linguistics adopted here to characterize the contributions to this volume is an inclusive one; a *mahayana* approach rather than a *hinayana* one. It contrasts primarily with more exclusively logical/formal approaches that have dominated linguistic practice since the sixties. Functional Linguistics is not 'newer' than formal linguistics; its roots are in fact much older, reaching far back into the history of linguistic speculation. Early in this century German functionalists like Allmann and Boost were discovering the functionalist principles of word order, for which they employed Greek terms like *thema* and *rhema*. In turn the Prague School linguists picked up this interest in functional word order and applied it to languages other than German. Other European schools of linguistics adopted these functional concerns, and for a period of time Halliday's work on Systemic Linguistics was almost synonymous with functional linguistics (cf. Halliday 1985). Work within Systemic Linguistics continues unabated, maintaining its focus with a yearly International Systemic Functional Congress. Following Halliday's direction, the bulk of the work in the Systemic School is applied, text-oriented, and sociological in its approach.

Functional developments in North America in the last decades since the mid 1960s have in large part taken place in research centers on the West Coast of the United States, hence the rubric "West Coast Functionalism" (cf. for example the work of Bolinger, Chafe, Davis, DuBois, Givón, Haiman, Hopper, Langacker, Talmy, Thompson, van Valin, and many others during the last two decades). Much of that work can be characterized as cognitive in its orientation, constraining discourse by the limits of cognition in the individual discourse participants. Other practitioners prefer to employ the social notion of the participants' negotiation in the production of discourse, and still others tend to reject such a dichotomy altogether. But what unites functional linguists is an implicit belief that language cannot be conceptualized or described separate from its functions in discourse; that autonomy of form or formal categories separate from function is a misguided myth, a myth that ultimately constrains progress in the understanding of language as a dynamic human phenomenon.

Bloomfieldian linguistics was not essentially a functional approach. Its virtual rejection of meaning in language analysis eventually led to its structuralist offspring, generative linguistics, as a natural logical development. But other developments out of Post-Bloomfieldian linguistics included proposals in the early sixties on structural semantics (e.g. Lamb 1964b; and Hockett 1964) that attempted to make semantics a central, rather than a peripheral, concern in linguistic analysis. Such proposals called for semantics to be given its equivalent status in a stratified grammar, conceived of as a network. The idea was to introduce propositional semantic structures as being systematically related to syntactic phenomena (treated by Lamb in the lexotactics). Mathematics was in the air and computers were exerting a growing influence on scientific thinking in linguistics. In part because of their narrow, sentence-defined scope, those attempts by Lamb and Hockett were not widely influential (cf. Hockett 1968); but the door had been opened, and Fillmore's Case Grammar, with its propositional input into a generative-tranformational syntax, came along toward the end of the decade. Subsequent work on generative grammar, including generative semantics, and the like, maintained the same scope limitations (to sentence-sized pieces of language form), ultimately also with unsatisfying results.

Lamb's formal adaptation of European functionalist concepts started in the sixties when he began a long period of collaboration with Michael Halliday. They first learned of their common interests at the Georgetown Roundtable in 1964, and they continued their discussions at the summer Linguistic Institute at UCLA in 1966. A number of publications have appeared in the literature since that time that emphasize the complementary nature of their work. A symposium at Rice University in 1984 featured, among others, papers by Lamb and Halliday and their co-workers, and focussed on a comparison of systemic analyses with various cognitive analyses of a common oral text captured on video (dubbed the Rhino Text by Michael Halliday). Halliday's functionalist work has influenced Lamb's theoretical work in a number of important ways, and vice-versa. Lamb's relational network notation took important cues from Halliday's systemic diagrams, and Halliday's notions of **given** versus **new** as well as **theme** versus **rheme** greatly influenced Lamb's thinking. Lamb's unpublished papers from the early seventies show an attempt to indicate the contrast between the given information from the new information in a proposition frame by diagramming the new discourse material using bold lines, but not until the 1984 symposium on Text Linguistics did he demonstrate his own notion of how the concepts could be applied to discourse analysis. By this time the notation had been applied by others (even though it was, unfortunately, no longer a widely familiar notation in linguistic practice due to the eclipsing predominance of MIT-based algebraic notations). But the notation's lack of currency among the current generation of MIT-trained linguists should not necessarily be taken as an indictment of its ultimate efficacy and heuristic value. A vast amount of recent work on neurolinguistics is corroborating Lamb's relational network claims that go all the way back to the 1960s.

There are a substantial number of linguists who find a relational network notation to be the most useful formal way to conceptualize (even if not to diagram) linguistic and cognitive structures (cf. much recent work on PDP, which is in some ways similar). Other linguists quickly reject such representations as reductionist and misleading. Two possible major advantages of the relational network notation are first, that the lines can cross, and second that the notation felicitously allows for both syntagmatic and paradigmatic relations to be combined in a single visual array. Because of separate realizational mappings from the semantic/discourse to the syntactic stratum, together with the encoding/decoding notion in processing information through the system, the need for movement rules is avoided, preserving the idea that synchronic linguistic structure consists of systems of relationships that are activated/created as needed in the production and processing of discourse. Any constraints on discourse are cognitive constraints, as against putative formal linguistic constraints. Thus the data in linguistic analysis includes cognitive as well as language discourse data: the unsaid as well as the said. Social constraints on discourse interaction are always combined with the cognitive constraints of the individual participants, which must also necessarily enable interpersonal negotiation in specific contexts of discourse. What makes the relational network notation potentially problematic is its possible misapplication as a predictor of behavior — a before-the-fact encoder — rather than an after-the-fact analysis of what has or might have occurred in a discourse. The relations are not intended to be seen as stored in memory with hard wiring; discourse conversants attempt to make sense of whatever has occurred. And the constancy of the role of analogy [i.e. metaphor in a broad sense] in the successful accomplishment of discourse can hardly be overemphasized. In a networkist's view relational networks actually generate insights into linguistic phenomena, and networkists are confident that they can, if called upon, adapt the notation to deal with additional powerful insights from other theoretical sources as necessary.

Despite the debate about notations, let it be said that the relational network notation developed by Lamb and his co-workers is not the theory, and the two need to be strictly distinguished. Although both rest on the same reticular metaphor, the one is an attempt to give a practical visual manifestation of some token of the other, and no more. As such, it can be either limiting or enabling or both, depending on the degree to which it is reified in its conceptualization. Lamb steadfastly maintains that the network notion of linguistic structure and the theory that it is based on are potentially so powerful that they will continue to inform work on language, and that their currency will increase as their efficacy becomes more widely known.

References

Lamb, Sydney M. 1958. Linguistic Prehistory in the Great Basin. *International Journal of American Linguistics* 24: 95–100.

Lamb, Sydney M. 1959. Some Proposals for a Linguistic Taxonomy. *Anthropological Linguistics* 1: 33–49.

Lamb, Sydney M. 1964a. The Classification of Uto-Aztecan Languages: A Historical Survey. In *University of California Publications in Linguistics* 34.

Lamb, Sydney M. 1964b. A Sememic Approach to Structuralist Semantics. *American Anthropologist.* 66(3, part 2): 57–78.

Lamb, Sydney M. 1998. *Pathways of the brain: The Neurocognitive basis of language.* Amsterdam & Philadelphia: John Benjamins.

Lamb, Sydney M. and Earl Douglas Mitchell. 1991. *Sprung from Some Common Source.* Stanford: Stanford University Press.

Halliday, Michael. 1985. An Introduction to Functional Grammar. London: Edward Arnold.

Hockett, Charles F. 1967. Language, Mathematics and Linguistics. The Hague: Mouton.

Hockett, Charles F. 1968. *The State of the Art.* The Hague: Mouton.

Biographical Sketch of Sydney MacDonald Lamb

David G. Lockwood
Michigan State University

This volume honors the career of Sydney MacDonald Lamb, who is currently Agnes Cullen Arnold Professor Emeritus of Linguistics and Cognitive Sciences at Rice University. Lamb was born in Denver, Colorado on May 4, 1929, as the third in a family of four children. His father, Sydney Bishop Lamb, was employed as a highway engineer for the state of Colorado. His mother was Jean MacDonald, whose family had moved directly to Colorado from Scotland around 1910. His childhood and early youth were spent in Denver, where he attended public schools. His academic performance was sufficient that, upon graduating from high school in 1947, he found himself the winner of a scholarship to attend Yale. This was won in a regional competition involving the various states of the Rocky Mountain area.

The breadth of Lamb's interests was reflected already in his undergraduate days. After considering majors in zoology, mathematics, and philosophy, he eventually decided on economics, in which he received a Bachelor of Arts in 1951. It was only in his senior year that he learned, through quite accidental circumstances, that there was such a field as linguistics. This came when he decided to begin the study of Russian. As it happened, this course was directed by the linguist William Cornyn, and his graduate assistant was Alexander Schenker, now a senior Slavic linguist on the Yale faculty. Through these two, he learned of the existence of linguistics, and the field so fascinated him that he decided very late to attend graduate school to study linguistics, specifically Slavic linguistics. At that time, only a few institutions in the United States offered graduate study in both general and Slavic linguistics, and, as it happened, the University of California at Berkeley was the only one of these where admissions for the following fall were still open, so that was where he went.

During his graduate career at Berkeley, he was advised by Professor Murray Emeneau, whose contribution appears in this volume. By the time he wrote his dissertation, Lamb had shifted his focus of interest from Slavic linguistics to general linguistics. So his 1958 "Northfork Mono Grammar" was written under the supervision of the late Professor Mary Haas. It was one of the many studies of the native languages of California and adjacent states that were prepared under her direction.

Two years before the completion of his doctorate, the Berkeley faculty thought highly enough of his work to offer him the post of Instructor in Linguistics, which he held from 1956 to 1958. In the latter year, he was promoted to Assistant Professor. The promotion resulted not only from the completion and successful defense of his dissertation, but from his initiative in securing National Science Foundation funding for a Machine Translation Project at Berkeley. Besides teaching, he served as Director of this project until he left Berkeley in 1964.

Obviously, the work in machine translation involved Lamb in the very new field of computational linguistics, which has remained a continuing interest of his. Beyond this, however, it was during this period that he began to achieve fame as the originator the linguistic theory known as stratificational grammar. The development of this model initially sprang from his dissertation, in which he had advanced the unorthodox idea that languages like Mono (also known as Monachi) required two levels of alternation instead of just one between the morpheme and the phoneme. Instead of treating allomorphic and morphophonemic alternation as alternative ways of describing this relation, he attempted to combine them in such a way that some cases required one, others required the other, and still others required both.

His approach to Machine Translation differed from some others of the period in that he sought to work from explicitly formulated grammars of each language involved. This work therefore provided an ample opportunity for the development and formalization of his ideas on the organization of linguistic structure. The model was first set forth in the 1962 version of his *Outline of Stratificational Grammar*, a publication prepared for students in his classes and sold through the on-campus bookstore in Berkeley. This early version of the stratificational model was used in some Berkeley dissertations of the period, in particular William Shipley's *Maidu Grammar* and M. A. R. Barker's *Klamath Grammar*, both issued in the series University of California Publications in Linguistics in 1964.

Beyond his interest in language description and mechanical translation, some of Lamb's earliest publications reflected an interest in the prehistory and genetic classification of languages — his 1958 article "Linguistic prehistory in the Great Basin" and the 1959 paper "Some proposals for linguistic taxonomy".

In 1964, Lamb joined the Yale linguistics faculty at the instigation of Bernard Bloch, who had seen him as a rising young scholar in the area of linguistic theory. This move had actually taken a couple of years to accomplish. The invitation was extended and accepted in principle in 1962, but Lamb was allowed extra time in order to work out a transition of management for the Machine Translation Project. In the meantime, stratificational theory was receiving greater attention through oral presentations and journal publications. Lamb also found that his ideas converged, at least in part, with the thinking of certain more senior linguists, particularly H. A. Gleason, Jr., who was developing what he later termed "Hartford Stratificationalism", and Charles F. Hockett. After the move to Yale, Lamb was able to interact with Gleason, then at the Hartford Seminary Foundation, on a more regular basis. It was just before this move that he began to develop his relational-network notation (initially based on the systemic network notation of Michael Halliday). So after the move, he realized that Louis Hjelmslev had been right in insisting in the 1940s that linguistic structure consists of relationships alone, rather than objects with relationships among them.

Beginning in 1966, Lamb also secured National Science Foundation funding for his Linguistic Automation Project at Yale. The work of this group grew out of that of the Berkeley project, but it had a broader focus than just Machine Translation. It is interesting to note that its work on the automation of Russian grammar was done with the aid of William Cornyn and Alexander Schenker, the same people who had taught Lamb Russian fifteen years earlier. This project ran until 1970, and it allowed Lamb to provide employment to several Yale graduate students, as well as to two linguists who had been students in his 1965 course in Stratificational Grammar at the Linguistic Institute in Ann Arbor. Peter Reich, now at the University of Toronto, worked for the project while finishing his Michigan doctorate in psychology. Ilah Fleming prepared an annotated bibliography of the stratificational literature, which was published in 1969. She went on to develop her own variant of the stratificational model, which she taught at the International Linguistics Center of the Summer Institute of Linguistics at Dallas before her retirement in 1992.

Yale dissertations written under Lamb's influence and/or direction include those of Adam Makkai (on English idioms), Henry Rogers (on Sherbro phonology and morphology), Yoshihiki Ikegami (on English verbs of motion), David Bennett (on English prepositions), William J. Sullivan (on Russian phonology and morphology), and William M. Christie (on the applications of stratificational theory to language change). All of these are contributors to the present volume. Lamb's own work in this period included in particular the 1966 textbook *Outline of Stratificational Grammar*, which systematically presented the relational-network notation in print.

During his years at Yale, Lamb moved beyond his initial modeling of linguistic structure as simply a system of relationships, and began to explore the relations between his model and what was known about the storage and acquisition of language by the human brain. By the early 1970s he had begun to refer to his model as "Cognitive Linguistics" in preference to "stratificational", though some have also called it "cognitive-stratificational" to distinguish his views from those of others who have independently used the term "cognitive".

Lamb's years at Yale ended in 1977 with his resignation, submitted for personal reasons. He did not immediately seek another academic position. Instead he worked as managing general partner of Semionics Associates, which he had begun as a side business in 1976. Operating from offices in Berkeley, California, this group developed a revolutionary kind of associative memory system for microcomputers, together with associated software.

His return to academics came about as a result of the efforts of James Copeland of Rice University, who had been a student in a Linguistic Institute course Lamb taught at UCLA in 1966. Copeland had long appreciated the value of his academic work, and invited him to serve as Andrew Mellon visiting professor in linguistics at Rice in the fall of 1980. A year later, Lamb was persuaded to return on a regular appointment in linguistics and semiotics, and he worked on organizing a Department of Linguistics and Semiotics at Rice, with a doctoral program added to the formerly interdepartmental undergraduate program. This new department came into being in the spring of 1982, with Lamb as its chairman. He continued to serve in that office until 1988. The inauguration of the department was celebrated by an international symposium on issues in linguistics and semiotics in March of 1982. Various other symposia on specific topics have continued as a fairly regular feature of the Rice program.

Among the several dissertations Lamb has directed at Rice are those of three contributors to the present volume: Chang-In Lee (1988), Cynthia Ford

Meyer (1991), and Timothy Pulju (1995). In recent years, Lamb has organized an interdepartmental program in Cognitive Sciences at Rice, and he served as Director of this program until his retirement in 1998.

Ever since its founding in 1974, Lamb has regularly attended meetings of the Linguistic Association of Canada and the United States. He served as a member of its Board of Directors in the 1976–1979 period, then as Vice President in 1982–1983, and President in 1983–1984. In 1995 he began a term as Chair of the Board of Directors of the Association. In this role he has been attempting to attract to the organization such groups as functional linguists, neurolinguists, and those interested in long-range comparative linguistics.

Lamb has been active in several other endeavors besides linguistics and related academic fields. These include membership in the Houston Philosophical Society (he was its president in 1992–1993), and in the Houston Folklore and Music Society (he was its president in 1997–1998). In connection with the latter interest, he has long been singing to the accompaniment of his own guitar as a way of entertaining students and friends. Since 1993, he has regularly entertained members of LACUS with his songs (some of them his own compositions) as a part of the organization's Annual Presidential Banquet. Billed as "The Singing Professor", he has also sung at some local clubs in Houston and in Berkeley, California.

While he has not had many book-length publications, the ideas of Sydney Lamb have made very important contributions to the linguistic literature over the past three decades. These ideas have often proven to be ahead of their time, and not all of those whose later thinking has approached his earlier ideas have even been aware that he preceded them along the same path, The writings of many contributors to this volume, among others, however, are full of references to this work, and these show the obvious importance of his personal influences over his current and former students, and colleagues. And surely the author of this sketch is not the only one whose career in linguistics has been profoundly enriched by Lamb's teachings.

Published Works of Sydney M. Lamb

David G. Lockwood   Sydney M. Lamb

This bibliography was prepared by David G. Lockwood with the assistance of Sydney M. Lamb. It includes all publications pertaining to linguistics and related fields. The ordering of items within a particular year is based on the order of completion, according to the best recollection of the author.

1958

Linguistic prehistory in the Great Basin. *International Journal of American Linguistics* 24: 95–100.

1959

a. Some proposals for linguistic taxonomy. *Anthropological Linguistics* 1: 33–49.
b. Review of: Colin Cherry, *On Human Communication*. (Cambridge, Massachusetts: M I T Press, 1957). *Romance Philology* 12: 286–289.

1960

A System for Analyzing Russian Texts (co-authored with Alfred Hudson and C. Douglas Johnson). Machine Translation Project Report, University of California, Berkeley.

1961

a. Advances in machine translation. *New Scientist* 9: 260–261
b. MT research at the university of California. *Proceedings of the National Symposium on Machine Translation*, edited by H. P. Edmundson, 140–154. Englewood Cliffs: Prentice-Hall.

c. On the Organization of Information in a Machine Translation Dictionary. (co-authored with William H. Jacobsen, Jr., Russell K. Gardiner, and John H. Wahlgren), Machine Translation Project Report, University of California, Berkeley.

d. Segmentation. *Proceedings of the National Symposium on Machine Translation,* edited by H. P. Edmundson, 335–342. Englewood Cliffs: Prentice-Hall.

e. A high-speed large-capacity dictionary system. (co-authored with William H. Jacobsen, Jr.) *Mechanical Translation* 6: 76–107.

f. The digital computer as an aid in linguistics. *Language* 37: 382–412.

1962

a. Outline of Stratificational Grammar. Berkeley: A.S.U.C. Bookstore.

b. On the mechanization of syntactic analysis. 1961 International Conference on Machine Translation. London: Her Majesty's Stationery Office, Pp. 673–686. [Reprinted in abridged form in *Readings on Automatic Language Processing,* ed. by David G. Hays, 149–157. New York: Elsevier, 1966.]

1963

a. *Chinese Character Indexes.* (Five Volumes, co-authored with Ching-Yi Dougherty and Samuel E. Martin) Berkeley: University of California Press.

b. Information Needs in Linguistics and Related Fields. Machine Translation Project Report, University of California, Berkeley.

c. Machine-Aided Translation, Machine Translation Project Report, University of California, Berkeley.

1964

a. *Concordances from Computers.* (Co-authored with Laura Gould) Berkeley: Mechanolinguistics Project, University of California.

b. Linguistic diversification and extinction in North America. *XXXV Congresso Internacional de Americanistas, Actas y Memorias.* Mexico City. 2: 457–464.

c. On alternation, transformation, realization, and stratification. *Georgetown University Monograph Series on Languages and Linguistics* 17: 105–122. [Reprinted in *Phonological Theory: Evolution and Current Practice,* ed. by Valerie Becker Makkai, 565–605. New York: Holt, Rinehart & Winston, 1972.]

d. *The sememic approach to structural semantics American Anthropologist* 66.3.2: 57–78. (= *Transcultural Studies in Cognition,* ed. by A. Kimball

Romney and Roy G. D'Andrade) [Reprinted in *Readings in Stratificational Linguistics*, ed. by Adam Makkai and David G. Lockwood, 207–228. University, Alabama: University of Alabama Press, 1973.]

e. The classification of the Uto-Aztecan languages: A historical survey. *University of California Publication in Linguistics* 34: 106–125. [Reprinted in *A Great Basin Shoshonean Sourcebook*, ed. by David H. Thomas, 106–125. New York: Garland Publishing, 1986.]

f. The nature of the machine translation problem. *Der Sprachmittler, Informationshefte des Sprachendienstes des Bundeswehr* Nos. 1–4. Bonn: Bundesministerium der Verteidigung, V R 5. [See 1965 for revised version.]

1965

a. The nature of the machine translation problem. (Revision) *Journal of Verbal Learning and Verbal Behavior* 4: 196–210.

b. An anthropologist's introduction to the computer. (co-authored with A. Kimball Romney). *The Use of Computers in Anthropology*, ed. by Dell Hymes, 159–188. The Hague: Mouton.

c. What computers may do with the printed word. *Computers for the Humanities*, 30–40. New Haven.

d. Kinship terminology and linguistic structure. *American Anthropologist* 67: 5.2: 37–64. (= *Formal Semantic Analysis,* ed. by E. A. Hammel) [Reprinted in *Readings in Stratificational Linguistics,* ed. by Adam Makkai and David G. Lockwood, 229–257. University, Alabama: University of Alabama Press, 1973.]

1966

a. *Outline of Stratificational Grammar,* Revised Edition.Washington, D. C.: Georgetown University Press. [Russian Translation: *Očerk Stratifikacionnoj Grammatiki*. Minsk, 1977.]

b. Epilegomena to a theory of language. *Romance Linguistics* 19: 531–573.

c. Prolegomena to a theory of phonology. *Language* 42: 536–573. [Reprinted in *Phonological Theory: Evolution and Current Practice,* ed. by Valerie Becker Makkai, 606–633. New York: Holt, Rinehart, and Winston, 1972, and also in *Readings in Stratificational Linguistics*, ed. by Adam Makkai and David G. Lockwood, 128–165. University, Alabama: University of Alabama Press, 1973.]

d.   The use of semantic information for the resolution of syntactic ambiguity. *Actes du Premier Colloque International de Linguistique Appliquée*, 13–36. Nancy, France: Faculté des Lettres et des Sciences Humaines.

e.   Linguistic structure and the production and decoding of discourse. *Speech, Language, and Communication* (*Brain Function* Volume III) ed. by Edward C. Carterette, 173–199. Berkeley and Los Angeles: University of California Press.

1967

a.   Review of *Current Issues in Linguistic Theory* (The Hague: Mouton,1964) and *Aspects of the Theory of Syntax* (Cambridge, Massachusetts: M I T Press, 1965) by Noam Chomsky. *American Anthropologist* 69: 411–415.

b.   *Type Lists, Indexes, and Concordances from Computers* (co-authored with Laura Gould). New Haven: Linguistic Automation Project, Yale University.

1968

a.   Lamb's reply to Teeter. *American Anthropologist* 70: 364–365.

b.   Review of: Paul Garvin. *Natural Language and the Computer.* (New York: McGraw-Hill, 1963) *Language* 44: 912–915.

1969

Lexicology and semantics. *Linguistics Today*, ed. by Archibald A. Hill, 40–69. New York: Basic Books. [Another version published for overseas distribution by the Voice of America, under the title *Linguistics* contains the same article on pages 44–54 (in the series *Voice of America Forum Lectures.*; this version includes a photograph and brief biographical sketch of each author).][Reprinted in Spanish translation (as Lexicología y Semántica) in *Antología de Temas de Lingüística*, ed. by Sara Bolano. Mexico City: Universidad Nacional Autónoma de México, 1978.]

1970

Linguistic and cognitive networks. *Cognition: A Multiple View* (Paul L. Garvin, ed) 195–222. [Reprinted in *Readings in Stratificational Linguistics*, ed by Adam Makkai and David G. Lockwood, 60–83. University, Alabama: University of Alabama Press. 1973.]

1971

The crooked path of progress in cognitive linguistics. *Georgetown University Monograph Series on Languages and Linguistics* 24: 99–123. [Reprinted in *Readings in Stratificational Linguistics*, ed. by Adam Makkai and David G. Lockwood, 12–33. University, Alabama: University of Alabama Press, 1973.]

1972

Some types of ordering. *Phonological Theory: Evolution and Current Practice*, ed. by Valerie Becker Makkai, 670–677. New York: Holt, Rinehart, and Winston. [Paperback reprint by Jupiter Press, 1978.]

1973

a.   Stratificational linguistics as a basis for machine translation. *Readings in Stratificational Linguistics*, ed. by Adam Makkai and David G. Lockwood, 34–59. University, Alabama: University of Alabama Press. [Russian Translation of Preliminary Version (presented at U. S.-Japan Joint Conference on Machine Translation, Tokyo 1964) appeared in *Naucno Texniceskaja Informacija* 10. 33–40. (Moscow 1964).]

b.   The Halliday-Lamb linguistic theory (co-authored with M. A. K. Halliday) *English in Australia* 24: 3–17.

1974

[Discussion with] Sydney M. Lamb. (based on a discussion with Herman Parret) *Discussing Language*, ed. by Herman Parret, 179–219. The Hague: Mouton.

1975

a.   Mutations and relations. *The First LACUS Forum, 1974,* ed. by Adam Makkai and Valerie Becker Makkai, 540–557. Columbia, South Carolina: Hornbeam Press. [Reprinted in *Linguistics at the Crossroads*, ed. by Adam Makkai, Valerie Becker Makkai, and Luigi Heilmann, 407–423. Padova: Liviana Editrice and Lake Bluff, Illinois: Jupiter Press, 1977.]

b.   Language. *The Great Ideas Today, 1975,* ed. by John van Doren, 58–71 and 94–97. Chicago: Encyclopedia Brittanica.

1976

On thrashing classical phonemics. (Co-authored with Ralph Vanderslice) *The Second LACUS Forum, 1975,* ed. by Peter A. Reich, 154–163. Columbia, South Carolina: Hornbeam Press.

1978

a.   Recognition memory (REM). *Notes on Linguistics* 6: 29–33 (April).
b.   An add-in recognition memory for S-100 bus micro-computers. *Computer Design* 17.8: 140–142 (Part I: An Introduction. [August]); 17.9: 162–68 (Part II: Structure and Specifications [September]); 17.10: 182–86 (Part III: Applications. [October]).

1980

a.   A new look at phonotactics. *Papers in Cognitive-Stratificational Linguistics,* ed. by James E. Copeland and Philip W. Davis. Rice University Studies 66.2: 1–18.
b.   Louis Hjelmslev's position in genetic and typological linguistics. *Typology and Genetics of Language,* ed. by Torben Thrane, Vibeke Winge, Lachlan Mackenzie, Una Canger, and Niels Ege. *Travaux du Cercle Linguistique de Copenhague* XX.49–63.

1981

On the aims of linguistics. *The Seventh LACUS Forum, 1980,.* ed. by James E. Copeland and Philip W. Davis, 17–27. Columbia, South Carolina: Hornbeam Press. [Reprinted with revisions in *New Directions in Linguistics and Semiotics,* ed. by James E. Copeland, 1–11, Rice University Studies, 1974.]

1982

Whitehead and Lamb: A New Network of Connection. (based on a seminar discussion also involving J. B. Cobb, D. R. Griffin, and John O. Regan.) Claremont, California: Claremont Graduate School, Seminar Series on "Issues in Communication".

1983

a.   Content-addressable memory uses 256 byte 'superwords'. *Mini-Micro Systems,* 16.11: 237–242 (October).

b. On determining the number of strata in linguistic structure. *The Ninth LACUS Forum, 1982,* ed. by John Morreall, 189–203. Columbia, South Carolina: Hornbeam Press.

1984

a. *Semiotics of Culture and Language.* (2 volumes, co-edited with Robin Fawcett, M. A. K. Halliday, and Adam Makkai.) London and Dover: Frances Pinter.
b. Semiotics of language and culture: A relational approach. *Semiotics of Culture and Language,* Volume 2: *Language and Other Semiotic Systems of Culture* ed. by Lamb et al., 71–100.

1985

a. Descriptive process. *The Eleventh LACUS Forum, 1984,* ed. by Robert A. Hall, Jr., 5–20. Columbia, South Carolina: Hornbeam Press.
b. Information and its representation in English texts. *Computing Power and Legal Reasoning,* ed. by Charles Walter, 145–155. St. Paul: West Publishing Company.
c. Language, linguistics, and linguists. (based on a panel discussion also involving Michael Gregory, M. A. K. Halliday, Walter Hirtle, David G. Lockwood, Andre Martinet, Jan Mulder, and Kenneth L. Pike. *Langues et Linguistique* 11: 1–36. (Sainte-Foy: Université Laval)

1987

a. Linguistics, semiotics, and the human information system. *Georgetown University Round Table on Languages and Linguistics,* 1986, ed. by Simon P. X. Battestini, 51–63. Washington D.C.: Georgetown University Press..
b. Semiotics in education: A dialogue. (Based on a seminar discussion also involving Thomas A. Sebeok and John O. Regan). Claremont, California: Claremont Graduate School. (Seminar Series on "Issues in Communication") [Chinese translation of excerpts published in Zhe Yue Yichong (Philosophical Translation) 2: 16–24. Beijing,
c. On the settlement of the Americas: The Linguistic Evidence. *Current Anthropology* 28: 101–102.
d. The influence of Kenneth L. Pike. Appendix 6 to Kenneth Lee Pike Bibliography, compiled by Ruth M. Brend, 51. Bloomington, Indiana: Eurolingua.

1988

In Retrospect: Using Language and Knowing How. (Based on a seminar discussion also involving M. A. K. Halliday and John O. Regan.) Claremont, California: Claremont Graduate School. (Seminar Series on "Issues in Communication"

1991

a. *Sprung from Some Common Source: The Prehistory of Languages.* (coedited with E. Douglas Mitchell.) Stanford: Stanford University Press.

b. Linguistic model and linguistic thought: The case of either-or thinking. *The Seventeenth LACUS Forum, 1990,* ed. by Angela della Volpe, 109–120. Lake Bluff, Illinois: Linguistic Association of Canada and the United States.

c. On the object of study of linguistic science. *Communications of the Workshop for Scientific Linguistics* 3: 32–34.

d. Objects, real and conceptual. *Communications of the Workshop for Scientific Linguistics* 5: 75–76.

e. Boundedness and continuity in time. *Communications of the Workshop for Scientific Linguistics* 5: 76–78.

f. Objects of study. *Communications of the Workshop for Scientific Linguistics* 5: 78–80.

g. The scientific status of linguistics. *Communications of the Workshop for Scientific Linguistics* 5: 80–81.

h. Are words real objects of illusory objects?. *Communications of the Workshop for Scientific Linguistics* 5: 81–83.

1992

Syntax: Reality or illusion? *The Eighteenth LACUS Forum, 1991,* ed. by Ruth M. Brend, 179–186. Lake Bluff, Illinois: Linguistic Association of Canada and the United States.

1993

a. Idioms, lexemes, and syntax. *Proceedings of the XVth International Congress of Linguists,* ed. by André Crochetière, Jean-Claude Boulanger, and Conrad Ouellon, 347–350. Sainte-Foy: Les Presses de L'Université Laval.

b. Sources of linguistic patterning. *The Nineteenth LACUS Forum, 1992,* ed. by Peter A. Reich, 23–44. Lake Bluff, Illinois: Linguistic Association of Canada and the United States.

1994

Cognitive linguistics meets neural science. *The Twentieth LACUS Forum, 1993,* ed. by Valerie Becker Makkai, 151–178. Chapel Hill, North Carolina Linguistic Association of Canada and the United States.

1995

a. Meaning in language and meaning in music. *The Twenty-First LACUS Forum, 1994,* ed. by Mava Jo Powell, 269–277. Chapel Hill, North Carolina: Linguistic Association of Canada and the United States.

b. *Language, Thought, and Mind.* Houston, Texas: Rice University Department of Linguistics. (Course packet)

1996

a. *Language, Thought, and Mind: An Invitation to Neurocognitive Linguistics,* Rice University Department of Linguistics (Course packet).

b. A word from the chair: Touching the bases of reality. *LACUS Newsletter* 2.1: 3–4

1997

a. A word from the chair: Reality and illusion. *LACUS Newsletter* 2.2: 4.

b. Bidirectional proccessing and expanded relational network notation. *The Twenty-Third LACUS Forum, 1996.* ed. by Alan K. Melby 109–124.

c. A word from the chair: The 'Old Curiosity Shop' school of linguistics. *LACUS Newsletter* 3.1: 3–4

1998

a. *Unity in Creativity.* Twenty-First Symposium in the series "Issues in Communication". Claremont Graduate University. (Based on a seminar also involving Aldo Casanova, Thomas Leaphard, Maggie Murray, Leonard Pronko, Len Rubenstein, Paul Soldner, Harrison McIntosh, and John O. Regan.)

b. Linguistics to the beat of a different drummer. *First Person Singular III*, ed. by E. F. Konrad Koerner. Amsterdam: Benjamins, pp. 97–130.

c. Mary Haas: Lessons in and out of the classroom. *Anthropological Linguistics* 39.620–622.

d. Review of *The Literary Mind*, by Mark Turner. *American Speech* 73.325–328.

1999

a. Bidirectional processing in language and related cognitive systems. *Usage-Based Models of Language*, ed. by Michael Barlow and Suzanne Kemmer. Stanford: CSLI Publications.

b. Local and distributed representation in network models of linguistic and conceptual structure. *LACUS Forum XXV*, ed. by Shin-Ja J. Hwang and Arle Lommel, pp. 317–330.

c. *Pathways of the Brain: The neurocognitive basis of language.* Amsterdam: Benjamins.

FORTHCOMING

a. Re-examining the family-tree theory of linguistic classification. *Language and Prehistory in the Americas*, ed. by A. R. Taylor. Stanford: Stanford University Press.

b. Neurocognitive structure in the interplay of language and thought. *Explorations in Linguistic Relativity*, ed. by Martin Pütz and Marjolein Verspoor.

c. Translation and the structure of language. *Early Years in Machine Translation*, ed. by John Hutchins. Amsterdam: Benjamins.

d. The mental representation of complex lexemes: Evidence from Chinese aphasics. (Coauthored with Xiuhong Zhang.) *LACUS Forum XXVI*, ed. by Alan Melby and Arle Lommel.

PART I

Functional Approaches to the Structure of Language
Theory and Practice

A. Cognitive Approaches: Theory

Chapter I

Valence and Phraseology in Stratificational Linguistics

Ernst-August Müller

Universität des Saarlandes

1. Introduction

From its inception stratificational linguistics has been concerned with the description of idioms and other phraseological units. By contrast, valence grammar has to this day largely ignored the existence of such stereotyped complex expressions. This is all the more surprising since it is verbal phraseological units that have valence properties far more interesting than those of simple verbs in so-called free constructions. On the other hand, stratificational linguistics has given very little attention to valence, a grammatical concept which in European linguistics has for decades served as a useful and extremely popular theoretical approach to verb description and sentence analysis.

In view of such a bilateral deficiency, some valence properties of a central type of verbal phraseological unit will be investigated here and the analysis will be integrated into the stratificational descriptive framework. The more general intention is to suggest an approach to the problem of how the functional category of valence can be accommodated within a less functionally oriented linguistic model as represented by the relational network system of stratificational linguistics.

2. Valence Properties of Prototypical Phraseological Units

Valence may be defined as the inherent capacity of verbs, adjectives, and certain nouns to take a specific number and kind of obligatory or optional syntagmatic complements, or "participants" as they are also called. The number of slots opened by the valence carrier is its numerical valence, and the morpho-syntactic and semantic types of the slot-filling complements represent its qualitative valence. Other linguistic elements in construction with the valence carrier, but not valence-bound, are called (free) adjuncts or circumstantials. As reflected in the literature,[1] valence is a very complex grammatical concept, being simultaneously a morpho-syntactic category, a language-specific semantic category, and a universal logical phenomenon. Discrepancies between these aspects of valence justify the distinctions.

It is in the field of phraseology that such discrepancies are most obvious, for here expression structure and content structure diverge most conspicuously. This article focuses on the valence of expressions like *miss the boat, smell a rat, twist somebody's arm*, and *follow in somebody's footsteps*. Because of their idiomaticity, i.e. their semantic non-compositionality, these belong to the core of phraseology and can be viewed as prototypical phraseological units.[2] In contrast to simple verbs, such idioms have a dual valence structure: an internal valence and an external valence.

2.1 *Internal valence*

The internal valence of an idiom relates to the valence properties of the idiom's verbal component, i.e. the valence pattern governed by its verbal nucleus. With most idioms, such valence properties coincide with those which the verbs have

---

1. E.g. Helbig 1982, Heringer et al. 1980, Tarvainen 1981, Welke 1988; Emons 1974, Matthews 1981, Allerton 1982, Somers 1987.

2. See Gläser (1986: 44–62) for a classification of English phraseological units in terms of central and peripheral types. Her proposal to classify so-called restricted collocations with phrasal idioms as two central types appears to be fairly counterintuitive, and might also be disputed on theoretical grounds. On account of their semantic compositonality, restricted collocations should perhaps be placed somewhere between the center and the periphery of the phraseological inventory. On the valence of a subtype of such non-idiomatic stereotypes see Müller 1985. An excellent typology-oriented study of German, English, and Dutch phraseology is Dobrovol'skij 1988, but like Gläser 1986 it totally ignores aspects of valence.

in non-phraseological constructions, so that the combinations regularly have a literal interpretation aside from their idiomatic meaning. In the sentence *Marvin twisted Susan's arm*, the verb *twist* is used as a bivalent predicator under both its idiomatic and its literal interpretation, just as in the non-phraseological construction *Carl twisted Jane's fingers*; the first complement slot is filled by the subjects and the second by the direct objects. In the expression *wear one's heart on one's sleeve*, the verb functions as a trivalent predicator in a manner no different from its function in the non-idiomatic *wear one's name tag on one's lapel*; the third valence slot is in each case filled by a complement which is realized as an adverbial prepositional phrase with a regular and semantically motivated choice of preposition.

However, there are a few fossilized expressions like *come a cropper* (chiefly in British English, henceforth BrE), *lead somebody a merry chase* (BrE) and *hear tell* as in *I hear tell he's left the city*, where the internal valence does not conform to the valence the verbs have in regular, non-phraseological syntax. In all three cases the verbs exhibit an abnormal qualitative valence; idiosyncratically, the verb *come* governs a direct-object complement, and the verb *lead* an indirect-object complement, while the verb *hear* is in construction with an immediately adjacent infinitive. Yet more frequent are cases where the internal valence is not coupled with a semantic valence that relates to a meaningful proposition. On a literal analysis, the truth conditions supplied by the constituents of *wear one's heart on one's sleeve*, not unlike those of *jump down somebody's throat, move heaven and earth, shoot the breeze* (American English, henceforth AmE) or *pay through the nose*, are absurd and situationally improbable to such a degree that these phraseological units have virtually no literal reading and lack the potential double exposure which is otherwise so characteristic of idioms.

The verbal subset of English idioms is structurally very heterogeneous, so that all valence patterns of regular syntax also seem to occur with idioms. They constitute their internal valence structure. It is the additional external valence that distinguishes idioms from free syntactic constructions.

2.2 *External valence*

The external valence of an idiom relates to the quantity and type of its variable complements which are governed by the expression as a whole. It is a property of a complex predicator with a unitary meaning.

2.2.1 *Univalent idioms*

Since they govern only the subject as a variable complement, the following phraseological units are externally univalent: *fill the bill, beat it, be all thumbs, be up the creek, fly off the handle, give up the ghost, have a screw loose, keep the wolf from the door, make a mountain out of a molehill.* The quantitative discrepancy between their external and internal valence is evident; externally they are univalent, but internally they are bivalent, or even trivalent like the last three examples.

Some externally univalent idioms internally provide additional variable positions which are occupied by pronouns coreferential with the subject participant, as *in let oneself go, keep one's nose clean* and *put one's foot in one's mouth.* Another subclass of externally univalent idioms is represented by constructions where the subject or head noun of the subject-NP is a fixed component and the variable complement appears elsewhere: *the ball is in somebody's court, somebody's eyes are bigger than his stomach, there is more to somebody/something than meets the eye.* Such predicative constructions resemble sentence idioms like *The penny dropped* and *The coast is clear,* but unlike those they provide a variable valence slot, and having *per se* only an incomplete sentence status, they should be grouped with phrasal idioms. Univalent idioms with a fixed subject and a variable object complement, which are not uncommon in other languages, do not seem to occur in English.[3]

2.2.2 *Bivalent idioms, complements, and adjuncts*

The following idioms are externally bivalent: *give somebody the cold shoulder, throw the book at somebody, be Greek to somebody, be in somebody's good books, pull the wool over somebody's eyes.* The expressions *put somebody in his place* and *give somebody his due* are bivalent constructions where the possessive pronouns co-refer to the second complement. Bivalent idioms where the subject head-noun is a fixed component are extremely rare; two instances concern the heart: *somebody's heart goes out to somebody* and *somebody's heart is not in something.*

---

3. Cf. German *jemandem* (= variable dative object) *geht der Hut hoch* 'somebody blows a gasket', *jemandem sind die Felle davongeschwommen* 'all of somebody's hopes were dashed', *jemanden* (= variable accusative object) *sticht der Hafer* 'somebody is feeling his oats, is cocky and ready for action'.

With the idioms considered so far, all variable constituents are obligatory complements in the external valence patterns. With some bivalent combinations, however, the second valence slot may be left unoccupied. Thus the idiom *ring a bell (with somebody)* includes a prepositional phrase as an optional complement which is normally omitted as in *This name will ring a bell*. Also the idioms *pay through the nose (for something),* and *show (somebody) a clean pair of heels* (BrE) have to be classed as optionally bivalent predicators, for the expressions permit the thing for which one has to pay too much money and the person one is very fast getting ahead of or away from to be unmentioned without impairing the integrity of the idiomatic constructions.

Phraseological units may, of course, always occur with free adjuncts, as in the sentence *The reporter threw the politician a curve in last night's interview by asking him an unexpected question* (AmE). Here the two prepositional phrases are not governed by the valence of the idiom *throw somebody a curve* (AmE); they are circumstantials, not inherently related to the semantics of the complex predicator. The delimitation of free adjuncts and other peripheral sentence elements from valence-dependent complements/participants, and also the rather language-specific distinction between obligatory and optional complements can more or less reliably be made on the basis of distributional criteria and various operational tests. These have been extensively discussed in the literature (e.g. Somers 1984, Welke 1988: 21–52). Since in verbal phraseology the distinctions are parallel to those in non-phraseological syntax, I feel that I may dispense with their discussion.

2.2.3 *Trivalent idioms and summary*

Idioms which are externally trivalent are rare. The expressions *spill the beans* and *open somebody's eyes* comprise optional trivalence: *X spilled the beans to Y about Z, X opened Y's eyes to Z*; in both idioms the prepositional phrases are optional complements. The phraseological units *put somebody in mind of something* (BrE) and *throw something (back) in somebody's teeth/face* are two of the few idioms with obligatory trivalence; in a sentence such as *This story puts me in mind of my brother* (BrE) none of the three complements *this story, me,* and *of my brother* can be omitted without destroying the construction. While trivalence is rare with idioms, quadrivalence, which in recent publications is generally regarded as the upper limit of (optional) valence (cf. *(W) translated (X) (from Y) (into Z)*), seems not to occur as an external valence pattern of idioms.

It can be stated that verbal idioms are characterized by external univalence or bivalence, and in a few cases by trivalence. As regards the quantitative correspondence between their external and internal valence patterns, the general rule obtains for univalent and bivalent idioms that their internal valence is numerically at least one grade above their external valence. However, this is not the case with trivalent, and not always with bivalent and univalent combinations. In the bivalent *ring a bell with somebody* and the trivalent *throw something in somebody's teeth/face* the prepositional phrase *with somebody* and the genitive premodifier *somebody's* occupy valence slots which are not in the valence pattern of the verbs *ring* and *throw*. While these idioms thus show a numerical congruity in their external and internal valence, they involve a non-numerical discrepancy that relates to the distinction between complements and free adjuncts or free attributes. Under a literal interpretation of these idioms, i.e. in terms of their internal valence, the constituents *with somebody* and *somebody's* would merely function as a free adjunct and a variable attribute respectively, cf. *Carl rang a bell with a gavel/ with a flourish/ (along) with Marvin* and *Carl threw the chewing gum in Marvin's teeth/face*.[4]

Moreover, some idioms have prepositional complements whose qualitative syntactic and semantic valence is only explainable on the basis of the idioms; with *spill the beans to somebody* and *scratch one's head over something* it is the idiomatic meaning that determines the choice of the prepositions *to* and *over* and the semantic roles of the participants. And finally some discrepancies of a purely semantic nature should be mentioned. In general, the semantic roles of variable idiom complements coincide with the roles which the constituents express under a literal interpretation. However, there are some semantically more opaque idioms where this is not the case. The subject participant in the sentence *He'll climb up the wall* is a prospective experiencer of a violent emotion under the sentence's idiomatic interpretation, while on its literal reading the subject denotes an agent who will intentionally perform a certain action. Similar semantic discrepancies hold for the indirect object of *show somebody a clean pair of heels*

---

4. On a non-binary, six-point, scale of complements and non-complements as proposed by Somers 1984, instrumental *with*-phrases are in a category closest to optional complements, but are still classed as non-complements, i.e. adjuncts, while the alternative *with*-phrases above are incontrovertible cases of free adjuncts realizing the semantic roles MANNER and CONCOMITANCE respectively. The attribute *Marvin's* in the second sentence is immediately dependent on its head noun and has only a distant dependency relation to the verb of the sentence.

(BrE) and the subject and the adverbial phrases of *ring a bell with somebody*. Under its idiomatic interpretation the subject of *ring a bell* is an inanimate cause, and under its literal interpretation it most naturally denotes a human agent, cf. *The name/melody* etc. *rang a bell* — *Somebody/the janitor* etc. *rang a bell*; the optional *with*-phrase always functions as an experiencer with the idiom, while in a literal construction it realizes other semantic roles as illustrated above.

In sum, comparing the grammar of idioms with the grammar of their homonymous literal constructions, we encounter quantitative discrepancies relating to the complement or free adjunct/attribute function of their constituents, and also discrepancies pertaining to the semantic functions of constituents, i.e. to qualitative semantic valence properties. Verbal idioms thus reflect the complexity and heterogeneity of valence to a much higher degree than simple verbs and their valence properties deserve an in-depth investigation. The related problems and potential solutions can only be indicated here. Since valence grammar has proved to be a useful approach not only to the linguistic description of languages, but also to their teaching as foreign languages, it should be an aim for applied linguists and lexicographers of English to compile an English valence dictionary where the valence properties not only of simple verbs, but also of idiomatic and non-idiomatic phraseological units are listed and explicated along with their major inherent discrepancies.[5]

3. A Stratificational Approach to the Valence of Idioms

According to Gerhard Helbig, the leading valence theorist in German linguistics, and arguably its most experienced lexicographer, a valence entry in a dictionary of verbal lexemes should include the following information:

(i) maximum number of semantic arguments governed by the semantic predicator which corresponds to the verbal lexeme;

(ii) inherent features of the semantic predicator of which some are irrelevant, others such as "action", "process", "state", "experiential" are relevant to its valence;

---

5. Cf. Helbig/Schenkel's (1991) valence dictionary of German verbs, which regrettably neglects phraseological units.

(iii) semantic roles of the arguments/complements such as "agent", "patient", "beneficiary", "experiencer";

(iv) common inherent features of potential arguments/complements such as "animate", "human", "abstract", "solid", "liquid", i.e. semantic collocational restrictions;

(v) number of obligatory and optional complements, i.e. numerical syntactic valence;

(vi) morpho-syntactic properties of complements, i.e. functional and formal categorization of the complements, morphological cases, choice of preposition(s), and word order (cf. Helbig 1983).

The above list reflects the complex character of valence; points (i) through (iv), which represent highly interdependent factors, relate to numerical and qualitative semantic valence of a more or less language-independent kind, while points (v) and (vi) pertain to language-specific numerical and qualitative syntactic valence, with the specification of morphological cases and word order clearly being the most idiosyncratic information.[6]

On the whole, a valence entry of a verbal idiom should provide similar information, but add lexical variants to the entry's lemma (cf. *chew the fat/rag*) and give information on the idiom's transformational potential, a property which in many cases seems to be coupled with its valence. Its internal valence could most economically be described by cross-referencing within the entry or the dictionary.

It is well known that stratificational grammar includes no lexicon or dictionary in a conventional sense, nor in the linguistic sense of a separate grammatical component, as is the case in most other descriptive language models; lexical information is spread over the whole of its relational network system. Figure 1 shows a simplified LEXICAL VALENCE ENTRY of the bivalent idiom *ring a bell with somebody* using the relational network notation of stratificational linguistics.

This figure incorporates a peculiar descriptive approach to semantics. While the tactic portion of the lexo-morphemic stratum continues to be described in

---

6. The description of the semantic properties of complements, cf. (iv), should perhaps be supplemented by information on restricted collocations, i.e. usage-conditioned, purely lexical co-occurrence restrictions holding between the verb and its variable complements (cf. Müller 1981). Being a highly language-specific property, this could be added as a seventh type of information.

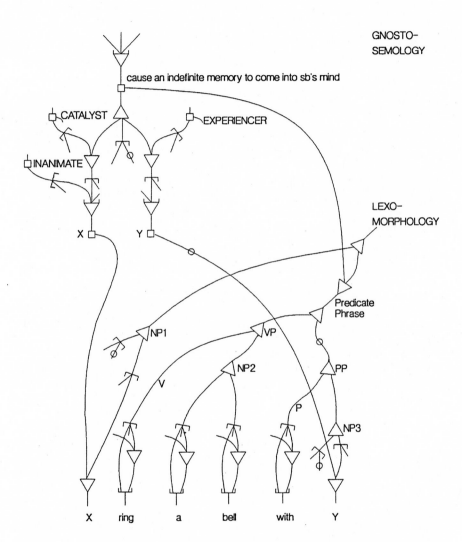

Figure 1. *The valence of the idiom **ring a bell with somebody** in relational network notation*

terms of constituent structure configurations, a type of semantic dependency has
been chosen here for the description of gnosto-semological structure.[7] Such a
format appears to be more adequate not only for the description of valence,
which is a special case of dependency, but also of semantics and discourse
structure in general. The square node, a notational device which James E.
Copeland (1983) uses for the description of discourse phenomena, also proves
suitable for explicating semantic dependency. Symbolizing the same type of
connectivity as an ordinary AND-node, a square node additionally signals a
special interpretative convention that holds for the relevant part in the linguistic
network system.

As can be seen in the upper half of Figure 1, square nodes are placed on
lines in the gnosto-sememic stratum and they connect to the lexo-morphemic
stratum by lines from their right side. These connection points correspond to
elements of a semantic proposition, i.e. sememes, which in stratificational
semantics are interpreted as conceptual nections. All sememes are conceived as
being neutral in terms of word class. In propositions, however, sememes that
function as predicates are represented as controlling those which function as their
arguments or act as modifiers of the predicating sememes.[8]

Dependency relations are not restricted to predicating sememes and their
dependents, but also hold within other, non-predicating, sememic arrangements,
which are realized as various syntactic constructions. What, in general, qualifies
a sememe as a controller is its relative autonomy *vis-à-vis* the dependent,
controlled element(s). It can be observed that predicators generally determine the
number and semantic properties of their arguments, while arguments normally do
not restrict the choice of possible predicators. Among Indo-European languages

---

7. The present approach draws its original inspiration from P. H. Matthews's discussion and
elaboration of valence and dependency grammar (Matthews 1981), and was first proposed in Müller
1985. It reinterprets the grammatical concept of dependency as a semantic notion; grammatical
dependency is viewed as a mere reflex of semantic dependency, with the two types mainly differing
in terms of linearity / non-linearity. Such a view is basically supported by Ronald W. Langacker's
approach to what he calls "conceptual dependence" (Langacker 1987: 298–310; 1991: 28 et passim).
However, my approach differs from his in some essential aspects, which for limitations of space
cannot be dealt with here.

8. Observe that the last point is in conflict with the practice of logicians, who normally interpret
predicator-modifying elements like adverbials as predicates of a higher order. The semantic
dependency approach — in line with Matthews's proposals concerning grammatical dependence —
is less abstract and more oriented towards linguistic surface structure.

this is reflected in the fact that verbal and other predicators typically require their dependent valence-partners to assume particular case forms or to combine with specific prepositions. So one can reasonably claim that a predicating sememe has a status which is relatively more autonomous than that of its argument sememe(s). The situation is different in the case of a dependency relation holding between a predicating sememe and its modifier and also in the case of dependency relations obtaining within various attributive sememic arrangements. Here the relative autonomy of the controllers is borne out by the properties of the elements they control; these unilaterally presuppose the existence of a controller and may typically be removed without the structural identity of the rest of the semantic arrangement being affected. It should however be emphasized that omissibility in this sense does not imply that the dependent elements represent communicatively less important information; in a text they may well have a degree of communicative dynamism exceeding that of their controllers, just as an argument sememe can be communicatively more important, more "rhematic", than its controlling predicator sememe. Whether a semantic element acts as a controller or is dependent is thus determined by predicational function and by the notion of relative semantic autonomy. Verbal valence represents a special case of predicational dependency. Those controlling relations which correspond to valence, i.e. the dependency relations between a linguistic predicator and its complement(s), will be called GOVERNING RELATIONS.[9]

In diagrammatic notation the controlling relation is expressed by placing a square that symbolizes a controller sememe above those that symbolize its dependent sememes, so that a predicating sememe controls or governs all sememes which are directly connected to it by downward lines. In those parts of a stratificational diagram where square nodes are used, the connecting lines thus not only indicate realizational relations or tactic arrangements, as elsewhere in the network, but simultaneously express the functions of governing and controlling by virtue of a hierarchical ordering of the elements. Besides square nodes, conventional AND, OR and AND/OR nodes continue to be used in the stratum.

---

9. Since we are concerned with verbal idioms, it would take us too far afield to discuss the valence of adjectives, nouns, and prepositions. It is sufficient here to note that the status of prepositions and (non-predicative) non-derived nouns as valence carriers is a matter of dispute among theorists and that in principle the present framework can accommodate a valence description of these other word classes without postulating any additional descriptive machinery (cf. Matthews 1981: 114–17, 156–59, 162).

We are now in a position to explain the valence characteristics of the idiom *ring a bell with somebody* in stratificational terms. Like all idiomatic phraseological units, this expression seems to correspond to a unitary concept of the content plane; in the diagram, it is glossed as 'cause an indefinite memory to come into somebody's mind'. What distinguishes our analysis from previous stratificational accounts (e.g. Makkai 1972; Sullivan 1980), is that such an idiomatic sememe is now realized via tactic nodes because in the revised stratificational system there is no longer a lexemic sign pattern between the sememes and the morphemes; the idiomatic sememe is viewed as a constructional meaning of a complex verbal lexeme (cf. Lamb 1983, 1984). In the diagram a line from the conceptual nection corresponding to this sememe enters a tactic nection that represents a predicate phrase within the lexo-morphemic stratum.

The valence of the idiom is explicated over two strata. As for its external valence, the idiom is bivalent: the idiomatic conceptual nection controls and governs the two variable co-sememes X and Y. This is the maximum number of semantic arguments conditioned by the valence of the semantic predicator. The functions of the co-sememes X and Y are specified by the role sememe CATALYST, a neutral term I propose for something or someone causing an event, and the role sememe EXPERIENCER. These roles are conditioned by the meaning of the idiom — a semantic interdependence which for ease of legibility is not explicitly shown in the diagram, but could be displayed by realizational lines that link the two role sememes with the componency of the idiomatic sememe. The selection restriction pertaining to the idiom's notional subject is captured in the diagram by the componential feature INANIMATE above the variable sememe X. Taken together, this constitutes the external semantic valence of the idiom, see points (i)–(iv) in Helbig's categorization of valence information. Within the lexo-morphemic stratum the two variable sememes are realized as nominal complements. By virtue of its intrinsic structure and by using information supplied by the gnosto-sememic stratum, the lexo-morphotactics introduces linear order and specifies that the one variable sememe syntactically functions as a subject (NP_1) and the other acts as an object (NP_3) of the determined preposition *with* inside an adverbial phrase. As previously noted, the distinction between optional and obligatory complements is a rather language-specific matter; it seems to have no direct correlate on the content plane (cf. Helbig 1982: 38; Allerton 1982: 76–8).[10] Therefore it is preferable not to relate it to semantic valence, but to syntactic valence, as expressed in the diagram. The optionality of the prepositional phrase *with Y* is indicated by small circles on the lines that connect it to the predicate phrase nection and to the sememe square Y. Taken together, this makes up the external syntactic valence of the idiom, see points (v) and (vi) in Helbig's categorization. The direct object *a bell* (NP$_2$) is displayed as not being a realization of a semantic argument, but as realizing — just like *ring* and *with* — an indeterminate part of a semantic predicate.[11]

Various details and additional expositions have been omitted from Figure 1. First, the valence-bound adverbial is in a substitutional relationship — at least in British English — with the expanded phrase *in somebody's mind*. And as illustrated by the quotation 'While his name may not ring any bells, you have heard his bass before ...' (*Guitar Player*, May 1984: 72), the idiom allows variation in the determiners and grammatical number of its direct object. Such systematic options could easily be handled by adding some lines and nodes in the diagram.

Now consider the sentence *Doubtless, this name immediately rang a bell with the senior citizens*. It contains three adverbials: as an optional complement the adverbial *with the senior citizens* is less strongly presupposed by the semantics of the idiom than the subject, while the adverbials *immediately* and *doubtless* are the least grammatically presupposed and count as free adjuncts in valence theory. In the literature such valence-independent constituents have generally been interpreted as higher predicates, in line with logicians' practice, and they have been accorded the status of valence carriers standing in need of complementation and governing the verb of the sentence plus its dependent complements (cf. Welke 1988: 74–9). Such an approach is beset with theoretical problems. The most serious one appears to be that because dependency rules can only make

---

10. As evidence for an interlingual discrepancy of this kind, let me cite one example from English and German involving the verb *watch* and its German equivalent *beobachten*:
   Peter was watching the card players —
   Peter beobachtete die Kartenspieler.
   Peter was watching —
   *Peter beobachtete.

11. Nominal elements of verbal idioms such as *a bell* in our example have been defined and treated as "integral complements" by Somers (1984, 1987). In my view this is quite problematic; being partial realizations of complex valence carriers, they should not be accorded any kind of complement status in the idioms' external valence patterns.

reference to terminal syntactic categories, the account is incapable of distinguishing different kinds of adverbials and their differential scope of grammatical modification. In the sentence the adverbial *immediately* modifies the verb phrase, i.e. the idiom within the predicate phrase, while *doubtless*, as a so-called content disjunct (Quirk et al. 1985: 612–31), obviously functions as a sentence modifier. The present dependency approach, which interprets all modifiers as dependent, controlled elements, is capable of clearly delimiting the different scopes of modification which these two adverbials have. In the gnosto-sememic trace of the sentence, the sememe corresponding to the adverbial *immediately* would, as the diagram suggests, be attached to the middle line directly below the idiomatic nection. This is only an optional controlling line connecting a modifier to its head. Unlike the semantic roles and certain inherent features of the complements, this modifier's componency and semantic role seem not to be in any way determined by the controlling sememe. While the optionality of the valence-bound complement *with the senior citizens* is indicated in the lexo-morphemic stratum, the optionality of an adjunct like *immediately*, being a less language-specific phenomenon, is explicated in the gnosto-sememic stratum. The figure, as it stands, does not take into account such peripheral sentence elements as *doubtless*, *allegedly*, or *predictably*. What constitutes a severe problem of formalization for conventional dependency rules and dependency trees (but see Matthews 1991: 90 *et passim*), can be tackled with ease by the present approach, due to the flexibility of the stratificational network notation. In the sentence's trace, lines would run downwards from the square nodes directly, or via an AND-node in the case of the idiomatic sememe, and merge into an upward AND-node above the square representing the sememe of the content disjunct *doubtless*. Multiple controlling lines thus specify that the scope of this adverbial, in contrast to that of *immediately*, extends over the entire remainder of the proposition.

Due to its qualitative semantic valence, which requires an inanimate subject, *ring a bell* is not ambiguous in an active construction; here its potential ambiguity is resolved by the immediate co-text so that the construction *Carl rang a bell*, unlike the ambiguous sentences *Carl missed the boat* or *Carl passed the buck*, cannot be interpreted idiomatically. This construction instantiates the regular, non-phraseological valence pattern of the verb *ring*, which represents the idiom's internal valence pattern. To keep the diagram transparent, the figure gives only an indication of the idiom's internal valence. Within the lexo-morphemic stratum, such valence properties coincide with those of its external valence as far as constituent structure is concerned. However, its corresponding gnosto-semology would reveal that in the internal valence pattern the constituent *a bell* is a complement filling an optional valence slot, which is marked by the role sememe OBJECTIVE, that the subject would be an animate CATALYST, and that any potential constituent introduced by the preposition *with* would be a free adjunct of the verb functioning in roles other than EXPERIENCER. In Figure 1 the short lines that come out of the upward AND-nodes above the lexemes *ring, a, bell,* and *with* suggest the connection to the gnosto-sememic structure of the idiom's literal meaning. By the additional means of ordered OR-nodes directly over the lexemes, the stratificational network notation is capable of integrating the description of the idiom's external valence, i.e. the valence of its common, clearly preferred and in most contexts single idiomatic interpretation, with the description of its internal valence, i.e. the valence pattern of its unusual, contextually marked, literal interpretation, into one relational diagram.[12]

4. Conclusion

Some valence properties of a central type of verbal phraseological unit have been explored. On account of their idiomaticity, these phraseological units have an external and an internal valence pattern, between which there are discrepancies

---

12. As previously noted, one aspect related to an idiom's valence is its transformational potential and defectiveness. The expression *ring a bell* represents one of the rarer cases of idioms where, for instance, the passive version preserves the idiomatic interpretability; compare the potential ambiguous passive *No bells were rung when he mentioned the name* with the exclusively literal interpretability of *My goat was gotten when they left the fence open* or *A rat was smelled when they entered the barn.* Interesting suggestions on how stratificational grammar can tackle such syntactic irregularities have been made by Coleman (1984). There seems to exist some correlation between the passivizability of an idiom and its semantic divisibility and perhaps also the degree of transfer motivation which relates the literal constituents to parts of the definitional paraphrase. This, in many cases, allows one to make a fairly safe prediction as to whether an idiom can or cannot appear in an idiomatic passive version. The present dependency approach to valence and phraseology precludes neither a simple decomposition of an idiomatic sememe nor its analysis into predicational structures at a higher, more abstract level and thus in principle is capable of describing such idiosyncrasies. Semantically 'monadic', i.e. basically univalent, idioms of the type *kick the bucket, fill the bill, chew the fat* generally disallow passivization and hardly any idiom permits one of its constituents to be the topic in topicalization constructions. While this can rather straightforwardly be explained and described in stratificational terms, the defectiveness of idioms in regard to other transformations remains a complicated explanatory, descriptive and also empirical problem, considering the fact that with native speakers the assessment of the transforms' acceptability is subject to considerable variation.

of various kinds. Suggestions have been made as to how the complex functional category of valence can be described in stratificational network notation. The description has been implemented by an approach to gnosto-semological phenomena which utilizes the notion of semantic dependency. The valence characteristics of verbal idioms are explicated in the gnosto-sememic and the lexo-morphemic strata, with the semantic valence properties being described in terms of semantic dependency relations. The omissibility of (optional) complements, which is a language-specific phenomenon, is indicated in the lexo-morphemic stratum, while the optionality of modifying adjuncts, which seems to hold across all languages, is explicated in the gnosto-sememic stratum. Although the description has primarily been exemplified by idiomatic complex valence carriers, it is also perfectly applicable to simple verbs and in principle to all valence carriers.

As early as 1966, Sydney M. Lamb wrote that "... semantic arrangements do not have immediate constituent structure in the usual sense, and they cannot in general be represented by tree diagrams" (Lamb 1966: 32). Surveying the stratificational publications which deal with semantic phenomena, one notices that in most studies their authors nonetheless group and hierarchically order semantic elements in accordance with the principles of syntactic constituent structure or in a rather intuitive fashion with little or no theoretical justification. So after a quarter century one is still left in doubt as to what the exact descriptive principles are or should be in stratificational semantics. The only notable consensus seems to be that there is no linear order in predicational or componential semantic structure, with linearization being effected at a lower descriptive level, i.e. by the lexo-morphotactics. Given this unsatisfactory situation in stratificational linguistics, the proposed semantic dependency format, whose basic outlines could only be presented here and whose usefulness I have tried to demonstrate for a relational valence description, might perhaps also prove to be an adequate approach to a unified overall account of semantic structure. Its fairly obvious descriptive advantages are that the directionality of grammatical modification in endocentric constructions, a classic descriptive problem for standard phrase structure rules, and also the head status of constituents within other subordinating constructions (cf. Matthews 1981: 146–67), the predicative or non-predicative function of constituents, and finally the semantic unity or continuity of syntactically continuous or discontinuous constituents can in most cases be neatly and economically elucidated in the model.

In a paper published in 1991, Lamb emphasized one aspect showing the superiority of relational network notation over the notational systems of most other contemporary linguistic theories. This type of formalization allows equally plausible analyses of a specific linguistic problem to coexist in the descriptive system. Perhaps stratificational linguistics might also permit syntactic constituency and semantic dependency to coexist as two descriptive principles in its relational model.

Acknowledgments

My thanks go to Peter Erdmann for commenting on an earlier version of this article, and to Virginia Brown and Roger Charlton for passing judgment on the currency and acceptability of the linguistic examples.

References

Allerton, D. J. 1982. *Valency and the English Verb*. New York: Academic Press.

Coleman, D. Wells. 1984. Idiomaticity and the autonomy of syntax in stratificational grammar. *Southwest Journal of Linguistics* 7: 26–46.

Copeland, James E. 1983. Linguistic creativity and the langue/parole distinction. *The Ninth LACUS Forum 1982*, ed. by John Morreall, 159–68. Columbia, South Carolina: Hornbeam Press.

Dobrovol'skij, Dmitrij. 1988. *Phraseologie als Objekt der Universalienlinguistik*. Leipzig: Verlag Enzyklopädie.

Emons, Rudolf. 1974. *Valenzen englischer Prädikatsverben*. (Linguistische Arbeiten, 22.) Tübingen: Niemeyer.

Gläser, Rosemarie. 1986. *Phraseologie der englischen Sprache*. Leipzig: Verlag Enzyklopädie.

Helbig, Gerhard. 1982. *Valenz – Satzglieder – semantische Kasus – Satzmodelle*. Leipzig: Verlag Enzyklopädie.

Helbig, Gerhard. 1983. Valenz und Lexikographie. *Deutsch als Fremdsprache* 20: 137–43.

Helbig, Gerhard and Wolfgang Schenkel. 1991. *Wörterbuch zur Valenz und Distribution deutscher Verben*. 8. Auflage. Tübingen: Niemeyer.

Heringer, Hans Jürgen, Bruno Strecker and Rainer Wimmer. 1980. *Syntax: Fragen – Lösungen – Alternativen*. München: W. Fink.

Lamb, Sydney M. 1966. *Outline of Stratificational Grammar.* Washington, D.C.: Georgetown University Press.

Lamb, Sydney M. 1983. On determining the number of strata in linguistic structure. *The Ninth LACUS Forum 1982,* ed. by John Morreall, 189–203. Columbia, South Carolina: Hornbeam Press.

Lamb, Sydney M. 1984. Semiotics of language and culture: A relational approach. *Semiotics of Culture and Language,* ed. by Robin P. Fawcett., M. A. K. Halliday, Sydney Lamb, & Adam Makkai., vol. 2, 71–100. London: Frances Pinter.

Lamb, Sydney M. 1991. Linguistic model and linguistic thought: The case of either-or thinking. *The Seventeenth LACUS Forum 1990,* ed. by Angela Della Volpe, 109–20. Lake Bluff: Linguistic Association of Canada and the United States.

Langacker, Ronald W. 1987. *Foundations of Cognitive Grammar. Volume I: Theoretical Prerequisites.* Stanford, California: Stanford University Press.

Langacker, Ronald W. 1991. *Concept, Image, and Symbol: The Cognitive Basis of Grammar.* Berlin and New York: Mouton de Gruyter.

Makkai, Adam. 1972. *Idiom Structure in English.* The Hague: Mouton.

Matthews, P. H. 1981. *Syntax.* Cambridge: Cambridge University Press.

Müller, Ernst-August. 1981. Towards a stratificational description of collocations. *The Seventh LACUS Forum 1980,* ed. by James E. Copeland and Philip W. Davis, 175–87. Columbia, South Carolina: Hornbeam Press.

Müller, Ernst-August. 1985. A stratificational approach to the valence of function-verb constructions. *The Eleventh LACUS Forum 1984,* ed. by Robert A. Hall, Jr., 171–81, Columbia, South Carolina: Hornbeam Press.

Quirk, Randolph, Sidney Greenbaum, Geoffrey Leech, and Jan Svartvik. 1985. *A Comprehensive Grammar of the English Language.* London and New York: Longman.

Somers, Harold L. 1984. On the validity of the complement–adjunct distinction of valency grammar. *Linguistics* 22. 507–30.

Somers, Harold L. 1987. *Valency and Case in Computational Linguistics.* Edinburgh: Edinburgh University Press.

Sullivan, William J. 1980. Some logical consequences of Makkai's idiomaticity as a language universal. *Papers in Cognitive-Stratificational Linguistics,* ed. by James E. Copeland and Philip W. Davis, 143–84. Houston, Texas: Rice University Studies.

Tarvainen, Kalevi. 1981. *Einführung in die Dependenzgrammatik.* Tübingen: Niemeyer.

Welke, Klaus M. 1988. *Einführung in die Valenz- und Kasustheorie.* Leipzig: Bibliographisches Institut.

About the author

Ernst-August Müller currently teaches at the University of the Saarland in Saarbrücken, Germany, where he has held a tenured position since 1982. From 1977 to 1982, he taught at the Free University of Berlin. His doctoral dissertation, from the University of Kassel in 1977, dealt with verbal phraseological units inspired by the stratificational work on idioms published by Syd Lamb and Adam Makkai. He later became acquainted with Lamb at LACUS meetings, and was visiting lecturer at Rice University during the 1983–1984 academic year. He currently divides his time between synchronic and historical linguistics.

CHAPTER 2

A Neural Network Model of Language Production

William M. Christie

Catawba College

Contemporary theoretical linguistics has been described, not altogether inaccurately, as an essentially masochistic enterprise. One first constructs an extremely powerful model of grammar, and then one invests one's energy in trying to apply constraints on the power of that grammar. Indeed, the history of theory over the past decade may well be thought of as nothing more than an extended attempt to constrain MOVE-α. In this paper, I wish to suggest a somewhat different approach to model building. Rather than begin with an extremely powerful model and then add particular constraints to it, I wish to examine a much less powerful, though still highly general model to see whether particular constraints might be found to be natural consequences of the nature of the model itself.

The model I will examine is a neural network of the kind described by Rumelhart and McCleland (1986) and others. It will be my general hypothesis that a neural network model can be specified that will embody, as a natural consequence of network design and language structure specification, the equivalent of appropriate constraints that must be stated separately in other more powerful models. I will first describe the general properties of the particular neural network model I am using. I will then describe a test performed on this model that shows that it automatically blocks a certain type of phenomenon generally described by a constraint on a movement rule. I will then discuss some of the theoretical considerations of structural description and network design that will bear on further investigations of this sort. It should be emphasized that the present essay cannot be regarded as a definitive description of an alternative grammatical model. I hope, however, that it will be found to be a provocative suggestion for a new direction in linguistic metatheory.

1. A Sequential Neural Network

Most neural networks of the type described by Hopfield (1982), Rumelhart and
McCleland (1986), and others will, after training, calculate on the basis of an
input vector a corresponding output vector that represents the state of the
network at the time of output. Networks of this type have been put to many
diverse uses, the majority of them being identification or discrimination tasks.
Some of these tasks have direct bearing on language perception (for example
Hampshire and Weibel 1989, Deng 1992), but they have been limited in their
applications to natural language because of the atemporal nature of the input and
output sets. Some recent attention has been paid to the storing of temporal
sequences (Fang, Wilson, and Li 1989, Reiss and Taylor 1991), but little has
been done in the design of networks that will produce a temporally ordered
sequence of output states on the basis of a single input state. This last-named
task, however, is crucial if one is to develop a neural network model for natural
language production.

The neural network model proposed here is a variation on the Brain-State-
in-a-Box (BSB) model described by Anderson (1977). It is a single-layer feedback network with input and output buffer layers. Each processing element in the
input layer is correspondingly connected to an element in the middle layer with
a fixed weight of 1. Each element in the middle layer is connected to all
elements in that layer (including itself) with a trainable weight. Each element in
the training layer is also correspondingly connected to an element in the output
buffer layer. For present purposes a training layer of 100 processing units has
been used. The activation rule is slightly different from that originally used by
Anderson. In the present model

$$s_j(t) = 1 \qquad \text{if} \sum s_i w_{ij}(t-1) \geq 0 \qquad \text{otherwise } s_j(t) = 0 \qquad (1)$$

where $s_j(t)$ is the activation state of processing unit j at time t, and w_{ij} is the
weight (range -9 to 9) of the connection between processing unit i and processing unit j. A modified Hebbian learning procedure is used for the network:

$$\Delta w_{ij} = s_i(t-1)\left[k_j(t) - s_j(t)\right] \qquad (2)$$

where $k_j(t)$ is the desired state of processing unit j at time t and $s_j(t)$ is the actual
state of processing unit j at time t. The implementation of these rules is shown
in the partial source code listing in the appendix.

2.   The Syntactic Test

A common difficulty with neural networks is superimposition of training. While a network can normally be trained to recognize a single input (or, in the case of partial match retrieval, a portion of a single input), a network will often have difficulty learning a second input, especially when either the second input or the second output partially overlaps the first. As a test of its learning abilities, the present network was given a set of activated processing units as input and was asked to learn a specified sequence of outputs. Each output state at each time interval consisted of simultaneous signals from two processing units in the output buffer layer. The network was then given a second input set which overlapped the first set. In the second training, one member of each output pair was identical to one member of each pair in the first training. For the other member of each pair, one new output element was substituted for one of the corresponding elements in the first sequence, and the remaining elements were reordered slightly. The sample sequence is shown in Figure 1.

Training 1: Input processing units 0, 1, 2, 3, 4, 5

Output at time t+	1	2	3	4	5	6
Processing units	220	221	222	223	224	225
	230	231	232	233	230	234
	det	N_1	*Aux$_1$*	V	*det*	N_2

Training 2: Input processing units 2, 3, 4, 5, 6, 7

Output at time t+	1	2	3	4	5
Processing units	220	221	222	223	224
	236	232	230	231	233
	wh	*Aux$_1$*	*det*	N_1	V

Figure 1. *Sample Sequences of Inputs and Outputs*

To make a connection with linguistic data, let **236** represent an appropriate *wh*-element, and let **232** represent the appropriate initial element from the **Aux**. Other correspondences should be clear from the figure. The interpretation of the target learning results would be as follows: Given a particular semantic input to the system (processing units **0, 1, 2, 3, 4, 5**), a well-formed string is produced as output (processing units **230, 231, 232, 233, 230, 234** in that order). With a partly similar semantic input (procesing units **2, 3, 4, 5, 6, 7**), a related well-formed string will be produced that will begin with a *wh*-element, contain appropriate subject-verb inversion, and lack one nominal element that the first string possesses.

It remains to note that processing units **220–225** function simply as timing elements, holding sequential slots in the clause string. These were deemed to be essential for proper processing of diverse sequences since the network as designed is a modified Markov process model with deterministic state transitions. In such a model, the repetition of any single element would, if that elment were the sole component of a particular state realization, produce a subsequent sequence that would be a mere repetition of the sequence that followed the first occurrence of that element. Given this arrangement, the network was able to learn the two sequences together with no difficulty. In other words, this sequential neural network is capable of learning the sequential structures involved in WH-MOVEMENT.

Now within the Extended Standard Theory there is a well-known constraint on WH-MOVEMENT that prevents this rule from applying to any constituent within a syntactic island. In Figure 2, Training 1 illustrates a possible sequence representing the occurrence of a nominal element, here labeled **230, 235**, within an island. The existence of the island is marked by the reinitiation of the timing sequence. Training 2 in the same figure shows the output sequence if the WH-MOVEMENT is allowed to move the sequence **230, 235** out of the island and replace it with an appropriate *wh*. This sequence should be blocked by the island constraint. Training was attempted with these two sequences, and the sequential neural network proved incapable of learning this pair of sequential structures.

In analyzing this pair of sequences, one can see that that the reinitiation of the timing sequence which marks the beginning of the island creates a situation in which the exact same combination of processing elements is activated at two distinct time intervals. A modified Markov model such as this one is incapable of distinguishing between these two occurrences and thus is unable to learn the version with WH-MOVEMENT. Therefore this particular movement constraint does not have to be stated separately. It falls out as a natural consequence of the model.

Of course, WH-MOVEMENT is not the only movement rule affected by this constraint, and this is not the only kind of island that is involved. It has been necessary to simplify somewhat for purposes of an initial investigation to determine whether a constraint such as this might fall out as a natural consequence of a more restricted model of grammar. The results obtained thus far suggest that this indeed may well be the case, and that further investigation is warranted.

Training 1: Input processing units 0, 1, 2, 3, 4, 5, 8, 9, 10

Output at time t+	1	2	3	4	5	6	7	8	9	10	11
Processing units	220	221	222	223	224	225	220	221	222	223	224
	230	231	232	233	230	234	236	237	238	230	235
	det	N_1	Aux_1	V_1	*det*	N_2	*wh*	Aux_2	V_2	*det*	N_3

Training 2: Input processing units 2, 3, 4, 5, 6, 7, 8, 9, 10

Output at time t+	1	2	3	4	5	6	7	8	9	10
Processing units	220	221	222	223	224	225	226	220	221	222
	236	232	230	231	233	230	234	236	237	238
	wh	Aux_1	*det*	N_1	V_1	*det*	N_2	*wh*	Aux_2	V_2

Figure 2. *Sample Sequences for Constituents in a Syntactic Island*

3. The Structural Description

From the foregoing description it is clear that this particular constraint arises from the general model as a consequence of the particular combination of processing elements assigned to represent a string constituent. One might express this differently by saying that the constraint is a consequence of the particular labels assigned to the string constituents. Since any tree can be equivalently represented by a properly bracketed string, and since appropriate labeling can represent the bracketing, it follows that constraints stated in terms of tree structure can equivalently be stated in terms of the labels assigned to the constituents.

The initial step, then, in further investigations of a model such as this should be a determination of the proper string labeling to capture a full range of constraints on all kinds of syntactic islands. What I have shown here is that one constraint applied to movement from one kind of island need not be stated separately in a grammatical description because it is a natural consequence of the model being used. It remains to be determined whether a full range, or at least a substantial part of that range of movement constraints can be accounted for in the same way.

There are also some significant issues to be investigated in the structure of the model itself. Two questions in particular need to be addressed. First, the model described in the present paper is, as noted above, a modified Markov process model with deterministic state transitions. As such it is context-free in its operations, though the number of processing elements that can be involved in defining any state is large enough to obscure this property somewhat. However, a change in the connections from the input buffer layer to the training layer, making these connections full and trainable rather than corresponding and fixed, could convert this into a context-sensitive Markov process model. Given the arguments advanced in Reich 1969, this alternative structure merits serious consideration.

Second, this model incorporates one particular form of output sequencing. Other possible forms were discussed in Christie 1991, and one of these alternatives, using laterally coupled suppressive elements, has recently been applied to the processing of acoustic signals (Deng 1992). This form merits further attention as a possible sequencing process for modeling language production.

4. Summary

In this paper it has not been my intention to present an elaborated alternative model for linguistic description. I have tried, rather, to suggest the direction in which such a model might be developed. In so doing I have tried to show, through the investigation of one example, that it may be possible for this model to simplify linguistic description by capturing as natural consequences of the system certain constraints that in other models must be stated separately. I have tried, in addition, to suggest the directions in which this investigation might profitably be extended and expanded.

Appendix

```
int matrix[100][100], net_size, state_former[300], state_current[300], state_new[300];
main()
{

run_network()
    {
    char ch;
    int cell, tmr1, tmr2 = 1, duration = 20;
```

```c
printf("This routine runs your network. Cells 0 through %d make up the input layer.\n\n",net_size-1);
printf(" Please enter, one at a time, the numbers of the cells in that layer that\n");
printf(" you wish to activate as system input. When you have finished, enter 999.");
gotoxy(2,9);
input_values();
gotoxy(2,11);
printf("Please enter the number of time intervals for which you want the network to\n");
printf(" fire. The default value is 20 time intervals. ");
duration = getnum();
if (duration == 0) duration = 20;
for(tmr1 = 0;tmr1<=duration;++tmr1) begin_run(tmr1);
return 0;
}


begin_run(tmr1)
    {
    int tm, cursor_position;

    printf(" The following cells fired at time t+%d:\n ",tmr1);
    for(tm = 0;tm<=3*net_size-1;++tm)
        {
        if(state_current[tm] == 1) printf("%d ",tm);
        cursor_position=wherex();
        if (cursor_position>77) printf("\n"" ");
        }
    printf("\n\n");
    change_values();
    return 0;
    }


change_values()
    {
    int tm1, tm2, tm3, val;
    for(tm1 = 0;tm1<3*net_size;++tm1)
        state_former[tm1] = state_current[tm1];
    for(tm2 = net_size;tm2<2*net_size;++tm2)
        {
        tm3=tm2-net_size;
        if(state_current[tm3] == 1) val=1;
            else val=0;
        for(tm1=0;tm1<net_size;++tm1)
            val=val+matrix[tm1] [tm3]*state_current[tm1+net_size];
        if(val>0) state_new[tm2]=1;
            else state_new[tm2]=0;
        val=0;
        }
    for(tm1=net_size;tm1<=2*net_size-1;++tm1)
        {
```

```
        if(state_current[tm1] == 1) state_current[tm1+net_size]=1;
            else state_current[tm1+net_size]=0;
        state_current[tm1]=state_new[tm1];
        }
    return 0;
}

clear_values()
    {
    int tmr1;

    for(tmr1=0;tmr1<=3*net_size-1;++tmr1)
        {
        state_former[tmr1]=0;
        state_current[tmr1]=0;
        state_new[tmr1]=0;
        }
    return 0;
    }

input_values()
    {
    int tmr1=2, cell;

    do
        {
        cell=getnum();
        state_former[cell]=1;
        state_current[cell]=1;
        state_new[cell]=1;
        tmr1=tmr1+3;
        gotoxy(tmr1,9);
        } while(cell!=999);
    return 0;
    }

train_network()
    {
    training_1()
    {
    int tm1, tm2, tm3, tm4, tm5, val, target[100][12], input, cell, control;

    for(tm1=0;tm1<100;++tm1)
        for(tm2=0;tm2<12;++tm2)
            target[tm1][tm2]=0;
    clear_values();
    clrscr();
    textattr(118);
```

```
gotoxy(32,1);
printf(" TRAIN NETWORK 1 ");
textattr(30);
clear_values();
printf("\n\n"" This routine will train your network to produce a sequence of outputs based on\n");
printf(" an input set that you will specify. The output cells are %d through %d.\n", 2*net_size,
    3*net_size-1);
printf(" Sequential output begins at time t+3 and continues through time t+14. Please\n");
printf(" enter, one at a time, your set of input cells in the range 0 through %d, ter-\n", net_size-1);
printf(" terminating entry by entering 999.\n\n"" ");
input_values();
gotoxy(2,11);
printf("Now enter the output sets, terminating each set by entering 999.");
for(tm1=0;tm1<12;++tm1)
    {
    tm2=23;
    gotoxy(2,13+tm1);
    printf("Output at time t+%d: ",tm1+3);
    do
        {
        gotoxy(tm2,13+tm1);
        input=getnum();
        if(input == 998) menu3();
        if(input!=999)
            {
            cell=input-2*net_size;
            target[cell][tm1]=1;
            }
        tm2=tm2+4;
        }
    while(input!=999);
    }

change_values();
change_values();

for(tm2=0;tm2<12;++tm2) /*12 time intervals*/
    {
    textattr(79);
    gotoxy(1,25);
    cprintf(" Training at time t+%d. ", tm2+3);
    tm5=1;
    do
    {
        control=1;
        for(tm3=0;tm3<net_size;++tm3) /*go through the target neurons*/
            {
            if(target[tm3][tm2] == 1) /*cell should fire*/
```

```
        {
        if(state_current[tm3+net_size] != 1) /*cell does not fire*/
            {
            control=0;
            for(tm4=0;tm4<net_size;++tm4)
                if(state_former[tm4+net_size] == 1) ++matrix[tm4][tm3];
            }
        }
    else /*cell should not fire*/
        {
        if(state_current[tm3+net_size] == 1) /*cell fires*/
            {
            control=0;
            for(tm4=0;tm4<net_size;++tm4)
                if(state_former[tm4+net_size] == 1) — matrix[tm4][tm3];
            }
        }
    }
if(control == 0) /*calculate what state_current is with the new matrix*/
    for(tm3=0;tm3<net_size;++tm3)
        {
        if(state_former[tm3]==1) val=1;
            else val=0;
        for(tm4=0;tm4<net_size;++tm4)
            val=val+state_former[tm4+net_size]*matrix[tm4][tm3];
        if(val>0) state_current[tm3+net_size]=1;
            else state_current[tm3+net_size]=0;
        }
    } while(control == 0);
change_values();
    }
  }
}
```

References

Anderson, J. A. 1977. Neural models with cognitive implications. *Basic Processes in Reading: Perception and Comprehension*, ed. by David LaBerge and S. Jay Samuels. Hillsdale, New Jersey: Erlbaum.

Christie, William M. 1991. A mathematical model of linguistic sequencing in neural networks. *Proceedings of the Fourteenth International Congress of Linguists: Berlin/GDR, August 10–August 15, 1987*, ed. by Werner Bahner, Joachim Schildt, and Dieter Viehweger. Berlin: Akademie-Verlag.

Deng, Li. 1992. Processing of acoustic signals in a cochlear model incorporating laterally coupled suppressive elements. *Neural Networks* 5.19–34.

Fang, Luyuan, William H. Wilson, and Tao Li. 1989. *Experiments on Signal Processing with Neural Networks*. International Joint Conference on Neural Networks, Washington, D.C..

Hampshire, J. B. II, and Alex H. Waibel. 1989. A novel objective function for improved phoneme recognition using time delay neural networks. *Proceedings of the International Joint Conference on Neural Networks* I.235–241.

Hopfield, John J. 1982. Neural networks and physical systems with emergent collective computational abilities. *Proceedings of the National Academy of Sciences of the USA* 79.2553–2558.

Reich, Peter A. 1969. The finiteness of natural language. *Language* 45.831–843.

Reiss, Michael, and John Taylor. 1991. Storing temporal sequences. *Neural Networks* 4.773–787.

Rumelhart, David E., and James L. McCleland. 1986. *Parallel Distributed Processing: Explorations in the Microstructure of Cognition*. Cambridge, Massachusetts: MIT Press.

About the author

William M. Christie is Dean of the College and Professor of Linguistics at Catawba College. He received his Ph. D. from Yale in 1973, writing his dissertation A **Stratificational View of Linguistic Change** *under the direction of Syd Lamb. He has also held teaching and administrative positions at the University of Arizona and at Furman and Wingate Universities. His research has concentrated on comparative and historical linguistics, especially diachronic theory, and on neural network modeling of syntactic systems.*

CHAPTER 3

From Reticula to Trees

A Computerizable Model of Transduction from Semology to Lexology

Earl M. Herrick

Texas A&M University – Kingsville

Stratificational linguists have usually concerned themselves with how the trace of an utterance is transduced from one stratal system to another, rather than with how the impulses of a trace are related to one another while they are passing through a stratal system and its levels. (The relationships which exist among the impulses that constitute a trace while those impulses are passing through a certain level of a certain stratal system will be referred to here as the "intra-level trace organization" or "ILTO" of those impulses.)

The only relationships among the impulses of a trace which stratification-alists usually show are those which can be shown by ORDERED AND and UNOR-DERED AND nodes in the tactics. These AND nodes suffice to show the ILTOs of some levels within some stratal systems. If, while they are passing through a certain level, the impulses of a trace are organized as a string or as a rectangular matrix with significant differences along either one or two dimensions, the ILTO of that level can be shown by ORDERED ANDs or by both ORDERED ANDs and UNORDERED ANDs in the tactics, in the ways shown in Figure 1. However, strings and matrices such as these are unable to describe the ILTOs of many levels of language. Several stratificationalists (e.g. Taber [1966; 1968] for semology, Lockwood [1976] for phonology, and Herrick [1976; 1984; 1987] for grapho-nomy) have described levels of language which have ILTOs that cannot be adequately shown by ORDERED ANDs and UNORDERED ANDs. Additional notation-al devices **within** such levels will therefore be needed. Moreover, the tactics of a stratal system can show only the ILTO of its emic level. Other notational devices will be needed for showing the ILTOs of its other levels.

The present paper offers a notation which can show the ILTOs of all the levels within the semological and lexological stratal systems. In a paper which H. A. Gleason, Jr. delivered at the 1964 meeting of the Georgetown University Round Table, on which occasion he and Sydney M. Lamb first presented stratificational theory to the linguistic community at large, he suggested that the characteristic organization of a language within its semology should be a reticulum and that the characteristic organization of a language within its lexology should be a tree.[1] (A tree can, of course, be mathematically regarded as a simplification of a reticulum.) The present paper will therefore describe a notation for reticula which can show the ILTOs of all the levels within semologies, and which can also serve as a notation for trees and can thereby show the ILTOs of all the levels within lexologies; it will also describe a computerizable model of this system of notation.

Taber (1966; 1968) was the first to show what the details of a semological reticulum might look like,[2] and Herrick (1987), in the process of describing the ILTO of a graphonomy, showed how Taber's reticulum can be modified so that it can be modeled on a computer. For those who may be interested, Figures 2 and 3 show how the notations for two relationships were changed when Taber's original reticulum (in Taber 1966, Figure 16, page 94) was successively converted into the reticula shown in Figures 6, 7, and 8 of Herrick 1987.[3] (In all of these reticula, referentials are shown by circles or by dashed lines which constitute logical extensions of circles, relationals are shown by rectangles, and valences are shown by lines. The referentials, relationals, and valences of a reticulum may be collectively called its "elements".) Figure 2 shows the notational changes that were made for one relationship, and Figure 3 shows the notational

---

1. In non-mathematical terms, a reticulum is a network. Gleason originally (1964) used the term "network", but he later said (Gleason 1969) that he preferred the term "reticulum" because "network" was being used for describing the realizations between strata.

2. Taber's work was originally published in 1966. In 1968, when it was reprinted, he added a preface saying that he did not have time to revise it, but describing some notational changes that he would have made if he had had time to do so.

3. The notations shown in Figures 2 and 3 are successive attempts to achieve a notation which is both explicit (in that all relationships are stated by labels, and no referentials or classes of referentials are implicitly assumed to stand in certain relationships to one another) and linear (in that such labels are never arranged alongside one another).

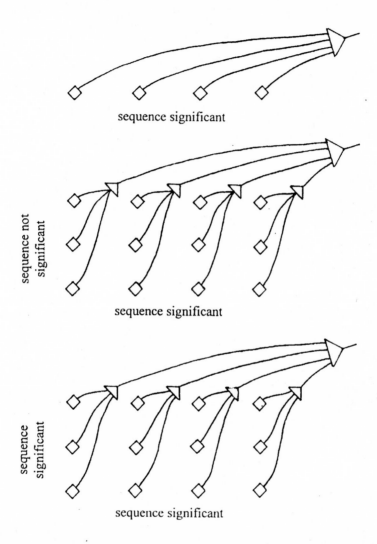

Figure 1.   *Intra-level organizations that can be described by* AND *nodes alone*

changes that were made for another relationship, together with a further change that is made in Figure 4 of the present paper. Changes like these, when applied to this 1966 reticulum of Taber's (and omitting his "story line"), produce the reticulum in Figure 4.

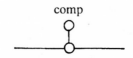

(a) Notation used in Taber 1966.

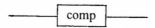

*(b) Notation used in Herrick 1977, figure 6, making
a change suggested by Taber 1968.*

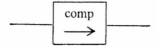

(c) Notation used in Herrick 1987, figure 7.

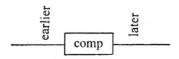

*(d) Notation used in Herrick 1987, figure 8, and
also used in the present paper.*

comp = completed action

Figure 2.   *Four notations that have been used for one relationship*

Herrick's 1987 paper, which was concerned with developing a stratificational model for graphonomies, introduced a notation for linguistic reticula which
differed in another way from Taber's notation. When analyzing the shapes of
characters in the graphonomy, some relationals were found which had to have
more than two valences. Such a relational is illustrated in Figure 5.

(a) Notation used in Taber 1966 and in Herrick 1987, figure 6.

(b) Notation used in Herrick 1987, figures 7 and 8.

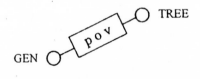

(c) Notation used in the present paper, figure 4.

GEN = gen = viewed generically
p o v = point of view

Figure 3.   *Two notations that have been used for another relationship, and a third notation for the same*

The linguistic data which this relational describes is the written character shown in 5(a). This character was described in Herrick 1987 (Figure 9) by a reticulum with valences that name all the places around the character's edge where it can have a significantly different shape; a part of this reticulum is shown in 5(b). An equivalent description of this character, using symbols like those in Figure 4 of the present paper, is shown in 5(c).

Once it is assumed that a relational can relate to more than two referentials, a new hypothesis for semological analysis becomes available. If a reticulum

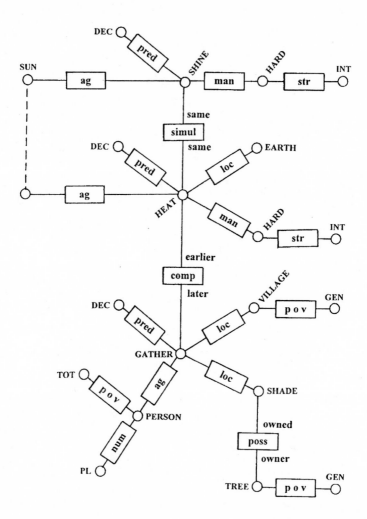

Figure 4.   (continued on next page)

contains a group of relationals with unlabeled valences, all of which are simultaneously joined to a referential, that group of relationals can be replaced by a
single relational which has valences with the same labels as the former relationals and which has one more valence, labeled "stem", that is joined to the

---

abbreviated symbols

ag = agent of event	PL = plural
comp = completed action	poss = possession
DEC = declarative	p o v = point of view
GEN = viewed generically	pred = predicate
INT = intensified	same = equal valences
loc = location	simul = simultaneous action
man = manner	str = strength
num = number	TOT = viewed in its totality

*the dashed line represents a circle which is extended so that
many lines of the diagram can conveniently reach it*

Figure 4.   *Reticulum with notation derived in the ways illustrated in Figures 2 and 3*

referential to which the former relationals were joined. Such a replacement is illustrated in Figure 6. The use of multi-valent relationals may also simplify the semotactics and the lexotactics, because the referentials that can be joined to the valence "stem" of a certain multi-valent relational may form a class to which those tactics will want to refer.

The reticulum in Figure 7 illustrates the use of multi-valent relationals. It is the same as the reticulum in Figure 4, except that it contains the two multi-valent relationals "event" and "entity", which have valences that replace several of the relationals in Figure 4. (There are, of course, some relationals, such as "posses-sion" and the temporal relationals "simultaneous" and "completed event", which by their natures can be joined to only two referentials and therefore can have only two valences.) A reticulum like that in Figure 7 should be able to show the ILTOs of all levels within the semologies of languages.

The shaped symbols used in Figure 7 are unsuitable for manipulation by a computer program, but a notation suitable for that purpose was introduced in Herrick 1987. There, all symbols were written as character strings of the same, fixed length, bracketed by slant lines and preceded by letters. Relationals were

d

(a) The linguistic data.

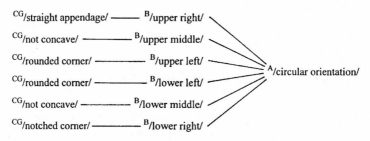

(b) Description of the data from Herrick 1987, figure 9.

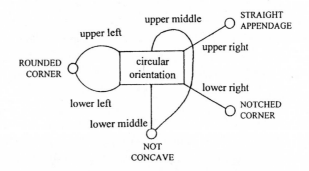

(c) Description like that used in figure 7 of the present paper.

Figure 5.   *A character of written language and two descriptions of it*

called "arachnes" and were written with "A";[4] valences were called "brachions" and were written with "B";[5] referentials were called by names that depended on the level of the language which they described, and they were written with appropriate letters. In an abstract discussion such as the present paper, referentials can

---

4. This term is based on the Greek word meaning 'spider'.

5. This term is based on the Greek word meaning 'arm'.

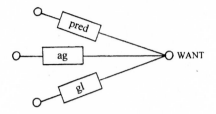

(a) With several relationals.

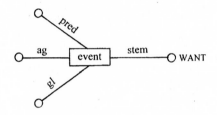

(b) With one relational and several valences.

Figure 6.   *Two equivalent reticula with different uses of relationals and valences*

all be called "hapses" and can be written with the letter "H".[6] Using this notation, the upper part of Figure 7 can be rewritten in the way shown in Figure 8.

A reticulum like the one in Figure 8 can be modeled on a computer by storing its symbols in a computerized data base organized in a way that represents the reticulum's own organization. In order to model a transduction to another linguistic level, that reticulum can be rewritten as another reticulum which has its symbols stored in another computerized data base organized in a way that represents the organization of that other linguistic level.

---

6. This term is based on the Greek word meaning 'junction'; its singular is "hapsis". This term may prove useful in theoretical discussions of abstract linguistic structures, or it can be used when only a partial analysis has been made for some linguistic material and the proper level for a referential is not yet certain. In an actual linguistic description a term and a symbol referring to the linguistic level on which the referential occurs will ordinarily be used instead.

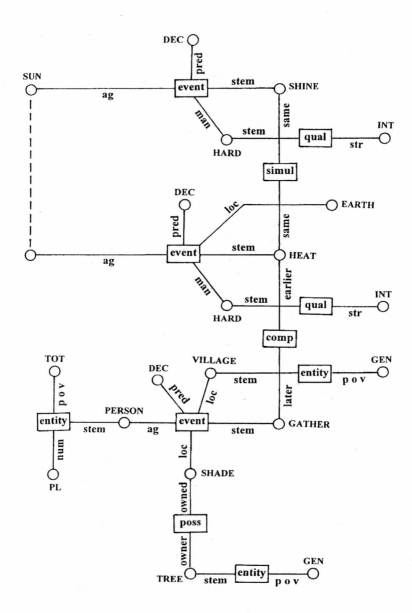

Figure 7.   (continued on next page)

---

abbreviated symbols

ag = agent of event	poss = possession
comp = completed action	p o v = point of view
DEC = declarative	pred = predicate
GEN = viewed generically	qual = quality
INT = intensified	same = equal valences
loc = location	simul = simultaneous action
man = manner	str = strength
num = number	TOT = viewed in its totality
PL = plural	

*the dashed line represents a circle which is extended so that
many lines of the diagram can conveniently reach it*

Figure 7.   *Reticulum with multi-valent relationals*

A reticulum like that in Figure 8 can model an ILTO within a semology; but, as Gleason (1964) has suggested, an ILTO within a lexology must be modeled by a tree. Because reticula and trees are mathematically similar, it should be possible to use many of the same relationals for describing both of them. In mathematical terms, a reticulum and a tree are both graphs, i.e. they are mathematical structures consisting only of points connected by lines. Both of these kinds of graphs are illustrated in Figure 9. A reticulum is a cyclic graph: if it contains a path which starts at one point and ends at another point and runs along certain lines, then it also contains another path which starts at the second point and ends at the first point and does not run along any of the lines that the first path ran along. A tree is an acyclic graph: if it contains a path which starts at one point and ends at another point and runs along certain lines, then the only path within it which starts at the second point and ends at the first point runs along exactly the same lines as the first path ran along.

During some step of the downward transduction of an utterance, presumably when the lowest level of the semology is realized by the highest level of the lexology, the ILTO of the utterance changes from a reticulum to a tree. Before this can happen, there must be defined within the utterance a "story line", which is a string of connected elements that will stay together and will eventually become the sequence in which the utterance is spoken or written. Just how this "story line" is defined is beyond the scope of the present paper. But, as the

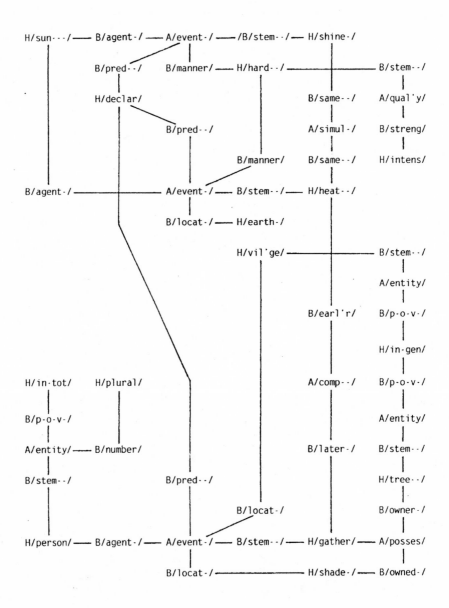

Figure 8.   (continued on next page)

abbreviated symbols

A/comp‑‑/ = completed action
A/qual'y/ = quality
A/simul‑/ = simultaneous action
A/posses/ = possession
B/earl'r/ = earlier
B/locat‑/ = location
B/pred‑‑/ = predicate
B/p‑o‑v‑/ = point of view

B/same‑‑/ = equal valences
B/streng/ = strength
H/declar/ = declarative
H/intens/ = intensified
H/in‑gen/ = viewed generically
H/in‑tot/ = viewed in its totality
H/vil'ge/ = village

Figure 8.   *Part of the same reticulum, rewritten with a notation using computerizable
symbols*

*(a) A reticulum
(a cyclic graph).*

*(b) A tree
(an acyclic graph).*

Figure 9.   *Examples of cyclic and acyclic graphs*

lowest level having a reticulum as its ILTO is realized by the highest level having
a tree as its ILTO, the elements which make up the "story line" will stay connected, and enough other connections within the reticulum will be broken so that the
cyclic reticulum will become an acyclic tree. These breaks will be made by
choosing appropriate referentials, making as many copies of each as there are
valences joined to it, and then joining a separate copy of it to each of those
valences. The same relationals and valences will show the ILTOs of these two
levels, and similar relationals can be used for showing the ILTOs of the other,
lower levels of the lexology.[7]

---

7. A semological reticulum and the lexological tree which realizes it are shown and discussed in
Herrick (1994), which should be read along with the present paper.

References

Gleason, H. A., Jr. 1964. The organization of language: a stratificational view. *Georgetown University Round Table* 15: 75–95.

Gleason, H. A., Jr. 1969. Contrastive analysis in discourse structure. *Georgetown University Round Table* 19:39–63.

Herrick, Earl M. 1976. Orderedness and 'AND' nodes. *LACUS Forum* 2: 200–210.

Herrick, Earl M. 1984. On the nature of the interfacial strata. *LACUS Forum* 10: 96–107.

Herrick, Earl M. 1987. A computerized model of transduction. *LACUS Forum* 13: 344–409.

Herrick, Earl M. 1994. Turning linguistic reticula into linguistic trees. *LACUS Forum* 20: 440–450.

Lockwood, David G. 1976. Alternatives to matrix models in phonetics and phonology. *LACUS Forum* 2: 141–153.

Taber, Charles R. 1966. *The Structure of Sango Narrative*. (Hartford Studies in Linguistics, 17.) Hartford, Connecticut: Hartford Seminary Foundation.

Taber, Charles R. 1968. Reprinting of Taber 1966, with a new preface.

About the author

Earl M. Herrick has taught at Texas A & M University – Kingsville since 1972. He believes he may be the only stratificationalist of his generation who never took a course from Syd Lamb. He wrote his 1966 M.A. thesis under H. A. Gleason at the Hartford Seminary, and then completed his doctorate under David Lockwood at Michigan State University in 1977. While at Hartford he first met Lamb at meetings of the Yale Linguistics Club. He has sometimes drawn diagrams for Lamb's publications and asked his advice on theory. His own stratificational work, however, still shows Gleasonian influences, such as a preference for weak tactics and strong realizations.

CHAPTER 4

Neurological Evidence for the Existence of an Autonomous Lexicon

Tim Pulju

Providence University (Taiwan)

1. Introduction

In the summer of 1965, Peter Reich pointed out to Sydney Lamb that Lamb's relational networks, which had been developed purely on the basis of linguistic evidence, were strikingly similar to neural networks (Lamb, personal communication). A few years later, John White, in his article "Language and the brain", which encapsulated Lamb's views as of 1969, emphasized the neurological parallels to stratificational linguistics as the most interesting and significant aspect of the theory. One example of the subsequent influence of neurology on the theory is the adoption by Lamb and others of a more delicate notation of one-way, rather than two-way, lines and nodes, a preference partly motivated by the fact that nerve impulses flow only one way through neurons (Lamb, personal communication).

Cognitive linguistics, then, has long been seen as a theory closely tied to neurology. It is therefore surprising to discover how little work relating to contemporary neurolinguistics has been done in the stratificational school. There are notable exceptions, of course, including Michel Paradis's excellent work on bilingualism (1977, 1978, 1979, 1980) and several papers by Marc Schnitzer (1978, 1982) and by Ilah Fleming (1967, 1982). Moreover, a cognitively-minded relational network linguist could justly claim that all of his work is in some sense neurolinguistic, for the reasons mentioned in the preceding paragraph. However, the term neurolinguistics, as commonly used, designates the science which attempts to correlate specific, usually macro-anatomical features of the brain with aspects of linguistic structure and function, often paying particular attention to the evidence of aphasias. It is this macro- rather than micro-anatomical approach to language and the brain which has been comparatively neglected in cognitive linguistics.

In this paper, I will apply neurolinguistic evidence to the problem of the lexicon in cognitive linguistics, debate regarding which has thus far been uninformed by such evidence. My primary purpose is to enrich this debate over the existence and nature of a lexicon in some sense separate from grammar. A secondary purpose is to provide an example of how neurolinguistics can and should contribute to cognitive linguistic modeling, an example which I hope will provoke fruitful use of neurolinguistic data in the future.

2.   The Lexicon in Cognitive-Stratificational Linguistics

The classic view of the lexicon in stratificational grammar is that presented by Sullivan's 1977 paper "A stratificational view of the lexicon", which integrates "arguments and discussion scattered throughout the [stratificational] literature" (11). Much of the article consists of criticism of then-dominant transformational theories about the lexicon; hence, much of the description of the stratificational "lexicon" is designed to show that the stratificational model is different from and superior to the transformational. This point is important to a proper understanding of exactly what Sullivan says about the lexicon, and we will return to it after a brief summary of his position.

The lexicon, in Sullivan's view, is simply "the realizational portion of linguistic structure" (20). "In fact, 'the lexicon' is not 'the' lexicon at all. It is several related lexicons" (21). Sullivan quotes (12) with approbation Gleason's statement that "it is highly doubtful that a dictionary in anything like the familiar form can be given any reasonable theoretic base. Language is simply not organized in such a way that all the features we expect in a dictionary can be brought together in any one place" (Gleason 1968: 58). And, as Sullivan points out, "the [generative] lexicon parallels what is developed in more normal lexicography" (12), making it theoretically baseless.

The standard stratificational viewpoint, then, seems to be that there is no such thing in language as a lexicon. But this is only a fair statement of the stratificational view if, by lexicon, we mean the autonomous lexicon of generative linguistics, full of a jumble of semantic, syntactic, morphological, and phonological data for each entry. The model leaves room for the existence of a lexicon in a more restricted sense, a glossary of sorts in which words are connected with meanings. In fact, Sullivan himself specifies what such a glossary-lexicon could look like, although he never refers to it as a lexicon *per se*, but rather as the portion of the network which serves as the source for lexical items such as names. This portion of the network is at the interface between the cognitive level, where meanings are diffusely stored in interconnections, and the sememic level, where single lines connected to various diffusely represented meanings enter into the linguistic system for eventual realization as lexemes (16). Fifteen years later, we can see that each of these individual network chunks linking a sememe to a complex conceptual structure could be characterized as a nection, the type of element which Lamb now considers the basic building block of relational networks.

Contrary to first impressions, then, there could be a certain type of lexicon in a stratificational model. Moreover, unlike the stratificational counterpart to the generative model, which is inextricably tangled in with the linguistic system as a whole, this differently-defined lexicon could be more easily regarded as a quasi-autonomous unit, although ultimately the entire network is interconnected, and any boundaries we hypothesize will be arbitrary.

Such are the outlines of Sullivan's model. But although it is the definitive stratificational statement on the lexicon, it is not the only one. Christie outlines a very different model in a paper published in December 1978, which, incidentally, makes no reference to Sullivan's paper of August 1977. In Christie's model, the lexicon is separated out from the grammar, which operates in terms of categories. Moreover, lexicon and grammar interface not at the top of the stratal system, above the semology, but at the bottom of the morphological stratum, below the morphotactics. For the most part, the particular arguments which Christie advances in favor of his model are not relevant to this paper, since even though he does bring in considerations of neuron availability, we are concerned here with localized function in macro-anatomically defined chunks of cortex rather than micro-neurological instantiation of networks. However, he does make the noteworthy claim (124) that his model

> explains the very common, intuitively valid, but otherwise unexplained
> traditional tripartite division of language descriptions into phonology, grammar,
> and lexis (the last including semantics). So many grammars have been written

in this fashion, and the results have seemed so natural, that it would indeed be
strange if that arrangement had no theoretical validity whatever.

We might add to this the statement that in cognitive linguistics, it would indeed
be strange if theoretically valid work had no neurological validity whatever.

A final cognitive-stratificational approach to the lexicon which deserves our
attention is that developed by Lamb over the past several years, in which the
centrality of the lexicon in language has been emphasized. My exposure to this
approach has been primarily through coursework and informal discussion with
Lamb; one written source which incorporates Lamb's current ideas is Lamb
(1992a). These ideas were already developing in 1984 when Lamb gave his
LACUS presidential address (Lamb 1985) which argued in favor of regarding the
vertical, realizational patterns of language as more primary than horizontal, tactic
structures. Lamb now argues that in fact, tactic patterns are illusory, and that
language consists of a collection of vertical elements, essentially Saussurean
signs with an elaborated structure intermediate between meaning and phonetics.
Since, as we have seen, the realizational portion of the linguistic system corresponds to the lexicon, broadly defined, Lamb's approach claims that a language
consists essentially of a lexicon, albeit a greatly expanded one including multitu-
dinous separate words, phrases, sentences, and larger texts. Such a model
emphasizes the extraordinary human capacity for remembering specific information over the narrowly defined syntactic creative ability central to generative
grammar.

Lamb's theory makes the lexicon autonomous by eliminating the horizontal
aspects of language, unlike Christie's theory, which simply separates the two.
Both contrast with the standard stratificational view which states that there is no
autonomous lexicon, although this statement is not necessarily true for all
possible definitions of the lexicon. The neurological evidence to which we will
now turn is not such as to strongly support any one of these three theories over
the others, but it does provide evidence in favor of the existence of a particular
relatively autonomous lexicon localizable in the brain.

3.   Object Naming and the Inferior Parietal Lobe

In 1964, at a Georgetown University conference also attended by H. A. Gleason,
Sydney Lamb, and Michael Halliday, neurologist Norman Geschwind presented

a paper detailing the neurological mechanisms underlying object naming. Although systemic linguistics thereafter had considerable positive influence on the development of stratificational grammar, neurolinguistics, unfortunately, did not. Almost thirty years later, I hope that cognitive linguistics can start to meet Geschwind's challenge to answer the question, "To what extent does the theory tie in with other, non-linguistic information, for example, the anatomical aspects of language?" (157)

Geschwind's paper was an attempt to provide linguists with some of the data needed to answer that question. Presentation of the theory of object naming is preceded by an explanation of the neuro-anatomical structures it involves. For simplicity's sake, the paper assumes the usual pattern of simple left hemisphere dominance for structural aspects of language. The pertinent structures within the dominant hemisphere are as follows (157–159, 165). 1) The limbic system, a phylogenetically and ontogenetically primitive area along the inner surface of the temporal lobe which controls motor and sensory responses connected with fear, anger, hunger, sexual arousal, and other functions essential for personal or species survival. 2) Three sensory regions of the cortex — visual, auditory, and somesthetic. 3) Three corresponding regions of association cortex, which in other primates principally connects the sensory cortex to the limbic system. 4) The inferior region of the parietal lobe, in particular the angular gyrus, which is an associative region connecting the three areas of sensory association cortex. Significantly, the inferior parietal region is exceptionally more highly developed in humans than in any other primates. Moreover, it develops late ontogenetically and may not be mature for four or more years after birth (165).

Geschwind postulates that object naming occurs in the area around the angular gyrus. Being able to associate a name with an object implies being able to relate an auditory signal, the spoken word, with the visual, tactile, and in many cases auditory information which are the essence of the word's meaning (163). Experiments show that not only can't a primate such as a monkey perform this word-naming task, it can't even relate two non-limbic stimuli to each other, since one sensory association cortex is not associated to another except via the inferior parietal lobe, which hardly exists in monkeys (162). Naturally, Geschwind does not cite ape-language projects conducted since 1964, but we can interpret their level of success as confirmation of his theory. Various great apes have shown ability to learn a sign language vocabulary of restricted size (Dwyer 1986: 235); this ability is unsurprising in primates whose angular gyri are more

developed than those of monkeys but much less developed than those of humans
(Geschwind 1964: 165).

Further evidence for Geschwind's theory comes from aphasic patients.
Large lesions in the angular gyrus result in voluble but not very communicative
speech. Speech is particularly deficient in object names while functors are more
commonly preserved. This is plainly a natural result of insult to the area where
contentive lexical items are stored. Speech remains voluble because the linguistic
form has not been damaged, only content substance (166).

Geschwind states clearly that his theory is not intended to explain the
learning and neurological storage of functors such as *if*. However, he hypothesizes that such words will involve very different neurological mechanisms (167–8).
We shall consider this conclusion, along with other implications of Geschwind's
paper, in the following section.

Geschwind's theory of object naming was only part of the overall neurological theory he advanced in the 1960s. This theory, in many ways a revival of the
ideas of Karl Wernicke and his followers, has become the basis for the standard
clinical classification of aphasias. The success of Geschwind's paradigm is
evidenced by its treatment in a recent neurolinguistics textbook (Caplan 1987:
67–78) and even more in the chapter on aphasias in a comprehensive modern
neurology text (Mayeux and Kandel 1991). Although much of his early work has
been superseded, of course, his fundamental theory of object naming as sketched
above remains well-supported and can obviously shed great light on the problem
of the lexicon in cognitive linguistics.

4.   The Lexicon Revisited

Geschwind's data support the existence of a quasi-autonomous lexicon, a lexicon
in which words are connected with their meanings, but not a lexicon in which
'entries' include syntactic, morphological, or phonological information. Such a
lexicon is clearly compatible with the restricted glossary-type lexicon described
by Sullivan as well as Christie's lexicon as distinct from grammar and phonology. Moreover, such a lexicon accords extremely well with Lamb's current model
of the individual linguistic system, as I will now show.

Figure 1 presents a network diagram similar to numerous diagrams which
Lamb has scrawled on various blackboards at Rice University over the past
several years. (I was unable to find a published example in Lamb's writings

which would serve the purposes of this paper as well as Figure 1; Figure 4–6 on page 66 of Lamb 1992 comes closest).

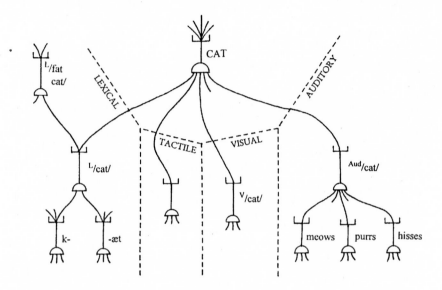

Figure 1.   *Connections of the lexical nection 'cat'*

In Figure 1, the single conceptual nection labeled 'cat' serves to connect a wide range of information from different modalities, both linguistic and sensory. The single nections at the 'top' of each individual modality themselves integrate numerous features within that modality. For example, sufficiently strong activation of *k-* and *-æt* would lead to activation of lexemic *cat*, while in the auditory system, recognition of purring and/or meowing would induce activation of the auditory nection 'cat'. Sufficiently strong activation of the lexical and/or auditory nections will of course activate the concept 'cat'. Furthermore, whenever a conceptual nection such as 'cat' is activated, it will in turn cause activation of connected nections in the sensory, linguistic, and also conceptual systems.

All of this is obvious to readers versed in cognitive linguistics. What should also now be obvious is the similarity of such diagrams to the neurolinguistic theory of object naming. In short, I contend that conceptual nections such as 'cat' in the diagram do correlate with actual neurological structures, and that these structures exist in or near the angular gyrus.

This is not to say that all of conceptual structure is physically to be found in the inferior parietal lobe. For example, it is difficult to conceive, linguistically, of a conceptual nection 'if' which would integrate visual, tactile, and other sensory information. Apart from phonological and graphemic characteristics, which are linguistic in nature, a functor such as IF does not have sensory characteristics. It would be strange, then, neurologically as well as linguistically, to locate the concept IF in a center which integrates linguistic and sensory information. The same is true for semantico-pragmatic items such as FOCUS or DEFINITENESS. Contentives other than nouns are more problematic. Geschwind's theory refers to object naming, yet verbs and adjectives (or events and qualities), for example, also have sensory connections. Are these nections located in the same general area as conceptual nections for objects? The data are unclear, and I will not speculate here on the answer. However, it does seem clear that the conceptual correlates of certain linguistic elements, such as the lexeme *if* or the sememe FOCUS, are not to be found in the lexicon which I have described.

5.   Conclusion

It is usually claimed that in stratificational/cognitive linguistics, there is no lexicon *per se*. But in fact, both cognitive linguistics and neurolinguistic theory lead us to conclude that there exists a quasi-autonomous lexicon relating certain contentive lexemes to their meanings. Here, cognitive linguistic theory is supported by the neurological evidence. For the future, it will be worthwhile to consider other aspects of cognitive linguistics in the light of neurolinguistics, as one way among many of refining and improving our linguistic theory.

References

Caplan, David. 1987. *Neurolinguistics and Linguistic Aphasiology*. New York: Cambridge University Press.

Christie, William M., Jr. 1978. Creativity, grammar, and the lexicon. *Forum Linguisticum* 3.118–125.

Dwyer, David. 1986. What are chimpanzees telling us about human language? *Lingua* 69.219–244.

Fleming, Ilah. 1967. Omission of the determined elements: a type of aphasic error. Paper read at the summer meeting of the Linguistic Society of America.

Fleming, Ilah. 1982. Some implications of aphasic data for linguistic modeling. Paper read at the Ninth LACUS Forum, Northwestern University.

Geschwind, Norman. 1964. The development of the brain and the evolution of language. *Report of the Fifteenth Annual (First International) Round Table Meeting on Linguistics and Language Studies,* ed. by C. I. J. M. Stuart, 155–169. Monograph Series on Languages and Linguistics, No. 17. Washington, D. C.: Georgetown University School of Languages and Linguistics.

Gleason, H. A. Jr. 1968. Contrastive analysis and discourse structure. *Contrastive Linguistics and its Pedagogical Implications,* ed. by James Alatis, 39–63. Monograph Series on Languages and Linguistics, No. 21,. Washington D. C.: Georgetown University School of Languages and Linguistics.

Lamb, Sydney M. 1985. Descriptive process. *The Eleventh LACUS Forum 1984,* ed. by Robert A. Hall, Jr., 5–20. Columbia, South Carolina: Hornbeam Press.

Lamb, Sydney M. 1992a. Outlines of a cognitive theory of language. Course packet for Rice University course LING 306, printed by Kinko's Copies, Houston, Texas.

Lamb, Sydney M. 1992b. Syntax: reality or illusion? *The Eighteenth LACUS Forum 1991,* ed. by Ruth Brend, 179–186. Lake Bluff, Illinois: LACUS.

Mayeux, Richard, and Eric Kandel. 1991. Disorders of language: the aphasias. *Principles of Neural Science,* 3rd edition, ed. by Eric R. Kandel, James H. Schwartz, and Thomas M. Jessell, Chapter 54. New York: Elsevier Science Publishing Co., Inc.

Paradis, Michel. 1977. The stratification of bilingualism. *The Third LACUS Forum 1976,* ed. by Robert J. DiPietro and Edward L. Blansitt, Jr., 237–247. Columbia, South Carolina: Hornbeam Press.

Paradis, Michel. 1978. Modèle neurolinguistique du bilinguisme. Unpublished dissertation, University of Montreal.

Paradis, Michel. 1979. Contributions of neurolinguistics to the theory of bilingualism. *Metatheory III: Applications of Linguistic Theory in the Human Sciences,* ed. by Robert K. Herbert, 180–211. East Lansing, Michigan: Department of Linguistics, Michigan State University.

Paradis, Michel. 1980. Language and thought in bilinguals. *The Sixth LACUS Forum 1979*, ed. by William C. McCormack and Herbert J. Izzo, 420–431. Columbia, South Carolina: Hornbeam Press.

Schnitzer, Mark L. 1978. Toward a neurolinguistic theory of language. *Brain and Language* 6.342–361.

Schnitzer, Mark L. 1982. The translational hierarchy of language. *Neural Models of Language Processes*, ed. by Michael A. Arbib, David Caplan, and John C. Marshall, 237–270. New York: Academic Press, pp. 237–270.

Sullivan, William J. 1977. A stratificational view of the lexicon. *Language Sciences* 46.11–22.

White, John. 1969. Language and the brain. *Yale Alumni Magazine*, December, 47–51.

About the author

Tim Pulju is presently Assistant Professor of Linguistics at Providence University, in Taiwan. He earned his Ph.D. at Rice University in 1995. His dissertation **Problems in the Reconstruction of Indo-European Stop Consonants** *was written under Syd Lamb's direction. Earlier, he received a B.A. in linguistics at Michigan State University, where he studied cognitive-stratificational linguistics under David Lockwood and Tagmemic linguistics under Ruth Brend. He continued to pursue his interest in the former with Lamb at Rice. His primary research interests are Indo-European studies and cognitive linguistics.*

CHAPTER 5

Luminous Loci in Lex-Eco-Memory

Toward a Pragmo-Ecological Resolution of the Metaphysical Debate Concerning the Reality or Fictitiousness of Words

Adam Makkai

University of Illinois at Chicago

1. Bloomfield's Warning

Toward the end of his book *Language* (1933), Bloomfield warns the reader saying that a truly scientific linguistics will remain impossible as long as massive amounts of data are not far more easily manageable than possible at present. We have to remember that this 'present' was the year 1933 when Hitler came to power in Germany and when computers were a dream at best in the minds of some advanced thinkers. The 1940s and the end of World War II, however, did usher computers into modern life, and just half a century after Pearl Harbor the MacIntosh and the IBM-compatible PC have become almost universally available in the industrialized countries. If one considers the birth of "theoretical linguistics" in the modern sense to coincide with Chomsky's publication of *Syntactic Structures* (1957) when computers were large and relatively slow, unwieldy devices that required punched cards being wheeled from room to room in clumsy carriages, one must agree that this kind of theoretical linguistics still had its roots in the dark ages.

Yet there is ample evidence that Chomsky was actually influenced by the computer (see Carr 1958 quoted in Maher 1980), although in later years he spared no effort denying this fact. The computer, even in its early, unwieldy form, nevertheless did offer a reasonable starting chance for building larger data bases, but linguists paid more attention to syntax than to lexical and morphological data bases which, compared to today's storage capacity, were rather limited in size and complexity.

We should not be surprised, therefore, that this early kind of syntactic theorizing required a large number of complex rules. Had alternative phrase structures, clause and sentence types been available in lexicalized form within a rapidly accessible and appropriately ample data base, fewer and simpler syntactic rules could have accounted for most of what occurs in twentieth century written and spoken English whether in the United States or in various countries of the Commonwealth.

As the noted journalist and attorney George Egry of Toronto — now residing in Budapest — remarked: "The tragedy of linguistics is that it got computerized **before the computer**" (Personal Communication).

2. "Taxonomy" as a Dirty Word

Chomsky considered it important not to be embarrassed by facts and data and so he spared no effort to denigrate classical linguistics as a "taxonomical enterprise" which had become outmoded and was therefore not worthy of the rank of scientific investigation. Yet in the meantime more and better small computers were created by the industry at a rapid rate.

In the late 1970s Oxford University Press took the decision to computerize the OED and a serious search for a university campus that had the right equipment with an unusually large data base began in earnest. For a variety of technical and economic reasons the choice fell neither on an American nor on a British university, but on the relatively-little-heard-of University of Waterloo in Ontario, Canada, about 90 miles from Toronto. The work was completed in 1989. The OED, with its nearly 500,000 entries is now available on one single compact disk; the purchase price at the time of this writing is $800 (US). A CD ROM drive needs to be attached to any IBM-compatible PC, and what was once a matter of owning several hundred pounds of large printed volumes, or the condensed version only legible with a powerful magnifying glass, both versions typically housed in libraries or in departmental seminar rooms, has become a simple search procedure in a data-base on the screen of one's private computer at home.

It would make sense, I think, that "taxonomy" should no longer be considered a dirty word, after all the sweat and fatigue factor has been elegantly removed from the linguist's problems in handling large masses of data.

But old habits and prejudices obviously die hard, and so the possibilities offered by the truly amazing progress made by data management systems still has not penetrated the consciousness of most linguists, especially those who still consider syntax to be the most important area of linguistic research.

3. How Many Words does Humankind Possess?

This question would have been a meaningless one just a few decades ago, but today it can be calculated — if not exactly, at least in terms of approximate order of magnitude.

Let us believe the estimate in the *Ethnologue* (Grimes, 1992) that there are 5,103 known languages on planet Earth, considering both the living and the extinct ones as of the year 2000. Let us further suppose that this number is slightly inflated due to the difficulties that arise in determining what is a dialect and what is a language, and let us further, for the sake of simplicity, round this number off to 5,000.

Certainly not all languages on Earth have as many words as English, which is one of the lexically richest tongues of humanity replete with Latinate-Romance, Greek, Scandinavian, Oriental and other loan words alongside its native Anglo-Saxon vocabulary. Nor is the number of entries in the OED exactly half a million, but let us be maximalistic for the purposes of this brief exercise in calculation and, in order to make it a bit easier and in order to err on the side of more work rather than less, let us imagine that the 5,000 languages on planet Earth have half a million words each. That would mean that we are confronted with a universal word stock of $5,000 \times 500,000 = 2,500,000,000$ that is two billion five hundred million (or twenty five hundred million) words, which is certainly a very large number, but still a relatively small one in astronomical terms or in comparison to the number of neurons in the average human brain.

Since an average modern-day CD can contain half a million entry words with all their required definitions and examples of first occurrence, etc., it follows that the 2.5 billion words of all of the world's languages together with all required definitions would fit on 5000 CDs. Now it so happens that an average CD weighs no more than 1.5 ounces, or in metric measurement, roughly

3 dekagrams. Five thousand CDs, therefore, would weigh $5000 \times 3 = 15,000$ dekagrams or 150 kilograms, which is roughly 330 pounds, the weight of about 5 average suitcases for air travel. (Recent international air travel regulations allow two 70–pound suitcases per person.) 4.7 70–pound briefcases, therefore, could accommodate the electronic storage of all words in all of the languages of the world at 1994–95 levels of the state of the art.

If we further posit — as is reasonably expectable — that CDs in the future will be even more compressed, we can easily foresee a time when 2 million words (with all of their definitions and examples) could go on a single CD. The physical bulk of the required storage space could thereby be significantly diminished to maybe even as little as 75 kgs (165 pounds) or less.

But surely half a million words are too many to consider. The new edition of the *Shorter Oxford English Dictionary* (Brown 1993) contains 97,600 head-words explained in 500,000 definitions with 87,400 illustrative quotations amounting to a total length of 7,500,000 words presented in two volumes (3,776 pages). This means that there are far more words in the *New Shorter OED* than are found in the *Petit Larousse illustré* — a highly respected major dictionary representing one of the world's great literary languages.

So let us try again. Maybe there are really no more than 4,500 languages in the world and each individual language — on the average — has no more than 75,000 words. If we can accept this as a compromise estimate, we can calculate the number of words in the world at 337,500,000, that is, under four hundred million. If CDs become even more condensed than they are today, they might easily accommodate 3 million headwords with all definitions and examples, so that 3 languages would fit on one CD. Rounding it out to the nearest full figure, one hundred condensed CDs could then have all of the words of all of the world's languages on them and such a package would weigh no more than 300 dekagrams (3 kgs, or roughly six pounds). If to this we add the fact that a great many languages have far fewer words than does even such a reduced estimate, we would end up with a data base that was certainly unthinkably large in 1933, but whose management one century later, in the year 2033 would seem to fall well within the skills of a student in the first or second year of high school.

The National Textbook Company of Lincolnwood, Illinois — a suburb of Chicago — put on the market recently on a single CD, usable with a CD ROM attachment to any IBM-compatible PC, a 12 language computerized dictionary that has English, German, French, Italian, Spanish, Japanese, Chinese, Swedish, Norwegian, Polish, Finnish and Czech on one of its options; the average word-stock per language is around 60,000 words. Multiplying the twelve languages represented we reach $60,000 \times 12 = 720,000$ words, or less than three quarters of a million. Yet, as is commonly known, William Shakespeare's vocabulary was not over 35,000 words! If a person were to be able to retain 60,000 words in all of the 12 languages used by the NTC, such a person would have nearly twice Shakespeare's vocabulary in each of a dozen languages, totaling 720,000 words! Is there any person alive today who has this capacity?

4. Why has it been so Difficult to Define the "Word"?

The question is frequently debated by linguists: Just what is a word, really? Scholars do generally agree that whereas 'words' exist in the sense that this is the body of material from which lexicographers build their lexicons, and certain recurring combinations which they utilize in order to illustrate how a given grammatical system operates.

There is more or less general agreement among linguists and lexicographers alike that words are, nevertheless, not "material objects" of any kind, since any physical tangibility of words is strictly an illusion due to writing, printing, toy blocks with words on them, etc.

Since words do confusingly often overlap with "morphemes", "lexemes" and "syllables" in many languages, they are extremely elusive and hard to define. This is further complicated by the fact that different writing systems impose different visual limitations on the already multiply-complex morpheme-lexeme-syllable trichotomy of speech (think of the Sanskrit habit of writing several grammatical words as one graphic unit on the one hand, and of the Chinese habit of using 2, 3, 4 or more root characters to express a single complex lexeme, to which we must add compounding in most known tongues.)

People in general like to reify concepts — there is a certain ease of familiarity stemming from an instinctive natural Gestaltism we all share to varying extents. Just as I don't think of my dog as a bundle of neurons, calcium, haemoglobin, etc., and not even as just another animal of a certain kind, but specifically as "my pet that has a name", my life experience, my speaking and my reading and writing habits have molded me to be thinking of *table, chair, telephone, pen*, etc. as "English words" which I recognize in speech and writing and which I have no difficulty in translating into a number of languages I happen to know.

Let us be sincere and admit that, our religions and philosophical attitudes aside, we are really very materialistic in our general outlook about ourselves and the world in general. Permit me to use a simple example:

Everybody knows that in theory money is a fiction. A $10 bill is really only a piece of printed paper that you can light with a match and burn — I saw this done during the great hippie demonstrations of 1968 in Chicago. The youthful demonstrators burning the cash were trying to illustrate the very point that paper currency is only worth as much as you think of it. Yet the "reality" of "$10" is very powerfully seductive; I, for one, am quite unlikely to burn such a bill, because I know that in Hungary it is worth 2,230 Forints and that my relatives can buy enough bread and potatoes for that sum to feed a family of four for a week. The tangibility of my $10 is incidental; its real value lies in what it can do for me here in the US or abroad, and this action potential of the currency is rooted in our cumulative experience of it. In other words, the typical $10 bill enjoys a certain psychological reality in our culture and in our memory.

Let us consider a transaction between two friends carried out verbally on a Sunday afternoon, when the banks are closed, as a gentleman's agreement. We had an older bicycle I was willing to sell to my recently-arrived Korean neighbor. He had no cash on him, nor his checkbook, but he said *I'll pay you $20 tomorrow*. I knew the man and so I trusted him. It was a "done deal" as we say. He got the bike and I was assured that when he gave me my $20 Monday morning, I would have enough cash to put gasoline in my car without having to go to the cash station first, which is farther away. My neighbor's **words amounted to cash** in this instance, and my movements on the Monday morning that followed were materially influenced by my knowledge of having the $20 in my pocket. An immaterial word referring to a piece of printed paper, worthless in itself, has materially influenced my timing and the pattern of my locomotion in Chicago.

Trivial as this incident may seem, it serves as an example of why and how the word *money* has come to be associated in people's minds with some sort of "physical reality"; the reason, of course, is that money is **an enabling medium for action in human societies**.

But then my neighbor's promise to pay me was also something that enabled me to plan my moves that Monday morning. Could it be that words are, in a very real and deep sense, quite like money?

I believe that they are, because they "stand for something" and most of the numerous "somethings" we deal with — whether it is water, bread, milk, the elevator or the building I am in — **affect our senses in such a way that it is convenient to think of them as materially real objects and events**.

I am anxious to emphasize that "they appear" to us in such a way, since in Thomist theology and in Berkeley's solipsistic exaggeration thereof, a case could be made that water, bread, milk and houses with elevators in them are all essentially spiritual entities created by various agencies of God who can produce both "real", (i.e., tangible) objects, and abstract notions in people's heads.

I would, therefore, like to propose that any debate about the "physical" — as opposed to the "psychological" — reality of words can be seen as having been rendered old-fashioned, on the one hand, by today's powerful computer industry and, on the other, by what we have come to understand by the term CONSCIOUSNESS and ECOLOGY OF MIND in the sense of Capra (1991) and Bateson (1987).

It seems to have become less intriguing to speculate whether words are "nections in a huge conceptual network" as Lamb maintains (1990, 1992); "items" one can juggle in linear syntaxes as the advocates of TGG still seem to think, or identifiable as chunks of alphabetic material, as a naive beginning student might believe.

All of these views of "words" have residual elements of partial truths in them, while they do all stem from the obvious fact that people experience their words as entities that — much like money — enable them to do things in their respective social settings. Whereas it seems not to matter at all whether one thinks of a chair and a table as "only matter that evolved by itself with the aid of some human interference" or as "organic matter created by God" — both the spiritualist believer and the atheistic materialist must rely on what they leave out of their respective accounts: They fail to recognize the fact that **words are primarily "loci" in a "memory"**, that is **elements of consciousness**. And consciousness, although tied to the human brain in physiological terms, is ultimately not explicable in materialistic terms. Artificial intelligence will, in all probability, never be able to make a machine possess consciousness. Bombs may be called "smart" meaning that they are guided by a computer system which greatly increases their accuracy in finding the intended target — but they surely do not worry about the moral issues involved in being or not being dropped on a designated human population. Real human consciousness, on the other hand, is recognizable by the fact that it is linked to a **conscience**, that is, the ability to tell right from wrong. It is no coincidence that "conscience" and "consciousness" are etymologically related.

Let us, then, for the time being, agree with Lamb's model of "nections" and "networks" as a working hypothesis. The words in these are specific intersections of lines.

5.   Words as "Loci" in a "Memory" or Elements of Consciousness

Let us think it out a bit further what it would mean for linguistics in general and lexicography in particular, if we could realistically conceive of words as "loci in a memory", that is, "places" or "locations" in retained conscious daily awareness.

Our first major problem is that we have no clear, generally agreed upon concept of what "memory" really is. We can somehow manage artificial "memory" in our calculators and our PCs, but these are not humankind's live, real **memory** in the full psycho-social sense of that term. Real human, psycho-socially anchored memory is simultaneously **visual** — we can recall a friend's face even after decades of not seeing the person — **auditory** — we recognize noises, tunes, sounds and personal voices for years on end — **olfactory** — we retain the smells of baked bread, perfume, flowers, a burning haystack or rotting meat — **tactile, emotional-evaluative, social** and **personal**.

Artificial memories of the customary kind in PCs have nothing comparable in complexity, and no matter how advanced computers become in the future, I do not think any man-made object will ever be able to replace real, natural "human memory".[1]

The analogy of the high-speed PC with a large data-base is, therefore, not an entirely useless starting point in our attempt at understanding what a lexical data-base might look like, and the <delete> command on one's PC is a handy, albeit oversimplified, material analogy of the event of "forgetting" in human bio-social and individual reality.[2]

---

1. The age of the "talking dictionary", however, has arrived. Words are visually illustrated in color; they are pronounced either in American or in British English covering 83 topics, and are accompanied by 200 colored pictures involving 5,000 words in two kinds of pronunciation and tests [Borsódi, Mándi, Szabóné and Szendrö, 1994] — and this comes from Hungary, a relatively underdeveloped country!

2. The automatic "back-up files" that one's PC creates could, at the cost of stretching a point, be compared to "submerged memory" or "previously conscious memory gone unconscious" which then must be recalled by teasing a patient out of amnesia by a variety of methods used by medical doctors and psychologists. This is an important point that I must return to below in my discussion of the

6.   Straddling the Strenuous Stratal Stretch of "Words"

Is *hot dog* a word? Is *White House* a word? It all depends on whether I can write or not. In pronunciation they sound like single words. We say *hót=dòg* and *whíte=hòuse,* and this particular stress pattern plus the "open transition" symbolized as the /=/ sign (cf. Hockett 1958: 134), augmented by the unpredictable, idiomatic sense of the compounds as 'frankfurter in a bun' and 'American Presidential Residence' gives the nonspecialist public the folk-impression that they are dealing with "words"; after all a word is something that sounds a certain way and means something by standing for something that we know. Here the linguist has the upper hand over the lay-person, of course, as it can be convincingly demonstrated that with different stress patterns and a closed juncture /+/ transition, these show up as the literal constructs *hôt+dóg* and *whîte+hóuse,* respectively.

The lay notion that a word is a string of "letters" which are "pronounced in a certain way" carrying their own meaning and corresponding to one of the familiar "parts of speech" has a fair amount of socio-psychological reality supporting it, resting on the set of monomorphemic lexemes whose membership includes items such as *water, book, tree, sun, hand, drink, eat, yes, no, I, you, he, she, it, we, us, they, come, go, sit, walk, run,* etc., even allowing for the fact that both verbal and nominal uses can be seen to cohabit within most of these — *I hurt my left hand* vs. *hand me the sugar, I don't drink beer* vs. *she poured me a drink,* etc. In lay consciousness and lay terminology one speaks of "the noun *hand*" vs. "the verb *hand*" and so forth, and this is what enables educated nonlinguists to read or write a newspaper article, engage in commerce, to survive in a modern, literate society.

---

concept of the SEMEME in contrast to the LEXEME.
For as we will soon see, the notion of "words" is most meaningfully alive for all natural language users because of what must be characterized as their TRISTRATAL EXISTENCE.

Table 1. *Some Common Acronyms*
1.   *United Nations Educational Scientific and Cultural Organization,* or
     UNESCO   /yùwnéskow/
2.   *National Aeronautics and Space Administration,* or
     NASA   /næsə/
3.   *University of California at Los Angeles,* or
     UCLA   /yûw + siy + el + éy/
4.   *University of Illinois at Chicago,* or
     UIC   /yûw + ay + síy/
5.   *National Biscuit Company,* or
     NABISCO   /nəbískow/
6.   *North American Air Defense Command,* or
     NORADCOM   /nòʜrǽdkam/
7.   *Surface to Air Missile,* or
     SAM   /sæm/
8.   *People United to Save Humanity,* or
     PUSH   /puʃ/
9.   *National Organization of Women,* or
     NOW   /naw/
10. *Association on Smoking and Health,* or
     ASH   /æʃ/
11. *Separated Widowed or Divorced,* or
     SWORD   /soʜrd/
12. *Pfooi On Everything Tomorrow's Saturday,* or
     POETS   /powɪts/
13. *Mothers Against Drunk Driving,* or
     MADD   /mæd/
14. *Répondez s'il vous plait,* or
     RSVP   /âʜr + es + viy + píy/

The forms *White House* and *hot dog* are thought of as "compound words" or
"complex words" that may be pronounced without a pause between them and
which have a "specialized meaning". That such lay parlance is hardly satisfactory
needs no elaborate discussion for an audience of professional linguists; what
seems remarkable, however, is that such traditional, ill-defined lay notions and
the teaching based on them should still be responsible for far more people
learning English this way than by any other method, some valiant efforts of an
increasing number of better trained ESL experts notwithstanding.

Let us take a look at the forms in Table 1 in order to illustrate the notion of "word" as it affects the consciousness of literate laity, and what, in turn, we may say about them from the point of view of Pragmo-Ecological Grammar [PEG], my evolving view of languages and linguistic structures which is based, to a large extent, on Lambian stratificationalism:

Form (1) in Table 1 is recognized by more people in its acronym garb than in the original; indeed most people stammer and keep searching their memory when asked to provide the full form of UNESCO. This acronym form, pronounced /yuwnéskow/, amounts to a separate word containing three syllables. Trying to find the morphemes *un, uni-* and *co-, con-, com* in it might seem tempting to some, but will yield mixed results as the *un-, uni* part will be justifiable in view of the original full form, but not at all in the case of *co-.* If any one should seek the morpheme *esco-* in the acronym (as in such Latin forms as *senesco* 'I age,' *recrudesco* 'I bleed again' etc.) they will be disappointed: this is pure coincidence.

UNESCO will be perceived as one word consisting of one morpheme, whose meaning is the full form *United Nations Educational Scientific and Cultural Organization,* which may be further defined in a quasi-encyclopedic entry discussing where the organization's headquarters are, what it does, etc. The acronym form is also a single lexeme, essentially a noun, which can be the subject or direct object of a sentence or its indirect object as in *UNESCO has its headquarters in Paris, France, Many people admire UNESCO, The UN gave UNESCO a new budget.* The verbal use of *UNESCO* sounds contrived, although I heard it once as *They UNESCOed away all the money,* meaning probably 'spent it unwisely' or 'illegally distributed while ostensibly under the auspices of UNESCO'.

The full form, too, is a noun phrase, and can as such be the Subject or the Direct Object or Indirect Object of a sentence, but the full form takes a long time to pronounce and is, therefore, avoided in most speeches and documents. I think it is extremely unlikely that the full form should be verbalized, but you can try. This full form consists of seven words, sixteen morphemes, but is only one lexeme. The definition of *UNESCO,* the acronym, should really coincide with the dictionary definition of the spelled-out full form, but the full form may be used as the first definition of an acronym to which the second one is then added. In other words the acronym has two explanations: (a) the full form, and (b) the definition of the full form itself.

(2) *NASA,* although shorter, can be dissected in a similar way. Here we have a one-word acronym of high frequency but without any chance to see familiar morphemes in the acronym; the "meaning" of the acronym is the full spell-out which, in turn, amounts to five words, ten morphemes while being a simple noun phrase lexeme.

(3) *UCLA* is one of those acronyms whose full form is hardly ever spoken although, of course, it is the first spelling-sense of the acronym; it is seen infrequently as a return address on printed envelopes and other official documents. The spell-out contains eight morphemes and amounts to one lexeme.

(4) *UIC* used to contain a fourth letter C as its original name was "University of Illinois at Chicago Circle" but this fourth letter — as indeed the entire word *Circle* — was dropped after the campus was united with the University of Illinois Medical School in the early 1980s. The remaining five words of the full form contain six morphemes and amount to a single lexeme.

(5) The National Biscuit Company's acronym /nəbískow/ absorbs the initial syllables of the words of the original full form, not just each initial letter. The resultant three syllables *na-, bis-* and *co-* look quasimorphemic, but only *bis-* has any morphemic reality to it, and that too, only if we dare analyze *biscuit* in French, meaning 'baked twice'. *Co-,* as an abbreviation for *company* occurs frequently enough on stationery and invoices to be acceptable as an entity in itself, but is certainly not the same morpheme as in *coeducation, cohabitation,* etc., and its resemblance to the *-co* form of *UNESCO* is entirely accidental. The full form consisting of three words, then, has only four modern English morphemes in it, since *company* is only historically 'with' and 'bread' from the Latin *con-(m) panis.* The acronym rhymes with *UNESCO* by accident, contains also four syllables and amounts to one spoken word.

(6) *NORADCOM* mixes the syllabic principle with the letter principle as *nor-* is the first part of the full form with *-com* its ending, the *-ad-* in the middle is a case of letter acronymy. The full form's five words can be broken down into seven morphemes if we count *defense* as *defend + N,* otherwise only as six; it too, amounts to a monolexemic noun phrase. The acronym's four syllables reveal no morphemic link to any relevant etyma; the form *-ad-* has no connection to 'advertisement' or to 'opposite of subtract'; the form /kam/ (written *com-*) has developed a life of its own in Space English (Cf. Makkai 1972a) and refers to 'commander' as in *the CapCom says he is ready to land* 'the Capsule Commander says he is ready to land'. The acronym *NorAdCom* is a trisyllabic word; its first-

degree definition being the full form whose larger meaning also engulfs the acronym itself.

(7) The word *Sam* is, in most of its daily occurrences, the common nickname for *Samuel*. When realizing the military weapon *Surface to Air Missile,* this is a letter acronym of the ordinary kind with the notable exception that the resultant syllable also realizes a man's nickname, which may be mere coincidence or deliberate or semideliberate playing with words, inasmuch as the *Surface to Air Missile,* due to its shape, may be associated with the notion of "masculinity". Although this is pure conjecture on my part, the fact remains that we do not have missiles called *Jane, Sue, Suzie, Mary, Katie,* etc. Here the four words of the full form contain six morphemes (with *sur-* and *-face* being available elsewhere as in *preface*; the form *miss-* is also an element in *missive);* the entire entry is one lexeme. The acronym /sæm/ is one word, one syllable, one morpheme and two lexemes since /sæm/ is best described as the same MORPHEMIC SIGN that leads to two separate lexemes (which have their own separate meanings anyway). Certainly the "word" /sæm/ 'surface to air missile' looks and sounds identical to the word /sæm/ 'nickname for Samuel.'

(8) With *People United to Save Humanity*, or as it is commonly referred to, *Operation PUSH,* we enter the mysterious and intriguing world of PUNNING ACRONYMS (Cf. Makkai 1974 and amalgamated into the longer chapter 'Towards a Musical Linguistics' in Makkai 1993.)

The same is true of the other forms that follow: *ASH* for 'Association on Smoking and Health'; *SWORD* for a group in New York 'Separated, Widowed or Divorced'; the Chicago based half-serious, half-joking group name *POETS* for 'Pfooi on Everything Tomorrow Is Saturday'; *MAD(D)* for 'Mothers Against Drunk Driving' and finally *RSVP* for the adopted French *Répondez s'il vous plaît.*

The remarkable feature of these "punning acronyms" is that they can be thought of either as single words, as words that stand for the name of a larger organization expressed as several words, or as a word whose meaning is linked in associative human memory with the purpose and function of the organization that both the acronym form and the full form describe.

7. Conclusions

It would seem that concept of "words", hazy and hard to define though it may be, is far too deeply rooted in the normal, waking consciousness of successful nonlinguist users of the English language — including, incidentally, carefully selected jury members on whose judgment the decision of someone's innocence or guilt and, therefore, their life or death, may depend — for us to abandon it. Linguistics should help the public, not ridicule it.

What laity calls a "simple word" is probably a monomorphemic lexeme identifiable rather obviously with a major part of speech, as one is taught in traditional pedagogic grammars. What laity calls "the meaning of a simple word" is the semantically always-complex SEMEME that stands behind or "sponsors" a given lexeme. If such a sememe is a common one — e.g., the meaning of *father, mother, milk* or *sun,* native speakers are not consciously aware of the DEFINITIONAL MEANING of such a form, but they can, nevertheless, immediately "translate" such a form into another language they know, say German, and come up with *Vater, Mutter, Milch* or *Sonne.* If the word needed to express a fairly clear notion does not come to mind or is actually unknown, laity says "how shall I put it?" (the person has the notion but cannot find the word for it).

The opposite occurs when you confront a person with a pronounceable or printed form, i.e., a "word", that is unfamiliar to them. Laity says "I don't know that word. What does it mean?" It is an interesting experiment in this context to ask intelligent nonlinguists and nonlexicographers what a common word such as *dog* or *water* means. Since they never had the need to look up such a common word in an English-to-English defining dictionary, they will laugh and seem embarrassed; they might try to talk around the subject or draw a simple figure on a napkin — reactions vary from individual to individual. If, by contrast, you should ask an educated native speaker — for instance a college senior — as to what is meant by saying that *"atrabilious floccification renders pusillanimous sesquipedalians intransigent"* they will take it as a vocabulary expansion assignment, and after looking it up at home, translate it into normal English as "melancholy (or pessimistic) belittling of things makes cowardly windbags stubborn".

Such a translation will not "naturalize" the words *atrabilious, floccification, pusillanimous, sesquipedalian* and *intransigent* to the extent that *sun, father, mother* and *milk* are unforgettable native citizens of his/her memory; a sentence full of long Latinate words like the example above remains, in all likelihood, just what it is, i.e., an example of unfamiliar English words; a joke, or a discussion point in an elementary linguistics class in a tertiary institute. Students do also typically forget the translation into normal English a few weeks after the assignment was given; some, of course, remember it and use it to taunt their parents and neighbors with.

As a non-native speaker of English who knew Latin, French and German before learning English at the age of 21, I knew the word *intransigent* before learning its English quasi-equivalents, *stubborn, unyielding, uninfluenceable, petrified in one's views*, etc. This fact in itself illustrates the point, I think, that words are "real" in a pedagogical sense: I can go to my old notebook and actually count the words I wrote down starting with January 1, 1957 (the day I landed in the USA), 1958, 1959 etc., all the way to the present. Twenty-one years late in arriving in the English speaking world, I, too, have, nevertheless, lived through the experience of no longer needing the conscious definitions of the most common words; I, too, can immediately translate *father, mother, milk* and *sun* into my native Hungarian as *'apa', 'anya', 'tej'* and *'nap'* without having to think of how a good dictionary must define them. And, to be completely honest about it, I must admit that sometimes I forget the Latinate test sentence above. (I have it written down in a dossier called "Teaching Materials'.)

Words are real to the extent that they **light up in memory** like a dim, a medium-bright, a bright, or as an extremely sharp light. The sharper the light, the more focused it is and thus it illuminates no surrounding **semantic court** around it. Such a semantic court may be thought of as the area needed for the **conscious multi-word definition** of a dimly lit locus in memory, where the dim light illuminates a larger area.[3]

I find the notions of "dimness" and "brightness" as quite true to nature and, therefore, believable. The frequent, familiar and short words compare to the "sharply focused flashlight on the wall"; the longer, rarer and much less familiar words may be compared to the situation when the flashlight illuminates a large area on the wall, but you have to go closer and look several times before you know what is actually there. This "going nearer and inspecting again" is, in a way, like the act of looking up unfamiliar words in the dictionary. Chances are that when a formerly dim and hard-to-see spot on the "wall" becomes more familiar (e.g. the holder of the flashlight knows where the switch is) we have a situation which is analogous to word learning: an unfamiliar word becomes more

---

3. Think of old-fashioned boy scouts' flashlights with adjustable focus as another available, though imperfect analogy. The sharper the focus, the smaller the area on the wall you can illuminate; the larger the area you want to point the flashlight at, the dimmer the illumination on the wall

and more familiar and so the user no longer needs to think of the word's definition when using it in an actual sentence.

Stratificational grammarians can illustrate this phenomenon by drawing thinner or thicker lines between "concepts" and pronounceable chunks of speech; a thin or staggered line indicating "first experience with a word" or "lowest degree of familiarity" may be drawn for the items *atrabilious, floccification, pusillanimous, sesquipedalian* and *intransigent*; once this contrived sentence becomes established in someone's usage — to whatever extent — the lines connecting the "concepts" to the pronounceable portions may become solid and thicker.

Both the general public and colleagues of other persuasions we need to serve with our insights and ideas tend to shy away from "stratograms". I have actually heard people characterize these as, "macaroni", "spaghetti", "jungle-gym equipment", etc.

Instead of insisting on a not-very-popular notation system, our more important goal should be the explanation of the insight that **words are a matter of consciousness**, and consciousness can be vague and general or sharply focused. This is why I have chosen to introduce a number of acronyms above, which have the virtue of illustrating rather convincingly the open-endedness of one's vocabulary. Should a good dictionary of English include /yunéskow/ *qua* UNESCO, or should it only be listed in its full form? What about *Surface-to-air missile* versus /sæm/? And how about the *National Aeronautics and Space Administration* versus /næsə/?

There is in reality, of course, no perfect dictionary. We must settle for what researchers in subatomic physics call the "theory of bootstrapping". Capra (1991: 331–332) writes:

> ... throughout the history of science, there has been a feeling that the foundations of knowledge were shifting, or even crumbling. The current paradigm shift in science again evokes such a feeling, but this time it may be the last time; not because there won't be any more progress or any more changes, **but because there won't be any more foundations in the future**. We may not see it necessary in a future science to build our knowledge on firm foundations, and we may replace the metaphor of the building **by the metaphor of the network. Just as we see reality around us as a network of relationships**, our descriptions, too — our concepts, models and theories — will form **an interconnected network representing the observed phenomena**. In such a

network, there won't be anything primary or secondary, and there won't be any foundations.

The new metaphor of knowledge as a network with no firm foundations is extremely uncomfortable for scientists. It was explicitly stated by Geoffrey Chew thirty years ago in the so-called bootstrap theory of particles. According to the bootstrap theory, nature cannot be reduced to any fundamental entities, like fundamental building blocks of matter, but has to be understood entirely through self-consistency. **Things exist by virtue of their mutually existent relationships, and all of physics has to follow uniquely from the requirement that its components be consistent with one another and with themselves.** *(Emphases added.)*

Capra's fascinating summary of modern physics seems to be the crown witness for the defense where Stratificationalism is on trial by the profession of linguistics. One more quote from p. 332. seems to be in order:

The material universe is seen as a dynamic web of interrelated events. None of the properties of any part of this web is fundamental; they all follow from the properties of the other parts, and the overall consistency of their interrelatedness determines the structure of the entire web.

One of the most important lessons one can learn from modern physics is that the observer's consciousness cannot be left out of the account of the investigation of subatomic particles. How much more then, must this be true about the observation of Language! A dictionary or a grammar starts and ends with the consciousness of the observer; only the ability and/or willingness of the lexicographer in question can determine whether to include **both** the acronym /yunéskow/ and the full form *United Nations Educational Scientific and Cultural Organization*, or just one or the other. No dictionary can, therefore, ever be complete, but we can "bootstrap" our way from less complete to more complete, and from less sophisticated to more sophisticated dictionaries. The same obviously goes about our understanding of the nature of the concept of the "word".

In terms of finding a believable metaphor for consciousness I have thought of turning to light. I am aware, of course, that one's knowledge of the meaning of a "word" is not a matter of physical light, but as visible phenomena go, "light" is perhaps an acceptable, if imperfect, metaphor for "consciousness".

As the title of this paper suggests, then, words/lexemes can be thought of as **luminous loci in lex-eco-memory.** I do not know if this analogy will work for readers of this paper, but if it does, we may have come a step closer to resolving a seemingly endless metaphysical debate concerning the "reality" or "fictive status" of words, and that is the best one can hope for just before the end of the twentieth century. Bad as it has been, it was nevertheless the age when we seriously began thinking about thinking itself. I will end this paper by sounding a few words of caution about the computer and computerization in general.

Whereas throughout this discussion I have been using the computer as an analogy for "memory" and lexical data bases, we must never think that real human consciousness is like a man-made computer. A computer is, in reality, a lifeless object that is totally devoid of real consciousness. All a computer does is allow or disallow a flow of electricity to pass a certain stretch between points "a" and "b". These points and stretches were first wires, then they became transistors, and now they are microchips in various states of miniaturization.

What would it be like if all of mankind's various words, measurable in the abstract as ten, thirty, or seventy pounds of compact disks in a suitcase — as I have done above — were to be internationalized and bar-coded? I think it would be the end of human culture and civilization as we know it. It would be a kind of death through artificial intelligence.

Think of the bar-coded price-tags in a typical North American supermarket. The can of tomato soup or potato chips one buys does not carry a price tag on it readable by human eyes and comprehensible by human beings. If the price is not also written out in the traditional way on a sign on the shelf, one often only finds out at the cash register how much an item actually costs. And this is the beginning of a nefarious trend in the computerization of not only language but the general environment around us. If the word *tomato* is substituted for by a series of thinner and thicker vertical lines and the price of, say, 89 cents is also similarly coded, such an artificial coding system can spread all over the world and wipe out all the natural human words for 'tomato' and the local currency equivalent of "89 cents". I am not denying that it would be quite interesting in a sense to possess a language-neutral international inventory of human concepts that would be accessible to all natural lexicographers the world over. I did allude to the theoretical possibility of such a universal concept inventory more than twenty two years ago in my book on idioms (Makkai 1972b:181–184). The paradox we are up against is this: the registration and storage of our "words" which are, if you can agree with this view, points of luminosity in consciousness, can only be carried out by killing the life out of the words we so care to embalm and preserve, just as if they were little corpses littering a huge battlefield. The international bar-coded look-up for the entry *sun* would lead the user to a particular sequence of thick and thin lines with a serial number, say #7,777. By activating No. 7,777 in the central bar-coded concept inventory one could "call up the word" in any or all of the languages that participate in the universal index. If I type in #1 for English the word *sun* appears, if I type in #55 for Hungarian the word *nap* appears, and if I type in #22 for Russian I get *solnce.* The bar-coded inter-language thesaurus would be what Shaumyan's applicative-generative grammar could use for its genotype lexicon. The individual language codes would call up the phenotype "transformations" of the "universal concept". Such a system would break down in its unrefined, initial phases because different languages attach different **scopes of boundary** in terms of denotation and connotation to their individual lexemes, and the central bar-coded depository may or may not be sufficiently sensitized to such differences. Thus even though #7,777 in language #1 (English) "brings up" the word *sun,* it says nothing about what a child, a high school student, a graduate student, a professor of astronomy, or an astrologer mean by "sun". If the language should be Aztec, the system, if unrefined, would fail to notify the user if the concept "sun" was a deity in the culture at hand or not.

Mechanized lexical data bases, whether on a monolingual, a heteroglottic, or a universal basis, are not to be seen as substitutes for human consciousness, but merely as a possible convenience offered by a multipurpose machine, such as the computer. The computer's so-called "memory" is not real human memory: it is merely a shorthand device to illustrate on a material level what a corpse, or a "mummy" of a once-live point of consciousness looks like when it is turned into a fossil. But just as fossils have their use for the paleontologist, large, computerized data bases can be very useful for the lexicographer of real languages.

What is really alive in the human being is the consciousness of a word, which includes its basic, denotative meaning, its various connotative, emotive, subcultural and other possible meanings. The spoken word is still "alive" as it passes between speaker and hearer and causes direct human action based on common human understanding. The moment we write the word down, we are pinning a dead butterfly to a collector's panel, spraying it with some preservative and putting it under a layer of glass. As long as this is individual, live handwriting, the word is still slightly alive. In a visually anchored Chinese character even more so, although most of Chinese writing has become phonetic throughout the millennia. Once the word is printed, it is as dead as the color of lead. Once such dead letters are collected in a dictionary, you have a veritable necropolis — one funeral mound on top of another. Through the human ability of reading — really a sort of "white magic", if you think of it — a literate, educated human being is capable of attributing meaning to a visual sequence of lifeless black marks on a white surface and can give it his or her live voice. This is how it happens that actors memorize their lines in a play, performing their parts as if they were producing spontaneous, live human speech in a given dialogue in an actual scenario. The cultures of past epochs speak to us through the vast cemeteries of dead letters. Yet a live performance of *Hamlet,* by an undoubtedly "dead author", is one of the most intellectually and spiritually stimulating experiences that one can have.

Why have I made this detour into the cold, commercial world of bar-coded prices and the printed literature of the past? Because the "reality" or "illusory nature" of "words" is perhaps best illustrated from the points of view thus reached: first, that of outright arbitrariness and, second, that of "literary scholarship". In the world of business, where dollars and cents and the fluctuating value of shares can cause elation or panic, the reality of the words *buy!* and *sell!* (also illustrated by hand signals to overcome the shouting in crowded stock exchanges) is observable as **immediate action**. In the world of literary scholarship, history, etc., the career of a professional person may depend on whether a word written five hundred years ago is correctly or incorrectly interpreted. If someone could actually prove by inventing a time-machine tape-recorder whether Wolfgang von Goethe's last words were indeed *mehr Licht!* 'more light!', such a person would gain the fame and respect of Champollion, who deciphered the Rosetta Stone.

Words are both "real" and "unreal". They can be as "alive" as a hug and a kiss and the simple utterance *I love you!,* or as abstract and obtuse as the contrived *atrabilious floccification may render pusillanimous sesquipedalians intransigent.* (Words that are "alive" tend to be Anglo-Saxon monosyllables and words that are obtuse and abstract tend to be Graeco-Latin polysyllables.) At least, that is how they affect our consciousness.

Words, therefore, are as real or as unreal as our consciousness is able to make them. The more words in a second or third or fourth language you can remember, the more "concepts" you are able to express or understand. Words can be reified and sold as vocabulary cards and they can be alphabetized as usual, or in the reverse in an *a tergo* dictionary. Words can be acquired or lost, both as luminous loci in memory, or as vocabulary cards or pocket dictionaries. Words can be socially elevated as *queen* from "woman" or socially degraded to mean "tavern wench". They can give rise to given names as *Gwen(dolyn),* and they can designate a specialty in medicine as *gyne(cology).* **All of this is within**

the ecosphere of words. Small wonder that a straight and simple definition of "word" is hard to come by. You can be sparing with your words or you can be verbose and prolix.

What you think of "words" may define you as a person.

References

Bloomfield, Leonard. 1933. *Language*. New York: Henry Holt & Co.

Borsódi, Mándi, Szabóné and Szendrő. 1994. *PICDIC: British and American English-Hungarian Picture Dictionary*. For multimedia PC with MS-Windows). Budapest, PICDIC< Inc.

Brown, Lesley (Ed.). 1993. *The New Shorter Oxford English Dictionary*. Oxford: Clarendon Press.

Capra, Fritjof. 1991. *The Tao of Physics. An Exploration of the Parallels Between Modern Physics and Eastern Mysticism*. (Third Edition, Updated.) Boston: Shambhalla.

Carr, John W., III (Ed.). 1958. *Computer Programming and Artificial Intelligence: An Intensive Course for Practicing Scientists and Engineers*. Ann Arbor: University of Michigan College of Engineering.

Chomsky, Noam. 1957. *Syntactic Structures*. The Hague: Mouton.

Grimes, Barbara (Ed.). 1992. *Ethnologue. Languages of the World*. Dallas, Texas: Summer Institute of Linguistics.

Hockett, Charles, F. 1958. *A Course in Modern Linguistics*. New York: MacMillan & Co.

Lamb, Sydney M. 1990. *Language and Illusion*. Rice University, Houston. (Teaching Materials printed by Kinko's.)

Lamb, Sydney M. 1992. *Language and Illusion*. Rice University, Houston. (Teaching Materials printed by Kinko's.) (Revision of 1990.)

Maher, J. Peter. 1980. The transformational-generative paradigm: a silver anniversary polemic. *Forum Linguisticum* 5: 1–35.

Makkai, Adam. 1972a. *A Dictionary of Space English*. Chicago: Consolidated Book Publishers.

Makkai, Adam. 1972b. *Idiom Structure in English*. The Hague: Mouton.

Makkai, Adam. 1974. A stratificational re-examination of acronymy in English. *Proceedings of the Xlth International Congress of Linguists, Bologna*, ed. by Luigi Heilmann, 345–363. Bologna: Società editrice il Mulino.

Makkai, Adam. 1993a. *Ecolinguistics: ¿Toward a New **Paradigm** for the Science of Language?* London: Pinter Publishers, and Budapest: Akadémiai Kiadó.

Makkai, Adam. 1993b. Idiomaticity as a reaction to "L'arbitraire du signe". *The Universal Process of Semeio-Genesis. Idioms: Processing, Structure, and Interpretation*, ed. by Cristina Cacciari and Patrizia Tabossi, 297–324. Hillsdale, New Jersey: Lawrence Erlbaum Associates, Publishers,

Shaumyan, Sebastian K. 1987. *A Semiotic Theory of Language*. Bloomington, Indiana: Indiana University Press.

About the author

*Adam Makkai is Professor in the Department of English and Linguistics at the University of Illinois at Chicago, where he has taught since 1967. He has also held visiting appointments in Singapore and Hong Kong. His 1965 Ph.D. is from Yale, and his was the first Yale dissertation to be influenced by Lamb. In rewritten form, it was published as **Idiom Structure in English** in 1972. In 1974 Makkai was the principal founder of the Linguistic Association of Canada and the United States. He served as its executive Director and Chairman of the Board until 1995, when Syd Lamb succeeded him.*

CHAPTER 6

The Logic of Anataxis

William J. Sullivan
University of Florida

1.   Preliminaries

1.1   *Introduction*

Historical linguists have long recognized a kind of reordering phenomenon in language, wherein elements that originally occur in one linear order shift to the opposite order.[1] This phenomenon is called metathesis. A good example of metathesis is the liquid metathesis in Slavic, in which tautosyllabic *Vr* or *Vl* shifts to *rV* or *lV*: compare Polish *gród,* Bulgarian *grad* '(walled) city, citadel' with Proto-Slavic **gord-* (cf. English *yard,* Latin *hortus* 'garden').

It has sometimes been claimed that metathesis is a synchronic phenomenon that accounts for apparent discrepancies in ordering. For example, in the verb phrase *have been broken* the constituent structure seems to be as in (1). T-AFFIX HOPPING, which involves metathesis, derives the order in (1) from the "under-lying" order in (2). Of course, the situation is more complex than presented in (1) and (2), but there is clearly something here that should be addressed.

---

1. This paper would not have been possible in its present form without Lockwood 1977, which was provided me by David Lockwood. Lockwood was also kind enough to go over an earlier draft and make several suggestions which improved the final product. Any remaining shortcomings are my own.

1. have be en break en
    └──┴──┘   ┘

2. have en be en break
    └──┘   └──┘

3. SD: have en be en break
    SC: 1 2 3 4 5 ⇒ 1 3 2 5 4

The question is whether there is an actual change in order in the use of language during communication. That is, do speakers conceive of *have been broken* in the order given in (2), then change the order as indicated in (3)? Or does the order only change in the description, i.e. is metathesis imposed on language by linguists? There is a third possibility: none of this is as it appears in traditional approaches.

This third possibility, if true, can only be captured and characterized effectively in a concept of language that is radically different from the traditional. Traditional descriptions are couched in theories that conceive of language as a collection of items and their arrangements or the processes that change one item into another. Sydney Lamb, following Louis Hjelmslev, conceives of language as a network of relationships interconnecting meaning and sound. In a relational network theory of this sort other definitions of the phenomenon can be developed and more plausible descriptions become possible. Before I demonstrate these descriptions and the conclusions that follow from them, I must outline Lamb's conception of synchronic "metathesis".

1.2 *Anataxis*

Sydney Lamb (1966: 64) suggests that the term *metathesis* be restricted to historical phenomena and that the synchronic phenomenon be called ANATAXIS. He defines anataxis as a subnetwork involving two strata in which the structural relations on one define the order AB and on the other the order B′A′.

Lamb's reasoning in this matter is clear. An actual change in order occurred between Proto-Slavic and Old Polish or Old Bulgarian. Conversely, the only change in order that can be shown in the synchronic examples is in the description. No psycholinguistic or neurological evidence can be shown to back up descriptions that claim actual reordering. Only one linear order actually exists: the one that is produced in sound. That linear order corresponds to the B′A′ order represented in the structural relations on the lower stratum. The AB order hypothesized for the structural relations on the upper stratum is never realized in sound.

The discussion to this point is almost entirely in the abstract. David Lockwood (1977) took these abstract considerations and produced a concrete taxonomy of examples. In the process he refined Lamb's thinking and improved on it. I turn to Lockwood's study now.

1.3 *Lockwood's anatactic relations*

David Lockwood (1977: 35–36) points out that Lamb's conception of anataxis permits a radically different description of a whole class of synchronic phenomena. Moreover, he notes a further advantage to Lamb's suggestions. "Anataxis ... can be applied not only to cases where the opposite linear order pertains on adjacent levels, but also to cases where a linear order is present on one level but lacking on an adjacent level, ... (a)s long as we make no arbitrary assumption that all elements must occur [only-WJS] in linear order..."

This gives three types of anataxis: ordinary anataxis (AB on the upper stratum and B′A′ on the lower), simultaneous anataxis (AB on the upper stratum and unordered or simultaneous on the lower stratum), and sequential anataxis (unordered or simultaneous on the upper stratum and A′B′ on the lower). He also identifies a difference between automatic and specificational anataxis. In the latter case, two orders exist and there is a difference in meaning between them, e.g. English *He is* vs. *Is he* or Russian *pjat' knig'* '5 books' vs. *knig pjat'* 'about 5 books'.

After identifying these types of anataxis, Lockwood considers their occurrence on the different strata of language and discusses the reasons for particular gaps. At this point I diverge from Lockwood's study in approach and sometimes in the conclusions I reach.

1.4 *The logic of anataxis*

The differences between my approach to anataxis and Lockwood's arise from a close study of the logic of anatactic relations. The logic of anatactic relations in different cases shows two things. First, ordinary anataxis is limited to the boundary between the expression and content sides in Hjelmslevian terms, i.e. between the morphemic and phonemic strata. Nowhere else are the conditions necessary for its occurrence found. All other apparent occurrences of ordinary anataxis can be described more simply as occurrences of sequential anataxis.

The second thing shown by a study of the logic of anatactic relations is that they are found between every pair of adjacent strata. They potentially include both sequential and simultaneous anataxis. The actual situation and several more general predictions become clear when concrete examples are considered in some detail. Before I turn to them, however, I must consider what a relational network theory of language predicts in the juxtaposition between meaning and sound, with particular regard to linear order.

2.   Stratificational Predictions on Anataxis

2.1   *Encoding from meaning to sound*

The basic stratificational assumption is that language (or, more properly, the linguistic system of a human being) is a relational network between meaning and sound. Here *meaning* is a cover term for the semantic system, which is the storage center that is the source of particular messages communicated linguistically. Similarly *sound* is a cover term for the phonetic medium.

As herein conceived, *sound* and *meaning* are inherently different. *Sound* is a physical object and can be measured directly by acoustic means. The articulatory movements by which it is produced and even some of the aural responses to it can be recorded and measured. Conversely, *meaning* is a system hidden in the brain. We know relatively little about it and cannot record or measure much about the normal operation of the brain. Much of what is written about the study of meaning in linguistic research is almost pure speculation and can be shown to be untrue by the neurological or cognitive sciences. Still, neurological and cognitive research points at centers encompassing the knowledge and memory stores containing the information generally referred to by *semantics*. These are what I refer to as *meaning*.

If centers of meaning exist in the brain, we can draw a number of inferences about them. First, the information is stored in the form of relational networks. Second, meaning networks and linguistic networks are formed of the same basic elements (neurons and synapses, dendrites and axons). But there is no reason to conclude that meaning and linguistic networks have the same gross architecture. In fact, the opposite conclusion is more likely.

Consider what is necessary for an information network. Let's call a piece of information believed to be true a *fact*.[2] Facts as defined include opinions and pure beliefs. Individual facts are stored in relation to other facts, which gives some idea of their significance. Groupings of facts are related to other groupings of facts, which gives a further idea of their significance. And so on. In short, every fact in the realm of "meaning" and its significance to a particular individual is present simultaneously with every other fact and its significance.

However, sound is strictly linear and is produced in real time. Therefore, the facts communicated in a message cannot be communicated simultaneously. Choices are made and linear order is imposed on the message. This linear order sometimes results from semantic or cultural or experiential factors. That is, we tend to describe a picture from left to right and top to bottom, and an event from beginning to end. But the details of linear order and the bulk of choices in order are imposed by the language (e.g. SVO clause order in English, VSO in Welsh). That is, language imposes a linear order in the course of encoding an essentially unordered message into sound. There are instances in which more than one linearization can be chosen. Moreover, it is reasonable that one choice is the normal or unmarked choice and the other is somehow marked. Thus, given an initially unordered grouping, the marked environment evokes the realization of the marked linearization. In the absence of the marked environment, the unmarked linearization is chosen. In Lockwood's classification, this is a specificational sequential anataxis.

In its simplest form, Lamb's relational network hypothesis predicts that the encoding process imposes linear order on unordered semantic substance. Apparent cases of metathesis are thus predicted to be a choice of alternate linearizations on a lower stratum realizing unordered upper stratum elements. These specified choices are merely marked cases of automatic sequential anataxis, which constitute the bulk of linearization.

2.2   *Encoding on the bottom of the content side*

Only automatic, non-specificational anataxis is manifested at the bottom of each side. In particular, the morphemic stratum, which is on the bottom of the content side, can only manifest automatic anataxis. Of course, simultaneous anataxis can only be automatic. However, there is another reason. The final linguistic ordering

---

2. I probably should call it a factoid, but I try to avoid pejorative suffixes.

of the content side is imposed on the morphemic stratum. It follows naturally that this ordering is what remains in the organization of message content. All marked sequences are imposed on the sememic or lexemic strata. What remains for the morphemic stratum is just the remaining unmarked sequences. All unmarked sequences are automatic.

2.3 *Encoding from language to sound*

The sound stream is temporally linear, as remarked above. But it is composed of acoustic elements like formants which are inherently simultaneous. That is, they cooccur in time. Moreover, it is physically impossible for our articulatory apparatus to produce a tonal sound with only a single formant. Thus there is a certain limited type of simultaneity in the phonetic substance. Nor is this simultaneity restricted to vowels. Consider that the basic part of phonetic substance is a pure vowel-to-vowel sound stream and that the consonants are modifications imposed on it. Then consonants overlap with vowels. The difference between consonants and vowels is that the vocalic phonation is the basic carrier wave of the sound stream and the modifications are limited to consonantal positions in the syllable. Either way the sound stream is a complex but temporally linear signal. Some of its elements are simultaneous with others, some occur only in sequential order.

It is possible that at this edge of language anataxis might be observed. In this case, however, stratificational theory predicts simultaneous anataxis. That is, some phonemic feature which has a specific sequential position in the syllable is realized simultaneously with at least one other syllable position. This type of anataxis is automatic. We could only conclude that it was specificational (conditioned) if examples which did not exhibit simultaneous anataxis could be observed and if they signaled something other than what the simultaneous examples signal. Lockwood (1977: 42) seems uneasy with this type of anataxis. He calls it "more difficult to demonstrate" precisely because the ordered realization never occurs. It is abstracted from the phonetic evidence in the process of analysis. The sequential position is therefore an inference rather than a hard datum. However, as I show in Sullivan 1974, it is both the simplest way to describe what happens and a means of maintaining a biunique level of phonemic contrast.

One further type of anataxis is predicted by stratificational theory. Though normally considered a speech error, the slip of the tongue known as a Spoonerism is a classic example of metathesis. That is, it produces *B ... A* when *A ... B* is expected. Admittedly an aberration, spoonerisms are certainly not the norm and are never mentioned in the context of metathesis.[3] It is also the only example of classical metathesis (ordinary automatic anataxis) I am aware of in synchronic linguistics. Yet because of the relational network architecture of stratificational theory and its attempt to model real-time encoding processes, stratificational theory predicts the possibility of both perseveration and anticipation. Combine the two and we have the "metathesis" found in a Spoonerism. A reasonable description of this phenomenon is presented in Dell and Reich 1977. For this reason and because it is an aberration I say no more about it here.

2.4 *Summary*

The relational network model of stratificational theory predicts three types of anataxis: automatic and specificational sequential anataxis and automatic simultaneous anataxis. Sequential anataxis is to be found at every stratal intersection: sememic to lexemic, lexemic to morphemic, and morphemic to phonemic. Simultaneous anataxis, however, is limited to the lower or sound end of language. It occurs at the intersection between morphemic and phonemic strata and between the phonemic and phonetic strata. By its logic, sequential anataxis may be automatic or specificational; simultaneous anataxis, however, can only be automatic.

Before showing how different examples of metathesis can be described as one of these three types with the predicted distribution, I review examples in Lockwood 1977 and summarize his observations and predictions.

3. Anataxis Revisited

3.1 *Lockwood's examples*

Lockwood 1977 carefully catalogues the types of anataxis found synchronically in contemporary languages. Because his excellent article is not generally available, I repeat the types and his examples here.

---

3. Except, of course, in Lockwood 1977.

Automatic Ordinary Anataxis (Lockwood 1977: 35)

Korean *jotha* 'is good' and *jokhesso* 'will be good' from the root *joh* 'good' and verbal suffixes *ta* 'present' and *kesso* 'future' (cf. *jop* 'narrow' and corresponding forms *jopta* and *jopkesso*).

Automatic Simultaneous Anataxis (Lockwood 1977: 36)

Welsh *i:fen* 'her head' from *pen* 'head' and *i: ... S* 'her', where *S* indicates a signal that evokes the spirant form of a following initial consonant.

Automatic Sequential Anataxis (Lockwood 1977: 37)

Russian *ruki* 'arm, G'; the entire noun phrase is in the genitive case in syntax, but the morphotactics relate genitive case to the ending *i*, which is suffixed to the stem *ruk*.

Specificational and Automatic Sequential Anataxis (Lockwood 1977: 37–38)

Russian *stolov pjat'* 'about 5 desks' vs *pjat' stolov* '(exactly) 5 desks', where the marked word order realizes the APPROXIMATIVE sememe and the unmarked word order appears otherwise.

Clallam *ck^{w}ut* 'shoot' and *cuk^{w}t* 'shooting', where a marked syllable structure realizes one aspect and Clallam imposes the unmarked syllable structure in the absence of this aspect.

Automatic Sequential Anataxis (Lockwood 1977: 40)

Polish affricates are unit phonemes but are realized by the feature sequence Cl-Sp (oral closure followed by spirant friction).

Lockwood gives more examples, but the above are typical. More important, he details patterns in the occurrences of types of anataxis. He also details patterned gaps in the occurrence of anataxis. These patterns constitute a second significant contribution of his article. I turn to them now.

3.2 *Lockwood's observations and predictions*

Lockwood's view of stratificational theory is not based on an explicitly logical framework. Yet it is implicitly logical in its underpinnings, so his view and mine are compatible. A number of the theoretical predictions he makes about the distribution of types of anataxis match the predictions I make on logical grounds in Section 2.3. Specifically Lockwood (1977: 40–41) predicts that both automatic and specificational sequential anataxis should occur on the lexemic stratum. He also states that the possibility of ordinary and simultaneous anataxis is "excluded by general theory". His thinking in this area parallels mine, though he does not go into the same detail. He correctly observes that there is no justification for assuming an underlying linear order and concludes that language must supply the order(s) that occur. Hence only sequential anataxis is predicted.

Lockwood (1977: 41–42) then discusses the morphemic stratum. He notes that only automatic sequential anataxis is attested with clear examples. This is consistent with his predictions for the lexemic stratum But he is troubled by the lack of clear examples for any specificational anataxis. I predict above that only automatic sequential anataxis should occur here. I return to this point below.

In the final step of the encoding process, i.e. on the phonetic stratum, Lockwood observes automatic simultaneous and sequential anataxis. As remarked above, he seems troubled by the simultaneous example. He notes that ordinary anataxis and specificational examples of simultaneous and sequential anataxis are "unattested and probably to be excluded by general theory". I predict that only automatic simultaneous anataxis is possible here.

Clearly there is great agreement between Lockwood's treatment and mine. Two things remain to be shown. First, I must show the logic of anataxis in those cases where both analyses agree, to demonstrate that the stratificational approach takes care of what is called synchronic "metathesis" and the ordinary imposition of linear order. Second, I must show how the general theory I describe predicts the distribution of different types and tell why my analysis differs from Lockwood's.

4.   Anataxis Redescribed

4.1 *Automatic sequential anataxis*

I begin with automatic sequential anataxis for several reasons. First, it is easy to describe, both verbally and in relational networks. Second, it is the quintessential type of anataxis. That is, both Lockwood and I predict that one of the major effects of the encoding process is the imposition of linear order on an unordered message. Thus automatic sequential anataxis can be observed all over language. Third, the logic of automatic sequential anataxis demands the intersection of two strata. This supports the existence of stratal boundaries in language, a conclusion reached by many stratificationalists at various times. It also answers a long-standing question generally asked in rhetorical fashion: if we don't assume linear order, how does it appear?

Using Lockwood's simplified example I describe automatic sequential anataxis in Figure 1.

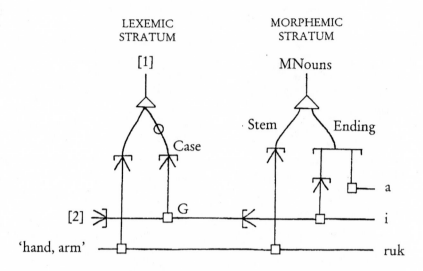

Figure 1.   *A relational network representing automatic sequential anataxis*

Beginning at the bottom left we see that a member of the syntactic class LNoun (lexemic noun) meaning 'hand, arm' is related to a set of syntactic positions [1] which require a marked case. If the case node is related to a member of a certain class of sememic functions like POSSESSOR or SOURCE [2], the marked case will be the genitive (G), as indicated. The lexeme 'hand, arm' is related one-to-one to a particular morpheme, which is ultimately realized as *ruk*. G has several possible realizations. That is, it is related to a whole set of endings. Which one is realized in a given instance is determined by other factors. Some of these (e.g. plural number) are semantic; others (e.g. stem class) are purely morphotactic. In this instance plurality is absent and *ruk* belongs to the *a*-stems, so the appropriate realization of G is *i*. At the same time the morphotactics imposes the linear order of stem before ending.

Note the appropriateness of this division of labor. The syntax needs only the information that the LNoun is related to G. It does not need the information about which G ending is appropriate to this particular lexeme or even that it is an ending, rather than a prefix or preposition or postposition. That information is crucial to the morphemic stratum but is irrelevant to the lexemic. The imposition of linear order in morphotactics as an example of automatic sequential anataxis is a minor if important detail here.

In short, Lockwood's automatic sequential anataxis is almost an *obiter factum*, provided in addition to a number of important characteristics of Russian. The·only difference is that the nature of these genitive cases is peculiar to Russian and automatic sequential anataxis is a true language universal.

4.2 *Automatic simultaneous anataxis*

Lockwood's example for automatic simultaneous anataxis is a typical exemplar of the Welsh mutation system. The Welsh morpheme for 'head' is *pen*. The morpheme for 'her' is *i:* plus an instruction *S* for the spirant mutation of the noun-initial stop.

The relational network is given in Figure 2.

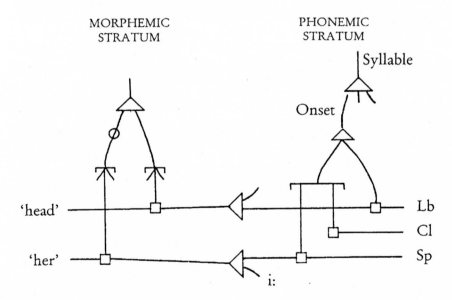

Figure 2.   *Relational network representing automatic simultaneous anataxis*

The diagram shows the boundary between morphemic and phonemic strata. Begin at the upper left. We have a morphemic phrase relating possessives and nouns, in that order. To the right of the morphotactics the possessive 'her' is related to two lines. The lower line is realized as *i:* the upper to what Lockwood calls *S*. In the relational network description, this line is directly related to syllable-onset position in the phonotactics. The first position of the 'head' morpheme is related to a diamond which is also directly related to onset position of that syllable. This diamond is always directly related to the feature Lb (labial). Syllable structure is related to this feature via the right-hand line from the AND node below ONSET. If the line to *S* is active, the left-hand branch from that AND node will choose the left-hand branch down from the ordered OR, and onset position will be realized by the features Sp and Lb (=[f]). If *S* is not active, e.g. in the absence of the possessive, the right-hand branch from the ordered OR will be active, and onset position will be realized by the features Cl and Lb (=[p]). Thus, though the possessor morpheme precedes the possessed morpheme in the morphotactics, the last part of the former and the first part of the latter are related to the same phonotactic position.

Up to this point Lockwood's description is directly translatable to mine, and there is no disagreement between his observations and my predictions. I turn now to the first place where I diverge from his work. It involves the case of automatic sequential anataxis in phonetics.

4.3 *Automatic sequential anataxis in phonetics*

Lockwood's example for automatic sequential anataxis in phonetics involves affricates in Polish: [c] is an unvoiced apicodental affricate. It is clearly a unit phoneme in Polish from both structural and phonetic vantage points. That is, its distribution across the syllable parallels but differs from that of stops and spirants, and it takes about the same amount of time in the sound stream as any other obstruent.

Lockwood describes this phoneme phonetically as beginning with the feature Cl (oral closure) followed by the feature Sp (spirant friction). His description is reasonable; in fact, it parallels the IPA description of an affricate as a stop-spirant sequence, such that /c/ = [ts], though Lockwood's description is phonetically more delicate. Recent work in autosegmental phonology has also adopted a parallel approach. Lockwood's reasons for adopting this approach are not given in Lockwood 1977, but they are sensible and both phonetically and typologically relevant. However, I find them phonologically unnecessary.

My approach to this problem parallels Roman Jakobson's. Jakobson's original approach to affricate phonemes is that they are phonetically similar to stops (they have oral closure and completely interrupt the sound stream) except in their manner of release. Stops have sudden, complete release but affricates have more gradual release. However, following Lamb (1966) I describe the mode of release directly. That is, the apicodental place of articulation has several possible affricates: [t$^\theta$] has a slit release, [t^l] a lateral release, and [c] a groove release. These differ from [t], which has a smooth release, and from [s], which has no closure.

In a temporal, purely phonetic sense, the release is linearly ordered, in that it applies to the end of the period of closure. But such linearity is the general case for the sound stream and plays no role in the phonology itself. That is to say, in real time the instructions for making oral closure (or spirant friction in the case of [s]) precede those for releasing it. But this holds for stops just as for affricates. Affricates differ, as observed above, only in the manner of release, and not in an occurrence of anataxis.[4] Thus anataxis is not involved here.

4.4 *Mixed specificational and sequential anataxis*

The examples of anataxis which have traditionally provided the superficially most convincing arguments for the synchronic relevance of metathesis involve situations where two different sequences are observed and the two are clearly related in some way, e.g. as in active and passive clauses.[5] Lockwood's example involves Russian number phrases: numeral before noun is the usual or unmarked sequence and noun before numeral is a marked sequence, suggesting that the numerical quantity is only approximate.

---

4. This type of linearization could be modeled mathematically by a switch matrix (see Lockwood 1975) or neurologically by a spreading activation model, a form of which was suggested to me as early as 1973 by Peter Reich. However, this question is beyond the scope of the present study.

5. For a description of the lexemic anataxis involved in active and passive and its interrelation with several other "movement" types see Sullivan 1980.

Following Lamb, Lockwood says that the marked word order realizes the APPROXIMATIVE sememe (hereafter PRX) as a taxon of arrangement.[6] I have no objection to this description. But the way it is phrased permits the derivational misinterpretation, i.e. that Lockwood's description assumes the unmarked order and derives the marked order from it in the environment of PRX.

This would be a complete misconstrual, however. In a stratificational description like Lockwood's the lexotactics provide two possible orders. The marked order is evoked in the presence of PRX; the unmarked order is provided in its absence. A relational network description is given in Figure 3.[7]

To see how this works, begin at the upper left of Figure 3. This is the semotactic structure that defines Russian quantity expressions. At the bottom are numbers and count nouns. At the top note that these expressions can be approximate, i.e. the uppermost AND optionally relates QUANT to the sememe PRX. The lexotactics provides a two-place, ordered number phrase. The left-hand (first) branch from the AND has two choices. If the sememe PRX is present, the lexotactics takes the (marked) left-hand branch of the OR and realizes the noun in first position. Then the numeral is realized in second position, via the right-hand branch of the AND: *stolov pjat'*. This is specificational sequential anataxis. In the absence of PRX, the left-hand branch from the OR cannot be taken. But it is possible to take the (unmarked) right-hand branch and realize the numeral in first position. Then the noun is realized in second position: *pjat' stolov*. This is automatic sequential anataxis. The two are related as indicated and produce one order or the other during encoding.

Another example of combined specificational and automatic sequential anataxis can be seen on the stratal boundary between morphology and phonology with the Clallam verb. Briefly, two verbal aspects are possible in the present tense. For one verb stem class, the difference between the two aspects is communicated by two different orderings of the phonemes in the stem. The

---

6. Lockwood (personal communication) warns that my use of PRX, which appears in my work on Russian locus expressions as the abbreviation for proximity, may be confusing here. He suggests the semantic distinction between APPROXIMATIVE in the present contexts and PROXIMAL in locus contexts. He is undoubtedly correct from a pedagogical point of view, but I am ignoring his admonition. If the principle of complementary distribution holds in semantics, there is no need to differentiate between the two. Moreover, there are two ways of saying 'approximately five tables' in Russian" *stolov pjat'* and *okolo pjati stolov,* with a metaphorical usage of the locus expression 'around five tables'. My impression is that the latter is more common in the standard colloquial language.

7. In this simplified description I omit interesting but irrelevant details involving case.

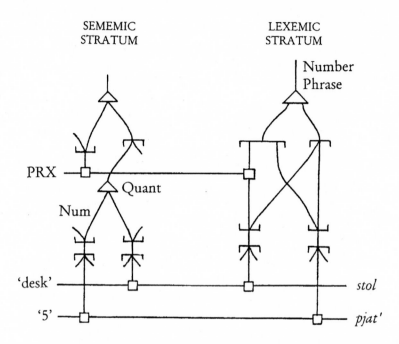

Figure 3.   *A relational network representing mixed specificational and sequential anataxis*

parallels to Russian number phrases are obvious. But here the anataxis is realized in the order of phonemes in the syllable.

A fully general description requires a knowledge of Clallam syllable structure much greater than I am likely to get.[8] As a result, what I present is *ad hoc*. But it represents the situation as I see it.

The relational network description is given in Figure 4. Excepting only the first phoneme and possibly the last, the order of phonemes in the native morphemes

8. Thompson & Thompson (1969:215, n. 2) state that "(o)nly a handful of elderly people still speak Clallam fluently."

of a language is generally predictable.[9] Thus the first phoneme is ordered relative to the rest, but they are not linearly ordered relative to each other. This is described in the stacked AND nodes at the bottom of Figure 4. I assume that the Clallam syllable has a consonantal onset, a vocalic peak, and a consonantal coda. Onset and coda may be monophonemic or diphonemic. The onset is diphonemic only in the Aspect 1 forms. The coda is diphonemic at need.

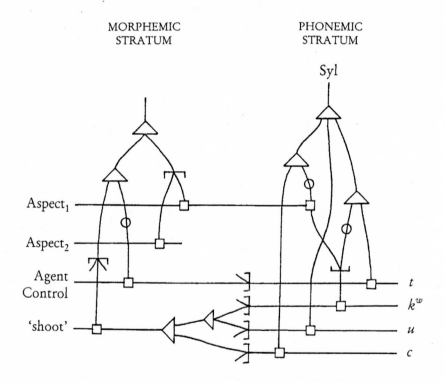

Figure 4.   A relational network representing mixed specificational and automatic sequential anataxis in the Clallam verb

During encoding the c is realized in first onset position. If Aspect 1 is present, the k^w is realized in second onset position. If not, second onset position

---

9. Michael A. K. Halliday suggested this to me in 1968. It proved to be true for Russian, which has a very complex syllable structure.

is vacant. The *u* is realized in peak position. If k^w is realized in second onset position in the environment of Aspect 1, first coda position is vacant; otherwise k^w is realized there. In either case *t* is realized in final coda position. Both orders are possible; one is marked for Aspect 1, the other appears in all other circumstances.[10]

4.5 *Automatic simultaneous anataxis*

Automatic simultaneous anataxis is found at the intersection between phonology and phonetics. It is the type of network that accounts for assimilation. My analysis of assimilation involves archiphonemic neutralization, a restricted syllabic environment for a particular feature in phonotactics, and a hierarchical difference in the tactic position of the "assimilated" feature.

The example Lockwood 1977 uses is from Sullivan 1974. In short, it concerns phonemic voice in Russian and regressive voice assimilation. The relevant facts are simple. A consonantal onset in a Russian syllable may begin with up to three obstruent phonemes. Voice is potentially phonemic for most Russian obstruents. But the position of contrast for voice is restricted to final position in the obstruent cluster. In prefinal position in an obstruent cluster the voice contrast is suspended, i.e. the obstruents represent the archiphonemes of neutralization between voiced and unvoiced phonemes. Thus we have an obstruent cluster of up to four positions: obstruent classes are related to the first three and voice to the fourth. At a subphonemic level voice is related to the hierarchically dominant position in a chain of obstruents, such that the phonetic output of voice is simultaneous with the phonetic output of the obstruents during encoding.

This phenomenon is diagrammed in Figure 5. The phonotactic portion (PT) of the network is at the left. At its top is an ordered AND node labeled VObstr. To the left VObstr is related to OBSTR, an AND node with three positions. The first position is related to the set of stops or the set of spirants. The second position is optionally related to the set of spirants. The third position is optionally related to the set of stops or the set of affricates. The right hand line is

10. The phonotactic details differ from those given in 1977. Whether Lockwood's description or mine or some third description is structurally more sound is a question that requires further information about Clallam syllable structure and cannot be answered at this time, if ever. In any case, resolving this issue is beyond the scope of the present study.

optionally related to voice (Y). Thus the phonotactics limits voice to a particular sequential position.

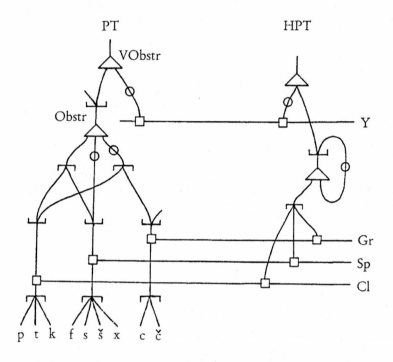

Figure 5.　*A relational network representing automatic simultaneous anataxis*

The hypophonotactic portion (HPT) is to the right in Figure 5. At its top is an unordered AND node which is related to voice and, simultaneously, to a series of obstruents, whose precise number and order is determined in the phonotactics. In this way a sequential phonotactic position is related to a hierarchically dominant hypophonotactic position simultaneous with the entire obstruent chain.

4.6 *Automatic ordinary anataxis*

The traditional example of automatic ordinary anataxis Lockwood uses is from Korean.[11] In it the final phoneme of roots ending in *h* show an apparent position switch with the initial phoneme of suffixes that begin with a stop. For example, the root for 'good' is *joh*. It combines with present- and future-tense suffixes *ta* and *kesso*. But instead of expected phonetic forms **johta, * johkesso* we observe *jotha, jokhesso*. The traditional assumption is therefore that the expected forms are underlying and there is a rule of metathesis to produce the actual forms.

In this case no such rule is necessary. In fact, this particular example is equivalent to the Welsh mutation problem I describe in Section 4.2. What happens is that the final *h* of the root morpheme combines with the initial stop of the suffix morpheme to produce an aspirated stop. There is no metathesis or change in order. We conventionally write aspiration following the consonant in transcriptions, and aspiration does affect the articulation of the following vowel. But it also affects the articulation of the preceding vowel and of the consonant aspirated itself. Thus it is in all ways (except for precise phonetic detail) parallel to the Welsh mutation.

I have heard of other cases of apparent metathesis of this sort, wherein the final consonant of one morpheme appears after the initial consonant of the following morpheme. I do not command any of these languages personally, but I can outline what happens in more general terms and provide an example from Hebrew.[12]

First, I assume that only two relevant specifications of ordering are provided to the phonology by the morphology: The order of morphemes and the order of realization of the first phoneme in each morpheme, relative to the rest of the phonemes in the morpheme (see Figure 4). Then the grouping of phonemes into syllables is imposed by the phonotactics. As a general rule, each phoneme is realized in the first position that allows fulfillment of all obligatory phonotactic relations. Assume that the last phoneme of the first morpheme can only be realized in syllable onset position. Assume further that the first phoneme in the

---

11. Lockwood (personal communication) agrees with my analysis of the Korean data and prefers the Hebrew example for its more clearly sequential realization. But the Korean data have been widely cited as an example of sequential anataxis (classical metathesis). It is a case of anataxis, but it is simultaneous rather than sequential.

12. I am indebted to Joellen Simpson of the University of Florida for pointing these data out to me.

second morpheme can be realized in syllable coda position. Then it would be available to fill coda position of the last syllable in the first morpheme. The last phoneme of the first morpheme would then fit into onset position of the first syllable of the second morpheme. All the phonemes to which both morphemes are related are realized phonetically, fulfilling all relations of both morphemes to sound. All syllable structure conditions are met, fulfilling phonotactic requirements. The output is well-formed, according to the language, and the apparent metathesis is predicted. This possibility is predicted by the stratificational assumption that language imposes linear order during encoding. Moreover, no special rules of metathesis are required. The relational network architecture can handle it all. But the specific conditions are fairly complex. Thus the phenomenon itself should not be common, and it is not.

One example of this kind of anataxis at the phonemic stratum appears to be present in some reflexive verbs in Hebrew. The reflexive morpheme *hit* is prefixed to *kibel* 'accept', *pina* 'remove', and *mina* 'appoint' to give *hitkabel, hitpana, hitmana*.[13] But if the verb begins with an *s*, as in *sipek* 'satisfy', the reflexive form is *histapek* rather than the expected **hitsapek*. The basic morphological order of the two morphemes is unchanged. The reflexive morpheme generally precedes the verb stem. It always begins before the verb stem begins and it ends before the verb stem ends. What makes it remarkable is that it doesn't always end before the verb stem begins. That is, its last phoneme sometimes comes after the first phoneme of the verb stem.

The Hebrew data are described in Figure 6. As with the Welsh example, the sequence of morphemes is given in the morphotactics at the upper left. The realization of these morphemes is given by the AND nodes (center, bottom), wherein the first phoneme is ordered relative to the rest. The key to this description is in the phonemes to which the morphemes are related and the way the phonotactics syllabifies them and imposes linear order on them. In particular, both stops and spirants can occur in syllable onset and syllable coda position. But all other things being equal, coda position prefers *s* to a stop (the ordered OR node). Thus the first phoneme in 'satisfy' is realized in coda position of the first syllable. The *t* can then be realized in onset position of the second syllable. Once again no reordering occurs. The correct order is imposed during encoding.

---

13. The difference of vowels shown in these examples is an instance of the well-known Semitic phenomenon of vowel alternation in morphology. Its detailed treatment is beyond the scope of this paper.

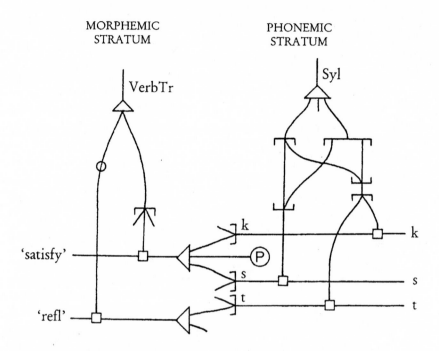

Figure 6.   *A relational network representing automatic ordinary anataxis in some reflexive verbs in Hebrew*

5.   Summary and Conclusions

A careful study of the logic of anataxis in the context of certain observations about the structure and workings of the human cognitive and neurological systems produces a number of findings. Several observations and conclusions stand out. I summarize these now, beginning with the observations.

–   The human knowledge store has all "facts" stored simultaneously.
–   These facts are probably stored in more or less hierarchically-ordered cognitive semantic structures.
–   There is no evidence that these facts are stored in a linearly-ordered fashion.
–   They provide the source for messages that are encoded into sound.

–   The sound stream produced when a linguistic message is encoded is strictly linear, in an informational sense.
–   Thus the linguistic system of a human speaker must be able to impose linear order on an unordered message-content during encoding.
–   Historical metathesis involves a reordering of linguistic elements, if the earlier stage is compared with the later stage.
–   Synchronic metathesis, dubbed "anataxis" by Lamb, has traditionally been described by rules which move or reorder linguistic elements, probably by analogy to historical metathesis.
–   However, there is no evidence that reordering actually occurs in the human linguistic system.
–   Descriptions of anataxis that resort to reordering rules are thus imposing reordering on the data.
–   Imposing an artifact on a description is a problem for all science, and such artifacts should be avoided if at all possible.
–   Accounting for anataxis without reordering rules avoids the artifact.
–   Lamb's relational network theory accounts for anataxis without reordering rules.
–   It accounts for anataxis
    –   as a part of its account for the way the linguistic system of a human being linearizes unordered content during the process of encoding a message into sound and
    –   as an inter-stratal phenomenon.
–   It predicts
    –   that anataxis can be found between every pair of strata, which gives possible lexemic, morphemic, phonemic, and phonetic anataxis;
    –   that only automatic and specificational sequential anataxis can occur on the lexemic stratum;
    –   that only automatic sequential anataxis can occur on the morphemic stratum;
    –   that automatic and specificational sequential anataxis can occur on the phonemic stratum;
    –   that simultaneous anataxis can only be automatic; and
    –   that simultaneous anataxis is found only on the phonemic and phonetic strata.
–   It describes the attested types of anataxis within these boundaries.

– It explains and justifies the predictions and the descriptions completely via the logic of the relationships in the relational network.

Beyond the normal apparatus of Lamb's stratificational theory, no additional descriptive artifacts are necessary. Moreover, the descriptions produced are neurologically and cognitively reasonable. That is, though the descriptions are neither neurological nor cognitive as such, they are compatible with what we know about neurology and cognition. It is difficult to imagine a description superior to that produced by Lamb's stratificational theory.

6. Afterword

Lamb's initial suggestion that stratificational theory had a relational network description for anataxis was made in print about 35 years ago. Lockwood's classification of types of anataxis and their distribution was made in print over 20 years ago. Lockwood's work is compatible with Lamb's original theoretical suggestions and with the models of stratificational theory current in the mid-1970s. My work is compatible with Lamb's original suggestions, with Lockwood's classification and his description, and with the models of cognitive-stratificational theory presently current. I doubt whether any such phenomenon could be cited in the case of the majoritarian theory of language. The fact that it is true of stratificational theory is a testimony to the basic soundness and fundamental nature of Syd Lamb's thinking. It is my hope (probably vain) that the rest of the linguistic community will at last recognize this fact.

References

Dell, Gary S., and Peter A. Reich. 1977. A model of slips of the tongue. *The Third LACUS Forum 1976*, ed. by Robert J. DiPietro and Edward L. .Blansitt, Jr., 448–455. Columbia, South Carolina: Hornbeam

Lamb, Sydney M. 1966. *Outline of Stratificational Grammar*. Washington, D.C.: Georgetown University Press

Lockwood, David G. 1976. Alternatives to matrix models in phonetics and phonology. *The Second LACUS Forum 1975*, ed. by Peter Reich, 141–153. Columbia, South Carolina: Hornbeam Press

Lockwood, David G. 1977. Anatactic relations in grammar and phonology. *Papers from the Annual Meeting of the Michigan Linguistic Society, October 15, 1976*, 35–41. Ann Arbor: University of Michigan Papers in Linguistics

Sullivan, William J. 1974. The archiphoneme in stratificational description. *Proceedings of the XIth International Congress of Linguists, Bologna, Italy*, ed. by Luigi Heilmann, 287–299. Bologna: Societa editrice il Molino

Sullivan, William J. 1980. Syntax and linguistic semantics in Stratificational theory. *Syntax and Semantics, vol. 13, Current Approaches to Syntax*, ed. by Edith Moravcsik and Jessica Wirth, 301–327. New York: Academic Press

Thompson, Laurence C., and M. Terry Thompson. 1969. Metathesis as a grammatical device. *International Journal of American Linguistics* 35: 213–219.

About the author

*William J. Sullivan is Associate Professor of Slavic and Linguistics at the University of Florida, where he has been since 1970. His 1969 Yale dissertation **A Stratificational Description of the Phonology and Inflectional morphology of Russian** was jointly directed by Alexander Schenker and Syd Lamb. Among his Yale classmates who are represented in the present volume are David Bennett and Yoshihiko Ikegami. Since its founding in 1974, he has been very active in the Linguistic Association of Canada and the United States, giving papers almost every year and contributing notably to the discussion of papers. His LACUS papers have included a notable series on Russian locus expressions.*

CHAPTER 7

The Dilemma of the Welsh Sentence Particle

Empiricism in Stratificational Linguistics

Toby D. Griffen

Southern Illinois University at Edwardsville

1.   Background: Empiricism and Stratificational Linguistics

One of the hallmarks of stratificational linguistics is the reliance upon empiricism required by its very form, in which no preexisting category or relationship can be maintained in the network — everything must be entered on the basis of the data. In developing the stratificational network, we thus start with few assumptions about the way that various relationships should interact, apart from the fact that whatever relationships emerge must be statable in the form of the three logical primes: AND, OR, and PRECEDENCE (see Reich 1973, Sullivan 1980: 324).

Nonetheless, there are certain assumptions that we tend to hold as axiomatic, particularly where markedness is concerned. We may represent a marked relationship as the ORDERED-OR node in the tactic pattern of Figure 1: Given condition A, category/relationship B will be realized; but if this condition is not present, then the unmarked category/relationship C will be realized. This approach, with the unmarked choice an actual category or relationship realized if certain conditions do not obtain, is broader than the zero realization in Lockwood 1972: 102 and different from the pseudo-node in Lockwood 1988: 68, but it does derive from the structure of the network. All things being equal, though, we would normally expect a zero realization to be the unmarked.

One of the most obvious candidates for markedness is the relationship between the unmarked declarative sentence, on the one hand, and the marked interrogative and responsive sentences, on the other hand. There is something basic to the assumption that interrogation and response are marked forms of

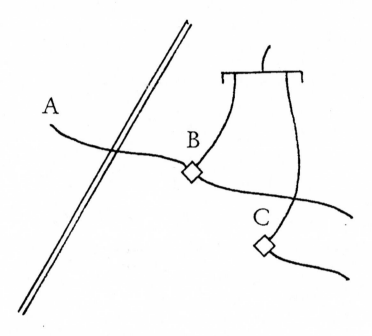

Figure 1.   *Markedness Tactics*

declaration. Indeed, this basic assumption even leads Lockwood to raise the possibility that the relationship between unmarked statements and marked questions may be universal: "Some aspects of markedness are undoubtedly universal — this is likely true of the marked status of questions as opposed to the corresponding statements — while other aspects may vary from one language to another" (Lockwood 1972: 102–3).

On the lexemic level of any language, then, we might expect some markedness relationship such as that in Figure 2. Given the appropriate sememic conditions, the interrogative lexeme ^{L}/I/ or the responsive lexeme ^{L}/R/ may be realized (may enter the realizational portion of the network). In the absence of these conditions, however, the declarative lexeme ^{L}/D/ will be realized as the unmarked.

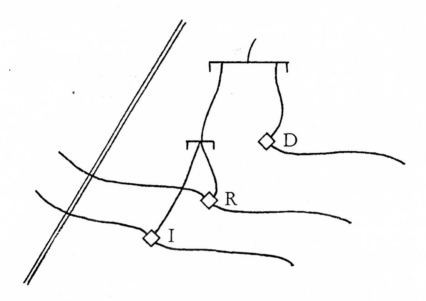

Figure 2.   *Unmarked declarative*

Between the lexemic and the morphemic strata, the assumption is that ^{L}/D/ will have the most basic syntactic order and the most basic morphological marking. To describe the interrogation of ^{L}/I/ or the response of ^{L}/R/, we expect to employ an alternative in the tactic pattern that would indicate a marked choice either of interrogation or of response.

If only one assumption be made by the empirical linguist, this would probably be the one. Not only is it suggested by Lockwood for stratificational linguistics (which normally avoids "universals"), but it can also be seen in other major linguistic models. The tagmemic appears to agree with this assumption in the classification of interrogation as a derived sentence type (compare Cook 1969, Pike 1982). Moreover, the generative has developed this assumption from

the very notion of the kernel sentence (Chomsky 1957) to movement traces
(compare Safir 1985) and other developments (see also Radford 1988).

2.   Data: Literary and Colloquial Welsh

Let us test the assumption that ^{L}/D/ is the unmarked relationship by examining
data from the development of the sentence particle in Modern Welsh. The Welsh
sentence or clause characteristically begins with a particle that indicates the type
of sentence or clause that follows — affirmative or negative; declarative,
interrogative, or responsive; conjunctive or disjunctive; etc. While there are
others within the system, we shall consider only the three major affirmative
sentence particles, as they appear before the verb in the basic verb + subject +
complement sentence order. Examples of each can be found in Table 1.

In Table 1, we find the appropriate variants of a simple sentence to illustrate
the sentence particles. We note, however, that there are two columns of Welsh
data — LW and CW. As pointed out by Fife (1986; see also Griffen 1980 in a
stratificational approach), the standard form of writing Welsh literature has
reflected a stage of the language that is by now somewhat archaic. In recent
years, a new standard called *Cymraeg Byw* 'Living Welsh' has been developed
from more or less standard elements of colloquial Welsh. There is still debate
over the use of this new standard, and the terms used for describing the alternatives are sometimes pejorative. Let us simply use literary Welsh (LW) for the
conservative written Welsh and colloquial Welsh (CW) for the innovative (but
realizing that this "colloquial" Welsh is indeed a written standard).

The standard LW is presented in such works as Richards 1938 and Williams
1980, and it is rather well summarized in the textbook of Bowen and Rhys Jones
1960. While the standard CW is still somewhat in flux, consistent presentations
can be found in the textbooks of Davies and Davies 1977, National Language
Unit of Wales 1988, and especially Rhys Jones 1977, which may be seen as a
revision of Bowen and Rhys Jones 1960. As pointed out by Fife (1986: 143–4),
one of the most valuable works for sorting out differences is Jones and Thomas
1977.

Table 1. *Welsh Sentence Particles*

Present Periphrastic

	LW	CW	English
D:	Yr wyf i'n darllen	Rydw/Rwy i'n darllen	I am reading
	Wyf i'n darllen		
I:	A (yd)wyf i'n darllen?	Ydw i'n darllen?	Am I reading?
R:	Ydwyf	Ydw	I am (= Yes)

Future Periphrastic

D:	Fe fyddaf i'n darllen	Fe fydda(f) i'n darllen	I shall read
	Byddaf i'n darllen		
I:	A fyddaf i'n darllen?	Fydda(f) i'n darllen?	Shall I read?
R:	Byddaf	Bydda(f)	I shall (= Yes)

Present-Future Inflected

D:	Fe ddarllenaf i	Fe ddarllena(f) i	I read
	Darllenaf i		
I:	A ddarllenaf i?	Ddarllena(f) i?	Do I read?
R:	Ie. Darllenaf Gwna(f)	LW: Yes.	I read
		CW: I do	

One aspect of the relationship between LW and CW that is of great value to the linguist is that these two represent accepted standardizations from different periods of Modern Welsh. They may thus be treated diachronically as two different synchronic structures of what Welsh speakers have perceived as the *langue*, in the sense of Saussure 1959.

The data in Table 1 illustrate that (1) The declarative sentence particle may be realized as zero (in literary Welsh). Alternatively, it may be realized as *Y* before consonants and as *Yr* or *R* before vowels when the periphrastic verbal phrase is used with the present or imperfect verb 'to be'; or it may be realized as *Fe* or as *Mi* (in the North) when the periphrastic verbal phrase is used with the future tense and also when the inflected verbal phrase is used. This latter particle (only) motivates the "soft mutation" or lenition of the initial consonant of the verb (seen in the table as the change from *b* [b] to *f* [v] in *fyddaf* and from *d* [d] to *dd* [ð] in *ddarllenaf*).

(2) The interrogative sentence particle is realized as *A* (in literary Welsh) or as zero (in colloquial Welsh). Both motivate the soft mutation.

(3) The responsive sentence particle is realized as zero. It does not motivate any mutation.

3.   Analysis: Stratificational Description

In the tradition of Christie 1977, Welch 1975, and others working in the stratificational description of diachrony (see also Griffen 1984), let us compare and contrast the network structures that obtain from the data on sentence particles in Table 1. These networks are presented in Figure 3 for LW and in Figure 4 for CW. On the lexemic stratum, the three relationships are represented with their appropriate initials (as in Figure 2); and on the morphemic stratum, the sentence-particle morphological representation of ^{L}/D/ is given as ^{M}/d/, that of ^{L}/I/ as ^{M}/i/, and that of ^{L}/R/ as ^{M}/r/.

The markedness relationships in LW are rather straightforward. On the lexemic stratum, ^{L}/D/ is realized if no condition in the realization portion (from the sememic stratum) requires another lexeme. If interrogation is required, then ^{L}/I/ is realized; and if response is required, then ^{L}/R/ is realized.

The morphemic stratum of LW reflects the lexemic markedness priorities. If there is no motivation for any particular sentence particle, then the unmarked relationship ^{M}/d/ is realized. This lack of motivation corresponds to the choice of the unmarked ^{L}/D/ on the lexemic stratum — if no marked choice is made on the lexemic stratum, then no marked choice is made on the morphemic. Given ^{M}/d/, if there is no further motivation, then the particle is realized as zero. If there is a motivation (such as emphasis), then there is a choice between relations that ultimately lead to *Y*, *Yr*, or *R* for the present and imperfect periphrastic tenses and to *Fe* or *Mi* and soft mutation (SM) for the future periphrastic and inflected tenses.

The motivation for a particular sentence particle in the tactic pattern of the morphemic stratum corresponds to the structure of the lexemic. Given ^{L}/I/, ^{M}/i/ is realized; and given ^{L}/R/, ^{M}/r/ is realized. Under ^{M}/i/, we find a conjunction of relationships that ultimately leads to *A* followed by soft mutation (in the OR-DERED-AND node). Of course, the realization of the relationships occurs on a lower, morphonic level (as designated by the single line on the diagram), and the orthographic representation is used here for clarity and simplicity.

For LW, we should note that there are two possibilities for the unmarked category on the morphemic stratum — ^{M}/d/ and ^{M}/r/. Both may be realized without any particle at all, certainly satisfying the zero criterion for the unmarked. Since there is no reason to introduce anataxis between the lexemic and morphemic strata, we can assume that ^{M}/d/ is the unmarked for the morphemic stratum as ^{L}/D/ is for the lexemic.

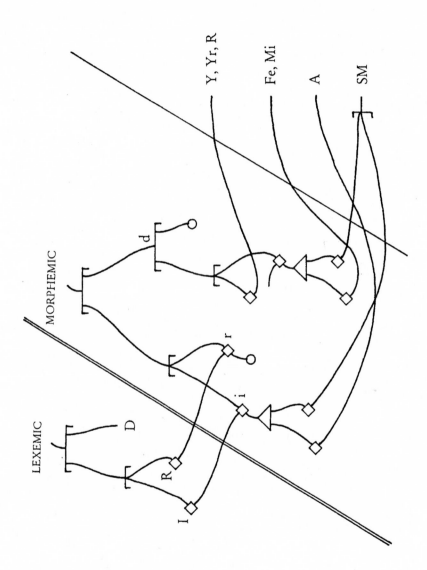

Figure 3.   *Unmarked Declarative in LW*

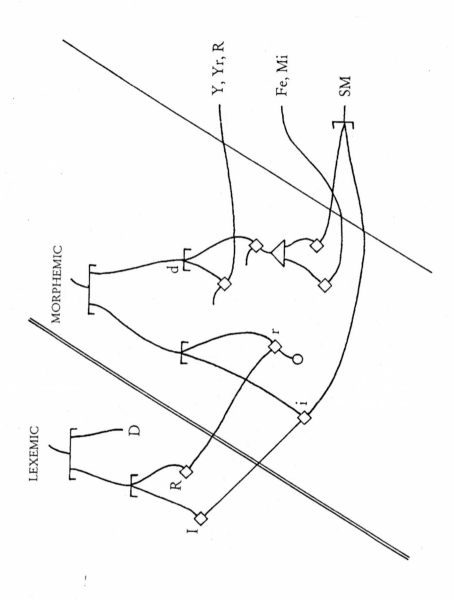

Figure 4.   *Unmarked Declarative in CW*

On the morphemic stratum of CW, however, there is a profound change. The zero realization is no longer the unmarked choice in the tactics of ^{M}/d/, for the particle must be realized (except as noted below in the conclusion). Even more important, the only zero realization is now in the branch of the tactic pattern containing ^{M}/r/. Given ^{L}/R/, there is simply no particle realized at all.

4.   Discussion: Revision and Analysis

In the foregoing diachronic stratificational analysis, the two synchronic stages are analyzed and compared and the differences are noted. The specific difference in the shift of the zero realization from ^{M}/d/ to ^{M}/r/ is taken to be the manifestation of the change. There is, however, one major problem: The analysis of CW is based upon the assumptions underlying the analysis of LW. Specifically, ^{L}/D/ and ^{M}/d/ are assumed to be the unmarked categories for their respective strata on the basis of the structure of LW. But what about the structure of CW?

The zero realization is morphologically unmarked (all things being equal), leading to the unmarked status of ^{M}/d/ in LW. Aside from our assumptions about declarative sentences, the only evidence we have of the unmarked nature of this relationship is the zero realization. If we were to apply the same analytic standards to CW as those applied to LW, then we would have to revise our analysis of the morphemic tactic pattern of CW as in Figure 5.

Morphologically, the relationships pertaining to ^{M}/r/ are less marked than are those pertaining to ^{M}/d/. From a morphological point of view, then, ^{M}/r/ should occupy the right-hand portion of the ORDERED-OR node. Thus, no motivating realizational line is necessary between ^{L}/R/ and this unmarked category. Consequently, a line is necessary between the ^{L}/D/ and the ^{M}/d/.

The rearrangement of the morpheme tactics in Figure 5 sets up a rather routine condition of anataxis, in which the unmarked relationship of the lexemic stratum corresponds to a marked relationship of the morphemic (and, of course, vice versa). But why does it have to be anatactic? After all, the only way of maintaining our assumption of the unmarked declarative sentence in the previous section was through the avoidance of anataxis.

Indeed, the very reason why the lexemic-morphemic relationship of the Welsh sentence particle is anatactic is that we have been assuming that the declarative sentence is inevitably the unmarked. If we do not make this assumption and we construct the lexemic stratum's tactic pattern on the basis of the

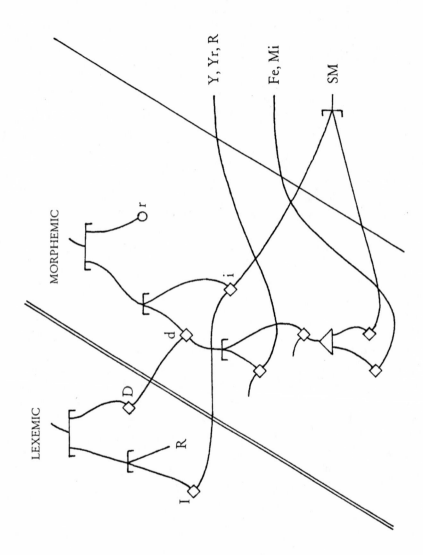

Figure 5.   *Unmarked ^M/r/ in CW*

evidence derived empirically, then the result is the rather disturbing network illustrated in Figure 6.

Not only is the responsive the unmarked sentence structure according to Figure 6, but if we did not have the responsive and had to decide between the declarative and the interrogative for the unmarked sentence order, we would have to chose not the declarative, but the interrogative. In the absence of the responsive, we would have to conclude that the verb of the Welsh sentence undergoes a mutation. The difference then between the declarative and the interrogative would be that the declarative is marked with a sentence particle, while the interrogative is unmarked. This is precisely how Davies and Davies pedagogically describe the difference for the inflected verb: "Questions are formed by dropping *fe*" (1977: 193).

5.   Conclusion: Return to Empiricism

Our findings relative to Figure 6 are indeed disturbing, for they describe a language in which the responsive sentence — not the declarative — is the unmarked on the basis of the sentence particles (and their mutations), which represent the only structural differences in these sentence types. And if the responsive sentence were somehow discounted, the interrogative would be considered the unmarked. The declarative sentence is thus the most marked of all!

If we examine the present periphrastic verb phrase as in Table 2, we find that the pattern of sentence particles is slightly different. While we see that the declarative sentence can indeed be morphologically unmarked for the sentence particle, we should note that the form of the verb itself is marked for the third person singular and plural — those instances in which the sentence particle may be realized as zero. Moreover, in the imperfect periphrastic, where there is no marked third-person verb form, the particle must be realized in the declarative — *Roeddwn i'n darllen* 'I was reading'; *Roedd hi'n darllen* 'She was reading'. Thus, the structure of the Welsh verb phrase as a whole maintains the apparent marking priorities evident for the sentence particle in Table 1.

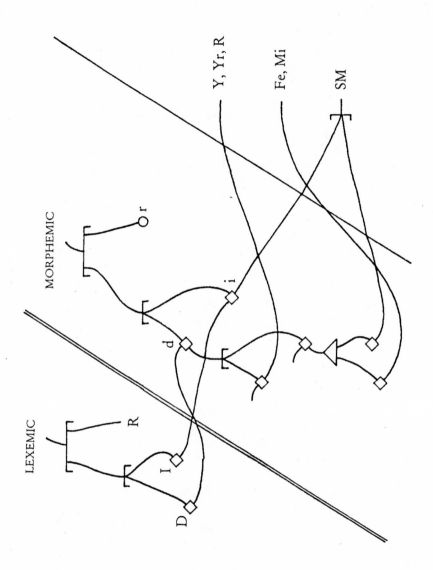

Figure 6.   *Unmarked ᴸ/r/ in CW*

Table 2. *The Present Periphrastic in CW*

Declarative	
Rydw/Rwy i'n darllen	I am reading
Rwyt ti'n darllen	You are reading
Mae e'n darllen	He is reading
Mae hi'n darllen	She is reading
Rydyn ni'n darllen	We are reading
Rydych chi'n darllen	You are reading
Maen nhw'n darllen	They are reading
Interrogative	
Ydw i'n darllen?	Am I reading?
Wyt ti'n darllen?	Are you reading?
Ydy e'n darllen?	Is he reading?
Ydy hi'n darllen?	Is she reading?
Ydyn ni'n darllen?	Are we reading?
Ydych chi'n darllen?	Are you reading?
Ydyn nhw'n darllen?	Are they reading?
Responsive	
Ydw	I am
Wyt	You are
Ydy	He/She is
Ydyn	We are
Ydych	You are
Ydyn	They are

If we are to maintain one sentence type as unmarked, and if we are to determine which sentence type is unmarked on the basis of the grammatical (the lexemic-morphemic) structure of the language (be it by sentence particle or by the form of the verb), then we may maintain the declarative sentence as unmarked for LW, but we must maintain the responsive sentence as unmarked for CW. The question now is: Must we designate one sentence type as unmarked?

The assumption that one sentence type — presumably the simple active declarative (kernel) sentence — must be considered as unmarked is not derived empirically from the grammatical evidence of Welsh, but supplied rather notionally from semantic/logical considerations. While this motivation for a basic, kernel, unmarked sentence type may suffice for an approach to linguistic analysis in which the semantic component is either not treated, treated as derivative (or interpretive), or incorporated into the syntax (as into a basic string), it is not necessary for stratificational linguistics, in which a particular sentence type may be marked or unmarked on the sememic stratum and unordered (void of markedness relationships) on the lexemic and morphemic strata.

The way around the dilemma posed by the Welsh sentence particles is to return to empiricism. If there is a good reason to treat the declarative sentence as unmarked on the sememic stratum, then we should construct our sememic stratal network accordingly. As for the lexemic and the morphemic, however, no use of the unmarked relationship is justified by the Welsh evidence. Thus, we should construct analytical networks both for LW and for CW as in Figures 7 and 8, respectively.

When we analyze and describe the lexemic and morphemic strata of Welsh purely on the basis of the empirically determined syntactic and morphological evidence, the networks turn out to be simpler in the economy metric. Moreover, the change between the conservative LW and the innovative CW can now be seen to be a minor adjustment in the morphemic tactic pattern.

The fact that the change itself can now be seen as something rather undramatic reflects the way Welsh speakers appear to have viewed the change. No mention is made of shifting markedness or anything so significant in Jones and Thomas 1977; no articles have appeared in *The Bulletin of the Board of Celtic Studies* or in *Studia Celtica* noting a dilemma posed by the unmarking of the responsive sentence and the marking of the declarative; no guidance is offered to students expecting the question to be a marked variant of the statement in CW texts (indeed, compare the earlier reference to Davies and Davies 1977: 193).

When we combine the empirical evidence from the language itself with the reception of the change by speakers, we are inexorably drawn to the conclusion that there is no grammatical reason why a question or a response must be viewed as inherently derived from a statement. Of course, stratificational linguistics can accommodate this finding simply by avoiding markedness notation on the lexemic and morphemic strata — by using UNORDERED-OR nodes. Other approaches, however, in which the one sentence type must be derived from the other through transformation or in which the elements are moved and traces are left to reconstruct a "common" (= declarative) structure may very well find that this empirical evidence still presents a significant dilemma.

This dilemma calls to mind Sydney Lamb's Presidential Address before the 1984 Forum of the Linguistic Association of Canada and the United States (Lamb 1985). He points out there that the problem common to item-and-arrangement and item-and-process models of grammar is that they are "varieties of a

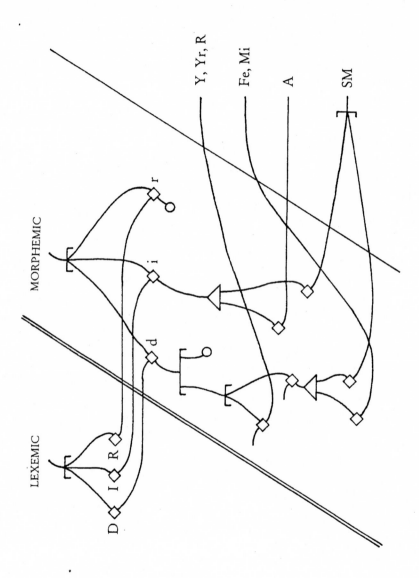

Figure 7.   *Unordered Sentence Types in LW*

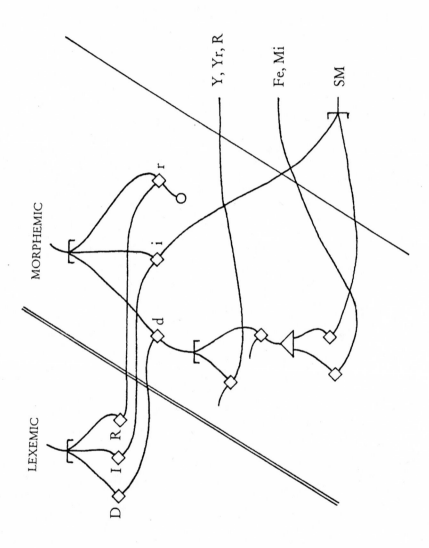

Figure 8.   *Unordered Sentence Types in CW*

horizontal approach to linguistic structure, and they thereby tend to neglect the vertical dimension. ...The horizontal approach involves looking at the relationships of units to other units of the same level" (Lamb 1985: 15). Lamb's stratificational model pioneered in his seminal work of 1966, however, leads to an alternative in which "syntactic constructions are treated as linguistic signs" (Lamb 1985: 18).

References

Bowen, John T., and T.J. Rhys Jones. 1960. *Welsh*. Kent: Hodder and Stoughton.

Chomsky, Noam. 1957. *Syntactic Structures*. The Hague: Mouton.

Christie, William M., Jr., 1977. *A Stratificational View of Linguistic Change*. (Edward Sapir Monograph No. 4.) Lake Bluff, Illinois: Jupiter.

Cook, Walter J. 1969. *Introduction to Tagmemic Analysis*. New York: Holt, Rinehart and Winston.

Davies, Cennard, and W. Basil Davies. 1977. *Welsh Course Handbook*. London: Linguaphone Institute.

Fife, James. 1986. Literary and colloquial Welsh: Problems of definition. *Word* 37:141–51.

Griffen, Toby D. 1980. Nationalism and the emergence of a new standard Welsh. *Language Problems and Language Planning* 4:187–94.

Griffen, Toby D. 1984. On the metaplastic negative in French, Welsh, and Swabian. *Forum Linguisticum* 8:39–49.

Jones, Morris, and Alan R. Thomas. 1977. *The Welsh Language: Studies in its Syntax and Semantics*. Cardiff: University of Wales Press.

Lamb, Sydney M. 1966. *Outline of Stratificational Grammar*. Rev. ed. Washington: Georgetown University Press.

Lamb, Sydney M. 1985. Descriptive process. *LACUS Forum* 11: 5–20.

Lockwood, David G. 1972. *Introduction to Stratificational Linguistics*. New York: Harcourt Brace Jovanovich.

Lockwood, David G. 1988. *Introduction to Stratificational Linguistics*. Rev. ed., version for LIN 831. East Lansing, Michigan: Unpublished.

National Language Unit of Wales. 1988. *Cymraeg i ddysgwyr: Welsh for Learners*. Rev. ed. Treforest: Foxgate.

Pike, Kenneth L. 1982. *Linguistic Concepts: An Introduction to Tagmemics*. Lincoln: University of Nebraska Press.

Radford, Andrew. 1988. *Transformational Grammar: A First Course*. Cambridge: Cambridge University Press.

Reich, Peter A. 1973. Competence, performance and relational networks. *Readings in Stratificational Linguistics*, ed. by Adam Makkai and David G. Lockwood, 84–91. University: University of Alabama Press.

Rhys Jones, T. J. 1977. *Living Welsh*. Kent: Hodder and Stoughton.

Richards, Melville. 1938. *Cystrawen y frawddeg Gymraeg*. Caerdydd: Gwasg Prifysgol Cymru.

Safir, Kenneth J. 1985. *Syntactic Chains*. Cambridge: Cambridge University Press.

Saussure, Ferdinand de. 1959. *Course in General Linguistics*. Trans. by Wade Baskin. New York: Philosophical Library.

Sullivan, William J. III. 1980. Syntactic and linguistic semantics in stratificational theory. Syntax and Semantics. Vol. 13: *Current Approaches to Syntax*. Ed. by Edith A. Morovcsik and Jessica R. Wirth, 301–27. New York: Academic Press.

Welch, Doris H. 1975. Latinate English verbs and nouns: A synchronic, diachronic, and panchronic description. *LACUS Forum* 1: 472–522.

Williams, Stephen A. 1980. *A Welsh Grammar*. Cardiff: University of Wales Press.

Abou the author

*Toby Griffen is currently Professor of Foreign Languages and Literature at Southern Illinois University at Edwardsville, where he has taught since 1977. He received his Ph.D. in Linguistics from the University of Florida in 1975. He first met Syd Lamb in 1974 at the first Forum of the Linguistic Association of Canada and the United States. He has presented a paper at nearly every LACUS Forum, and is currently series editor for its annual Forum volumes. His publications focus on phonology, historical linguistics, and Welsh linguistics. They include **Aspects of Dynamic Phonology, Germano-European: Breaking the Sound Law**, and **Names from the Dawn of British Legend**.*

PART I

B. Related Approaches: Theory

CHAPTER 8

The Development Of Adequate Formalism In Linguistics

Winfred P. Lehmann

University of Texas at Austin

1. The Current Status of Formal Representation in Linguistics

Formal representation of language is now standard in our science. Instead of discursive description of structures, graphic notations comparable to those in presentations and interpretation of data in the physical sciences are virtually required. As the recipient of this volume, who has long been concerned with computation stated, and then demonstrated: "In analyzing and describing linguistic relationships it is a matter of practical necessity to employ some system of precise and simple notation". But since, as he went on to say, "some linguists have been saddened by the increasing use of algebraic notation in linguistics" (Lamb 1966a: 8), it may be of interest to examine the development of adequate formalism and its use in the history of our science.

Pursuing first, briefly, the "saddening", we may recall that earlier linguists were faced with a similar situation. It is remarkable that Lamb's reasons for using formal notation ("Languages are such complicated systems" [Lamb 1966a: 8]) virtually duplicate Brugmann's in his defense of his procedures: "das Objekt der Grammatik, die Sprache, [ist] eine sehr komplizierte menschliche Tätigkeit, bei der die verschiedenartigsten Faktoren in gegenseitiger Abhängigkeit zum Ganzen zusammenwirken, bei der im Grunde alles durch alles bedingt ist"[1]

---

1. In English translation: "The object of grammar, language, [is] a very complicated human activity, in which the most varied factors work together in mutual dependence upon the whole, and in which everything is at the bottom conditioned by everything else".

(1904: VIII). In response to critics of his procedures, Brugmann, like Lamb, compared the procedures in the fields of "medicine and the natural sciences" (1904: V). Brugmann's use of formal notation was not as pervasive in his works as is that in publications today. But the confrontation with protesting colleagues scarcely differs.

While with Lamb we may associate use of notation with progress in the field, and while that may be ascribed to specific individuals, it may be instructive to examine formal notation of the past, with some attention to its perceived advantages and shortcomings. Lamb supports its use in the interests of completeness and precision. On the other hand, any formal representation involves some simplification, whether through disregard of data and accordingly loss of information, or inadequacy in fit to the data.

Lamb discusses three types of formal notation: two-dimensional graphic, algebraic, and tabular. The first two he puts on a similar basis, assuming each to be preferable "for some types of work with linguistic structures", but also crediting the graphic or diagrammatic as providing "a more direct portrayal of structural relationships than the algebraic, and it may be considered the primary notation" (1966a: 8). Tabular notation he admits as "convenient for some purposes", referring to Newell's use of it for the lexicon (1966: 87ff.) and the "morphicon" (100 ff.) in the appendix to his *Outline* (Newell 1966). Interestingly, we find all three types employed in probably the earliest, and most widely represented, situation that claimed widespread attention in modern linguistics, so that all three types have a long and distinguished tradition of use.

2.   Formal Notation as Applied in Historical Phonology

In 1818 Rasmus Rask used primarily a tabular notation to present characteristic data clarified in successive versions of what came to be known as Grimm's law. His presentation may be conveniently examined in English translation (Lehmann 1967: 29–37). Rask provided "tables" of forms in several Indo-European dialects, preceding each set of forms with a formula indicating the change concerned, as may be illustrated by a sample in which the first word is Latin or Greek, the second Icelandic:

p to f, e.g.: *platus* (broad) *flatur* (flat), *pater fadir.*

In spite of its simplicity, the presentation led Jacob Grimm to revise quickly the first volume of his Germanic grammar, and to supplement the tabular notation with an algebraic (see Lehmann 1967: 46–60). In contrast with Rask, Grimm set up formulae in which the first column indicated the Greek sound, the second the Gothic, the third the Old High German, e.g.

P   F   B(V).

These algebraic formulae were followed by "the necessary examples for the proposed nine comparisons" (Lehmann 1967: 52).

Grimm also utilized more abstract classification for his nine entities in Germanic and the three realizations of each: Tenues, Aspiratae, Mediae. These abstractions soon were employed in the two-dimensional graphic or diagrammatic notation given in Figure 1 that has been widely reproduced:

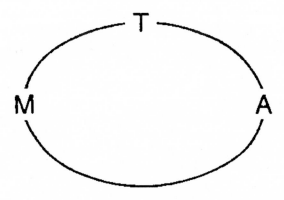

Figure 1.   *Notation showing the relation between Tenues, Aspiratae and Mediae*

The diagram has been elaborated, as by Prokosch (1939: 51). The elaboration was prompted by failure of the earlier representation to compensate for its lack of completeness and precision. These shortcomings have been so widely discussed that it is scarcely necessary to do more than mention them. But in view of many comments on the comparative method, especially in connection with "distant comparison", it is also important to point out firmly that Grimm listed all examples available to him of the sounds in question as well as "exceptions or instances where the proposed comparisons fail"; that is to say, he included all examples of patterns with any of the consonants, those in Greek or Latin as well as those in the Germanic dialects.

In contrast with Grimm's admirable procedures, the representations of current linguists, especially those in the generative school, do not account for all manifestations of the structures comprehended by the proposed rules; instead, they limit their attention to specific patterns.

Rather than incompleteness in the data concerned, Grimm's description of the consonants suffered from incompleteness as well as from imprecision in their identification. For example, **M** or Mediae included voiced fricatives as well as voiced stops.

Moreover, the environments of the consonants were not taken into consideration. Observation of these led to more precise statements, as by von Raumer and others on the "exceptions" involving lack of change after Germanic fricatives, as in *night*, German *Nacht*, cf. Latin *noctem*, or the lack of fit in words with aspirates in successive syllables of Sanskrit or Greek cognates, as in *bind*, cf. Sanskrit *bandhati* < PIE **bhendh-*, or the change of a **T** to an **M** rather than to an **A**, as in Gothic *fadar*, cf. Latin *pater*. The statements of these linguists were still largely discursive.

The algebraic notation, subsequently employed in all historical treatments of phonology, was made possible by Schleicher's reconstruction of Proto-Indo-European forms. Formulae representing derivation from earlier forms that was indicated by means of an arrowhead pointing to the later forms gradually replaced formulae in which the sounds in question were simply placed contiguously, as by Grimm. We may also note that this formalism was later adopted to indicate syntactic derivation of components from assumed larger components. In spite of the change in type of formalism and in use, it is important to remember that the first major contribution in modern linguistics, Grimm's clarification of the relationships of the Germanic obstruents with those in other Indo-European dialects, made use of formal representation.

3.   Formal Representation as Applied in Stating Genealogical Relationships

Schleicher is much better known for introducing notation to indicate relationships among languages and dialects. For this purpose he made use of the tree diagram, which recently has been widely used to indicate relationships between constituents of sentences. The use of such diagrams was not original in linguistics; they were also employed in illustrating relationships among manuscripts, as of the medieval epics, and may well have been prompted by the earlier representation classifying individuals into families, for which the tree diagram seems highly apposite. It is also of interest that Schleicher's use of the family tree for languages was more precise than the tree structures often provided in handbooks, for as he stated "the length of the lines shows the duration of the periods, their distances from one another, the degrees of relationship" (Lehmann 1967: 94). Yet those "lengths" were determined by Schleicher's views and by data available to him. Those data were rapidly supplemented, so that soon his line lengths no longer seemed accurate.

But the chief problem with Schleicher's "two-dimensional graphic notation" was found in its lack of precision for representing the complexities of relationships among dialects and languages, especially languages in contiguous areas; for such areas permit modifications of relationships that are not genealogically determined. A recent examination of the data used for determining the relationships among the "older Germanic languages" may be found in Robinson (1992: 247–64). Examining 31 features, 17 from phonology, 14 from morphology, though none from syntax, Robinson concludes "once one abandons the rigid dichotomies of the *Stammbaum*, one is dealing with a fluid, changeable situation in which dialect communities may alternately diverge, diverge only in part, converge, converge only in part, and otherwise behave like human groupings rather than biological species trees" (1992: 263). In view of the disclaimer, it might be pointed out that a major specialist in ecology has recently published a work which aims to get across the view "that one of the things to remember about ecosystems as well as species is that nothing stays the same; all is process" (Wilson 1992). Yet specialists in the humanities, including linguists, still propose ideal situations, e.g. language L, that are static and when appropriately treated can be provided with "a complete specification of an infinite set of grammatical sentences of L and their structural descriptions" (Chomsky 1961: 6).

The recognition of "changeable situations", not only in a relatively small group like the society speaking Germanic languages, but also in larger groups led to the introduction and widespread acceptance of Johannes Schmidt's wave theory (1872). In supporting his notation Schmidt pointed to wave-like spread of characteristics already when the Indo-European languages were contiguous, or in the term of Diakonoff, when they made up a dialect continuum. Further, such characteristics were identifiable among languages and sub-groups that were positioned on separate lines or branches of Schleicher's tree, as when Germanic and Lithuanian exhibit the same method of formation of the numerals for eleven (one-left) and twelve (two-left) even though Baltic by Schleicher's notation remained part of a Balto-Slavic unity long after this separated from Germanic. Many other such characteristics shared among contiguous, though presumably long separated, sub-groups have been cited. For such situations Schmidt's two-dimensional graphic notation in accordance with the wave theory seemed superior to Schleicher's family tree.

But, as has been pointed out, social groups speaking a given dialect or language may be abruptly separated from earlier neighbors, as through migration or intrusion of other speakers between them. For example, the Afro-Asiatic languages in Ethiopia as well as the far earlier Akkadian, were taken to areas in which OV speakers were socially dominant; similar examples may be cited from the sub-continent, as of Sinhalese. Rather than maintain consistently the characteristic VSO structure of the Afro-Asiatic family the separated languages adopted many OV characteristics. While the effects support the wave theory regarding the spread of characteristics among contiguous social groups in contact, such spread from Sumerian into Akkadian and the like is across family lines. Accordingly, the representation as proposed by Schmidt, even with modifications by others, only with difficulty represents the complex relationships among the members of the Afro-Asiatic language family or even the Indo-European, which was not extended so widely. Later Indo-Europeanists then proposed different models in attempts to depict the relationships among the sub-groups. (See Lehmann 1992: 41–48 for examples). Study of the relationships among languages is accordingly a further area of linguistics in which formalism was applied, found useful and subsequently maintained.

4.   Formal Notation as Applied in Morphology and Syntax

Morphology has almost entirely been presented in tabular form, that is, in paradigms, when not treated discursively. An exception to these procedures may be noted in the treatment of roots. In 1879 Saussure proposed an elegant system for Indo-European root structure. This system was subsequently elaborated, especially by Benveniste (1935: 147–73; see also Lehmann 1993: 93–94, 125). The Indo-European root is now depicted as consisting of three elements: CvC, in which v in basic forms is [e]. Further formulae indicate possible extensions: CvC-C, CC-vC(C) or CC-n-vC. The formulae indicate the possible forms of roots, or their extensions, in Proto-Indo-European. They have been very important in identifying roots, reconstructing accurate examples of them, and in determining earlier forms, as when a laryngeal has been lost. The system received support when the earlier data available in the Anatolian languages became known.

As a further result, these formulae have assisted in distinguishing between the forms of verbs and those of nouns in the proto-language. They accordingly have met the goal of such symbolization as noted by logicians like Carnap in providing "brevity and perspicuity".

In the same year in which Benveniste's system was published, Kuryłowicz advanced a somewhat different system (1935: 121–30). His system did not provide as much clarity as had Benveniste's. It has generally been disregarded. But I cite it here as another example of the use of symbolic notation in dealing with morphology. More such examples could be reviewed, especially those used by Hirt and others in attempting to clarify the ablaut relationships among morphemes in Proto-Indo-European. Similarly, efforts have been made to provide "canonical forms" for other language families, especially for the Semitic root system. But the examples cited may be adequate to indicate that linguists have employed, and found profitable, formal notation in the treatment of morphology.

Syntax generally has received discursive representation in historical linguistics, with the exception of relatively recent treatments (Lehmann 1974: 11–12 *et passim*). The procedures remain to be adopted generally.

Formal representation in the historical study of language was accordingly developed early, but applied only to some topics of concern. While languages continued to be presented much as they were a century ago, e.g. in the massive compendia produced at the turn of the century by Brugmann, to be followed by those of Hirt and Meillet, more extensive formal procedures were being developed by logicians that came to be widely adopted by linguists.

5.   The Development of Symbolic Logic and its Impact on Linguistic Research

Around the middle of the nineteenth century an abstract language was developed, initially for examining mathematical procedures. Known today under the term *symbolic logic*, as "a system of signs and of rules for their use" it is comparable in many respects to natural languages. Its development and extended uses are well-known, so that they do not require exposition here. Carnap may be consulted for a concise presentation, as of "Language B" (1958: 78–92 and following). Distinctions applied in computational linguistic research, as between semantic and syntactic systems, formational and transformational rules, as well as the "region of *pragmatics*" are clearly presented there. These and the procedures in general are the result of developments carried out by mathematicians like George Boole (1854) and Gustav Frege, curiously with no attention to work on natural languages even though the titles of some of their major works, e.g. Frege 1879, include the term for language. Only when attempts were undertaken to develop means for communicating through computers by means of natural language did the need arise for a system comparable to that developed far earlier in mathematics.

The advantages of such a system were discussed in a symposium organized by the American Mathematical Society in 1960 (cf. *Structure ... n.e.* 1961). Like the symposium itself, many of the participants were supported by military organizations. For example, Chomsky's work was supported, "in part by the U. S. Army (Signal Corps), the U. S. Air Force (Office of Scientific Research, Air Research and Development Command), and the U. S. Navy (Office of Naval Research). It was also supported in part by the National Science Foundation" (1961: 6). "Mechanical translation" is mentioned only once in the course of the volume — by Yngve, who states that his model was "designed for use in a mechanical translation system" (131). It scarcely needs mention that the military, and the intelligence agencies — who at the time funneled funds for such work through the National Science Foundation — were primarily concerned with the activity that went largely unmentioned by the participants.

As in the introduction of new methods in any science the early attempts to use computers for treatment of natural language were cumbersome and severely limited. Moreover, they are surprisingly undocumented. Fortunately, some of the major figures in those efforts are still active, among them Lamb, so that there are possibilities for their approaches to be documented.[2] Among other problems with regard to the new procedures was the lack of funding except for an application that had been proposed by physical scientists as one of the uses for the newly developed machine after the conclusion of World War II left it with few apparent opportunities. That application is translation with the help of computers, or as it came to be more widely known, machine translation.

When one reviews the treatises on the various projects that were inaugurated, arguments for shifting away from discursive presentation of language are more prominent than the procedures themselves, as suggested in the first section of this essay. Moreover, translation involves many fields: information on the material to be translated, whether in the sciences, human affairs, or *belles lettres*; understanding of the purpose of the work, whether formal or informal, technical, popular; extent of freedom desired in the result; and finally, various sub-fields of linguistics, including lexicographical control of various registers, as well as knowledge of the two or more languages concerned. These and other topics, including the luddite concerns of human translators, seemed to require greater attention in presentations by early specialists than did a concise statement of the adoption of procedures with a "logic of relations" that would represent those of natural language. A concise presentation of the activities at the time is available in Delavenay (1960).

Finally, vocal figures who proclaimed procedures that would permit improved formalization of natural language, especially syntax, also rejected computational verification of their "theories". In contrast with chemistry, where computational attention is labeled theoretical chemistry, prominent linguists expressed disdain for computational approaches. Even worse, a major figure proclaimed that "linguistic theory is primarily concerned with an ideal speaker-listener, in a completely homogeneous speech-community, who knows its language perfectly and is unaffected by such grammatically irrelevant conditions as memory limitations, distractions, shifts of attention and interest, and errors (random or characteristic) in applying his knowledge of the language in actual performance" (Chomsky 1965: 3). Fairly obviously the output of such a creature would have no interest for anyone seeking a translation, while attracting many younger scholars to vapid research. Since Chomsky acquired tremendous prestige, in part for sociological reasons beyond the scope of this essay, most

---

2. Also see Yngve's article in the present volume [editors' note].

linguists scorned machine translation, and with it development of formal means for testing and verifying linguistic theory.

Apart from the rigorous system for expressing relationships among linguistic elements, the chief innovation taken from the procedures of mathematics and symbolic logic was the notion of transformation (Harris 1952). With his attention to ideal language Chomsky's use of "transformation", in his words "bears little formal resemblance to this [i.e. Harris's] conception" (1961: 16). The requirement to deal with actual language determined the use of the notion as stated and pursued by Harris. Its use is central in the formalization applied in machine translation projects.

6.   Formalization as Proposed by Traditional Linguists

In a series of essays published from 1945 to 1962 that were preceded by earlier treatments Erwin Koschmieder dealt with formalization in linguistics; recognizing that many of these appeared in works that might be difficult of access, he made them generally available in a collection of 1965. Even so they were generally disregarded, possibly in view of the monolingualism of American linguists at that time and later. There is no reference to any of the articles in the 1961 work: *Structure of Language*....

Among Koschmieder's articles, the most pertinent for this discussion is one of 1956 entitled "Die Mathematisierung der Sprachwissenschaft" (1965: 124–39). Others deal with the "relationships between language and logic", (1951) "the problem of translation", (1955) and special situations in syntactic treatments. Another asks whether "the symbolic system of logistics (= symbolic logic) is a language" (1955); Koschmieder answers in the negative. In view of previous disregard, including among German linguists who adopted "generative linguistics", there is little point in doing more than calling attention to Koschmieder's essays once again, and suggesting that they might be useful still in providing perspective for formal approaches.

The many works of Zellig Harris, culminating in his book, *A Theory of Language and Information — A Mathematical Approach* (1991), probably have had greater influence on formalization in linguistics than have any other works by traditional linguists. Harris may be included in this tradition because of his stated continuation of the "distributional (combinatorial) methods of Edward Sapir and of Leonard Bloomfield" (1991: vi).

Harris's argumentation in favor of a mathematical approach to language is tight, and extensive, so that it cannot be summarized briefly (cf. esp. 1991: 146–60). Moreover it is based on attention to many languages. In supporting his approach with reference to these, Harris makes the highly welcome statement that "one cannot rely on episodic examples; it is necessary to survey the full range of data in a language, in a way that establishes their regularities" (1991: v). Presumably this is a gentle way to indicate that the trick sentences or restricted samples favored by generative linguists have little value. Other conclusions reached by Harris are equally important for achieving a complete grammar of a language or control over it, whether according to time-honored procedures or with the use of computers, as we may note briefly.

In a short section asking: "Can meaning be utilized?" (1991: 40–43) Harris states unequivocally that "for an adequate knowledge of meanings in language, we need to know the constructions, in addition to an unspecified amount of semantic information garnered from the situations in which earlier-heard words and sentences had been said" (41). That is to say, the so-called knowledge-based approach to computational control of language, without attention to the meaning conveyed by morphology and syntax is misguided.

Further, Harris denies vigorously that "the forms — the words and construc-tions — of language, and the meanings which they carry, can be described each independently of the other" (40). That is to say, efforts to achieve translation or any other simulation of human control over language by means of statistical analysis are hopeless. Unfortunately, efforts are also under way that attempt such procedures.

In concluding this reference to Harris's last, and presumably final views on linguistic procedures to analyze, describe and understand language, I add that the descriptions proposed or achieved by any set of assumptions can only be verified by means of computerization. Descriptions of constructions that have been falsified in subsequent publications by generativists and others might be cited to provide ready support for this conclusion. Experiences from successive computer-ized descriptions of a given language could also be noted here. But in a brief review of the efforts to introduce formalism into linguistic description there is only space to call attention to considered judgements of one of the outstanding linguists of recent times.

As is well-known, the grammarian on whom generative linguists have drawn most widely and deeply, Otto Jespersen, also published a work at the end of his career that employed formalism in the treatment of syntax (1937). While the work was reprinted in 1969, with an introduction interpreting Jespersen's formalism and its presumed shortcomings in accordance with generative theory at the time, Jespersen's "seemingly abstract formulas" have "deterred ... his fellow-students" from note of them. Those formulae then do not warrant attention here. But they illustrate that long before "generative" linguistics was inaugurated, formalism was applied in the treatment of syntax.

Samuel R. Levin, the editor of the reprinted work states that "Jespersen cannot, of course, be credited with having developed a theory of generative grammar, that is, an explicit system of rules from which the structural description of sentences can be automatically derived" (1968: vi). It would be difficult to claim such achievement for anyone else as well. Moreover, the efforts to treat language by one specific theory, whether or not the empty term *generative* is applied, have unfortunately reduced the advantages of applying formalism in the scientific study of language, as we note briefly below.

7.   Formalism in Early Computational Approaches

Only a few of the approaches by early computational linguists will be considered here. Simple attempts merely to annotate texts with symbols that might be interpreted by the computer will not be cited. We may recall that projects under pressure to produce operational machine translation systems developed them in accordance with computer hardware and software at the time, using minimal annotation of words and sentences in the hope that the results would be acceptable.

The most successful among such projects was that at Georgetown University. The resulting Russian-English translation system is still maintained, with modifications. Peter Toma, the leading programmer of the project, also went on to produce the machine translation system labeled SYSTRAN, which relies heavily on a large coded lexicon. In spite of its shortcomings, the system is widely used.

The leading theoretical linguist in the Georgetown project, Paul Garvin, advocated an advance to a syntax-based system. The project also involved leading linguists for improving its procedures, among them Charles Hockett and Martin Joos. But social matters brought an end to the Georgetown project, so that further research was carried on only privately by its leading Russian linguist, Michael Zarechnak.

Sheltered by the demands on the Georgetown group, other projects were able to devote more time to the theoretical bases of appropriate systems than to producing operational systems. Among these were projects directed by specialists who were not linguists.

The most prominent of these was located at the Massachusetts Institute of Technology, and was directed by Victor Yngve, a physicist. Yngve made many contributions to computational linguistics, including a programming language labeled COMIT and theoretical articles, of which "The Depth Hypothesis" may have received most attention (1961). His use of formalism had a general effect in the field. But he did not produce an operational machine translation system, nor a large formal description of any language. In time he turned his attention to other matters.

At the same time, projects were established that based their efforts on specific theories of language. Two of these may be reviewed briefly.

8.   Research Based on Stratificational Theory

Lamb may be signaled for following a principled theory of language while carrying out research towards machine translation. As his theory he adopted a stratificational system, viewing language as comprising three major portions: semology, grammar and phonology, consisting with their subdivisions of six strata. Lamb frankly admits that the theory is not original. As predecessors he cites Hjelmslev's glossematics, and credits Hockett, in this way placing himself in the tradition that is labeled "structural" and associated with Leonard Bloomfield. His chief contribution he sees in providing "a more precise specification of the relationships on which the concept of stratification is based" (1966: 2).

The precise specification is in many ways admirable. But the approach directed Lamb's use of formalism and led to enormous complications and redundancy. For example, in one version of the theory, the morpheme /-er/ is seen as a manifestation of either of two lexons: /-er$_1$/ is the comparative suffix, /-er$_2$/ the agent suffix. Either could be attached to the lexon /good/, the first yielding the word *better,* the second the word *-gooder*, as in *do-gooder*. Lamb's diagram exemplifying the patterning, like others in his monograph, is very complex (1966a: 17). As the simple example of /-er/ may indicate, identifying every item in a stratum and thereupon specifying the processes that are involved as the items proceed through other strata to their ultimate expression requires enormously intricate formalization. No operational machine translation resulted.

The second presentation of Lamb's theory is admittedly hasty, an "interim document" (1966a: iii). Lamb never published, however, a version to replace it. He may take comfort in the adoption by a second generation generativist, Jerrold M. Sadock, of virtually the same system (1991). Sadock's system, proclaimed on the back cover to be a "radical departure from the derivational model of grammar that has prevailed in linguistics for thirty years ... [embodies as] principal innovation ... the postulation of a uniform set of interface conditions that require the several orthogonal representations of a single natural language expression to match up in certain ways". In the text we are informed by Sadock that his proposed "grammar consists of parallel organizational principles [and follows] quite a traditional point of view". The "organization" involves "more or less independent sections" labeled "phonology, morphology, syntax, and semantics" (1991: 5). Claiming to have a theory that is "explicit and formal and that makes clear and testable predictions", Sadock provides examples that in many ways are comparable to those of Lamb. But like all generative publications, his book deals only with selected "problems" rather than with entire languages; and like these, it limits its formalism to sentence structures, simply annotating the lexicon with "information as to the structural properties of each lexical item with respect to the several autonomous components" (1991: 29). There is no indication that Sadock's model has been tested computationally.

9.   Research Based on Dependency Grammar

Study of machine translation at the Rand Corporation came to rely on a theoretical approach labeled DEPENDENCY GRAMMAR. A statement of the theory was published in David G. Hays 1964. In the article Hays confronts the dependency model with the immediate constituent model. Hays follows Harris in pointing out "the essential insight formalized by IC theory: ... there are composite expressions (phrases) that have the same distribution as minimal syntactic units". By contrast, "the insight formalized by dependency theory is that particular occurrences of minimal units are directly related to one another" (1964: 511).

To provide an example of formalism in accordance with dependency theory Hays uses the sentence: *Children eat candy neatly.*

$*V_a(N_{pl}(childr,S(en)), eat, N(candy),D_b(neat, L(-ly)))$.

Formalism representing relationships in the sentence with reference to verbs, is comparable to the verb classification that Hornby et al. identified and stated in their dictionary (1963). In subsequent computational approaches, such classes were replaced by frames, which are now central in determining computationally the structure of sentences.

Before observing the use of framing in current formalism we might note that Hays does not mention the massive work which is considered the classic presentation in accordance with dependency theory: *Éléments de syntaxe structurale*, by Lucien Tesnière (1959). We might also note that Tesnière did not refer to an earlier scholar, Johann Werner Meiner (1723–89), who was recently identified as a protagonist of dependency grammar (Naumann 1990). While relatively simple, like Grimm's algebraic formulae or Schleicher's graphic notation, such procedures illustrate long-standing use of formalism in our field.

At the conclusion of his article Hays examines the advantages and disadvantages of "IC and dependency theories, or between transformation and stratification", in this way comparing dependency theory with Lamb's stratificational grammar (524–25). Leaning towards his chosen theory, he finds little to decide between the two on the basis of semantic or of "psycholinguistic material". And he states that "recent formal work in linguistics has drawn attention to the inadequacy of sentencehood data" (1964: 525).

The capability of testing theories for their adequacy may be one of the major advantages of computational linguistics. Experience has demonstrated that an approach comparable to dependency theory is valuable in identifying and describing phrases, as well as the relationships between them. IC theory, on the other hand, is useful for comprehending the structure of clauses and sentences. Long concerned largely with the immediate constituent approach, Zellig Harris recently stated: "the crucial property of language is that the presence of words in a sentence depends on how other words in the sentence depend on yet other words in it" (1991: 54). For computerized recognition of such dependencies, a properly coded lexicon is required. Yet computers, as well as human speakers must first identify sentences in texts, as well as their major components, so that the dependencies can be examined within the sequences in which their relationships apply. Restricted adherence to either IC theory or dependency theory therefore fails to grasp the essence of language and leads to inadequate formalism. It is scarcely necessary to add that no machine translation system was produced with sole reliance on dependency theory.

10. Computational Research in Accordance with a Semiotic Theory of Language

In examining more extensive formalism for representing natural language, we may briefly sketch steps towards production of the METAL system, which after more than three decades of development at the Linguistics Research Center of the University of Texas has adequate capabilities to "observe" and "describe" as well as translate texts, largely in technical fields. Other operational systems may have followed similar steps, but because of the lack of generally available documentation the course of their development cannot be treated here.

In view of widespread misunderstanding of scientific work on language it may be useful to add that the METAL system was produced by a large number of specialists in linguistics and computation, originally at the University of Texas, subsequently also at Munich and other sites in Europe. The specialists were supported not by universities nor by federal agencies designated to fund "pure" research but by organizations interested in practical applications, initially machine translation, thereupon extended to information management. The system is extensive enough to investigate the adequacy of descriptions proposed for many elements and constructions in language. Such a computational system then furnishes linguistics with comparable procedures to those of sciences like physics, chemistry and biology, as well as those with practical aims, as in various engineering applications. Descriptions of languages need no longer be buttressed by introspection or *Sprachgefühl*, or by observation of its use, as in language acquisition, but can be verified experimentally.

Supported initially to explore the feasibility of machine translation rather than to produce an operational system, after several years of research the project did not select a specific linguistic theory such as those mentioned above. Instead, language was viewed as a semiotic system, in accordance with the position of Charles Sanders Peirce. Long established findings on language were followed, such as those now recognized by some generative grammarians. The grammar was "divided into more or less independent sections", much like those of Sadock as stated in Section 6. In view of computer capabilities, no effort was made to include a phonological component in the system; rather, representation of language was provided through traditional spelling. Formalization was carried out in the tradition of symbolic logic, as presented by Carnap, among others. Under this approach, the grammar was extended as further constructions and elements were included for control, as was the lexicon.

The procedures at an early stage of the research may be noted in the abstract of the Center's quarterly report of July 31, 1960, which summarized the fifth three-month period of its activities.

> Conventions have been explained for coding a multi-level phrase structure grammar with transformational properties which are supported by specific analysis and synthesis processes. Programming aids for the compilation and verification of such grammars have been described. The compiling procedure will be a research cycle with the following basic functions: (1) corpus revision, (2) grammar revision, (3) grammatical analysis of corpora, (4) analysis revision, (5) computation of rule frequencies in recorded analyses, (6) computation of analysis probabilities, and (7) synthesis of transformations of analyses. Coding errors and other imperfections in the grammars will also be displayed by the cycle. Heuristics for choices between alternatives in analysis and synthesis have been planned. The projected methods of grammar compilation and verification are thought to be more efficient than trial translations.

Later as well, methods were employed that proved effective in managing the texts, rather than for promoting a selected theory. That is, the use of specific formalism was guided by its success or failure.

Grammatical description of the time is illustrated in the sixth report by means of trees with labeled nodes. An example is provided there for the sentence: *The nature of sound no longer holds a secret for the physicist* (LRC Quarterly Report VI: 10–11, October 31, 1960). While some of the grammatical labels may differ from those subsequently adopted, the sentence is displayed in accordance with standard immediate constituent analysis. At that period of computational research into natural language, lexical analysis was carried out largely to describe morphological characteristics. Classification for syntactic and semantic properties was left for the future.

Advances in control of natural language succeeded in accordance with scientific procedures as applied in other fields, whether in the physical or the historical sciences. Data were examined in accordance with theoretical assumptions. Grammars, often referred to as theories of languages, were produced with successively improved adequacy. Improvements were introduced after testing and evaluating existing grammars through application to further sequences of texts.

Like the grammars, formalism was continually upgraded. As control of the structure of sentences increased, greater attention was given to treatment of the lexicon. Its extension was also guided by previous work, such as the twenty-five "verb patterns" determined by Hornby as given in his dictionary of English

(Hornby et al. 1963). As an example we may cite "Verb Pattern 16" with an illustration: "Verbs marked VP 16 may be followed by a noun or pronoun, and a clause introduced by a conjunction ... [as in] *Please advise me whether these seeds should be sown now*" (1963: xxii). Developed by Hornby from 1937 to 1940, a tabular formalism was available for English verbs, much as a tabular formalism was produced for the Germanic consonants in the early days of comparative linguistics, as noted in Section 2. In such classification a given verb may belong to more than one class; *advise*, for example, belongs to five. Tabular formalism has subsequently been replaced by algebraic formalism in lexical rules that are now referred to as frames. Five frames would be designed for *advise*. The frames are assigned probabilities, in accordance with procedures indicated in the quotation from the fifth quarterly report. Intricate formalism has in this way been developed for the lexicon as well as for the grammar.

While the formalism for control of syntactic structures is in accordance with immediate constituent theory, framing for verbs as the central units of clauses reflects the approach applied in dependency theory. In this way the formalism developed to control natural language represents an extension of previous approaches designed to secure the understanding and mastery of language, not excluding sentence diagramming as was long practiced in elementary education. Practices were subsequently modified in accordance with the procedures developed in symbolic logic. The procedures in turn were prompted by efforts, employed already by Aristotle, to achieve accuracy in communication. In this way, steps to control language computationally have resulted in improved formalism. That formalism is highly complex, cumbersome to depict in an essay, and best conveyed through computer communication.

The strategies employed in computational linguistics to achieve computerized control of natural language approximating that of its speakers in selected uses, specifically the expression of technical information, have then resulted in increasingly improved formalism. Moreover, by successful control of increasingly difficult segments of language, the procedures so employed have produced a secure foundation on which to achieve further improvements. In a sense, the strategy is comparable to that of human speakers, who first master partial control of formal elements and simple information, and thereupon proceed to control of more complex form and content. Verification of assumptions concerning human control of natural language by relating it to that of computer control remains to be carried out. The success of computational control of natural language is at present best demonstrated by use of the system.

Acknowledgments

This paper was produced under partial support by Siemens Nixdorf Informationssysteme for the Linguistics Research Center of The University of Texas.

References

Benveniste, Emile. 1935. *Origines de la formation des noms en indo-européen.* Paris: Adrien-Maisonneuve.

Boole, George. 1854. *An Investigation of the Laws of Thought.* London.

Brugmann, Karl. 1904. *Kurze vergleichende Grammmatik der indogermanischen Sprachen.* Strassburg: Trübner.

Carnap, Rudolf. 1958. *Introduction to Symbolic Logic and its Applications.* Trans. W. H. Meyer, J. Wilkinson. New York: Dover.

Chomsky, Noam. 1961. On the notion 'rule of grammar,' *Structure of Language and its Mathematical Aspects*, 6–24. Providence: American Mathematical Society.

Chomsky, Noam. 1965. *The Aspects of the Theory of Syntax.* Defense Documentation Center. Defense Supply Agency. Also published by the MIT Press, with omission of the first *the* in the title.

Delavenay, Emile. 1960. *An Introduction to Machine Translation.* London: Thames and Hudson.

Frege, Gottlob. 1879. *Begriffsschrift. Eine der arithmetischen nachgemachte Formelsprache des reinen Denkens.* Halle.

Harris, Zellig. 1952. Discourse analysis. *Language* 28: 1–30.

Harris, Zellig. 1991. *A Theory of Language and Information. A Mathematical Approach.* Oxford: Clarendon.

Hays, David G. 1964. Dependency theory: A formalism and some observations. *Language* 40: 511–25.

Hornby, Albert. S., Edward V. Gatenby, A. H. Wakefield. (1963, 2nd ed.) *The Advanced Learner's Dictionary of Current English.* London: Oxford University Press. (subsequently upgraded)

Jespersen, Otto. 1937. *Analytic Syntax.* Copenhagen: Munksgaard. Repr. 1969. New York: Holt, Rinehart & Winston.

Koschmieder, Erwin. 1965. *Beiträge zur allgemeinen Syntax.* Heidelberg: Winter.

Kurylowicz, Jerzy. 1935. *Etudes indoeuropéennes.* Krakow: Gebethner & Wolff.

Lamb, Sydney M. 1966a. *Outline of Stratificational Grammar*. Washington, D.C.: Georgetown University Press.

Lamb, Sydney M. 1966b. Epilegomena to a theory of language. *Romance Philology* 19: 531–73.

Lamb, Sydney M. 1967. Review of Noam Chomsky, *Current Issues in Linguistic Theory* and *Aspects of the Theory of Syntax*. *American Anthropologist* 69: 411–15.

Lehmann, Winfred P. (ed.) 1967. *A Reader in Nineteenth Century Historical Indo-European Linguistics*. Bloomington: Indiana University Press.

Lehmann, Winfred P. 1974. *Proto-Indo-European Syntax*. Austin: University of Texas Press.

Lehmann, Winfred P. 1987. Reflections by the computer. *Georgetown University Round Table on Language and Linguistics 1986*, ed. by Simon P.X. Battestini, 232–38. Washington: Georgetown University Press.

Lehmann, Winfred P. 1992. *Workbook for Historical Linguistics*. Dallas: Summer Institute of Linguistics.

Lehmann, Winfred P. 1993. *Theoretical Bases of Indo-European Linguistics*. London: Routledge.

Naumann, Bernd. 1990. Die "dependenzgrammatischen" Überlegungen Johann Werner Meiners (1723–1789). *Neuere Forschungen zur historischen Syntax des Deutschen*, ed. by Anne Betten, 439–50. Tübingen: Niemeyer.

Newell, Leonard E. 1966. Analysis of an English text. Appendix to Lamb 1966a: 71–106.

Prokosch, Eduard. 1939. *A Comparative Germanic Grammar*. Philadelphia: Linguistic Society of America.

Robinson, Orrin W. 1992. *Old English and its Closest Relatives*. Stanford: Stanford University Press.

Sadock, Jerrold M. 1991. *Autolexical Syntax. A Theory of Parallel Grammatical Representations*. Chicago: University of Chicago Press.

Schmidt, Johannes. 1872. *Die Verwandschaftsverhältnisse der indogermanischen Sprachen*. Weimar: H. Bohlau

Structure of Language and its Mathematical Aspects. (no editor) 1961. Providence: American Mathematical Society.

Tesnière, Lucien. 1959. *Eléments de syntaxe structurale*. Paris: Klincksieck.

Wilson, Edward O. 1992. *The Diversity of Life*. Cambridge: Harvard University Press.

Yngve, Victor H. 1960. A model and an hypothesis for language structure, *Proceedings of the American Philosophical Society* 104: 444–66.

Yngve, Victor H. 1961. The depth hypothesis. *The Structure of Language and its Mathematical Aspects*, 130–138.

Yngve, Victor H. 1962. COMIT as an IR Language, *Communications of the Association for Computing Machinery* 5: 19–28.

Yngve, Victor H. 1964. Implications of mechanical translation research, *Proceedings of the American Philosophical Society* 108: 275–81.

About the author

*Winfred P. Lehmann is Louann and Larry Temple Centennial Professor Emeritus and Director of the Linguistics Research Center at the University of Texas at Austin, where he has worked since 1949. He received his Ph.D. from the University of Wisconsin in 1941, with specialization in Germanic and Indo-European linguistics. These have remained his chief fields of teaching and publication. Two of the more recent of his many significant books are A **Gothic Etymological Dictionary** (1986) and **Theoretical Bases of Indo-European Linguistics** (1993). Work on machine translation undertaken beginning in 1957 first brought him into contact with Sydney Lamb, who was doing related work at Berkeley in the same period.*

CHAPTER 9

Parsing with a Chart and its Efficiency

Chang-In Lee
Paichai University
cilee@mail.paichai.ac.kr

1. Introduction

Syntactic processing involves analyzing a sentence to construct its syntactic structure according to a given grammar. Context free grammars have been used extensively for describing the syntax of programming languages and natural languages. Parsing algorithms for context-free grammars play a large role in designing compilers and interpreters for programming languages and understanding natural languages. Numerous parsing algorithms have been proposed. Parsing algorithms for a general context-free grammar can be classified largely into two categories: backtracking algorithms and non-backtracking algorithms with a chart (Aho and Ullman 1972, Allen 1987, and Winograd 1983). A sentence can be parsed in polynomial time by the latter, while the former may require exponential time. In this paper, the latter will be discussed. A chart is used as a data structure in order to maintain all the information for syntactic processing.

Recently, many successful experiments for real engineering and scientific problems are reported in the massively parallel processing environment: the outstanding results in solving fluid dynamic problems on SIMD type machines such as CM-2 (Oran et al. 1990 and Satti et al. 1990) and the report of Sandia National Laboratory on MIMD type machines such as NCUBE 10 (Yang et al. 1990). In addition, many successful massively parallel machines are being built by many computer manufacturers, and their peak performances are superior to those of vector computers from CRAY, Fujitsu, and NEC (Almasi and Gottlieb 1989, and Quinn 1987).

However, natural language processing may not take advantage of recent advances in computer architecture. Most syntactic parsing algorithms used to be designed for sequential execution. In addition, the existing parallel approaches to syntactic processing may not be suitable for the computer architectural environment due to a lack of clear job-scheduling onto the processors. We believe that syntactic processing is the most time-consuming part in all of natural language processing (Lee 1987, 1988) and requires parallel processing suitable for the massively parallel environment to speed up natural language processing. This paper proposes two parallel parsing algorithms which work well on the MIMD computational model.

2.   Parsing Algorithms with Charts

In this section, we will introduce two sequential parsing algorithms to be used as the basis for designing the parallel parsing algorithms in Section 3. Before discussing parsing algorithms, the terminologies for describing a grammar and a chart will be introduced. In this paper, terminal and nonterminal symbols are represented by lowercase and uppercase letters, respectively. Strings of either terminals or nonterminals are represented by Greek letters. Let $G=(N,?,P,S)$ be a context-free grammar (CFG), where N is the finite set of nonterminals, ? is the finite set of terminal symbols, P is the finite set of productions and S is the distinguished symbol in N. Let $w = a_1a_2...a_n$ be an input string in $?^2$. An object of the form $(A \leftarrow X_1X_2\langle...\rangle X_kX_{k+1}\langle...\rangle X_n,i,j)$ is called an active arc for w if $A \leftarrow X_1X_2\langle...\rangle X_n$ is in P and $0 = i = j = n$. The state of the parsing process is recorded in a structure called a chart, which is composed of active arcs.

First, we shall describe Earley's algorithm, which is called a top-down CFG parser with a chart (refer to the following algorithm in Aho and Ullman 1972, and Earley 1986).

Algorithm 1 (Earley's Algorithm)
    Input: $G = (N,\Sigma,P,S)$ and $w = a_1a_2\langle...\rangle a_n$ in Σ^*
    Output: The chart
    Method:
    1.   For $S \leftarrow \alpha$ in P, add $(S \leftarrow \cdot\alpha, 0, 0)$ to the chart.
    2.   repeat
         a.   For each completed arc, $(B \leftarrow \gamma\cdot, 0, 0)$,
                add $(A \leftarrow \alpha B\cdot\beta, 0, 0)$ for all $(A \leftarrow \alpha \cdot B\beta, 0, 0)$ to the chart.

     b.   For each $(A \leftarrow \alpha B\beta, 0, 0)$, add $(B \leftarrow \cdot\gamma, 0, 0)$ for $B \leftarrow \gamma$ in P.
         until (no new active arcs)

3. $j = 1$

4.   repeat

     a.   For each $(B \leftarrow \alpha \cdot a\beta, i, j\text{-}1)$ such that $a = a_j$.
         add $(B \leftarrow \alpha A \cdot \beta, i, j)$ to the chart.

     b.   repeat
        i)   For each $(A \leftarrow \cdot\gamma, i, j)$.
        add $(B \leftarrow \alpha A \cdot \beta, k, j)$ to the chart for all $(B \leftarrow \alpha \cdot A\beta, k, j)$.
        ii)   For each $(A \leftarrow \alpha B\beta, i, j)$.
        add $(B \leftarrow \cdot\gamma, i, j)$ to the chart for all $B \leftarrow \gamma$ in P.
       until (no new active arcs)

     c. $j = j + 1$

5.   until $(j \rangle n)$

The basic idea of Earley's algorithm is to keep all possible derivations of the sub-strings of an input sentence as active arcs in the chart and to guarantee that the successful ones will be read. The above statement can be formalized in Theorem 1:

Theorem 1:

    If the chart is constructed as in Algorithm 1, then there is an active arc, $(A \leftarrow \alpha \cdot \beta, i, j)$, if and only if $\alpha \Rightarrow^* a_{i+1} \langle ... \rangle a_j$ and there are strings γ and δ such that $S \Rightarrow^* \gamma A\delta$ and $\gamma \Rightarrow^* a_1 \langle ... \rangle a_i$.

    Proof) Refer to the proof in Aho and Ullman 1972.

Second, we will describe a bottom-up parsing algorithm with a chart. For simplicity, the completed arc, $(A \leftarrow \alpha \cdot, i, j)$, will be denoted by $(A \cdot, i, j)$, in Algorithm 2 from Allen 1987.

Algorithm 2

    Input: $G = (N, \Sigma, P, S)$ and $w = a_1 a_2 \langle ... \rangle a_n$ in Σ
    Output: the chart
    Method:

1.   Push all $(a_1 \cdot, i\text{-}1, i)$ into a stack for $i = 1, \langle ... \rangle n$

2.   repeat

     a.   Pop a completed arc, $(\delta \cdot, i, j)$, from the stack,
         where a single terminal or nonterminal symbol is.

    b.   For all A ← δβ in P, add (A ← δ·β, i, j) into chart.
            If β is an empty string, push the completed arc, (A·, i, j), into the stack
    c.   For all (A ← α·δβ, k, i) add (A ←αδ·β, k, j) into the chart
            If β is an empty string, add (A·, k, j) into the stack
            until (stack is empty)

The basic ideas in these two algorithms are quite similar to each other because they are based on the bottom-up processing feature. So, Earley's algorithm is also called a mixed-mode algorithm.

3.   Syntactic Parsing with a Chart

In the sequential parsing algorithms above, a parser scans an input string in a unidirectional way: left-to-right or right-to-left in a multiple processors environment, a parser may scan an input string in a bi-directional way. That is, an input string can be divided into two portions, and the first portion will be parsed in the left-to-right scanning manner, while the second portion is parsed in the right-to-left scanning manner.

Let us describe the main idea of parallel algorithms in this paper. Let a morphological processing of a sentence generate a list of lexical categories corresponding to words in the sentence. After this processing, the divide-and-conquer technique works as follows. First, the list generated by the morphological processing may be divided into two portions. Any divisions are applicable, but half division is recommended to save average parsing time because the synchronization overheads between processors may be reduced by allocating balanced loads. Second, each portion will be independently processed in parallel: the first portion will be parsed in the left-to-right scanning manner, while the second portion is processed in the right-to-left scanning manner. Each portion generates its own chart. Each active arc in these charts has starting and ending input positions, and a mark denoting the present status in a specific grammatical rule. When the starting position of one active arc is identical with the ending position of the active arc and the states of the active arcs are the same, these active arcs are said to be connectable. Initially, let a combined chart be empty. Then, the connectable active arcs in the two charts generated above and a combined chart will be recursively combined until no connectable active arcs exist in the charts generated above in order to build a complete syntactic structure.

In order to distinguish the active arcs generated by the first portion from those generated by the second portion, the symbol $\uparrow$ will be used as a meta-symbol instead of a dot such as the form $(A \leftarrow X_1X_2\langle...\rangle X_k \uparrow X_{k+1}\langle...\rangle X_n, i, j)$. We may get Theorem 2 through the same approach used in Section 2.

Theorem 2

If the chart is constructed as in Algorithm 1 with the right-to-left scanning manner, then there is an active arc, $(A \leftarrow \alpha \uparrow \beta, k, l)$, if and only if $\beta \Rightarrow^*$ $a_{k+1} \langle...\rangle a_l$ and there are γ and δ such that $S \Rightarrow^* \gamma A\delta$ and $\delta \Rightarrow^* a_{l+1}\langle...\rangle a_n$.

Proof) Refer to the proof in Aho and Ullman 1972.

A parallel algorithm will be constructed by applying the above idea to Earley's algorithm in Algorithm 3.

Algorithm 3

Input: $G = (N, \Sigma, P, S)$ and $w = a_1a_2\langle...\rangle a_n$ in Σ^*
Output: chart = chart1 U chart2 U chart3
Method:
1.   Divide w into $w_1 = a_1\langle...\rangle a_t$ and $w_2 = a_{t+1}\langle...\rangle a_n$, where $1\leq t \leq n$
2.   Generate chart1 for w_1 and chart2 for w_2 by algorithm 1.
3.   Combine the chart1 and chart2 into chart3 as follows:
    a.   For each arc pair, $(A \leftarrow \alpha\cdot\beta, k, l)$ in chart1 and $(A \leftarrow \alpha\uparrow\beta, k, l)$ in chart 2, add $(A \leftarrow \alpha\beta\cdot, i, j)$ to chart3.
    b.   repeat
        i)   repeat
              For each completed arc, $(A \leftarrow \alpha\cdot, i, j)$ in chart3, add $(B \leftarrow \alpha A\cdot\beta, i, j)$ to chart3, for all $(B \leftarrow \alpha\cdot A\beta, i, j)$ in chart1 and add $(B \leftarrow A\cdot, i, j)$ for all $B \leftarrow A$ in P to chart3.
              until (no new completed arc in chart3)
        ii)   For each pair, $(A \leftarrow \alpha\cdot\beta, i, k)$ in chart3 and $(A \leftarrow \alpha\uparrow\beta, k, j)$ in chart2, add $A \leftarrow \alpha\beta\cdot, i, j)$ to chart3.
        iii) repeat
              For each $(A \leftarrow \alpha\cdot, i, k)$ in chart3,
              add $(B \leftarrow A\beta\cdot, i, j)$ to chart3 for all $(B \leftarrow A \uparrow \beta, k, j)$ in chart2, and add $(B \leftarrow A\bullet, i, j)$ for all $B \leftarrow A$ in P to chart3.
              until (no new completed arc in chart3)
        until (find $(S \leftarrow \alpha\cdot, 0, n)$)

Theorem 3 shows that Algorithm 3 generates a sufficient chart to get the syntactic structure of an input string when there exists at least a derivation from a distinguished symbol to the input string.

Theorem 3

When the charts, chart1 and chart2, are constructed as in Algorithm 3, there is at least a combination, $(A \leftarrow \alpha\beta\cdot, i, j)$, of $(A \leftarrow \alpha\beta, i, t)$ and $(A \leftarrow \alpha\uparrow\beta, t, j)$ in chart2 if and only if $\alpha\beta \Rightarrow^* a_{i+1}\langle...\rangle a_j$ and there are strings γ and δ such that $S \Rightarrow^* \gamma A\delta$, $\gamma \Rightarrow^* a_1\langle...\rangle a_i$, and $\delta \Rightarrow^* \alpha_{j+1}<...>\alpha_n$.

Proof) (Only if) By Theorem 1 and Theorem 2, $\alpha \Rightarrow^* a_{i+1}\langle...\rangle a_t$, $\beta \Rightarrow^* a_{t+1}\langle...\rangle a_j$ and there are strings γ_1, γ_2, δ_1, and δ_2 such that $S \Rightarrow \gamma_1 A\delta_1$, $\gamma_1 \Rightarrow^* a_1\langle...\rangle a_i$, $S \Rightarrow^* \gamma_2 A\delta_2$, and $\delta_2 \Rightarrow^* a_{j+1}\langle...\rangle a_n$. Since $\alpha\beta \Rightarrow^* a_{i+1}\langle...\rangle a_j$ and $A \leftarrow \alpha\beta$, there exist γ_2 and δ_t such that $\gamma_2 = \gamma_1$ and $\delta_1 = \gamma_2$.

(If) since $\alpha\beta \Rightarrow^* a_{i+1}\langle...\rangle a_j$, there is an index, t, such that $\alpha \Rightarrow^* a_{i+1}\langle...\rangle a_t$, and $\beta \Rightarrow^* a_{t+1}\langle...\rangle a_j$. Since there are strings γ and δ such that $S \Rightarrow^* \gamma A\delta$, $\gamma \Rightarrow^* a_1 \langle...\rangle a_j$ and $\delta \Rightarrow^* a_{j+1}\langle...\rangle a_n$ there exist $(A \leftarrow \alpha\cdot\beta, i, t)$ and $(A \leftarrow \alpha\uparrow\beta, t, j)$.

In Theorem 3, the if-condition says that there exists at least one pair of connectable active arcs from Chart 1 and Chart 2 when there exists a correct syntactic structure of an input string given a grammar, and the only-if-condition says vice versa. The chart with complete syntactic information for parsing will be generated by the recursive combinations of connectable active arcs as described in Algorithm 3. This is obvious from Theorem 1, Theorem 2, and Theorem 3. Now, we describe the parallel parsing algorithm related to the sequential bottom-up parsing algorithm with a chart.

Algorithm 4

Input: $G = (N, \Sigma, P, S)$ and $w = a_1a_2\langle...\rangle a_n$ in Σ^*
Output: chart = chart1 U chart2 U chart3
Method:

The same theoretical arguments may be applied to the above algorithm, but these will be omitted to remove redundancies.

4. Examples

This section shows how the parallel algorithms proposed work on an input sentence given a grammar. An example is taken from Allen 1987 in order to compare the results with those from sequential algorithm in the reference. A simple grammar and a simple lexicon are given in the following.

Grammar 1

1.	S	←	NP VP
2.	NP	←	ART ADJ NOUN
3.	NP	←	ART NOUN
4.	NP	←	ADJ NOUN
5.	VP	←	VERB NP

Lexicon 1

1.	can	AUX, NOUN, VERB
2.	hold	NOUN, VERB
3.	large	ADJ
4.	the	ART
5.	water	NOUN, VERB

Now, let us take Grammar 1, Lexicon 1, and a simple sentence, *The large can can hold the water.*, as inputs of Algorithm 3. Assume that the subsentence, *The large can can*, is assigned to processor 1 and the sub-sentence, *hold the water*, to processor 2. Then, the following chart will be generated.

⟨Chart 1 generated by Processor 1⟩

(S   ←   NP VP, 0, 0)
(NP   ←   ART ADJ NOUN, 0, 0)
(NP   ←   ART NOUN, 0, 0)
(NP   ←   ADJ NOUN, 0, 0)
(NP   ←   ART ·ADJ NOUN, 0, 1)
(NP   ←   ART ·NOUN, 0, 1)
(NP   ←   ART ADJ ·NOUN, 0, 2)
(NP   ←   ART ADJ NOUN·, 0, 3)
(S   ←   NP ·VP, 0, 3)
(VP   ←   AUX VERB NP, 3, 3)
(VP   ←   VERB NP, 3, 3)

(VP ← AUX ·VERB NP, 3, 4)
(VP ← VERB ·NP, 3, 4)

⟨Chart 2 generated by processor 2⟩

(S ← NP VP↑, 7, 7)
(VP ← AUX VERB NP↑, 7, 7)
(VP ← VERB NP↑, 7, 7)
(NP ← ART ADJ NOUN↑, 7, 7)
(NP ← ART NOUN↑, 7, 7)
(NP ← ADJ NOUN↑, 7, 7)
(NP ← ART ADJ↑ NOUN, 6, 7)
(NP ← ART↑ NOUN, 6, 7)
(NP ← ADJ↑ NOUN, 6, 7)
(NP ← ↑ART NOUN, 5, 7)
(VP ← AUX VERB↑ NP, 5, 7)
(VP ← VERB↑ NP, 5, 7)
(VP ← AUX↑ VERB NP, 4, 7)
(VP ← ↑VERB NP, 4, 7)
(S ← NP↑ VP, 4, 7)

⟨Chart 3 combined by chart 1 and chart 2⟩

1. Step 3–a in Algorithm 3
   (VP ← AUX VERB NP·, 3, 7)
2. Step 3–b in Algorithm 3
   (S ← NP VP·, 0, 7)

When the same inputs and assumptions used in the above sample are applied to Algorithm 4, the following chart will be generated.

⟨Chart 1 generated by processor 1⟩

(NP ← ART ·ADJ NOUN, 0, 1)
(NP ← ART · NOUN, 0, 1)
(NP ← ADJ ·NOUN, 1, 2)
(NP ← ART ADJ ·NOUN, 0, 2)
(NP·, 1, 3)
(NP·, 0, 3)
(S ← NP ·VP, 0, 3)
(S ← NP ·VP, 1, 3)

(VP   ←   AUX ·VERB NP, 2, 3)
(VP   ←   VERB ·NP, 2, 3)
(VP   ←   AUX ·VERB NP, 3, 4)
(VP   ←   VERB ·NP, 3, 4)
(VP   ←   AUX VERB ·NP, 2, 4)

⟨Chart 2 generated by processor 2⟩

(NP   ←   ART ADJ↑ NOUN, 6, 7)
(NP   ←   ART↑ NOUN, 6, 7)
(NP   ←   ADJ↑ NOUN, 6, 7)
(↑ NP, 5, 7)
(VP   ←   AUX VERB↑ NP, 5, 7)
(VP   ←   VERB↑ NP, 5, 7)
(NP   ←   ART ADJ↑ NOUN, 4, 5)
(NP   ←   ART↑ NOUN, 4, 5)
(NP   ←   ADJ↑ NOUN, 4, 5)
(VP   ←   AUX↑ VERB NP, 4, 7)
(↑ VP, 4, 7)
(S   ←   NP ↑ VP, 4, 7)

⟨Chart 3 combined by chart 1 and chart 2⟩

1.   Step 3–a in Algorithm 4
     (VP   ←   AUX VERB NP·, 3, 7)
2.   Step 3–b in Algorithm 4
     (S   ←   NP VP·, 0, 7)
     (S   ←   NP VP·, 1, 7)

5.   Conclusion

The ultimate goal of computer processing may be characterized as fast and intelligent processing. The computer architectures also have been developed in order to accomplish this goal since a computational model has been proposed by Von Neumann. For a decade, massively parallel computers have been designed by collecting large processing elements that can communicate and cooperate to solve large problems fast. Many parallel processing algorithms for solving large-scale engineering and scientific problems also have been developed in order to utilize these computers effectively (Hwang and Briggs 1984, and Quinn 1987). However, intelligent processing may have been the main emphasis and fast processing has been of only minor theoretical interest in natural language processing.

Since syntactic processing is the most time-consuming part in natural language processing, the fast algorithm design of syntactic processing may speed up the whole processing (Lee 1987, 1988). This paper proposes two parallel parsing algorithms which work well on the MIMD computational model as a first step in accomplishing whole parallel treatment in natural language processing. These algorithms can also be used to design compilers using a context-free grammar. In future research, we may apply the ideas in Section 3 to different algorithms or extend them to algorithms with greater parallelism. For example, it may be possible to apply the idea used to derive parallel algorithms in Section 3 to Knuth's LR(k) algorithm in order to obtain a parallelism, and to extend the algorithms in Section 3 to those with more processors participating.

References

Aho, Alfred V. and Jeffrey D. Ullman, 1972. *The Theory of Parsing, Translation and Compiling.* Englewood Cliffs, New Jersey: Prentice-Hall.

Allen, James. 1987. *Natural Language Understanding.* Menlo Park, California: Benjamin/Cummings.

Almasi, George S., and Allan Gottlieb. 1989. *Highly Parallel Computing.* Redwood City: Benjamin/Cummings.

Earley, J, 1986. An Efficient Context-Free Parsing Algorithm. *Readings in Natural Language Processing*, ed. by Karen S. Jones, Barbara J. Grosz, and Bonnie L. Webber, Los Altos, California: Morgan Kaufmann.

Hwang, Kai and Faye Briggs, 1984. *Computer Architecture and Parallel Processing.* New York: McGraw-Hill.

Lee, Chang-In. 1986. A general linguistic automatic system — Illustrated with Korean and English, *The Fourteenth LACUS Forum 1987*, ed. by Sheila Embleton, 231–242. Lake Bluff, Illinois: LACUS.

Lee, Chang-In. 1988. A dynamic model of comprehension with application to Korean and English. Ph.D. Dissertation. Rice University. Hanshin.

Oran, E. S., J. P. Boris, R. O. Whaley, and E. F. Brown. 1990. Exploring fluid dynamics on a connection machine. *Supercomputing Review* 52–60.

Quinn, Michael J. 1987. *Designing Efficient Algorithms for Parallel Computers.* Reading, Massachusetts: Addison Wesley.

Saati, A., S. Biringen and C. Farhat. 1990. Solving Navier-Stokes equations on massively parallel processors: Beyond the 1 GFΩTP performance. *International Journal of Superconducting Applications* 4, 1: 72–80.

Winograd, Terry. 1983. *Language as a Cognitive Process. Vol 1: Syntax.* Reading, Massachusetts: Addison Wesley.

Yang, Y. K, et al. 1990. Analysis of up-to-dated profound information on the supercomputing development and utilization. *SERI, KAIST* September.

About the author

Chang-In Lee is currently Assistant Professor of English Literature and Language at Paichai University in the Republic of Korea. Her Ph.D. is from Rice University, where she met Syd Lamb, taking several of his courses on cognitive-stratificational linguistics between 1985 and 1989. In her dissertation, she set up a Korean grammar and implemented a comprehensive system illustrated with Korean and English. Her subsequent publications deal with parsing and semantic representation based on her background in Lamb's grammar.

CHAPTER 10

Language as Human Action

Jonathan J. Webster

City University of Hong Kong

1. Introduction

Language is neither complete homogeneity nor is it total heterogeneity. M. A. K. Halliday describes it as being neither an ideal order, nor the absence of order. It is "a human artifact having some of the properties of both" (1975: 42). In the past, some linguists, most notably Chomsky, have attempted to idealize the situation by maintaining a distinction between competence and performance. Chomsky explains his notion of "grammatical competence" as "the cognitive state that encompasses all those aspects of form and meaning and their relation, including underlying structures that enter into that relation, which are properly assigned to the specific subsystem of the human mind that relates representations of form and meaning" (1980: 59). However, the psychological evidence available reveals the human cognitive system to be a far less simple and efficient system for processing language than that suggested by the grammars of Chomskian linguistics. Bechtel and Abrahamsen (1991: 235) suggest that grammatical competence, or as they refer to it "linguistic competence", be thought of "as one of many possible levels of description of linguistic functioning, in which most of the aspects of the functioning itself have been abstracted out; the products of that functioning remain, and have regularities that the grammar describes". If whatever falls outside of this idealized norm — otherwise referred to as linguistic or grammatical competence — is ignored, then obviously one cannot claim to be modeling the human cognitive system. What then are the alternatives for those interested in modeling the human cognitive system without losing sight of heterogeneity in actual linguistic behavior?

2.   Language as Human Activity

If linguistic theory is intended to match real world data and not distort it, then some convenient fictions need to be corrected. I believe R. B. LePage (1980) points us in the right direction when he proposes a theory in which (i) idiosyncratic behavior is subsumed in communally-agreed; (ii) context bound verbal relationships are subsumed in context free; (iii) semantically-based verbal relationships are subsumed in syntactically-based; (iv) analogical processes are subsumed in logical; (v) properties of an open system are subsumed in those of a closed system; and (vi) concrete instances are subsumed in abstract. LePage's theory of language is basically socio-psychological. It is one which envisages each individual in a community observing the behavior of others extrapolating from observed variability towards idealized models of invariable rules.

LePage criticizes those who

> tend to assume as innate, or as properties of all human languages, logical concepts which probably should instead be thought of as reflecting unachievable goals **towards which** human languages aim. All that need be postulated as innate is the capacity to extrapolate from analogy towards logical targets in infinity. (1980b)

Rather than idealize language as some innately logical, designed entity, the functional empiricist views language as a system evolving out of speech encounters in which "people create meaning, by exchanging symbols in shared context of situation" (Halliday 1984: 11). Semantically-based verbal relationships exist along a vertical or semiotic dimension. Given the semiotic encoding of the context of situation, Hasan argues, "we can predict the crucial semantic elements of the embedded text as well as the permitted range for the over-all message form" (1981: 110). This ability to make predictions — that the listener and reader have a good idea of what to expect — follows from "the organization of a text, and in particular the relation of a text, as a semantic unit, to a clause as the primary lexicogrammatical unit through which it is realized" (Halliday, 1981: 43,44). Clauses make it possible to create text, explains Halliday, because a clause "has itself evolved by analogy with the text as model, and can thus represent the meanings of a text in a rich variety of different ways" (1981: 44). A clause is related to text along two axes (Halliday, 1981: 39), one being composition — clause as constituent of the text, the other being realization — clause as instantiation of the text. Halliday describes a clause as "a text in microcosm, a 'universe of discourse' of its own in which the semiotic properties of a text reappear on a miniature scale".

The clause as primary lexicogrammatical unit evolves by analogy with the text as model, the text as intersubjective event is the realization of the context of situation. The context of situation includes my sense of self in society, my sense of who I am in relation to others. Halliday (1975: 29) maintains that "the 'fuzziness' of language is in part an expression of the dynamics and tensions of the social system ... [The social structure] is an essential element in the evolution of semantic systems and semantic processes". Language is an activity which is creative and dynamic. It is also the process by which we attempt to integrate ourselves into society. We speak as we have been spoken to based on our perception of who we are and to whom we are speaking, where, when and why. The speech situation is the individual's own construct. That construct includes the individual's sense of identity, defined idiosyncratically and in relation to others, as well as social role. "The normal pattern", explains Richard Hudson, "is for each individual to learn their language from their particular network of friends and relations, and to try hard to make their own language as similar as possible to these models"(1984: 32). Subjective knowledge becomes inter-subjective, idiosyncratic behavior is subsumed in communally-agreed.

3.   Accounting for Heterogeneity in Language

Accepting the principle of heterogeneity in language, argues Bolinger, prompts a new attitude toward the object of study:

> Prime attention to the overarching system and more or less incidental attention to the local detail follows naturally from the assumption that grammar is homogeneous and self-confirming. In a formal deductive system everything is explained when everything fits. There is no need to worry about missing a detail or two because sooner or later any mistake or oversight will show up in a grinding of the gears. It even seems rather petty to insist on full and precise documentation in each separate province of the realm. The power of the system as a whole to reveal a flaw is so great that mastering the grand design outweighs any small help that can be picked up from one of its many neighborhoods. But once homogeneity is denied, this security is gone. Separate — and, yes, *ad-hoc* — explanations for each part become essential. It is no longer safe to assume that the system will correct itself. Unquestionably it will in many ways; certainly there are local regularities as well as universal ones; but

the corrective remedies must be sought **after** one has canvassed as thoroughly as possible in each neighborhood, approaching its indwellers on their own terms. (1976: 12–13):

Computer-aided corpus data-collection has made it possible to do what Bolinger suggests and go canvassing for linguistic data. In the article "Computers and Dictionaries", Willem Meijs writes:

> The great traditional grammarians (Poutsma, Kruisinga, Jespersen) were ardent data-gatherers, as their voluminous grammars amply demonstrate. While the transformationalists' simple substitution of linguistic intuition for data-collection went to other extreme, they did have a point in their criticism of the traditional form of data-collection as being flawed by a bias for the unusual, the irregular: in the traditionalists' search for special "interesting" phenomena the larger generalities were all too often over-looked. Computer-aided corpus linguistics has made it possible to overcome this traditional bias towards the extraordinary, and develop a more balanced view of the "spread" of linguistic phenomena — lexical as well as syntactic ones — and their relative contributions to the language as a whole. (1992: 146):

Given the availability of computer resources for collecting and managing large amounts of language information, it is not surprising to see an increase in the number of studies dealing with finding probabilities based on text frequencies. In the article "Corpus Studies and Probabilistic Grammar" (1991), Halliday refers to his work on Chinese grammar in the 1950s, in particular his use of text frequencies to assign "crude" probabilities to the terms in the grammatical system. His basic assumption, then and now, is that the linguistic system is inherently probabilistic with frequency in the text being the instantiation of probability in the grammatical system. He describes the grammar of a language as a network of choices, "each choice consisting of a small number of alternatives related by probability; these probabilities appear to form a pattern related to the construing of information" (1991: 41). In fact, Halliday argues that a probabilistic model could help in a number of areas from explaining how children acquire language, to giving us a better understanding of variation across registers.

4. The Analogical Alternative

Accepting that there is indeed probabilistic behavior in language, Royal Skousen poses the question of how should we account for this behavior. He cites as an example a situation where there are two possible outcomes in a given context, s and t. The probability of s occurring is 1/3, the probability for t is 2/3. The learner, however, is only exposed to a sequence of s's and t's. Skousen asks:

> How does the learner discover the probability from the statistics? Does the learner make an estimate of the probability and continually revise that estimate as additional examples of s and t occur? And having learned a probability, how does the speaker use that probability to predict the s outcome one third of the time? (1989: 79)

To avoid the problems of learning and using probabilities, Skousen proposes an analogical approach to account for language behavior. In place of a system of rules, Skousen's analogical approach relies on an extensive data set derived from actual language data. The data set for a given context x is constructed by looking through a collection of examples for examples similar to x. On the basis of this data set, called the analogical set, an outcome is randomly chosen. In his book, *Analogical Modeling of Language*, (1989), Skousen discusses the application of his approach to the problem of predicting non-deterministic language variation. Skousen gives the example of colloquial Egyptian Arabic which has two terms of address that mean 'my brother'. There are at least eight social and discourse factors that can affect the probability of choosing one form of address over the other. Whereas rule-based approaches have had little success in predicting the behavior of such non-deterministic multivariate data, Skousen's analogical approach readily predicts the outcome for any given context. Considering the failure of rule-based approaches to account for heterogeneity in language behavior, plus the fact that speakers cannot make explicit the rules that govern their own behavior, Skousen concludes that "rules don't actually exist" (1989: 100) except in the minds of linguists.

5. Both Rule-like and Non-rule-like Behavior

Rumelhart, co-author of *Parallel Distributed Processing* (PDP), which Bechtel and Abrahamsen refer to as the "'bible' of the connectionist enterprise" (1993: 2), similarly rejects an "explicit rule" account of language in favor of

> a *unified* account in which the so-called *rule-governed* and exceptional cases
> were dealt with by a unified underlying process — a process which produces
> rule-like and rule-exception behavior through the application of a single
> process ... both the rule-like and non-rule-like behavior is a product of the
> interaction of very large number of "sub-symbolic" processes. (1984: 60) (cited
> in Bechtel and Abrahamsen, 1991: 237)

The connectionist model, also referred to as parallel distributed processing
(PDP), or neural network model, is described by Bechtel and Abrahamsen as
follows:

> a network of *elementary units* or nodes, each of which has some degree of
> *activation*. These units are *connected* to each other so that active units excite
> or inhibit other units. The network is a *dynamical system* which, once supplied
> with initial input, spreads excitations and inhibitions among its units. (1991: 2)

Neural networks share certain similarities with relational networks in Stratificational Grammar (STRAT). Both are attempts at capturing what is known from
neurophysiology about how the brain works. STRAT provides a relational
perspective supported by a relational notation. The linguistic system is regarded
as a relational network system consisting of nections and their interconnections.

The major processes associated with a relational network are described by
STRAT's inventor, Sydney Lamb, as

(1)   transmitting activation along lines and through nodes;
(2)   bringing latent nections into active participation in the network;
(3)   building new connections among nections already actively connect-
        ed;
(4)   changing activation thresholds;
(5)   changing the strengths of connections.   (1991: 112),

STRAT's inventor, Sydney Lamb, acknowledges the notation's fringe status in
contemporary linguistics, but argues it is not too late for those who have so far
failed to recognize its beauty to realize that they have been missing out on
something of value, something which can free them from illusions about
language (1991: 110–111).

Lamb first introduced the network notation associated with STRAT in a
lecture at the 1965 Linguistic Institute at the University of Michigan. However,
it was just about this time that neural network research was being forced un-
derground. Robert Hecht-Nielson describes the events leading up to what he calls
"the quiet years" in neurocomputing research:

By the mid 1960s it was clear that neurocomputing's era of first successes was drawing to a close. The final episode of this era was a campaign led by Marvin Minsky and Seymour Papert to discredit neural network research and divert neural network research funding to the field of "artificial intelligence". The campaign was a success, although the victory was largely illusory, since neurocomputing was already a moribund field. The campaign was waged by means of personal persuasion by Minsky and Papert and their allies, as well as by limited circulation of an unpublished technical manuscript (which was later de-venomized and, after further refinement and expansion, published in 1969 by Minsky and Papert as the book *Perceptrons*.) (1990)

It was not until the 1980s that neural network research began to make a comeback and recover some of its lost legitimacy. Bechtel and Abrahamsen offer five reasons for this revival of interest in neural networks (1991: 16–17):

1. new approaches to network modeling;
2. the credibility of certain researchers who became involved in neural network research, e.g. John Hopfield, the physicist;
3. increased interest among cognitive scientists in neuroscience and neural networks because they provided a neural-like architecture for cognitive modeling;
4. general interest in finding a fundamental explanation for the character of cognition;
5. the limitations of symbolic models. (1991: 16–17)

The generativist approach in linguistics, which is symbolic and algorithmic, possesses similar limitations with symbolic models in cognitive science. Generativists have deliberately ignored the exceptional and the idiosyncratic. They have focused on rule-like behavior, and ignored the non-rule-like. STRAT offers a relational network-based alternative to symbolic-based theories which operate under the illusion of language as a well-defined, homogeneous, logical system.

6. Conclusion

Recent advances in computerized data collection and processing, including the introduction of massively parallel processing render the analogical and relational network-based approaches viable alternatives for modeling human language behavior as it really is, and hopefully, for achieving a better understanding of ourselves. To quote Sydney Lamb, whose insight into language as human action can best be described as ahead of its time:

> As we learn more and more about the structure of this puzzling, beautiful, and complex human information system we may become better and better equipped to understand what that **real** world is really like. (1981: 27)

References

Aijmer, Karin and Bengt Altenberg (eds.). 1991. *English Corpus Linguistics*. London: Longman.

Bechtel, William and Adele Abrahamsen. 1991. *Connectionism and the Mind*. Cambridge, Massachusetts and Oxford: Basil Blackwell.

Bolinger, Dwight. 1976. Meaning and memory. *Forum Linguisticum*, 1: 1–14.

Chomsky, Noam. 1965. *Aspects of the Theory of Syntax*. Cambridge, Massachusetts: MIT Press.

Chomsky, Noam. 1980. *Rules and Representations*. New York: Columbia University Press.

Cook, V. J. 1988. *Chomsky's Universal Grammar*. Oxford: Basil Blackwell.

Garmen, Michael. 1990. *Psycholinguistics*. Cambridge: Cambridge University Press.

Garvin, Paul. 1978. An empiricist epistemology for linguistics. *The Fourth LACUS Forum 1977*, ed. by Michel Paradis, 331–351. Columbia, South Carolina: Hornbeam Press.

Gleason, H. A. Jr. 1976. Continuity in linguistics. *The Second LACUS Forum 1975*, ed. by Peter Reich, 3–16. Columbia, South Carolina: Hornbeam Press.

Gleason, H. A. Jr. 1981. Grammar, grammars, and grammarians. *The Seventh LACUS Forum 1980*, ed. by James Copeland and Philip W. Davis, 3–13. Columbia, South Carolina: Hornbeam Press.

Halliday, M. A. K. 1975. Language as social semiotic: towards a general sociolinguistic theory. *The First LACUS Forum 1974*, ed. by Adam Makkai and Valerie Becker Makkai, 17–46. Columbia, South Carolina: Hornbeam Press.

Halliday, M. A. K. 1981. Text semantics and clause grammar: some patterns of realization. *The Seventh LACUS Forum 1900*, ed. by James Copeland and Philip W. Davis, 31–60. Columbia, South Carolina: Hornbeam Press.

Halliday, M. A. K. 1985. *Introduction to Functional Grammar*. London: Edward Arnold.

Halliday, M. A. K. 1991. Corpus studies and probabilistic grammar. *English Corpus Linguistics: Studies in Honour of Jan Svartvik*, ed. by Karin Aijmer and Bengt Altenberg, 30–43. London: Longman.

Hasan, Ruqaiya. 1981. What's going on: a dynamic view of context in language. *The Seventh LACUS Forum 1980*, ed. by James Copeland and Philip W. Davis,. 106–121. Columbia, South Carolina: Hornbeam Press.

Hecht-Nielson, Robert. 1990. *Neurocomputing: The Technology of Non-Algorithmic Information Processing*. Reading, Massachusetts: Addison-Wesley.

Hudson, Richard. 1984. *Word Grammar*. Cambridge: Cambridge University Press.

Lamb, Sydney. 1981. On the aims of linguistics. *The Seventh LACUS Forum 1980*, ed. by James Copeland and Philip W. Davis, 17–27. Columbia, South Carolina: Hornbeam Press.

Lamb, Sydney. 1991. Linguistic model and linguistic thought. *The Seventeenth LACUS Forum 1990*, ed. by Angela Della Volpe, 109–120. Lake Bluff, Illinois: LACUS.

LePage, Robert B. 1980a. Projection, focussing, diffusion, or, Steps towards a sociol;inguistic theory of language illustrated from the Sociolinguistic Survey of Multilingual Communities. *York Papers in Linguistics* 9: 9–31.

LePage, Robert B. 1980b. Theoretical aspects of sociolinguistic studies in pidgin and creole languages. *Theoretical Orientations in Pidgin and Creole Studies*, ed. by Albert Valdman and A. R. Highfield, 331–397. New York: Academic Press.

Longacre, Robert. 1979. Why we need a vertical revolution in linguistics. *The Fifth LACUS Forum 1978*, ed. by Wolfgang Wölck and Paul Garvin, 247–270. Columbia, South Carolina: Hornbeam Press.

Meijs, Willem. 1992. Computers and Dictionaries. *Computers and Written Texts*, ed. by Christopher S. Butler, 141–166. Oxford: Basil Blackwell.

Rumelhart, David E., James L. McClelland and the PDP Research Group. 1986. *Parallel Distributed Processing: Explorations in the Microstructure of Cognition*, Volume 2: *Psychological and Biological Models*, Cambridge, Massachusetts: MIT Press.

Skousen, Royal. 1989. *Analogical Modeling of Language*. Dordrecht: Kluwer Academic Publishers.

About the author

Jonathan Webster is Associate Professor in the Department of Chinese, Transla-tion, and Linguistics at the City University of Hong Kong. His 1981 Ph.D. is from the State University of New York at Buffalo. Prior to coming to Hong Kong, he served at the National University of Singapore for six years. His main research interest is in the area of language information sciences, with particular attention to developing World-Wide Web access to linguistic databases. Currently he is designing a bilingual Chinese-English lexical database to provide Word-Wide Web access to lexical information for Chinese and English. He has become acquainted with Syd Lamb through meetings of the Linguistic Association of Canada and the United States.

CHAPTER 11

Some Hermeneutic Observations on Textlinguistics and Text Theory in the Humanities

Robert E. Longacre

University of Texas at Arlington

1. Introduction

Homo Sapiens is an incessant creator of texts, both oral and written. Primarily, texts serve basic communication needs — as seen in any social milieu which is characterized by written exchanges as well as face-to-face relations, or for that matter as seen in the feverish interchange of memoranda which characterizes a modern corporation or a university. Casual *ad hoc* texts, rather than disappearing as a culture becomes technologically sophisticated, **proliferate** to a degree that is both amusing and alarming. We could perhaps voice a prophecy:

> This is the way the world ends,
> This is the way the world ends,
> This is the way the world ends,
> Drowned deep in paper.

Nevertheless, cultures of the past, and we hope our own as well, can produce **privileged** texts which are of more than ephemeral significance. In fact, the study of the humanities has traditionally revolved around the study of such texts, from the medieval student's preoccupation with Aristotle, to the University of Chicago's plan, which equated an adequate liberal arts education with the knowledge of the "great books of the Western world". Such texts presumably are a privileged few which survive as the embodiment of ideas and values that persist across time and outlive the cultures in which they originated.

But the study of the Humanities also perforce involves the study of more ephemeral texts — as, for example, the papers presented at a conference, class lectures, textbooks, and the like.[1]

The relevance of ephemeral texts to the Humanities can further be seen in text-theoretical studies of such ephemeral texts. This is exemplified in the sort of text studied by contributors to the journal *Text*: conversation between doctors, psychiatrists, and patients (Freeman and Heller [eds.] 1986), courtroom discourse and conversation between lawyers and clients, along with legal documents such as insurance policies and court decisions (Danet [ed.] 1984), the language of a church service (Borker 1986), the language of prejudice and discrimination (van Dijk & Wodak [eds.] 1988). Add to this a recent volume (Mann and Thompson 1992) on the textual structure of an appeals letter, and an article which studies the textual structure of a linguistic article (Farmer 1981).

2.   Textlinguistics

Textlinguistics has developed in the last decades of this century as a way of getting at the meaning of a text through a study of its linguistic structure in the language in which it is written. While it is believed that certain text features are universal among the languages of the world, it is also believed that the particular working out of these strategies is language-specific. Thus, for example, while all languages have a way of indicating the storyline of a narrative, the specific verb system and clause structure of a language delimit the means by which this is done. The goal of the textlinguist is to confront the morphosyntax of a language with the structure of texts in that language to the mutual elucidation of both. This leads not only to a better understanding of the linguistic structure of a language, but also to a kind of text hermeneutic.

A textlinguistic analysis can fruitfully begin with an attempt to identify the framework of a discourse in terms of text type (Longacre 1983). Contingent temporal sequence in accomplished time and a slate of participants determine a narrative discourse — whether the EVENTS and the ACTORS are concrete and personal or abstract and impersonal (as in some historical writing — Ricoeur 1984, vol. I). Contingent temporal sequence in projected time with an appropriate

---

1. This article is a reworking of a paper which was read at the Tenth Annual Conference of the Association for Integrated Studies at Arlington, Texas, October 1986.

agent constitutes procedural how-to-do-it discourse; contingent temporal sequence in accomplished time constitutes, with appropriate agents, procedural how-it-was-done discourse. Various kinds of behavioral discourse exist: eulogy, promissory speech, exhortation, of which the latter is very common; in these, there is no contingent temporal sequence (except in limited context) and certain actions of an agent are praised, promised, or inculcated. Expository (including descriptive) discourse has neither temporal nor agentive orientation; rather it has some sort of logical/spatial development and heavy thematic structuring. Text typology is basic, not simply because humans are inveterate classifiers — although that is relevant — but because text analysis proceeds best by comparing **like** texts.

Having roughly isolated the text type which provides the framework of the discourse (which may contain many embedded texts of diverse types), the text analyst does well to raise the question of what a text is all about, i.e. its macro-structure. The macrostructure of a discourse (van Dijk 1977, 1980) provides a control as to what is included or excluded from mention in the text; what is developed in detail or merely summarily mentioned; and may affect the order of presentation in regard to big chunks of the discourse. It can also control some rather subtle details that we do not have time and space to develop here.

The textlinguist is now ready to focus on the linguistic structure of the text. Here a good beginning point is the examination of the verb forms and clause structures that characterize the text. Certain of these verb forms and clause types are highly relevant to the forward progress of the text. Each text type in a given language will have a way of encoding its main line of development. There will also be subsidiary lines of development. Thus, in a story in which action verbs dominate, explanation and description are subsidiary lines of development, while in an explanatory discourse where the main line is expository/descriptive, the action verbs that characterize the main line of a story come in only in subsidiary anecdotes and illustrations. Eventually the textlinguist should be able to make for any discourse type in any language a scalar arrangement of verb forms/clause types in terms of nearness (or degrees of departure from) the mainline of development (Longacre 1989).

The textlinguist must also be concerned with what nouns and pronouns do within a text. In a story nouns/pronouns/agreement references within the verb (as well as null reference) have to do with participant reference: first mention, integration into the story, routine tracking, reintroduction after absence from the story, narrator comments on a participant, local contrast between participants, and local thematicity. Themes as well as participants occur in stories, and participants occur as well as props. In a procedural discourse, the anyone-qualified agent acts on props to produce something (or to stage a ritual event). In a behavioral discourse, especially the hortatory type, the targeted audience is second person, and there may occur a proliferation of constructions to express mitigation of commands; noun phrases identify involvement with other participants or impingement on others, or occasional split of the target audience ("you men do x; you women do y"); or noun phrases may identify props used in implementing commands/suggestions. In explanatory/descriptive discourse, nouns provide characterization of the environment, whether human, non-human, props, or topological features. At any rate, whatever the discourse type, the use of noun versus pronoun versus reference in the verb (in an inflected language) versus null must be accounted for in terms of text structure and text semantics.

Particles and conjunctions must also be accounted for, as well as other prominence/cohesive features not included above, e.g. repetition/back reference (reprise) in adverbial clauses; and use of parallelism and paraphrase.

Certainly it is also part of the textlinguist's job to catalogue the ways in which a high point or cumulative development of a text is marked. I have written considerably about "peak marking" in other places (1983, 1985, 1990) and will not again elaborate this idea here.

Finally, a textlinguistic analysis can plug in all the above to come out with a presentation of the constituent structure of a text. An attempt is made in such a presentation to account for the function of every sentence, every part of a sentence, and every group of sentences in the plan of the whole. In regard to the functioning of parts of the constituent sentences, sentence-level grammar of any one of several varieties can be plugged in — but may need some restatement in the light of discourse perspective. The relation of sentence to sentence and of one group of sentences to another group of sentences requires some kind of logical calculus adapted to describing natural languages. Several such catalogues exist (Beekman, Callow, and Kopesec 1981; Longacre 1976, 1983, 1996; van Dijk 1977; de Beaugrande and Dressler 1981; Halliday and Hasan 1976; Mann and Thompson 1987). No linguist can do microanalysis without such a catalogue — although the macroanalysis into "big chunks" is more obvious and less problematic.

Especially valuable in microanalysis is the attention to verb forms/clauses in a scalar scheme such as that suggested above. In microanalysis the sentences whose main verbs/main clauses rank higher should predominate constituent-wise over those sentences whose main verbs/main clauses rank lower. Here, in the analysis of local spans (paragraphs), the concepts of DOMINANCE and ANCILLARI-NESS replace those of independent and subordinate on the sentence level.

The upshot of all this is a system of interrelated guidelines for the under-standing of a text.[2] What is the author trying to make prominent or background, dominant or ancillary? What does he connect up well or decide to leave in implicit connection? What logical relations are implied? How do fine-grained details — use of one verb form rather than another, or of a noun rather than a pronoun — have to do with the whole? How do all these details relate back to the postulated macrostructure and to the analysis of local spans? A textlinguistic analysis will not automatically deliver to us the meaning and intent of a text and its parts, but it should constrain within plausible bounds our possible interpreta-tions of it.

I posit the formulation in (1):

(1)   TL $\rightarrow$ ^{H} $\rightarrow$ Text

i.e., "Textlinguistics provides a partial hermeneutic of the text".
Textlinguistics, practiced somewhat as above might with profit be applied to some of the "great books of the Western world" referred to above. Could we, for example, get a new and fresh look at Plato by applying a textlinguistic methodol-ogy to the Greek text of the *Dialogues* and of the *Republic*?

3.   Text Theory

Textlinguistics was, however, scarcely conceived and born before it was expand-ed to text theory — the interdisciplinary study of text or at least the study of text against the background of an enriched and much more sophisticated kind of textlinguistics. It became, for example, immediately evident that cognitive and social aspects of text had to be studied whatever interdisciplinary milieu devel-oped. Thus, Teun van Dijk's early partnership with Walter Kintsch, a psycholo-gist, was no fortuitous concourse of personalities. Their experimental work on macrostructures via progressive attrition of text retention on the part of Dutch school children (1977) was of considerable early significance to text theory. Nor

---

2. I refrain here from going into the role of reported speech and variation in quotation formulas to textlinguistic analysis. Janice Ware and I read a joint paper on this frontier question of discourse analysis in 1987; cf. Longacre 1994.

is it an accident that early work on dialogue relations in the United States was carried out by sociologists (e.g. Sacks 1984 and others).

The journal *Text* itself was founded in the hope, which time has justified, of having an interdisciplinary journal devoted to text theory. As mentioned above, special issues, such as those on medical discourse, legal discourse, and the language of prejudice and discrimination have demonstrated the value of the cooperation of the textlinguist with practitioners from other disciplines. It is not always possible to find one person who is competent in two such fields, but joint research and discussion and joint authorship must often be resorted to in order to bridge between two disciplines or professions.

Two conferences at my home university, the University of Texas at Arlington, attempted to encourage such an interdisciplinary milieu. The first, in 1980, took as its topic "Linguistics and the Humanities". Results of this conference were published in three successive issues of *Forum Linguisticum* (1982–1983). The second such conference, in 1985, took as its topic "The text as a focal concern in the humanities". The results of this conference were published in the linguistics journal *Word* (Brend, 1986) and consequently some of the more interdisciplinary papers were not included.

Textlinguistics and text theory can also with profit be applied to Biblical Studies — especially in the somewhat inbred field of Old Testament Studies. While some have talked of a "return from the desert of criticism", textlinguistics and text theory can lead the way in such a return, i.e., a facing away from the questions of putative sources and a facing towards the text itself.

A rather striking example of the latter emerged in a paper by Nicolas Bailey (1992). Nehemiah Chapter 3 is an account of the rebuilding of the walls of Jerusalem by returned Jewish exiles in the fifth century B.C. Critics have latched onto certain differences in the style and grammar of Neh. 3:1–15 and 3:16–32 and have suggested that two authors/sources are involved.[3] At this point Bailey observes that the geography and archaeology have something to say. Crucial is the question of the extent of the city which Nehemiah walled in and the location of the walls. Contemporary Israeli archaeologists have elucidated this problem, and in the process have elucidated our text for us.

The Jerusalem of Solomon's day was essentially the Jebusite stronghold that David captured, plus an extension to the higher land immediately to the north,

---

3. In the English text, Chapter 3 ends with v. 32 and Chapter 4 begins. In the Hebrew, Chapter 3 continues through 4.6 of the English text.

culminating in Solomon's temple mound, which was somewhat smaller than we find today (it having been enlarged by Herod). The whole city then was a narrow walled strip extending over two hills and running from north to south. In Hezekiah's time a refugee population from the north had extensively settled the Western Hill, which Hezekiah proceeded to wall in with his "Broad Wall". This somewhat rectilinear city was destroyed by the Chaldeans in 587 B.C. The question is how much of the wall did Nehemiah rebuild?

Current archaeological investigation suggests that he essentially restored the walls along the line of the Solomonic City; in fact Nehemiah 3:8b could properly be translated: "They left out part of Jerusalem as far as the Broad Wall" — although it is not so translated in even as up-to-date a version as the New International Version.

What then? Essentially Nehemiah enclosed the old city running across the two hills, and including the City of David, the Ophel, and the temple mound. His men began their work at the north end and work crews are described as situated to the south one after the other. The Hebrew text of 3:1–15 says "X restored R, and **on his hand** Y restored S, and **on his hand** Z restored T". But on reaching the southern tip of the narrow oblong city and on rounding the tip the descriptive phraseology changes as the work parties are now described as disposed from south to north. Here the Hebrew text of 3:16–32 runs: "X restored R, and **after him** Y restored S. And **after him**, Z restored T". While the precise rationale of *on his hand* versus *after him* (where *him* refers to the leader of a working group and his followers) is not clear, it seems abundantly clear that the shift in phraseology refers to a shift in descriptive perspective. But this shift of perspective is intelligible if and only if the topography is grasped and the results of current archaeological studies are taken into account. Again, the full understanding of the Neh. 3 text (and an appreciation of its unity) depends not just on the study of the text itself, but on adding insights from geography and archaeology to the study of the text. In the process, the rather strained translation of Neh. 3:8b (in contemporary English versions) can be replaced by a more adequate one — indicating in so many words that Nehemiah did not try to wall in the whole city of the last days of monarchical Judah but intentionally "abandoned" part of it.

While it is a commonplace that the study of one text can be elucidated by the study of a similar related text, text theory suggests that we go further afield and that texts in separate disciplines be allowed to elucidate each other. But whether texts are closely related or relatively distant, a kind of INTERTEXTUALITY is involved.

Let me suggest in (2), therefore, a formulation in which this element of intertextuality is accounted for hermeneutically:

$$(2) \qquad \text{Text}_i \leftarrow {}^H \rightarrow \text{Text}_j$$

i.e., "a given text may be partially elucidated by reference to another text(s), even if not in the same discipline". I have drawn the hermeneutic arrow here as bidirectional, since the mutual elucidation can work in both directions.

4.   Text Theory and the Arts

But what of the implications of text theory for the arts, e.g. music, dance, visual arts, and architecture? Semiotics has made a beginning in this regard, but — as a comprehensive and sprawling discipline — it lacks an adequate theory of text.[4] An adequate theory of text must come by way of textlinguistics and text theory.

But is it not naive and *ad hoc* to make text the measure of everything? Assuredly yes. What then? Let us consider some bidirectional relations of the sort: "X as text; text as X". Thus, if music can be regarded as a kind of text, cannot a text also be compared to a musical composition? And if a painting can be considered to be a kind of text, why cannot a text be considered to be a kind of painting? And if architecture is a kind of "frozen text", why cannot a text be regarded as a kind of building/complex of buildings?

4.1   *Text theory and music*

Textual concepts are not difficult to apply to music. Musical compositions have passages that can be considered to be *introduction, inciting incident, development, climax*, and *denouement* much as in a narrative. A composition has parts which advance it and parts which serve as background. We might with some propriety

---

4. Sydney Lamb is to be commended for inaugurating at Rice University a joint department of linguistics and semiotics. The conference held at the program's inauguration resulted in a volume of articles (Copeland 1984) of considerable relevance in this connection. I mention also in this regard the Halliday festschrift volumes (Steele and Threadgold [eds.] 1987).

search, therefore, for the mainline of development in a composition. Furthermore, one germinal motif (like the opening bars of Beethoven's Fifth Symphony) can be compared in some ways to the macrostucture of a text. In addition, some compositions are spontaneous (improvised) and others are pre-planned — much like unplanned and planned texts. Finally, musical idioms throughout the world, (including the vast world of non-Western music) vary in ways much like the variation observed in texts in different languages.

But what of text as music? A disconcerting aspect of some current text-analysis (including possibly my own!) is the tendency to over-specificity because of dissection according to a particle-oriented view of reality (Pike 1959). Indeed some text analyses are so static that one suspects that a kind of *rigor mortis* has set in. But music is a kind of flowing and less discreet continuum. Taking seriously musical analogies to texts would encourage us to view a text more as a dynamic production. Indeed, such an approach to text-analysis is specifically advocated by de Beaugrande and Dressler as "the procedural approach". Here is where the analogy to music can help save text analysis from *rigor mortis*.

The musical sequence: theme — countertheme — recapitulation, much used in Western music has a rather exact counterpart in text structure, especially in Semitic inclusio/chiastic patterns (Arabic and Hebrew literature), but has also been observed in South American Indian languages (Waltz 1976) and in Australian aboriginal languages (Sayers 1976). Furthermore, the idea that one theme can be dominant while another is echoed or backgrounded (or even nascent), while easily documentable in music, can also be extended to texts. Thus, any one of Arthur Hailey's novels equals (1) a storyline, plus (2) exposé of an institution or industry. The storyline (1) usually predominates, but the background thematic material (2), which is quite pervasive, sometimes becomes dominant for a while as well — or conflates with the storyline.

There is at least one kind of discourse type, the familiar essay, that is often comparable to theme plus variations in music. Such an essay on a topic Q rarely presents a valid logical partitioning of the theme, rather Q_i, Q_j, Q_k ... are presented in succession as variations on the theme. This is illustrated for example in Charles Krauthammer's *Time* essay, "Vacationing on a Return Ticket" where a vacation is presented as an example, often a flight into irresponsibility — and a few examples of such irresponsible jaunts are presented. But always the traveler has a return ticket in his pocket and never intends to live with the situation that he is visiting. Here, I believe that the musical analogue might lead to a perception of the text structure in terms of theme plus variations.

4.2 *Text theory and painting*

A painting of the more pictorial/anthropomorphic sort can be compared to a text in terms of backgrounding and foregrounding. The whole has an overall macrostructure to which the details must conform. For this reason such paintings are inevitably interpretations or even reconstructions of reality. Furthermore, such a painting has a hierarchical/constituent structure. Certain figures/features are elaborated as sub-wholes which fit into the main whole.

But even the better sort of abstract art is, I suspect, not all that different. A good abstract composition must also have cohesion and prominence. It must subordinate some features to others. It must have a macrostructure of sorts — no matter how difficult it may be to state such a notion in words. And why should we expect it to be stateable in words?

But what of text as painting? Let us return here to an idea voiced in Section 2, where we focus on the linguistic structure of a text in a textlinguistics framework, and mention the feasibility of scalar arrangement of the verb forms/clause types of a discourse type in a given language. The claims were made there that (1) such a scalar arrangement could reflect progressive degrees of departure from the mainline of a story; and (2) this could partially guide microanalysis in that higher-ranking verb forms/clause types in the scale could also be shown to be dominant in the constituent structure of local spans. I have even made the claim (1981) that an optical analogy, the color spectrum, is of relevance here.

Thus, in a story in English, the storyline (active verbs, cognitive events, contingencies) dominates and can be color-coded as red. Background activities and cognitive states can be color-coded as red-orange. Flashbacks — events reported out of sequence, can be color-coded as yellow-orange. Setting (descriptive and explanatory material) can be color coded as yellow. Irrealis sentences — things that didn't/should have/might have happened — can be color-coded as green. And, finally, intrusive author evaluations can be color-coded as blue.

Thinking this way, we conceive of an author as painting a story with various sorts of verb forms/clause types. We can push the analogy further by color-coding a part or all of a story in this fashion, then throwing away the verbal component, and studying the resultant color design. Some such project was once attempted between myself as discourse analyst and Carolyn Dyk, an artist colleague.

4.3 *Text theory and architecture*

What of a building as text? Here the thought of a building as a cohesive whole with lines that lead the eye to its most prominent feature (and avoidance of distracting detail) is not so different from that of a text. Here such facts as that the Parthenon is not built on straight lines but with lines almost imperceptibly bowing outward, is again similar to a requirement of text development: Make everything to the smallest detail subservient to the main thrust of the whole.

But what of text as building? I heard it once remarked that the sermon of a certain preacher kept us so long in the vestibule that we scarcely had time to appreciate the sanctuary — saying in effect that the introduction was much too long and that the body of the sermon was relatively underdeveloped. Or a writer may announce his intention of building only a rude scaffolding in the first part of his work and erecting the main building in the second part. The center of a chiasm in literature can be compared to the keystone of an arch. In fact, running metaphor in terms of architectural motifs often characterizes the discussion of text — even the frequent claim: "I lay a foundation here for what is to follow". Perhaps comparing a text to a building is one of the "metaphors we live by" (Lakoff and Johnson 1980).

Francis Thompson uses the metaphor text-as-building towards the end of the second of his "Sister Songs": a pair of long poems written to two children, Monica and Madeline, who were children of his patron, Wilfred Meynell. He writes at the end of the composite poem:

As, poised upon this unprevisioned height
      I lift into its place
The utmost aery, traceried pinnacle.
So; it is builded, the high tenement,
      — God grant! — to mine intent:
Most like a palace of the Occident,
      Upthrusting maze on maze
      Its mounded blaze ...

Down a few lines he likens his poem to a castle guarded by a dragon:

Yet wail, my spirits, wail!
So few therein to enter shall prevail.
Scare fewer could win way, if their desire

> A dragon balked, with involuted spire
> And writhen snout spattered with yeasty fire.

In the next line he sighs for the "appointed knight" who will blow the horn at the portal and gain admission — perhaps the poet-reader who will understand his poetry.

Taking up again the figure of the building, he refers to his poem again as something perceived by glancing through a window:

> Receding labyrinths lessening tortuously
> ·In half obscurity
> With mystic images, inhuman, cold
> That flameless torches hold ...

But, when the one comes who can blow the horn, then

> Straight
> Open for him shall roll the conscious gate;
> And light leap up from all the torches there,
> And life leap up in every torchbearer ...
> As for the appointed knight,
> He threads securely the far intricacies.
> ....
> Until he gain the structure's core, where stands —
> a toil of magic hands —
> The unbodied spirit of the sorcerer ...
> ...
> It rests exempt, beneath the edifice
> To which itself gave rise;
> Sustaining center to that bubble of stone
> Which, breathed from it, exists for it alone.

Thus ends Thompson's prolonged passage (51–52) in which he compares his poem to a vast, but rather inaccessible structure sustained at the heart by his spirit and waiting for the arrival of the "appointed knight" who can find his way in.

I have tried to illustrate the "X as text" and "text as X" analogies from domains of the arts in which X is first music, then painting, then architecture. I do not believe that the analogies are superficial. They cut across **worlds**: the world of texts in general (Text-W) and the world of the various Arts (Arts-W).

I believe that just as text theory must be interdisciplinary, with one text illuminating another text across disciplinary lines, so must semiotic theory in general, i.e. one field of study can illuminate another field. I propose therefore a third and final correlation in (3):

(3) Text-W $\leftarrow$ ^{H} $\rightarrow$ Arts-W

i.e. "the study of texts and the study of the arts can mutually illuminate each other".

References

Bailey, Nicolas A. 1992. Nehemiah 3:1–32: An intersection of the text and the topography. *Journal of Translation and Textlinguistics* 5: 1–12.

de Beaugrande, R., and W. Dressler. 1981. *An Introduction to Textlinguistics*. London: Longmans.

Beekman, John., John Callow, and Michael Kopesec. 1981. *The Semantic Structure of Written Communication*. Fifth Edition. Dallas: Summer Institute of Linguistics.

Borker, Ruth. 1986. 'Moved by the Spirit': constructing meaning in a Brethren breaking of bread service. *Text* 6: 3 (special issue). *The Audience as Co-author*, ed. by Alessandro Duranti, and Donald Brenneis, 317–337.

Brend, Ruth (ed.) 1986. *The Text as Convergence of Concerns*, Second UTA conference on linguistics and the humanities. *Word* 37: 1–2.

Copeland, James A. (ed.). 1984. *New Directions in Linguistics and Semiotics*. Rice University Studies. Houston Texas: Rice University.

Danet, Brenda (ed.) 1984. *Studies of Legal Discourse*. *Text* 4: 1–3 (special issue).

van Dijk, Teun A. 1977. *Text and Context: Explorations in the Semantics and Pragmatics of Discourse*. London: Longmans.

van Dijk, Teun A.. 1980. *Macrostructures: an Interdisciplinary Study of Global Structures in Discourse, Interaction, and Cognition*. Hillsdale, New Jersey: Lawrence Erlbaum Associates.

van Dijk, Teun A., and Walter Kintsch. 1977. Cognitive psychology and discourse. *Current Trends in Textlinguistics*, ed. by W. U. Dressler. Berlin and New York: de Gruyter.

van Dijk, Teun A. and Ruth Wodak (eds.) 1988. *Discourse, Racism and Ideology*. *Text* 8: 1–2 (special issue).

Farmer, Jeff. 1981. The discourse analysis of a piece of transformational-generative argumentation. *Journal of the Linguistic Association of the Southwest* 3: 266–280.

Freeman, Sarah and Monica Heller (eds.) 1987. Medical discourse. *Text* 7.1 (special issue).

Halliday, M. A. K. and Ruqaiya Hasan. 1976. *Cohesion in English*. (English Language Series 9.) London: Longman

Krauthammer, Charles. 1984. Holiday: Living on a return ticket. *Time*, August 27.52

Lakoff, George and Mark Johnson. 1980. *Metaphors We Live by*. Chicago: University of Chicago Press.

Longacre, Robert. 1976. *An Anatomy of Speech Notions*. Lisse: Peter De Ridder Press

Longacre, Robert. 1981. A spectrum and profile approach to discourse analysis. *Text* 1: 337–384.

Longacre, Robert, (ed.) [under Adam Makkai] 1982–1983. *Linguistics and the Humanities. First UTA Conference on Linguistics and the Humanities, Forum Linguisticum* 7.1,2,3 (August 1982, December 1982, April 1983).

Longacre, Robert. 1983. *The Grammar of Discourse*. New York: Plenum Press.

Longacre, Robert. 1985. Discourse peak as zone of turbulence. *Beyond the Sentence*, ed. by Jessica Wirth, 82–98. Ann Arbor: Karoma.

Longacre, Robert. 1989. Two hypotheses regarding text generation and analysis. *Discourse Processes* 12: 413–60.

Longacre, Robert. 1990. *Storyline Concerns and Word-Order Typology in East and West Africa. Studies in African Linguistics*, Supplement 10. Los Angeles: UCLA.

Longacre, Robert. 1994. The Dynamics of Reported Dialoque in Narrative. *Word* 45, 125–143.

Longacre, Robert. 1996. *The Grammar of Discourse*. Second Edition, New York: Plenum Press.

Mann, William C. and Sandra A. Thompson. 1987. *Rhetorical Structure Theory: A Theory of Text Organization*. Marina del Rey: University of Southern California, Information Sciences Institute.

Mann, William C. and Sandra A. Thompson (eds.) 1992. *Discourse Description, Diverse Linguistic Analyses of a Fund-Raising Text*. Amsterdam: John Benjamins.

Pike, Kenneth L. 1959. Language as particle, wave, and field. *The Texas Quarterly* 2: 37–54.

Ricoeur, Paul. 1984–1985. *Time and Narrative* (3 volumes). Chicago: University of Chicago Press.

Sacks, H. 1984. Notes on methodology. *Structures of Social Action: Studies in Conversational Analysis*, ed. by J. Heritage and J. M. Atkinson, 21–24. Cambridge: Cambridge University Press.

Sayers, Barbara. 1976. *The Sentence in Wik-Munkan: A Description of Propositional Relationships*. Pacific Linguistics series 13, no. 44. Canberra: The Australian National University.

Steele, Ross and Terry Threadgold (eds.) 1987. *Language Topics: Essays in Honour of Michael Halliday*. 2 volumes. Amsterdam: John Benjamins.

Thompson, Francis. no date. *Complete Poetical Works of Francis Thompson*. pp. 18–58. New York: The Modern Library (original collection and arrangement by Wilfred Meynell, 1913).

Waltz, Nathan E. 1976. Discourse functions of Guanano sentence and paragraph. *Studies in Indigenous Languages of Colombia, Panama, and Ecuador*, ed. by Robert Longacre and Frances Woods, 21–146. Dallas: Summer Institute of Linguistics Publications #52.

About the author

Robert E. Longacre is Professor Emeritus at the University of Texas at Arlington, where he taught from 1972 to 1993. He completed a doctorate in Linguistics at the University of Pennsylvania in 1955. His primary influences in linguistics came from Zellig Harris of Pennsylvania and Kenneth L. Pike, whom he met at a session of the Summer Institute of Linguistics in 1945. He worked as a field investigator under the SIL from 1946 to 1972, preparing a New Testament translation into the Trique language of Mexico. He has traveled to many parts of the world as a consultant in linguistics and translation. Though he sees himself as reacting somewhat against stratificationalism, he still feels his linguistic work has been enriched by growing up professionally in the same world with Sydney Lamb.

CHAPTER 12

The Schemata for Motion and Action

A Typological Consideration

Yoshihiko Ikegami
University of Tokyo

1.   Introduction

My Yale University Dissertation (1969), prepared under Professor Sydney Lamb, was entitled "The Semological Structure of the English Verbs of Motion: A Stratificational Approach" (published as Ikegami 1970). It was an attempt to apply the theory of semology in stratificational grammar to the description of the semantic structure of the verbs of motion in English. Part III of the dissertation, entitled "The Extension of the Notion of the Verb of Motion", however, departed from this general theoretical framework and explored how the structural patterns encoding motion are transferred and applied to other conceptual domains, such as donation, perception, action, causation, and change of state.

With the strongly formalistic orientation which dominated the linguistic scene during the ensuing quarter of a century, an idea like the extension of the notion of motion has rarely, if ever, been seriously discussed. As a very few exceptions, one could perhaps cite Gruber (1976) and Jackendoff (1983, 1990). Limitation of space forbids me to discuss and comment on the works of these two authors, which were, naturally enough, strongly influenced by the basic tenets of transformational grammar.[1]

---

1. As examples of more congenial attempts, one may refer to Anderson (1971) and Lyons (1977: 15.7). The interest in the localist theory, however, generally tended to center around the definition of cases (exactly the kind of topic actively explored by the nineteenth century localists), while my interest has been to apply localistic ideas in attempting to define a set of basic patterns for the semantic structure of the verbs (see especially, Ikegami: 1973, 1984).

2. Image Schemata for Motion

What I propose to do in the present paper is to reconsider the problem of the
conceptual transfer of the notion of motion, not in terms of (putatively discrete)
semantic features and the ways they are combined into "larger" units, but in
terms of (essentially non-discrete, holistic) image schemata, which, in recent
cognitive linguistic literature, have been shown to underlie a number of important
semantic transfers from certain cognitively basic domains (closely associated
with our concrete bodily experiences) to relatively more abstract domains (not
directly associated with our concrete bodily experiences) (cf. Lakoff 1986,
Johnson 1987, Langacker 1991: Ch. 1).

I will in particular be concentrating on the imagic mapping from the domain
of motion to that of action. In contrast to the transfer from motion (via abstract
motion or change of state) to causation, which dominated the discussion in
componential semantics since Gruber, the question of the motion-action relationship has, to my knowledge, rarely been seriously addressed. The cause for this
neglect apparently is that the notion of causation clearly involves the notion of
change and once the notion of abstract motion is introduced as one standing for
change in general, one can quite straightforwardly relate the notion of motion
with that of causation. By contrast, it appears that the notion of change is not
immediately associable with that of action, since the characteristic feature
associated with action is that of an object being "affected" rather than "changed".

3. "Action" as an Extension of "Motion"

There is, nevertheless, good linguistic evidence which shows that "action" can be
conceived of as an extension of "motion" just as "causation" can be, and that,
moreover, the conceptualizations of these two notions are closely parallel to each
other. Japanese offers particularly transparent examples testifying to the plausibil-
ity of such construal, as was suggested in my Yale dissertation (Ikegami 1970:
Pt. III) and discussed more explicitly in Ikegami 1973: 42–43 and 1984: 59.

I.   Pattern 'DO X TO Y'
      Mary ni kisu o   suru (literally, 'do "kiss" to Mary')
      Mary-to kiss-ACC do
      'kiss Mary'

II.   Pattern 'MAKE Y TO X'
    Mary o   kofuku   ni suru (literally, 'do Mary to happiness')
    Mary-ACC happiness to do
    'make Mary happy'

The contrast is quite systematic. Thus for X in Pattern I, one can use lexical items like *aisatsu* ('greeting'), *akushu* ('hand-shaking'), *itazura* ('trick'), *kisu* ('kiss'), *setsumei* ('explanation'), *yakusoku* ('promise'), and so forth, while for X in Pattern II one can use lexical items like *anzen* ('safety'), *hadaka* ('naked-ness'), *kenko* ('healthiness'), *kofuku* ('happiness'), *shikaisha*('(the state of being a) chairperson'), *tsuma* ('(the state of being a) wife'), and so forth. It is easy to see that we have a contrast between an "action" term for X in Pattern I and a "state" term for X in Pattern II. Pattern I thus encodes transfer of an act to Y, namely "action", while Pattern II represents change of state undergone by Y, namely "causation".

4.   Marking of "Affected" and "Goal"

There thus seems to be sufficiently good reason to assume that the linguistic encoding of action derives from that of motion. If we choose to proceed on this assumption, however, there are two points in particular which are to be account-ed for.

One point concerns the marking for the affected in action. As we have seen above, the affected in action corresponds to the goal in motion. The correspon-dence is quite transparent in the Japanese examples discussed above and also in such English expressions as *give him a blow/kick/lift* or *give it a thought/try*. In typical action sentences, however, the affected is not marked as the goal (encoded as dative or its equivalent) but as the patient (encoded as the accusative or its equivalent). This conversion from goal to patient is a point to be accounted for.

The other point to be considered concerns the marking of the goal in the encoding of motion. The normal marking for the goal is quite expectedly dative or its equivalent, but there are cases in which a verb of motion is accompanied with a complement noun phrase in the accusative case (which then cannot formally be distinguished from a direct object in the accusative accompanying a verb of action). This is again quite commonly attested in Japanese, as in *kosu o aruku* (lit. 'course-ACC walk') 'walk along the course', *yama o noboru* (lit.

'mountain-ACC climb') 'climb up the mountain', *yuka o hau* (lit. 'floor-ACC crawl') 'crawl over the floor', *sora o tobu* (lit. 'sky-ACC fly') 'fly in the sky', and so forth. It is indeed the case that English can also have *walk the course, climb the mountain, crawl the floor, fly the sky*, etc., but these are "marked" uses, associated with a higher degree of transitivity. Thus an English expression like *walk the course* is described as evoking a situation in which a professional golfer walks over the course "before a big tournament ... looking at the lie of the land from every angle" (Dixon 1991: 282). The course is here turned into an object to be examined and the verb *walk* is nearly a verb of action rather than of simple motion. The Japanese expressions, by contrast, are unmarked and the accusative case cannot be replaced by any other oblique case without either producing an unacceptable (or at least awkward) expression or manifestly changing the meaning of the expression.

5.   Motion Mapped onto Action

With the preliminary considerations given above, let me now address the question of how the schema for motion is mapped onto that of action, what different options are available in the mapping, and how they are encoded. Crucial to my discussion is the realization that the cognitive distinction between "bounded" and "unbounded" entities (Talmy 1988; also for cultural implications, see Ikegami 1989) plays an all-important role in the schematization of motion and action.

Motion, by definition, is change in locus. A change may or may not be oriented toward a certain goal. When the motion is goal-oriented, it is BOUNDED; when not, it is UNBOUNDED. Another way of characterizing the two types of motion is to say that a motion is essentially goal-oriented, but that the goal can be either a BOUNDED entity (or an individuum) or an UNBOUNDED entity (or a continuum). In the former case, the motion too is necessarily BOUNDED. In the latter case, it is UNBOUNDED, since with a continuum as goal there is no definite point at which the motion is viewed as having reached the goal. Just as the "unbounded" goal extends itself indefinitely, so the motion will have to be indefinitely extended. The notion of the goal then will naturally be turned into that of the path along which the motion proceeds.[2]

Schematically, we start with a contrast between motion toward an unbounded goal and a bounded goal, as in Figure 1.

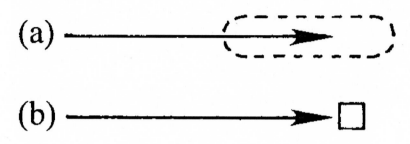

Figure 1.   *Motion toward an unbounded goal compared with motion toward a bounded goal*

The first type of motion is reinterpreted as motion along/through a path, as in Figure 2.

The two types of motion are contrasted with each other in terms of the different loci on which the cognitive focus is laid. A bounded entity is naturally more cognitively salient than an unbounded entity. Hence the goal is more liable to be focused on if it is a bounded entity than if it is an unbounded entity. In the

2. As a concrete illustration, compare the meanings of the German preposition *in* in the two phrases, *in das Zimmer eintreten* 'to enter the room' and *in die Luft steigen* 'to rise into the air'. One can construe the former phrase (which involves a BOUNDED goal) in terms of MOTION — GOAL, but the latter phrase (which involves an UNBOUNDED goal) can very well be construed in terms of MOTION — PATH. Because the sky is typically conceptualized as an UNBOUNDED entity, the contrast between goal and path is neutralized.

As another piece of evidence which shows a close relationship between the notion of the path and that of the unbounded continuum, consider the distinction between the German prepositions *von* (literally 'of') and *durch* (literally 'through') as markers of the agent in the passive sentence. While *von* is typically used for 'Urheber' ('author'), *durch* is typically associated with 'Ursache' ('cause'): cf. *Der Kranke wurde von einem Spezialisten operiert* ('The sick person was operated on by a specialist') and *Er wurde durch eine geschickte Operation gerettet* ('He was saved by a skillful operation') (Schmidt 1974: 10).

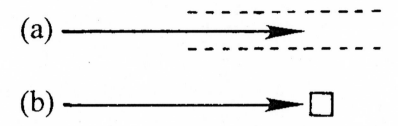

Figure 2.   *Motion toward an unbounded goal (reinterpreted as motion along a path) compared with motion toward a bounded goal*

latter case, there is only the process of motion *per se* to be focused on. Thus the (a) type of motion tends to be "process-oriented" and the (b) type "goal-oriented".

An action is typically directed to a goal. Only the (b) type of motion, therefore, serves well as a schema for action.[3] The (b) type of motion is "goal-oriented" rather than "process-oriented", as discussed above. There is, however, a sense in which one can say that the action schema has an even greater focus laid on the goal than in the case of the second type of motion schema. In a typical instance of motion, one will conceive of a concrete entity in motion. In an action, by contrast, the entity in motion is abstract, as discussed and illustrated in Section 3. Since an abstract entity is less likely to be focused on than a concrete entity, we have a situation here in which the goal is still more likely to monopolize the focus than in the case of the goal in motion (in which case the entity in motion is equally qualified to be focused on — or certainly more, because an entity in motion is generally more likely to be focused on than an entity *in statis*). In fact, in the conceptualization of an action (specifically, a goal-directed action) the cognitive focus is so much concentrated on the goal that the notion of the process tends to be backgrounded.

There is one further modification to be introduced in the schema for action and this also concerns the goal. The goal in motion is something that is simply

---

3. The remaining possibility of the (a) type of motion serving as a schema for action will be discussed in Section 8.

"reached", but the goal in action is not only reached but "affected". The shift from "being reached" to "being affected" is easily understood if we think of a person as the prototypical goal: the person is a locus where "being reached" leads most readily to "being affected" — a contact with a certain part of the whole may have an effect of affecting the whole. This entails a change in conceptualization — a change from the goal reached (by motion) to the patient affected (by action) and the change in conceptualization is encoded by marking the patient as accusative rather than as dative.[4]

6.   Morphosyntactic Realization of Schemata

We have so far identified the following three schemata and have shown how they are related to each other:

I.	(a)	MOTION	–	PATH
	(b)	MOTION	–	GOAL
II.		ACTION	–	PATIENT

These three types are morphosyntactically not marked in the same way in different languages. In English, for example, the basic contrast is I (a) and (b), on the one hand, and II, on the other:

I.   (a)

       (intransitive) verb + preposition + objective case

    (b)

II.   (transitive) verb + objective case

The rationale behind this division is clear enough: 'motion' (I (a) and (b)) vs. 'action' (II). Over and above this basic distinction, it must be added that English has a tendency to use some verbs of type I (a) transitively (cf. examples like *walk the course, jump the stream, swim the channel*, etc., already referred to). This point will be discussed later in Section 7.

---

4. Note that with the reconceptualization of the goal as the patient, the stage is now set for a further development, namely, for a schema for causation.

Japanese, by contrast, has a very different system of marking. Below, the *o*-case and the *ni*-case are approximate equivalents of the accusative and the dative, respectively.

I. (a)   *o*-case + verb
    (b)   *ni*-case + verb

II.   *o*-case + verb

The fact that 'motion + path' (I (a)) and 'action + patient' (II) are morphosyntactically marked in the same way has long puzzled traditional Japanese linguists. Intuitively, the *o*-case is typically associated with the patient role in action, while the same marking is also applied to the path role associated with "intransitive" motion. The rationale for marking the path role in the same way as the patient role, however, will not be very difficult to detect if we may assume that the accusative case serves, as the least marked case directly associated with the verb, to indicate an entity most closely and directly involved in the process denoted by the verb.[5] Thus the "motion — path" schema is characterized, as we argued in Section 5, as "process-oriented", with the cognitive focus on the process of motion *per se*. The path here is closely and directly involved in the motion *per se* and accordingly qualifies to be marked in the accusative. By comparison, the goal is a more external entity in relation to the process of motion and is hence appropriately marked obliquely.

German is particularly interesting in this respect, since the language has two sets of contrastive marking at its disposal: preposition vs. no preposition, on the one hand, and the accusative vs. the dative, on the other:

I. (a)   (intransitive) verb + preposition + the accusative case
    (b)   (intransitive) verb + preposition + the dative case
          (intransitive) verb + preposition + the accusative case

II. (b)   (transitive) verb + the accusative case

German, like English, thus makes a basic distinction between "motion" (I (a) and (b)) and "action" (II) in terms of the contrast between no use and the use of a preposition. But an interesting feature to be noted is that the accusative rather

---

5. Another way to capture the same situation is to stipulate, as Halliday (1985) does, that the noun phrase in the object position following the verb specifies how far the process denoted by the verb "extends". Notice that the term *extend* can conveniently be applied both to the goal and the range of the process.

than the dative is selected for the prepositional object to encode the path in 1 (a) — which reminds us of the use of the accusative in Japanese (with this difference, of course, that the accusative case is directly governed by the verb in the latter): cf. *durch den Tunnel fahren* 'to travel through the tunnel', *über die Brücke gehen* 'to go over the bridge', *sich um die Sonne drehen* 'to turn around the sun' (all of which will be encoded by the accusative (*o*-case) + verb in Japanese).[6] The encoding of 'motion — goal' also shows an interesting split in German. On the one hand, we have the goal obligatorily marked in the dative for prepositions like *zu* 'to' and *nach* 'toward': e.g. *zur Schule gehen* 'to go to school', *nach Deutschland fahren* 'to travel to(ward) Germany'. There are, on the other hand, a set of prepositions with which the goal is encoded in the accusative: e.g. *an die See gehen* 'to go to sea', *auf den Berg steigen* 'to climb up the mountain', *ins Wasser fallen* 'to fall into the water', *vor den Altar treten* 'to step before the alter'. It seems to me that the coexistence of two different ways of marking "motion — goal" here reflects a situation in which two contrasting typological principles for marking are at work in the conceptualization of the "motion" — "action" domains, as will be discussed in the next section.

7.   Typological Considerations

My suggestion is that there are languages with which the motion schema (prototypically, of the "process-oriented" type, I (a)) is more dominant than the action schema, on the one hand, and languages with which the action schema is more dominant than the motion schema, on the other. As we have noted in Section 5, the motion schema is essentially process-oriented rather than goal-oriented, while the action schema is clearly goal-oriented. Depending on which schema is relatively more dominant in the language in question, either the process-oriented character of the motion schema is superimposed on the action

---

6. There are certain cases of interesting discrepancy. Thus in German, expressions like *über den Wolken fliegen* 'to fly over the clouds', *über der Stadt kreisen* 'to circle over the city', and *an dem Haus vorbeifliegen/vorübergehen* 'to fly/go past the house' involve a prepositional object in the dative rather than the accusative, while the corresponding Japanese expressions use the o-case (equivalent to the accusative). Presumably, German requires "contact" between the trajector and the landmark for the accusative to be used. Cf. also expressions like *über die Grenze /über Hamburg fahren* 'to travel over the border/over Hamburg' with an accusative object, to which the corresponding Japanese expressions behave in a parallel way.

schema or the goal-oriented character of the action schema is superimposed on the motion schema. Japanese serves as a good example of a language of the former type. As already pointed out (Ikegami 1984), verbs of motion in Japanese (except perhaps *iku* 'go' and *kuru* 'come') do not freely collocate with a goal phrase: e.g. ?? *eki e hashiru* (lit. 'station-to run') 'run to the station', ?? *kishi e oyogu* (lit. 'shore-to swim') 'swim to the shore'.[7] Clearly parallel to this process-oriented character of Japanese verbs of motion is the equally process-oriented character of Japanese verbs of action (as fully discussed in Ikegami 1985): it will not necessarily sound contradictory if one says *Moyashita kedo, moenakatta* (lit. '(I) burned (it), but (it) burned not') '*I burned it, but it didn't burn' (where what is actually meant is 'I tried to burn it, but it didn't burn'). It is found that in quite a number of cases, Japanese verbs of action, in contrast to the semantically-corresponding English verbs of action, do not necessarily imply the achievement of the intended goal, and an interesting point is that apparently no reverse case is found. The semantic focus of the Japanese verbs of action is on the process, which may or may not lead to the achievement of the goal.

English, on the other hand, is a good example of a language in which the action schema with its focus on the goal is dominant. Its verbs of action tend to imply goal-achievement. For example, the sentence, *I helped John (to) solve the problem* generally implies that John was able to solve the problem, but the same implication does not exist for the corresponding Japanese sentence. The focus on the notion of goal-achievement helps the English action verbs to be readily causativized, as in *sing a baby to sleep, dance the girl weary, laugh a person into silence* (some of which may not be literally translatable into German). It is certainly this dominance of the action schema that allows quite a few English verbs of motion to be transitivized (as in *walk the course*, discussed in Section 4) by having the goal turned into the patient.

8. Conclusion

It will have been noticed that there is one logically possible schema that I have not referred to yet. We have found it convenient to distinguish between two

---

7. One way to improve the Japanese expressions is to support the action verbs with the verb *iku* 'go' or *kuru* 'come': e.g. *eki e hashitte iku* (lit. 'station-to running go') 'go running to the station', *kishi e oyoide kuru* (lit. 'shore-to swimming come') 'come swimming to the shore'.

cases for the motion schema, depending on whether the goal is a "bounded" entity (an individuum) or an "unbounded" entity (a continuum). The same distinction should logically apply to the action schema. The action schema we have already posited (namely II) is the one in which the patient is conceived of as a "bounded" entity. What happens if the patient in action is an "unbounded" entity? The situation will be very much like that of I (a) in motion. The action here has no definite goal and hence no implication of the achievement of the goal with which the action is characterized as having been completed. The action will then become very much like what may be called an activity — an ongoing process of acting which will prototypically be associated with encoding in terms of an intransitive verb.

We thus have four schemata:

I. (a) MOTION   –   PATH   (PROCESS-oriented)
    (b) MOTION   –   GOAL   (GOAL-oriented)
II. (a) ACTION   –   PATIENT   (GOAL-oriented)
    (b) ACTIONAL PROCESS   (PROCESS-oriented)

We have seen that for motion the process-oriented type is prototypical, while for action the goal-oriented type is prototypical. Languages may differ as to which of the two prototypical types — the process-oriented type of motion or the goal-oriented type of action — is dominant, and depending on the option in this respect, the favorite type of either action or motion is selected in a way coordinated with the option of the dominant prototype. The coexistence of two types of marking for the goal in the motion schema in German can thus be considered as the double superimposition of two dominant schemata, one deriving from the "motion-path" schema (which leads to the marking of the goal in the dative, as the goal is less integrated with, and is therefore more external to, the notion of motion) and the other coming from the "action-patient" schema (which leads to the marking of the goal in motion in the accusative, just as the goal (reinterpreted as patient) of action is, because the patient is closely and directly involved in, and is in fact part of, the notion of action.

References

Anderson, John M. 1971. *The Grammar of Case: Towards a Localistic Theory.* Cambridge: Cambridge University Press.

Dixon, R. M. W. 1991. *A New Approach to English Grammar, On Semantic Principles*. Oxford: Clarendon Press.

Gruber, Jeffrey S. 1976. *Lexical Structures in Syntax and Semantics*. Amsterdam: North-Holland.

Halliday, M. A. K. 1985. *An Introduction to Functional Grammar*. London: Edward Arnold.

Ikegami, Yoshihiko. 1970. *The Semological Structure of The English Verbs of Motion: A Stratificational Approach*. Tokyo: Sanseido.

Ikegami, Yoshihiko. 1973. A set of basic patterns for the semantic structure of the verb. *Linguistics* 117.15–58.

Ikegami, Yoshihiko. 1984. How universal is a localist hypothesis? A linguistic contribution to the study of 'cognitive styles' of language. *The Semiotics of Culture and Language*, ed. by Robin Fawcett et al., Vol. 1, 49–80. London: Frances Pinter.

Ikegami, Yoshihiko. 1985. 'Activity'-'accomplishment'-'achievement': A language that can't say 'I burned it, but it didn't burn' and one that can. *Linguistics and Philosophy: Essays in Honor of Rulon S. Wells,* ed. by Adam Makkai and Alan K. Melby, 265–304. Amsterdam: John Benjamins.

Ikegami, Yoshihiko. 1989. Homology of language and culture: A case study in Japanese semiotics. *The Nature of Culture*, ed. by Walter A. Koch, 388–403. Bochum: Brockmeyer.

Ikegami, Yoshihiko. 1991. DO-language and BECOME-language: Two contrasting types of linguistic representation. *The Empire of Signs: Semiotic Essays on Japanese Culture*, ed. by Yoshihiko Ikegami, 258–326. Amsterdam: John Benjamins.

Jackendoff, Ray. 1983. *Semantics and Cognition*. Cambridge, Massachusetts: MIT Press.

Jackendoff, Ray. 1990. *Semantic Structures*. Cambridge, Massachusetts: MIT Press.

Johnson, Mark. 1987. *The Body in the Mind: The Bodily Basis of Meaning, Imagination, and Reason*. Chicago: University of Chicago Press.

Lakoff, George. 1986. *Women, Fire, and Dangerous Things: What Categories Reveal about The Mind*. Chicago: University of Chicago Press.

Langacker, Ronald W. 1991. *Concept, Image, and Symbol: The Cognitive Basis of Grammar*. Berlin: Mouton de Gruyter.

Lyons, John. 1977. *Semantics*. 2 vols. Cambridge: Cambridge University Press.

Schmidt, Werner. 1974 (1964). *Der Gebrauch der deutschen Präpositionen.* München: Hueber.

Talmy, Leonard. 1988. The relation of grammar to cognition. *Topics in Cognitive Linguistics*, ed. by Brygida Rudzka-Ostyn, 165–205. Amsterdam: John Benjamins.

About the author

Yoshihiko Ikegami is now Professor Emeritus at the University of Tokyo, where he taught for 30 years, and is continuing his teaching at Showa Women's University. He received his doctorate at Yale in 1969, with Syd Lamb as director for his dissertation **The Semological Structure of the English Verbs of Motion: A Stratificational Approach** *(published as a book in 1970). He has also written on a variety of topics in semantics, poetics, and semiotics. He has been a guest professor at Indiana University, the University of Munich and the Free University of Berlin, and has held research fellowships in Germany, the United States and Great Britain.*

CHAPTER 13

The Iconicity of Consonant Alternation

Roger W. Wescott
Drew University

Scepticism concerning the iconicity of vowels and of the tones that they carry is now rare enough to make it unnecessary to amass evidence demonstrating that iconicity. It is, for example, widely conceded that high front vowels have a diminutive connotation in most languages and that high pitch has the same connotation in languages characterized by lexical tone.

Scepticism concerning the iconicity of consonants, however, remains appreciable. At a recent linguistic conference, for example, a distinguished European scholar cited the English adjective *big* as a counter-example of iconicity, noting that its vocalism is diminutive — but overlooking the fact that its consonantism, acoustically grave and articulatorily labio-velar, is augmentative. In terms of phoneme count, *big* is predominantly augmentative in connotation (and, if cognate, the bases of the words *boggle*, *bogey*, and *bugaboo* are wholly so.)

1.   Primary, Secondary, and Tertiary Iconism

But, before advancing arguments in support of consonantal iconicity, we would do well, I think, to distinguish at least three types of iconicity in speech. The first of these is PRIMARY ICONISM, exemplified by utterances that resemble or imitate extralinguistic reality. Such iconism includes not only onomatopes of the sort dystactically represented as *bzz* and eutactically as *buzz* but also by technical terminology that illustrates what it designates. Examples of such illustration are phonological terms like *dental*, which contains four dentals, and *stop*, which contains two stops.

The second type of iconicity is SECONDARY ICONISM, exemplified by an utterance that resembles or imitates another utterance and, in so doing, conveys a similar meaning. Examples of such iconism are so-called phonesthemes, including both alliterative types like the asyllabic onsets of *gleam*, *glow*, *glitter* and rhyming types like the nucleus-and-coda sequences in *lash*, *gnash*, *thrash*. (From an expressive standpoint, it makes no difference that the *gl-* phonestheme is a Proto-Indo-European allomorph of the base whose syllabic form occurs in *gold*, *yolk*, and *yellow*, while the *-ash* phonestheme developed only in the 14th century by lexical assimilation to the 13th century verb *dash*.)

The third type of iconicity is TERTIARY ICONISM, exemplified by utterances in which one phoneme or syllable repeats another in the same base or word. In English, such iconism takes two forms: reduplication, or syllabic replication, as in infantilisms like *booboo*, *doodoo*, *googoo*; and palindromy, or syllabic margin repetition, as in *pip*, *tit*, *kick*.

2. Palindromes and Pentesthemes

English palindromes are often products of a process of palindromization. This process of derivation takes four forms:

progressive additive:	e.g., mom < ma
progressive replacive:	e.g., peep < peek
regressive additive:	e.g., Nan < Ann
regressive replacive:	e.g., Bob < Rob

Observation of speech-acquisition by children further suggests that there is a sequential relation between reduplication and palindromy, which may be typologically represented as follows:

stage 1:	single open syllables, like *pa*
stage 2:	repeated open syllables, like *papa*
stage 3:	single palindromic syllables, like *pap*
stage 4:	single heterophonic syllables, like *pat*

One striking aspect of palindromes is the frequency with which they exhibit mutual synonymy. Such synonymy appears not only within languages, where we encounter semantic equations like *pop=dad*, *tit=boob*, and *cack=poop*, but also between languages. Examples from Indo-European languages are in Table 1.

Table 1. *Translingual synonymy of palindromes*

Italian *ninna*	~	English *lullaby*
Cuban Spanish *tatagua*	~	Latin *papilio* (both meaning 'butterfly')
Latin *lolium*	~	English *cockle* (a weed)
Greek *tétīks*	~	Latin *cicāda*
Kurdish *pepū*	~	English *cuckoo*
Proto-Indo-European **tet-er-*	~	English *cackle*

Such correspondences extend even to languages from different phyla, as in the cases of Estonian *sõsar* ~ English *nun*, and Hebrew *dad* ~ English *teat*.

Perhaps because of their inherently repetitive and substitutive nature, palindromic forms are particularly prone to compounding, as in the surname *Babcock*; to reversal once compounded, as in *poplolly* = *lollipop* (where the first word means "mistress" and the second "candy" but both connote sensual self-indulgence); and to chaining, as in the sequence *lollipop* ~ *poppycock* ~ *cocka-mamie* (where all three terms suggest silliness of some sort). Like simple palindromes, compound palindromes also tend toward translingual synonymy, as in Italian *pappaceci* ~ English *nincompoop*.

A deviant type of English palindrome to which, to the best of my knowl-edge, no label has as yet been applied by other linguists, is what I call a "pentestheme". Pentesthemes may be broadly defined as five-phoneme sequences that follow the formula: obstruent plus continuant plus vowel plus continuant plus obstruent. Examples are: *shrimp*, *whisk*, *tweak*. A narrower definition would restrict such forms to more nearly palindromic shapes, deviating from full palindromy only to the extent that English phonotactic restrictions require them to. Examples are: *primp*, *clank*, *tweet*.

Not surprisingly, an iconic form may be of more than one type. The British regionalism *lolly*, "tongue", for example, exhibits primary iconism by virtue of its lingual consonantism and tertiary iconism by virtue of its basal palindromy. (A non-Indo-European analog is Estonian *nina*, "nose".) And the verb *cuck*, meaning "immerse", exhibits secondary iconism by rhyming with *duck* and tertiary iconism by palindromy.

3. Problems of Icon Selection

Since the illustrations of iconicity that have been selected thus far are nearly all Indo-European and mostly English, it may be that they will be regarded as manifestations of linguistic ethnocentricity. They are so only in the sense that, because the iconic lexicon of any spoken language tends to be both minimal and peripheral, examples of it are considerably easier to cite from those languages of which one is a speaker or of whose vocabularies extensive dictionaries have been compiled.

4. Glide Alternation

Because the iconicity of vowel alternation is, as noted above, more generally accepted than that of consonant alternation, we might do well to begin our consideration of consonant categories with glides, or semi-vowels. Employing a Tragerian phonemicization of English (Smith and Trager 1951), we find that those glides which are phonetically most vowel-like are the ones that precede consonants or pauses. In all such cases where the palatal and the labio-velar glide appear to stand in phonosemic contrast, the /y/ seems to connote what is bright, joyful, near, or present, while the /w/ seems to connote what is dim, depressing, far, or absent. Table 2 presents a few examples.

Table 2. *Examples of iconism involving /y/ and /w/*

y-form	w-form
gleaming	gloaming
glee	gloom
these	those
bind	bound

In hypocoristic suffixes, the phonosemic contrast appears to be that of diminutive versus augmentative, as in the onomastic pair *Danny* vs. *Danno* or the colloquial pair *kiddy* vs. *kiddo*. Among forms representing non-linguistic vocalization, the opposition appears to be that of high pitch versus low pitch, as in *hee-hee* vs. *ho-ho*.

The same alternation seems to have occurred in Proto-Germanic, to judge by the opposition between Old English *sīcan* and Swedish *sucka*, both meaning 'sigh'. (Presumably the former verb was diminutive and the latter augmentative. If so, the latter was cognate with Proto-Indo-European *swen-, 'sound', *swagh-, 'resound', *sward-, 'laugh', and *swer-, 'buzz': Watkins 1969).

In contemporary English, pre-vocalic glide alternation is less common, though pairings like *yow* ~ *wow* may be semantically neutralized examples of it. In Proto-Indo-European (or Pre-Indo-European), the phonemic opposition between frontal and labio-dorsal velars may reflect an analogous semantic contrast. The form KYEW, whence PIE *kwon-, 'dog', and *ekwo-, 'horse', may originally have meant 'slender domesticated animal'; while KWEW, whence PIE *gwow-, 'cattle', and *owi-, 'sheep', may have meant 'plump domesticated animal'.

5.   Horizontal, Vertical, and Diagonal Alternations

Most consonant alternations can be divided into "horizontal" types, involving shift in articulatory position, and "vertical" types, involving shift in articulatory manner. Examples of horizontal alternation in English are given in Table 3.

Table 3. *Examples of horizontal alternation involving labial, alveolar and velar consonants*

p/t/k:	chirp = chirt = chirk
b/d/g:	bash ~ dash ~ gash
m/n/ŋ:	damn ~ darn ~ dang

Predictably, alternant pairs are commoner than alternant triads. Among such pairs, alternations involving acoustically grave obstruents are commoner than those involving acoustically acute obstruents. Examples of labial/velar alternation are in Table 4.

Table 4. *Examples of horizontal alternation involving labial and velar consonants*

p/k:	damp = dank
b/g:	bumble = bungle
m/ŋ	bam = bang

Sometimes the alternation is replicated in such a way as to produce a palindromoid effect, as in *burble = gurgle*.

Generally speaking, labial and velar consonants convey a more derogatory connotation than do apical and palatal consonants. A surprising number of slur-words in English illustrate this pattern. Exemplificatory ethnic nicknames are:

Mick, *Spic*, *Wop*, *Kike*, *Gook*, and *Bohunk*. In Bini, a Congoid language of south-central Nigeria, bases beginning with a voiceless labio-velar stop often convey disparagement. Examples are given in Table 5.

Table 5. *Examples of labio-velar derogation in Bini*

kpa	to vomit
kpọ̀ọnkpọ̀ọn	bug-eyed
kpùkpùukpù	cowering
àkpà	fool
ọ̀kpò	hemorrhoids
òkpá	nose-bleed (Melzian 1937)

Horizontal stop-alternation can be cited even from Proto-Indo-European. The examples in Table 6 are from Pokorny (1959).

Table 6. *Horizontal stop alternation from Proto-Indo-European*

*appa	father
*atta	father or mother
*akka	mother or wet-nurse
*pen-	to strain
*ten-	to stretch
*ken-	to exhaust (Schwartz 1947)
*bher-	to carry
*dher-	to hold
*gher-	to grasp (ibid.)

Vertical consonant alternations involve movement from voiceless occlusive manner to voiced sonorant manner or vice-versa. English examples are:

> drip(ple)   dribble   drivel   drool   (from *driwel-)
> god(-damn it)   con(-sarn it)   gol(-durn it)   cor(-dim it)

In the *dr-* series, the form with /p/ seems to indicate maximal discontinuity, and the form with /w/ maximal continuity, of flow, the /b/ and /v/ forms providing intermediate stages in a gradient seriation. In the *g-/c-* series, the gradation from /d/ to /r/ seems to represent a progressive diminution in the strength of the profanity involved.

Proto-Indo-European appears to have exhibited similar vertical seriations, as in Table 7.

Table 7. *Vertical alternations in Proto-Indo-European*

*p(e)u-	to fertilize (cf. Latin *pūbēs*, genitals)
*b(e)u-	to gestate (cf. Latin *bucca*, cavity)
*bh(e)u-	to mature (cf. Latin *futūrus*, coming to be)
*uter-	womb (as in Latin *uterus*)
*uder-	belly (as in Sanskrit *udáram*)
*udher-	udder (as in English)
*ek-	I (as in Old Lithuanian *eš*)
*eg-	I (as in Latin *ego*)
*egh-	I (as in Sanskrit *ahám*)

The longest vertical column in PIE was apparently the apical. Predictably, more alternations can be reconstructed in this series than in any other. Examples are given in Table 8.

Table 8. *Alternations which involve apical consonants in Proto-Indo-European*

t/d:	*stā-, to stand	~	*sed-, to sit
t/dh:	*tragh-	~	*dhragh-, to pull
t/s:	*ten-, stretched	~	*sen-, aged
t/n:	*tEm-, then	~	*nEw-, now
t/r:	*pet-, to fly	~	*per-, to travel

Some consonant alternations are neither horizontal nor vertical but diagonal. "Bishop's moves" of this sort seem to presuppose intermediate alternations that were once either horizontal or vertical but have subsequently been lost. English examples fall into four categories, depending on whether the presumed diachronic movement was down and back, down and forward, up and back, or up and forward. Each of the four is illustrated in Table 9.

Table 9. *Changes which involve both vertical and horizontal moves*

1.	↘	: hath > has
2.	↙	: cackle > chuckle
3.	↗	: hell > heck
4.	↖	: yes > yep

The surmise that there have been lost intermediaries is strengthened by cases in which three clearly related forms exhibit simultaneously horizontal and vertical alternations. One such follows:

Bett(e)	
Beth	Bess

Here, the relation of /θ/ to /s/ is horizontal, while that of /t/ to the other two is vertical.

In some cases the decision whether to classify an alternation as diagonal or not depends on one's preference for phonemic or for phonetic patterning. The consonantal relation between the initial obstruents in the pair *pooey = fooey*, for example, is vertical if one classifies *f* broadly as labial but diagonal if one classifies it narrowly as labio-dental.

In a few cases, consonantal alternation occurs at the phonetic but not at the phonemic level. In English, such alternation is most plentiful in the apical column. An example is the series [tt~t~d~ɾ] occurring in the allomorphs of *ten* in the numerals *fourteen*, *fifty*, *ninety*, and *thirty*, respectively.

If, in addition to recognizing the alternation of consonants with one another, we also recognize their alternation with phonic zero, the range of such alternation is greatly extended. The commonest variety of consonant/zero alternation is the kind that results from utterance-abridgment of the sort encountered in nicknames. The simpler form of such hypocorism is exemplified by "stump-words" like *Sue* for *Susan*. A more complex form involves not only the elimination of syllables but the reduction of consonant-clusters in the syllables retained, as in *Kit* from *Christopher*. Proper names, however, are also capable of generating "excrescent" consonants, usually between nasals and oral continuants, as in *Thompson* from *Tom's son* or *Henderson* from *Henry's son*.

6.   The "Accordion Principle"

The fact that consonants may be either added or deleted in some forms gives rise to what I call "the accordion principle", whereby certain words come to have both expanded and contracted allologs. An example is the Middle English verb *mew* which, in the mid 16th century, lost its prenuclear glide to produce *moo* and, in the late 16th century, gained a terminal lateral to produce *mewl*. Other such "accordion" verbs are:

quell	quelch	squelch
cosh	quash	squash
crush	crunch	scrunch

As it happens, all three of these allologous words are optional sigmatics, capable of preposing a voiceless sibilant to their intermediate forms. This sibilant, known to Indo-Europeanists as "s-movable", seems to have been common in English and pre-English for at least three millennia. Table 10 provides examples of such sigmatic forms, with indications of their attested or postulated antiquity. Although in most cases the forms with *s* developed later than those without *s*, as in *spudgy*, a recent slang variant of *pudgy*, in some cases the reverse has clearly occurred, as in *tummy* from *stomach*.

Table 10. *Sigmatic forms of Indo-European forms*

antiquity	s-form	base form
Proto-Indo-European	splint	flint
Proto-Germanic	smelt	melt
Òld English	slime	lime
Middle English	smash	mash
Modern English	stamp	tamp

As we have already noted in our discussion of palindromes, consonant alternants may be either additive or replacive. Terminal *p*, for example, is additive in the case of *chirp ~ chirr* but replacive in the case of *skip ~ skim*. In a few cases, such as *guess ~ get*, a consonant may be analyzed either way. (If additive, this terminal *s* would have to be regarded as a contraction of *-t(i)s-*. In either case, the meaning of *get* would be "understand" or the like.)

7.   Phoneme Alternation as Affixation

When additive, optional consonants may be regarded as affixes. If they are external to the base and accompanied by a stressless vowel, so that they form part of a discrete syllable, our inclination so to regard them is certainly stronger. Examples of such affixes are the frequentative suffixes in the apparently cognate verbs *tiddle*, 'fondle', and *tidder*, 'procreate'. Other such affixes are the mutually apophonic prefixes in the slang pairs in Table 11.

Table 11. *Mutually apophonic prefixes in slang words*

Consonant	Prefixed Form	Unprefixed Form
p	pizazz, "zest"	zazzle, "sex appeal"
b	baluke, "worthless person"	luke, "nothing"
f	phedinkus, "fraud"	dinkus, "contrivance"
v	vaboom!	boom!
m	mahoola, "nonsense"	hooey, "nonsense"
k	kathob, "vague entity"	thob, "to be credulous"
g	gazook, "tramp"	zook, "prostitute"
c	chewallop, "bang"	wallop, "to hit hard"
j	jamake, "liquor"	make, "loot"
š	shebang, "wild party"	bang, "thrill"
y	yazunk, "plop"	plunk, "to throw down"

Allologies like those of *spurt* and *sputter*, however (especially with regard to the base-form *spout*), clearly suggest infixation in alternation with suffixation. If this alternation, along with the alternation in *blab ~ babble*, may be so analyzed, then it seems that all English sonorants are capable of forming infixes — some only before the syllabic peak, others only after it, and a few in either position. Examples of such infixes, in alternation with phonic zero, are given in Table 12.

Table 12. *Sonorant infixes in English*

infix	infixed word	uninfixed word
(V)y	cheep (=chirp)	chip
w(V)	twitter	titter
l(V)	blam	bam
(V)l	dolt	dote
r(V)	crow	caw
(V)r	purp	pup
(V)m	clamp	clap
(V)n	clink	click

Here, as elsewhere, the English pattern, however peripheral it may seem to the "core" grammar of the language, seems to perpetuate an ancient Indo-European pattern. Examples from PIE are in Table 13.

Table 13. *Sonorant infixes in Proto-Indo-European*

infix	infixed base	uninfixed base
(V)y	peik-, to fleece	pek-
(V)w	bheug-, to flee	bheg-
l(V)	klEu-, to hear	kEu-
r(V)	bhreg-, to break	bheg-
(V)n	ghend-, to take	ghed-
n(V)	men(e)gh-, large	megh-

In addition to the above infixes, colloquial English offers a number of bound and stressless disyllabic forms, which, because they seem to link bases in compounds, I prefer to call "interfixes". These forms themselves comprise a vertical apophonic series, as in Table 14.

Table 14. *Vertically apophonic interfixes*

interfix	compound
/p/	lollapalooza
/b/	hullabaloo
/m/	thingamajig

An even more anomalous set of vertical apophonic series is provided by the rhyme-tags on English echo-compounds. Some of these tags seem to have no intrinsic meaning and to serve, as their name implies, solely to echo the preceding forms with which they rhyme. Others, however, seem to contain meaningful bases, as in Table 15.

Table 15. *Examples of English echo compounds*

apophonating consonants	echo compounds
p	Georgy-Porgy
b	hurly-burly
m	holy-moly
w	palsy-walsy
t	hotsy-totsy
d	okey-dokey
l	Turkey-Lurky
k	hootchy-kootch(y)
g	hurdy-gurdy
j	heebie-jeebie

In a few cases, interfixes and rhyme-tag onsets seem to have been combined to expand a slang form from one syllable to three. An example is *razz(a)ma-tazz* = *razzle-dazzle*.

Some of these non-canonical affixes can occur in any or all positions. An example is /(ə)m(ə)/, which is found, in one or another of its allomorphs, in the words *mahoola*, *clamp*, *dingamabob*, *pell-mell*, and *stickum*.

8.   Fossilized and Productive Alternations

An alternative mode of classifying consonant alternations is to divide them into fossilized and productive types. An example of vertical seriation that was apparently productive in Proto-Into-European but has become fossilized in English is *foal~ pod ~ bud* (from PIE pEu- ~ bEu- ~ bhEu-). Another is the series represented by the bases of the verbs *holler ~ call ~ yell* (from PIE kEl- ~ gEl- ~ ghEl-). Needless to say, such fossilized series are not confined to English. A phonologically comparable series in Latin is *ceres*, '(goddess of) grain' ~ *granum*, 'grain' or 'seed' ~ *herba*, 'grass' or 'plant' (from PIE *ker- ~ *g(e)r- ~ *gher-).

An example of a productive alternation is that between velar stops and prepalatal fricatives, which has yielded an expressive "paradigm". In this paradigm, which developed in late Middle and early Modern English, the first member represents instantaneous or iterative action and the second, continuative or resultative action, as in Table 16.

Table 16. *Expressive velar stop/prepalatal fricative alternations*

punctive/iterative	continuative/resultative
hack	hash
crack	crash
smack	smash
stack	stash

Even more productive, however, is the pattern of consonantal alternation that I have elsewhere christened "zazzification" (Wescott 1978). Zazzification is the replacement in slang, mostly during the past two centuries, of other consonants or consonant clusters by z. Examples are given in Table 17.

It will be noted that, in about half these cases, a stressed vowel is also replaced by the diphthong /uw/, a process elsewhere termed "ooglification" (Wescott 1977). Ooglification, likewise confined to slang, may itself be treated as a form of consonant insertion, analogous to "kee-rect" for *correct*, where /iy/ replaces /ə/.

Table 17. *Examples of zazzification*

replaced consonant	zazzified form	presumptive source
p	snazzy 'stylish'	snappy
t	jizzum 'semen'	jit
k	fooze 'to copulate'	fuck
b	zonkers 'crazy'	bonkers
d	foozle 'to trick'	befuddle
g	bazook 'Asian'	gook
g	zigzig 'to copulate'	frig ~ fugg
θ	gazinkus 'gadget'	thing
s	foozle 'fogey'	fossil
š	swizzle 'stir'	swish
m	scuz 'dirt'	scum
n	zigaboo 'negro'	nigger-boy
r	snooze 'doze'	snore
l	gazoony 'oaf'	loony

Some patterns of consonant alternation seem to exist in both fossilized and productive forms. One such is the lingual alternation of laterals with vibrants. A fossilized example in English is *lamb ~ ram*, which appears to go back at least to Proto-Germanic. Here the lateral connoted diminution in size or age. A productive example is *zilch ~ zero*, which is no older than World War II. Here, the lateral connotes trivialization of a formal or technical term.

9.   Sonorant Alternatives

When the dyadic sonorant alternation just illustrated is expanded to yield a triadic pattern, the third member of the series is perforce the only other apical sonorant available — namely, the apical nasal. In this triad, which appears in a surprisingly large number of languages and language-families, the lateral is usually diminutive, the vibrant augmentative, and the nasal neutral. A productive example of this alternation in English is the onomastic series *Molly ~ Minnie ~ Mary*. A fossilized example is the verb series *wallow ~ wander ~ wriggle*. (An Amerindian analog, which monogeneticists might well hold to be not only synonymous but cognate, is the triad comprised of Yucatec *walak*, 'turn', Sahaptin *wina-*, 'go', and Tarascan *wirian-*, 'run'.) A fossilized example in Afro-Asiatic is the contrast in words for 'dog': Proto-Semitic *kal-, Proto-Chadic *kan-, and Proto-Cushitic *kar-. A plausible surmise is that, in Proto-Afro-Asiatic, all three forms co-existed, the lateralized form having meant 'little dog' and the rhotacized, 'big dog', but that, when the pattern lost its productivity, each branch retained only one form and discarded its two variants. The same educated guess can be hazarded about three New England Algonquian words for 'dog': Nipmuck *alum*, Quinnipiac *arum*, and Cowesett *anum*. (If the New World *aN-root is related to the Old World *kaN- root, their relation may parallel that of English *ear* and *hear*, derivable from pre-Indo-European *xous- and *kous-, respectively.)

Sonorant alternations seem to lend themselves more readily than others to cross-patterning of vertical and horizontal types. A good example of this, if we accept the etymology which treats the nasal in *Henry* as having undergone anticipatory assimilation from labial to apical position, is the following:

	l	
m	n	ŋ
	r	

	Hal	
Hamlin	Hen(ry)	Hank
	Harry	

10. Alternational Processes

A different way of classifying consonant alternations is in terms of the processes that produce them. Some of the commoner ones in English are:

occlusion, as in *Dick* from *Rich(ard)*
affrication, as in *jabber* from *gab(ber)*
fricativization, as in *Hodge* from *Roger*
lateralization, as in *Sally* from *Sarah*

advancement, as in *map* from *nap(kin)*
retraction, as in *mutter* from *natter*

unvoicing, as in *tarnation* from *damnation*
voicing, as in *beep* from *peep*

A striking form of the last process named above is the "stretch voicing" of palindromic forms, as in Table 18.

Table 18. *Examples of "stretch voicing" forms from English*

bubby (young boy)	from *puppy*
dodder	from *totter*
gaggle	from *cackle*

11. Subphonemic Processes

Besides these phonemic alternations, there also occur purely phonetic shifts (whose analogs, in languages other than English, are sometimes fully phonemic). Examples are:

gemination, as in [ɛ́nnĭ] for [ɛ́nĭ], "any"
glottalization, as in [ʌ́ʔòw] *vis-à-vis* "oh"
pharyngealization, as in [hʌ́ʕrĭ] for "hurry"

In all three of the preceding cases, the effect of the special phonic modification seems to be emphatic or exclamatory.

12. Reconstructed Alternations

If we follow Morris Swadesh in assuming that consonant alternation was commoner in prehistory than in historic times, we can discern phonic as well as semantic correspondences among certain lexical clusters. One such cluster is the reconstructed Proto-Indo-European vocabulary of trees (Friedrich 1970). If we go beyond Friedrich in postulating a pre-Indo-European proto-root meaning "food-tree" (that is, a tree producing fruit, nuts, or syrup), we can reasonably cite specific variants, as in Table 19.

Table 19. *Proto-Indo-European terms which refer to trees which produce food or fruit ('food tree')*

1.	ker-	cherry
2.	gr-obh-	hornbeam
3.	ar- (from pre-IE xer-)	nut-tree
4.	kl-en-	alder
5.	al-iso- (from pre-IE xel-)	maple
6.	kn-(e)u-	nut-tree

To do this, of course, we must reconstruct the doubly hypothetical form KEN, where K is construed as k ~ g ~ x, E as e ~ a ~ o, and N as l ~ n ~ r. But, if vertical alternations of the k ~ g ~ x type are accepted, it may be that horizontal alternations of the P ˜ T ˜ K type should also be accepted. In that case, we could enlarge the proto-root and rewrite it as PEN ˜ TEN ˜ KEN, enabling it to subsume such Proto-Indo-European roots as per- 'oak', bher- 'birch', and dor- 'tree'.

Acceptance of prehistoric consonant alternations of this sort make it possible for us further to descry cognations in modern languages which we would otherwise overlook. Examples of such potential cognate pairs in English are: *take ~ do*, *hound ~ cur*, *hen ~ goose*, *kid ~ goat*, *gleam ~ green*.

On the other hand, although the recognition of apophonic possibilities among consonants enlarges the range of potential cognations discernible, it can sometimes overwhelm us with an embarrassment of etymological riches. The verb *slurp*, for example, can easily be related to *lap*, *slop*, *slur*, and other forms, both in English and in cognate languages. (All things considered, however, I would myself prefer the problems of linguistic abundance to those of linguistic paucity.)

13. Sequence Reversals

One form of consonant alternation whose reality as a pattern remains in doubt is sequence-reversal. Such reversal, known as metathesis, is common enough in two-consonant clusters, such as dialectal English *ax* for *ask*. Nor is it rare in cases where a vowel intervenes, as in *dog-gone* for *god-damned*, where connotation changes though denotation remains unchanged. Sometimes it even involves the order of morphemes, as in English *peep-bo=bo-peep*, 'hide-and-seek', or Bini *kángún=gúnkán*, 'lean, emaciated'. The point at which such sequence reversal becomes dubious is the semantic one that involves reversal of meaning. An example of the questionable co-reversal of order and meaning is the opposition of the wide-spread Congoid root NAM, 'animal', and the Indo-European root that appears in English as *man*. To treat this as a primal but fossilized pattern, we must assume linguistic monogenesis.

14. Marked and Unmarked Features

A cursory overview of the material above makes it clear, I believe, that English, like most other languages, abounds in consonant alternations. But the phonological organization of these alternations is considerably clearer than their semantic organization. In general terms, we may safely say that voiceless stops tend to be unmarked and that vertical deviations from them — as in voiced stops, voiceless fricatives, or nasals — tend to be marked and, by virtue of that fact alone, emphatic. Beyond this, it is harder to go with any certainty. In Indo-European languages, at least, there is a tendency for voiced obstruents to be negative or derogatory in relation to voiceless obstruents. Examples are modern English *dowdy* and *jeer* in contrast to older words like *tidy* and *cheer*, or Latin *sub*, 'under', and *gelidus*, 'cold', in contrast to *super*, 'above', and *calidus*, 'warm'. And sibilants, whether additive, as in *(s)melt*, *(s)lime*, and *(s)mash*, or replacive, as in *zap*, *zonk*, *zoom*, tend to be intensive in force.

What can we say, however, about those cases in which voiceless stops have apparently replaced or supplemented other, more vowel-like consonants? In English, at least, additive stops like the final surd in *snort* as against *snore* seem to connote brevity or abruptness. And replacive stops, like the initial surd in *Peg* for *Margaret* connote not only abridgment in size but also (at least partial or temporary) absence of femaleness. Here the consonantal opposition seems to parallel that of *pa* and *ma*.

15. Interpretive Problems

Nevertheless, most consonant alternations are associated with shifts in meaning that are elusive — subtle at best and, at worst, undetectable. The probable reason for this is the world-wide tendency to supplant internal and replacive flexion of the *man/men* type with additive and external flexion of the *fan/fans* type. The result of this trend has been a noticeable reduction in vowel alternations and an even more drastic reduction in consonant alternations.

Because of the increasing rarity of consonant alternation in most languages, evidence for it is becoming increasingly inferential in nature. The alternation that seems obvious to one investigator seems dubious to another and illusory to a third. In this respect, residual iconicity resembles unconscious motivation and clairvoyance: its reality appears to vary directly with the zeal with which it is sought. It should hardly surprise our colleagues, then, that those of us who seek it usually find it!

Appendix: Glossary

accordion principle: expansibility and contractability
allolog: free allomorph
Amerindian: American Indian, native American
apical: dental or alveolar
apophony: phoneme alternation
Congoid: Niger-Congo or Congo-Kordofanian; Guineo-Bantu
"core" language: micro-language; grammaticized language
diagonal alternation: phoneme alternation involving change of both articulatory position and articulatory manner
dyad: pair, group of two
echo-compound: compound whose second base or word rhymes with its first
excrescent: added as a transitional phoneme between other phonemes
fossilized: unproductive, inoperative
frequentative: iterative, repetitive
grave: acoustically labial or velar
horizontal alternation: change of articulatory position
hypocorism: nickname
iconism: mimesis, imitativeness

interfix: affix between bases or words in a compound

metathesis: transposition, inversion

"ooglification": substitution of the complex nucleus /uw/ for another vowel or diphthong in English slang

palindromoid: exhibiting partial palindromy; a quasi-palindrome

palindromy: identity of syllabic onset with syllabic coda in a base

pentestheme: English palindromoid containing five phonemes

phonic iconism: sound-symbolism

post-nuclear: following the syllabic peak

pre-Indo-European: Indo-Hittite; late Proto-Nostratic

pre-nuclear: preceding the syllabic peak

primary iconism: resemblance to extra-linguistic reality

rhotacized: converted into a vibrant

rhyme-tag: second base in a compound, rhyming with the first base

secondary iconism: phonic resemblance to synonyms or near synonyms

sigmatic: capable of acquiring a preposed sibilant; a form so capable

sonorant: nasal, lingual, or glide

"stump" word: word with one or more syllables eliminated

tertiary iconism: repetition of sounds within words

triad: trio, group of three

vertical alternation: change of articulatory voice or manner

vocalism: vowel sequence; vowel inventory

"zazzification": replacement of a consonant or consonant-cluster by /z/ in English slang

References and Additional Bibliography

Antilla, Raimo. 1972. *An Introduction to Historical and Comparative Linguistics.* New York: Macmillan.

Diffloth, Gerard. 1972. Notes on expressive language. *Proceedings of the Chicago Linguistic Society*, 8, ed. by Paul M. Peranteau, Judith N. Levi, and Gloria Phares, 440–447. Chicago: Chicago Linguistic Society.

Friedrich, Paul. 1970. *Proto-Indo-European Trees: The Arboreal System of a Prehistoric People.* Chicago: University of Chicago Press.

Jespersen, Otto. 1922. *Language: Its Nature, Development, and Origin.* London: Allen and Unwin.

Melzian, Hans. 1937. *A Concise Dictionary of the Bini Language of Southern Nigeria.* London: Kegan Paul.

Pokorny, Julius. 1959. *Indogermanisches etymologisches Woerterbuch.* Bern: Francke.

Schwartz, Benjamin. 1947. *The Root and its Modification in Primitive Indo-European*. New York: Columbia University dissertation.

Swadesh, Morris. 1960. *Tras la huella linguistica de la prehistoria*. Suplementos Cientificos, 2a serie, num. 26. Mexico D.F., Mexico.

Swadesh, Morris. 1970. The problem of consonantal doublets in Indo-European. *Word*. 26: 1–16.

Swadesh, Morris. 1971. *The Origin and Diversification of Language*. Chicago: Aldine.

Trager, George L., and Henry Lee Smith. 1957. *An Outline of English Structure*. Studies in Linguistics, Occasional papers 3.

Watkins, Calvert. 1969. Indo-European roots. *The American Heritage Dictionary*, 1505–1550. Boston: Houghton Mifflin Co.

Wescott, Roger W. 1977. 'Ooglification' in American English slang. *Verbatim*. 4.5.

Wescott, Roger W. 1978. 'Zazzification' in American English slang. *Forum Linguisticum* 2: 185–187.

Wescott, Roger W. 1980. *Sound and Sense: Linguistic Essays on Phonosemic Subjects*. Lake Bluff, IL: Jupiter Press.

Wescott, Roger W. 1983. Consonantal apophony in English. *In Honor of Charles F. Hockett*, ed. by Frederick B. Agard et al. Leiden: Brill.

About the author

Roger W. Wescott is Professor Emeritus of Linguistics and Anthropology at Drew University. He received his doctorate from Princeton in 1948. Earlier he had been a Rhodes Scholar at Oxford. He first became acquainted with Syd Lamb at a meeting of the Linguistic Society of America in the late 1950s, and he followed his ideas on language taxonomy and linguistic structure with interest in later years. Both he and Syd were also founding members of LACUS. Wescott was President of LACUS (1976–1977), and also of the International Society for the Comparative Study of Civilizations (1992–1995).

PART I

C. Functional Language Description

CHAPTER 14

Grammar and Daily Life

Concurrence and Complementarity

M. A. K. Halliday

Macquarie University and University of Sydney

Let me first say what I mean by "grammar" in the title of the paper. I mean the lexicogrammatical stratum of a natural language as traditionally understood, comprising its syntax and vocabulary, together with any morphology the language may display: Lamb's "lexical system", in his current (1992: Chapter 5) "three-level architecture" — in commonsense terms, the resources of **wording** in which the meanings of a language are construed. And here I have in mind particularly the evolved, spontaneous grammar that construes the discourse of daily life. This is not to exclude from the picture the elaborated grammars of scientific and other metalanguages; but these can only be understood as what they are: an outgrowth, supported by design, of the original grammar that is learnt at mother's knee and on father's shoulders.

Now English is not very efficient at creating technical nomenclature, since it tends to confuse the study of a phenomenon with the phenomenon itself. So while the term "grammar" is commonly used in the way in which I have defined it, to mean the wording system, the central processing unit of a natural language, it is also used indiscriminately to mean the **study** of that system: $grammar_2$ meaning 'the study of $grammar_1$'. And even this is not part of any consistent pattern. We do, for example, distinguish *society* from the study of society, which is called *sociology*. We used to distinguish, in parallel fashion, between the *psyche* and its study, *psychology*; but here the process has been reversed, so that we now use *psychology* to refer to the original phenomenon — hence *criminal psychology* means the criminal psyche, rather than psychological theories that are thought up and used by criminals. Since the study of language is called *linguistics*,

I have been calling the study of grammar *grammatics* in order to make the distinction clearer. A grammatics is thus a theory for explaining grammar.

But is not a grammar itself also a theory? Clearly it is. A grammar is a resource for meaning, the critical functioning semiotic by means of which we pursue our everyday life. It therefore embodies a **theory** of everyday life; otherwise it could not function in this way. A grammar is a theory of human experience: or rather, let us say, it **includes** a theory of experience, because it is also something else besides. Like any other theory, a grammar is something to think with. It is through grammar that we make sense out of our experience, both of the world we live in (what we experience as taking place "out there") and of the world that lives in us (what we experience as taking place "in here", inside our own consciousness), construing a "reality" such that the one can be reconciled against the other. (Matthiessen, 1991; Halliday and Matthiessen, in press.)

During the past twenty years leading neurobiologists, notably Harry Jerison and John Allman, have been investigating the way the brain evolved; and they explain its evolution as the evolution of the organism's resource for constructing reality. Changes in the ecological environment require changes in the representation of experience (Edelman, 1992; Lemke, 1993). One critical step was the evolution of the cerebral cortex, which transformed the mammalian map of the external environment. The second was the evolution of language, which added a new dimension to reality, that of introspective consciousness; this latter step is associated with the development of the prefrontal zone of the cortex, allowing a major reorganization of neural circuitry (see the summary in 'Secret life of the brain', *New Scientist*). Linguists can show that the corresponding unique feature of human language, distinguishing it from semiotic systems of other genera and species, is that it has a grammar, an abstract stratum of coding in between the meaning and the expression. Grammar is what brings about the distinctively human construction of reality; and by the same token, grammar makes it possible for us to reflect on this construction.

As a teacher I have often said to my students that they should learn to "think grammatically". By this I mean that they should use the unique power of the human brain to reflect on the way their experience is construed in their grammar: use grammatics to think about what grammar thinks about the world. I suggest they might do this with problems of any kind, such as relationships with family and friends, or whether to go for the job that pays more or for the one they would more enjoy. Let me give a small example of what I mean by thinking grammatically. You're feeling a bit down. What's the matter, someone asks. "I have a headache." So how does the grammar construe your unfortunate condition? Of course, **you** construed it, using your grammatical potential; but you did so quite unconsciously, in the way that it has been done countless other times by countless other people, so it is reasonable to talk about the condition being construed "by the grammar".

In *I have a headache* the grammar construes a kind of thing, called an *ache*; it then uses a part of the body to classify this thing, setting up a taxonomy of aches including *stomachache*, *backache* and various others. (Not all the parts of the body are allowed to *ache*, however; you cannot have a *footache* or a *thighache*.) The grammar then sets up a configuration of possession between the ache and some conscious being, in this case the speaker *I*. The speaker becomes the owner of one specimen of that complex class of things. It is not a proto-typical form of possession; the possessor does not want the thing possessed but cannot get rid of it — cannot give it away, or put it back where it came from. Why then does the grammar not favour *my head aches*; or *my head's aching*? — in which the aching is a process, a state of being, rather than a thing, and the entity involved in that state of being is my head rather than me. The grammar has no trouble in constructing the clause *my head aches*; yet it is not the most usual way in which the experience is worded. Why is *I have a headache* preferred instead?

In English, as in many other languages (though not all), there is a particular meaning associated with being the first element in the clause. What is put first is being instated by the speaker as the theme of the coming message; it is the setting for the information that follows (Fries 1995). This pattern of the clause, a structure of "Theme + Rheme", was apparently identified by the earliest rhetorical grammarians of ancient Greece, the sophists, who seem to have recognized in the thematic organization of the clause a potent resource for constructing legal and political discourse. In modern times it was first investigated in detail by Mathesius, the founder of the Prague school; it is a particularly prominent feature of English, appearing not only in the clause but also as a "fractal" pattern in both smaller and larger structures — inside word groups, both nominal and verbal, on the one hand and extending over a nexus of clauses on the other. The following example, taken from natural conversation, shows thematic predication of a whole clause complex (from Svartvik & Quirk, 1980: 304):

–   … in my last year at college I said to myself: "You want to do applied chemistry, right? What industries are now just being born which will

blossom in the next quarter of a century, which is going to be my
working lifetime?" And I said "Plastics, sure as the nose on your face.
I'm going to get into this." ... ...

—   I'm dazzled, you know. ... It's being able to see your working life will
span a period in which so-&-so is the topmost industry which I find so
dazzling.

Now if I say *my head aches*, the first element in that clause is *my head*: I have
constructed a message in which *my head* is enunciated as Theme. My head is
instated as what I want to elaborate on. But it isn't; I'm the one that's suffering,
so the Theme of the clause should more appropriately be 'me'. How does the
grammar accommodate this alternative? Most naturally, by making 'me' the
Subject, since there is a strong association of these two functions in English. The
'ache' becomes a thing separated from myself, something that I possess, with my
head identified as its location: *I have an ache in my head*. Better still, if my head
is used as a classifier, the ache and its location become a single complex thing;
and this now occupies the culminative position in the clause: *I have a headache*.
The flow of information here is very different from that of *my head's aching*.

If this was just a feature of the grammar of localized aches and pains, it
might remain a curiosity, a special effect rather than a principle. But this pattern
has evolved in English as the prototypical form for construing bodily qualities
and states; rather than *her hair is long*, *his throat is sore*, we tend to say *she has
long hair*, *he has a sore throat*, putting the person rather than the body part into
the thematic role.[1] And in certain other languages where initial position is
thematic we also regularly find the person, rather than the body part, lodged at
the beginning of the clause. The overall patterns are of course different: in
particular, there may be no strong bond between Theme and Subject, and this
makes it clear that the relevant function is that of Theme. We can give examples
from Chinese, Russian and French. In Chinese it is possible to say *wodi tou teng*

---

1. Notice on the other hand that in the interrogative this pressure is much less strong: we readily say
does your head ache? *is your throat sore?* as well as *have you got a headache/a sore throat?* This is
because in the interrogative the grammar preempts the thematic slot to signal that the clause is, in
fact, a question, by putting at the beginning the part of the verb that selects for 'yes or no', the Finite
operator, *does/is: does your head ache?* signals 'my message is concerned with whether it does or
not'. As a result there is relatively little thematic weight left over; the difference in information flow
between *is your throat sore?* and *have you got a sore throat?* is very much less noticeable than that
between the agnate declarative pair *my throat's sore* and *I've got a sore throat*, where the full thematic
weight is felt on either *my throat* or *I*.

'my head aches', where as in the English *wodi tou* 'my head' is a single element in the clause and so functions as the Theme. The preferred form, however, is *wo tou teng* 'me the head aches', where the 'head' is detached from the personal pronoun; *wo* 'me' and *tou* 'head' are now independent elements in the clause and only the first one, *wo*, is thematic. Again, this is the typical pattern for all such expressions in Chinese: *ta toufa chang* 'her the hair (is) long', *ta houlong tong* 'him the throat (is) sore' and so on. In Russian, likewise, one can say *moja golova bolit* 'my head aches'; but this also is not the preferred form. Russian however displays a different pattern: *u menja golova bolit* 'at me the head aches', where again it is the 'me' that has thematic status. In French instead of *ma tête me fait mal* 'my head is hurting me' one can use possession as in English: *j'ai mal à la tête* 'I have an ache at the head'. French also has a further device, of detaching the Theme altogether from the structure of the clause, and announcing it as a key signature at the beginning: *moi j'ai mal à la tête* 'me I've got an ache at the head'. Neither Chinese *wo* nor Russian *u menja* nor French *moi* is Subject; what they have in common is the status of Theme.

At this point we might think once more of the sufferer and say to him or her: pity you've got a headache. But try de-construing this, in the grammar, and then re-construing it — rewording it — as *my head aches*; or better still *my head's aching*, which makes it an external rather than an internal phenomenon. This is rather less self-centered: it is no longer a fact about me, and my inner self, but an external fact about my head. This won't make the headache go; but it does put it in its place. It has now become a problem of my head, which is just one part of my physical make-up. One might offer this as a form of logotherapy, a kind of grammatical acupuncture. But here I am merely referring to it as an instance of "thinking grammatically".

Thus the grammar enables us, unconsciously, to interpret experience; and the metagrammar, or grammatics, enables us to reflect consciously on how it does so. The grammatics, of course, is part of a more general theory of meaning: of language as a semiotic system, and of other semiotic systems brought into relation with language. Without such a general theory, the excursion into other languages is no more than a piece of tourism; it assumes significance only when we can show how this small corner of experience is construed in relation to the meaning potential of each language as a whole.

But this requires much more than a purely local explanation. Taking a fragment of the grammar of daily life, and exploring it cross-linguistically in this way, still leaves it as an isolated fragment, detached from its environment in the overall system of the language. Yet this is the critical environment to take into account. The grammar construes a unitary semantic space, elastic and many-dimensioned; and whatever aspect of the grammar we are considering (such as the selection of person as Theme, in the examples above), there will usually be various other grammatical features, many of them not obviously related in any formal sense, which are associated topologically within this semantic space (cf. Martin & Matthiessen, 1992). Such features may cluster into a recognizable syndrome, needing to be interpreted not piecemeal but as a whole: this is the principle of "frames of consistency" as formulated by Whorf. Illustrations of this phenomenon may be found in Hasan's (1984) 'Ways of saying, ways of meaning', where she shows how the grammar of Urdu construes experience as collectively shared; and in Martin's (1988) account of "grammatical conspiracies" in Tagalog. If we are comparing the different "realities" of one language with another, it is the syndrome rather than the single feature that is likely to be significant.

Side by side with such frames of consistency, however, there are also frames of inconsistency: regions where the grammar construes a pattern out of tensions and contradictions — where the different "voices" of experience conflict. To put this another way, the grammar's theory of experience embodies complementarity as well as concurrence. Metaphorically the grammar is repre-senting the fact that human experience is too complex, and has too many parameters, to be construed from any one angle alone. It is the combination of these two perspectives — concurrence and complementarity — that is the salient characteristic of the grammar of daily life.

Let me first try to illustrate the complementarity, and then use this as a point of departure for exploring concurrence, looking at a more general syndrome of features within which the earlier, more particular example might be located. Many grammars (perhaps all) make a rather clear distinction between the two fundamental modes of human experience referred to above: between what we experience as taking place in the world outside of ourselves and what we experience as processes of our own consciousness — seeing and hearing, liking, disliking, fearing, hoping, thinking, knowing, understanding and the like. In English, the conscious or "mental" processes differ from the other, "material" kind in various respects: (1) they have a less exact present time; (2) they presume a conscious being taking part; (3) they do not fall within the scope of "doing", and (4) they can "project" — that is, they can construe any meaning as taking place in someone's consciousness (as "direct or indirect thought"). In addition, these "inner" processes display another feature not found with the grammar of processes of the external, "material" type: they are bi-directional. Processes of consciousness can be construed with the conscious participant, the Senser, either as object (active Complement), as in *it frightens me*, or as active Subject, as in *I fear it*; likewise *it pleases/convinces/strikes me*, *I like/believe/ notice it*, and so on. These are two different and in fact contradictory constructions of the same class of phenomena. Inner experience is complex and difficult to interpret; the grammar offers two complementary models, one with the Senser in the more active role (by analogy with material processes), one with the Senser appearing to be acted upon. Each of these brings out different agnate forms; the grammar of daily life, in English, accommodates both.

In late Middle to early Modern English the common verbs of consciousness such as *like* and *think* changed their allegiance from the one pattern to the other: from 'it likes/thinks (to) me' to *I like it, I think so*. This happened at about the same time as the emergence of the pattern discussed earlier: *I have a headache*, &c. For very general processes of consciousness the grammar came to favour the type of construction in which the Senser, the participant credited with consciousness, was the Theme. What was explained above as a preference for a person rather than a part of the body as the starting point for bodily states and conditions is part of a broader picture whereby the grammar of all inner processes and physiological states tended to orient the message towards the human, or human-like, participant — perhaps with 'I', the individual self, as the prototypical member of this class.

This in turn leads us to another feature. At the same period of history another shift took place affecting processes of the external kind, those experienced as happening "out there". In earlier English the grammatical Subject in such processes had been overwhelmingly the active participant, whether human or not (in fact the distinction between human and non-human, or conscious and non-conscious, plays no part in the construction of these processes of the external world). Thus in *an arrow pierced his eye* the *arrow* was the natural Subject, and remained Subject even if the narrative required the thing acted on to function as Theme. To use a constructed example, the pattern was that of:

The king fell to the ground; his eye an arrow had pierced.

with the Actor remaining as Subject even when displaced from initial position in the clause. Subsequently, as already noted, this bond between Subject and Actor was deconstructed and replaced by a different bond, that of Subject with Theme; this gave the modern pattern:

The king fell to the ground; his eye had been pierced by an arrow.

This change led to an increase in the frequency of passive verbs, which was followed by a change in the tense system as passive tenses caught up with the active ones; and various other changes took place besides. What this new alignment of grammatical forces amounted to was that relatively **less** prominence was being given to the structure of the experience — which partner is the doer and which the done-to, so to speak; and relatively **greater** prominence to the structure of the message — which part is the theme, and which part is the new information to be attended to. Without trying to go into all the components of the picture, let me refer briefly to three related developments.

First, the grammar developed a battery of resources such that any representation of a process can be construed in all possible patterns of information flow; given 'an arrow pierced his eye' we have not only *his eye was pierced by an arrow* but also *what pierced his eye was an arrow, what the arrow pierced was his eye, what the arrow did to his eye was pierce it*, and so on. These evolved as different ways of dividing the clause into a thematic portion and the rest. But the construction of the message is more fluid and more complex than that simple formulation suggests. The flow of information is made up of two distinct currents: a linear movement from Theme to Rheme, and an oscillation between Given and New which is not encoded in the sequence but in which the "New" — the part presented by the speaker as 'to be attended to' — tends to build up at the end. And just as various features in the grammar conspire to construe the Theme, so various others come together in construing the resources for the New; and this leads in to the second of the three developments being mentioned here.

Secondly, then, another feature of Modern English grammar is the motif of the "phrasal verb"; we can say *he invented the whole story*, but we prefer *he made the whole story up*; similarly *you left the important part out* (instead of *you omitted …*), *they've taken the furniture away* (instead of *they've removed …*), and so on. This is the grammar's way of making the **happening** the main item of news. The news tends to come at the end of the clause; but the happening is typically a verb, and if there are two parties to it — an Actor and a Goal, say — it is hard to get the verb at the end: we cannot say *he the whole story invented* (we can say *the whole story he invented*; but that changes the thematic balance by **marking** the Theme). What the "phrasal verb" construction does is to split the verb into two parts, so that the second part of it can come at the end: *he made the whole story up* is the grammar's suppletion for **he vented the whole story in.*

Thirdly, there is an analogous pattern whereby one of the other elements in the clause — one which could but would not necessarily come at the end — is marked out for news value by having a preposition added to it. If you want to tell me that you supported your brother financially you could say *I gave my brother a lot of money*; but if the observation is made to explain why you now need to borrow from me, you say *I gave a lot of money to my brother.* The preposition *to* makes explicit your brother's role as a participant in the process, and is added just in those positions which are prominent in the information flow (likewise if the brother appears as a **marked** Theme: *to my brother I gave a lot of money*). It is precisely this same principle which adds *by* to the Actor when the clause is passive: *his eye had been pierced by an arrow/by an arrow his eye had been pierced.*

All the features I have sketched in here are features of the grammar of daily life: some more global, some more local, but all of them characteristic of unconscious, spontaneous, everyday linguistic encounters. These, and others that could be added, form a syndrome, a concurrence of related developments, that has helped to shape the meaning potential of Modern English, giving the language its characteristic flavour — that "certain cut", in Sapir's terms, which makes each language unique. What all these have in common is that they tend towards giving greater prominence to the organization of discourse as a flow of information, making more explicit how each element is to be construed as part of a message. As a corollary to this, much less prominence is given to the experiential patterning, much of which is in fact left implicit once the concern with the message begins to take over. Most of these effects are fairly recent in history; they reflect the changing social conditions of the language over the past five hundred years. Or rather: they do not **reflect** them — they help to bring them about. These features in the grammar construe the kind of discourse that can be addressed to a stranger, who does not necessarily share the same expectations and norms of interaction. They can be written down in a book that is going to be printed in thousands of copies and read by people who have never met the author and do not even know who he is. In other words, they are features of a **standard** language: a form of discourse in which the flow of information will typically be rendered explicit rather than being taken for granted. (Interestingly, many of these changes appear not to have taken place in the surviving British rural dialects.)

Effects like these are not the result of sudden catastrophic changes. They are trends and tendencies in a long process of evolution; and at any given time they are quantitative — changes in the relative frequency with which this or that pattern is selected from within the system. The grammatics is thus a theory of probabilities, in which possible/impossible is only a special case of more and less probable — and a rather uninteresting case, because meaning is a product of choice and when something becomes impossible there is no more choice. So, for example, *I have a headache* is an instance of what is now the more probable of two agnate constructions; but in using that form the speaker is still choosing — choosing, among other things, to map *I* rather than *my head* on to the Theme. If *my head aches* had become obsolete, we could still have used the grammatics to explain why the structure is as it is; but the grammar would have taken over, and the significance of using *I have* ... in any particular instance would have been lost. Hence the semantic features being construed in this way would gradually disappear — just as the semantic feature construed by selecting *you* instead of *thou* in Elizabethan English disappeared after *thou* had ceased to be an available alternative, although we can still use this history to explain why *you* became the sole second person form.

What is it that gives language its elasticity, the facility for constantly adapting, reshaping and extending its semantic potential? The answer lies, as Lamb recognized from the start (cf. Lamb, 1964), in its stratal pattern: a language is an orchestration of interrelated levels of semiosis. Lamb no longer favours the term "stratificational grammar" (1988: 4), but the stratal principle has always been critical to his thinking. What is relevant here is that Lamb always "insisted that there has to be a level of meanings that is separate from the lexico-grammatical level" (1988: 6). This embodies the evolutionary perspective that I remarked on above: the evolution of lexicogrammar was the major innovation that transformed protolanguages into languages of the adult human kind.

Lamb now talks of the higher stratum as the "conceptual system" (1992: 98), and prefers to interpret this from outside language itself. As he remarks, the question "whether or not [the conceptual system] should be considered part of language is ... relatively uninteresting": it is absurd to draw boundaries around phenomena under study and then use these boundaries to justify one's intellectual stance. Such metalinguistic boundaries are like the boundaries drawn by language itself, which as he says (1992: 121) "both help us and hinder us in our efforts to understand the world". It is these arbitrary features of segmentation and of categorization, imposing syntagmatic and paradigmatic boundaries on our construction of experience, that lead to many of what Lamb calls the "thinking disorders" which arise both in everyday life and in scholarly life (both in language and in metalanguage). Such "disorders" arise at the interface between these two strata: "the semantically generated infelicities of thinking arise because of differences between concepts and the lexemes which express them" (1992: 162).

I myself take the alternative approach, of treating Lamb's "conceptual system" as part of language. This is because I do not think the lexicogrammar is arbitrary in its construction of meaning. The grammar has to impose discontinuity on the flux of experience; but the human condition — our total relationship to our environment — is complex and many faceted, so there will be indefinitely many ways of doing this, and hence differences between one language and another, and within one language at different stages in its history: some random, some resonating with variation and change in human culture. But even within one experiential domain, at any one moment in time, the grammar has to contend with conflicting and often contradictory demands; so this same interface accommodates complementarities — in a sense analogous to that in which Nils Bohr used the term to extend Heisenberg's uncertainty principle in quantum mechanics. The grammar is unable to reduce some aspect of experience to a single construction and so introduces two distinct perspectives, two construals which are mutually contradictory and yet depend on each other to provide a theory of daily life. An example would be tense and aspect as complementary theories of time. These contradict each other: either time is a linear flow out of past through present into future, or else it isn't. Yet many languages, perhaps all, insist that it both is and is not: in very different mixtures and proportions, but each amounting to a plausible theory for coping with the everyday world. Some of these complementarities display the further property that one of the two perspectives is construed configurationally, the other iteratively (as multivariate and univariate structures), thus foregrounding respectively the synoptic and the dynamic points of view. For example, the way the grammar constructs taxonomies of things involves both locating them in configurations of properties and modifying them by means of iterative bracketing. The construction of time in English also exemplifies this point: the system of aspect is activated once at a time, while the system of tense allows for successive reentries: present, past in present, future in past in present and so on. The essence of semiotic complementarity is that it is both objective and subjective: some domain of experience is being construed both as two phenomena and as two points of view on the one phenomenon. (The complementarity of lexis and grammar in the lexicogrammatical stratum is a metacomplementarity within the system itself.)

One very pervasive complementarity is that in the grammar of agency, where the problem to be solved is: how are the processes in the external world brought about? One theory, as construed in the grammar of daily life, is that of "Actor, +/− Goal" — a "doer", plus, optionally, something else that is "done to". Thus:

> Don't disturb Mum: she's sewing.
> −   What is she sewing?
> −   She's sewing her old jacket.

Mum is the doer and the jacket is the done-to. This is a configurational model; there is no re-entry to the choice of agency. Then there's a snap, and the grammar takes up the story again:

> Bother! the thread snapped.
> —   What snapped it?
> —   The machine snapped it.
> —   Yes? Who made the machine snap it?
> —   I did, of course.
> —   What made you make the machine snap it?
> —   My own impatience, I suppose.

and so on. This second theory says that there is a Medium, an entity through which the process is actualized (here the thread), plus, optionally, something else as Causer that brings it about. This is an iterative model; here the agency relation is construed in such a way that it can recur.

Thus there are two ways of looking at a process: one according to which participant a acts, and the action may (or may not) extend to another participant x (a is the constant, x the variable); the other according to which participant x "eventuates" (that is, permits the process to eventuate), and the event may (or may not) be brought about by another participant a (x is the constant, a the variable). The first of these (let us call it type A) is the transitive theory of processes, the second (type X) is the ergative; and probably all languages embody some tension between the two. Transitive and ergative are two points of view on the same phenomenon, that of the nature of material processes and the relationship of the participants to the process and to each other; but they are also two distinct phenomena — some processes pattern ergatively and others transitively (cf. Halliday, 1967–68; Davidse, 1992). This constitutes another strand in the pattern of changes that have been taking place in English: type X has tended increasingly to prevail over type A.

Let us follow this up in a related corner of the grammar. When I last worked in the United States I was living in Orange County; I frequently traveled on the local bus services, and there was a notice on the buses which read:

> Federal law prohibits operation of this bus when any passenger is forward of the standee line.

If you are standing, on the bus, you are a *standee*. Why not a *stander*? You are a passenger, not a passengee (and if you cannot get on the bus you may be a bystander); but once you are a standing passenger you become a standee, and you have your standee line, and must keep behind it. What kind of participant is construed in the grammar as an *-ee*?

There are familiar ones like *nominee*, *trainee*, *appointee*, and more recent instances of this type like *superannuee* and *oustee*, all of which are modeled on the pattern of *employee* 'person employed'. This forms one term in the transitive opposition *employer/employee*; the latter form was derived from the French passive participle and matched up with the English active termination *-er*, giving 'the one who is acting'/'the one who is acted upon'; cf. *trainer/trainee*. Here the *-ee* is functioning as participant *x* in type A.

Then there are some instances where rather indirect relationships are involved: *biographee* 'person whose biography is being compiled', *amputee* 'person who has had a limb amputated' (note that it does not refer to the limb; the *-ee's* are all human), *transplantee* (I have a letter beginning "I am a heart transplantee"), *ticketee* (in airline parlance); and various banking terms like *advisee, favouree, assignee* and so on. These are modeled on words like *referee* 'person to whom a dispute is referred for decision', *refugee* 'person to whom a place of refuge is offered'.

Then, with *escapee* 'person who escapes' as an early model, we now have *conferee* and *attendee* 'person attending a conference or lecture', *retiree* 'person having retired', and *returnee* 'person trying to get back to original country'. All these are like *standee*. When we examine them, we find that they pattern ergatively: the *-ee* corresponds to the function of the Medium in the process, to participant *x* in a process construed as type X. There is no implication that these are functioning as the Goal: a *standee* is not someone who has been or is being stood. If these were following type A we would have *stander, returner, retirer, attender* and so on. The pattern is given in Figure 1:

(type A)	-er	(process)	∅
	-er	(process)	-ee
	a		*x*

(type X)	∅		-ee	(process)
	-er	(process)	-ee	
	a		*x*	

Figure 1. *Pattern for transitive and ergative interpretations of -ee*

In itself, each instance is trivial. It does not matter whether we write *stander* or *standee*: the message will get across. But that, in another perspective, is just the point. The word *standee* is an instance of a very general pattern, through which our experience is ongoingly construed and reinforced; and as such it has a dual significance. On the one hand, as an instance it perturbs, however minutely, the overall probabilities of the system. System and instance are not two separate phenomena; they are the same phenomenon seen by different observers, observing from different time depths; and, especially where the grammar is unstable (as in the present-day English transitivity system), the cumulative effect of such instances is very noticeable. On the other hand, the word *standee* represents one perspective within a complementarity; to understand it we have to adopt (unconsciously, as always) a particular stance towards the phenomena we experience as taking place outside ourselves. In this perspective, where standing is grouped with being trained (*standee, trainee*) rather than with training (*trainer*), agency is interpreted as 'causing' rather than 'doing to': the variable is not 'does the action carried out by *a* extend to another entity *x*?' but rather 'is the process involving *x* caused by another entity *a*?' And this is quite a different way of looking at the processes of daily life.

A language is not only a mode of reflection; it is also a mode of action. Besides its ideational function, as a theory for construing our experience, it also has an interpersonal function, as a praxis for enacting our social and personal relationships. These two "metafunctions" are inseparably interlocked in the system of every language: the grammar does not allow us to perform in one mode without at the same time performing in the other.[2] In other words, while we are constructing reality we are also acting on it through our semiotic interactions with other human beings. And this brings me back to the point from which I began, in defining grammar as the spontaneous, natural grammar with which we lead our everyday lives. It is important not to set up a disjunction here. The most abstract theory of modern physics is also a "grammar" of experience — as Lemke (1990) has shown, a scientific theory is constituted of systems of related meanings: hence as well as being something to think with, it is by the same token also something to act with. We recognize this as a feature of scientific theories: they are not ideologically neutral, and this critically affects the domains of scientific praxis. The grammar of daily life is not neutral either. I have tried to suggest elsewhere (1990) some of the features of our everyday grammar that seem to me to condition our attitudes, to each other, to other species, and to the natural environment — certain aspects of the grammar are ecologically quite unfriendly. By the same token, however, those who "think grammatically" are enabled thereby to act grammatically, whether in developing forms of praxis for educational and other professional tasks, or in combating sexism, racism and other prevailing inequalities. To be a linguist is inevitably to be concerned with the human condition; it takes a linguist of the stature of Sydney Lamb to explain how so much of what constitutes the human condition is construed, transmitted, maintained — and potentially transformed — by means of language.

References

Davidse, Kristin. 1992. Transitivity/ergativity: the Janus-headed grammar of actions and events. *Advances in Systemic Linguistics: recent theory and practice*, ed. by Martin Davies & Louise Ravelli, 105–135. London & New York: Pinter Publishers.

Edelman, Gerald M. 1992. *Bright Air, Brilliant Fire: On the matter of the mind.* New York: Basic Books.

---

2. Thus the grammar signals metaphorically that meaning is a social process. We might put this together with the recent neurobiological finding by Robin Dunbar, that species living in large social groups have proportionally larger cortices. "Dunbar's explanation is that large group sizes demand greater social cohesion and hence more advanced skills for communicating..." (*New Scientist* no. 1850, p. 8).

Fries, Peter H. 1995. Patterns of information in initial position in English. *Discourse in Society: Systemic functional perspectives*, ed. by Peter H. Fries and Michael Gregory, 47–66. Norwood, New Jersey: Ablex.

Halliday, M. A. K. 1967–68. Notes on transitivity and theme in English. *Journal of Linguistics* 3: 37–81 and 199–244 and 4: 179–215.

Halliday, M. A. K. 1990. New ways of meaning: a challenge to applied linguistics. *Journal of Applied Linguistics* (Greek Applied Linguistics Association) 6: 7–36. Reprinted in Martin Pütz (ed.), *Thirty Years of Linguistic Evolution*, 59–95. Amsterdam & Philadelphia: John Benjamins. (1992)

Halliday, M. A. K., and Christian Matthiessen. in press. *Construing Experience through Meaning*. London & New York: Cassell.

Hasan, Ruqaiya. 1984. Ways of saying: ways of meaning. *The Semiotics of Culture and Language*, ed. by Robin P. Fawcett, M. A. K. Halliday, Sydney M. Lamb and Adam Makkai, Vol. 1, 105–162. London & Dover, New Hampshire: Frances Pinter.

Lamb, Sydney M. 1964. On alternation, transformation, realization, and stratification. *Report of the Fifteenth Annual (First International) Round Table Meeting on Linguistics and Language Studies*, ed. by C. I. J. M. Stuart, 105–122. Washington, D.C.: Georgetown University Press.

Lamb, Sydney M. 1988. (discussion in) M. A. K. Halliday, Sydney Lamb & John Regan, *In Retrospect: Using Language and Knowing How*. Claremont, California: The Claremont Graduate School (Issues in Communication 12)

Lamb, Sydney M. 1992. Outlines of a Cognitive Theory of Language: a work in progress (prepublication draft)

Lemke, Jay L. 1990. *Talking Science: language, learning, and values*. Norwood, New Jersey: Ablex (Language and Educational Processes)

Lemke, Jay L. 1993. Discourse, dynamics, and social change. *Cultural Dynamics* 6: 1–2 (*Language as Cultural Dynamic*): 243–275.

Martin, J. R. 1988. Grammatical conspiracies in Tagalog: family, face and fate — with regard to Benjamin Lee Whorf. *Linguistics in a Systemic Perspective*, ed. by James D. Benson, Michael J. Cummings and William S. Greaves, 243–300. Amsterdam: John Benjamins (Current Issues in Linguistic Theory 39)

Martin, J. R. & Christian Matthiessen. 1992. Systemic typology and topology. In *Literacy in Social Processes*, ed. by Frances Christie, 345–383. Darwin, N.T.: Centre for Studies in Language Education, Northern Territory University.

Matthiessen, Christian. 1991. Language on language: The grammar of semiosis. *Social semiotics 1.2: 69–111.*

New Scientist no. 1850, 5 December 1992 'Secret life of the brain' (Supplement No. 4)

Svartvik, Jan & Randolph Quirk (eds.). 1980 *A Corpus of English Conversation.* Lund: C.W.K. Gleerup (Lund Studies in English 56).

About the author

Michael Halliday is Professor Emeritus at Sydney University in Australia, whose Linguistics Department he headed from its founding in 1976 until his retirement in 1987. After he retired from Sydney University, he also became Honorary Visiting Professor at Macquarie University. He received his Ph.D. from Cambridge University in 1955. Before going to Australia he taught at Cambridge, Edinburgh, University College London, and the University of Illinois at Chicago, and held visiting professorships in the United States and elsewhere. He first met Syd Lamb in 1964, when they were both speakers at the Georgetown University Roundtable and found many common interests and outlooks. His principal interests include English semiotics and grammar, child language, and text linguistics.

CHAPTER 15

Translation and Text-Analysis[1]

Katharina Barbe
Northern Illinois University

Translation studies is a particularly vast field, being placed, as it is, at the intersection between many different disciplines (Hewson and Martin 1991: 229).

1. Introduction

The primary goal of translation is to enable an audience in a Target Language (TL) to understand a text or discourse which was originally not intended for them. The primary goal of text-analysis is to further the understanding of phenomena inside one language.[2] In both approaches, the inter-language translation and the intra-language text-analysis, similar mechanisms are at play. In this paper, I want to discuss the similarities between translation and text-analysis. In addition, the analysis of German data and their translation into American English (AE) demonstrate the unique position translation has, not only as an inter-language and inter-culture means of study, but also as a tool of text-analysis. Translation helps to discover problems that can then be approached in analysis.

The field of contrastive linguistics lends further support to the use of translation as inter-language comparison. "The phenomena to be accounted for in

---

1. A different version of this paper was presented at the Conference on Pragmatics and Language Learning, University of Illinois, Champaign-Urbana, on April 4, 1992 and covers literature up to 1992 only.

2. I understand text-analysis to imply the pragmatic analysis of spoken as well as written communication. In this paper, I am looking at spontaneous spoken communication. In my analysis, I follow Schegloff and Sacks (1973).

contrastive linguistics come most forcibly to attention in the course of careful translation" (Gleason 1968: 40). Wandruszka (1969) compared texts with their translations into other languages, to describe either a single language in more detail or similarities and differences between the compared languages. What language signifies for a speaker, what language achieves for him/her, is predominantly noticeable when different languages are compared (my translation of Wandruszka 1969: 7). This sentiment is shared by other linguists and translation theorists like Hartmann (1981), Roos (1981), and Snell-Hornby (1986). The combination of translation and text-analysis with contrastive linguistics, thus, can provide deeper insights into a pragmatic language description.

2. Translation and Text-analysis: A Comparison

Translation "is rendering the meaning of a text into another language in the way that the author intended the text" (Newmark 1988: 5).[3] To do so, we start either with single words, collocations, clauses, sentences, paragraphs, or the whole text. Regardless of the translation-method employed, the whole text is the ultimate criterion (cf. also Newmark 1988: 55).

The translator, just like the analyst, has to understand the text, show its intentions, recognize its attitude and discourse style (cf. Newmark 1988: 13). Words translated in isolation, just like words analyzed in isolation, provide a distorted picture. "For the translator the main problem lies in the frequent discrepancy between lexemes viewed in isolation and their usage as words in context" (Snell-Hornby 1988: 96). The context is decisive in translation as well as in the analysis of discourse phenomena.

> ... translation begins with the text-in-situation as an integral part of the cultural background, whereby text-analysis proceeds from macro-structure of the text to the micro-unit of the word, this being seen, not as an isolatable item, but in its relevance and function within the text (Snell-Hornby 1988: 2).

Both translation and text-analysis involve the re-creation of text; the translator re-creates in the TL, the analyst in some meta-language. The analyst as well as the

---

3. There is a lot of discussion about this point, e.g.: what are the author's intentions? Are the author's intentions more important than each reader's interpretations? Nevertheless, I think, this statement captures well the intentions of most translators.

translator need to be aware of all the possible relationships which hold in the text, from single words to the whole text. "Anything re-stated is in fact a translation. Creation, interpretation, re-creation, translation, and adaptation are more closely related than one might think" (Delisle 1988: 63). A successful text-analysis is even a pre-requisite for a good translation. Moreover, the relationship between translation and text-analysis is mutually beneficial. "Better than any analysis of a single language, translation demonstrates the fact that in discourse a word can have a completely different meaning from the one normally associated with that word taken in isolation" (Delisle 1988: 47).

3.   Data-Analysis

In the following, the intra-language analysis of each example precedes the examination of the information provided by the translation. The primary data for this study, a conversation among close friends, was recorded during an engagement party in Berlin, Germany. In the course of their conversation, the participants, all in their early 20s, talk about the engagement, in (1) referred to as *Sache*, which was a big surprise for most of them.

(1)   Stefan: *War 'ne richtige adhoc Sache irgendwie, wa*
                   Was a real adhoc thing somehow
        Martha: *Ja, spontaaan, nich Anna? Haha!*
                   Yeah, spontaneous, wasn't it, Anna?
        Helga: *Ganz spontan*
                   Truly spontaneous

The "incompleteness" of Stefan's utterance, i.e., the omitted subject, the truncated *ne* (from *eine*), the *wa*-tag (a sign of Berlin dialect, Berlinerisch in the following) give evidence of informal speech. I use the terms "truncated", "incomplete", etc., with reservation. They imply that utterances can be complete or incomplete. Usually, each utterance is as complete as the conversation and the intentions and abilities of the speakers require. Stefan has a certain discourse purpose in mind which even requires this "incompleteness".

Martha's remark also lacks a surface subject. Nevertheless, just like Stefan's, her remark suffices in the colloquial context. Had Martha spoken very formally in a grammatically complete and correct manner, the other participants would have considered that a violation of the "party-discourse-mode". With her remark, which was understood as ironic, she teases Anna. With her use of a *nich*-tag, Martha intends her remark to be taken like a punch line. She neither wants nor expects any response from Anna. However, she expects agreement with her proposition from the other participants.

On the discourse level the irony is based on the *adhoc — spontan* relationship and on the lengthening of *spontaaan*. However, these clues are not conclusive. It is doubtful that an outsider will be able to deduce that spontaneity is not one of Anna's characteristics. In this instance, the most important signal is not a linguistic one, it is prior knowledge of Anna's inflexibility. Then the irony becomes more obvious: Anna's known inflexibility is juxtaposed with *adhoc – spontan*. Anna does have some possible responses, among others; (a) noticing the irony, she could be offended and express this sentiment, (b) she could decide not to notice the irony and take Martha's query as a question, and answer accordingly, (c) she could come up with some smart repartee, or (d) she could just not react at all, which is what she did. An observer of the exchange, Helga, notices the irony and expresses agreement with Martha.

The translation of this exchange into colloquial AE seems to be without problems on the basis of the constituent words. The omission of the subject *das* in Stefan's and Martha's utterances is easily translated, without loss of the colloquial flavor. The "incompleteness" of the participants' utterances are signs of colloquial language not only in German but also in AE. The omission of the subject is also possible in AE without major distortion of the meaning. However, just like a text-analyst, a translator has to account somehow for unfinished sentences, interruptions, repairs, false starts, etc. All are signs of spontaneous conversation and consequently must appear in the TL-version to preserve the flavor of the utterance.

Having the requisite background-knowledge, a TL-speaker can also understand the irony in the translation. Although irony is generally described as a very culture-specific phenomenon, at least in this instance, German and American culture have a similar understanding of irony.

But, upon further examination, the translation of Stefan's utterance becomes puzzling. A translator has to decide if *War 'ne richtige adhoc Sache irgendwie, wa* is a question or a comment. With the tag *wa* Stefan tries to elicit agreement, which is, however, not necessarily a requirement for a question. Stefan's utterance should be disambiguated when intonation is considered. However, Stefan does not use question intonation, even though he stresses *wa*. But how does he want his remark to be understood? To explain further, let us look at the following examples:[4]

(2)   *War heute schön*
         Was nice today

(3)   *Ist alles fertig*
         Everything is ready / Is everything ready

(4)   *Sind alle fertig*
         Everybody is ready / Is everybody ready

Items (2), (3), and (4) are also ambiguous as to their discourse function. If said very forcefully, with a rather flat intonation, i.e., without the typical question-intonation, they can elicit either (a) some type of comment, (b) agreement or (c) disagreement.

(2a)   *Wieso?*
         Why?

(2b)   *Fand ich auch*
         I agree

(2c)   *Ganz und garnicht*
         Not at all

(3a)   *Toll*
         Great

(3b)   *Ja*
         Yeah

(3c)   *Nein*
         No

(4a)   *Endlich*
         Finally

(4b)   *Ja, wir können jetzt gehen*
         Yes, let's leave now

(4c)   *Nein, hetz mich doch nicht immer so*
         No, what's the hurry

---

4. Examples (2)–(4c) are constructed.

(2a), (3a), and (4a) are responses to a statement, in terms of either a doubting question (2a), a sign of praise (3a), or of impatience (4a). (2b), (2c), (3b), (3c) and (4b), (4c) are responses to assumed yes/no-questions. Thus, we find that there exist some "non-questions" in German, all using a form of *sein* ('to be'), which do not fit into any model developed so far.[5]

Similarly, the following example also includes "non-questions".

(5)   Stefan: *Ja, anstossen könn wa ooch noch ma*
                    Let's drink to their health again
        Anna: *Am liebsten mit andern Gläsern wa Stefan?*
                    Preferably with other people's glasses, right Stefan
        Stefan: *War des deins? Keine ansteckenden Krankheiten,*
                    Was this yours. No communicable diseases,
                    gloob ick jedenfalls
                    at least I hope so

Anna's utterance shows the traditional question intonation, which she even intensifies with the *wa*-tag. She expects some apology or at least acknowledgement from Stefan.

Stefan in turn replies with what appears to be a question. *War des deins?* shows all the signs of a yes/no-question complete with the rising intonation and first position of the verb. Stefan, however, asks the "question" **after** the "response", implied in Anna's statement, had already been given. Usually, we expect an answer to follow a question, not to precede it (cf. Schegloff and Sacks 1973). Stefan does not expect an answer at all.

Stefan's utterance can also not be considered a rhetorical question, even though it fits the description of a rhetorical question, namely, a question "without intent to elicit information" (Frank 1990: 730) but trying to elicit agreement. The question here rather functions as an expression of surprise coupled with an apology. It could perhaps be considered as an "echo-question" in terms of Green (1989: 155). Stefan's question and the examples provided by Green (e.g., "He did what?") both share the element of surprise. However, apology is not included in the definition of "echo-questions". Stefan's apology is insincere, because he invalidates it immediately by teasing Anna: He assures Anna that he does not

---

5. Lakoff (1973), Baumert (1977), Kiefer (1983), Levinson (1983), Green (1989), e.g., deal primarily with English. However, publications dealing with German questions did not discuss these types of questions, Bühler et al. (1973), Wunderlich (1975), Braun (1987), Brinker and Sager (1989).

have any diseases and that she can safely keep drinking from the glass in question, thereby alluding to her known fear of germs.

The translation of (5) also does not pose any major hurdles, except again for those "non-questions".

In the following example, Carl is talking about a better place for the tape-recorder, which was prominently displayed.

(6) Carl: *Auf's Klo hinstelln, ha! Das muß sich automatisch ein-schaltn Mensch*[6],
Put {it}[7] in the john. It has to turn itself on automatically,
die Leute dürfen das ... natürlich nichts davon wissen.
people should ... of course not notice it.
Ja, oh, da komm Sachen raus
Yeah, a lot of stuff is going to come out
Martha: *Natürlich sonst würdense ja nich uffs Klo jehn.*
Of course, otherwise they wouldn't go to the john.

Carl omits the subject (*man* or *du*) as well as the object (*es / das Tonbandgerät*) in *Auf's Klo hinstelln, ha!* Object omission is not possible in English in this instance, but the subject does not need to be expressed. There must then be some criteria that govern incompleteness: When is an incomplete sentence still pragmatically acceptable?

Carl achieves the colloquial flavor not only by ellipsis but also by his choice of words. He chooses *Klo* instead of the more polite *Bad* or *Toilette*. *Klo*, a synechdoche, does not only signify the bathroom as a whole but also the commode itself (in British English we could perhaps translate *Klo* with *loo*). Nevertheless, Carl meant his suggestion to be taken seriously. He did not intend the interpretation Martha gave to his utterances. However, the ambiguity of *rauskommen* — 'come out', 'get out', or 'find out' left a place for Martha to jump in. Carl intended 'find out' but his audience "misunderstood" 'come out'. After a bathroom visit it can jokingly be said *Did everything come out OK?*

---

6. *Mensch*, translated in other contexts with 'human being', is used here as an exclamation, somewhat like an intensifier, remotely comparable to *you guys, oh man,* or *you all.* Often used interchangeably with *Mann* in utterances like *Mensch, das mußt du doch wissen* 'you really should have known this' or *Mensch, war der doof* 'man, that guy was really stupid', it can also be paraphrased with *weißte* 'you know' or *wirklich* 'really'. *Die Leute* 'the people' could conceivably also be 'nobody' or 'everybody.'

7. { } indicates that the object needs to be expressed in English.

Example 6 constitutes another instance of irony. Carl becomes an ironist against his will, whereas Martha intends her ironic remark. In order to understand the irony here, no prior knowledge of the speakers involved is necessary. Except for the incompleteness, the exchange translates easily.

With (7) Stefan reacts to the previous exchange:

(7)   Stefan: *Fäkalästhetiker wo is der Wodka?*
                    Fecal aestheticist, where is the vodka?

He combines a comment to the Carl/Martha exchange with a request to the hostess by juxtaposing a nonce-lexeme with a seemingly unimportant question all in one breath. Stefan, intentionally or unintentionally, uses a technique common to sitcoms, which usually involves a revolving door. The addressee leaves through this door as if nothing had happened, only to return incredulously, wanting to re-check the last utterance. The same thing happened here. Only at some time later in the conversation does one participant catch on to the outrageousness of the utterance and then attempt to "publicize" it.

A translator will not find the term *Fäkalästhetiker* in any dictionary, not even in a dictionary of contemporary German. Translation of *Fäkalästhetiker* requires a nonce-form also in the TL, i.e., it leaves the translator to exercise his or her lexical creativity. The translation of nonce-forms has not been discussed in detail in the relevant literature. Newmark (1988: 140) considers these neologisms "the non-literary and the professional translator's biggest problem" and defines them "as newly coined lexical units or existing lexical units that acquire a new sense".

Nonce-forms are not only culture-specific but also very situation-dependent and personal. Like idioms, many nonce-creations have been integrated into the language and are now no longer recognizable as such. But, because of the obvious taboo-connotations involved, it is doubtful if Stefan's creation would ever find its way into mainstream German.

Up to now, we were able to discover two areas, "non-questions" and nonce-lexemes, with the help of translation. Example 8 highlights yet another problem, the use of American English (AE) in German.

(8)   Martha: *Da hat er da mit so dussligen Fremdwörtern arjumentiert, ja*
                    nich jescheckt
                    He argued with such silly foreign words, didn't get it

Martha complains about the inappropriate use of *Fremdwörter* by a fellow student, who, she thought, wanted to sound intellectual. But then she turns around and uses *Fremdwörter* herself. She juxtaposes *Fremdwörter* with *arjumentieren* and *jescheckt* (*arjumentiert* – Berlinerisch version of the standard *argumentiert*; *jescheckt* – Berlinerisch version of past participle of *schecken* – *gescheckt.*) *Gescheckt / gecheckt* is a recent loan from AE (*check*) with the meaning of 'fathom' or 'examine' (Küpper 1987). *Argued* has been incorporated into the English language and would no longer be considered a "foreign word" at least to the same extent as *argumentieren* in German is still considered a *Fremdwort* (DUDEN Fremdwörterbuch 1984).

'Foreign words' seems to be an inadequate translation of *Fremdwörter*, mainly because foreign words do not play as prominent a role in English as they do in German. *Fremdwörter* can be considered an institution in German. "The important thing is the association behind the word. The English equivalent of the German who talks in *Fremdwörtern* is the man who uses Latinized language" (Snell 1978: 198). It is most important for a speaker using *Fremdwörter* that he/she know either where to put the stress, in loans of Latin or Greek origin, or how to pronounce them, in loans of English origin.[8]

Utterance (8) can be translated into AE. However, no possible translation will show the same SL-connotations for *jescheckt* in the TL. Even though we can find a few German loans in AE (for example, *ersatz* and *angst*), the context of the use and the prestige of foreign languages in the U.S. (predominantly, French, German, and Spanish) are not comparable to the prestige and the use of AE in Germany. Historical circumstances (like the continued presence of American soldiers in the now former West Germany and West Berlin) as well as American leadership in pop-culture and technology prove responsible for AE prestige. The Germans have even coined a word for the extended usage of AE — *Amerikanismus*, which is defined as a loan specifically from AE (DUDEN 20).

Numerous *Amerikanismen* can be found in newspapers and magazines. *Die Bodyguards bewachen einen Mythos* 'the bodyguards guard a myth' (Spiegel 32/92:178) in an article about Bobby Fischer. An article about TV and Computers

---

8. Küpper (1987) has the following entry next to English loans – *Englisch aussprechen*, i.e., 'use English pronunciation'. For loans from Latin or Greek consider the following (stressed syllable bold face): *Philosoph – Philosophie – Philosophieren – Philosophikum.*

uses *hightechnischen Raum* 'high-tech area', *Computerfreaks*, 'hackers'[9] and *Mailboxen* 'mailboxes' (*Zitty* 17/92:206). An advertising-executive describes an advertisement for a cigarette as *lonesome hero mit Loch im Schuh* 'lonesome hero with a hole in the shoe', and criticizes himself with *aber ich weiß natürlich, daß das Bullshit ist* 'but, of course, I know it's bullshit' (*Zitty* 17/92:199). *Langeweile und Coolheit* 'boredom and detachment' are juxtaposed (*Zitty* 17/92:200). These phenomena have been studied extensively,[10] but not, however, from the point of view of what to do with them when translating into AE.

4. Discussion

This survey has illustrated that translation can support the analysis of texts/discourse in some instances, and, in the discussion of queries, even furthers the understanding of the text. Thus, we can divide the usefulness of translation for text-analysis into two areas:

I.   translation furthers understanding
II.   translation supports previous conclusions

Particularly in the discussion of what I have called "non-questions", translation played a role in the discovery of these phenomena. "Non-questions" as well as tag-questions and rhetorical questions, as they appeared above in (1) – (5) deserve further attention. A detailed pragmatic analysis should illustrate the special features of these questions, and compare "non-questions" with question-types previously studied.

Furthermore, a contrastive study of the definitions and possibilities of "incompleteness" should prove valuable not only to the translator but also to the analyst. We have found so far that subject omission is possible in AE and German in the cases discussed above. Object omission, however, was only possible in German. Does this hold true in other instances, for different grammatical features? Can the same features be omitted in German and English?

Nonce-forms also deserve further study, even though no unified approach can be possible due to the nature of these forms. However, as the translation of

---

9. Computerfreak is a term which does not exist in English in this combination. *Computer* and *Freak* do exist, their combination, however, is probably best re-translated as 'hacker'.

10. Carstenson (1971), Braun (1979), Viereck (1980), and many others.

nonce-forms makes us aware, translation is not only a bi-lingual and bi-cultural matter but also a personal one.

We have also run into major problems concerning the translation of *Amerikanismen*. As *Amerikanismen* find their way more and more into German, they are not only found in advertisements, newspapers, and magazines but also in recent German literature. Thus, the translation of *Amerikanismen* becomes a legitimate area of inquiry which merits further investigation. Surprisingly, as Dagut (1976) has noted, the pertinent translation literature has so far neglected the discussion of metaphors, and with it, of nonce-forms, even though they constitute the translator's biggest problem.[11]

In the cases of irony discussed above, the translation supports previous conclusions. Irony is a highly cultural phenomenon. The discussion of irony in conversation poses similar problems in German and AE, which indicates similar cultural experiences. Examples 1 and 2 show that ironic instances can cross culture boundaries. Furthermore, they point to some commonality in the treatment of irony in the two cultures. Irony has been variously described in linguistic-pragmatic terms (Roy 1978, Kaufer 1981, Sperber and Wilson 1981, Wilson and Sperber 1992, Barbe 1989, Littman and Mey 1991, and others). However, a contrastive study of irony has, as of yet, not been attempted.

5.   Conclusion

I have shown the similarity and the relationship between translation and text-analysis. Text-analysis is the basis for translation; translation, then, can re-influence text-analysis by helping to discover problems which merit further investigation. Translation, thus, functions here not only to distribute knowledge across language boundaries, but also to expand our knowledge about the Source Language.

> ... when translation is properly understood as something more than mere decoding, we realize that it suggests ... other ways of being in the world (Tyler 1978: 70).

---

11. Dagut presents a list of major works including Nida (1964) and Mounin (1967), for example. Unfortunately, the same holds true for more current texts, see Bassnett-McGuire (1980), Hatim and Mason (1990), Gutt (1991), and Hewson and Martin (1991).

References

Barbe, Katharina. 1989. *Irony in Conversational German: A Linguistic Approach.* Ann Arbor, Michigan: University Microfilms International. (Rice University Ph. D. dissertation).

Bassnett-McGuire, Susan. 1980. *Translation Studies.* London: Methuen.

Baumert, M. 1977. Classification of English question-answer structure. *Journal of Pragmatics* 1. 85–92.

Braun, Peter. (ed.) 1979. *Fremdwort-Diskussion.* München: Wilhelm Funk.

Braun, Peter. 1987. *Tendenzen in der deutschen Gegenwartssprache.* Stuttgart: Kohlhammer.

Brinker, Klaus., and Sven F. Sager. 1989. *Linguistische Gesprächsanalyse.* Berlin: Erich Schmidt.

Bühler, Hans. et al. 1973. *Funk-Kolleg Sprache II.* Frankfurt am Main: Fischer.

Carstenson, Broder. 1971. *Spiegel-Wörter.* Spiegel-Worte. München.

Dagut, M. B. 1976. Can "metaphor" be translated? *Babel* 22/1. 21–32.

Delisle, Jean. 1988. *Translation: An Interpretative Approach.* Ottawa, Canada: University of Ottawa Press.

DUDEN "Rechtschreibung der Deutschen Sprache" 20. 1991. Mannheim: Dudenverlag.

DUDEN "Fremdwörterbuch". 1984. Mannheim: Bibliographisches Institut.

Frank, Jane. 1990. You call that a rhetorical question? *Journal of Pragmatics* 14. 723–738.

Gleason, H. A. 1968. Contrastive analysis in discourse structure. *19th Annual Round Table Meeting on Linguistics and Language Studies*, ed. by James L. Alatis, 39–63. Washington, D.C.: Georgetown University Press.

Green, Georgia. 1989. *Pragmatics and Natural Language Understanding.* Hillsdale, New Jersey: Lawrence Erlbaum.

Gutt, Ernst August. 1991. *Translation and Relevance.* Oxford: Basil Blackwell.

Hartmann, R. R. K. 1981. Contrastive textology and translation. *Kontrastive Linguistik und Übersetzungswissenschaft. Akten des Internationalen Kolloquiums Trier/Saarbrücken 25–30.9.1978* ed. by Wolfgang Kühlwein, Gisela Thome, Wolfram Wilss, 200–208. München: Fink.

Hatim, Basil, and Ian Mason. 1990. *Discourse and the Translator.* New York: Longman.

Hewson, Lance and Jacky Martin. 1991. *Redefining Translation*. London: Routledge.

Kaufer, David S. 1981. Understanding ironic communication. *Journal of Pragmatics* 5. 495–510.

Kiefer, Ferenc. (ed.) 1983. *Questions and Answers*. Dordrecht: Reidel.

Küpper, Heinz. 1987. *Pons Wörterbuch der deutschen Umgangssprache*. Stuttgart: Ernst Klett Verlag.

Lakoff, Robin. 1973. Questionable answers and answerable questions. *Issues in Linguistics: Papers in Honor of Henry and* Renee *Kahane*. ed. by Braj. B. Kachru, Robert Lees, Yakov Malkiel, Angelina Pietrangeli, and Sol Saporta, 453–467. Chicago: University of Illinois Press.

Levinson, Stephen. 1983. *Pragmatics*. Cambridge: Cambridge University Press.

Littmann, David C. and Jacob L. Mey. 1991. The nature of irony. *Journal of Pragmatics* 15. 131–151.

Mounin, George. 1967. *Die Übersetzung: Geschichte, Theorie, Anwendung*. München: Nymphenburger.

Newmark, Peter. 1988. *A Textbook of Translation*. New York: Prentice Hall.

Nida, Eugene. 1964. *Toward a Science of Translating*. Leiden: Brill.

Roos, Eckhard., 1981. Contrastive analysis and the translation of idioms. *Kontrastive Linguistik und Übersetzungswissenschaft Akten des Internationalen Kolloquiums Trier/Saarbrücken 25.–30.9.1978*. ed. by Wolfgang. Kühlwein, Gisela Thome, Wolfram Wilss, 230–238. München: Fink.

Roy, Alice Myers. 1978. Irony in Conversation. Ann Arbor, Michigan: University Microfilms International.

Schegloff, Emanuel A. and Harvey Sacks. 1973. Opening up closings. *Semiotica* 8. 289–327.

Snell, Mary. 1978. *German – English Prose Translation*. München: Hueber.

Snell-Hornby, Mary. (ed.) 1986. *Übersetzungswissenschaften – Eine Neuorientierung*. Tübingen: Francke.

Snell-Hornby, Mary. 1988. *Translation Studies – An Integrated Approach*. Amsterdam: Benjamins.

Snell-Hornby, Mary. 1990. Linguistic transcoding or cultural transfer? A critique of translation theory in Germany. *Translation, History and Culture*. ed. by Susan Bassnett and Andre Lefevere, 79–86. London: Pinter Publishers.

Sperber, Dan and Deirdre Wilson. 1981. Irony and the use-mention distinction. *Radical Pragmatics*, ed. by Peter Cole, 295–318, New York: Academic Press.

Der Spiegel 32. 1992.

Tyler, Stephen. 1978. *The Said and the Unsaid*. New York: Academic Press.

Viereck, Wolfgang. 1980. *Studien zum Einfluß der englischen Sprache auf das Deutsche*. Tübingen: Gunter Narr.

Wandruszka, Mario. 1969. *Sprachen: vergleichbar und unvergleichlich*. München: Piper.

Wunderlich, Dieter (ed.). 1972, *Linguistische Pragmatik*. Wiesbaden: Athenaion.

Zitty 17. 1992.

About the author

*Katharina Barbe is currently Associate Professor of German Language and Linguistics and Director of the Division of German, Russian and Other Languages in the Department of Foreign Languages at Northern Illinois University. She received her Ph. D. from Rice in 1989 and took various courses from Syd Lamb in her studies. Her articles have appeared in the **LACUS Fora**, **Journal of Pragmatics, Meta, Perspectives,** and **The German Journal** of the Association for Language Learning. In 1995 she published the monograph **Irony in Context** in the Benjamins series **Pragmatics and Beyond**. Her research interests include translation studies, linguistic pragmatics, and second language acquisition.*

CHAPTER 16

Cognitive Networks in Conversation

Cynthia Ford Meyer

The Woodlands, Texas

1. Introduction

It is most fitting that the linguist whose name has become practically synonymous with networks should see the effects of his contribution spread in network
fashion to adjacent areas of the discipline, for like the traditional notions of
rationalism and empiricism, the notion of network operates on two levels. It is at
once a theory of the human mind and a practical approach to scholarship, the
ideas of one scholar leading from and to those of others in unforeseen ways and
fully appreciated only when viewed in the context of such relationships.

Our task here is not to provide a comprehensive review of the sources of
Sydney Lamb's thinking in Hjelmslev, Halliday and others (but cf. Meyer 1991,
ch. 2) or of the spreading applicability of his views to areas such as translation
(e.g. Fleming 1986), language description (e.g. Lockwood 1987), discourse
studies (e.g. Copeland and Davis 1980) and so forth. Instead, this paper introduces a single area of study which has yet to be fully explored in relation to
Lambian thinking, but which holds considerable promise for contributing to and
benefiting from cognitive network theory. That area is the analysis of conversation.

2. Background

Accurate conversational data has become available only recently in the long
history of linguistics by the invention of audio recording. Owing to enduring
Saussurean prejudice against *parole*, it has come to the serious attention of

linguists more recently still, mainly through the back door of Conversation Analysis, an endeavor of sociologists interested in the ways speakers use conversation to achieve such social tasks as taking turns speaking (Sacks et al. 1974), controlling the topic of conversation (Jefferson 1984), giving and receiving compliments (Pomerantz 1978), and even ending a phone conversation (Schegloff and Sacks 1973).

In linguistics proper, Chafe pioneered in the study of recorded spontaneous oral language (1976, 1980), recognizing in spoken monologue important clues to cognitive function, albeit without choosing a network orientation. Following his cue, a number of linguists have lately come to look more and more to spontaneous oral language in place of written texts or made-up examples (e.g. Thompson 1990, Fox and Thompson 1990). In contrast to the socially oriented Conversation Analysts, Chafe and those following him have shifted the major focus to grammatical and cognitive issues. They define their tasks as understanding information flow and explaining grammatical patterning in terms of underlying cognitive and social principles (e.g. Thompson 1990).

As for Lamb, he has long had the overarching goal of representing "the speaker's internal information system which makes it possible for him to speak his language and to understand utterances received from others" (Lamb 1973: 13). His way of defining his goal and his faith in network representation as both the key insight and the key problem have set him on a track somewhat different from that of Chafe's intellectual heirs and colleagues who construe quite differently both cognition itself and the questions to be asked about it in relation to language usage. Like their views, however, Lamb's has much to gain from the consideration of conversation.

For these cognitive approaches, conversational data, as opposed to much oral monologue and practically all written texts, offers the double advantages of increased spontaneity, hence a certain transparency of cognitive function which is lacking in carefully planned discourse, and of oral interaction among interlocutors, hence a significant amount of overt stimulus-response data. This second advantage was first recognized by the Conversation Analysis school, which though socially inclined, could not help but notice some cognitive phenomena as well:

> What two utterances, produced by different speakers, can do that one utterance cannot do is: by an adjacently positioned second, a speaker can show that he understood what a prior aimed at, and that he is willing to go along with that. Also, by virtue of the occurrence of an adjacently produced second, the doer

of a first can see that what he intended was indeed understood, and that it was
or was not accepted. (Schegloff and Sacks 1973: 299)

Within the Lambian school, as in much post-Saussurean work, the bulk of the
attention has focused on short data samples, constructed for the purpose in
English or collected from other languages. Actually occurring oral language
samples have been treated more rarely and more tentatively.

Dell and Reich (1980) extracted slips of the tongue from spontaneous oral
language and gave plausible cognitive network accountings. Reich (1985)
identified and accounted for unintended puns from similar data. These efforts
exploited in an ingenious way one of the signal characteristics of conversation,
its disfluencies, or more accurately in the case of the puns its superfluencies. The
chief shortcoming of this line of work was perhaps that it stopped before mining
conversational data further and more systematically for cognitive clues in
keeping with the overarching Lambian goal. For example, while disfluencies are
singled out and accounted for, interactive aspects of conversation as a whole, as
pointed out by Schegloff and Sacks (1973: 299), are not addressed. Likewise,
Lamb's own rare foray into the analysis of conversational data (1984) dealt
exclusively with a short narrative monologue portion and not in any systematic
way with the conversation as a whole, i.e. some of the most promising characteristics of conversational data for cognitive studies were left unexamined.

In summary, there remains much room for the application of cognitive
network theory to the data of conversation. In what follows, we survey a
selection of phenomena and issues in order to demonstrate the potential benefits
of such study and to invite further investigation.[1]

3.   Cognitive Networks in Conversation: A Sampler

From a Lambian vantage point, conversation can be approached in a systematic
way as a process in which several cognitive systems interact with each other by
means of the speech signal and change as a result. That is, interlocutors talk to
each other and learn from talking. The recorded and transcribed speech signal,
the relic of the interaction, provides clues as to cognitive organization and the

---

1. See Meyer 1991 for more comprehensive treatments of these areas.

on-line cognitive processing of the conversation partners as they work both to produce utterances and to interpret the utterances of others.

The cognitive systems of the interlocutors can be represented as networks of relationships. Conversational data can be studied with the goal of discovering details of how these cognitive networks are organized and operate and how they are related to each other and to the speech signal, and in turn, the network notion should be able to offer explanations for phenomena identified in conversational data.

The data used in the following examples is purposely taken from a very simple type of conversation, one involving only two interlocutors, and one in which the major purpose of the interaction is the exchange of factual information. While acknowledging that much conversation is more complex than this sample and that conversation often involves purposes other than information exchange, we nevertheless find it useful to focus on this type of conversation because it provides a manageable starting point for studying a range of cognitive issues. It is a spontaneous unscripted sample which, without being overly complex, is nevertheless complex enough to provide an interesting window into the basic cognitive processes characteristic of conversing individuals.

In the conversations, LeRoy, whose utterances are transcribed against the left margin, interviews one of his parents, Walter or Lucinda, depending on the excerpt, concerning his or her experiences on the Oklahoma frontier around the turn of the century.[2] Walter and Lucinda's utterances are indented in the transcription.[3]

---

2. I am grateful to LeRoy Ford for making available these several hours of recordings which he made over thirty years ago as a family archive. Full transcriptions are given in Meyer 1991.

3. Other transcription conventions are as follows: Relative pitch is marked with raised numerals 1 to 4 signaling low to high pitch respectively. Accent marks show stressed syllables. Pauses of x seconds are shown in double parentheses as are transcriber comments. The notation following the excerpt number identifies its source. LeRoy's turns are numbered in the right margin. Lucinda and Walter's responses are numbered after a decimal point in the right margin. Single parentheses mark transcriber doubt. Dashes mark brief hesitations or incomplete intonation contours. Periods and question marks indicate complete intonation contours with the intonation typical of the type of statement or question, e.g. yes-no vs. *wh*-question.

3.1 *Phenomenon 1: Doubletake and repair*

Characteristic of conversation is misunderstanding, and hopefully the eventual repair of the misunderstanding. In narrower terms, the misunderstanding shown in Excerpt 1 is a doubletake, in which Lucinda gives one response and then changes it after further consideration. In broader terms, misunderstanding can be classified as a conversational breakdown. Dell and Reich's slips of the tongue (1980) provide another example, and such breakdowns often provide a window into the cognitive processing of the speaker, for it is where a system makes mistakes that it sometimes best betrays its hidden mechanisms.

Excerpt 1: Lu3B

Well that's when- you and your dad- [3]móved up there[1]	. 66
[2]Yeah[2.] ((2))	.1
No it's when- me 'n [3]yóur dad moved up there[1]. ((3))	.2

In Excerpt 1, Lucinda shows a misunderstanding of LeRoy in line 66.1 and corrects herself in line 66.2. LeRoy, in 66 seeks confirmation that the events under discussion occurred during a certain move. He marks his intent with stress and high pitch on the word *moved*, i.e. the part of the proposition that is under question. The part of the proposition that he is sure about and, as it turns out, wrong about, i.e. that the participants were Lucinda and her father, is not marked for Lucinda's special attention by pitch or by stress. Lucinda answers two times, first confirming LeRoy's idea in 66.1, and then, after a two second pause, revoking her confirmation and issuing a correction. The participants were not Lucinda and **her** father as LeRoy had thought, but Lucinda and **LeRoy's** father, her husband.

This excerpt reveals something interesting about Lucinda's cognitive processing in response to LeRoy's request for confirmation. It appears that processing advances in some sort of sequence through the network as she compares her internal representation of the questioned event to that which LeRoy seems to have. Further, it appears that the sequencing is directed by the intonation on the stimulus question. Lucinda's initial confirmation (66.1) suggests that she processed and responded to the stressed part of LeRoy's utterance first, before completing the processing of the earlier, unstressed portion of the utterance, the incorrect part which was concerned with the participants in the proposition.

3.2 *Phenomenon 2: Sequencing of conversational topics*

As interviewer, one of LeRoy's tasks in these conversations is to select topics for discussion. Although he did not refer to written notes in the interviews, the topic sequence as it unfolded was far from random, and its patterning reveals a great deal about the organization of and accession of information in LeRoy's cognitive system.

In Excerpt 2, we consider first the underlined portion of LeRoy's turn 14 and ask why this of all possible interview questions is chosen at this point. Here it seems clear that LeRoy's motivation for selecting the burning of buffalo chips as a topic stems from Lucinda's earlier comment (underlined in 10.1 and 10.2) about picking up pieces of wood to make a campfire out of. Her mention of "little pieces of wood" and "campfire" causes LeRoy to activate the portions of his network representing the corresponding concepts in his system. LeRoy has in his cognitive system the concept of "buffalo chips", which is closely associated with these concepts in this way. "Pieces of wood" and "buffalo chips" are related as separate particulars or subdomains of a single domain that can be characterized as "what campfires are made of". Activation from the concepts "pieces of wood" and "campfire", therefore, easily spreads along this association pathway preparing "the burning of buffalo chips" as a handy new topic when one is needed.

Likewise, Lucinda's contribution of the story about Willie's reading in school (14.2 ff.) is motivated by a close association in her system between "burning buffalo chips" and the figurative sense of "cows chopping wood" (underlined in 14.5).

Two conclusions come from this discussion. First, the selection of successive topics in these conversations is governed by the organization of the cognitive networks. More specifically, the more accessible information is in a network, the more likely it is to be topicalized. Previous activation of closely associated information, as in this example, is one facet of accessibility.[4] Second, we see that selection of topics grows out of the interaction of the conversation. Lucinda's utterances help activate portions of LeRoy's system that likely would not have been activated were he left to himself, and vice versa.

---

4. There are other factors which condition accessibility as well. For further discussion, see Meyer 1991, Chapter 3.

Excerpt 2: Lu2A

When you stopped to camp at ^{3}níight^2 — did all the kids have ^{3}chóres to do^3?	10
Well we'd — go aróund 'n <u>pick up little pieces a wóod</u> — ((1))	.1
to make the ^{3}cámp ^{1}fire out of^1.((1))	.2
Who put up the tént? ((1))	11
Oh dáddy used to done most a ^{3}thát^2. ((3))	.1
Did you put up a tent every time you stópped? ((1))	12
^{2}No^2 — not ^{3}éver^1 time. ((1))	.1
Did you sleep out in the ^{3}ópen sometimes^3?	13
^{1}Yeah^2. (**(4)**)	.1
When you were at the ^{3}fárm^1 at **uh** — ^{3}Érick^1 — <u>did you ever burn ^{3}búffalo chíps^3</u>? ((1))	14
^{3}Óh ^{1}yes^2. ((Chuckle))	.1
LéRo — uh Wíllie said a little reading in ^{3}schóol^1–	.2
Aunt Léla 'd láugh about. ((1)) ((Chuckling))	.3
He said the reáson he liked Okla^{3}hóma^2–	.4
the wínd pumped all the wáter — 'n <u>the cóws chopped all the ^{3}wóod^1</u>. ((Chuckling))	.5
Thát was the reading he said in ^{3}schóol^1.	.6
'N shé just láughed 'n laughed 'n laughed. ((Trailing off intonation))	.7

3.3 Phenomenon 3: Disfluencies at the establishment of topics

If we now consider the bold-faced portions of lines 13.1 and 14 in Excerpt 2, we can learn something else about LeRoy's cognitive processing in the conversation and at the same time see in another way the usefulness of breakdowns to cognitive study.

Line 13.1 ends with a four-second pause, and line 14 has the filled pause *uh*. Such phenomena may be accounted for in social terms. Jefferson (1985: 216), for example, analyzes the utterance *uh* as a floorholder which helps a speaker to prolong his turn without interruption. Likewise, the four-second pause may be LeRoy's way of encouraging Lucinda to elaborate on her answer.

Looking at this phenomenon from a cognitive vantage point, a different and complementary analysis emerges. It turns out that disfluencies such as filled pauses, hesitations, false starts, and long pauses, are not at all randomly distributed, but tend to cluster at points of topic change where activation must spread through relatively large areas of network. Disfluencies are much less frequent within stretches of conversation that continue on an established topic. It appears that the selection of a new topic takes time and effort, resulting in disfluent production. Within an established topic, however, activation moves easily among closely associated nections of information, and more of LeRoy's processing capacity is free to concentrate on smooth production.

3.4 Phenomenon 4: Misunderstanding & understanding of new topics

Excerpt 3 shows the usefulness of yet another type of conversation breakdown and repair for cognitive study. In 29, LeRoy introduces a topic which is likely motivated in his system by an association between the texture of a clay-like material called "keel" (27.10) and the texture of sorghum taffy. The connection between keel and taffy is not so obvious at this point to Walter, however. That association may not be present in his system, and if it is present, it may not be activated. At any rate, he does not immediately follow the topic change (29.1), and LeRoy must pose the question again (30).

In contrast, we can find many examples of new topics that are likely to be equally unexpected by the interviewee, but which nevertheless succeed without a breakdown. In Excerpt 4, LeRoy introduces the topic of "when Oklahoma became a state" at the beginning of the interview. Lucinda would have no motivation to be thinking about this topic already at this point, yet it is established without misunderstanding on her part. Key here are strategies that LeRoy uses and which are absent from the sorghum taffy example. For instance, he formulates his question twice in slightly different ways, giving Lucinda more time to process the topic. He also uses multiple sentence stress as well as the lexical cues "about" and "do you remember" which serve to alert Lucinda to the imminent task of locating a certain topic in her cognitive system. Strategies such as this aid the addressee in orienting to a new topic. They are common at major topic shifts, and when absent, often result in the type of misunderstanding illustrated above. Within an established topic, they are rare, but their absence does not typically result in misunderstanding.

Excerpt 3: Walter 3A

We'd get that ^{3}kéel^2–   27.10

. . . .   27.11–28.1

You could shárpen it up — turn it around any shape you ^{3}wánted^2.   28.2

(you know) it just come in ^{3}chúnks^1 and you — ((1))

you could ^{2}cút it up — ^{2}stríp it up^2 'n. ((2))

Did you all ever make sórghum ^{3}táffy^3?   29

Huh?   29.1

Did you all ever make sórghum ^{3}cándy^3? ((2))   30

^{1}Yeah^2. Used to make sórghum ^{3}cándy^2.

These examples illustrate an important aspect of the interaction of cognitive systems in conversation. Since the two cognitive systems involved are distinct, they must constantly work, via the speech signal, to coordinate their notions of topic. LeRoy's use of various strategies to orient the interviewee to new topics suggests that he maintains an idea of the interviewee's cognitive status, i.e. what he knows and is thinking about at any given time, and is sensitive to that status as he introduces new topics and continues established ones.

Excerpt 4: Lu2A

Do you remémber mama anything about when Oklahóma became a státe?   1
Do you remember any of the tálk about it?

Oh of cóurse I re^{3}mémber^2 but^2 — ((2))

We 'uz all seem like ^{3}próud^1. ((5))

But Í don't remémber much about it áll. ((Chuckling))

You don't remémber — about reading any pápers or anything abóut it?   2

No-

3.5 Phenomenon 5: Retellings of personal experience

A particularly fascinating phenomenon captured in LeRoy's interviews involves the double tellings of single experiences. In Excerpts 5 and 6, Lucinda describes on two occasions roughly ten years apart a single experience from her early life. Such alternate tellings suggest a number of insights concerning the storage of the memory in Lucinda's cognitive system and its expression in conversation. Only a few of these will be mentioned here.[5]

First, observation of the two tellings in Excerpts 5 and 6 reveals Lucinda's sensitivity to LeRoy's cognitive state at the time. In the 1952 version, LeRoy's elicitation of the story (78) suggests that he is not familiar with it. In the 1960s version, in contrast, LeRoy's elicitation (94) makes clear that he has heard the story before. Lucinda's two versions show sensitivity to LeRoy's different states of knowledge. For example, in the 1952 version, Lucinda carefully describes for LeRoy the location of her mother's burial and the reason for that location (79.5–79.6). In the later version, she mentions the burial place in a subordinate clause (94.3) as a detail that she expects LeRoy to remember.

Second, marked differences in the organization of the two tellings and the disfluent delivery of each suggest that this memory is stored mainly in a non-linguistic sensory form which must be transformed into linguistic expression at each telling. The disfluencies can be attributed to the difficulty of finding adequate linguistic expression for this personal, ineffable, and according to LeRoy, rarely verbalized experience. In contrast, others of Lucinda's twice-told experiences, which we do not have space for here, are more similar to each other in expression and show fewer disfluencies. For such experiences, a linguistic encoding seems to have been worked out over numerous tellings. This linguistic encoding is itself stored, resulting in more similar tellings and also freeing up more processing capacity, resulting in fewer disfluencies.

---

5. See Meyer 1991, Chapter 5 for a more complete account including other examples.

Excerpt 5: Lu40 (Lucinda's salvation experience, 1952 version.)

((4)) Do you remember the- tíme that you were ^{2}sáved^3?	78
^{3}Oooohh- ^{2}yes^3. ((2))	.1
Where ^{3}wás it^2?	79
^{2}Well^2– ((4))	.1
Í ^{3}don't ^{1}know it ^{3}séem ^{1}likes kinda pe^{3}cúliar^2 – ((3))	.2
that it ^{3}háppened^1 that a ^{1}wáy^2–	.3
but uh-((5))	.4
whén they ^{3}búried ^{1}mother^2 they buried her up on our ^{3}pláce^1. ((1))	.5
We didn't háve no graveyard there ^{3}thén^2.	.6
That was down by- ^{2}(Cóllums)^3?	80
^{2}Yeah^3. ((6))	.1
And uh- Í'd been up to her ^{3}gráve^2 ⁻	.2
'n uh- I'd- I got ^{2}dówn^2 'n –	.3
'n I- I just ^{3}práyed^1.	.4
I don't know- ((1)) how ^{4}cóme^2 but ^{3}ányway^2 ⁻ ((2))	.5
I was up there by my^{3}sélf^1.	.6
'n as I was comin ^{2}báck^2 ⁻ ((3))	.7
from there – down there in the ^{3}pásture^1 – ((5))	.8
What'd you ^{3}féel^1 like?	81
^{2}Well^3 – Í ^{3}don't ^{1}know^2 it just ^{3}séem ^{1}like that – ((5))	.1
Thát's somethin' you can't hardly ^{3}téll ^{1}ísn't it^3? ((Chuckle))	.2
((Chuckle)) I guess it ^{3}is^1.	82
((Chuckle))	.1
It's pretty ^{3}wónderful ^{1}though^1 ^{3}ídn't it^2?	83
^{2}Yeah^3. ((3))	.1

Excerpt 6: Lu2A (Lucinda's salvation experience, 1960s version.)

I remember you téllin' one time bout when you were sáved. ((2))	94
What uh- do you remémber about ^{3}thát^1? ((1))	.1
Oh Í just felt like uh –	.2
I needed sómethin' (comin') –	.3

and I went to- óut to where momma was búried 'n –   .4

kneeled down in práyer.   .5

I thóught (there) where her héad was –   .6

but Í don't know whether – it was her héad or her [3]féet[1]. ((1))   .7

'N I – ((8))   .8

Go ahéad. ((2))   95

'N as I come back to the hóuse –   .1

séem like I can see them fenceposts nów.   .2

Everthing looked so góod to me. ((2))   .3

But I didn't know the Bíble or (quote it). ((9))   .4

4. Conclusion

As the preceding examples have shown, the application of cognitive network notions to the study of conversational data shows significant promise. It has potential both to advance cognitive linguistic theory, shedding new light on aspects of network organization, operation, and interaction, as well as to advance the study of conversation through offering network accountings for a variety of conversational phenomena. These include topic sequencing, topic coordination strategies, aspects of the form of retold experiences, and a number of conversational disfluencies and breakdowns.

Lamb's pioneering efforts have blended Hjelmslev's notion of relationships with the notion of cognition to produce a systematic and still fertile approach to understanding the mind and its workings. However, Lamb's work may best be understood not as an isolationist theory, but, in true Hjelmslevian fashion, in relationship to other ideas and goals, that is, as a strategic location in a network much larger than itself. The developing link between network theory and the study of conversation forms a promising portion of that growing network.

References

Chafe, Wallace. 1976. Givenness, contrastiveness, definiteness, subjects, topics and point of view. *Subject and Topic*, ed. by Charles N. Li, 25–56. New York: Academic Press.

Chafe, Wallace. 1980. The deployment of consciousness in the production of a narrative. *The Pear Stories: Cognitive, Cultural, and Linguistic Aspects of Narrative Production*, ed. by Wallace Chafe, 9–50. (*Advances in Discourse Processes,* Vol III). Norwood, New Jersey: Ablex.

Copeland, James E. and Philip W. Davis. 1980. A stratificational approach to discourse and other matters. *The Sixth LACUS Forum 1979*, ed. by Herbert Izzo, 255–263. Columbia South Carolina: Hornbeam Press.

Dell, Gary S., and Peter A. Reich. 1980. Slips of the tongue: The facts and a stratificational model. *Papers in Cognitive-Stratificational Linguistics*, ed. by James Copeland and Philip Davis, 19–34. Rice University Studies, vol. 66, no. 2. Houston: Rice University.

Fleming, Ilah. 1986. *Communication Analysis: A Stratificational Approach.* Unpublished Manuscript.

Fox, Barbara and Sandra Thompson. 1990. A discourse explanation of the grammar of relative clauses. *Language* 66: 297–316.

Jefferson, Gail. 1984. On stepwise transition from talk about a trouble to inappropriately next-positioned matters. *Structures of Social Action: Studies in Conversation Analysis*, ed. by J. Maxwell Atkinson and John Heritage, 191–222. Cambridge: Cambridge University Press.

Lamb, Sydney. 1973. Stratificational linguistics as a basis for machine translation. *Readings in Stratificational Linguistics* ed. by Adam Makkai and David Lockwood, 34–59. University, Alabama: University of Alabama Press.

Lamb, Sydney. 1984. Constructing the content of a text. Paper presented at the 1984 Rice Symposium on Linguistics and Semiotics: Discourse Semantics and Text Semantics.

Lockwood, David. 1987. Clitics in a stratificational model of language. *The Thirteenth LACUS Forum 1986*, ed. by Ilah Fleming, 236–245. Lake Bluff Illinois: LACUS.

Meyer, Cynthia. 1991. *Talk of Times Past: On the Interaction of Cognitive Systems in Conversation.* Unpublished Ph.D. dissertation, Rice University.

Pomerantz, Anita. 1978. Compliment responses: Notes on the co-operation of multiple constraints. Schenkein 1978: 79–112.

Reich, Peter. 1985. Unintended puns. *The Eleventh LACUS Forum 1984*, ed. by Robert A. Hall, Jr., 314–322. Columbia, South Carolina: Hornbeam Press.

Sacks, Harvey, Emanuel A. Schegloff, and Gail Jefferson. 1974. A simplest systematics for the organization of turn-taking for conversation. *Language* 50: 696–735. Reprinted in Schenkein, 1978: 7–55.

Schegloff, Emmanuel, and Harvey Sacks. 1973. Opening up closings. *Semiotica*,
    8: 289–327.
Schenkein, Jim. (ed.). 1978. *Studies in the Organization of Conversational
    Interaction.* New York: Academic Press.
Thompson, Sandra. 1990. Discourse and grammar. *Text* 10: 113–115.

About the author

*Cynthia Ford Meyer received her Ph.D. in linguistics from Rice University in 1991.
Her dissertation, written under the direction of Syd Lamb, applied his ideas on the
individual cognitive system to conversational data, viewing conversation as the
ongoing interaction of cognitive systems. Prior to her studies at Rice, she received
a B. A. in Spanish and a B. S. in Education from Texas Christian University, and
taught for five years in public elementary schools. She remained at Rice after her
doctorate as a visiting lecturer and scholar until the birth of her son in 1992. She
is presently a homemaker in The Woodlands, Texas.*

CHAPTER 17

Some Stratificational Insights Concerning the English Noun Phrase

David G. Lockwood
Michigan State University

1. Introduction

One of Sydney Lamb's most essential contributions to linguistics has been the extension of the difference of "levels" applied by some Neo-Bloomfieldian linguists (e.g. Hockett 1961) to distinctions between phonology and morphology/syntax from such a simple bistratal model to apply to a larger number of strata within linguistic structure. Though in Lamb's own work the number of strata has varied from six (1966) down to just two (personal communication, 1970s), it has usually included at least a distinction between semology — the structure of linguistic meaning — and one or more properly grammatical strata. The present paper shows how a separation of semology from lexology (roughly equatable with a classical conception of syntax) can aid in the solution of problems in the analysis of the noun phrase in English.

2. Point of Departure

Anyone studying the English noun phrase is fortunate in having available a very thorough empirically-based study by Peter Fries (1970). Although its author states that "it does not go into detail sufficient to make it an exhaustive treatment of the English noun phrase" (vii), it is still the most thorough study of the subject known to the present author, and is therefore capable of serving as an admirable point of departure for further studies like the present one.

Using a tagmemic model, Fries summarizes his analysis by referring to nine constituents. Of these, only the Head is obligatory, and four of the remaining eight, all referred to as "modifiers", are repeatable. Figure 1 presents the essentials of this treatment, using Fries's own terms, but cast into the relational network notation of stratificational linguistics. Here the optionality of a constituent is indicated by a small circle on the line leading to its label, a notational device introduced in Reich 1968. The indefinite repeatability of a constituent is shown by the coordination element, represented by a upper semicircle, as first presented in Lamb 1966.

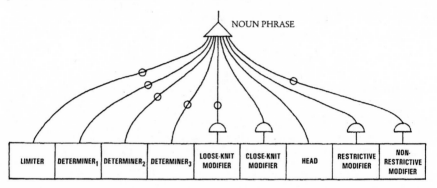

Figure 1.   *A stratificational recasting of P. H. Fries's tagmemic treatment of the English noun phrase*

The manifestations of various functions labeled on this diagram are summarized in the Appendix, which is also based on Fries's chart and examples presented later. The material in this figure and Appendix will serve as the basis for the discussion which follows.

3.   Stratificational Reinterpretation

A preliminary revision of Fries's analysis is given in Figure 2. This figure differs from Figure 1 in a number of ways. Some of these are purely terminological, but one is more essential.

The terminological differences involve the names chosen for several of the functional constituents. Fries used the term "determiner" for three successive functions, distinguishing them by numbers in the order of their potential occurrence.

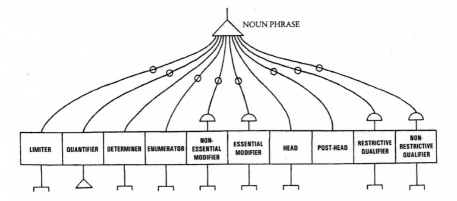

NOUN PHRASE

| LIMITER | QUANTIFIER | DETERMINER | ENUMERATOR | NON-ESSENTIAL MODIFIER | ESSENTIAL MODIFIER | HEAD | POST-HEAD | RESTRICTIVE QUALIFIER | NON-RESTRICTIVE QUALIFIER |

Figure 2.   *A preliminary revision of Fries's analysis from Figure 1*

Here the terms QUANTIFIER, DETERMINER, and ENUMERATOR are suggested as more distinctive and useful labels. Rather than terming the pre-head modifiers "looseknit" and "closeknit", it is suggested that we might rather term them the NON-ESSENTIAL MODIFIER and the ESSENTIAL MODIFIER, respectively.[1] Finally, following the usage of Halliday and Hasan (1976: 39–43), the term QUALIFIER is adopted for each of the post-head adjuncts.

The more essential revision beyond Fries involves the number of constituents recognized: an additional constituent, termed the POST-HEAD, has been added between the HEAD and the RESTRICTIVE QUALIFIER. This additional position is needed in a stratificational account to deal with the fact that some of Fries's "looseknit modifiers" occur at least partly after the HEAD as shown by the examples in Table 1.

Table 1. *Examples of discontinuous "looseknit" modifiers (Fries 1970: 64)*

(a)	an easy dial to read
(b)	the larger machine of the two
(c)	the most difficult problem to solve

1. Further alternatives suggested in the work of Halliday and Hasan (1976) are EPITHET and CLASSIFIER. These terms have the advantage of brevity, but they have not been adopted here because the latter is so frequently used for a rather different function in the grammars of some languages, this being probably the most widespread use of the term among general linguists.

This difference of treatment stems essentially from differences between the models being used. Tagmemics has long emphasized that its "slots" are general functions not based purely on matters of position.[2] So the same slot does not have to be in the same physical position in every occurrence. Data of this sort certainly amply illustrates this point. The post-head phrases are certainly semantically most immediately associated with the adjectives preceding the heads. So following the tagmemic view, Fries posited just a single slot with a potentially discontinuous manifestation. The stratificational alternative set forth here does not deny the unity postulated in such an analysis. Its account of the matter, however, places the unity in the semology, where the realizate of *to read* (in example (a) of Table 1), for instance, would be subordinated directly to that of *easy*, with the whole then functioning as a semological attribute of the realizate of *dial*. The actual arrangements of all words, however, must be treated in the lexology in the type of stratificational model used here. For this reason, the additional position is necessary, since neither transformational operations nor quasi-transformational operations such as tagmemic "permutations" (Longacre 1964: 27–34) are found in stratificational models.

4.   Further Refinement

Another aspect of Fries's "looseknit modifier" not considered in relation to Figure 2 is the so-called "permutation" of the modifiers with Enumerators (Fries's "Determiner 3"). This is said to indicate a kind of emphasis, as illustrated in the data of Table 2. In the relational network model, such significant differences of order are matters of SPECIFICATIONAL ANATAXIS (see Lockwood 1977). They are handled by introducing an option in the syntax which is controlled by a factor of emphasis in the semology. The configuration needed in this instance is shown in Figure 3. Fries also notes a further restriction on the selection of the marked (emphatic) order: it can only be taken with simple modifiers like those in the examples. Most likely this matter could be handled in the semology. It would involve presenting the emphatic element as an alternative

---

2. See, for instance, the discussion of tagmatic slots versus tagmemic slots in Section 7.321 of Pike 1967 (218–222). It is emphasized that physical order is a rigid property of a tagmatic slot, but not of a tagmemic one.

to further attribution. Other cases of such meaningful differences of order can be treated analogously in a stratificational model.

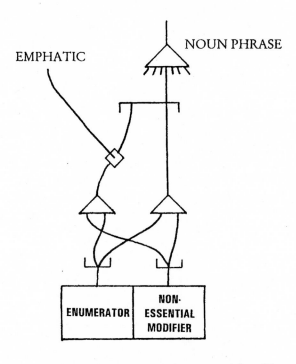

Figure 3.   *Alternative orders of enumerator and non-essential modifier*

Table 2. *Emphatic order of "looseknit" modifiers before enumerators (Fries 1970: 67)*

| (a) | the bíg three balls |
| (b) | The gréen six balloons |

5.   The Determiner Position and its Further Relations

5.1 *Optional versus obligatory determiner*

It is not altogether clear whether the determiner should be considered an obligatory constituent in the English noun phrase. On the surface, it is of course clear that not all noun phrases contain an overt word of the determiner class. At the same time, it appears that a phrase headed by a singular, common count noun must have an overt determiner, so instead of **tree, *horse, *old man* we would find rather *a horse, a tree, an old man*, if no more specific determiner were appropriate. Since we can get the plurals of the above examples as perfectly good noun phrases, the hypothesis arises that the zero determiner is in fact the plural of the indefinite article. On this basis, we can set up the determiner as an obligatory constituent with common nouns and provide for the zero realization of the indefinite article in plural contexts and in the case of mass usage.

The obligatory nature of the determiner has already been shown in Figure 2. To get the zero forms in a stratificational description we can provide alternation in the lexemic alternation pattern for the indefinite article lexeme ^{L}/a(n)/, as suggested in Figure 4, conditioned by the contexts in which the head either is plural or is a mass noun.

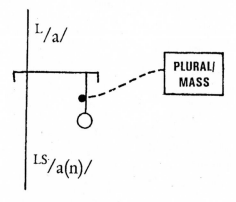

Figure 4.   *Zero as an alternate form of the definite article*

In the case of mass nouns, it is of course true that virtually any mass noun can be treated as a count noun, in which case they convey an extra element of meaning: forms like *a sand, those milks* can be paraphrased as *a kind of sand, those kinds of milk*. We can get contrasts, furthermore, in such cases as *They sell good milk* (mass) and *They sell a good milk* (count). This sort of contrast can best be clarified by reference to the semology: we can recognize that entities such as milk are unmarkedly mass in English, but in special circumstances such entities can be combined with a sememe of countability. In the lexology, we could then say that ^{S}/milk/ alone is realized as a lexeme ^{L}/milk$_M$/, classified as a mass noun, while in combination with ^{S}/COUNTABLE/ the same sememe is realized as ^{L}/milk$_C$/, classified as a count noun. Below the lexotactics the separate ^{L}/milk$_M$/ and ^{L}/milk$_C$/ would be realized as a single lexemic sign ^{LS}/milk/. When the need to apply a similar analysis to a whole class of sememes and corresponding lexemes is considered, however, the same essential information can be captured more economically via the structure in Figure 5. Here lexemes of a class including ^{L}/milk/ are treated as mass nouns if unmarked, but as count nouns if the sememe they realize is accompanied by ^{S}/COUNTABLE/. The latter is realized not as a separate lexeme, but as a specification to the lexotactics affecting whether the mass or count structure is taken.[3] The count/mass distinction seen here, furthermore, would form part of the lexotactically-based conditions for *a(n)* versus zero as allolexes of the indefinite article lexeme ^{L}/a/.[4]

This kind of treatment is further complicated, however, by the fact that there is another candidate for the plural/mass form of the indefinite article, namely *some*, i.e. the unaccented from of this word, as in *sŏme books, sŏme water, sŏme butter*. This unaccented *sŏme*, furthermore, is capable of contrasting with the zero form mentioned above. To see the evidence for this contrast, we can consider one of the important functions of the English indefinite article, that of introducing a new participant into the discourse. In introducing a joke or anecdote, for instance, an English speaker might use the phrase *Once there was a _____* to introduce a participant in the situation being narrated. In such a context as this, as summarized in Table 3, *sŏme* rather than zero would be the determiner used in either a plural or a mass context. So based on this data, it would seem proper to consider this unaccented *sŏme* rather than zero to be the form of the indefinite

---

3. This phenomenon may be termed SPECIFICATIONAL REALIZATION, to use a term introduced in Lockwood 1977.

4. The present discussion does not purport to be a complete treatment of the classification of English nouns in relation to the use of determiners. A classic example of a fuller classification is found in Chapter 12 of Bloomfield's *Language* (1933: 204–205).

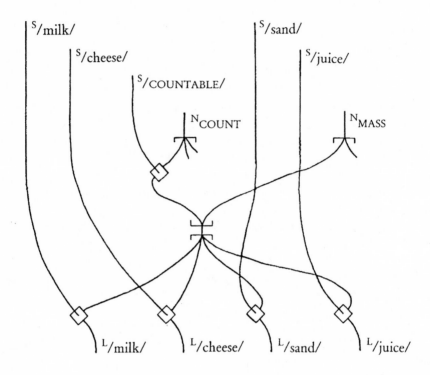

Figure 5.   *Sememes in relation to lexology for unmarked mass entities optionally relatable to count nouns in unmarked usages*

article in plural and mass contexts. The fact remains, however, that *a(n)* is in complementation with both *sŏme* and zero, and in some contexts it seems we could use either of the plural/mass variants with equal ease. Consider Table 4, parts 1 and 2. Examples 1 b/c and 2 a/b might be seen as evidence of free variation between *sŏme* and zero. Certainly the members within each pair cited mean approximately the same thing, though many observers may feel that there is at least a subtle distinction between such examples.

Table 3. *Examples of phrases introducing participants*

PARTICIPANTS EXPRESSED BY COUNT NOUNS

Singular
a.   Once there was a farmer.
b.   Once there was a fierce wolf.
PLURAL
c.   Once there were sŏme farmers.
d.   Once there were sŏme fierce wolves.

PARTICIPANTS EXPRESSED BY MASS NOUNS
e.   Once there was sŏme grain.
f.   Once there was sŏme pure gold.

In the examples at 3 b/c in Table 4, we can, in fact see a solid case for contrast. These two utterances would typically occur in distinct contexts, not at all in free variation. 3c assumes that the hearer knows what unicorns are and the speaker is asserting the past existence of particular individuals of that species. 3b, on the other hand, asserts the existence of the general category of unicorns at some time in the past. It assumes that the hearer either (1) has never heard of unicorns or (2) does not believe that such a species ever existed.

Table 4. *The contrast between zero articles and the unstressed* **some**

(1a)   There is a mouse in the basement
(1b)   There are mice in the basement.
(1c)   There are some mice in the basement.
(2a)   There is water in the basement.
(2b)   There is some water in the basement.
(3a)   Once there was a unicorn.
(3b)   Once there were unicorns.
(3c)   Once there were some unicorns.

As it turns out, this characterization fits very well with two distinct contexts identified for the indefinite article in the work of Copeland and Davis (1981), in connection with what they term "identifiability". This work used a stratificational relational network model of human cognition to distinguish various discourse contexts. Within the framework, it established a hierarchy of identifiability from GIVEN to NOVEL (see Table 5), which governs the use of pronouns versus more explicit expressions with definite or indefinite articles in referring to the participants associated with particular events. This scheme, in fact, identifies two separate situations for the use of the indefinite article. In the situation labeled NOVEL, the whole class of entities, termed the DOMAIN, not to speak of the individual members of this class, is assumed to be unknown to the hearer. In the situation labeled NEW, however, the domain is assumed to be known to the hearer, though not conscious at the time of utterance, and only the particular representatives of the domain are treated as unknown.

Table 5. *Type of identifiability (adapted from Copeland and Davis 1981, Table 1, p. 128.)*

	Domain		Particular		
NOVEL	Non-Ident	(Non-Consc)	Non-Ident	(Non-Consc)	*a(n)*
NEW	Ident	Non- Consc	Non-Ident	(Non-Consc)	*a(n)*
COMPUTABLE	Ident (SM)*	Non-Consc	Ident (SM)	Non-Consc	*the*
RECOVERABLE	Ident (EM)*	Non-Consc	Ident (EM)	Non-Consc	*the*
SOME	(Ident)	Consc	Non-Ident	(Non-Consc)	*one/some*
GIVEN	(Ident)	Consc	(Ident)	Consc	*pronoun*

In relation to the unicorn examples (Table 4. 3), then, it seems that we can say that English has two indefinite articles, one appropriate to NOVEL contexts, with a zero form in plural and mass contexts, and a second appropriate to NEW contexts, with *sŏme* as its plural/mass form. This situation is diagrammed in Figure 6. This treatment does not imply, it should be noted, that the lexemes labeled ^{L} /some/ and ^{L} /a/ relate exclusively to NEW or NOVEL contexts. It allows for the possibility that other usages might be revealed by deeper investigations. This is indicated by the upward OR nodes below the labels NEW and NOVEL. The difference between zero and *sŏme* already observed in Table 4 (1b/c and 2 a/b) may, after fuller investigation, reveal one such alternative function.

All of this further implies, of course, that such a phrase as *Once there was an X* can be ambiguous between the NOVEL and the NEW context. Consider, for instance, the sentence *Once there was a king of France.* If one says this to someone for whom it is assumed to be NOVEL, its meaning would correspond to the activation of a new domain, connecting with such known domains as 'KING′' and 'FRANCE′'. But addressed to someone assumed to have sufficient education to know the institution of royalty did indeed exist in past periods of French history, it would rather suggest that the speaker intends to say something about some particular individual who held that title, so it would be NEW rather than NOVEL. Most commonly, the following context would make it clear which meaning was intended. So if this clause were to be followed by something such as *but royal institutions have been abolished there for over a century now* the NOVEL interpretation is clearly indicated. A different follow-up, such as *his name was Louis the Fat*, on the other hand, would indicate the NEW interpretation.

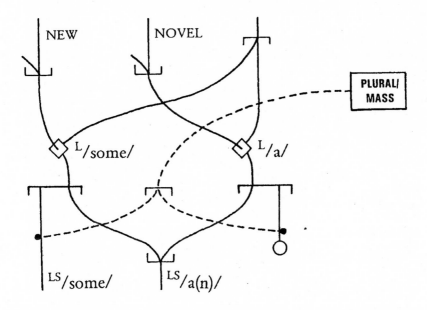

Figure 6.   *The two indefinite article lexemes of English*

In view of these considerations, one amendment to Copeland and Davis's discussion of NOVEL versus NEW seems to be warranted. According to their discussion (1980: 127), in a NOVEL context the listener is directed to activate both a domain and a particular characterized by it. While this may be true in some contexts, the use of *There was once a King of France* to merely assert the existence of royal institutions in that country at some past time does not seem to require one to go on and speak of any particular individual who held that office. So it appears that the distinctive part of this difference involves whether a new domain is to be established (as with NOVEL) or not (as with NEW).

This leads to the conclusion that the determiner category is lexotactically obligatory in the ordinary English noun phrase. The apparent exceptions involve the zero realization of the indefinite article ^{L}/a/ in various contexts.[5]

5.2 *The expression of possession*

Next, we need to consider the expression of possession, as in the data given in Table 6.[6] The basic observation to be drawn from this material is that such expressions as *John's* and *my* in the determiner position are semologically related to the corresponding post-head expressions such as *of John's* and *of mine*. Fries treated these latter as "definite possessive phrases" occurring in his Restrictive Modifier position — what has here been termed the Restrictive Qualifier. The conclusion here is that each correlated pair of such expressions would have the same semological realizate, a construction combining a possessive sememe ^{S}/Poss/ with some kind of entity sememe. Such a construction would then be functioning semologically as an attribute to some other entity, in these examples, ^{S}/house/.

Table 6. *Examples of determiners and possession expressions*

(a)	John's house	(a′)	my house
(b)	a house of John's	(b′)	a house of mine
(c)	some house of John's	(c′)	some house of mine
(d)	this house of John's	(d′)	this house of mine
(e)	that house of John's	(e′)	that house of mine
(f)	any house of John's	(fc')	any house of mine

Based on this data, we can say that the non-possessive forms of the determiner take precedence over the possessive ones. Then, since the determiner is not a repeatable element of the noun phrase, a possessive expression combined with a determiner has to come in a different position, namely in that for the

5. For an alternative view, arguing that the zero is not the plural of the indefinite article, see Carlson 1977. Thanks are due to Professor Barbara Abbott of Michigan State University for drawing the author's attention to this paper.

6. The semantics of possession is beyond the scope of the present study. It is obvious (as pointed out in Fleming 1988:10, for instance) that what is traditionally termed "possession" may involve various real-world relations, including ownership, temporary custody, kinship, whole-to-part relation, and others.

restrictive qualifier. Figure 7 sketches the general situation for such possessive expressions, but it omits the realizational details needed for the pronominal forms, with their distinctions between *my* versus *mine*, *your* versus *yours*, and so on. This treatment shows a shared portion ending in the enclitic postposition '*s*. This element is taken to directly realize the possessive sememe. The basic construction is shown as occurring either in the determiner position, or in the restrictive qualifier position. When in the latter position, it is obligatorily preceded by the determined preposition *of*. Since the determiner element is obligatory according to this treatment, a signal for one of the possessives will have to be realized in the determiner position if there is no semological signal corresponding to one of the non-possessive determiners. When a non-possessive is signaled, on the other hand, it will take precedence over the possessive, and then the latter will have to be realized in the restrictive qualifier position.

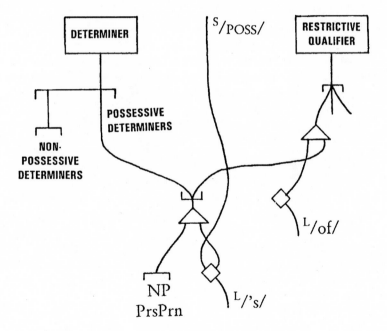

Figure 7.   *Possessive expressions in determiner and restrictive qualifier positions*

At first glance, such examples as those in Table 7 seem to be counter-examples to the claim made in connection with Figure 7, since they have no determiner, but they still have the possession expression in the restrictive qualifier position. When the determiner is treated as syntactically obligatory, as in Section 5.1, however, these examples fit right in, because the plural heads will condition the zero form of the indefinite article. It simply means that the possessive in the restrictive qualifier position without an overt article is treated as a case of the zero realization of ^{L}/a/, showing that this zero element can force the possessive phrase into the secondary position just as much as an overtly realized determiner can.

Table 7. *Possessive qualifiers without overt determiners*

(a)	friends of Uncle Jack's
(b)	servants of theirs
(c)	dogs of our neighbors'
(d)	interesting ideas of hers

It should also be mentioned that the occurrence of the simple definite article *the* with the postposed possessive seems to be rather restricted. Consider the examples in the Table 8. The (a) and (b) examples are readily acceptable, but example (c) with the definite article seems strange outside some special context. On the other hand, such an example as (d) seems perfectly fine. The crucial difference between (c) and (d) seems to be the occurrence of further qualification in the latter example, making it precise just what friend is meant. Otherwise, (c) would more likely be paraphrased as (e), and (f) seems to be a virtual synonym of (d). Whatever significant restrictions are operative here can be treated as a matter of semology. They would not belong to the syntax of the noun phrase itself, which is here treated in the lexology.

Table 8. *Data for restrictions on the use of **the** with possessive qualifiers*

(a)	A friend of mine visited.
(b)	This friend of mine visited.
(c)	?The friend of mine visited.
(d)	The friend of mine from Chicago visited.
(e)	My friend visited.
(f)	My friend from Chicago visited.

5.3 *All* and *Both*

One additional phenomenon concerning the noun phrase is exemplified by the data in Table 9. Semologically, it appears that *both* can be reasonably viewed as a portmanteau realization of the sememes ^{S}/all/ and ^{S}/two/, so that the word takes the place of the non-occurring phrase **all two*. Figure 8 diagrams the essential situation. The absence of an overt article in (e) and (e') simply reflects the zero form of ^{L}/a/.

Table 9. *Data for the occurrence of* **all** *and* **both**

(a)	all the seven heros	(a')	both the heros
(b)	all those ten reports	(b')	both those reports
(c)	all these many books	(c')	both these books
(d)	all the ladies	(d')	both the ladies
(e)	all four little girls	(e')	both little girls

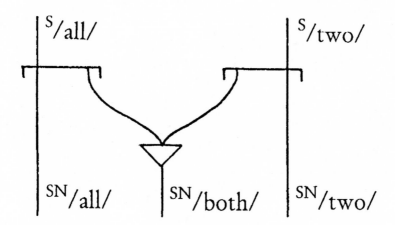

Figure 8.   *A sememic portmanteau analysis relating* **both** *to* **all** *and* **two**

It should be noted in this connection that *all* and *both* can also be used with a different construction involving the preposition *of.* The items in Table 10, for instance, are essentially paraphrases of the corresponding items in Table 9. Syntactically, however, these phrases have *all* or *both* as heads with the prepositional phrases as qualifiers. Semolexemically, on the other hand, they would have to be closely related. The exact nature of any semological difference between these close paraphrases is not, however, evident at present.

Table 10. *Data for the occurrence of* **all of** *and* **both of**

(a″)	all of the seven heros	(a‴)	both of the heros
(b″)	all of those ten reports	(b‴)	both of those reports
(c″)	all of these many books	(c‴)	both of these books
(d″)	all of the ladies	(d‴)	both of the ladies

6.   Conclusion

This paper has attempted to demonstrate the value of Lamb's distinction between semology and lexology (as discussed particularly in Lamb 1964) as an aid to our understanding of various phenomena related to the English noun phrase. It further demonstrates how the stratificationally inclined linguist can profitably use material developed in other frameworks as a starting point for further refinements. This means that stratificational models are not so completely distinct from various other models to rule out profitable interactions between their proponents and the proponents of these other views.

Acknowledgments

The original version of this paper was presented in April of 1984 at a colloquium sponsored by the Applied Linguistics Research Working Group of the English Department of Glendon College, York University in Toronto, Canada. A revised version was presented three times during 1985: in April at the International Linguistic Center of the Summer Institute of Linguistics and also at Rice University, and in November at Michigan State University. Thanks are due to all those who offered comments at these presentations.

Appendix: A Summary of the manifestation of noun-phrase elements according to the analysis of Fries 1970.

Function	Manifestation Class	Examples
limiter	(limiting adverb)	only, just, even
determiner 1	quantity phrase	all, almost half, practically all, exactly one tenth
determiner 2	indefinite article	a
	definite phrase	the, that very, these
	possessor phrase	my, your, his, John's own, my own wife's brother's wife's
determiner 3	cardinal numeral phrase	over seven thousand, at least six, sixty three, up to three
	quantifier phrase — count	very many, awfully few, too few to be of any use
	quantifier phrase — mass	little, very much, too little to help, as much as we could carry
	number words	several, most
	numeral comparison phrase	far fewer, very many more than we expected, a lot more than Bill
looseknit modifier	adjective phrase	green, almost rectangular, entirely different, generally very good
	nominal adjective$_2$	three dimensional, peaceful, deep rooted, religious
	-*ing* phrase	leading, rapidly growing, continuing, existing
	-*en* phrase	unwritten, then unforeseen, now lost, constantly heard, dreaded
	material noun phrase	iron, high carbon steel, cut stone, beach glass, plastic
	manner adjective phrase	steady, generally very slow, second biggest, truly big
	adverbial adjective	extreme, near, comparative, particular, utter, perfect
	adjective word	former, present, weekly, daily, certain, particular, main

Function	Manifestation Class	Examples
closeknit modifier	restricted noun phrase	car (doors), three ring notebook (paper), consumer product (line)
	denominal adjective	ballistic (missiles), nuclear (treaty), criminal (lawyer)
	ing-word	Breathing (organs), conditioning (shampoo), jamming (transmitters)
	en-word	airborne (navigation)
head	common noun	boy, girls, location, butters, bread
	restricted noun phrase	(labor day) traffic accidents, (Bendix) automated radar
	complex noun expression $_{that}$	fact that he left early, philosophy that adults have to do dull jobs
	complex noun expression $_{to}$	duty to help them out, determination to live, ability to argue
	complex noun expression $_{of}$	stimulus of discomfort, city of Ephesus, idea of the reactor
	semipartitive expression$_1$	number of identifiable specimens, interior of the body
	close appositive phrase	carrier Wasp. opera Faust, poet Burns, Authors Hemingway and Steinbeck
	title phrase	President Adams, Doctor J. Bronowski, King George, Mister Smith
restrictive modifier	adjective phrase	very easy to solve, generally subject to the will of the people
	locational phrase	right here, just below the water level, right up above all of us
	non-locational prepositional phrase	after my own heart, from the Franks, of airbreathing animals
	definite possessive phrase	of John's, of theirs, of the old man's
	-ing phrase	originating elsewhere, parading through the streets
	-en phrase$_{passive}$	thus measured in the head, partly derived from the skin

Function	Manifestation Class	Examples
(restrictive modifier, continued)	*-en* phrase$_{active}$	(economics) come to life, (teacher) newly arrived from Germany
	active infinitive phrase	(children) to succeed him, (delights) to be found there
	relative clause	(man) that came, (time) when he knocked the helmet off a policeman
non-restrictive modifier	relative clause	(estates,) which pass to the eldest son, (children,) whose father died yesterday
	-en phrase$_{passive}$	(model,) shown above, (brain-power,) proven since 1888
	-en phrase$_{active}$	(man,) finally come to life, (buffalo,) vanished from the plains
	-ing phrase	(man,) standing in the water, (plane,) exceeding all requirements
	locational phrase	(reference,) just here on page 323, (man,) on the right
	non-locational prepositional phrase	(article,) by A. H. Benade, (dials,) for clocks
	adjective phrase	(people,) deeply interested in our welfare, (ore,) not very good
	extended noun phrase	(retina,) the receptor organ for light, (transepts,) or cross aisles

References

Bloomfield, Leonard. 1933. *Language*. New York: Holt, Rinehart, & Winston.

Carlson, Greg N. 1977. A unified analysis of the English bare plural. *Linguistics and Philosophy* 1.413–457.

Copeland, James E. and Philip W. Davis. 1981. Identifiability and focal attention in an integrated view of discourse. *The Seventh LACUS Forum, 1980* ed. by James E. Copeland and Phillip W. Davis, 122–137. Columbia, South Carolina: Hornbeam Press.

Fleming, Ilah. 1988. *Communication Analysis: A Stratificational Approach. Volume II: A Field Guide For Communication Situation, Semantic, and Morphemic Analysis*. Dallas: Summer Institute of Linguistics.

Fries, Peter H. 1970. *Tagmeme Sequences in the English Noun Phrase*. (SIL publications in linguistics and related fields, No. 36.) Norman, Oklahoma: Summer Institute of Linguistics

Halliday, M. A. K. and Ruqaiya Hasan. 1976. *Cohesion in English*. (English language series, no. 9.) London: Longman.

Hockett, Charles F. 1961. Linguistic elements and their relations. *Language* 37.29–53.

Lamb, Sydney M. 1964. The sememic approach to structural semantics. *American Anthropologist* 66:3, Part 2.57–78.

Lamb, Sydney M. 1966. *Outline of Stratificational Grammar*. Washington, D.C.: Georgetown University Press.

Lockwood, David G. 1977. Anatactic relations in grammar and phonology. *Papers from the Annual Meeting of the Michigan Linguistic Society, October 15, 1976*. Ann Arbor: University of Michigan Papers in Linguistics, pp. 35–47.

Longacre, Robert E. 1964. *Grammar Discovery Procedures*. (Janua linguarum, series minor, 33.) The Hague: Mouton.

Pike, Kenneth L. 1967. *Language in Relation to a Unified Theory of the Structure of Human Behavior*. (Janua linguarum, series major, No. 24.) The Hague: Mouton.

Reich, Peter A. 1968. *Symbols, Relations, and Structural Complexity*. Linguistic automation project report, May. Yale University.

About the author

David G. Lockwood is Professor of Linguistics at Michigan State University, where he has taught since 1966. His Ph.D. is from the University of Michigan, where he first met Syd Lamb, taking his Stratificational Grammar course at the 1965 Linguistic Institute. He began his own stratificational courses at Michigan State in 1968, leading to his 1972 textbook **Introduction to Stratificational Linguistics,** *which drew heavily on Lamb's advice. Most of his subsequent publications, including his 1993 textbook* **Morphological Analysis and Description: A Realizational Approach** *are based on some kind of stratificational model.*

CHAPTER 18

Some Peculiar Adjectives in the English Nominal Group

Peter H. Fries

Central Michigan University and Hangzhou University

1. Introduction

When I met Syd Lamb some 30 years ago, I was just embarking on an analysis of the English nominal group (later published in Fries 1970b). Now, some thirty years later, I am in the process of returning to the analysis of the English nominal group, and thought it might be fitting to submit a portion of this present analysis to a volume of papers collected in his honor.

A great deal of work has been devoted to the description of the English nominal group, ranging from the classic major grammars of Jespersen, Kruisinga and Poutsma to more modern works of people such as Halliday (Halliday (1985), Halliday and Hasan (1976), and Kress (1976)), Huddleston (1984), Jackendoff (1977), Quirk et al. (1985), and others. Leonard Newell (endorsed by Sydney Lamb and published in Lamb (1966)) used the stratificational model to describe this part of English grammar. It is, perhaps, not surprising that considerable fundamental agreement has developed concerning the basic outlines of the structure of the nominal group, but that this agreement is accompanied by significant areas of disagreement. Let me take five analyses (one is presented in Figure 1, and four are presented in Table 1 A-D) as representative of several major strands of recent work.[1]

---

1. Each of these charts may be taken as representing the work of several authors. Thus, Bache [1978] presents a model which is quite similar to that described in Quirk et al. [1985]. One interesting strand of work which is not represented in these charts is the approach taken by R. M. W. Dixon (1991). In this work Dixon categorizes adjectives according to certain semantic and grammatical criteria and

Table 1. *Models of the English Noun Phrase*

A. Newell* 1966

Determiner	Ordinal Number	other	Adj₁	Adj₂	N	Post N Mod	Rel
John's					hat		
a			great big		tube		
about six					feet		
the	first			large	lizards		that we found
any		other			treefrog		that pops up
the					class	of that Mr. Donello	

B. Halliday (1976 and 1985):

Deictic			Numerative		Epithet		Classifier	Thing	Qualifier
Pre-Deictic	Deictic	Post-Deictic	Ordering	Quantifying	Interpersonal	Ideational	Classifier	Thing	Qualifier
both	those			two	splendid	old	electric	trains	with pantographs
	the		first	two				people	to come
	a	certain			old			man	

* This representation of Newell's analysis is my interpretation of certain aspects of his diagram and discussion on pages 78–82.

C.   Quirk, Greenbaum, Leech and Svartvik (1985)

Determinative			Modification Zones				Head	PostModifier		
Predeterminers	Central Determiners	Post Determiners	Precentral	Central	Post-Central	Pre-Head		Appositive	Restrictive	Non-Restrictive
	the						news	that the team had won		
	this		first	important	long	French	novel			which was read in this course
all	this				costly	social	security			
	a		certain		grey	church	tower		poking up through the trees	
	the	first					people		to come	

D.   Huddleston (1984)

Determiners			Modifier	Head	Complement	Modifier	Peripheral-dependent
I	II	III					
all	her	many	good	ideas			
	a few			remarks			
	the	few		remarks			
all	the			girls		with red hair	which he made
	the			destruction	of Carthage		

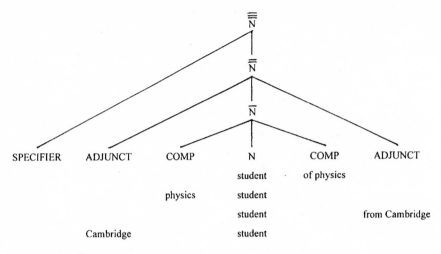

Figure 1. $\bar{X}$ analysis of the structure of the noun phrase

First, it is clear that there is general agreement that the structure of the nominal group should be described in terms of its functions.[2] The various

---

then uses this categorization to predict the normal ordering of adjectives within the noun phrase. This approach resembles the old order class approach taken by Hill, Chatman and others in that it is claimed that certain adjectives appear in a certain order in the English noun phrase. The approach differs, however, in that the basis for categorizing the adjectives is at heart a semantic basis, not simply a formal one (indeed, the ordering of adjectives does not play a significant role in Dixon's justification for his classes. The result is that his classes are at heart functional classes, but the functions are lexically determined on the basis of the meanings of the individual adjectives. I have ignored his work in this chapter, since he does not have much to say about the group of words which are the focus of this chapter.

2. Quirk et al. are somewhat ambiguous about how they wish readers to understand their wording. They divide modifiers into what they call "pre-modification zones". I believe they choose the term zone with the express purpose of indicating that the boundaries between the various modification zones are not definite or easy to locate. The inventive reader may also infer that they mean to imply that words may shift between zones in various uses. Thus a word such as *nervous* belongs in the Prehead zone in its most transparent sense (as in *nervous systems*), but belongs with the central adjectives in a phrase such as *nervous people*. One consequence of their use of the word *zone*, however, is to de-emphasize the functional nature of the distinctions they make. The use of the term *zone* as well as the consistent mention of position in their descriptions of the modification zones (*central, pre central, pre head*) emphasizes the relative order of the zones, and de-emphasizes their different functional natures. In spite of their consistent de-emphasis of function in their description, I believe that their concept of zone is basically a functional one.

columns in each table and the end points on the branches in the tree diagram all have functional implications.[3] Thus, all of these linguists are able to treat different occurrences of the same word in different ways provided that they see that the word functions differently. Thus the word *certain* in Examples 1 i-iii could be considered to function in different ways, despite the fact that in each case it is an adjective.

1.   i.   who is this E. Andrews on the **'certain'** list?
         ii.   ... the bed that sagged in a **certain** place
        iii.   If an evil which is certain and extensive and immediate may rarely be compensated for by a problematic, speculative, future good, by the same token, not every present, **certain**, and immediate good (or lesser evil) that may have to be done will be outweighed by a problematic, speculative, and future evil.

One can see from Figure 1 and Table 1 that these grammarians all distinguish between the determiners and the modifiers. In addition, most of these analyses explicitly describe at least three sorts of determiners, while they may only describe one pre-modifier and one post modifier. Some similarities of analysis are, in fact, concealed. Thus, Halliday seems to be the only linguist who posits only one post modifier in the nominal group. However, he discusses non-restrictive modifiers (the equivalent of Huddleston's Peripheral-dependents) as hypotactic clauses in clause complexes, thus even he distinguishes between the two types of roles which Huddleston describes as (post) modifier and peripheral dependent.

     Other differences in the analyses are real.[4] Thus, Halliday finds two functions, Post Deictic, and Ordering Numerative, which do not appear in the Huddleston or Jackendoff analyses. Quirk et al. agree with Halliday that addition-

---

3. The tree in Figure 1 represents my reinterpretation of features of the analyses presented by Jackendoff 1977, and Radford 1988, and is derived from their work. These linguists do not generally put names for functions (e.g. Complement) on their trees. However, since in their model, functions are derivable from tree shapes, it is reasonable to emphasize the functional implications of their analyses (and their comparability to the other analyses) as I have in Figure 1.

4. One real difference between the analyses presented in Table 1 and the analysis in Figure 1 is the difference in number of constituents and constructions assigned. The analyses presented in Table 1 are "flat" in that the noun phrase contains relatively few constructions within it. The "nested" analysis presented in Figure 1 uses constituency as a means of assigning different functions. The difference between the "flat" approach and the "nested" approach will be ignored in this chapter.

al functions are needed, but label the functions differently, and indeed group most of Halliday's Post Deictics with their Modifiers. Huddleston and Jackendoff do not see these words as playing special roles within the nominal group at all. They treat these words as sub modifiers of the number if they precede a number as in 2 i.–iv.

2.	i.	the first two people	the [first [two]] people
	ii.	another two candidates	[another [two]] candidates
	iii.	the inner two members	the [inner [two]] members
	iv.	the extra two sails	the [extra [two]] sails

If these words do not precede a number (as in 3 i-iv) they are considered modifiers of the nominal group.

3.	i.	the two first people	the [two [first [people]]]
	ii.	two other candidates	[two [other [candidates]]]
	iii.	the two inner members	the [two [inner [members]]]
	iv.	the two extra sails	the [two [extra [sails]]]

The issue then arises of how best to describe words such as *first, other, inner, extra, certain, specific,* etc. What are their syntactic and semantic features? Are these features sufficient to warrant setting them up as a separate group?[5] Finally, if we determine that they warrant a separate nominal group function, then should that function be grouped with the modifiers or with the determiners?

Candidates which are worth exploring include the words in List 1. I have placed the words in rough semantic categories so that the range of meanings which are at risk is more obvious.

List 1 includes words which express a great range of meanings. Perhaps the major semantic thread that unites these words is the fact that none of them indicates a quality or property of the referent of the head noun which they modify. (Compare the semantics of the more traditional modifiers such as red, large, blue etc.) Instead, these words help identify the reference of the noun (as

---

5. One issue which must be considered before any final decision can be made on these words is the issue of whether they should be treated as direct constituents of the noun phrase (as Quirk et al. and Halliday do), or should be considered sometimes to submodify constituents of the noun phrase which contains them (as Jackendoff, Radford and Huddleston do)? The analysis in this chapter assumes a non-embedded approach to these words (similar to those of Quirk et al. and of Halliday). I intend to justify this approach in another article.

List 1. *Candidates for a separate nominal group function*

Range	various, numerous, countless, sundry
Ordination	
Specific ordinals	first, second, third, etc.
Relative ordination	next, last, subsequent, preceding
Superlatives	the **best** two people, the **fastest** two swimmers[6]
[the] Comparative [of]	the **bigger** man of the three
General Comparison	other, same, different, similar, identical,
Relations	
external to speech act	inner/outer, upper/lower, top/bottom, remaining, middle, previous, opposite, past, remaining, earlier, additional, extra, further, final, original
internal to speech act	above, latter/former, earlier, previous, remaining, aforementioned, final
Identifiers	certain, particular, specific, given, said,
Limiting	sole, only, mere
Focusing	main, primary, principal, prime
Extent	complete, entire, whole, full, total
Modalities (truth)	virtual, accused, hypothetical, putative, possible, probable, alleged, purported, true, proverbial
Modalities (temporal)	former, late, present, old, previous
Modalities (frequency)	customary, likely, normal, standard, usual, exceptional, expected, habitual, ordinary, typical, occasional
Intensifiers	a **particular** humiliation, a **relative** handful, a **perfect** fool, an **utter** fool, **sheer** terror
Other	famous, infamous, notorious, well-known, necessary, obvious, odd, regular, respective, special

---

6. Superlatives often merge with simple intensifiers. Examples 1. i-iii are true superlatives. These are clearly used in a different way from the superlatives in Examples 2. i-ii. Examples 3. i-iii), however, are ambiguous out of context, and often the context does not provide sufficient information to differentiate the two interpretations.

1.	i.	We had the most interesting evening of all last night.	
	ii.	We saw the most beautiful picture of all last night.	
	iii.	We went to the best party of all last week.	
2.	i.	We had a most interesting evening last night.	cp. very interesting
	ii.	We saw a most beautiful sunset last night.	cp. very beautiful
3.	i.	We had the most interesting evening last night	
	ii.	We saw the most beautiful picture last night.	
	iii.	We went to the best party last week.	

in *specific*),[7] or indicate restrictions on the validity of the head noun as a descriptor of the referent (as in *hypothetical, former,* or *utter*). Are there any grammatical features which distinguish these words from the other more obvious determiners and modifiers? The following grammatical features have been used in a number of arguments on related issues.[8]

2.   Grammatical Features Used to Distinguish Modifiers in the Nominal Group

2.1 *Relative order of the dependent in the nominal group.*[9]

This test has two important aspects.

a.   Can the dependent precede cardinal numbers or general quantities? If it can, then it is more determiner-like.

b.   Can the dependent follow central adjectives? If it can, then it is more modifier-like.

2.2 *Entry into partitive constructions*

May the dependent function in a partitive construction? Partitive constructions require an *of*-construction which contains a definite nominal group as head. See several in Examples 4i-ii.

---

7. Quirk et al. include *certain, definite,* and *sheer* under the heading "emphasizers", while terms such as *absolute, entire,* and *extreme* are described as amplifiers. In this context it is not clear how emphasizers differ from amplifiers, nor is it clear why the words were assigned to the classes they were. *Sheer,* for example seems to have much more in common semantically with *absolute* and *perfect* than it does with *certain* and *definite*. Monumental though the Quirk et al. work is, we would still like to read more from them.

8. While the wording of this following section would change radically had we decided to take the "embedding" approach advocated by Huddleston and Jackendoff, the issues which are being addressed here are also relevant for that analysis.

9. I use the term dependent here to avoid calling the word being tested either a MODIFIER or DETERMINER before that decision has actually been made. One of the issues which must be decided is whether *certain* in a phrase such as *a certain two people* is to be interpreted as a determiner or as a modifier (or as some third option). Regardless of which decision we make after we have applied all the tests, we can say that *certain* is a dependent in this phrase.

4.   i.   several of the passengers were injured.(cp. several passengers)

       ii.   *Several of passengers were injured.

If the dependent may function in a partitive construction, then it is more determiner-like. If it cannot, then it is less determiner-like.

2.3 *Function as Head of elliptical nominal groups*

May the dependent function as head of an elliptical nominal group as *some* and *two* do in Examples 5. i. and ii.?

5.   i.   **Some** came

      ii.   Those **two** came

Most determiners may function as heads of elliptical nominal groups, while many central adjectives do so only with difficulty. As Halliday and Hasan (1976: 150 ff.) point out, ellipsis is used in the context where some part of a previous expression is presupposed and another part is repudiated. It is clear in this context that the repudiated information must deal with some experiential aspect of the referent. That is, we can say 6i. but not 6ii..

6.   i.   We wanted three dogs but got **two** [dogs].

      ii.   *We wanted those three dogs but got these three **poor**

In 6ii *poor* should be interpreted as having an interpersonal meaning similar to its meaning in 7.

7.   **Poor** Freddie was in trouble again.

2.4 *Function as Modifier of the substitute **one/ones***

May the dependent (pre-)modify the substitute *one/ones*?[10] Both determiners and experiential epithets may premodify the substitute *one/ones* as in Example 8. i-v. However, classifiers may not premodify the substitute *one/ones*. Thus, this test does not distinguish determiners from epithets, but it does indicate one way in which these two functions differ from other dependents of the nominal group.

---

10. See Halliday and Hasan (1976:91–98).

8. i.   a certain man   a certain one
    ii.   a **small** man   a big man and two **small** ones
    iii. a **chemistry** book   *a biology book and two **chemistry** ones
    iv.   a **text** book   *two trade books and a **text** one
    v.   a **physics** student *a chemistry student and two **physics** ones.

Like the previous test, this test again selects items which can be repudiated. Such items are experiential in meaning.

2.5 *Gradability*

Is the dependent gradable? Gradability may be expressed by two grammatical means.

a. Gradability may be expressed using a comparative or superlative construction
    Central adjectives are typically gradable via comparative and superlative constructions. Determiners do not allow grading via comparative or superlative constructions. (See Examples 9.i.-ix.)

9. i.   the **bigger** boy (of the two)
    ii.   the **older** folks
    iii. the **more infirm** people
    iv.   the **biggest** boy of the group
    v.   the **most sickly** people of the group
    vi.   *the **more any** group
    vii. *the **most any** group
    viii. *the **more several** people
    ix.   *the **most several** people

b.   Gradability may be expressed using an adverbial element
   i.   Intensifying adverbs
        Central Adjectives which have appropriate meanings accept intensi-
        fying adverbs as dependents, as in Example 10 i-ii.[11] Determiners
        do not accept intensifying adverbs as dependents, as in Example
        11.i-ii.

10.   i.   a **very big** catalog
      ii. a **rather dark** room

·11. i.   *****somewhat any** feature
      ii. *****rather any** feature

   ii. Approximative adverbs
        Many Determiners and most central adjectives (with appropriate
        meanings)[12] accept approximative submodifiers as in Examples 12.
        i-iv.

12.   i.   an **almost unique** feature
      ii.   a **practically unique** feature
      iii. **almost any** feature
      iv.   **practically any** feature

---

11. Of course certain meanings are considered not to accept degree modification. Thus, modifiers
such as *pregnant* and *unique* are thought not to accept modification by intensifiers. It is of interest,
however, that the forces of everyday conversation often push these words into situations where degree
modification is relevant, as in 1 and 2:
1.   Our company offers you a very unique solution to your communication problems.
2.   While I was waiting a very pregnant woman walked into the office.
Of course, these examples are frowned on by those speakers who insist that they are logically
inconsistent.

12. Words which are perceived to indicate some threshold typically accept approximative modification. Thus color terms and specific dimensions accept approximative modification (as in 1, while
inherently comparative terms and terms which do not refer to some threshold do not (as in 2).
1.   i.   the almost red color
     ii.   an almost unique feature
2.· i.   *an almost long spear
     ii.   *an almost pregnant woman

2.6 *Function as Complement*

May the dependent occur as Complement in an attributive relational clause with the same meaning? Central Adjectives typically may occur as Complement in an attributive relational clause as in Examples 13. i-ii.

13.   i.   the bag is **blue**   cp.   the **blue** bag
       ii.   an elephant is **large**   cp.   a **large** elephant

Determiners typically do not occur as Complement in an attributive relational clause as in Examples 14. i-iii.

14.   i.   *a person you meet is **any**   cp.   **any** person you meet
       ii.   *the chairs are **all**[13]   cp.   **all** chairs
       iii. *a/the chair is **all**   cp.   **all** the chair

2.7 *Conjoinability with other elements of the nominal group*

May the dependent conjoin with other elements of nominal group? Conjoining is of interest because in general only similar items may be conjoined. Indeed, a number of linguists have proposed that only items which belong to the same form class may be conjoined.[14] That requirement is clearly too strong if we interpret *form class* to refer to 'surface' form. since it does not allow for examples such as 15.i-iii.

15.   i.   **State** and **federal** control of trade
       ii.   **sensory** and **motor** ability
       iii. **visual, auditory, gustatory** or **pain** perception

The examples in 15 demonstrate that a similarity of grammatical function is sufficient to allow two items to be conjoined. However, notice that the similarity of function includes both the similarity of 'surface' grammar (the conjoined modifiers function as modifiers in the nominal group) as well as a similarity of

---

13. Certain varieties of English in Pennsylvania use *all* as complement in an attributive relational clause to mean roughly 'all gone'. (The milk is all.) In this usage, however, *all* is not simply equivalent to a determiner which is being used predicatively.

14. Radford (1988:76), for example, suggests that coordination is subject to the constraint that only identical categories can be conjoined idiomatically.

participant role relationships. Thus, in Example 15.i, *state* and *federal* can each be seen as referring to an institution which can act as Agent for *control*.

Clearly the factors which may allow or prevent coordinatability include more than simple grammatical factors. Pragmatic factors which affect coordinatability may involve issues such as whether one can find in the real world more than one item which may stand in the same relationship with the head. For example, we have a special term for a hypothesis which we know to be false, but which we adopt for our present purposes. We call it a 'working hypothesis'. However, I am unable to think of a special term for hypotheses which I am committed to and wish to test further. As a result, I am unable to think of truly acceptable coordinations which involve *working* in that construction. (**Working and serious hypotheses* does not sound very plausible to my ears.) On the other hand it is quite easy to think of other phrases in which *ing*-verbs coordinate with central adjectives (e.g. *his **eager** and **loving** eyes.*). Thus the problem does not seem to be with the structures involved but rather with the particular pragmatics of the individual phrase. Since the requirements for successful conjunction are so complex, a positive answer to this test is more significant than a negative one.

As in test A, we must distinguish two major aspects of this test.

a.   Does the dependent coordinate with central adjectives? If so, it is more modifier-like

b.   Does the dependent coordinate with determiners? If so, it is more determiner-like.

2.8   *Occurrence in broken phrases*

May the dependent occur in broken phrases? In written English, a broken phrase is one in which a single comma occurs between two dependents in a nominal group. As in previous tests, this test has two possible implications.

1.   Broken phrases may be associated with conjunction. Thus, phrases such as those in 16. i-ii may be considered paraphrases of coordinations such as those in 17.i-ii.

   16.   i.   that **cool, detached** way
         ii.   a **likable, happy** little girl

   17.   i.   that **cool and detached** way
         ii.   a **likable and happy** little girl

As a result, we can say of Example 16.i that *cool* and *detatched* are linked in the broken phrase. I will refer to the broken phrases illustrated in 16 as conjunctive broken phrases.

2. Other examples of broken phrases do not seem to be linked to coordination. These broken phrases seem to be used more for the management of information presentation. Thus, Examples 18. i-ii are difficult to relate to coordinations such as those in 19. i.-ii.

18.   i.   a **certain**, **selective** homogenization   [B G57 1210]
       ii.   **numerous, apparently true** terminal bronchioles[B J12 0220]

19.   i.   *a **certain and selective** homogenization
       ii.   ***numerous and apparently true** terminal bronchioles

I will refer to the broken phrases illustrated in 18 as information-management broken phrases.

If a conjunctive broken phrase links a dependent with a central adjective, this will be interpreted as indicating that the dependent is modifier-like. If a conjunctive broken phrase links the dependent with a determiner, then the dependent will be interpreted as determiner-like. In the case of non-conjunctive broken phrases, no implications will be drawn regarding the status of the dependent as modifier or determiner.

2.9 *Repeatability*

Can a single nominal group contain more than one instance of the function? There are two major reasons why a single function might occur more than once within a single phrase. First, the function may be modifier-like. In that case, the additional instances of the function merely add information as in Examples 20. i-ii.

20.   i.   a **long bony** hand
       ii.   a **sharp difficult** corner.

In these examples, *long* and *bony* (in 20i) and *sharp* and *difficult* (in 20ii) each add separate information concerning the Head of the nominal group.

By contrast, another reason a function may be repeated is that the filler is strongly interpersonal. In that case, the repetitions do not add experiential information, but rather act as a sort of intensification of a meaning that is already present. Examples 21. i-ii demonstrate this feature.

21.   i.   the **very very** large book
       ii. a **red red** sky.

In each case, the repetition of *very* or *red* does not add new features, but rather the repetition intensifies the degree to which the perception is emphasized. In earlier work (Fries 1970a and 1970b) I referred to this phenomenon as reduplication, thinking that the repetition of the exact lexical item was an essential characteristic. However, it is clear that all that is necessary is a repetition of the same sort of interpersonal meaning, as in 22.

22.   a **very damn** large book

While I have suggested that there are two reasons for the possibility that a function may occur several times within a single construction, these motivations are strongly restricted within the determiner system. Only one predeictic, deictic, ordering or quantifying numerative may occur in a single nominal group without some conjunction. Examples such as 23. i-ii are ungrammatical.

23.   i.   *the **many sixty** books
       ii. * **a my** house

If a dependent may form part of a repeated function with the effect of added information (as in Example 20) then it is more modifier-like. If the dependent may occur with sharply limited potential for repetition, then it is more determiner-like.[15] If the meaning of a repetition of the function is intensification, then the dependent is neither like a prototypical modifier nor a prototypical determiner.

The tests and the conclusions they lead to are summarized in Table 2. If one thinks of the prototypical determiner (e.g. *any*) and the prototypical central adjective (e.g. *red*) these dependents would fit the grammatical tests as suggested in Table 2.

---

15. Using the ability for a function to repeat as a test for the type of function must be done carefully, since some dependents may be nested as in Example (1).
1.   the **inner inner** doors vs. the **outer inner** doors.

Table 2. *Comparison of prototypical determiner and central adjective*

Grammatical Test		Answers	
		Prototypical Determiner	Prototypical Adjective
A.	Relative Order		
	a. Pre Number	Yes	No
	b. Post Adjective	No	Yes
B.	Partitive	Yes	No
C.	Head of Elliptical NG	Yes	Some?
D.	Premodify *one*	Yes	Yes
E.	Gradable		
	a. comp/superlative	No	Yes
	b. intensification	No	Yes
	c. approximatives	Some	Some
F.	Predicative function	No	Yes
G.	Conjoining		
	a. With Central Adjective	No	Yes
	b. With Determiner	Yes	No
H.	Broken Phrases		
	a. Coordinating with Central Adj	No	Yes
	b. Info. Mgmt.	Yes	Yes?
I.	>1 instance in NG		
	a. Added features	No	Yes
	b. Meaning intensification	No	No

How do the words given in List 1 behave according to these tests? The Brown and the LOB corpora were examined for all occurrences of the words in List 1. Where neither the Brown nor the LOB corpus had examples of a certain sequence type, the corpus of the Macquarie Dictionary was checked.[16] Where no examples of a particular construction were found, I attempted to construct my own examples based on examples found in the data. Space prevents an exhaustive treatment of each word, or even of each group. However, let me illustrate these tests with a few samples taken from four of the groups given in List 1.

---

16. Time prevented a careful, exhaustive search of the Macquarie Dictionary corpus, Such a search would clearly have improved the reliability of my statements concerning the ungrammaticality of certain word combinations.

3.   Range (*various, numerous, countless, sundry*)

3.1   *Relative order of dependent*

a.   Range dependents do not co-occur with numbers.

24.   i.   ***various/sundry/numerous** two hundred people*
ii.   **two hundred various/numerous people*
iii.   *?two hundred sundry people*

Examples such as 25 do not provide counter evidence since *countless* submodifies *thousands*

25.   There are **countless** thousands of them.   [LOB B14 0930]

In this behavior, countless resembles *many* in 26.

26.   there are **many** thousands of them

b.   Range dependents may precede *other*, etc.

27.   i.   **various** other classes at the show   [Brn E05 0090]
ii.   **sundry** other touches of realism   [Brn C02 1160]
iii.   **numerous** other wealthy members of Cairo society
[Brn F09 1250]
iv.   **countless** other people

c.   Range dependents may not follow central adjectives.

28.   i.   **various/countless/numerous/sundry** large bowls
ii.   ***large various/countless/numerous** bowls

3.2   *Entry into partitive constructions*

Range dependents may function in partitive constructions.[17]

---

17. For obvious semantic reasons, these words do not occur as definites in partitive phrases. See the examples in (1)
1.   i.   *the **countless** of television viewers in the Denver area
ii.   *the **numerous** of his listeners who paid attention
iii.   *the **sundry** of the other people who liked it
iv.   *the **various** of the other listeners

29.   i.   **various** of the other places   [LL 22b 0010]
       ii.   **numerous** of his listeners
       iii. **sundry** of the other people
       iv.   *****various** of other places
       v.   *****numerous** of listeners
       vi.   *****sundry** of listeners

But note 29.vii.

       vii. **countless** of television viewers in the Denver area

[Brn A13 0050]

3.3 *Function as Head of elliptical nominal groups*

Range dependents may function as head of an elliptical nominal group.

30.   i.   his willingness to take cruel advantage of all and **sundry**

[B G28 1530]

       ii.   **Various** came
       iii. **Countless** came
       iv.   **Numerous** came

3.4 *Function as Modifier of the substitute one/ones*

Range dependents may (pre-)modify the substitute *one/ones*.

31.   i.   **Various/numerous** ones were eliminated on different grounds.
       ii.   ?**Countless** ones were eliminated.

3.5 *Gradability*

Range dependents are not gradable (with the exception of *numerous*)

a.   via comparative or superlatives

32.   i.   ??His **more/most numerous** listeners were in Australia.
       ii.   ??Australia provided his **more/most numerous** listeners.
       iii. *His **most countless/sundry/various** listeners were in Australia.

b.   via intensifiers

33.   i.   his **rather/very numerous** listeners
       ii.   *his **rather/very countless/sundry/various** listeners

c.   via approximatives

34.   i.   *his **roughly numerous** listeners
       ii.   *his **approximately countless** admirers
       iii. *his **almost various** advocates

3.6 *Function as Complement*

Range dependents may occur as Complement in attributive relational clauses.

35.   i.   Today's earthquakes are most **numerous** in …
                                                        [Brn F21 1460]
       ii.   the honors that have come to Greer Garson are **countless**.
                                                        [Brn A29 0610]
       iii. The reasons given by owners … are **various**.
                                                        [LOB H05 0770]

3.7 *Conjoinability*

a.   Most Range dependents may not conjoin with central adjectives.

36.   i.   ?all these **countless and distant** evocations
       ii.   ?these **sundry and important** issues

      However, *numerous* may conjoin with central adjectives

37.   i.   It evokes **numerous and distant** resonances from the entire
             body of Mann's work   [Brn G15 0510]
       ii.   there are **long and numerous** quotations,   [Brn G46 0580]
       iii. **numerous and varied** "catchpenny attractions"
                                                        [LOB F43 1480]

b.   Range dependents do not conjoin with determiners.

38.   i.   *all and numerous** people
       ii.   *many and sundry** people

3.8 *Occurrence in broken phrases*

1. Range dependents may not occur in coordinating broken phrases linked to central adjectives

2. Range dependents may occur in information-management broken phrases.

    39.   i.   composed of **numerous, apparently true** terminal bronchioles and occasional, poorly developed respiratory bronchioles

                                                                        [Brn J12 0220]

            ii.   *composed of **numerous and apparently true** terminal bronchioles and occasional, poorly developed respiratory bronchioles

3.9 *Repeatability*

Can a single nominal group contain more than one Range dependent with an additive meaning or with a meaning of intensification?

    No, Range dependents do not co-occur in a single nominal group either with an additive meaning or a meaning of intensification.

    40.   i.   *****various numerous** issues arose
            ii.   *****numerous various** issues arose
            iii.   *****various sundry** issues arose

4. Identifiers (*certain, particular, specific, given, said*)

4.1 *Relative order of dependent*

a. Identifiers may precede or follow cardinal numbers or general quantities. *Certain* is unusual in that it may not follow cardinal numbers or general quantities.

    41.   i.   a **particular** two people
            ii.   these **particular** two people
            iii.   a **certain** two people
            iv.   a **specific** two people
            v.   the **given** two lines
            vi.   the **said** two defendants

42.   i.   these two **particular** people
      ii.   one **particular** word   [Brn G37 0540]
      iii. *two **certain** people
      iv.   two **specific** people
      v.   the two **given** lines
      vi.   ?the two **said** defendants

b.   Identifiers may precede but not follow central adjectives

43.   i.   a **certain** large stone   *a large **certain** stone
      ii.   no **specific** important effects   *no important **specific** effects
      iii. a **given** important effect   *an important **given** effect

4.2 *Entry into partitive constructions*

Of the identifiers, only *certain* may function in partitive constructions.

44.   i.   **Certain** of the passengers were injured.
      ii.   *(a) **particular/specific/given/said** of the passengers were injured
      iii. *The **particular/specific/given/said** of the passengers were injured

4.3 *Function as Head of elliptical nominal groups*

Of the identifiers, only *certain* may function as head of an elliptical nominal group.

45.   i.   **certain** [friends] came
      ii.   ***particular/specific/given/said** [friends] came

4.4 *Function as Modifier of the substitute **one/ones***

Most Identifiers may (pre-)modify the substitute *one/ones*.

46.   i.   a **specific/particular/certain** one
      ii.   ??the **said** one
      iii. *the/a **given** one

4.5 *Gradability*

Is the dependent gradable?

a. Identifiers do not accept grading via comparative or superlative construc-
    tions.

    47.   i.   more **personal and specific** statements[Brn F12 0030]
          ii. ***more certain** people arrived
         iii. *the **more said** defendants

b. Identifiers do not accept grading via adverbial elements expressing intensification.

    48.   i.   *These products meet your **very/rather particular** needs
          ii. *A **rather certain** person walked up to us.

c. Identifiers do not accept grading via adverbial elements expressing approximation.

    49.   i.   *These products meet your **almost specific/definite** needs.
          ii. *a **practically certain/particular** person walked up to us.

4.6 *Function as Complement*

Identifiers may not occur as Complement in an attributive relational clause.

    50.   i.   *a/the person is **particular**[18] vs. one **particular** person
          ii. *a/the person is **certain**   vs. a **certain** person
        iii. *the/any amount is **given**   vs. any **given** amount
        iv. *the premises are **said**   vs. the **said** premises

4.7 *Conjoinability*

Identifiers may not conjoin with other elements of the nominal group.
    [No examples exist in the Brown or LOB corpora]

    *A **particular and important** statement.

4.8 *Occurrence in broken phrases*

1. Identifiers do not occur in coordinating broken phrases linked to central
    adjectives.

2. Identifiers may be found in noncoordinating broken phrases.

---

18. Note that though the words *particular, certain,* and *given* all may occur as Complements, they do
not express an identifying meaning.

51.   i.   a **certain**, selective homogenization of attitudes and values

[B G57 1210]

        ii.   working on a **given**, complicated piece of legislation

        iii. one **particular**, detailed account of this phenomenon

Compare 52.

52.   i.   *a **certain** and selective homogenization of attitudes and values

        ii.   *working on a **given** and complicated piece of legislation

        iii. *one **particular** and detailed account of this phenomenon

4.9 *Repeatability*

Identifiers rarely co-occur within a single nominal group. When they do, the effect is an additive effect (not an intensifying effect).

53.   i.   ?a **certain specific** item

        ii.   *a **specific certain** item

        iii. ??these **said specific** needs

        iv. *these **specific said** needs

        v.   *a **certain particular** item

        vi. *a **particular certain** item

        vii. *the **specific particular** item

        viii.*The **particular said** item

5.   **Limiting Dependents**   (*sole, only, mere*)

5.1 *Relative order of dependent*

a.   Limiting modifiers may precede cardinal numbers. They may follow numbers only with difficulty.

54.   i.   the **sole** two issues

        ii.   a **mere** 10 yards

55.   i.   ??the two **sole** issues

        ii.   ??10 **mere** yards   [*mere* has different scope]

b.   Limiting modifiers may precede but not follow central adjectives.

    56.   i.   a **mere** useless gibbering stop-the-war-at-any-price pacifist.

                                             [LOB G13 1650]

          ii.   the **sole** large, well-kept building in the town

Compare 57.

    57.   i.   *a useless **mere** gibbering stop-the-war-at-any-price pacifist.

          ii. ??two practical **primary** results of science

          iii. *the large, **sole**, well kept building in the town

          iv. *the large, well-kept **sole** building in town

5.2 *Entry into partitive constructions*

Limiting dependents may not function in partitive constructions.

    58.   *(the) **mere/sole/only** of his friends came to the party

5.3 *Function as Head of elliptical nominal groups*

Limiting dependents do not function as head of an elliptical nominal group

    59.   Bill made many good points. *Jane made a **mere/sole.**

5.4 *Function as Modifier of the substitute* ***one/ones***

Only one limiting modifier (*only*) may (pre-)modify the substitute *one/ones* with no problems of acceptability.

    60.   i.   the **only** one

          ii. *a/the **mere** one

          iii. ?the **sole** one

5.5 *Gradability*

Limiting dependents are not gradable,

    61.   i.   *a **more mere** ten yards

          ii. *my **very sole** point

          iii. *his **almost only** point

5.6   *Function as Complement*

Limiting dependents do not occur as Complement in an attributive relational clause.

    62.   i.   *the reason is **sole/only**   cp.   the **sole/only** reason
           ii.   *the thought is **mere**   cp.   the **mere** thought

5.7   *Conjoinability*

Sole and *only* may conjoin with central adjectives and with focusing dependents.

    63.   i.   it must be abandoned as the **sole** or proper means for presenting the Christian understanding of existence   [Brn D02 0150]
           ii.   their **prime** and indeed **only** consideration   [LOB F28 1910]
          iii.   that **prime**, if not **sole**, source of knowledge. [Brn C02 1910]

5.8   *Occurrence in broken phrases*

Limiting dependents never occur in conjunctive broken phrases and they rarely occur in information-management broken phrases.

    64.   i.   ?their **sole**, regular support
           ii.   *a **mere**, little slip of a thing

5.9   *Repeatability*

Nominal groups may contain more than one limiting dependent only with difficulty. If more than one occurs, the repetition will have an intensifying interpretation.

    65.   i.   ?their **only sole** purpose
           ii.   *their **mere only** purpose
          iii.   *their **only mere** purpose

6. Intensifiers (*particular, relative, perfect, utter*)[19]

6.1 *Relative order of dependent*

a.   Intensifiers may follow but not precede cardinal numbers or general quantities,

    66.   i.   his two **relative** failures
           ii.   *his **relative** two failures

b.   The Brown and LOB corpora contain one example of an Intensifier which precedes a central adjective.

    67.   For **sheer** luxurious warmth in the middle of winter

                                                              [LOB H30 0640]

    Brown and LOB also contain several examples of intensifiers which precede denominal adjectives (Quirk et al's prehead modification zone).

    68.   i.   matters of **particular** medical interest   [LOB H06 0370]
           ii.   this makes these results of **particular** statistical interest.

                                                              [LOB J14 0700]

           iii. **sheer** emotional and physical exhaustion.   [LOB G29 0470]

    Brown and LOB corpora contain one example of an intensifier following a central adjective.

    69.   He had a mean, unbroken **sheer** bastard in his outfit,

                                                              [Brn K03 0300]

    The difference in ordering with respect to central adjectives (see Examples 66 and 68) seems to be closely related to whether the central adjectives are or are not to be included within the scope of the intensifier.

6.2 *Entry into partitive constructions*

Intensifiers may not function in a partitive construction.

    70.   i.   *__particular__ of the humiliation
           ii.   *(a/the) **relative** of the handful

---

19. As in examples 1–3.
    1.   a *particular* humiliation,
    2.   a *relative* handful,
    3.   a *perfect* fool, an *utter* fool

6.3 *Function as Head of elliptical nominal groups*

Intensifiers may not function as head of an elliptical nominal group.

71. *John is certainly a fool, but Bill is an **utter**/a **particular**.

6.4 *Function as Modifier of the substitute* **one/ones**

Intensifiers may not pre-modify the substitute *one/ones*.

72. i. *It was a humiliation. In fact it was a **particular** one
    ii. *Only a handful showed up. Actually the handful was a **relative** one.

6.5 *Gradability*

Intensifiers are not gradable

73. i. *We suffered an **even more particular** humiliation the next day.
    ii. *John is an **extremely utter** fool.
    iii. *John is an **almost utter** fool[20]

6.6 *Function as Complement*

Intensifiers do not function as complements in attributive clauses.

74. *a/the handful is **relative**   vs.   a **relative** handful

6.7 *Conjoinability*

No examples exist in the Brown or LOB corpora in which intensifiers are conjoined with other elements of the nominal group. Indeed it is unlikely that Intensifiers may coordinate with central adjectives.

75. *an **extreme** and embarrassing humiliation

---

20. A phrase such as *almost an utter fool* is not simply an approximative (*almost*) serving as dependent on the Intensifier (*utter*), hence that phrase is not analyzed here.

6.8 *Occurrence in broken phrases*

The Brown and the LOB corpora have no examples of Intensifiers in broken phrases of any sort. In fact, I have few examples of Intensifiers co-occurring with other dependents in the nominal group. Like Truth Modalities, Intensifiers do not convey information which is sufficiently separate from the information conveyed by the head to be given status as a separate "chunk" of information.

6.9 *Repeatability*

A single nominal group may contain more than one intensifier. If it does, the interpretation will be one of intensifying the effect, not of adding new meanings to the combination.

76. i.   ?He is an **utter perfect** fool
     ii.   He told us some **sheer utter** nonsense
     iii. forced on us by **sheer desperate** necessity   [LOB B25 0510]

7. Conclusion

Let us now turn to a discussion of the general pattern of grammatical features of these words. Table 3 summarizes these general patterns. For purposes of comparison I have also included some representative determiners and central adjectives. Rows representing these words are shaded. Since adjectives which derive from the interpersonal metafunction have a different potential for modification than experiential adjectives, I have included one of each.

Table 3 demonstrates that, with one exception, the groups of words under consideration have quite different grammatical properties from either the determiners or the central adjectives. The exception is the category of words which I have labeled Range. Range dependents have many of the characteristics that the non-specific numeratives (*many* and *several*) have. Indeed, in the case of *countless* the similarity is even greater than Table 3 would indicate, because all three words (*several*, *many*, and *countless*) may serve as dependents in comparative phrases as in 77i-iii.

77.   i.   **many more** people arrived after that
      ii. **several more** people arrived after that
      iii. **countless more** people arrived after that.

In addition, like *many* and *several*, *countless* may submodify large numbers. Thus one may say any of 78i-iii.

78.   i.   There were **many thousands** of them.
      ii. There were **several thousand** of them.
      iii. There were **countless thousands** of them.

When we turn to the other categories of dependents in Table 3, their status is less obvious. On the one hand, the pattern of answers for each group differs both from the patterns of answers for the determiners in the shaded area at the top of the table, and at the same time these same patterns all also differ from the patterns of answers for the central experiential adjectives in the shaded area at the bottom of the table. In particular, it is worth noting that few of the members of these groups may conjoin with central adjectives or occur in conjunctive broken phrases linked to an adjective. Similarly, few of the dependents described in Table 3 function as Complement in an attributive relational clause. Finally, few of the dependents described in Table 3 are gradable in the way that the central adjectives typically are.

On the other hand, these groups of words share few grammatical features which distinguish them as a group from the determiners and the central adjectives. Certainly many of these words (but not all) may precede numbers within a nominal group. In addition, most of these words may follow numbers. About half of the groups of words may function in partitive constructions or as heads of elliptical nominal groups. Few of them are gradable, occur as Complement in an attributive relational clause, conjoin with central adjectives or occur in conjunctive broken phrases linked to central adjectives.

As mentioned earlier, one feature that distinguishes these words is the semantic feature that they do not indicate attributes of the head (compare the central adjectives), or types of head (compare Quirk et al's fillers of the prehead modification zone, and Halliday's classifier function). Rather, these words seem to "be concerned with the status of the set of instantial representatives of a nominal group as representatives of the general experiential category". (Matthiessen 1995: 702) Looking at the semantic relations more delicately, these words seem to concern the identity of the referent (see especially the various types of ordination and the identifiers) or they may act as modalities on the

Table 3. *Patterns of grammatical features by semantic group*

	Grammatical Tests					
	A Rel Order			**B** Part	**C** Ellipt	**D** Prn
Word Group	prec. #	foll#	foll. adj.	Const.	NG	one
Determiners						
any	yes	no	no	yes	yes	yes
many	—	—	no	yes	yes	??
several	—	—	no	yes	yes	??
cardinal number	—	—	cntrst	yes	yes	?
range	—	—	no	yes	yes	yes
specific ordinals	yes	yes	no	yes	yes	yes
relative ordinals	yes	yes	no	yes	yes	yes
superlatives	yes	yes	no	yes	yes	yes
comparatives	yes	yes	no	yes	yes	yes
general comparison	yes	yes	some	no	yes?	yes
other relations	yes	yes	some	few	yes	yes
identifiers	yes	most	no	one	one	most
limiting	yes	no?	no	no	no	yes
focusing	yes	yes	no	no	no	yes
extent	yes	yes?	yes?	one	one	some
truth modalities	some	yes	no	no	some	yes?
temporal modalities	few	yes	some	no	no	most
frequency modalities	most	yes	no	no	yes	yes
intensifiers	no	yes	yes	no	no	no
interpersonal adjective						
poor	no	yes	no	no	no	no
central adj						
red	cntrst	yes	yes	no	some?	yes

E Gradable			F Comp	G Conjn	H Brkn Phrs		I >1 instance	
comp.	intens.	approx.		w. adjs.	conj.	info. mgt.	add. feats.	intens.
no		yes	no	no	no	yes	no	no
	yes	no	yes	no	no	yes?	no	no
no	no	no	yes	no	no	yes	no	no
no	no	large #	yes	no	no	yes?	no	no
one	one	no	yes	one	no	yes	no	no
no	no	yes	yes?	no	no	yes	no	no
no	no	yes	yes?	no	no	yes	no	no
no	no	yes	yes?	no	yes	yes	yes	no?
no	no	no?	yes?	no	yes	yes?	yes	no?
some	no	few	yes	no	no	yes	yes	no
no	no	no	no	no	no	yes	yes	no
no	no	no	no	no	no	yes	no	no
no	no	no	no	yes?	no	some	no	yes?
no	no	no	no	no	no	yes	no	yes?
no	no	one	one	some	yes	most	no	yes?
no	no	no	some	some	no	no	no	no
no	no	no	no	no	no	few	no	no
yes	yes	some	no	no	no	some?	yes	no
no	no	no	no	no	no	no	no	yes
no	no	no	no	no	yes	yes	no	yes
yes	yes	yes	yes	yes	yes	yes?	yes	*no*

accuracy of the head noun (see especially the intensifiers, and the various types of modalities). We might generally categorize these two types of meanings as textual-oriented meanings and interpersonal-oriented meanings.

This semantic categorization shows a general correlation with the grammatical characteristics of the groups of words on Table 3. I have placed the textual-oriented items in the rows toward the top of the table and the interpersonal-oriented items toward the bottom of the table. Certainly there is no sharp simple distinction between the two groups, but there does seem to be a trend which distinguishes them. In particular, the textual-oriented items seem to precede numbers more easily than the interpersonal-oriented items. They also function more easily in partitive constructions, as heads of elliptical nominal groups, and modifying the substitute *one/ones*. The textual-oriented items also function more easily as attributes in attributive relational clauses. In most cases, no more than one instance of a textual item of a given type may be found within a single nominal group. When a nominal group does contain more than one textual-oriented word, then the combination adds features much as a sequence of central adjectives might. Finally, textually oriented items may be found in broken phrases which seem to be managing information.

By contrast, many interpersonal-oriented items cannot precede numbers at all. In general they do not function in partitive constructions, as heads of elliptical nominal groups, nor do they modify the substitute *one/ones*. Their inability to occur as head of elliptical nominal groups and as modifiers for the substitute *one/ones* can be related to their status as interpersonal modifiers and the fact that they convey little experiential meaning. The interpersonal-oriented items do not usually function as Complements in attributive relational clauses, nor are they usually gradable. The tests which probe other interpersonal traits also distinguish the textual-oriented groups from the interpersonal-oriented groups. None of the textual-oriented items are repeatable in a single nominal group with the interpretation of intensification. On the other hand, nominal groups may contain more than one interpersonal item with the resulting interpretation of intensification. Similarly, few of the interpersonal-oriented items are found in any broken phrases at all. In other words, their informational status seems to differ from that of the textual-oriented words. These characteristics link the interpersonal-oriented items more closely to the interpersonal modifiers such as *poor* (e.g. *Poor Freddie was in trouble again.*)

In sum, we can say that while the class of words which we have been discussing does not exhibit strong positive distinctive characteristics which unify it, its members are distinct syntactically and semantically from the central adjectives and from the determiners. Further, the members of the class fall into two general subcategories, the textual oriented words and the interpersonal-oriented words, which are more unified. We seem to be dealing with a squish in Ross's (1972 and 1973) sense, however the squish has four foci: the central adjectives, and the determiners at each extreme, and then the textual-oriented modifiers, and the interpersonal-oriented modifiers in between.

Acknowledgments

This chapter was researched and written during a sabbatical leave from Central Michigan University. It has benefitted from the help of many people. Pam Peters, Andrew McVeigh, and Steve Cassidy have been most helpful in obtaining examples from the various corpora with which they are working. Richard Tardiff has made the corpus of the Macquarie Dictionary available to me, and Chris Nesbitt has even created a search program that I could use on my own copies of the Brown and LOB corpora. I received many helpful comments from the Sydney Linguistic Circle, when I presented a preliminary version of this paper. In addition, this paper has benefitted from discussions with Peter Collins, Ruqaiya Hasan, Rodney Huddleston, David Lee, James Martin, Christian Matthiessen, Pam Peters, and Peter Peterson.

References

Bache, Carl. 1978. *The Order of Premodifying Adjectives in Present-Day English.* Odense: Odense University Press.

Dixon, R. M. W. 1991. *A New Approach to English Grammar on Semantic Principles.* Oxford: Clarendon Press.

Fries, Peter H. 1970a. On repeatability and reduplication. *TESL Reporter* 3,4:1–2.

Fries, Peter H. 1970b. *Tagmeme Sequences in the English Noun Phrase.* Summer Institute of Linguistics Publications in Linguistics and Related Fields. Publications No 36. Norman Oklahoma: Summer Institute of Linguistics.

Kress, G. R. (ed.). 1976. *Halliday: System and Function in Language.* London: Oxford University Press.

Halliday, Michael. 1985. *An Introduction to Functional Grammar.* London: Edward Arnold.

Huddleston, Rodney. 1984. *Introduction to the Grammar of English.* Cambridge: Cambridge University Press.

Jackendoff, Ray. 1977. *X Bar Syntax: A Study of Phrase Structure.* Linguistic Inquiry Monograph 2. Cambridge, Massachusetts: MIT Press.

Lamb, Sydney. 1966. *Outline of Stratificational Grammar.* Washington, D.C.: Georgetown University Press.

Matthiessen, Christian. 1995. *Lexicogrammatical Cartography: English Systems.* Tokyo: International Language Sciences Publishers.

Newell, Leonard E. 1966. Stratificational analysis of an English text. Appendix in Lamb 1966.

Quirk, Randolph, Sydney Greenbaum, Geoffrey Leech, and Jan Svartvik. 1985. *A Comprehensive Grammar of the English Language.* London: Longman.

Radford, Andrew. 1988. *Transformational Grammar: A First Course* Cambridge: Cambridge University Press.

Ross, John Robert. 1972. Endstation Hauptwort: The category squish. *Papers from the Eighth Regional Meeting, Chicago Linguistic Society,* ed. by Paul Peranteau, Judith Levi and Gloria Phares, 316–328.

Ross, John Robert. 1973. Nouniness. *Three Dimensions of Linguistic Theory,* ed. by Osamu Fujimura, 137–257. Tokyo: TEC

About the author

Peter Fries is currently Professor of English and Linguistics at Central Michigan University (in Mount Pleasant) where he has taught since 1971. He received his Ph.D. from the University of Pennsylvania in 1964, and first taught at the University of Wisconsin-Madison. He also worked with Kenneth L. Pike during the 1960s and early 1970s. He first got to know Syd Lamb well during the summer of 1970, when Syd made an extended visit to the Summer Institute of Linguistics at Norman, Oklahoma, where Fries was teaching at the time. In 1991 he taught at Hangzhou University in China, where he was made Adjunct Professor. Fries's principal interests include research on English grammar and on discourse analysis.

CHAPTER 19

The *ist-* Prefix in Alabama

Heather K. Hardy   Philip W. Davis
Northern Illinois University   *Rice University*

1.   General Introduction

Alabama is a Muskogean language that was spoken historically by people indigenous to what is now the southeastern United States, and is currently spoken by their descendants residing on the Alabama-Coushatta Indian Reservation east of Livingston, Texas. It is a fairly representative SOV language, with a semantically complex system of direct and indirect participant marking consisting of pronominal arguments affixed to verbs, direct marking on nominals, and a verbal switch-reference system (Davis and Hardy 1984, 1988; Hardy and Davis 1993). Like the other Muskogean languages, Alabama includes in its extensive verbal morphology a number of prefixes that can be (somewhat loosely) labeled **applicative** (see for instance Munro 1989). By far the most productive of these are the dative prefix *im-* (Hardy 1991 and In preparation) and the *ist-* prefix that is the focus of this paper.

Muskogeanists have traditionally referred to the *ist-* prefix and its cognates throughout the Muskogean family as the **instrumental** (e.g. Booker 1980). Although the derivation of instrumental nouns from verbs and the sanctioning of an instrumental argument of a verb are among its more obvious uses, the functions of the *ist-* prefix in Alabama range far beyond this limited use and pervade the grammar, suggesting an advanced degree of grammaticalization in this language.

We begin with a brief description of basic morphosyntax relevant to this discussion before we examine the range of functions of the *ist-* prefix.

Consider examples 1–4:[1]

(1)   *icho-n   ibi-li-ti.*
      deer-N shoot:at-1sI-Asp
      'I killed a deer.'

(2)   *cha-hoopa-hchi.*
      1sII-sick-Asp
      'I'm sick.'

(3)   *a^n-ɫakfi-k   cha-chifipka-ti.*
      my-brother (woman speaker)-K 1sII-trip-Asp
      'My brother tripped me.'

(4)   *yusti-fa-n   aɫɫa-l-ah-o.*
      Houston-Loc-N go-1sI-Fut-Asp
      'I'm going to go to Houston.'

A comparison of the pronominal marking on the verbs in (1–4) shows that the subjects of some intransitives (S) are marked like transitive agents (A) (e.g. a *-li* suffix for first person), while other intransitive arguments prefix a marker that is identical with that used for a transitive object (e.g. a *cha-* first person prefix). Alabama has an "active/agentive" pronominal marking system (cf. Mithun 1991) for referring to speech act (nonthird - person) participants. The choice between two pronominal sets is determined by the semantics of CONTROL (Hardy and Davis 1993, Klaiman 1991). The suffix *-k* on the agent in (3) and the *-n* on the patient (in 1) and oblique noun (in 4) suggest a nominative vs. oblique (or nonnominative) case pattern, and although that is perhaps the most common

---

1. Examples are cited in the practical orthography developed by Hardy and Cora Sylestine; values are phonetically as expected except that ch = [č], the *n* written before [k] is [ŋ], and raised ^{n} is nasalization on a preceding vowel. Abbreviations are as follows: For person markers, the Arabic number indicates person, followed by lower case *s* for singular or *p* for plural, followed by the Roman numbers for pronominal type: I, II, IID (allomorph of II used with Dative), or Iirr for the irrealis first person agentive. Adv = adverbial modifier; Art = article; Asp = aspect; Contr = contrastive; Cs = causativizer; Dat = dative; Dem = demonstrative; Distr = distributive; Evid = evidential; Foc = focus; Frn = foreign; Fut = future; Ggr = geminate grade; Hgr = h-grade; Loc = locative; Lgr = lengthening grade; Mid = middle; NegImp = negative imperative; Nom/Mid = nominal/middle; Sbjn = subjunctive. Morphemes whose semantics defies a simple gloss will be represented by capital letters; for instance, the nominal/sentential suffixes *-t*, *-k*, and *-n* whose semantics are the topic of several papers by the authors (Davis and Hardy 1984, 1988) are glossed T, K, and N, and the prefix discussed here is glossed as IST. < > is used to set off infixes from roots. Three lower case bracketed letters following an example indicates the text code of the text from which it is taken.

distribution, it is an oversimplification of a semantically more complex system. Nominal participants are marked with one of three suffixes (or are unmarked), the choice being semantically determined by relationship between the participant and the proposition (Davis and Hardy 1984, 1988). Arguments not provided for in the lexical specification of the basic verb are generally indicated by one of a number of applicative prefixes.

In addition to *ist-*, the most common derivational prefix of this sort is the dative marker *im-*, which indicates the addition of a recipient, benefactive, goal/source, or experiencer participant as in (5) and (6).

(5)   *minerfa-n   i^n-fat-chi-nnàa!*
        Minerva-N Dat-tell-2sI-Neg:Imp
        'Don't tell (it to) Minerva!'

(6)   *wanda-k   chi-n-libatl-o.*
        Wanda-K 2sII-Dat-cook-Asp
        'Wanda just cooked it for you.'

The dative is also used productively on verbs to mark the involvement of a possessor or other participant that may indirectly 'experience' an event without being directly (physically) affected by it in the manner of patients — an ethical dative sense.

(7)   *mobìl-ka-k a-m-alwahka-ti.*
        car-Frn-K 1sIID-Dat-break-Asp
        'My car broke down on me.'

In contrast with the roles of the *ist-* prefix, as we will see, the kinds of roles expressed by the dative, then, show its typical association with human participants. For nonthird persons a dative argument is referenced with a pronominal marker from the noncontrol (II) set as in (6). The dative prefix is subject to phonologically determined allomorphy and the II pronominal marker has a special allomorph in the first person, used when it co-occurs with the dative and indicated here by the gloss IID shown in (7).

As has been noted by others (cf. Munro and Gordon 1982) the dative prefix *im-* is associated typically with human (or at least animate) participants and its functions (recipient, benefactive, possessor, experiencer) make it clear why. The *ist-* prefix, by contrast, refers typically to inanimate, indeed often abstract, entities. As Lupardus notes in passing, the *ist-* prefix often co-occurs with a following dative marker (1982: 104).[2]

2.   The Functions of *ist-*

2.1 *Background*

The *ist-* prefix occurs in several allomorphs produced by regular phonological processes in the language (described elsewhere in e.g. Hardy and Montler 1988b, Montler and Hardy 1990, 1991): [ist] or [st] before vowels, and [is] or [s] before consonants.[3] In her 1982 description of Alabama, Lupardus identifies the *ist-*prefix as an 'instrumental'; although she provides examples that hint that 'instrumental' may be but one of its functions, she does not discuss any other uses (103–108). She cites Swanton (1922–23: 37) and Booker (1980: 241), who suggest that the prefix has its origins in a complex construction involving the verb *isi* 'take, get' suffixed with *-t* (in this use a same subject subordinating suffix) which presumably preceded the matrix verb. Swanton, who worked with the Alabama in 1906–1913, documents its function in deriving instrumental nouns, but of its use on verbs says "it more often preserves the sense of 'he took it and', 'she took it and'" (cited in Lupardus 1982: 103). Munro and Gordon (1982: 111–112) report that the oldest Chickasaw speaker they have worked with still uses the complex verb construction and in fact prefers it to the cliticized form. Comparison of their description of Chickasaw usage with Swanton's description from seventy-five years ago suggests that the advanced degree of grammaticalization of this prefix in contemporary Alabama may be a fairly recent phenomenon, given that the onset of grammaticalization may date to Proto-Muskogean times.

---

2. Such an association would seem to follow from its origin in the verb 'take'.

3. The forms without the initial [i] occur only in rapid casual speech, and the pronunciation [s] is rare before fricatives and never occurs before /s/ or /h/.

2.2 *The instrumental function*

Like some of the other applicative verb prefixes, the *ist*-prefix functions to derive deverbal nouns, typically concrete nouns that refer to implements or materials used in performing the action of the base verb, as in (8)–(10):

·(8)   *st-afinap-ka*   cp. *afinapli* 'to lock, bar'
        IST-lock-Nom/Mid
        'key; crowbar'

(9)   *st-aaboh-ka*   cp. *aabohli* 'to scrub'
        IST-scrub-Nom/Mid
        'soap'

(10)   *ist-ita-pas-ka*   cp. *pasli* 'to wipe'
        IST-on:ground-wipe-Nom/Mid
        'broom'

Sometimes it is used (in conjunction with the dative) to derive terms for body parts for which there is no simple root as in (11)–(12):

(11)   *ist-in-chak-ka*   cp. *chakli* 'to chop at repeatedly'
        IST-Dat-chop:at-Nom/Mid
        'spurs or beak (of a cock)'

(12)   *ist-il-limit<il>ka*   cp. *limitka* 'to swallow'
        IST-Dat-swallow<Nom/Mid>
        'esophagus'

Rarely, *ist-* derives nouns referring to objects produced in performing the action of the verb, as in (13):

(13)   *ist-oo-pat-ka*
        IST-in:liquid-put:in (pl.obj.)-Nom/Mid
        'dumplings'
        (Compare to *istoopatli* 'spread out [several objects] in liquid with something else' [from *patàali* 'spread out one object].)

Typically, these 'instrumental' nouns also require nominal derivational morphology — some allomorph of the nominal/middle morpheme (Hardy and Montler 1991) as seen in (8)–(13).

When the implement or means by which an action is performed is to be referred to — whether specifically mentioned in the same clause, previously mentioned, or implied — the *ist-* prefix must be used with the verb, as in (14)–(16):

(14)   *icho-n bih-o-n   ist-ibi-li-ti.*
deer-N gun-Foc-N IST-kill-1sI-Asp
'I killed the deer with a gun.'

(15)   *itto-káhchot   ist-abititlìichi-t ...*
wood-for:instance IST-weight:down<Fgr>-T
'They would weight it (deer hide) down with a piece of wood, for example,' [pth]

(16)   *is-ho-po-batl-áa^{n}hosíi-m-o-n*
IST-Distr-1pII-whip-almost-Sbjn-Foc-N
ho-po-batl-áa^{n}hos-t-ool-o.
Distr-1pII-whip-almost-Asp-Evid-Asp
'They were about to whip us, they were supposed to have whipped us.' [nia]

(17)   a.   *talikcho-n asikopli-ti.*
rope-N   knot-Asp
'S/he tied a knot in the rope.'

        b.   *ittakòopa-n ist-asikopli-ti.*
box-N   IST-knot-Asp
'S/he tied up the box (with something).'

The instrumental object is mentioned in (14) and (15); in (16) and (17) no implement is specifically mentioned, but in (16) the contrast of *isbatli* in the first clause with *batli* in the second suggests the anticipated thrashing with the use of clubs, perhaps, as well as fists. When used with the *ist-* prefix as in (17) the verb 'tie a knot in' means 'to tie up with' or 'tie a knot onto'.

It is quite easy to see how the earlier verbal construction meaning 'take (an object) and VERB', presumably motivated by the kinds of restrictions on number of noun phrases per clause described by Munro and Gordon (1982), came to be grammaticalized with an applicative function referring to instrumental arguments. We begin the discussion of the extension of this function to other uses by observing the frankly spatial sense of the original construction: an object at some spatial remove from the agent is brought into the spatial domain of the event. But consider example (18):

(18) *am-ifa-k ibisaani-n is-sa-chifipka-ti.*
my-dog-K nose-N IST-1sII-poke-Asp
'My dog poked me with his nose.'

Example (18) shows that the original sense of taking an object at a distance to perform an action (still transparent in Swanton's time) has been metaphorically extended to include attached body parts, to whose role in the performance of an action the speaker wishes to call attention.

In grammatical terms, then, we can say that an oblique argument is "brought into" the representation of a narrative event. We examine how this sense of semantic peripherality manifests itself in the extended functions of the *ist-* prefix.

2.3 *The associative function*

The *ist-* prefix is commonly used to implicate the existence of an object that is somehow associated with the mentioned participant, but removed from the focus of the narrated event. For instance, *ist-* is used to implicate the presence of a container if its contents are mentioned (19), or some content if a container is mentioned (20).

(19) a. *nipo-n maalichi-li-ti.*
meat-N throw:away-1sI-Asp
'I threw the meat away.'

b. *nipo-n is-maalichi-li-ti.*
meat-N IST-throw:away-1sI-Asp
'I threw the meat (in its package) away.'

(20) a. *ittakòopa-n maalichi-li-ti.*
box-N throw:away-1sI-Asp
'I threw the (empty) box away.'

b. *ittakòopa-n is-maalichi-li-ti.*
box-N IST-throw:away-1sI-Asp
'I threw the box (and its contents) away.'

Example (21b) seems to treat the body metaphorically as a container from which something (in this case a gallbladder is referred to) is removed.

(21)   a.   *mobìl-ka-n   oh-a-m-isi-ti.*
           car-Frn-N Distr-1sIID-Dat-take-Asp
           'They took my car from me.'

     b.   *ist-oh-a-m-isi-ti.*
           IST-Distr-1sIID-Dat-take-Asp
           'They took it out of me.'

But the sense of association is not limited to a container and its contents and can refer to any kind of physical contiguity where one member is central and in the foreground, the other peripheral and in the background, as a branch to a tree or a flower to a stem.

(22)   a.   *itto-n   kotaffi!*
           tree/wood-N break
           'Break the stick (i.e. lying on the ground).'

     b.   *itto-n   is-kotaffi!*
           tree/wood-N IST-break
           'Break off the branch (i.e. attached to the tree).'

(23)   a.   *alpooba-n tipli-l-o.*
           flower-N   pick-1sI-Asp
           'I picked the flowers.'

     b.   *alpooba-n is-tipli-l-o.*
           flower-N   IST-pick-1sI-Asp
           'I picked the flowers.'

In (23a), the gardener is collecting only the flowers, while in (23b) more than the flowers may be removed, or it is emphasized that the separation occurs at the stem attached to the flower. A more thoroughgoing pruning of the plant which removes the stems as well the flowers is possible here, but not in (23a). This usage referring to physically attached entities is reminiscent of the extension to actual body parts referred to in (18).

The previous examples have involved transitive verb stems with external controlling agents, but compare (24)–(26).

(24)   a.   *tinikb-o.*
           bend-Asp
           'It bent (by itself).'

     b.   *is-tinikb-o.*
           IST-bend-Asp
           'It bent.'

(25) a. *acha-hoota-ti.*
          1sII-vomit-Asp
          'I vomited.'

      b. *st-acha-hoota-ti.*
          IST-1sII-vomit-Asp
          'I vomited it up.'

In (24b), a pipe, say, is bent under the weight or force of something in it or attached to it, such as ice. Example (24a) by contrast has a middle sense: the pipe just bends by itself, perhaps by warping. The *ist-* prefix in (24b) implicates some external factor in the realization of the bent pipe. The addition of *ist-* to the word for 'vomit' in (25b) implies the specific contents purged from the stomach, such as medicine or bad food. Impersonal verbs which lack arguments entirely require the use of *ist-* to specify what might be called means or manner.

(26) a. *maali-hchi.*
          blow (of wind)-Asp
          'It's windy.'

      b. *stokhatka-n is-maali-hchi.*
          dust-N   IST-blow (of wind)-Asp
          'The wind is blowing dust.'

      c. *híipli-t   is-maali-hchi.*
          snow<Lgr>-T IST-blow (of wind)-Asp
          'The wind is blowing snow.'

Example (26b) has an accompanying noun 'dust', while (26c) has another verb 'to snow'. (The addition of a patient argument requires yet another applicative.) This sense of accompaniment can be seen in more common uses as well.

(27) a. *iischoba-fa-n ila-l-ah-o.*
          church-Loc-N come-1sI-Fut-Asp
          'I'm coming to the church.'

      b. *oolimpa ist-il-aa-lòo.*
          food   IST-come-1sIirr-Fut
          'I'll bring food.'

(28) *iischoba-fa-n ist-achi-ɬ-aa-lòo.*
      church-Loc-N IST-2sII-go-1sIirr-Fut
      'I'll take you to church.'

The use of the *ist-* prefix with the intransitive verb *ila* 'come' derives the stem 'bring' or 'come with' (27). A more obviously comitative flavor is felt with human undergoers, as in (28).[4] To this point, the range of senses of *ist-* is not unlike that of the English preposition *with*: instrument, associative or comitative, and the suggestion of external cause, influence, or means.

The sense of metaphorical accompaniment has been grammaticalized in the derivation of ordinal numbers from cardinals, and in other expressions of spatial or temporal order.

(29)   a.   *táɬàapi*
              five; be:five

        b.   *an-o-k   is-táɬàapii-mool-o.*
              I-Art-K IST-be:five-Adv-Asp
              'I'm fifth.'

(30)   *sn-o-k   ist-ánnòok-o.*
        You-Art-K IST-finished<Ggr>-Asp
        'You're last.'

The peripheral or extraneous entity that is presented as merely associated with the proposition in question does not have to be an actual object, but may in fact be another proposition, either expressed or implied.

(31)   a.   *biniili-l-o.*
              visit-1sI-Asp
              'I visited.'

        b.   *is-biniili-l-o.*
              IST-visit-1sI-Asp
              'I visited (as well).'

(32)   a.   *roy-ka-n   i^n-haalo-li-ti*
              Roy-Frn-N Dat-hear-1sI-Asp
              'I heard Roy.'

        b.   *roy-ka-n   ist-i^n-haalo-li-ti*
              Roy-Frn-N IST-Dat-hear-1sI-Asp
              'I overheard Roy.'

---

4. The language provides a distinct comitative prefix *ibaa-* used exclusively with human participants and much less frequently than *ist-*. The *ist-* seems to suggest greater responsibility on the part of the agent, the difference perhaps between 'take' and 'go with', both of which contrast with a third (complex) construction using a verb meaning 'together' and thus implying co-subjects. (See Hardy, In preparation).

Example (31a) would be the usual way to indicate one had gone out for the primary purpose of visiting (without mentioning whom), while (31b) suggests the visiting was incidental to the primary activity of, for instance, collecting for charity. The visiting happens spontaneously as an adjoined activity which accompanies the primary reason for the speaker's presence. The continued sense of extraneousness is seen in a second context for which (31b) is appropriate. In this instance, visiting is the purpose of the speaker's presence, but the speaker is accompanied by a non-visiting companion, e.g. an infant who is carried along on the occasion. The contrast between 'hear' and 'overhear' in (32) suggests the same sense of an event performed incidental to one's main purpose. Examples (31)–(32) show that the sense of extraneousness need not inhere in some one participant of the proposition. •

We begin to see a metaphorical extension from the concrete (remote physical object brought into contiguity) to the more abstract (related propositional contents) — from 'with' to 'with respect to', and we now turn to examine these more abstract senses in detail.

2.4 *Associated propositions: cause, reason/purpose, topic*

Several examples we have already seen suggest the possibility of a semantic extension from mere association or contiguity to a causal relationship. For instance, in (24) the use of *ist-* with the middle verb 'bent' to mark the presence of some entity connected to the subject led to the interpretation that it might be the cause of the warping; the mention of the specific matter purged from the stomach implies it is the cause of vomiting (25b).

Alabama has a morphological causative that differs semantically from its cognates in some other Muskogean languages in that it is for the most part limited to direct physical causation.[5] The *ist-* prefix as used in cases such as (27) is semantically very close to a causative such as (33b):

(33) a. *waliika-ti.*
        run:away(Mid)-Asp
        'It ran away.'

---

5. Kimball (1991) refers to this construction in Koasati, the language closest to Alabama, as a *compulsive* to capture this more restricted sense.

    b.   *mobìlka-n walii-lichi-li-ti.*
        car-N   run:away-Cs-1sI-Asp
        'I drove the car.'

When the associated nominal signaled by *ist-* is human, however, the sense is of a more indirect cause than that expressed by *-chi*; (28) does not imply that the undergoer was physically picked up and transported, but rather performed the action herself along with the actor, who perhaps is a facilitator. This sense of a less direct causal relationship is echoed by the use of *ist-* on a variety of (typically) emotion, mental, or communication verbs to indicate the source, reason, or topic of the experience in question.

(34)   a.   *in-cha-palatk-o.*
          Dat-1sII-angry-Asp
          'I'm mad at him/her.'
       b.   *st-in-cha-palatk-o.*
          IST-Dat-1sII-angry-Asp
          'I'm mad at him/her about it.'

In (34b), I am mad at him/her for some specific reason; perhaps she has received preferential treatment or won a prize which I wanted. The person referred to in 34b is not the first cause of my anger; something else is.

(35)   *náasholìiba-n is-ho-cha-paapiłk-o.*
        thing-stolen-N IST-Distr-1sII-lay:blame:on-Asp
        'They blamed me for the theft.'

(36)   a.   *ilaawoota-tiská-nnàa!*
          brag-2sI-Neg:Imp
          'Don't brag!'
       b.   *chim-mobìlka-n ist-im-ilaawoota-tiská-nnàa!*
          your-car-N   IST-Dat-brag-2sI-Neg:Imp
          'Don't brag about your car to your brother!'

(37)   a.   *heła-k   yahka-hchi.*
          Heather-K cry-Asp
          'Heather's crying.'
       b.   *heła-k   is-chi-yahka-hchi.*
          Heather-K IST-2sII-cry-Asp
          'Heather's crying about you.'

The communication verbs in (35)–(36) use the *ist-* prefix to refer to the topic of the speech act, which is the ultimate reason for its being uttered. But, as (35)–(37) suggest, the reason is actually an implied proposition. It is the occurrence of a theft, referred to by a nominalized clause in (35). It is the virtues of the car in (36b) or the fact that one brother possesses one and the other doesn't that inspires the bragging. Something has happened to someone or it is because of their actions that Heather cries in (37). The participants that are actually mentioned in these cases evoke a proposition in which they are implicated and it is that proposition that is offered as a less direct cause of the response in question. English glosses such relationships with a range of prepositions, such as 'about', 'over', 'for' and, more generally, 'with respect to'.

The backgrounded propositional content implicated by *ist-* can be mentioned specifically in constructions such as the purpose clause in (38) and the cause clause in (39):

(38)   *clinton-ka-n   is-ho-bann-o,   mikk-aahii-y-o-n.*
        Clinton-Frn-N IST-Distr-want-Asp be:chief-Fut-Dem-Foc-N
        'They want Clinton for President.'

(39)   a.   *cha-łikaay-o.*
              1sII-wet-Asp
              'I'm wet.'

        b.   *a-l-lokbaa-y-o-k   is-cha-łikaay-o.*
              1sIID-Dat-hot-Dem-Foc-K IST-1sII-wet-Asp
              'I'm sweating because I'm hot.'

The connotation of a causal relationship is often compelling, as when a speaker responded to (40b) by saying "it's like it makes you want it, maybe because you're so hot and thirsty":

(40)   a.   *isilk-o-n   cha-bann-o.*
              drink-Art-N 1sII-want-Asp
              'I want something to drink.'

        b.   *isilk-o-n   is-cha-bann-o.*
              drink-Art-N IST-1sII-want-Asp
              'I really want/need a drink.'

The *ist-* prefix has actually been lexicalized as the only way of forming a direct causative for a number of verbs. There is a (nonproductive) plural suffix *-chi* which is homophonous with the causative and which forms the (third person) duals of a number of motion verbs, as well as occurring with a number of verbs indicating repetitive motion or noise. Verb stems that include this suffix form their causatives with the *ist-* prefix, as in (41)–(42).

(41)   *chasàalichi*   'to rattle'
       ischasàalichi   'to make something rattle'

(42)   *wachàalichi*   'to squeak'
       iswachàalichi 'to make something squeak'

We should note in this context that the motion verbs in (27)–(28), discussed earlier in this section, all have these irregular dual forms ending in *-chi*. The possibility of ambiguity with the dual form, as well as the semantic connection we are suggesting, may have led to the use of the *ist-* prefix in the formation of the only type of causative stem possible for such verbs.

A number of other verbs marked as semantic middles with the *-ka* stem suffix idiosyncratically form their causatives with *ist-* rather than the usual causative.

(43)   *maapka* 'to be taut'   *smaapka*   'to stretch taut'

(44)   *falanka* 'to wake up' *isfalammi*[6]   'to wake someone up'

One middle verb has two causative forms, one derived with *ist-* alone, the other the productive causative form derived from the *ist-* causative.

(45)   a.   *ayapka*   'to get away from, overcome, get the better of'
       b.   *istayapka*   'to cheat out of something, take away from'
       c.   *istayaplichi* 'to let someone take it away from one/make someone take it away from someone else'

Its use with the semantically unusual verb in (46) shows the more indirect sense of causation not possible with the productive causative suffix.

(46)   *chiliita* 'to beg to go, want to go'
       ischiliita 'to urge, encourage, or force to go'

---

6. Middle verbs of this stem shape show an alternation between a stem in *-ka* and a transitivized stem in *-li* or *-lichi*. Example (37) fails to take an alternate stem suffix and (38) requires *ist-* in addition to the *-li* suffix (shown here in its assimilated form. (See Hardy and Montler 1991 and Hardy In preparation for further discussion.)

2.5 *Associated propositions: comparison and others*

We have seen in Section 2.4 a number of ways in which the *ist-* prefix signals something other than a simple nominal argument of the main verb. The *ist-* prefix is often used to implicate the relevance of some propositional content (often left unstated) extraneous to the one that is foregrounded, and that the general sense of 'with respect to' is often interpreted as a causal relationship. Its versatility can be seen as we examine yet another of its functions in implicating a semantic content beyond that of the foregrounded event.

In this vein, we find that *ist-* is involved in the semantics of comparison. (See Hardy and Davis 1988 for a detailed discussion of comparatives in Alabama.) This is understandable when we realize that peripherality to a proposition may be entailed in the semantics of comparatives. For example, in a comparison such as

(47)   I danced better than you.

two narrated events occur: 'I danced' and 'You danced.' And where they differ, that is, with respect to participants 'I' versus 'you,' it is asserted that one participant bested the other with respect to the shared content. In contrast to this, in a different type of comparison such as

(48)   I drank more tea than milk.

only one narrated event occurs, although with some internal complexity (i.e. the coordinate patient): 'I drank tea and milk.' And (48) claims further that 'tea' exceeded 'milk' in the speaker's drinking. Such a difference is overtly reflected in Alabama by the use of *ist-* and a complex verb construction:

(49)   a.   *is-chi-n-káhno-n   bitli-li-ti.*
                IST-2sII-Dat-good<Hgr>-N dance-1sI-Asp
                'I danced better than you.'
        b.   **chi-n-kahno-n bitli-li-ti*

In (49a), the first clause *is-chi-n-káhno-n* asserts that there is something with respect to which the addressee as standard is compared and that it is 'better'.[7] The *ist-* sets that compared content outside any narrated event involving the addressee, and the second clause *bitli-li-ti* identifies that propositional content as 'I danced.'

---

7. The h-grade intensive aspect required in comparatives incorporates the sense of 'more', hence 'good' plus 'more' or 'better' (Hardy and Montler 1988a).

(50) a. *tii-ka-k   kafi-n   im-mayya-n   isko-l-o.*
          tea-Frn-N coffee-N Dat-more:than-N drink-1sgI-Asp
          'I drank more tea than coffee.'
      b. **tii-ka-k kafi-n ist-im-mayya-n isko-l-o*

In (50a), the first clause asserts that 'tea exceeds coffee,' and the absence of *ist-* portends an equal degree of involvement in some narrated event, which is identified by the second clause *isko-l-o* 'I drank.' This contrast is confirmed by syntactic contexts which allow *ist-* to be present or absent, and which show the expected contrast:

(51) a. *holikfa-n aayampo-n im-mayya-n   ischoopa-l-o.*
          shirt-N   pot-N   Dat-more:than sell-1sI-Asp
          'I sold more shirts than pots.'
      b. *holikfa-n aayampo-n st-im-mayya-n   ischoopa-l-o.*
          shirt-N   pot-N   IST-Dat-more:than sell-1sI-Asp
          'I sold the shirts for more than the pots.'

Sentence (51a) is like (50a): 'shirts' and 'pots' are being sold simultaneously and their comparison is in the constitutive amounts. In (51b), two separate narrated events occur: 'I sold the shirts' and 'I sold the pots.' And now the comparison implied by *mayya* 'exceed' is interpreted in the less event-determining (more "extraneous") way of "price", rather than the more essential content of "amount". The fact that *ist-* should imply two narrated events is certainly appropriate to the domain of comparison, but as we have seen in 2.4 it is not confined to it. And this independence finally convinces us that it is indeed *ist-* itself which is responsible for this content. Compare:

(52) a. *heła-n   i^n-fayli-li-n   aasiil-o   mobila-n.*
          Heather-N Dat-leave-1sI-N wash-Asp car-n
          'I let/left it with Heather to wash the car.'
      b. *heła-n   ist-i^n-fayli-li-n   aasiil-o   mobila-n.*
          Heather-N IST-Dat-leave-1sI-N wash-Asp car-n
          'I left it up to Heather to wash the car.'

In (52a) there is an activity of washing in which the speaker is participating; but, for whatever reason, the speaker interrupts his activity, leaving Heather to finish the job. The two events, *fayli* 'stop/cease/leave' and *aasiili* 'wash' are comingled. But in (52b), the speaker never gets his hands wet; that is, he abandons the task before it is begun, and the two events are now separate entities. They do not combine to create a single, however complex, narrated event. First, the speaker leaves something up to her and it is identified in the proposition that Heather washes the car; the two are distinct, though not unrelated, narrated events.

In (49)–(52), the clause with suffixed *-n* sets the backgrounded content against which some declaration is asserted. (See Davis and Hardy 1984, 1988 for a detailed discussion of the semantics of *-n*.) In (49), the background is the content that '(I am) better than you' and the foreground is the identification of how I am better. In (52), the background is that I have left something to Heather and the foreground identifies what that was. The relationship and contrast between foreground and background is not of a fixed sort; both may be asymmetrical modulations of a single conceptual unit, or the two may be kept more distinct. And this latter is the content of *ist-* here, a peripherality of separation.

This generalized sense of *ist-* as indicating 'with respect to' some associated but peripheral propositional content, as we suggested in 2.4, is found outside complex constructions such as comparatives. Consider (53)–(55).

(53)   *máaloolo.*
       right-Evid-Asp
       'That's right.'

The verb *máali* has a range of meanings, the most basic of which seems to be to indicate agreement, that something is 'right' or 'correct'. It has another usage shown in (54).

(54)   A: *cha-hoyapli-hchi.*
            2sII-tired-Asp
            'I'm tired.'
       B: *an-óo-k   máal-ool-o.*
            I-Contr-K right-Evid-Asp
            'I am too.'

(55)   *sn-óo-k   is-máal-ool-o.*
       You-Contr-K IST-right-Evid-Asp
       'You're the same (way).'

Example (55) with *ist-* refers to whatever propositional content with respect to which the addressee is judged as being the same (e.g. being tired).

We have shown a range of functions of a morpheme that originated in a separate clause having the narrow sense of taking an object at a spatial remove in order to perform some foregrounded event. We note here the duality of this conception: an object is at once asserted to be at a distance and peripheral to, but yet relevant to some task at hand. The claim of relevance or association with the foregrounded event becomes highlighted in an iconic way as the construction becomes grammaticalized: what was once related by a separate clause is now 'part' of the foregrounded event. The sense of spatial remove that Swanton suggests was still the focal meaning of *ist-* seventy-five years ago appears only sporadically in contemporary usage, as in (56b).

(56) a. *heła-n   fayli-l-o.*
          Heather-N leave-1sI-Asp
          'I left Heather.'

      b. *heła-n   is-fayli-l-o.*
          Heather-N IST-leave-1sI-Asp
          'I took Heather somewhere and left her.'

The speaker of (57) noted both the instrumental interpretation and the allative for (57b). In one case the dative is interpreted as indicating a possessor, in the other a benefactive argument.

(57) a. *roy-ka-n   im-iltoono-l-o.*
          Roy-Frn-N Dat-work-1sI-Asp
          'I'm working for Roy.'

      b. *roy-ka-n   st-im-iltoono-l-o.*
          Roy-Frn-N IST-Dat-work-1sI-Asp
          'I used Roy's stuff to work.'
          'I went to get someone to work for Roy.'

Speakers explain the difference between (58a) and (58b) by saying that in (58b) the speaker has gone to the door and checked and then reports on the weather.

(58) a. *akmi-hchi.*
          freeze-Asp
          'It's freezing.'

      b. *ist-akmi-hchi.*
          IST-freeze-Asp
          'It's freezing.'

Such interpretations attest to the diverse application of this morpheme as it interacts with contexts. In the proper context, the form *ist-i^n-fayli* (compare to (52)) may also exhibit the peripherality of 'spatial remove':

(59) a. *am-poskoohaasi-n heła-n   i^n-fayli-l-o.*
          my-children-N   Heather-N Dat-leave-1sI-Asp
          'I left my children with Heather.'

      b. *am-poskoohaasi-n heła-n   ist-i^n-fayli-l-o.*
          my-children-N   Heather-N IST-Dat-leave-1sI-Asp
          'I took my children over to Heather's and left them.'

3. The Grammaticalization of *ist-*

The range of concepts expressed through *ist-* and the attentuation of its spatial
sense suggest an advanced stage of grammaticalization (cf. Heine, Claudi, and
Huennemeyer 1991). This observation is supported by the existence of a number
of minimal pairs in which the difference in meaning attributable to the presence
of *ist-* does not relate in any obvious way to the range of common uses described
here — that is, it is lexicalized to a considerable degree.[8] Compare the binary
contrast in (60) and the ternary one in (61).

(60) *choopa*   'to buy';   *ischoopa*   'to sell'
      talaami 'to be dirty'; *istalaami* 'to be ugly'
      balàaka 'to lie down'; *isbalàaka* 'to be lined up'

(61) *nàaho*   'to exist';   *in-nàaho*   'to have (dative)';
      is-nàaho 'to be rich'

In one case *ist-* is used along with the dative to derive an idiom from a noun, in
a manner suggesting a metaphor similar to an American English idiom popular
in the sixties — *It's my bag; Papa's got a brand new bag.*

(62) a. *sokcha*   'bag, sack'
      b. *isti^{n}sokcha*   'to be a fan of, an enthusiast of'

In fact, there is a small number of verbs that clearly must have been poly-
morphemic at one time, but which have undergone base loss, so that no bare
stem remains, as in (63)–(64).

(63) *istibitchi*   'to joke' (*ibitchi)

---

8. Our assessment of amount of lexicalization is based on the extensive lexical corpus of Sylestine,
Hardy, and Montler 1993.

(64)   *istimposaachi*   to be jealous of' (*imposaachi, *posaachi)

Finally, *ist-* has become grammaticalized in the formation of a number of aspectual auxiliaries which follow main verbs and are themselves grammaticalizations of independent directional/positional verbs. For instance, consider (65)–(67):

(65)   *iisa*   'to be located (plural)

        istíisa   'continue (Lgr, used with plural verb)

(66)   *aɬa* 'to go'

        istaɬa   'start; to go on a certain way'

(67)   *ila*   'to come'

        istíila   'during a period until a certain time'

4.   Conclusion

We have shown that the traditional gloss 'instrumental' for the *ist-* prefix implies a much narrower range of functions than those for which *ist-* is currently used in Alabama. We suggest that the two general senses that derive from *ist* — remoteness or extraneousness on the one hand and association or relevance on the other — can be traced to the semantic duality of the original verbal construction with 'take and'. A verb such as 'go', which is often the source of an allative marker or a directional prefix such as *ilt-* 'go and' in Alabama, incorporates only the sense of movement towards some distant point. A verb like 'take', however, includes not only the sense of movement towards a location at a distance, but also the taking up of an object at that location such that it is now 'with' the actor, that is, both a sense of distance and peripherality as well as a sense of association, contiguity, and relevance. The majority of current uses of *ist-* seem to emphasize the sense of relevance and association rather than removal, and to the degree that relevance and association can be realized in grammar in a multiplicity of domains, it is not surprising that the *ist-* prefix is ubiquitous in the grammar of Alabama. What remains to be shown is the path of grammaticalization that *ist-* has taken and how it compares to the development of the cognate prefixes in other Muskogean languages.

Acknowledgments

This paper is an extensively revised version of a paper presented to the Linguistic Association of the Southwest (LASSO) in October 1987, Dallas, Texas. Hardy (in preparation) provides a more extensive discussion of the grammaticalization of the *ist-* prefix.

We wish to express our appreciation for the patient assistance of Cora Sylestine, Wanda Poncho, Vincent Celestine, and Dorcas Bullock in providing the information that is the basis for this paper. We dedicate this paper to the memory of our friend and colleague, Cora Sylestine. We wish also to thank the following organizations for financial assistance in support of research conducted over a number of years: the Department of Linguistics and Semiotics of Rice University, the Organized Research Program of the University of North Texas, the Melville Jacobs Fund, the National Endowment for the Humanities (RT209103–88), and the National Science Foundation (BNS90222141).

References

Booker, Karen M. 1980. Comparative Muskogean: Aspects of Proto-Muskogean verb morphology. Lawrence: University of Kansas Ph.D. Dissertation.

Davis, Philip W. 1991. Language and intelligence: the coherence of linguistic semantics. *Studies in English Linguistics and Literature* 16.139–48.

Davis, Philip W., and Heather K. Hardy. 1987. Nominal-sentential morphology in Alabama. *Southwest Journal of Linguistics* 7.87–101.

Davis, Philip W., and Heather K. Hardy. 1988. The absence of noun marking in Alabama. *International Journal of American Linguistics* 54.279–308.

Hardy, Heather K. 1991. The dative in Alabama. Paper presented to the Linguistic Association of the Southwest, October 15, Austin, Texas.

Hardy, Heather K. In preparation. Grammar of the Alabama language.

Hardy, Heather K., and Philip W. Davis. 1988. Comparatives in Alabama. *International Journal of American Linguistics* 54.209–31.

Hardy, Heather K., and Philip W. Davis. 1993. The semantics of agreement in Alabama. *International Journal of American Linguistics* 59.453–472

Hardy, Heather K., and Timothy R. Montler. 1988a. Alabama radical morphology: H-infix and disfixation. *In Honor of Mary Haas*, ed. by William Shipley, 377–409. New York: Mouton de Gruyter.

Hardy, Heather K., and Timothy R. Montler. 1988b. Imperfective gemination in Alabama. *International Journal of American Linguistics* 54.379–415.

Hardy, Heather K., and Timothy R. Montler. 1991. The formation of the Alabama middle voice. *Lingua* 85. 1–15.

Heine, Bernd, Ulrike Claudi, and Friedrike Huennemeyer. 1991. *Grammaticalization: A conceptual framework*. Chicago: University of Chicago Press.

Kimball, Geoffrey. 1991. *Koasati grammar*. Lincoln: University of Nebraska Press.

Klaiman, M. 1991. Control and grammar. *Linguistics* 29.623–651.

Lupardus, Karen Jacque. 1982. The language of the Alabama Indians. Lawrence: University of Kansas Ph.D. Dissertation.

Martin, Jack B. 1991a. Lexical and syntactic aspects of Creek causatives. *International Journal of American Linguistics* 57.194–229.

Martin, Jack B. 1991b. Possessor raising and possessor construal in Muskogean (and French). Manuscript.

Mithun, Marianne. 1991. Active/agentive case marking and its motivations. *Language* 67.510–546.

Montler, Timothy R., and Heather K. Hardy. 1990. The phonology of Alabama agent agreement. *Word* 41.257–76.

Montler, Timothy R., and Heather K. Hardy. 1991. The phonology of negation in Alabama. *International Journal of American Linguistics* 57.1–23.

Munro, Pamela. 1989. Chickasaw applicatives. Manuscript.

Munro, Pamela, and Lynn Gordon. 1982. Syntactic relations in Western Muskogean. *Language* 58.81–115.

Swanton, John R. 1922–23. A Sketch of the Alabama language. Ms. 4127, National Anthropological Archives, Washington, D.C.

Sylestine, Cora, Heather K. Hardy, and Timothy Montler. 1993. *Dictionary of the Alabama Language*. Austin: University of Texas Press.

About the authors

Heather K. Hardy is presently Professor and Chair of the Department of English at Northern Illinois University. Prior to that, she taught for more than a decade at the University of North Texas. She received her B. A. from Rice in 1974, and her Ph. D. from UCLA in 1979. She was visiting Assistant Professor at Rice in 1982–83, during Syd Lamb's chairmanship. Her interest in Amerindian language began when she was an undergraduate and has continued throughout her career. She treated Tolkapaya Yavapai in her dissertation, and her work on the Muskogean language Alabama since 1980 has produced a co-authored dictionary and many papers.

Philip W. Davis is Professor of Linguistics at Rice University, where he has taught since 1969. He has been Syd Lamb's colleague since the founding of the Rice department in 1982. He received his Ph. D. from Cornell University in 1965. From 1965 to 1969 he taught at Simon Fraser University. During that period he began fieldwork on a Salishan language, and has been involved in fieldwork and language description since that time. The present paper arose from a collaboration on Alabama with Dr. Heather K. Hardy which began in 1983.

CHAPTER 20

Attention to Microspace

Plotting the Connections of a Cultural Theme

John Regan   Joe Stephenson
Claremont Graduate University   *Albuquerque, New Mexico*
Nancy Pine
Mount St. Mary's College

1. Overview

Lamb's contributions to the understanding of cognition and cultural information systems span diverse theoretical and applied domains. Fundamental to these contributions is his development of the scholarly world's recognition of the interconnected, network nature of knowledge — the nondiscrete characteristics of the cultural and, specifically, the linguistic informational system. In addition to his demonstration of the actuality of this integration and his refinement of a notational system for its description, Lamb has initiated a range of applications from computers to education. Our report concerns the latter application.

Lamb's work provides a concrete, although frustrating, point of view from which to study the diversity of a culture, a topic which has, in the socio-political environment of the late twentieth century, become an issue of vigorous axiological and political world discourse, particularly in the education establishment.

In the monograph, *Whitehead and Lamb, A New Network of Connection* (Regan et al, eds. 1982), some directions of the educational applications of Lamb's work have been discussed. In the present research, our interest centers in encouraging educators' recognition of a procedural, methodological issue related to any study of cultural forms:

From the network of relationship theory viewpoint, any part of a culture is, in fact, connected to all the rest; therefore there cannot be, logically, any linear, one-dimensional pursuit of the "meaning" of an event or word. Rather, the reality of cultural information is more a galaxial one. Hence from this view which we accept, the tracing of the "meaning" of words, behaviors, or events, can move in a very considerable number of alternative directions. Which of these directions is chosen, what first step is primary, secondary, etc., is neither obvious nor, actually, is there a sequence. The explication of this methodological fact is, we propose, of considerable importance to end-of-century educational theory and practice. The following section introduces our discussion of a five-year study of one aspect of one cultural group present in American schools.

2.   Noticing a Nonlinguistic, Cultural Event

We notice and puzzle over an event in another culture as we might over an unfamiliar lexical feature we hear in discourse. But what strategies can we use to find that event's connections with the rest of the whole contextual informational system? In encounters with another society, observers may note a detail and suspect that cross cutting this "unit" lie masses of interacting cultural and linguistic informational networks. But how does an investigator systematically follow those networks of relationships from a first observation? How is the path followed so that the next steps taken (so that those observations) will lead further into the whole culture? How can the first data base, begun by that first noticed event unit, be expanded so as to point out next productive directions of the search for relationships?

When travelers in another society or — as is our interest — educators in an ethnically diverse school system notice an event which is unlike that which they have experienced in their own cultural context, they may puzzle at it, considering it simply as an interesting fragment of daily experience. Or, they may, over time, persist in looking for related events until by accumulation of those events, an outline of a previously unrecognized, cultural pattern begins to become apparent.

For example, one member of our research team was stopped for some twenty minutes in dense, six-lane traffic on a Beijing overpass. At a fork in this overpass, six lanes were packed with motionless cars. One vehicle on the extreme left moved several inches towards the researcher's car as a signal of intent to get into the right fork. However, the driver of the researcher's car inched up his vehicle to prevent this possibility. More interestingly, each of the Chinese passengers, by very slight nods and vocalizations, indicated a basic nonverbal assent for this action. After that observation, in numerous locations and events (in diverse allomorphic variations and contexts) the essence of this cultural unit was seen repeatedly: "only give way when the other (be it car, bike, or person) has definitely blocked the path". When we gave verbal descriptions of such events, Chinese associates would react knowingly, their comments revealing a recognition of the rule.

In a stratificational model of non-separable networks, there is little room to claim causes, effects, or origins; co-presence is all that can be suggested. And as cultural themes and dispositions interact in multiplicities of nonlinear ways, consequently, the tracing of the correlations of an observation is a baffling and difficult task.

What observational and notational strategies exist for both the extrapolation from such a nonverbal event, and for the identification of the cultural impetus to that fraction of behavior? It is most unlikely that the lines of closest connection of such an observed cultural fragment would lie in the time sequence in which the examples were experienced by our observer. So where to go next in a search of a pattern for this event? If this observation were considered to be a first thread to pursue into the cultural matrix, where would the exploration of that topic go next to get further grasp on the theme? Where into the broader domains of the society's meaning and behavior might such a starting observation lead? Could such a single observation lead to others? If so, which others? There is the problem. What would the logical proximity of a subsequent observation be to the original one? And finally the larger question: Could the data eventually collected by disciplined observation and testing be extrapolated to a rule or cultural trait? If so, at what point in the data gathering would that rule or trait be established. And how many noticings make the meaning?

As Lamb's work with language has demonstrated, tracing the relations and associations of a linguistic feature is complex. In addition to all those he records, pursuing the networks of connection of nonverbal units (such as the above example and those below) presents further problems.

3. The First Part of Our Observing

In addition to linguistic information, a culture's nonverbal knowledge, including the peoples' visual knowledge, is a network of inseparable interrelationships. So, too, any evidence, or any fragment of such a subsystem network could be pursued to a final ethnography of the entirety. A first observation could be used as the basis from which eventual conclusions about a culture were made. These problems of discovering the next logical steps in the construction of the "meaning" of a nonverbal unit is the issue with which we have wrestled. This problem began for us in the following simple, commonplace events:

Like many outsiders to a culture experiencing a puzzling difference in a way of life, one of our research group was struck by an event in which a Chinese associate insisted on taking his hands from the bicycle which he was riding down a hill and wildly sketching his name in the air with his finger. Puzzled by this insistence on writing the Chinese name which the visitor had already heard numerous times (and which he could easily pronounce and spell), the Westerner asked why — at such an inappropriate location and situation — this insistence on visual air writing.

The answer came immediately; there were six entirely different ways to write this bicyclist's name in Chinese. To this piece of information were added two other points, and these together suggested a connection that intrigued the observer:

1. Nearby was an inscription on a wall that was, according to the biker, presented in Mao's handwriting. Each character of this three foot high inscription, was crafted by an artisan whose employment was just this sort of task.
2. Furthermore, the badge that the Chinese was wearing was in Sun Yat Sen's script which the bicyclist could easily recognize and reproduce.

The Westerner puzzled about this set of statements related to an apparent Chinese attention to the complex, geometric nature of the 40,000–50,000 characters of the Chinese writing system. In the next days, this in-the-air or on-the-hand, sketched writing was noticed on the street, in offices and meeting halls. With only the barest of features — indeed, even from backward or sideways positions — these transient, geometric movements were immediately understood by the Chinese interactants. When and by what means was this visual acuity learned? What would young children's abilities and visual enculturative experiences in such a cultural context be?

And increasingly arose the question: Where next would we go to observe other features of this theme? Where would the next level of relevant meaning show? How proxemically or logically close on the lines of connections from that first event was any next detail or component of such a relationship network? The steps in the logic of events follow.

4.   **Chronology of Related Observations**

1.   A university student, discussing the brilliance of a work of Chinese literature, spoke about the beauty of one of the written characters selected from some
dozen possibilities by the classic writer. "I love the look of that character" the
student said, and other students around the room nodded in agreement. Certainly,
these shapes had for the Chinese a special importance that included both a sense
of and interest in a type of architectural beauty that we westerners did not
recognize. Increasingly we found evidence of special attitudes regarding these
complex geometric characters. Attitudes not matched in Western experience.

Then other observations occurred, for example:

2.   A Chinese commented that he found the shape of one character of a name
card "very nice". We subsequently showed informally the same name card to a
total of 59 Chinese, asking each person which of the five characters were the
most appealing. Each of the 59 promptly gave a response. Furthermore, to our
surprise, when asked to rank the other four characters on the name card, again,
each of the 59 Chinese (across different social levels) complied, frequently
giving reasons for their individual choices. A similar question to similar people
in the United States about the very same name (though on an English script card)
always drew puzzled, curious responses. And never was a choice made. Such a
question about the pleasantness of letters or words seemed ridiculous to all of the
Westerners.

3.   Discussing his young daughter, a Chinese father mentioned that he had used
five criteria to select her name at birth. Among the criteria for the name-choice
was the character's shape itself. The father replied that the characters of the
given name needed to "balance" the family name, i.e., to match the simplicity of
the surname. Subsequently, we discussed this topic with many Chinese parents,
and found frequently reported that they had indeed made a choice of names
based on design — for example, simplicity, complexity, balance, etc. Sometimes
at first our question was not understood. But then perhaps this type of decision
about names is made as a judgment deep within the non-verbal awareness. In
further studies we found more evidence of this.

For example, at one home the parents replied that shape factors had *not*
been considered. Later in the evening, however, a page of the parents' original
48 choices was brought out — six rows of eight characters. Of these, one quarter
had been eliminated with an X. When we asked why this one and that one had

been crossed out, we were often told (and with some embarrassed laughter) that indeed the shapes had not fitted well. Other examples of this were observed with other families.

So in what ways are these events related? What was their proximity to a theme, a topic cluster like that of which the first bike-event was an example? Where exactly was each event that we had noticed located in the galaxial meaning universe? Did the "units" placed together point to an origin or source of this apparent focused Chinese interest and involvement in two-dimensional, geometric forms? We needed more information. But Lamb's model warned against assuming that the networks constituting meaning lay in any linear cause/effect association, or that a simple path to the heart of the meaning system would be found.

5.   Associated Observation/Data Collection

We heard of school children memorizing and repeating aloud the 100 most common Chinese names one at a time while alternately visually focusing on the different characters for those names, for example, looking at 'Li' or 'Wang' and saying those names in unison as each of the array of different characters were pointed out by the teacher. Also, we had heard of the necessity of children and adults practicing looking up characters in a dictionary and telephone book by the character's geometric likenesses (and hence engaging in a type of architectural microspace memory experience). Would this practice in visualizing for the purpose of "looking up" words set in process skills that somewhere in the universe of Lambian interconnectedness would have an outcome?

We turned to a more formal type of data-gathering while continuing to record any chance observation opportunities:

1.   We tested young children to estimate their visual memory and noticing-acuity concerning this narrow band of two dimensional shapes called characters. Now, one year on from the original observation, we were hypothesizing that accompanying Chinese attention to such a form of visual, two-dimensional detail, perhaps other dispositions, habits, etc., were to be found in a child's develop-ment. We first designed a simple reproduction memory test using five characters. These characters' meanings, we were assured, even the bright, first-grade children would certainly not know. Hence, these shapes, although recognized as "writing" to the children had no semantic meanings for them. They were simply

graphical shapes, part of the seen world of everyday life — the visual semiotic. Each character, written boldly on separate pieces of 5″ × 8″ paper, was held up to the group for 10 seconds, one at a time, then removed. At a signal, the children reproduced the character. First, with these Grade 1, then younger children, and later with Western children of a much wider age range, some 250 children were tested.

The results were impressive. With speed and accuracy, in unexpected evenness (linear, horizontal straightness) and precision the Chinese Grade 1 children reproduced these shapes from memory. Some children were seen moving their bodies, embedding the shape's general form and direction of lines. The results suggested that the children had developed (through their six years of looking at their environment) sophisticated, microspace-noticing strategies. However, testing of Western children revealed a very different result indeed. We tried this test from Grades 1 and 2 up to Grade 6 in Australia and the United States. The results were uneven, large, disordered shapes scattered across the paper, and quite unlike the originals shown for the 10 seconds. When we asked Western adults to do this looking/memory test. The results were like those found among the grade school children — sometimes worse. Many of the Westerners reported using mnemonic strategies (e.g., "there's a roof in it") a method not mentioned by Chinese who seemed rather to see and know the shape as a whole.

A Chinese looking at the results of American adult efforts to reproduce these five shapes was astonished with what he regarded as the "chaos" of the results. We finally reminded him, with some defensive ego, that the Westerners were not accustomed to seeing such shapes. "But all they have to do is look and remember", he replied, stating an attitude and opinion echoed many times among the Chinese with whom we discussed this issue. The Chinese apparently thought any such shape was surely quite easily reproduced once it had been looked at.

Were there then, indeed, skills that the Chinese children had that came from frequent focused, two-dimensional, equally-spaced, visual semiotic, micro-noticing? Certainly children's enormous motor and perceptual efforts — to understand and to make the huge number of characters necessary for literacy — would surely encourage different habits than would the experience of Western orthographic learning. When we tested other forms of this ability in younger ages in both Chinese and Western societies, we continued to find dramatic differences between the two populations. The Chinese children indeed were more practiced in that noticing skill. But did that practiced noticing produce — in a Whorfian-like form of association — other skills or behaviors and at earlier ages? What if very young Chinese and American children were not asked to remember and reproduce shapes, but rather were invited to create "writing". We devised a second formal probe to explore this possibility.

2.   Through native speaker representatives we told, in words and action, some two hundred children ranging in age from under two-years to five-years in seven different geographic areas of China to "pretend to write a letter" to their parents. After numerous trial runs of this probe and numerous fine-tuning efforts (which in themselves unexpectedly produced valuable data related to our interest), we finally designed precise instructions.

There were astonishing features to the results. At very young ages, even two years of age, some children produced tiny, linear, discrete, box-like shapes analogous to the character system. In some, we needed to enlarge the page on which the "writing" was done to be able to see the detail. This doubling and more of size was necessary in order to see completely the box-like shapes densely impacted and compacted in a tiny, narrow, linear band. Looking at these enlargements was astonishing.

And there was more to surprise us. Before we introduced a time limit on the task, some very young Chinese children worked on these small shapes for 15–20 minutes with amazing persistence and care. Western children's productions tended to be quickly accomplished and were continuous, bigger, more oval-shaped, filling more of the page and rarely arranged linearly. To be able to appreciate completely these children's results, we recorded every micro-feature of a character and produced a comprehensive and extensive grid of components that included each micro-variation of line, angle, and position. The resulting chart could be, therefore, used in later testing to evaluate these children's approximations of characters and to illustrate the extent of their learning from environmental exposure.

3.   To estimate the speed and accuracy of pre-kindergarten children's noticing of micro-variations in characters, we gave a further test using three sets of 10 identical characters repeated five times with photocopied, and hence identical units. In each set there were two rows with one of the 10 characters having a minor difference, perhaps a tiny fragment — a dot or a line omitted from one. The test scores themselves, in comparison with those of Western children, indicated a more accurate noticing by the Chinese. But more interesting was the fact that many of the Chinese children's "errors" indicated a highly-detailed attention to the most minute page print imperfections which we had not noticed (for example, a spot from the photocopy screen on the reprinted test page).

Again, kindergartners' evidence of disciplined, lengthy perusal of the test shapes was astonishing.

4. We next set out to test children's awareness of a single component of writing. We speculated that much younger children than those we had tested, for example 1½–2 years old (whose linguistic level was such that they might not understand what to do if we verbally asked them to "write a letter"), would also have learned basic architectural aspects. We selected the correct "upright position" and designed a test that could be used in China and the West. Again, after numerous mis-starts and subsequent adjustments, we presented Chinese and Western children, one at a time, with three sets of different shapes, pictures, characters, and letters placed on 2″ × 2″, laminated surfaces. The sets were of (i) pictures of commonplace objects, (ii) characters, and (iii) letters. The pictures were the first group scattered on the table. These we used so as to give the preverbal children the idea of the game, namely turning the pictures right side up. Each set of 5 cards was, one at a time, scattered on a table to be placed "right side up". We showed what to do with the pictures. As we did, we role played, stating, for example, "Now this pig should stand upright", "Oh, this chair is upside-down! That's not right!" We found indeed that the Chinese knew significantly better than the Westerners what side was the correct side up for characters (and the Western children were better at orienting the letters). Hence, at an even earlier awareness of this two-dimensional system which is seen in the general daily life environment, there was identifiable learning. We took this result as a further indication of the early visual learning that goes on in human growth and, importantly, as an area of potential future, visual semiotic research.

5.   We next gave kindergarten to second-grade children a copying test that included (a) the original five unfamiliar characters used in the first visual-memory test, (b) five English alphabet letters, and (c) five invented shapes. These graphical forms, placed together in one line on the board, were displayed in the front of the classroom. The children were given as long as they liked to copy these. There were in this test's results only 42 slight malformations and only one reversal in the more than 2,800 copies. However, an unexpected result, and one of considerable interest to us, was the following: In one class of 52 children aged 6 years, when we returned in the afternoon to pursue other tests, the teacher proposed that we see how much of the morning's task the class still remembered. An interesting proposal, we thought.

The children were given the same sized piece of paper on which in the morning they had copied the three sets of shapes. They were asked to write the same unfamiliar Chinese characters which they had earlier directly copied from the board now erased. Although we expected minimal success in this task, in fact, there was more like a 90 percent recall and only 28 very slight deviations in the 260 attempts. We considered this further suggestive evidence that these children were becoming sophisticated in a domain of visual memory of shape not specifically emphasized in Western culture. Naturally, the Chinese would be expected to be better at this sort of task. But that, of course, is the point. We have begun preliminary replication of these tests with Japanese children in Japan, where there are similarities but also differences related to the orthographic system. We look forward to identifying what may be similarities and differences.

6.   Further Observations of a Culture's Attention to Variations in Graphical Details

As we proceeded, unexpected side inputs of evidence contributed to our growing sense that the "meaning" of the first observational event was rich and diverse beyond our imagining.

1.   For example, a week after a request to a Chinese associate for his name to be written in Chinese, one of our group finally received it. Why had that simple request for writing a name taken all that time? Could not the associate, as would a Westerner, have done it right then and there at the time of the request? The answer was "no", and the reason for that negative was intriguing. The Chinese associate "had been thinking through" some 50 character alternatives to the **approximation** of the Western name (further evidence of mental visual cogitation that was unlike our own skills which we practice). But why was an "approximation" of this name necessary? Why could it not be exactly (as it is in English) reproduced? There were dozens of alternative characters for the same-sounded name part. The Chinese had been looking through all the alternatives so that our colleague was not given a name that read as something insulting but rather aptly appropriate. But the sounded name would be the same.

We examined this topic from various angles. What had been the alternative shapes, the characters which the Chinese friend had considered for our colleague's name? Among those mentioned was one with a regal, aristocratic meaning. Had **that** one been chosen, the name would have been pronounced the same, but the name's meaning would have been very different. However, in a socialist nation, that character option had been rejected for politically sensitive reasons.

2.   A Chinese research associate in China had been considering changing his name. He had gone to a person who specialized in problems caused, as it was believed, by individuals' given names. This specialist inspected the alternative meanings of the different shapes behind the heard name and told our associate that a name with "more water in it" was needed. He had been told earlier that his name, its visual form, was related to a health problem and our colleague consequently studied some 150 characters, none of which would have changed the actual *sound* of his name but only the meaning. Finally he decided to keep the character that he had despite the effort put into his exploration. None of the alternatives seemed quite right for him. Still, in this process, he had been perusing mentally for some months those tight, equally-spaced forms and looking for some feature that would help his problem.

3.   A young woman, speaking about her exploration of feminist literature, claimed that male biases were in the Chinese writing system and were visually based. These biases, unlike *he* or *she, doctor* or *woman doctor,* etc., problems in English would not be heard in speech — only remembered from the visual form. Here was a topic we needed to study, so our team devised a probe of this topic. On the top of separate pages was written one character with "woman" in it which had negative meanings. These included 'envy', 'treacherous', 'chaos', 'improper', 'suspicion', 'ill will', 'enmity', 'grudge', 'trouble', 'blunder', 'corrupt', 'jeopardize', 'obstruct', 'finicky', 'slave', 'give pleasure' or 'amuse', 'compliance with'. Each included a "side" that was the character for female. Looking at these characters on the top of each page, a person would see that they each had, in terms of shape, something (this female "side") in common. Each character had on its left-hand side this similar form. And this was apparent even if that character's meaning ('woman') was not known.

Hence, embedded into the visual representation of these derogatory words (but not their audible spoken form) was the meaning for 'woman'. We showed Chinese the separate pages. On the top of each was one of the negative 'woman' words. Underneath each of the top negative words were 10 different lists of characters. We asked the Chinese to select the one character from the list which reminded them of the word above. We speculated (and were correct) that this visual meaning 'woman' carried over into the awareness of the Chinese speaker when thinking of those derogatory words despite the fact there was no logical or semantic connection.

Whereas, again, in English a gender-bias element such as *he* or *man* could be readily eliminated or replaced, within the Chinese visual character system, the bias component was inextricably embedded in the whole Chinese word-character unit.

4.   As we continued to identify examples of this interest in the vast two-dimensional character forms, Chinese attitudes, customs and opinions about the nature of such forms in the population became apparent. There was a whole range of negative and positive values, etc., about words, actions, gifts, etc., that connected back to written form. These went deep into the Chinese social practices and often had their basis in the extensive repertoire of homonymous characters. Hence, we suggest a generally literate person would in a visual way understand these, and this awareness would extend a bias into the avenues of the spoken realm.

We encountered in the substratum of many people's awareness opinions about characters these architectural forms linked to attitudes about motor and perceptual sharpness. These were evidences of a meta-awareness of the system. Some of these recorded in conversations are listed below:

- "Characters are geometric forms";
- "The rules of manual construction of a character are analogous to performing mathematic operations";
- "Our characters, which we practice in our schools, are, in fact, types of formulae";
- "Chinese learn to write, character by character, and this requires discrimination of large numbers of different visual forms together with long hours of practice";
- "Learning to write Chinese characters is like practicing with a stroke design whereby understanding of multifarious visual forms and space is used to produce just the exactly-right character within a constraint of space";
- "Chinese concentrate on the visual strokes' design and notice the strokes' detail in building their frame of character within relative heights and widths";
- "Geometry also is the branch of mathematics dealing with the properties and relationships of lines, angles, surfaces, and solids — and the properties and relationships among those lines, angles, surfaces";
- "We think of characters as being space defined by lines".
- "Each character is a rectangular white space with lines balanced within it".

5.   Deviations from a character's exact form were frequently rejected, even to the point of dismissing as "meaningless" the clearly obvious characters. Indeed,

even with children's attempts, the expectancy of precision and accuracy about characters was surprisingly vigorous. For example, we asked a Chinese about the possibilities of replacement of a character's component. In one case each of the components had a distinct meaning. We asked about reversing the pattern on the right rather than the left side of the unit. Would not a parent or friend guess the meaning intended by recognizing both "word parts" but reversed accidentally in position? The answer was energetically negative. There was no tolerance for such error, no acceptance of "cute" mistakes.

6.   We saw no children's approximations of writing like those sketched notes to parents in the West often displayed abundantly on doors and cupboards as evidence of child-like play.

7.   When we asked Chinese adults their opinions of samples of our Western children's "pretend-to-write" tests, they stated (choosing words diplomatically) that they would be embarrassed to have their child perform like those samples. On the other hand, Western parents chose neutral or positive words to describe these same imperfect Western children's approximation. When we reversed our question showing the Chinese samples to Western adults, we received negative descriptions ("mechanical", "mathematical", and "tight") to describe the Chinese child's results.

8.   Adding other questions to our interviews on these topics, we asked what the parents, looking at these samples, would expect such children to be like later in school. What in later work life did these adults think these children might chose as professions?

The Chinese parents' comments followed the same patterns as those indicated above, so did the Westerners' — predictions of success for the one and outlandish, artistic, or menial careers for the other.

9.   Close to the surface of awareness is a rich Chinese interest in the forms of their writing, a highly specific meta-knowledge of their writing form and its neatness. Indeed, the Chinese page is itself symmetrical with straight edges — each character a whole semantic meaning in equally-spaced units fitting across the page, creating an interlocked visual harmonious unit.

10.   In the United States, we were intrigued by the skill of the Chinese children in being able to visualize (from minimal, transient clues) the complex, orthographic shapes. What in American schools would be the learning styles of early preschool children growing up in a society accustomed to these equally-spaced, linear-boxlike graphic phenomena coming from a system with 40–50,000

different forms? Did such dispositions that were interlocked with memory, etc., affect other behaviors? To explore these questions we recruited extensively experienced non-Asian teachers of Chinese children in the United States. We had open-ended discussions over a six-month period with them.

Of course, it is commonplace to hear of Chinese and Asian children being model students, excellent in certain subjects. But setting all this comment aside, we wondered what culturally-based traits these children, as immigrants, might carry into their American school environment. The elementary school teachers we chose to ask had no knowledge of our interests or work, merely that we were studying ethnic groups in schools. They were asked, in informal, brainstorming sessions, to talk in general about their elementary school Chinese pupils. The following summarizes the comments we recorded in three sessions of four hours over a six-month period in open, unstructured discussions. Configuration of skills and dispositions the teachers might trigger among themselves was noted down and discussed with our team of observers. A full account of this project is contained in the report to the Kluge Foundation (Regan 1992).

- a dislike of tasks requiring general estimates and approximation, rather than precise calculation;
- a similar aversion to "rounding off" rather than giving the exact answer as it was;
- a detailed accuracy of drawings, for example, the almost perfect replication of figures (including, as in one example, the accidental ditto paper lines which crossed a page);
- skill in miniaturization, small motor skills;
- persistence in length of time on micro-tasks;
- detailed accuracy of memory of two-dimensional forms;
- interest in formulaic phenomena;
- interest in precision of geometric forms and formulae;
- insistence that an answer is correct if the numbers were right despite clerical omissions;
- speed and accuracy of mental arithmetic;
- skills in separateness of parts rather than contiguity;
- interest in the importance of linear phenomena;
- desire to do more math, to get other work done so that they could return to math and, hence, the teachers' giving of math exercises as a reward;
- the formal, non-standard look of letters, e.g., artificial hooks or loops linking them (characters are not joined, occupy separate, even spaces);

- rejection of teachers' imperfect efforts to write characters as "not being Chinese writing".

But surely, we speculated, the consequences of such a massive micro-system of shape was not all of positive advantage to the people who used it. Were there not perhaps perceptual disadvantages? Would not the eye of each reader need to be constantly alert to notice very precise details and, therefore, what of, for example, the situation of a person who is dyslexic and whose problem in English orthography is that of b's, d's, g's, etc., moving and flipping so that the words become incomprehensible? An unexpected first result of our investigation into such reading problems in China was that there seemed to be fewer, rather than as we anticipated, exponentially more cases. Reserving final judgment of this topic until further results, we became interested in the possibility that the visual learning of characters became such that the complexity of each unit is embedded as a semantic whole rather than, as is the case of letters, a result of non-semantically meaningful fragments.

If there exists — as there does in the Chinese writing system — a massively greater number of figures than those in the system practiced by the children in the American schools who learn a 26-letter alphabet, then presumably Chinese parents and teachers will tend to look for, emphasize, and reward different skills than those which the Western parents do. And, we suspect, there will be a type of "back up" into attitudes and behaviors from these different emphases. What, indeed, of the adults' wider-spread expectations of an exactness of replication (if a dot cannot be left off a character, an angle turned and still preserve acceptance — comprehensibility)? In English writing, there can be multiple errors while leaving the meaning still clear and where redundancy of signals is tolerated, "small" differences could be readily overlooked as unimportant. In such a cultural context, perhaps "approximation" might be more acceptable?

Where time and energy needs to be spent on learning such a system as Chinese writing, approximations might be regarded more negatively than in a society where redundancy of clues would allow more playful approximation, while yet retaining meaningfulness.

Such realities of the actual semiotic form of literacy — the orthography itself — acted on by parents could, in corners and crevices of daily life and interaction, become their own initiating impulses to behavioral adaptations. As we survey our multiple projects and results to this point, we are disposed to conclude this is the case. Nevertheless, claiming causes and effects between semiotic systems (such as an orthography and systems of other behaviors) is problematic.

Despite such elusiveness of a clear-cut result in our methodological search, there is indeed a practical conclusion to our speculation. Namely, acknowledgment for educators operating in a multicultural society of this fact: the wisdom in being cautious in coming to conclusions about what (in a complex interlock of nondiscrete cultural information) causes what results.

There is much that our line of research needs to address. For example, there is the question of whether the skills and abilities of the Chinese children (and those skills different forms in Western children) are found in texts of non-character shapes. However, our meta-interest is less in the area of the abilities produced by the practice with the orthography (or some other manifestation of a cultural habit) than in the methods of pursuing a cultural theme.

7.   Conclusion: The Proximity Problem of What is Related to What?

Something is going on in Chinese children's visual learning that is different from that which occurs in the learning of their North American counterparts. We have identified some components of this difference and we hypothesize a pervasive presence in both literate and illiterate Chinese of a disposition, an interconnected network of interests, opinions, skills, attitudes, practices, expectations, motor abilities, awarenesses that are related to the ubiquitous micro-graphical forms. Children's early, unique grasp of, and sensitivity to, features of the geometric details of Chinese graphical units is part of their society's "learning how to mean," as Halliday puts it. The subtle, non-verbal behaviors and events that constitute sources of this socialization are yet to be recorded.

Ethnographers practicing observational strategies become skilled trackers of cultural themes and patterns. To this general skill, Lamb's theoretical position brings an added feature, and, principally, an efficiency. This position provides a procedural, metaphoric template for the study of information networks beyond that of the more recognized and established linguistic systems. In addition, accompanying the stratificational propositions of Lamb's work are implicit precautionary assumptions concerning leaping to whole cultural meanings from what might seem, to a casual observer, to be a discrete unit.

We have documented our observations, identified and commented on problems and opportunities of studying the visual cultural information system which is one feature of non-verbal knowledge. However, there remain those same issues and questions which we outlined in the opening section. Our sequence of probes from the original event and later for encountering events in that vast network of relationships was not determined by a logic of proximity of one behavior being next in line with another, but rather by the opportunities circumstance placed before us. This strikes a researcher as not being as clean as it should be. But the network is an interactional context, so this strategy is not as "messy" as it might appear. In our work's developing frame of examination of the visual meaning-network related to the visual micro-space character system, each new datum source which we identified we placed as one more node in an interaction spreading, in terms of our discoveries, in galaxial formats from that original bike-ride event. Nevertheless, we find no rules or procedures of tracing a network we can state at this point, but rather simply a prerequisite attitude that we regarded as necessary to the determination of an approximation of "meaning" of an event.

Our form of encounters with the visual sub-theme within the visual semiotic progressed from participant observation to formal testing, was criss-crossed with further observations. But again this sequence followed the logic of immediate necessity rather than a pre-established, absolute *sine-qua-non*, obligatory, logical strategy. Indeed, any of the recorded or other cultural observation entry points could have led an analytical, persistent observer into a completeness of this semiotic domain and eventually a cultural description, a recording of the complexity of a way of life. Such a view is basic to any understanding of a people whose total cultural knowledge always constitutes a coherence.

There are indeed unique problems for those working in the nonlinguistic domains where analysis and recording categories are still not agreed upon. Issues of relationships, explored by Lamb concerning the linguistic information system, present special problems to researchers examining such nonlinguistic phenomena as those which we have pursued as a result of a query on a bike ride. The reason is that observers' unfamiliarity with the nature of the units make nonverbal events, their components, and categories less available for, or accessible to research, than is the case with the more taxonomically-developed linguistic systems.

Indeed the establishing of categories for this type of nonverbal exploration is a problematic matter. In a symposium exploring Lamb's theoretical assumptions, a striking piece of prose by J. M. Barrie illustrated from a viewpoint outside of semiotics, both the "network" viewpoint of multi-media connected relationships and, consequently, the difficulties of looking for discrete connections of any one section. Furthermore, this viewpoint expresses the complexity of delineating informational associations in either the child's mind, or indeed the microspace universe.

> I don't know whether you have ever seen a map of a person's mind. Doctors sometimes draw maps of other parts of you, and your own map can become intensely interesting, but catch them trying to draw a map of a child's mind, which is not only confused, but keeps going round all the time. There are zigzag lines on it, just like your temperature on a card, and these are probably roads in the island, for the Netherlands is always more or less an island, with astonishing splashes of color here and there, and coral reefs and rakish-looking craft in the offing, and savages and lonely lairs, and gnomes who are mostly tailors, and caves through which a river runs, and princes with six elder brothers, and a hut fast going to decay, and one very small old lady with a hooked nose. It would be an easy map if that were all; but there is also first day at school, religion, fathers, the round pond, needlework, murders, hangings, verbs that take the dative, chocolate pudding day, getting into braces, say ninety-nine, three-pence for pulling out your tooth yourself, and so on; and either these are part of the island or they are another map showing through, and it is all rather confusing, especially as nothing will stand still. (Barrie 1928: 13)

In like manner, neither are those customs, skills, etc., which we have explored discrete pieces. Rather they intrude into other behavioral networks of the culture member's knowledge. The result is that (like Barrie's analogy) placed all together, they constitute a moving, three-dimensional web of embedded connections, a galaxy of meaning in which cross-pathway patterns and customs infuse the totality in nonstatic ways.

From that first observation about a name of a bike rider to structured and planned tests, we were surrounded by evidence of a special and well-developed, pervasive, mostly nonverbal Chinese interest in a small band of visual material. We noticed in the Chinese child and adult subtle skills and awarenesses of diverse micro-variations in the actual form. We saw indications of thinking spatially. At times we saw small variations — miniscule, unintended finger movements when a Chinese would be silently thinking through a character sentence. And we recorded a wide-ranging variety of the use of these special types of visualization being engaged in daily. But despite this work we have noted but a fragment of what exists in the Chinese culture related to this thematic interest. Hence, we conclude that the Lambian "messiness" viewpoint is salutary for educators dealing with the issues of living, appreciating, and working in a multicultural society.

Could a system such as an orthography have an influence in interacting with the users of that system? In such a possibility concerning his central focus, language, Lamb takes a cautious interest. His broader perspective of cultural knowledge favors the perspective that any strand of a network could equally well serve as a starting point; there is no single source of influence or beginning of a cultural theme, whether that theme involves the semiotic system of movement proxemics as in the overpass example or microspace. Suggesting, as we have, connections among early learning of one sign-system — the orthographic — and the wide-ranging behaviors of the people who use that system, is proposing somewhat a Whorfian-like view. However, again from a strictly stratificational standpoint, there would be neither a certain or a best place in the network from which to begin to explore an observed difference, or a way to identify an origin of a cultural theme.

So it is that, while any one strand of the totality of information of a people, or an individual, if followed thoroughly, would surrender to the investigator the entire information system, nevertheless, despite all the complexity or "messiness" (to again use Lamb's metaphor), there are identifiable domains. One of these is a networked knowledge of the seen world. We have explored a small corner of this in the studies reported above. We, too, could have begun from a quite different entry-event, but the fact is that some cultural moments are more interesting to an observer, and hence, are more "obvious". Some details (such as the traffic example) come to a researcher's attention in a more memorable way through their being part of a situation which has more personal texture. We used the bike-ride context as the ground foundation from which to discuss one thread of China's meaning.

At this juncture in our work, we see the study of the visual semiotic as an area of broad scope containing research themes extending from complex forms of visual creativity (like those practiced by an Albert Einstein, or a Stephen Hawking), to such micro-noticing features as those on which we have reported. But before understanding of the network nature of a cultural information system could achieve the results of which it is richly capable, generations of detailing features of visual learning is necessary. To this end, while puzzling about rules of connections and inter-relationships, we have attempted to make a contribution.

Certainly, what a child knows includes diverse semiotic systems, including the meta system we call the visual: what an object can be used for, who uses it, its feel, shape, where it is usually found, what it looks like, its size, color, and texture. Each of these is an area of knowledge, it is one part on the "maps showing through", as Barrie might say, and each constitutes an interconnected drawing upon data from multiple semiotic universes.

The domain of visual information systems, where our interests have been located, is one area of increasing importance for education, for Lamb himself, and for semiotics in general. Although the emphasis of stratificational work lies principally in the study of the linguistic information system, Lamb's interests and later work includes this additional, nonlinguistic complexity of visual knowledge/culture.

Simple cause-effect descriptions do not touch the reality of a people's information, nor are quick applications of observations about culture likely. In this report we propose to our field of education that the pursuit of understanding of cultural uniqueness and excellence is itself without further requirement a practical result in a society where increasingly the presence of socially diverse groups is part of the reality of everyday life.

For educators and others, relationship theory contains a practical reminder of necessary precautions against assuming linear, cause-effect associations. A culture's information system is a cohesive, interlocking reality. Too anxious to find the inner essence of the totality of things, an observer like Goethe's Faust about ultimate knowledge might assume that the examples gathered derived directly from the atomic core of the Chinese orthographic system. But this system itself and its emphases might be results of, not causes, might add to, or be part of, myriads of other connections. The meaning and relationship of a cultural event, like a word, lies in every feature of the self-supporting, interlocking system of knowledge. In a stratificational view, an inextricable combination of causes and effects lies within the enmeshed interacting features of a people's implicit/explicit informational system. This view is problematic for those wanting swift comprehension of cultural behavior. However, as writers from Machiavelli to Henry Lee Smith, Jr. have advised, description of the way things actually are constitutes the wisest basis for any conclusion.

References

Barrie, J. M. 1928. *Peter Pan*. London: Hodder and Stoughton. (Republished in 1968 by Puffin Books.)

Regan, John O., Sydney M. Lamb, John B. Cobb, Jr, and Donald R. Griffin. 1982. *Whitehead and Lamb: A New Network Connection*. Second in a series of seminars: Issues in Communication. Claremont, California: The Claremont Graduate School.

Regan, John. 1992. Diversity and Excellence: An Exploration of Parallel Realities. A report to the Kluge Foundation. Claremont, California: Institute for Education in Transformation at The Claremont Graduate School.

About the authors

John Regan is professor at the Center for Educational Studies in the Claremont Graduate University. He also has honorary professorships with several universities in China. His 1965 doctorate is from the State University of New York at Buffalo, where he studied under Henry Lee Smith, Jr. and George L. Trager. He first met Syd Lamb during the 1971 Linguistic Institute at SUNY Buffalo, and has since been involved in his views, along with those of Halliday, whom he had met earlier. Under these resulting interactions, Regan has developed the study of applied semiotics and cross-cultural comparison of non-verbal human development.

Joe Stephenson works for the Albuquerque, New Mexico, Public Schools in the evaluation of preschool children suspected of having disabilities. In his 1991 doctoral dissertation, written under John Regan at the Claremont Graduate University, he applied concepts from linguistics and cultural anthropology to the qualitative analysis of interviews with mothers of special education students. From 1991 to 1993, he served on the faculty of the Department of Counseling and Special Education at Central Michigan University. His connection with Syd Lamb is through Regan and LACUS. He continues research on children's acquisition of gestures and other forms of non-verbal communication.

Nancy Pine is Assistant Professor of Education and Director of Elementary Education at Mount St. Mary's College in Los Angeles. Her 1993 Ph.D. from Claremont Graduate University compares graphical knowledge of three-year-old children in China and the United States. Her continuing research investigates semiotic development of children from different cultures. Syd Lamb's ideas have influenced her work in cross-cultural learning since he spoke at a Claremont Graduate School seminar on Issues in Communications. She has published articles and given talks internationally on visual semiotic development in young children and on research methodology. One of her papers won the LACUS predoctoral prize.

CHAPTER 21

Toward Kawaiisu Poetics

Dell Hymes
University of Virginia

1. Introduction

It is a pleasure to be able to join in honoring Sydney Lamb. We were colleagues at Berkeley at the beginning of the 1960s, a seminal period for the work of both of us, and one that remains fresh in mind. Syd has been concerned with Uto-Aztecan throughout his career, and I hope that what follows will be a useful addition to its literature.

2. General Approach

In the last decade or so it has been possible to identify discourse relations of a new kind in a number of Native American languages, and in some other languages as well. It appears that oral narratives, and perhaps other forms of oral discourse, are composed of lines and groups of lines in regular ways. Two main types of patterning have been recognized so far. Chinookan, Sahaptin, Kalapuya, Cowlitz and Chehalis Salish, American English, and some other languages use relations of three and five. Kwakiutl, Takelma, Zuni, Irish English, and some other languages use relations of two and four. Intonation contours, initial particles, quoted speech and other features enter into identifying one or more lines as what can be called a "verse". Sequences of three and five, or two and four, verses constitute stanzas. Stanzas in turn enter into longer sequences which may be considered "scenes" and "acts".

The pattern of relations informs a narrative at every level. The patterning makes it possible to be precise about the place of a particular line or feature in a narrative, and to recognize ways in which a narrative has proportion and point.

The patterning of relations is not mechanical. The relations are not only numerical; they are also rhythmical. There is a sense of a rhythm in the development of action, of what Kenneth Burke has called "arousal and satisfaction of expectation". Often the recurrent reaching of a certain kind of ending point is significant. In general, recognition of the patterning in a particular text depends upon form/meaning covariation, covariation between markers, sequences and what makes sense.

The competence of narrators appears to involve a weaving together of a sequence of incident, and a sequence of relations of this kind. The process is not mechanical. The usual relations offer alternatives at each point — to complete a passage in a third verse, say, or a fifth, or in three or five pairs; to build a scene of three stanzas, or of five; alternatively, to develop a passage in pairs of verses, or in sequences of four; and so on. There may be special relationships and exceptions, which can not be reduced to expected pattern. Often enough, where the usual relations involve three and five, pairing may be used for emphasis; where the usual relations involve two and four, three and five may provide emphasis. Some narrators indeed are evidently able to choose either of the two kinds of relation in telling a story in a certain circumstance. (Some of the issues are discussed in Hymes 1992, 1993a, and 1993b).

3.   Uto-Aztecan and Kawaiisu Materials

Work of this kind is little developed in Uto-Aztecan. Loether has made a start with Western Mono, analyzing closely two stories (Loether 1991). I have found indications that a quotative element and some other particles enter into marking such relations in a Hopi narrative told by Helen Sekaquaptewa (Hymes 1993a). I hope that it and this discussion of a set of related Kawaiisu stories will be useful to others who pursue such possibilities in greater depth and detail.

Only two of the texts that follow are in Kawaiisu itself. They are versions of the same story, "Coyote and the Wasp", both told to Klein by Mrs. Carmen Peebles in January 1982, the first rehearsed, the second not. Klein (1988) reproduces his phonetic transcription of both, to which reference should be made. He appends a version of the same story, told in the language but transcribed only in English, not later than 1949 (Zigmond 1980). I am grateful to Klein for examining my effort to discover rhetorical, or poetic, relations in the rehearsed performance, and finding it reasonable (personal communication 1989). I have since modified what he saw, but the kind of patterning remains the same.

In this paper I examine the three texts published by Klein, and two others that Zigmond published. There are connections among them, and the somewhat larger corpus increases confidence that such patterning is characteristic of Kawaiisu narration. To be sure, stories in English might have three and five part relations in virtue of the prevalence of such relations among American speakers of English. Their use in these stories, however, seems characteristically Indian. The three step sequences noted in connection with the first story, "Coyote and Ladybird", are an example. I hope, therefore, that the large body of such narratives published by Zigmond will not be neglected, and that the English versions here will encourage analysis of the rest. It seems likely that they can provide insight into personal and community narrative style.

All five texts involve Coyote and someone who sings a song. The first two express a theme widespread in North America, namely, that a trickster cannot master a song. In Hopi and Zuni there is a story in which Coyote keeps forgetting a woman's winnowing song (cf. Hymes 1993a). In this Kawaiisu story it is a woman's song which evidently confers power to dive and come up again. The same narrator, Emma Williams, is involved in both. In the text obtained by Cappannari, the singer is Ladybird and the location is Bodfish. In the text obtained by Zigmond, the singer is Wasp and the location is Isabella, also on the east bank of the Kern River, less than two miles away. I venture the speculation there are two such versions, because Mrs. Williams, and/or whoever told her the stories, liked the plot and doubled it. The same seems to have been true for the Kathlamet Chinook. The second version of "The war of the ghosts" which Franz Boas obtained from Charles Cultee, as a check on linguistic accuracy, is not in fact just a repetition. It varies the action a bit, and locates it in a community on the other side of the Columbia from the first (Boas 1891).

In these two stories, the singer, Ladybird or Wasp, is a woman. In the three versions of "Coyote and Wasp" that follow, Wasp is male.

Story 1: "Coyote and Ladybird"

Emma Williams: Sadie Williams, recorded by Stephen Cappannari

Across the river from the Bodfish Post Office, there is a spring.   (A)
Ladybird was diving into it.
She had pretty long hair.
Before diving,
    she sat on a little rock   5
        and sang,
    "činakapuri činakapuri hu hu nakari".
Coyote heard the song,
    and he sneaked up
        and watched her from behind a bush.   10

Then he came over   (B)
    and asked her what she was doing.
Ladybird said,
    "Nothing.
    "I'm just sitting here."   15
She sang again,
    dove into the water,
        and then got back on the rock.

Coyote said,   (C)
    "Let me try that".   20
He sang, too.
Then he dove into the water.
He never came up.
His hair floated on the surface.

The song (line 7) is the same as that sung by Wasp in Story 2. Zigmond takes this to support the view that the "ladybird" of the story is not a kind of bird, but, like wasp, an insect, the one variously called "ladybird", "ladybug", "ladybeetle", "ladyfly" (1980 : 133, n. 1).

The presence of three- and five-part relations is suggested by the three sequences of three successive acts (lines 4–7, 8–10, 16–18). The presence of such relations is also suggested by the last stanza. Its five lines (verses) appear to make use of a pattern found in several widely disparate languages (Philadelphia English, Finnish, Chinookan) in which three- and five-part patterning is clear. In such traditions a sequence of five elements can consist of two three-step sequences, with the third element serving as pivot, completing the first sequence, and beginning the second. Here the third element, "Then he dove into the water", completes three steps of action on Coyote's part, and initiates the outcome. The fact that it is the only line with an initial particle in English (*then*) may reflect this role. Notice that the other initial *then* initiates the three verses of the second stanza.

This pattern of interlocking can be called just that, "interlocking", adding "pentad" for the five units. (Other pentads would be sets of five lines or verses without interlocking).

The story moves forward with three successive stanzas that end in a focus on Coyote. Stanza (A) describes Ladybird, (B) Coyote and Ladybird, (C) Coyote. All this contrasts with Mrs. Williams's telling of the cognate story of "Coyote and Wasp" (Story 2), which has a different rhythm and proportions.

Story 2: "Coyote and Wasp" 1

Emma Williams, recorded by Maurice Zigmond

Wasp lived near the site of the power house in Isabella.　　　(A)
Every day she would take a bath in the spring pond.
When she came to the pond,
　　　she would sit on a rock beside the water.
She would sing a song:　　　　　　　　　　　　　　　　5
　　　"činakapuri činakapuri uuhuunaakari",
and at the end of the song, she would say,
　　　"činak",
　　　　　　dive in,
　　　　　　　　and swim to the other side.　　　　　10

Coyote was walking along.　　　　　　　　　　　　(B)
He heard the song.
He listened to see from what direction it was coming.
He went that way,
　　　hid behind a tree,　　　　　　　　　　　　　15
　　　　　　and watched Wasp.
Then he came up to her
　　　and asked what she was doing.

She wouldn't tell him at first,　　　　　　　　　　(C)
　　　but he kept asking questions,　　　　　　　　20
　　　　　　so she began to tell him.
She showed him how she sang,
　　　said *"činak"*,
　　　　　　and jumped into the water.
After he watched her several times,　　　　　　　　25
　　　he wanted to try it.

Coyote put down his bow and arrow,   (D)
    got on a rock,
        sang in his big voice,
            said *"činak"*, loudly,   30
                and jumped in.
He didn't come up.
Wasp kept watching the place where he would come up.
She could see his hair under the water,
    but he never came up.   35
He drowned.

The opening lines tell about Wasp, where she lives, what she would do every day. Such an opening is frequent in many traditions. There appear to be five main elements to the account as a whole: where she lived, that every day she would take a bath in the pond, she would sit on a rock, she would sing a song, what she would do at the end of the song. My sense of the sequence is that its five main elements do not involve an interlocking pentad, but a leisurely enough progression, under the sign of *every day* — from the second verse, we already expect Wasp to enter the water, as she does in the fifth.

I take the three things Wasp would do after her song as going together as an immediate triad of successive action within a single verse. Lines 22–24 are a parallel. Indeed the two stanzas are parallel. (A) is about Wasp, (B) about Coyote, (C) returns to what Wasp does, (D) focuses on what happens to Coyote.

This overall rhythm, Wasp, then Coyote, Wasp, then Coyote, bespeaks awareness of two and four part relations. Perhaps it is motivated by a sense of the story as a dyadic relation between the two actors. There is indeed a nice balance, between what Coyote does and what Wasp sees, within the last stanza. At the same time the three stanzas after the first proceed steadily as if concerned with successive moments regarding Coyote (see below on both these points).

Coyote is introduced as he is in many traditions, going along. There appear to be three successive ending points: he asks what Wasp is doing, he wants to try it, he drowns.

The first of these three stanzas appears to have an interlocking pentad. The first three lines show a triad of onset, ongoing, outcome with a perception as the outcome: Coyote is walking along, he hears the song, he listens for the direction. That immediate outcome, listening, initiates a second triad within the stanza. Six actions are distributed among three verses, whose main elements are that Coyote listens for the direction, goes that way, asks Wasp what she is doing.

Within these three steps, the intermediate step, the fourth verse, is itself a triad with perception as the outcome: He went that way, hid behind a tree, watched Wasp. This strengthens a sense that such relations are part of Kawaiisu narrative tradition. The use of *Then* with the fifth verse seems to mark the outcome of the stanza as important. Notice that the last verse of the next stanza (C) begins with *After*. *Then* and *After* appear to correlate the two outcomes as successive points in time.

The third stanza has also a triad of action in its middle verse: She showed him how she sang, said *"činak"*, and jumped into the water.

The last stanza opens with five lines of successive action, the dramatic highlight for Coyote. The lines do not seem to involve interlocking, but to sweep ahead. The following verses elaborate one outcome: not come up, Wasp watching where he would come up, seeing his hair but not come up, drowned. In number they balance the opening five lines, but in a contrasting mode: not a surge of successive acts, but reiteration of a chord, *not come up* three times, resolved by *drowned*. There is a related contrast in mode in Wasp's watching. It is a triad of perception, but of perception not completed by its intended object: she keeps watching where he would come up, she sees his hair, he does not come up. Moreover, Wasp's watching is distributed among two verses, in contrast to preceding triads, which have moved stepwise within the same level of organization, lines within a verse. Similarly, the stanza as a whole has a three-step progression in relation to Coyote — he jumped in, he didn't come up, he drowned — but it also is distributed across verses. The effect in each case is to subordinate a sense of action in successive steps, in contrast to the first five lines of the stanza, and to the ending of "Coyote and Ladybird", focused on Coyote.

Rhythm appears to echo sense. The sense of stasis in the last half of the stanza (in terms of number of lines) recalls the "everyday" quality of the opening of the story. Coyote's watching and questioning and attempted emulation are no more than an interruption in this woman's life. They do not change it.

Story 3: "Coyote and Wasp" 2

Louisa Marcus, recorded by Maurice Zigmond

[i] [Coyote gets Wasp to fly with his blanket]
Wasp was flying up into the air from a flat rock.   (A)
He sang a song:
        *"ulalai tapičik*ʷ*e?ani ta...o...sak*ʷ*ik"*,
                flew into the air.

and returned to the rock.   5
Coyote saw him from behind the brush.

Coyote came over to Wasp.   (B)
"What are you doing?" he asked.
"I am not doing anything", said Wasp.
"You're lying", said Coyote.   10
"You were doing something."

Coyote put his rabbitskin blanket around Wasp.   (C)
"When you go up in the air,
    you will look pretty," said Coyote.
Wasp flew up   15
    and came down.

[ii] ["Try it again", Wasp does not return, Coyote dies]
Coyote said,   (D)
    "It's pretty.
    It's pretty.
    Try it again."   20
Wasp went up a second time.
He flew away
    and never came back.

Coyote was watching him.   (E)
He yelled at him   25
    and told him to bring down the blanket.
Wasp kept going straight on
    and never came back.

Coyote was cold.   (F)
He kept following the sun,   30
    trying to keep warm.   }
He reached the top of the mountain.
The sun went down.   }
Coyote was very cold.
He died.   }   35

This is the only text Mrs. Marcus told Zigmond. She would speak a few phrases in Kawaiisu, and then she or perhaps someone else translated into English, which Zigmond then transcribed, She was the great grandmother of Klein's consultant, Carmen Peebles, who sought to recreate the performance style she had experienced as a child, using Zigmond's collection as a stimulus to plan and rehearse a number of texts (Klein 1987: 467).

Mrs. Marcus's narrative has two scenes, one for each of Wasp's flights with Coyote's blanket. The two outcomes, success and failure, are formally contrasted in this way. (In content, of course, as in the versions that follow, there are three flights in all, the first being that which attracts Coyote.)

The relations among the three stanzas in each scene follow the logic one expects in a tradition using such relations, a pattern of onset (or initial state), ongoing, outcome. In [i] Coyote sees what Wasp does, demands to know what he does, gets him to fly with his (pretty) rabbitskin blanket. In [ii] Coyote, repeating that it's pretty, gets Wasp to do it again, but Wasp does not come back; Coyote yells at him to return, but he does not; Coyote, cold without his blanket, dies. The turning point is the middle stanza, in which Coyote makes a demand: tell me what you are doing, come back. The outcome follows.

In the second scene the relation is clear: Wasp ignores what Coyote yells, and Coyote dies of cold. The relation is not clear in the first scene. Perhaps Wasp is understood to admit that he flies up, before Coyote puts his blanket around him. Perhaps what is stated is all that happens, and Wasp admits nothing. Perhaps what is understood is that he cannot keep Coyote from putting the blanket on him, when Coyote is right at hand, and so does what Coyote wants. On this view, Wasp refuses what Coyote demands in the middle stanza of both scenes. That would be all the more reason for Coyote not to press his luck a second time, to let the story end with the one scene. In any case, on either account, Wasp is a willing partner only once.

As to form within stanzas: Notice that in (A) the second verse is a three step triad of action with the essentials of what Wasp does — sing, fly, sit on the rock. It occurs just once here, but is elaborated four times by Mrs. Peebles in her rehearsed performance. In (B) it has seemed to me that the Coyote's quoted speech in lines 10 and 11 counts as two verses, separated by *said Coyote* at the end of the first. If not — if other Kawaiisu narratives do not support the inference, if it was perhaps a stylistic trait particular to Louisa Marcus, from whom we have no other stories to check —, then the stanza is the only irregular one, four verses instead of three or five, among those examined.

In stanza (E) the five lines could be five verses. I have followed Zigmond's punctuation and the grouping it implies, yielding three. The relations of lines to verses are consistent with those in stanzas (C) and (D).

At the end Mrs. Marcus makes use of a device found often enough in other traditions with relations of three and five, namely, sets of pairs. (For examples in Kathlamet Chinook and Kalapuya, see Hymes 1985, 1987).

I have indicated the pairing of verses by putting closing braces to the right at the end of each pair.

There are various connections one might track among the lines of this last stanza — Coyote being cold, and very cold; following the sun, reaching the top of the mountain; the sun being up, the sun going down — but the one cogent sequence does seem to inhere in taking the verses two at a time. Lines 29 and 30–31 identify an initial stage: cold and following the sun to keep warm. Lines 32 and 33 identify a second, intermediate stage: reach the top of the mountain, the sun goes down. (The sun is setting in the west, Coyote reaches the highest point from which its warmth could still be felt, but in a race that cannot be won.) Lines 34 and 35 identify a third, concluding stage: very cold, die.

Story 4: "Coyote and the Wasp" 3

Carmen Peebles, unplanned retelling to Sheldon Klein

"How does it go?"
The wasp was sitting on a rock.   (A)
Fly up and come back down [again].
Oh I forgot about the song it sang.

        (Anne P.: "Sit and sing")   5

WELL THEN, I'll say he was singing   (A')
    he'd fly up,
        (and then) sit back down [again].
AND SO the coyote was watching him,
    while it was doing this.   10
AND SO the coyote came to the little wasp.
    "I have a pretty blanket — to make it,
        out of rabbit fur.
    You can put it on,
    when you fly up and land again it'd be pretty."   15
The wasp said, "OK", and put the blanket on.
He flew up and he sit back down again.

AND SO the Coyote,   (B)
    "Again, one more time".
He flew up again,   20

```
          (and) the wasp started flying away.
      (And) the coyote,
              started hollering "Bring back,
                  my blanket".

      BUT the Wasp,                                    (C)   25
              flew away,
          and the Coyote when it got night,
              died,
          because he got cold,
              because his blanket was gone.                30
```

In this unplanned retelling, Mrs. Peebles appears to make a false start. After two lines,

> "The wasp was sitting on a rock.
> Fly up and come back down"

she interrupts herself,

> "Oh I forgot about the song it sang",

and Anne Peebles interjects,

> "Sit and sing".

What Mrs. Peebles next says appears to be a fresh start:

> "Well then, I'll say he was singing, he'd fly up..."

Continuous telling of the story appears to begin with this line.

What follows is well formed, if three and five part grouping is to be expected in Mrs. Peebles's narratives.[1] I have indicated the first start with (A), and the fresh start with (A').

There are three stanzas, neatly disposing of the essentials of the story, in an onset, ongoing, outcome relation. In the first stanza, the wasp flies, Coyote watches, proposes that wasp fly with his rabbitskin blanket, Wasp agrees, flies

---

1. It may be accidental, but it is interesting that Mrs. Peebles's comment afterwards itself takes the shape of five lines (Klein 1987: 479):

> "I forgot the song that went to that.
> It just went phoox! out of my mind.
> My grandmother told it.
> Great grandmother.
> She must not meant me to sing her song."

up and returns. In the second stanza, Coyote tells Wasp to do it again, Wasp does and flies away, Coyote shouts for him to bring back his blanket. In the third stanza Wasp nonetheless flies away, and Coyote dies, because of the cold without his blanket.

Notice that the first stanza has initial particles for the first three of its five verses, but the second and third stanza have an initial particle only for the opening verse of each ("And so", and "But" [*nágyʌsây*]). This may be an example of more explicitly marking an opening part.

Notice that Wasp explicitly agrees to fly with the blanket the first time round (line 16), and that there is no confrontation, no accusation of liar, as in Mrs. Marcus's telling.[2] There is only the yelling to come back when Wasp does fly away. At the outset Mrs. Peebles's Coyote is all persuasion. Here we have indication of a difference in conception, either of Coyote, or of Coyote in relation to particular situations and alters.

Mrs. Peebles's final stanza has a certain similarity to the final stanza in Mrs. Marcus's telling. It too makes of use of a kind of three-part grouping of pairs. Here the pairs are short lines, not verses, recoverable because of access to Klein's notation of the end of each largest intonational unit. Each of the lines in (C) is so marked. The parallelism of the last two lines (because..., because...) is rather like a closing couplet at the end of Shakespearean scene.

Story 5: "Coyote and the Wasp" 4

Carmen Peebles, rehearsed telling to Sheldon Klein[3]

---

2. Line 16 might have been taken as more than one line, because of the occurrence of quoted speech within it, but it is marked as all within a single major intonational unit by Klein.

3. The English translation published by Klein includes the exact words given by Mrs. Peebles in translation (Klein 1987: 468). For the sake of analysis, the English that follows diverges in certain respects. Nothing published by Klein is omitted, but the apparent status of some elements is indicated.

Occasionally an initial *and* in the published translation seems not to be overtly, or at least not initially, marked in the Kawaiisu. I have put such a word in parentheses. (For (*and*), See "Coyote and the wasp" 3, lines 21, 22, and "Coyote and the wasp" 4, lines 12, 22, 23, 24. For (*then*), see line 8 in "Coyote and the wasp" 3 and lines 14, 33, 38, 39 in "Coyote and the wasp" 4.

Occasionally an initial particle in the Kawaiisu does not have a published translation. I have supplied "And so" for that easily recognizable word in "Coyote and the wasp" 4, line 16, and "but" for *ʔešá*, untranslated in lines 52 and 65. Both are structurally significant markers.

Occasionally a form recognizable as "again" is untranslated; cf. lines 12, 23, 58. The form for "come back and sit down" is variously translated, sometimes with both these English elements, sometimes not. Apparently it is thought of as a single action, perhaps having more than one aspect.

[i] [Wasp sings, flies, sits]

This was told a long time ago by my great grandmother. (A)
It's about the coyote,
    and the wasp.

Once this wasp was sitting on a rock. (B)
It would fly away 5
    (and) come back
        (and) sit,
    on the little rock.

AND SO as it was doing this (C)
    sometimes it would sing. 10
It would fly
    (and then) come back and sit down [again].

AND SO it would sing again, (D)
    (then) he'd fly again.
        He kept doing that. 15
[And so] ..... it sat down,
    that little wasp.

"Yûlá·Bʌlii·, tápʌčikʷê·nʌnee·" (E)
(That was the song it sang.
    Something about the end of it, tie me up. 20
    I still don't know what that means.)[4]
(And) fly up,
    (and) come back and sit [again] on the little rock.

[ii] [Coyote gets Wasp to fly with his blanket]

(And) the coyote was watching him (A)
    but not where the wasp was aware of it. 25
AND SO after a while the coyote went over to the little wasp.

"What are you doing?" he asked. (B)
"I'm not doing anything", said the little wasp.

Finally, in order to make salient their role in marking verses, initial particles have been put in small capitals.

4. In Chinookan there are terms for *ant* and *wasp* that involve a verb stem 'to notch'. The idea is that their middles are as if "notched", because once tied tightly around (in a myth). Such an idea might lie behind what Mrs. Peebles says about Wasp's song in this story: "Something about the end of it, tie me up". Klein finds this plausible.

"You're lying", said the coyote.   (C)
AND SO after saying that, after a while the coyote sort of buttered up
    the little wasp...   30
    made overtures so the wasp would like him...
    not suspect anything.[5]
AND SO (then) the coyote said,   (D)
    "I have a ...
    (Oh, I blanked out, wait, wait, wait, oh")[6]   35
    "I have a rabbit blanket, a pretty one", he said.
    "You could put it on", he said to the little wasp.
AND SO (then) the little wasp put it on.

AND SO (then) the coyote said,   (E)
    "When you fly up and sit back down this would be pretty.   40
    The rabbit looks pretty."

AND SO,
    the little wasp put it on,
        flew away
            and sat back down again.   45

[iii] [Wasp flies again, does not come back, Coyote dies]

"It's pretty   (A)
    it's pretty
        the blanket"
            the coyote said.
"One more time fly away again", he said.   50

AND SO the little wasp flew again.   (B)
BUT the wasp went the other way flying off.

The coyote was standing there watching him.   (C)
He called the wasp.
"Bring back my blanket",   55
    he said.

---

5. Lines 30–32 are an English explanation, not a translation. "And so after saying that after a while
the Coyote" is followed by no more than one or two words, presumably equivalent to "sort of
buttered up."
    The word for 'Wasp' does not occur.

6. Notice the threefold repetition of *wait*. If initial and final *Oh* were a unitary frame, there would be
five elements in all.

IN SPITE OF IT ALL the wasp kept going
    he didn't come back [again].

AND SO it got evening   (D)
    the coyote got cold.   60
He went up on the little mountain
    and the sun was going down.

AND SO the coyote was shivering as he was standing,   (E)
    on the little mountain.
BUT the sun,   65
    went down
        and the coyote because he was freezing died.

The three scenes of this prepared telling fit nicely an onset, ongoing, outcome pattern. We meet Wasp [i], we hear Coyote persuading Wasp to fly with his blanket [ii], we find Coyote left without his blanket to get cold, shiver, and freeze to death [iii].

In the first scene Mrs. Peebles introduces us to Wasp, leisurely and pleasurably. After a formulaic introduction (A), his habitual three-part action, to sing, to fly up, to sit down on the little rock, is repeated four times. This is done with varying detail and relation to verse form. I identify it in parentheses as a (triad of action), in order to distinguish the ordered presence of three elements from a sequence in which three elements themselves constitute a structural unit, such as a verse or stanza. I reserve "triad" (unmodified) for the latter.

This scene suggests an enjoyment in contemplating what Wasp does of a sort that seems to shine through the initial scene of another myth, set north of Kawaiisu territory in southern Oregon, wherein Frances Johnson introduces Coyote trapping gophers every day (Hymes 1995).

The presentation of what Wasp does four times, rather than three or five, may be connected with the choice of pairs of verses as the building blocks of almost every stanza. A sensitivity to two- and four- part relations may inform this rehearsed telling, along with the three- and five- relations among stanzas and scenes. Such a sensitivity stands in strong contrast to the complete pervasiveness of three and five part relations in the unprepared telling just considered.

Whereas Mrs. Marcus (Coyote and Wasp 3) had Coyote accuse Wasp of lying, and Mrs. Peebles in her unrehearsed version had Coyote cajole Wasp, this full version has both, accusation first, cajolery second. In both tellings by Mrs. Peebles Wasp himself dons the rabbit blanket, in contrast to that by Mrs. Marcus, in which Coyote puts it on him.

In the course of persuasion, Coyote is marked as speaking three times (33, 36, 37) in relation to one verse of response by Wasp (38). This 3 : 1 relationship, of course, sums to four, in keeping with the two-part relations among verses in stanzas generally. That it is a resource, not an accident, is indicated by its use again in (c) of the next scene (53, 54, 55–6 : 57–8).

In the unrehearsed telling Mrs. Peebles had Coyote simply tell Wasp "Again, one more time", but here in scene [iii] there is further inducement as prelude, "It's pretty, it's pretty".

The end of the scene, and myth, maintains the pattern of pairs of verses. This is not evident in stanza (D), where only the first verse is marked (line 59), but in stanza (E) both verses are marked (lines 63, 65). In this rehearsed telling Mrs. Peebles has in mind content much the same as that in Mrs. Marcus's telling ("Coyote and Wasp" 3). This is striking, since her unrehearsed telling does not. Compare

AND SO it got evening   (D)
    the coyote got cold.   60
He went up on the little mountain
    and the sun was going down.
And so the coyote was shivering as he was standing,   (E)
    on the little mountain.
BUT the sun,   65
    went down
        and the coyote because he was freezing died.

to Mrs. Marcus's

Coyote was cold.   (F)
He kept following the sun,   30
    trying to keep warm.   }
He reached the top of the mountain.
The sun went down.   }
Coyote was very cold.
He died.   }   35

But if Mrs. Marcus's telling was the stimulus, Mrs. Peebles's has added telling detail. Notice the three-step sequence of Coyote "cold", "shivering", "freezing" (Da, Ea, Eb), and that of "it got evening", "the sun was going down", "the sun went down" (Da, Db, Eb), each integrating the four-verse group with a different verse (b = c) between the first and last. There is also an effect of chiasmus from the repetition of "on the little mountain" in the middle stanzas (Db Ea), matched with the two explicit actions of Coyote — went up, was standing.

Yet overall there is a four-step progression matching the overt form. Three of the verses (Da, Db, Eb) pair the situation of the sun and the situation of Coyote. The third verse (Ea) has only the situation of Coyote, shivering as he was standing on the little mountain. This is in effect a moment of suspense, or merely a pause, before the inevitable next state for sun and Coyote both. The intricacy prevents the ending from seeming routine.

It is rather as if two musical lines begin and end together (Da, Eb), moving somewhat independently between (Db, Ea).

4. Conclusion

The last narrative is the longest, and the most thoroughly marked by initial particles. This is not surprising, given that it was told in Kawaiisu without interruption, and with opportunity for reflection beforehand. What is surprising is the consistent use of pairs of verses as building blocks of stanzas. This cannot have come from a review of the telling by Louisa Marcus, since that telling is not so organized. Mrs. Peebles must have had recollection of such a style of narration independently.

Mrs. Peebles's use of paired verses is the more remarkable, because the other four narratives examined all use groups of three and five. On the other hand, Mrs. Peebles's use of groups of three and five stanzas in both her tellings of the story is in keeping with that by Mrs. Marcus, and the first narrative involving Emma Williams. At the level of relations among stanzas, it is the second narrative involving Emma Williams that stands out, for it clearly makes use of pairs, and in what appears a clearly motivated way. Evidently two- and four- relations were available to at least some Kawaiisu narrators.

These choices and other features of the five narratives are displayed in the profiles in the Appendix. Analysis of the entire body of texts may make clear what is personal preference, and what is part of a community range of styles widely shared.

In the interim, I hope this exploration shows that Kawaiisu will repay such study, enriching what can be known of Native American narrative art.

Appendix: Profiles

In these profiles some of the features that enter into the recognition of verses are indicated. Initial time expressions are cited (e.g, "Then", "Every day", "After"). Quoted speech or song is indicated by "–". Turns at talk, and song, seem always to constitute verses in Native American narratives. When separated by expressions of saying, the words of one actor can count as more than one verse. (Such seems to be the case with lines 11 and 12 in "Coyote and Wasp" 2). The term "interlocking pentad" is discussed in the text.

Table 1: Profile of "Coyote and Ladybird"
Emma Williams: Sadie Williams, recorded by Stephen Cappannari

Scene/Stanza	Verses	Lines	Features
A	abcde	1, 2, 3, 4–7, 8–10	Triplets (d e)
B	abc	11–12, 13–15, 16–18	Then, "–", triplet
C	abcde	19–20, 21, 22, 23, 24	"–", . Then, inter-locking pentad

Table 2: Profile of "Coyote and Wasp" 1
Emma Williams, recorded by Maurice Zigmond

Scene/ Stanza	Verses	Lines	Features
A	abcde	1, 2, 3–4, 5–6, 7–10	Formulaic, Every day, when, "–", "–" (triplet)
B	abcde	11, 12, 13, 14–16, 17–18	Interlocking pentad, with triad, Then
C	abc	19–21, 22–24, 25–6	triad, triad "–", After
D	abcde	27–31, 32, 33, 34–5, 36	pentad, chord

Table 3: Profile of "Coyote and Wasp" 2
Louisa Marcus, recorded by Maurice Zigmond

Scene /	Stanza	Verses	Lines	Features
i	A	abc	1, 2–5, 6	triad with "–"
	B	abcde	7, 8, 9, 10, 11	"–" (four verses)
	C	abc	12, 13–14, 15–16	"–"
ii	D	abc	17–20, 21, 22–23	"–", second time
	E	abc	24, 25–26, 27–28	
	F	ab cd ef	29, 30–31; 32, 33; 34, 35	

Table 4: Profile of "Coyote and the Wasp" 3
Carmen Peebles, unplanned retelling to Sheldon Klein

Scene/ Stanza	Verses	Lines	Features
		1	Query
A	abc	2, 3, 4, 5	Self-interruption 4, Interjection
A'	abcde	6–8, 9–10, 11–15, 16, 17	Well then (triad), And so, And so "–", "–"
B	abc	18–19, 20–21, 22–24	And so "–", ..., "–"
C	abc	25–26, 27–28, 29–30	But, night, couplet

Table 5: Profile of "Coyote and the Wasp" 4
Carmen Peebles, rehearsed telling to Sheldon Klein

Scene/	Stanza	Verses	Lines	Features
i	A	ab	1, 2–3	long time ago, formulaic?
	B	ab	4, 5–8	Once (triad of action)
	C	ab	9–10, 11–12	And so (triad of action)
	D	ab	13–15, 16–17	And so (triad of action)
	E	ab	18, (19–21), 22–23	"–" (triad of action)
ii	A	ab	24–25, 26	..., And so
	B	ab	27, 28	"–", "–"
	C	ab	29, 30–32	"–", And so
	D	abc: d	33–34, 36, 37; 38	And so "–" (3), And so
	E	ab	39–41, 42–45	And so "–", And so (triad of action)
iii	A	ab	46–49, 50	"–", "–"
	B	ab	51, 52	And so, But
	C	abc : d	53, 54, 55–56, 57–8	..., ..., "–"
	D	ab	59–60, 61–62;	And so
	E	ab	63–64, 65–68	And so, But

References

Boas, Franz. 1901. *Kathlamet Texts*. Bureau of American Ethnology, Bulletin 26. Washington, D.C.: Government Printing Office.

Hymes, Dell. 1985. Language, memory, and selective performance: Charles Cultee's 'Salmon's myth' as twice told to Boas. *Journal of American Folklore* 98: 391–434.

Hymes, Dell. 1987. Anthologies and narrators. *Recovering the Ground*, ed. by Brian Swann and Arnold Krupat, 41–84. Berkeley & Los Angeles: University of California Press.

Hymes, Dell. 1992. Use all there is to use. *On the Translation of Native American Literatures*, ed. by Brian Swann, 83–124. Washington: Smithsonian Institution Press.

Hymes, Dell. 1993a. Helen Sekaquaptewa's Coyote and the birds': Rhetorical analysis of a Hopi Coyote story. *Anthropological Linguistics* 34: 45–72.

Hymes, Dell. 1993b. In need of a wife: Clara Pearson's 'Split-his-own-head' [Tillamook]. In American indian. *Linguistics and Ethnography in Honor of Laurence C. Thompson*, ed. by Anthony Mattina and Timothy Motler, 127–62. (University of Mouton. Occasional publication in linguistics, 10) Missoulu: University of Montana.

Hymes, Dell. 1995. Reading Takelma texts: Frances Johnson's "Coyote and Frog". *Fields of Folkore. Essays in honor of Kenneth S. Goldstein*, ed. by Roger D. Abrahams, 90–159. Bloomington: Tricksten Press.

Klein, Sheldon. 1988. Narrative style in variants of a Kawaiisu myth text. *In Honor of Mary Haas*, ed. by William Shipley, 467–81.

Loether, Christopher Paul. 1991. Verbal art among the Western Mono. Ph.D. dissertation, UCLA. Ann Arbor: University Microfilms International Dissertation Services.

Zigmond, Maurice L. 1980. *Kawaiisu Mythology. An Oral Tradition of South-Central California. Ballena Press Anthropological Papers No. 18,* ed. by Lowell John Bean & Thomas C. Blackburn. Socorro, New Mexico: Ballena Press.

About the author

Dell Hymes is Commonwealth Professor of Anthropology Emeritus at the University of Virginia, where he has been since 1987. He earned his Ph.D. in Linguistics at Indiana University in 1955, with a dissertation on Kathlamet Chinook. After five years at Harvard, he moved to Berkeley, where he met·Syd Lamb and became interested both in his approach to structure and his ideas on language classification. After five years at Berkeley, Hymes was at the University of Pennsylvania from 1965 to 1987, the last twelve years as Dean of the Graduate School of Education, to which he helped introduce applied linguistics.

CHAPTER 22

The Effect of Rate of Speech on Laryngeal Timing in Medial Stops in Mongolian

Henry Rogers

University of Toronto

Entia non sunt multiplicanda præter necessitatem.

Every week Syd Lamb began our class in Linguistic Theory at Yale with a Truth of the Week. As callow graduate students, we felt a bit superior when this week's truth contradicted last week's. Later, we came to see this sort of change as evidence of an active, fertile, and above all scientific mind. For me, the most memorable and useful of these weekly truths has been Occam's Razor: entities should not be multiplied without necessity.

1. Introduction

Phonologists find a binary classification of stops into voiced–voiceless useful for many languages. Indeed, the absence of some such contrast is noteworthy. Phoneticians, however, have long been aware of the considerable variation in the phonetic activities constituting "voiced" and "voiceless". This paper examines the role of laryngeal timing in distinguishing such stops in medial position in Mongolian.

In particular, the question of changes in laryngeal timing caused by different rates of speech is examined. Löfqvist (1991) has argued that the changes in timing cannot be described by an across-the-board proportional change in timing; his claim is tested using the Mongolian data.

Mongolian is an Altaic language, more closely related to the Tungus languages and more distantly to the Turkic family. The consultant for these data is a native of eastern Inner Mongolia (politically a part of China). He is a speaker of the Khorchin [xortʃin] dialect, marginally different from the standard Khalkha [xɑlxx] dialect. He is currently a graduate student at the University of Toronto, having received an M.A. in Mongolian Studies from the University of Inner Mongolia.

The phonemic inventory for Mongolian (Bosson & Unenšecen 1962; Luvsanvandan 1964; Poppe 1970; Street 1963) is shown in Table I.

Table 1. *Phonemic inventory of Mongolian*

(p)	t	(tʃ)	(k)		i			u
b	d	dʒ	g		e	ø	ɤ	o
	s	ʃ	x				ɑ	ɔ
m	n		ŋ					
	r				iː	yː		uː
	l				eː	øː	ɤː	oː
w		j					ɑː	ɔː

The stops /p/ and /k/ are rare in Mongolian, found mostly in borrowed words; they do not occur medially. Affricates are not considered in this study; the parentheses around /tʃ/ indicate that, although it occurs in most dialects, it is replaced in Khorchin by /ʃ/. Thus, /d/ and /t/ form the only pair of stops in Mongolian that exhibit a voiced–voiceless contrast.

2.   Method

The data for this study consist of two-syllable words with a single intervocalic /d/ or /t/. Each word was pronounced in a frame /tɑ: — — gɤddʒɪ/ 'You say — — '. The randomized list of items was pronounced twice at a normal rate of speech and twice at a fast rate. Both rates were self-selected by the consultant. The recordings were made on three separate days within a two-week period. The list consisted of twelve items, giving 24 examples at each rate. Some recorded items were discarded as unmeasurable with the result that not all totals add up to 24.

Medial stops were chosen for investigation for two reasons. First, they have been less commonly studied than stops in initial or final position. Second, medial position allows both the onset and release to be measured readily, whereas measurements of the onset of an initial stop or the release of a final stop are often difficult to make. All words have the same stress pattern with stress falling on the initial syllable.

The data were recorded using a Marantz PMD430 recorder with a TOA HY3 headset microphone. The recordings were digitized using a MacAdios 411 at 20.8 kHz, 12 bits. The software Signalyze was used to make the measurements of timing.

3. Results

Figure 1 is a schematic diagram showing a VCV sequence and labeling various portions of it which were measured. Time goes from left to right. The lower line labeled "glottis" is zigzag for voiced portions and straight for voiceless portions. The next line above, labeled "coronal closure", is a single line during the closure for the stop and divided into two lines when the articulators are apart during the vowels.

Four basic measurements were made from the beginning of the preceding vowel to the onset of voicing in the following vowel. These are described below and are illustrated in Figure 1.

VD: duration of the preceding vowel
VCT: voice cessation time; voicing at the beginning of the closure
VlessCl: voiceless portion of closure
VOT: voice onset time; continuation of voicelessness after closure

Other measurements composed of the basic ones can also be made:

ClD: closure duration (= VCT + VlessCl)
VlessD: voiceless portion of consonant and vowel (= VlessCl + VOT)
TotalC: total consonant duration (= ClD + VOT)
TotalD: total duration from beginning of vowel to onset of voicing after stop
            (= VD + TotalC)

Note that in all cases for both /d/ and /t/, there is some voicing at the beginning of the closure (VCT), although most of the closure is voiceless (VlessCl). This voicelessness always extends into the following vowel, creating VOT.

The onset of the vowel is measured at the point where a wide-band spectrogram shows the onset of a second formant; when a sonorant precedes the

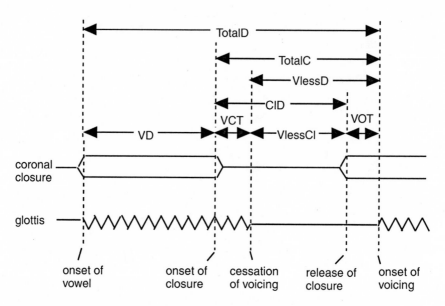

Figure 1.   *Diagram of VCV sequence showing measurements*

vowel, vowel onset is generally not measurable. The onset of closure is measured at the point where a wide-band spectrogram shows an end to the second formant. The cessation of voicing is measured at the last zero-crossing of the waveform consistent with the frequency of F_0. The release of closure is measured at the release burst of the waveform. The onset of voicing after the closure is measured at the beginning of low-frequency striations indicating glottal pulsing.

Table II shows the number (N), mean ($\bar{X}$), and standard deviation (s) of the measurements. The mean and standard deviation are given in milliseconds. A statistical t-test was performed comparing the means of /d/ and /t/ for each measurement. The likelihood that the difference in means occurs by chance is shown as a proportion p below each pair. Similar tests were performed comparing the measurements of the stops for normal and fast speech; for these, the value of p is shown at the right of each pair. An asterisk is appended to those values of p which are less than 0.050. In these cases, the difference between the means is considered significant and unlikely to have occurred by chance.

The smaller number of measurements for VD is due to the difficulty of determining the precise onset of a vowel after an initial sonorant. Further, only

Table 2. *Measurements in milliseconds*

		Normal Rate			Fast Rate			
		N	$\bar{X}$	s	N	$\bar{X}$	s	
VD	/d/	14	87.0	20.1	10	79.2	13.8	p = 0.274
	/t/	15	108.5	26.9	6	64.9	12.3	**p < 0.001***
			p = 0.021*			p = 0.054		
VCT	/d/	21	37.0	10.1	24	52.1	10.8	**p < 0.001***
	/t/	21	34.4	13.6	16	39.9	13.0	p = 0.226
			p = 0.491			**p = 0.004***		
VlessCl	/d/	21	66.3	19.3	24	40.6	12.9	**p < 0.001***
	/t/	21	70.0	20.7	16	58.2	17.1	p = 0.066
			p = 0.549			**p = 0.002***		
VOT	/d/	21	19.6	6.7	24	16.3	4.5	p =0.065
	/t/	21	48.4	34.0	6	38.9	31.7	p =0.387
			p = 0.001*			**p = 0.012***		
ClD	/d/	21	103.3	14.4	24	92.6	13.1	**p = 0.013***
	/t/	21	104.4	14.0	16	98.0	9.9	p = 0.112
		p = 0.792				p = 0.145		
VlessD	/d/	21	87.2	19.1	24	56.8	11.1	**p < 0.001***
	/t/	21	118.4	43.5	16	91.9	36.4	p = 0.051
			p = 0.006*			**p = 0.002***		
TotalC	/d/	21	122.8	16.1	24	108.9	12.5	p = 0.103
	/t/	21	152.8	39.8	16	136.9	30.3	p = 0.176
			p = 0.004*			**p = 0.002***		
TotalD	/d/	14	212.0	32.4	10	187.8	12.0	**p = 0.020***
	/t/	16	269.7	47.9	6	192.3	26.7	**p < 0.001***
			p = 0.001*			p = 0.713		

* p < 0.050

values of VD for phonologically short vowels were included. As mentioned later, the few examples with phonologically long vowels show patterns generally consistent with those of the short vowels.

4.   Discussion

The differences between /d/ and /t/ are shown graphically in Figure 2. At the normal rate, the preceding vowel is significantly shorter before /d/ than before /t/. This is a very unusual finding. Keating (1985) reports the reverse relationship as common, where a longer vowel occurs before a voiced stop. She also reports some languages as having no difference, but nowhere does she find the relationship which we see in Mongolian with a longer vowel before a voiceless consonant. Note that this difference is lessened to a nonsignificant status ($p = 0.054$) in fast speech. The data for the few examples of long vowels are consistent with the findings for the short vowels.

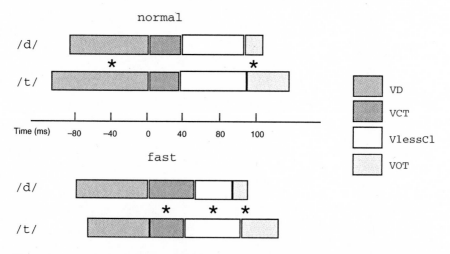

Figure 2.   *Differences between /d/ and /t/. Asterisks are placed between elements that are significantly different*

The VCT for all cases is approximately the same (34–39 ms), except in fast speech for /d/, where it is significantly longer than in slow speech. This lengthening of VCT is discussed below.

The VlessCl shows a significant difference between /d/ and /t/ only at the fast rate.

VOT is significantly shorter for /d/ than for /t/ at both rates of speech; this is the expected result (Lisker and Abramson 1964).

The ClD is not significantly different at either rate. The literature (see Crystal & House 1988 for an overview) gives conflicting reports on the relationship of the duration of the closure and voicing. It appears that voicing, phonological environment, place of articulation, as well as other contextual elements may affect the duration of stops. For Mongolian medial stops, the length of the closure does not appear to distinguish /d/ and /t/ at either rate of speech.

The total amount of voicelessness (VlessD) is significantly greater for /t/ than for /d/ at both rates of speech.

The total duration of the consonant (TotalC) is shorter for /d/ than for /t/ at both rates of speech. At both rates, this difference is primarily due to the VOT. The overall duration (TotalD) is significantly shorter for /d/ than for /t/ at the normal rate, but the difference is not significant at the fast rate.

A separate study of comparable data (Rogers 1992) argues that at the normal rate VOT is the most salient cue for distinguishing /d/ from /t/. Even though VCT and VlessCl are also distinctive at the fast rate, it is VOT which can consistently serve to distinguish /d/ from /t/ at both rates of speech.

Figure 3 shows a graphic representation comparing the measurements found in the normal and fast rates of speech for /d/ and /t/.

VD is shortened significantly only for /t/.

VCT is actually lengthened for /d/ at the fast rate. The other values of VCT are about the same. To explain this unexpected lengthening, we must look at what controls the duration of voicing at the beginning of a stop. The voicelessness of the /t/ is explained as the result of a voiceless gesture, in which the vocal cords separate precluding any vibration. The timing of the voiceless gesture with respect to the stop articulation is part of the general motor control coordinating speech activities.

For a /d/, however, the situation is different. The vocal cords remain close to each other in a position in which voicing can occur. Voicing is dependent, however, not only on the position of the vocal cords but on a suitable airflow. During a vowel, the airflow is relatively unimpeded and voicing occurs. After the closure in the oral cavity is completed, airflow continues, causing voicing, called here VCT. After a short period of time, however, the supraglottal pressure increases to a point where the airflow from below is insufficient to sustain

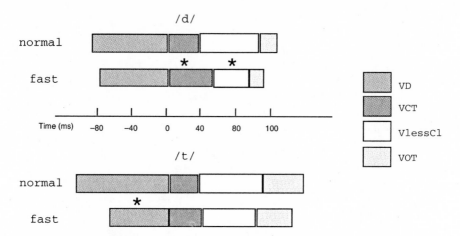

Figure 3.   *Differences between normal and fast speech. Asterisks are placed between elements that are significantly different*

voicing; this point represents the end of VCT. Thus, the timing of the voiceless-ness of /d/ is a result of aerodynamic forces operating within the vocal tract.

Westbury (1983) presents a model showing that the duration of VCT during a voiced stop depends on the volume of the upper vocal tract; this volume can be actively or passively altered. Active enlargement can be made by pulling the tongue down and forward, by pulling the rear pharyngeal wall back, or by raising the velum (Bell-Berti 1975). The supralaryngeal volume can be altered passively as well by varying the compliance or tension of the walls of the vocal tract. As air is pushed upwards, a more compliant wall yields to a greater extent, passively allowing the cavity to expand; a less compliant wall yields less, allowing a smaller increase in cavity volume.

Westbury's model predicts that the wall compliance should be tense for a VCT of 39 ms, the mean value for Mongolian /d/ at a normal rate, assuming no active volume change. For a VCT of 52 ms found in fast speech, the walls would have to have a greater degree of compliance. In fast speech it is reason-able to assume that the shorter time allows less muscular tension to develop; as a result, we expect more compliant walls in faster speech and consequently a longer voicing duration. We can thus account for the longer VCT of /d/ in fast speech in Mongolian as the expected result of faster speech with a more compliant vocal tract. The VCT of /t/ is not lengthened in fast speech, because its timing is determined by the speech motor control system and not by aerodynamic forces.

The shortening of VlessCl for /d/ is due to the lengthening of the VCT. For /t/, there is no significant difference for VlessCl at normal or fast rates. The results for VOT show a nonsignificant shortening for both /d/ and /t/.

In general, we see that in fast speech each basic component is shortened slightly, cumulatively producing the overall shortening in TotalD, significant for both /d/ and /t/. The significant exceptions to this statement are that VD for /t/ is strongly shortened, and VCT for /d/ is lengthened.

Table 3. *Duration of fast rate expressed as a percentage of normal rate*

	/d/	/t/
VD	91.0	59.8
VCT	140.8	115.99
VlessCl	61.2	83.1
VOT	83.2	80.4
ClD	89.6	93.9
VlessD	65.1	77.6
TotalC	88.7	89.6
TotalD	88.6	71.3

From Table 3 we see that the overall duration for the consonants at the fast rate is virtually the same, 88.7% of the duration at the normal rate for /d/ and 89.6% for /t/. However, on closer inspection, the individual components show considerable variation in the amount of shortening found in fast speech. This variation occurs both for the measures within /d/ and /t/ and for the measures between them. For example, within /d/, VD is shortened about 9% and VOT about 17%, and VCT is actually lengthened. Within /t/, VD is shortened by 40%, whereas VOT is shortened by only 20%. Comparing /d/ and /t/, only VOT among the basic components shows a similar level of shortening — 17% and 20%, respectively.

Löfqvist (1991) has argued that proportional timing is not a characteristic feature of speech. Proportional timing would mean that as the rate of speech is varied, the duration of each element is changed by a constant proportion; i.e., VC, VCT, VlessD, and VOT would all be shortened by the same percentage for both /d/ and /t/ in fast speech. Table III clearly shows there is not an absolute proportional shortening applied to all components in fast speech. The Mongolian results are thus consistent with Löfqvist's (1991) claim.

5.   Conclusion

Mongolian is a rather "voiceless" language in the sense that all stops have very long voiceless periods. The difference between /d/ and /t/ at both normal and fast rates of speech lies largely with the VOT; an unexpected observation is the longer vowel length before /t/ in normal speech.

The process of speaking faster shortens most elements slightly. The vowel before /t/, however is shortened dramatically, and the VCT of /d/ is lengthened, a result explained by the greater wall compliance of faster speech. These data do not support the notion of proportional timing in speech.

References

Bell-Berti, Fredericka. 1975. Control of pharyngeal cavity size for English voiced and voiceless stops. *Journal of the Acoustical Society of America* 57: 456–61.

Bosson, James and B. Unenšecen. 1962. Some notes on the dialect of the Khorchin Mongols. *American Studies in Altaic Linguistics*, ed. by Nicholas Poppe, 23–44. Indiana University Publications, Uralic and Altaic Series 13. Bloomington, Indiana: Indiana University.

Crystal, Thomas H., and Arthur S. House. 1988. The duration of American-English stop consonants: an overview. *Journal of Phonetics* 16: 285–94.

Keating, Patricia A. 1985. Universal phonetics and the organization of grammars. *Phonetic Linguistics*, ed. by Victoria Fromkin, 115–32. New York: Academic Press.

Lisker, Leigh and Arthur S. Abramson. 1964. A cross-language study of voicing in initial stops: acoustical measurements. *Word*. 20: 384–422.

Löfqvist, Anders. 1991. Proportional timing in speech motor control, *Journal of Phonetics* 19: 343–50.

Luvsanvandan, S. 1964. The Khalkha-Mongolian phonemic system. *Acta Orientalia Hungariæ* 17: 175–85.

Poppe, Nicholas. 1970. *Mongolian Language Handbook*. Washington, D.C.: Center for Applied Linguistics.

Rogers, Henry. 1992. Laryngeal timing in Mongolian. *Proceedings of the 1992 Canadian Linguistic Association*, 241–8. Toronto.

Street, John C. 1963. *Khalkha Structure*. (= Research and studies in Uralic and Altaic languages, No. 25), Bloomington: Indiana University Press.

Westbury, J.R. 1983. Enlargement of the supraglottal cavity and its relation to stop consonant voicing. *Journal of the Acoustical Society of America* 73: 1322–36.

About the author

Henry Rogers is currently Associate Professor and Associate Chair of Linguistics at the University of Toronto, where he has recently served as Acting Director of the Centre for Computing in the Humanities. His 1967 doctoral dissertation was produced at Yale under the direction of Syd Lamb. It applied a stratificational model to **The Phonology and Morphology of Sherbro**, *a Niger-Kordofanian language of Sierra Leone. It was the first full-scale treatment of these areas using a relational network notation. He has recently authored* **Theoretical and Practical Phonetics** *(1991). Besides phonetics, his research interests include writing systems and Scots Gaelic.*

PART II

Functional Approaches to the History of Language and Linguistics

A. Language Change: General Studies

CHAPTER 23

Change — Linguistic and Societal

Robert Austerlitz

Columbia University

Cultural (societal) change will here be compared with linguistic change: how they are launched and their mechanisms. The basic assumption is that both language and society form systems which consist of sub-systems and that these systems are simultaneously stable and in disequilibrium. Disequilibrium engenders change. Parcels of language which can change are, for example, words (and stems and roots), e.g. *imp*, affixes (*pre-*, *-s,* -[iš]), plain sounds without meaning (*i, m, p*), and the order of elements (*Pym saw the imp* as against *The imp saw Pym*). Any and all of these can but do not necessarily have to change in time. The causes of change are still under discussion. Two favorites are analogy and the correction of unsystematicity, respectively *George* to *Georgette*, *kitchen* and *lunch(eon)*, to *kitchenette* and *luncheonette* on the one hand and *more/less jam* vs. *more/fewer people* giving *less people* on the other, under the aegis of systematicity. Change takes place in time, i.e., history. The history of a given language can be studied by comparing it, piece by piece, to related languages, to unrelated languages (by appealing to linguistic universals), or by reconstructing the language internally (*comb* vs. *unkempt*, *thumb* vs. *thimble*), or the combination of any of these. Sub-systems can compete with each other: *ice* has the adjective *icy* with [s] but *grease* can have either [s] or [z] in *greasy*. Vestiges of a rule whereby medial [s] was voiced to [z] under certain conditions are still audible in *easy, lazy, thousand*, and in the British pronunciation of *philosophy* with medial [z]. The change of *louse* with medial [s] to *lousy* with medial [z] can thus be thought of as regular but the change in meaning from 'louse' to 'bad, unacceptable' is not regular. The adjective should have the meaning 'having lice'. How do we say 'having lice'? We say *lousy* with medial [s] because *lousy* with medial [z] has already been pre-empted by the meaning 'bad'. The change from voiceless to voiced is still operative in a subset of nouns when they alternate with their cognate verbs, as in *mouth* (noun with [θ] vs. *mouth* (verb with [ð]), *tooth* vs *teethe*, *breath* vs. *breathe*, *house* (noun, with [s]) vs. *house* (verb, with [z]). However, if a new verb such as **to mouse* were to be created it would most likely have medial *s* as in *grouse* and not *z* as in the verb to *house*.[1] That is what is meant by **systems in competition.** It is important to note that all of this, including competition, is subconscious.

There is a distinction between [dž] as in *virgin* and [ž] as in *version* in contemporary English. The latter sound does not exist in initial position, except perhaps in the still foreign word *genre*; it is restricted to a few, mostly modern, words in final position: *garage, rouge, mirage*. But [ž] is strong medially: *usual, seizure, leisure, measure, Asia* (but British *Asia* with [š]). It is so strong medially that it is insinuating itself into the [dž]-class, viz., *Azerbaijan, Beijing, adagio, parmigian*. These are all [dž]-words in the host languages and were [dž]-words in English when they entered. Why are they changing? Because of the strength of medial [ž]. Do these words share a feature which makes them susceptible to change? Yes. It is their exotic meaning; unprofessionally it could be said that they are "pseudo-French". — Stress is attracted to the first syllable in nouns (*an íncrease in taxes*) and to non-first in verbs (*they will incréase the taxes*), but the former is winning in verbs: *they prótested.* (C. H. Rounds, p.c., December 1992, suggests that *prótest* is intransitive and *protést* transitive, as in *The students were prótesting* vs. *The students were protésting the vote.*) In any case, the system is in flux. — In English weak verbs, the preterit and the past participle are formed by agglutination, without schwa: *blessed* -[st], *learned* -[nd], *winged* -[ŋd], but the adjectival form, especially when it is ceremonial, has schwa: *Blessed* -[əd], *learned, winged* (as in the statue). An individual hostess, V.E.S., was heard to say, in jest: *Would you like it slicèd?* with schwa. (On this, see below.) — *It looks like it's going to bring down the house* with *like* (vs. an older *as if*) and *You look like you didn't sleep all night* (vs. *as if you hadn't*) are now probably accepted by all but older speakers. However, *Do not refer to anyone as an Indian unless you are positive that they really are one* (from the *Culturegram* on Venezuela, 1982,

---

1. Editors' note: Though many speakers probably do not have a verb to mouse, it is listed in dictionaries and most are probably at least aware of the related agent noun, as in *That cat is a good* **mouser**. Professor Austerlitz's general point is valid, but a different example should be substituted. Unfortunately, Professor Austerlitz passed away before the editors could contact him for a refinement here.

issued by Brigham Young University) may arouse the grammatical tentacles of those for whom *anyone* cannot agree with *they*. Similarly (from the radio): *It allows **a person** to simply show **their** ID card and walk in*, for those for whom *a person* cannot agree with *their*. Are these also unconscious chains or are they on the borderline: partly unconscious and partly induced by conscious, politically induced engineering? (The change from *simply to show* to *to simply show* is older and must have been spontaneous, i.e., unconscious.)

As Table 1 shows, the pronoun *thou* served as the subject in the singular (as *I* still does). *Thou* was unmarked for case (subject vs. object) and it was unmarked for number (singular vs. plural). The object in the singular was *thee* (as *me* still is); it was marked for object. The subject in the plural was *ye* (marked for plurality but not for case; cf. *we*) and the object in the plural was *you* (marked for case and marked for plurality). Thus *thou — thee — ye — you* formed a little system just as *I — me — we — us* still does. In the course of time, presumably in order to express politeness, in a wave which swept over much of Europe, *you* came to usurp the functions of the four forms. What is strange here is that the most heavily loaded form (plural, object) took over the function of the other, less loaded, three. Was this an unconscious change? Was it conscious to a certain degree, sired by the need to express politeness or generated by imitating another culture, which already expressed politeness?

Table 1. *Analysis of second person pronouns*

	unmarked singular	marked plural
subject	thou	ye
unmarked	– –	– +
object	thee	you
marked	+ –	+ +

One may thus wish to reckon with a continuum, ranging from completely unconscious change in language to partially unconscious change in language, to completely conscious change in society. Laws are the most obvious instances of change, e.g., laws concerning flag burning, women's suffrage, driving on the right, choice of building materials, introduction of the kiwi fruit, introduction of rhymeless poetry, rules in rationing. A change in musical scale may be conscious or unconscious, at times governed by the introduction of a new musical instrument. The introduction of cubism seems to have been conscious change. Was the introduction of cross-cousin marriage conscious or unconscious? Was the first person who wore black to indicate mourning doing it consciously or not? How do fashions and fads spread (marinated chicken and melted cheese), consciously or unconsciously? The initiator of a fad may have acted consciously: in ... *demotic prose and populist stance* ... (*Newsweek*, January 18, 1993) *demotic* has lost some of its original meanings. The transfer was probably unconscious, but the first author who effected the transfer (*demotic* as a style in Modern Greek or an Egyptian writing system) probably did it consciously. — Not so long ago those who spoke about the Ukraine spoke about *The Ukraine*, with an article. At present the article can hardly be heard or seen: *In Ukraine* .... How did this come about? By conscious linguistic engineering. The article was thought to suggest that ***The** Ukraine* was part of a larger unit (such as Russia); *Ukraine* without the article suggests that it is a country like any other. (Note that neither Ukrainian nor Russian has an article like *the*.)

The main question being discussed here is: which changes are instinctive, subliminal, uncalculated, spontaneous, and unconscious and which changes are engineered, planned, premeditated, the result of committee work, or consciously telic? The definition of *conscious* can simply be 'aware of what one is aiming at, as in committee work'.

There are occasional changes in language which involve memory. In the *hapax legomenon* cited above — *would you like it slicèd?* — the speaker was aware that the listener projected the exceptional form *slicèd* — [səd] against the normal, expected form *sliced* — [st]. Memory provided the back-drop. The *hapax* was creative and entertaining and allowed to fade into the background. This was a change which did not propagate.

In the case of the second person *you*, which now has four functions in English, the change must have been unconscious. This is all the more significant because the old *you* was both plural and the object (note the two plus signs in Table 1). The new *you* thus destroyed an entire paradigm, thus contributing to the new topological profile of Modern English. In fact, Modern English is unique in that its pronouns for the 2nd person singular and for the 2nd plural are homophones. In this way Modern English also lost a device for politeness; cf. Modern French, where *vous* is 2nd plural, 2nd singular-polite, and 2nd-plural-polite.

Are puns relevant here? In *He has more dollars than cents/sense* there is ambiguity. The speaking community agrees to be entertained, but this is not an instance of linguistic change. Furthermore, the process is conscious. Similarly, rhyme (... *shame* / ... *same*) is not an instance of change. It is difficult to say whether rhyme and the other devices (parallelism, alliteration, assonance) are conscious. They are conscious insofar as they draw attention to the substance of language, but they are not as conscious as societal change.

Can society willfully impede or retard change in language? Yes, it can. This is called prescriptive grammar. In *He is taller than I am* (or *than I*) the progress of the language (which by now dictates *He is taller than me*) is being impeded. Here society is conservative and combats the will of the people.

Can society willfully change language? Yes; see language engineering above. In *Everyone will bring their notebook*, *their* does duty for *her or his*, which is too clumsy and ultimately stands for *his* which is thought to be biased. Language engineering can be thought of as an act of conscious interference with the natural state of language or with the natural progress of language, i.e., change. *Everyone will show* **their** *ID* as against *his* may be an instance of natural evolution or it may be an instance of interference with language. Likewise: *Ukraine* as against *The Ukraine*. Who is interfering? Society.

A word generally containing more than two syllables which looks like a compound but is not a compound sometimes begs for an internal explanation, e.g. *hospital*, reinterpreted as *horse pistol* (note the identical stress pattern: strong, weak, weak). In *asparagus*, reinterpreted as *sparrow grass* the initial, stressless syllable (*a-*) is sacrificed. Both words, when reinterpreted, make sense, sometimes with humorous overtones. Conversely, *shamefaced* seems to consist of *shame* and *faced*, historically, but does not. It was *shamefast* 'fast in modesty' in Old English, cf. *steadfast*. These reinterpretations are folk etymologies, conscious attempts at finding remedies for unintelligibility by the community of speakers (note the polysemy of *fast*). Here, when a reinterpretation survives, language changes consciously. In *worship* the elements have melted together to the point of unrecognizability: *worth(y)* plus *-ship* from *shape*. This is not a folk etymology. — Calques are word-to-word translations from one language to another: *Thursday* (which is from Old English, which is from Old Norse) is a calque on *Jovis diēs* 'Jupiter's day'. Old Norse *Thor* was identified, by cultural covenant, with the Roman god Jupiter. Furthermore, the Latin form is a calque on Greek *Diòs hēmérā* 'Zeus's day'. Calques, then, are conscious and transparent at the time when they are being created but can and generally do lose transparency in the course of time. Transparency here means that consciousness is involved.

So much for language. The cultural (or societal) changes listed below are listed at random. The question still is: is the given societal change conscious or not? Women in the clergy, change of calendar, introduction or reintroduction of the miniskirt, educational policy, rotation of crops, change in military regulations, transfer from pottery making to basket weaving, avoidance of the triton in composition (C to F#), avoidance of spilling salt at table for fear that it brings bad luck (cf. Judas at the Last Supper), not shaking hands over a threshold (in Scandinavia), flag burning, marinating, the spread of maize, rationing in time of need, adoption of chopsticks. These are all based on conscious ratiocination, though the spread of maize may be an exception: it may have been an unconscious transfer.

Ultimately, linguistic change is initiated and sustained by one or another segment of society (working, middle, other), for non-linguistic reasons: association with another class (imitation), disassociation with one's own class (camouflaging). The *mechanism* of linguistic change is subconscious or unconscious. In contrast, both the idea of and the mechanism of societal change are fully conscious. The interesting cases are on the borderline: linguistic changes which are consciously brought about and their mirror image: instinctive social changes, if there are such changes. The first (engineered) category are in fact changes in the social channel, with the difference that in the case of non-observance there is only mild censorship or mild punishment. In any case, language does not change because a group of people convene to decide that, say, an original initial [f] will or should be replaced by zero, as in Spanish *hierro* 'iron', from Latin *ferru-*. (*h* in Spanish is silent.) In contrast, societal change is launched and implemented by one or more persons (despot, parliament, fashion designer, or voting majority).

One moral issuing from all this is that when students of society study change in society they should not rely on linguistic change as a model or should rely on it with utmost caution. Language, i. e. linguistic behavior, is like breathing and walking. Society is more like speaking (in public).

About the author

Robert Austerlitz died September 9, 1994. He was Professor Emeritus of Linguistics at Columbia University, where he received his Ph.D. in 1955 and taught from 1958 to 1993. Though he was especially known as a Uralicist, his interests extended more broadly to the languages of Eurasia, and he did field work with a number of groups there and in native America. His special recognitions included the presidencies of the Linguistic Society of America and the American Oriental Society and several visiting professorships. His acquaintance with Syd Lamb began in the 1960s and strengthened with his frequent attendance at meetings of the Yale Linguistic Club.

CHAPTER 24

From First to Second Person
The History of Amerind *k(i)

Joseph H. Greenberg

In diachronic typology there are instances in which it is possible for a language of a particular type A to change to type B but not directly. In such cases a language of type A must go through some other type (or in the general case, types) C before it can change into type B. We may then say that the types A and B are weakly, rather than strongly, connected.

A common example is the following. A language must first go through a singular/plural differentiation before it can enter the type singular/dual/plural. This is commonly done in one of two ways. The plural becomes restricted to the dual and a new plural develops with the meaning 'three-or-more'. A second common way is for the new dual to develop from the plural by the addition of a new marker which is then usually suffixed to the old plural. This new marker often develops from the numeral expression for 'two'. An instance of this is Lithuanian in which a dual developed which is not the historical continuation of the Proto-Indo-European dual, namely *mu-du* 'we two' and *ju-du* 'you two'.

Except for its exemplification in Greenberg (1987: 55–6), such an indirect connection has never been noted before, to my knowledge, between first and second singular pronouns. In such instances, of course, the first person pronoun of one language will be cognate with the second person of another language but a semantic change from first to second person or vice versa will not have occurred.

The manner in which this comes about is that a first person inclusive dual or plural either becomes a first person plural general pronoun, without an inclusive-exclusive distinction, a normal and very frequent change, or much more rarely it becomes confined to the second person rather than the first.

Table 1. *"Philippine system" of pronouns*

	Singular	Dual	Plural
1st Incl. .	−	+	+
1st Excl.	−	−	+
1st w/o distinction	+	−	−
2nd Person	+	−	+
3rd Person	+	−	+

If a language has a first person inclusive/exclusive distinction it frequently has first person dual inclusive but has no exclusive first person dual, or in fact any other dual form. In such systems the first person inclusive plural sometimes shows by its form that it is the plural of the first person inclusive dual. Systems of this kind are common in the Austronesian languages of the Philippines. When complete they have eight members, and when arranged in terms of conventional categories the system appears to be highly asymmetrical and irregular as can be seen from Table 1.

Such systems have been convincingly realigned by certain Austronesianists (e.g. Thomas, Conklin) by treating the first inclusive dual as a separate person (fourth or inclusive person). We can then rearrange these eight forms as in Table 2.

Table 2. *Philippine System Reanalyzed*

	Singular	Plural ("and others")
1	+	+ (exclusive plural)
1+2	+ (i.e. dual)	+ (inclusive plural)
2	+	+
3	+	+

This has also been expressed in terms of three features each with plus and minus values +/− ego, +/− tu, +/− others. I believe that all linguists with a knowledge of the Carib languages will recognize this analysis and indeed Franchetto (1990), in an analysis of Carib pronouns arrives at precisely these three features, presumably in ignorance of Philippine systems.

Such systems are very fragile historically. The most common course of events is for the inclusive dual to be lost and the first person inclusive to become the ordinary first person plural, thus leading to the common six person type, three persons and two numbers.

If we compare Philippine languages with Carib, however, we note two major differences. Unlike Austronesian languages, Carib, like many other Amerind languages has bipersonal markers, here prefixed on the verb, indicating the person and number of the verb, subject and object. A second difference is that whereas the feature +/– "other" is covert in Philippine languages e.g. second plural is not distinguished from second singular by an overt plural marker, in Carib it is, most commonly by the suffixation of -komo, -kon, so that the conditions for the analysis described above are indeed transparent.

A further relevant fact about Carib languages is that the same marker kV- occurs both for first person inclusive, frequently a dual, and in the bipersonal marker system, first person acts on first, and first person acts on second. Thus the meaning of kV-, most frequently ki or ku, is first person in association with second person.

A remarkably similar system is found in the Algic languages, especially Algonkian. The first person inclusive plural is once more kV- along with a suffix for the plural. Moreover, as discussed in detail in an article by Hockett (1966), this kV- is implicated along with other various supplementary marks in all bipersonal forms in which first person acts on second, or second on first, just as in Carib. However, there is one respect in which the development of kV- in Algic languages is different from the common one. We have seen that the usual further development of first person inclusive form is to first person plural. From here it can also become a first singular marker. However in Algic languages the kV- rather becomes the source of the second person marker as shown in the now-famous comparison of Wiyot, Yurok and Algonkian by Sapir in which there is a fourfold agreement among the languages in the set n- first person, k- second person, w- third person, m- indefinite person.

However Algonkian, by its use of kV- in forms indicating the action of first on second person and second person on first and as a first person plural inclusive by the addition of a plural marker, contrasts with the first person exclusive based on Pan-Amerind first person singular n with the plural marker *nan (as recon-structed by Bloomfield). For the second person plural we have k- prefixed and *waaw suffixed. We thus have the double use of k as first and second person with k- as second singular, k- ... -nan as first person inclusive and k- ... -waw second person plural while n- ... -nan is first person exclusive. But what of m- the Pan-Amerind second person marker? It has apparently disappeared from Algonkian but there are abundant survivals in the verb both in Wiyot and Yurok so that it can be reconstructed for Algic.

A further remarkable typological agreement between Algic and Carib concerns the first person exclusive plural which is, as it were, the odd man out in the whole system. In Carib it can, in its independent pronominal form, be reconstructed as *amna* or the like. Syntactically it acts just like a noun and takes third person agreements on the verb. In Wiyot the independent first person plural exclusive pronoun *hinod*, which is of course not cognate with *amna*, takes the verb in the third person singular indefinite (Teeter 1964: 36). The verb by itself can indicate a first person plural exclusive subject, or an indefinite subject. It is disambiguated by the presence of *hinod* e.g. *toʔl-uy* 'one talks, we (excl.) talk', but *hinod toʔl-uy* can only mean 'we (excl.) talk'.

There is one further aspect of the comparison of Algic and Carib which is of interest here. In Algic, as has been seen, Pan-Amerind *n* functions as the first person singular pronoun and, with a pluralizer, as first person exclusive plural. Further, whereas Pan-Amerind second person *m* has been displaced in the second person by the first person inclusive (i.e. 1+2 person) in the possessive (and elsewhere in Algonkian), it survives abundantly in Wiyot and Yurok. In Carib, however, the widespread Ge-Pano-Carib pattern *i-* 'first person', *a-* 'second person' has replaced *n-* and *m-* in the first and second persons in the nominal possessive. However in the bipersonal forms of the verb both *n-* and *m-* are found in an interesting distribution. Here my main sources are the early surveys of Carib morphology found in Adams (1893) and de Goeje (1907, 1909) and the very stimulating article by Franchetto which covers the verb intransitive and transitive bipersonal markers for a number of Carib languages based on more recent sources (1990).

These data lead to the reconstruction of third person acting on second as *a-* but second person acting on third as *m-*. In some instances in Carib, for example in Apalai, *m-* has spread analogically to be both third acts on second and second on third but this is clearly historically secondary unlike first person *i-*, second person *a-* which appears to be a Ge-Pano-Carib innovation. I suspect, however, that it might be Amerind and a further diligent search, not attempted here, might reveal scattered survivals elsewhere.

My conjecture is that the coincidence of Algic and Carib can hardly be accidental and that Proto-Amerind had a Philippine type pronominal system. Given the historical fragility of such systems and the vast time period which has elapsed, its survival, although of course in two variants, in only two widely separated families is not surprising.

Moreover, this assumption has explanatory value in two regards. We have seen that the usual course of development of first person inclusives is to become simply first person plural pronouns and then sometimes to generalize as first person pronouns displacing the singular. In fact, in Amerind alongside of, or instead of, *n-*, the most common first person pronoun is *k* which is found in Andean, Macro-Carib, Oto-Mangue, Kiowa-Tanoan, Hokan and Penutian.

If indeed this fairly widespread *k-* first person pronoun does derive from general Amerind inclusive dual or plural, there should be found instances in which it is confined to the plural in contrast to *n* or *i* of the first person singular. There is in fact one strong example of this in Oto-Manguean already pointed out in Greenberg (1987: 124). In Rensch's reconstruction of Proto-Oto-Manguean we find as no. 123 (Rensch 1976: 223) *(h)ka(h)* all of whose glosses are first person pronouns. Rensch never gives meanings for his reconstructed forms. The above form is based on a *k /n* Ablaut alternation which has very little support in any other etymologies and is phonetically implausible. In the Oto-Pame subgroup we find only forms in *k* for which Rensch's reconstruction is *ka. All the glosses are first person plural inclusive. Amuzgo, another branch of Oto-Manguean has a reconstructed form *hka(h)* and has as translations 'I', 'we (inclusive)' and we (exclusive). On the other hand Mixtec of San Miguel has *naa* 'I' which is said to derive from Proto-Mixtecan *nah, Proto-Popolucan has a reconstructed form *na with the meaning 'I' in two of the languages cited and first person plural exclusive in the other. Isthmus Zapotec has *naʔa* 'I' deriving from *nah. We thus have two branches which have *k* forms with predominantly first plural inclusive meanings and three branches with *n* forms with the semantic value 'I' in almost all cases. If, as posited by Rensch, the *n* and *k* forms have a single origin in Proto-Oto-Mangue, it is a remarkable coincidence that they should have sorted themselves out by an internal process into agreement with the general Amerind pronominal pattern, *n* 'first person singular' and *k* 'first person plural inclusive'.

Sapir, whose comparative studies of Hokan are still the only broad comparisons of these languages we have in print, in his study based on Yana (1917), on Subtiaba (1925), and his paper on Hokan-Coahuiltecan (1920), has entries for first person pronouns based both on *k-* and *n-*. In fact *i-*, to which at least tentatively I would assign an original absolutive meaning, is also widespread. Often several of these alternatives *n-*, *k-*, and *i-* occur in the same language with different functions. It is my impression that *m-* 'second person' is more common in Amerind languages than *n-* 'first person'. This is because its only common rival is *a-* in Ge-Pano-Carib in South America. That both *a-* and *m-* occur in Carib has been seen above.

In the following portion of this paper I investigate the distribution of *k-* as a first person marker in the Hokan-Coahuiltecan group where, as we have seen, its presence was noted by Sapir, language by language. If indeed Hokan first person *k-* derives from a first person inclusive plural (ultimately dual), we would expect that in some instances it is confined to the plural in contrast to *n* and *i*. The results of this inquiry are summarized in Table 3 which indicates for each Hokan language and for some Coahuiltecan languages for which the sparse data on those languages give information, the presence of *n*, *k* and *i* for first person and *m* for second person. In this table the languages are arranged in a general north-south direction.

As noted above, if Hokan first person *k* does arise in the manner hypothesized here, we should find instances in which *k* recurs as a plural as against *n* singular while the opposite distribution would count against it. We proceed in a general north-south direction, evaluating briefly the evidence from each language and each language group.

The Shasta first person singular independent pronoun is recorded by Bright as *ya-ʔa* and the second person singular as *mayʔi*. The first presumably derives from Proto-Amerind *i*. There seems to be no evidence for *n* or *k* in the first person.

The Achumawi-Atsugewi group has the overall designation Palaihnihan. Olmsted (1964), in his treatment of Palaihnihan phonology, compares the first independent pronouns Achumawi *it* and Atsugaewi *ak*, *akh* and reconstructs Proto-Palaihnihan **ekh*. For the plural of the same person he reconstructs *Eku* on the basis of Achumawi *ittu* and Atsugaewi *akuir*. The second person singular is reconstructed as **mi-*. We seem then to have only a *k* form in the first person. Chimariko clearly has *n* 'first person' and *m* 'second' deducible from the independent pronouns *nout* 'I', *noutowa* 'we two (exclusive)', *mamut* 'thou', *mamutowa* 'we two (inclusive)', *nacidut* 'we (plural)'. Dixon (1910), our source for Chimariko, was unable to elicit a second or third person plural. The suffixed nominal possessive *-i* 'my' no doubt reflects general Amerind *-i*. The second singular possessive is *-mi*.

Table 3. *Reflexes of first person *n, *i, *k and second person *m in Hokan and Coahuiltecan pronouns*

	First Person			Second Person
	n	i	k	m
Shasta		+		+
Palaihnihan			+	+
Chimariko	+	+		+
Karok	+		+	+
Washo	+	(+)		+
Yana	(+)	+	+	+
Pomo		+	(+)	+
Chumash		+	+	(+)
Salinan			+	+
Esselen	+			+
Yuman	(+)			+
Seri		+	(+)	+
Chontal			+	+
Jicaque			+	
Subtiaba			(+)	
Yurimangi	+			
Coahuiltecan	+		+	+

For Karok we have the excellent detailed grammar of Bright (1957). The nominal possessive prefixes show the *n/m* pattern e.g. *nanitta:t* 'my mother', *mitta:t* 'thy mother'. The first plural also shows *n-* with a vowel change *nanuttat* 'our mother'. The verb possesses a highly complex morphology involving bipersonal prefixes which differ for the indicative positive, indicative negative and imperative. A suffix *-ap* appears in some forms along with the prefixes. The intransitive verb subject markers are identical to the transitives with a third person singular object. Macauley (1992) has sought to interpret *-ap* as an inverse marker but admits that not all occurrences of *-ap* can be interpreted in this fashion. In addition she has interpreted the prefixes *kan-* and *kin-* as first singular involved (that is, acting or being acted on by second and third persons) and *kin-* as first plural involved. The *-n* is puzzling, but *ka-* and *ki-* might be interpreted as *k-* first person and *ki-* specifically in its involvement of first plural is suggestively similar to the posited *ki-* 'first inclusive' that has been proposed here and in Greenberg (1987) for Amerind.

Washo has both independent first person pronoun *le* and *l-* verb subject and possessive marker. That Washo *l* derives from *n* is well known. In addition it may contain *i-* first person in the bipersonal form *m-i*, 'I ... thee'. The second person *m* is further attested in *mi* 'thou'; *mi-u* 'you', (cf. *le-u* 'we') and *m- ~ -um* 'thou'(verb subject)

The Yana pronominal system is described and analyzed in some detail by Sapir (1917: 23–6). Yana has three dialects Northern, Central and Southern. The Southern is the most different, but not drastically so. The basic pronominal elements, all suffixed, contain an initial *nV-*. possibly of demonstrative origin, from which we may abstract. In the first singular we have *-ndja, nidja* (Southern Yana *-ndji, nidji*); *nu-ma* 'thou'; *ni-gi* 'we, our'. These form the independent set when suffixed to a base *ai'-* e.g. *ai'nidja* 'I' (Northern Yana) and are possessives when suffixed to nouns and subjects when suffixed to verbs. It is clear that *-gi* 'our, we' coincides with the first person plural marker that has been posited here and *-ma* is the almost ubiquitous *m* second person of Hokan and other groups. It is possible that *-i* first person is present in Southern Yana *dj-i, dj-* being, as has been noted, a demonstrative element. If so then we may have *-i* first person as argued by Sapir (ibid. 24–25) where *-i* is said to be an old first person, also found in the isolated Yana form *mau-s-i* 'I am about to' (cf. *mau-s* 'he is about to'). Sapir equates this with Chimariko *-i* as in *masomas-i* 'my red salmon'. It may be added that in Macauley's article on *-ap* as an inverse marker in Karok there is included (1987: 199) a reanalysis of the subject-object markers of Yana in which the passive *wa*, which is compulsory in some combinations, is reanalyzed as an inverse marker. In her table it is clear that *ki-* is common to all subject-object combinations in which the first plural is subject or the first plural is object.

We next consider the Pomo languages, a group of fairly divergent dialects. The Proto-Pomo forms of the pronominal system have been reconstructed in McLendon (1976). There seems to be no trace here of the *n-* 'first person' nor for that matter *i-*. The first person singular stem is reconstructed as *ha?a* in Proto-Pomo. The second person *m*, however, is clearly present. In Sapir's Hokan comparisons the first person *k* appears as the possessive *ke* found in southwestern (Kashaya) Pomo *?K^{h}e* and central and northern *k^{h}e*. According to McLendon's analysis this would be the violently shortened form of *-baq^{h}e* the common possessive suffix. The full form for 'my' is **ha?aw+i+at+baq^{h}e* in which *-i-* is an oblique case marker and *at* and *baq^{h}e* are both possessive markers. For northern Pomo we must assume a borrowing from central Pomo or Kashaya since the pronominal possessive *baqʰe* is not found in that dialect. This is possible but by no means completely plausible. The main weakness of the McLendon reconstructions is the assumption of complete unity in Proto-Pomo (i.e. the absence of any variant forms) and the complete analyzability of every pronominal form in the proto-language. At this point, one would, I believe, be justified in asserting that a first person possessive *$*kʰe$ is by no means excluded as a variant in Proto-Pomo and in this case it might be a continuation of the widespread *k-* first person found in other Hokan languages.

The languages this far considered are all in a general sense Northern Californian. In Southern California, Mexico, and Central America we first consider Chumash, a language spoken in a number of dialects in the area of Santa Barbara and San Luis Obispo. For the independent first person singular pronoun the existence of the *n-* form is well attested, e.g. Santa Ynez *noi*, Santa Barbara and Santa Cruz *noo* and San Buenaventura *no*. The plural however is formed from *ki-* as we see in Santa Ynez and Santa Barbara *kiku*. The second person is *pii* (Santa Ynez, Santa Barbara) and *pi* (San Buenaventura and Santa Cruz), which might be derived from forms in *m-*. Chumash has a set of bound pronominal prefix forms which, as so often is the case, are identical as pronominal possessives and verb subjects but suffixed when an object is present. These form a highly symmetrical system in which *k-* functions as the first person, *p-* as the second and *s-* as the third. These form duals *kis-, pis-, sis-* and plurals *ki-, pi-, si-*. Chumash, as can be seen, gives clear evidence for *k-* first person plural versus *n-* first person singular in the independent pronouns with *k-* generalized to all first persons in the bound forms. It thus provides important evidence in favor of the thesis presented in this portion of the paper.

Salinan, spoken south of Chumash, has two reported dialects, Antoniano and Migueleño, treated in some detail in Mason (1918). Both show forms in *k* both for the singular and plural first person while *m* occurs in the second person. To the south of Salinan we find Esselen, concerning which our knowledge is very restricted. Kroeber (1904) has summarized our information. The independent first person pronoun is *enni, enne* and the possessive suffix *-nis* is 'my'. The second person shows clear evidence of *m* in *-mis*, 'thy'. The independent second person pronoun is *name, nemi*. I find no indications of a first person *-i* or *-k* in our sparse materials.

South of this, we find the extensive Yuman group. The basic first person form in these languages has a palatal nasal *nʸ* which possibly derives from *n*, while the second person has *m*. I see no indication of either first person *i* or *k*.

The next language to be considered, Seri, is spoken in Northwestern Mexico. A recent study by Marlett (1990) concerns the person and number inflections of this language. The general possessive prefixes are given as *ʔi-* 'my', *mi-* 'thy'. With kinship terms we find *ʔi-* and *ma-,* respectively. Whether *ʔi-* here is the common Amerind (and Hokan) *i* is not, however, quite certain in view of the plural forms *a-* 'first person', *ma-* 'second person' employed when the next segment begins with *y.* In other words *i-* here may rather be part of a pattern of number contrast *i* (singular) versus *a* (plural) and in fact the stem of the first person may rather be *ʔ.*

The Chontal independent pronouns clearly show *i-* first person and *m-* second person. Our most reliable source is no doubt Waterhouse (1962) who gives *iyaʔ* 'I'; *imaʔ* 'thou'; *iyank'* 'we'; *imank'* 'you'. There are two dialects of Chontal, mountain and coastal. Waterhouse's study is one of the coastal dialect. A detailed, although doubtless phonetically flawed study is that of Belmar (1950) of the mountain dialect. Here we find a whole series of conjugations which seem to have no parallel in Waterhouse's grammar. A series of these have *ka-* in the first person (first and second), *ki-* (third), *ku-* (fourth). The seventh conjugation has *na-* 'I'; *ma-* 'thou'; *nin-* 'we'. The vowel variations probably are due to different stem vowels. Belmar's ninth conjugation is identical to the nominal possessives which are formed from an article *la-* followed by a person marker, e.g. *lai-* (= my); *lo-* (= thy); *li-* (= his, her).

Jicaque has two dialects, an eastern and western. Except for some entries in Conzemius (1922) all our information is on the eastern dialect. The pronouns only seem to occur in unbound form. In the eastern dialect *-p* is clearly not part of the pronominal morpheme, as in *na-p* 'I'; *hi-p* 'thou'; *ku-p* 'we'. This is further confirmed by the western form *na-k* 'I' and *hi-k* 'thou'. Jicaque is one of the very few Hokan languages for which second person *m* is not attested. The contrast *na-* 'I', *ku-* 'we' obviously supports the thesis advanced here. Von Hagen (1943) also gives a form *maska* 'let's go' with variant *masnukup.* This suggests a stem *mas-* 'to go'. The *-kup* of the second form is obviously the second person independent pronoun. If this analysis is correct then *-ka* in the first of these is a first person plural hortatory.

In Subtiaba a first person *-k* appears to be the only one of the morphemes under consideration to recur. Sapir (1925) has, to my mind, argued convincingly, both on internal and comparative grounds that *u* < **ak.* Thus Subtiaba *isu* 'bee' corresponds to Mohave (Yuman) *-isaka* and *Enyu* to Salinan *t-enak* where *t-* is a third stage article. Within Subtiaba *ra:bu* 'man, person' < *ra:bak* matches *ra:ba-gu* 'woman'. In Subtiaba the pronominal elements are suffixed to a base *ik-* to form the pronouns e.g. *ika* 'thou'. Hence first person singular *iku'* < **(ik-)ak)*

Finally I consider the Coahuiltecan languages, of which only Tonkawa is known in more than a fragmentary way. The first person singular *n* is well attested: Coahuilteco *na-*; Karakawa *nayi*, and Comecrudo *na*. Second person *m* is found in Coahuilteco *mai* 'thou' and possibly Karankawa *emna* 'thou' or 'you'. A first person plural is found in Maratino *ko*. Swanton had proposed *xo-* Coahuilteco 'our', which could be compared to first singular *na-* providing another example of the *n* /*k* first person distribution. However, Troike's reanalysis (1963. 298) rather gives as possessive prefixes *na-* 'my ' *naxo-* 'our'. Finally the *k-* 'first person' appears in the verbal object prefix, *ke-* 'me' of Tonkawa.

These results are summarized in Table 3 although incompletely since singular and plural uses are not specified. Items in parentheses are to be considered doubtful.

The chief conclusions to be drawn from this table and from the data in the article are that *m* is much more widely found as second person in Hokan than *n* as first person, that *n*, *i* and *k*, all of which can be explained on comparative grounds, account for almost all instances of the first person pronoun and that although there are a few instances of *k* as plural and *n* or *i* as first persons, Pomo (?), Chumash, Yana, Jicaque) there are no examples of the opposite distribution. A similar study should, of course, be made on other subgroups of Amerind in order to test the hypotheses set forth in this paper.

References

Adam, Lucien. 1893. *Materiaux pour servir à l'établissement d'une grammaire comparée des dialectes de la famille Caribe*. Paris: Maisonneuve.

Bloomfield, Leonard. 1946. Algonquian. *Linguistic Structures of Native America* ed. by Harry Hoijer et al., 85–129. New York: Viking Fund Publications in Anthropology 6.

Belmar, Francisco. 1905. El Chontal. *Lenguas Indigenas de México*, 118–216. México: Imprenta Particular.

Bright, William. 1957. *The Karok Language*. University of California Publications in Linguistics 13. Berkeley, California: University of California Press.

Bright, William. 1964. Shasta. (See Shirley Silver, University of California Publications in Linguistics 34: 170.)

Conklin, Harold C. 1962. Lexicographical treatment of folk taxonomies. *Problems in Lexicography,* ed. by Fred W. Householder and Sol Saporta, 119–128. Publications of the Research Center in Anthropology, folklore and Linguistics, Indiana University, No. 21. (Part of *International Journal of American Linguistics* 28).

Conzemius, Edward. 1922. The Jicaques of Honduras. *International Journal of American Linguistics* 2: 163–170.

Franchetto, Bruna. 1990. Ergativity and Nominativity in Kuikuro and other Carib Languages. *Amazonian Linguistics,* ed. by Doris L. Payne, 408–27. Austin: University of Texas Press.

Goeje, Claudias H. de. 1909–1949. Études linguistiques Caraibes. (Mededeelingen der Koninklijke Nederlandsche Akademie van Wetenschappen.) Amsterdam: J. Müller.

Greenberg, Joseph H. 1987. *Language in the Americas.* Stanford: Stanford Press.

Hockett, Charles F. 1966. What Algonquian is really like. *International Journal of American Linguistics* 32: 59–73.

Kroeber, Alfred. 1904. Esselen. *The Languages of the Coast of California South of San Francisco,* 49–68. University of California Publications in American Archaeology and Ethnology 2. Berkeley, California: University of California Press.

Macauley, Monica. 1992. Inverse marking in Karok: the function of the suffix *-ap. International Journal of American Linguistics* 58: 182–201.

Marlett, Stephen A. 1990. Noun inflection in Seri. *International Journal of American Linguistics* 56: 503–41

Mason, J. Alden. 1918. *The Language of the Salinan Indians.* University of California Publications in American Archaeology and Ethnology 14: 1–154. Berkeley, California: University of California Press.

McLendon, Sally. 1976. The Proto-Pomo Pronominal System. *Hokan Studies: Papers from the First Conference on Hokan Languages, held in San Diego, April 23–25, 1970,* ed. by Margaret Langdon and Shirley Silver, 129–154. Janua Linguarum, Series Practica, No. 181.) The Hague: Mouton.

Olmsted, David 1964. A History of Palaihnihan Morphology. University of California Publications in Linguistics 35.

Rensch, Calvin R. 1976. *Comparative Otomanguean Phonology.* Indiana University Publications, Language Science Monograph Vol. 14. Bloomington, Indiana: Indiana University.

Rivet, Paul. 1942. Un dialecte Hoka Columbien. *Journal de la Societé des Américanistes* 34: 1–59.

Sapir, Edward. 1917. *The Position of Yana in the Hokan Stock.* University of California Publications in American Archaeology and Ethnology 13: 1–34.

Sapir, Edward. 1920. The Hokan and Coahuiltecan Languages. *International Journal of American* Linguistics 1: 280–90.

Sapir, Edward. 1925. The Hokan Affinity of Subtiaba in Nicaragua, *American Anthropologist* 27. 402–35, 491–527.

Silver, Shirley. 1964. Shasta and Karok: A binary comparison. *Studies in California Linguistics,* ed by William Bright, 170–181. (University of California Publications in Linguistics 34.) Berkeley and *Los Angeles, California: University of California Press.*

Teeter, Karl V. 1964. *The Wiyot Language.* University of California Publications in Linguistics 37. Berkeley, California: University of California Press.

Thomas, David. 1955. Three analyses of the Ilocano Pronoun System. *Word* 11:204–208. [Reprinted in *Readings in Philippine Linguistics*, ed. by Andres Gonzalez, Teodoro A. Llamzon, and Fe Torres Otanes, 611–615. Manila: Linguistic Society of the Philippines. 1973.]

Troike, Rudolf C. 1963. A Contribution to Coahuilteco Lexicography. *International Journal of American Linguistics* 29: 295–299.

von Hagen, V. Wolfgang. 1943. *The Jicaque (Torrupan) Indians of Honduras.* New York: Museum of the American Indian, Heye Foundation.

Waterhouse, Viola. 1962. *The Grammatical Structures of Oaxaca Chontal.* Publications of the Research Center in Anthropology, Folklore, and Linguistics, Indiana University, No. 19. (Part 2 of *International Journal of American Linguistics* 28.)

About the author

Joseph H. Greenberg is Professor Emeritus of Anthropology and Linguistics at Stanford University, where he went in 1962 after previous positions at the University of Minnesota and Columbia. He received his Ph. D. in Anthropology at Northwestern University in 1940. His chief work has been in language universals and the genetic classification of languages. His first extended contact with Syd Lamb was in 1986, when he spoke at the Rice University Symposium on language classification. He was already aware of Syd's agreement with him on the classification of

North American languages, and Lamb later served as the publisher's reader for his manuscript of **Language in the Americas** *(published in 1987).*

CHAPTER 25

The Grammaticalization of Lexicalized Manual Gesture in Tarahumara

James E. Copeland
Rice University

1. Introduction

Any informed attempt to understand and describe a language synchronically inevitably comes to involve reasonable inferences about the origins and development of its lexical/grammatical forms. In the absence of written records we are never sure about earlier states of affairs and paths of development, and even *with* written records the data and conclusions are subject to interpretation and disagreement. Still, we continue to do historical work, applying the methods of historical linguistics and seeking reasonable hypotheses that are based broadly on comparisons, typological generalizations, and universals of language. Not just anything goes. We insist that work, in order to be credible, must be based on well-established principles of language change and methods of reconstruction. Ever since the Neo-grammarians, the troika of sound change, analogy, and borrowing have been seen as the major mechanisms of language change. But during the last decade the mechanism of *grammaticalization* has increasingly taken its place as a fourth major mechanism, expanding the scope of inquiry, and licensing a whole new body of research. The term reaches back to Meillet, and refers to the view that *grammatical elements in a language typically have their genesis in the lexicon*. A strong version of the theory postulates that **all** grammatical elements arise unidirectionally from lexical elements. In principle, the theory states that some words, or word sequences, gradually lose their independent lexical status, are bleached of their semantic meaning, ritualized by repetition, reduced phonologically, and come to code grammatical functions. In the later stages of the process, lexical items may first become cliticized, clitics may become bound forms, and bound forms may be lost by incorporation or by reduction to zero. In a similar process, lexical items may become fused with contiguous morphemes, disappearing as separate elements, and retaining but a wispy historical trace of their original status as content lexemes. At any given synchronic stage, a language exhibits elements and patterns that are at various stages of the grammaticalization cycle; some words are emerging from word complexes, some grammatical elements are emerging from lexical elements, some grammatical elements are being further reduced. Lexical and grammatical structure can thus be seen as dynamic rather than static, and any attempt to understand the phenomenon thus requires an understanding of the ongoing micro-history of the language. Exclusively synchronic constructs like *morpheme* stop short of this goal in language description.

In this connection I want to trace a phonological shape *ma* in Tarahumara, a Uto-Aztecan language spoken in Northern Mexico (cf. Lamb 1959). The free form *ma* is often clearly the reflex of an earlier pan-Uto-Aztecan word for hand. In Tarahumara it has been replaced (as the name for the body part) by the term *seka-ra*, so that nowhere in Tarahumara does the isolated form still occur as the word for 'hand'. The form is reconstructable for the family by application of the method of EXTERNAL COMPARATIVE RECONSTRUCTION. But the phonological traces of **ma* (together with its morpho-phonological variants *pa ~ ba ~ ma ~ wa ~ a*) are widely represented in the lexicon and grammar of Tarahumara, and they are sometimes found in places that do not necessarily line up with our expectations. The presence of the scattered phonological traces of **ma* internally within the language is detectable only by the method of INTERNAL RECONSTRUCTION. It will be apparent that only the application of the two methods of reconstruction, in tandem, facilitates an understanding of the history of **ma* and its synchronic functions in the language.

The suggestions that I want to make here about the history and current identities of *ma* will be based on principles of semantic change, and grammatica-lization theory (Greenberg 1991). As stated above, these processes do not always result in the total loss of a form, i.e. reduction to phonological zero, but may result only in the loss of separate phrasal or morphemic status (incorporation). Examples abound (for example, in English the word *handy* is, in spite of its bimorphemic history, a form that most of us would analyze synchronically as a single lexical morpheme). This process is a major source of words in the world's languages (cf. Hopper 1990). The evidence is from both internal and external reconstruction.

2.   Lexical Adaptations of */ma/

First let us consider some examples of the incorporation of *ma* in lexical forms of Tarahumara, before proceeding to examples of its grammaticalization. Lexical adaptations of **ma* in Tarahumara encompass a number of semantic fields, including among others, *measuring, counting, body parts, manual instruments, events*, and *deixis*. In its synchronic *lexical* reflexes, **ma* no longer ever occurs as a free form. In all of its occurrences as a recognizably incorporated phonological part of a referential form, it has colexicalized with an adjacent form, resulting in the emergence of a single lexical morpheme. Let us now consider some examples.

2.1   *Measures of quantity*

Consider first the occurrence in Tarahumara of the reflex of **ma* in derivations expressing measures of quantity. The hand obviously provides a handy instrument for measuring small quantities or expanses. Some of these measures have been lexicalized in derivations that earlier involved the word for hand in Tarahumara:

(1)   *makomí* 'handful'

(2)   *maka-ri* 'a span' (**measure: width of the back of the hand**)

Likewise in the decimal numeric system of Tarahumara, for example in the words for five, ten, etc., the traces of **ma* can be observed, as in Table 1.

Table 1. *Some numerals in Tarahumara*

Cardinals		Ordinals	
1. *mari*	'five'	1a. *mari-sa*	'fifth'
2. *makoi*	'ten'	2a. *makói-sa*	'tenth'
3. *makoi biré*	'eleven'	3a. *makoi siné*	'eleventh'
4. *ki-makoi*	'nine'	4a. *ki-makói-sa*	'ninth'
5. *makoi ma-ri*	'fifteen'	5a. *makoi mari-sa*	'fifteenth'
6. *mari-sa makoi*	'fifty'	6a. *mari-sa makói-sa*	'fiftieth'
7. *makói-sa makoi*	'hundred'	7a. *makói-sa makói-sa*	'hundredth'
8. *mari-sa makói-sa makoi*	'five hundred'		

The element *ki-* in *kimakoi* is historically a morpheme used in counting. Its traces are apparent in forms like *ki-pu,* 'how many', and probably also in the word *peikia, (*pe-iki-a)* 'three'. It often functions now as an attenuator, as in *ke'me* 'hardly', (*iki-'me*). In the word for 'nine', with a meaning of 'something like; almost', it serves to diminish the co-occurring value, deriving 'nine' from 'ten'. Likewise consider some additional numeric expressions given in Table 2.

Table 2. *Additional numeric expressions in Tarahumara*

1.	**mak**ói-niga	'in a group of ten'
2.	**mak**ói-sa	'ten times'
3.	**mak**ói-bi	'only ten times'
4.	**mak**ói-na	'in ten parts'
5.	**mak**wa-ná	'in ten places'

In all of these expressions of measurement, the erstwhile free lexeme **ma* 'hand' has lost its status as an independent lexical form and become merely part of a larger morph. Essentially it has been reduced to being a mere phonemic syllable, and is recognizable to us as a reflex of **ma* only by internal reconstruction. Thus in the numerals, the phonological sequence *ma* is no longer recognizable as a separate morph in Tarahumara.

2.2 Entities: Body parts

Similarly, incorporation is apparent in all of the nominal reflexes of **ma*. As the general Uto-Aztecan word for 'hand', it has been replaced by *seká-ra*, but the words for 'finger' and 'palm' still manifest the fused *ma* sequence: *makusa-ra*.

(3)   **ma**kusa   'finger'

(4)   **ma**hta-ga-ra 'palm' of the hand

2.3 Entities: Manual instruments

Likewise the phonological reflex of **ma* is found as a desemanticized sequence in many lexical items for *objects* that instrumentally involve use of the hand.

(5)   **ma**htaka   'metate'

(6)   **ma**htasura   'grinding stone' (mano)

In attempting to make sense of the synchronic forms in the language as being products of their history it is apparent that these forms contain fused or weakened traces of the earlier form *ma, meaning 'hand'. It is also quite clear that Tarahumara speakers no longer directly associate the syllable ma in these words with the body part.

The diachronic explanation involves, for example (cf. Figure 1), the metonymic extension of the term for the EXECUTOR ma (hand) of the EVENT batuma (grinding) to designate the INSTRUMENT mahtaka used in the process (grinding stone).

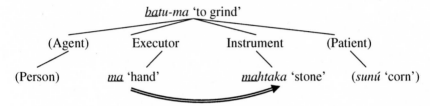

Figure 1. *Description of the diachronic change in interpretation of */ma/ in mahtaka*

2.4 Objects metonymically associated with 'hand'

Similarly, other objects that are metonymically associated with 'hand' in the culture show incorporated reflexes of *ma,* for example:

(7)   **makáwa-ra**   'cuff (of a long sleeve blouse), sleeve band'

A few terms are also attested in Tarahumara for similarly derived names for *qualities* and *manners,* for example:

(8)   **makarí**   (ma-a'ká-arí) 'open handed(ly)'

2.5 Verbal events with the hand as instrument

Many lexical verbs, that code events involving use of the hand(s) as Executor of an action, still show lingering phonological and semantic echos of *ma* in coalesced forms as historical residue. Here, as was the case above with numerals and manual objects, it is also doubtful that the semantic resonance of ma 'hand' is still cognitively identifiable for speakers, as it must have been in the original derivational coinages. Some examples are given in Table 3:

This is only a sample list of such verbs. Most of them are examples of what T. Givón has referred to as INSTRUMENTAL INCORPORATION, but a preferable label for the Tarahumara data might be EXECUTOR INCORPORATION (in many cases there is a physical instrument involved in addition to the hand as Executor). This is a frequently identified phenomenon in Uto-Aztecan languages (Givón 1996).

Table 3. *Lexical verbs with echos of* **ma**

Pointing:	1. **ma**howa	'to point to, to point out' ☞
Placing:	2. **ma**na-ma	'put, place (with the hand)'
	3. **ma**na-ma	'make (corn) beer (grinding)'
	4. **ma**ní	'place, arrange (with the hand)'
	5. **ma**naso	'manually scattered, disarrayed'
	6. **ma**co-ma	'place the hand (in something)'
Grabbing:	7. **ma**ko-ma	'clutch with the hand, seize'
Carrying:	8. **ma**to-ru	'carry (holding on the shoulders)'
	9. **ma**, **me**a	'bring, fetch, carry'
Clapping:	10. **ma**ta	'applaud, clap'
Hitting:	11. **ma**coco-ma	'pound (with the fist)'
Grinding:	12. **ba**tu-ma	'to grind (by hand)'
Extracting:	13. **ma**'ci-bu-ma	'to take out, extract (by hand)'
Giving, paying:	14. **ma**hteta	'hand over, give payment in kind'
Thanking:	15. **ma**htatera ba	'give thanks (gesture of gratitude)'
Requesting:	16. **ma**htetera ba	'please! (polite request)'

In the case of *mahowa*, 'to point', which is shown diagrammatically in Figure 2, the name for the hand as Executor of the pointing event is extended to the event itself and becomes part of the name of the event.

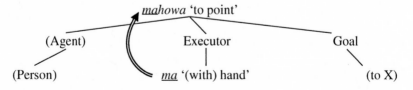

Figure 2. *Description of the relation of* **ma** *to the meaning of* **mahowa**

3.   Deictic Pointing (from physical gesture to verbal gesture)

Now we come to the main point of this paper. Psychologically, the hands constitute a disproportionately large share of our internal image of our own body. As humans we are tremendously aware of hands, and we use them powerfully in our verbal communication. Manual gestures are ritualized differently in different cultures, so that in learning an alien language we inevitably also have to learn the accompanying gestural code. Universally we use the hands gesturally to code **sizes** and **shapes**, and **motions** and **locations** and also importantly in **deictic** functions to **point to** and to **demark boundaries**.

Physical deixis (e.g. pointing with the hand) is often accompanied by concomitant **verbal deixis**. The importation of gestural (pointing) functions into verbal language by extension of the medium of reference from manual to **verbal** is apparently a cultural universal, but the paths that such transfer takes are quite language specific. Once the verbal expression **for hand (the Executor** of gesture) is functionally associated with the physical gesture, a new lexeme has been coined by metonymic association. Such lexemes are then subject to the same inexorable processes of relexification and grammaticalization that lexemes from any other source undergo.

In Tarahumara, the free form *ma*, when used with **hand pointing** (represented here as: + ☞), functions as a deictic to identify shifting spatial referents. On the surface, the **hands** would seem universally to be a logical association as a source notion for the coding of deixis. But studies have not yet identified large numbers of the world's languages that have exploited the words for hand or finger to create demonstratives. At least in Tarahumara this seems clearly to be the case as in Example 9.

> 9.   *ma!* + ☞
>   Here!/There!

The strong tendency of grammaticalization to be unidirectional predicts that **spatial deixis** is always the source of **temporal deixis**. The mechanisms that are adopted for coding spatial reference are typically extended by analogy for coding temporal reference. Thus we have Tarahumara:

> 10.   *ma!* [+ ☞]
>   Now!

In the temporal usage, the speakers are somewhat less likely to accompany the verbal expression with a manual gesture (hence the use of brackets in Example 10 to indicate optionality), but frequently they do. It might also be interesting to note, for example, that the Tarahumaras frequently point with their **lips** to identify a locative referent, but the term for 'lips', *cum'*, has **not** been extended to code these deictic functions in the language as has the word for hand.

3.1 *The grammaticalization of deictic elements*

Up until now we have considered diachronic extensions of the use of the reconstructed word for hand in patterns of lexicalization. We now turn to instances of **grammaticalization** involving the same etymon **ma*. It is important to keep in mind that each of the examples presented here is taken from real spoken texts in cultural contexts.

We have seen that novel linguistic forms may result from the incipient association of iconic **physical** deixis (gestural) with **verbal** deixis (lexical). The novelty is seen in the recruitment of the extant word for hand, as the Executor of the deixis, subsequently then to code the deixis itself. Once lexicalized, the forms of the word for hand are subject to further extension and grammaticalization. Thus we can identify various grammaticalized reflexes of **ma* in Tarahumara that have emerged to code aspectual functions. The metonymic extension of the spatial **deictic** *ma* to code **temporal** reference, can be seen for example in the aspectual uses of *ma* that mark progressive and perfective aspect. The point of reference is to a temporal boundary, either pre- or post- speech time that has been selected for salience in the proposition. The form *ma* is used metaphorically **to point to** the boundary in question. The notion of aspectual boundary is of course itself a metaphorical extension from a physical (spatial) source. Traces from the Tarahumara data indicate a chain of developments. Some of these are schematized as in Figure 3–5, but first let us consider further evidence.

3.2 *Grammatical pointing to temporal boundaries: Tense/aspect*

For propositions that are narrated in PRESENT TIME and PAST TIME, the free form *ma* functions to code tense/aspect distinctions in the verb phrase for states and events in reference to SPEECH TIME (ST). The metonymic use of the linguistic form *ma*, still distantly echoing the metaphoric manual gesture, **points** in each case **to** the temporal boundary that has been or is to be crossed. highlighting and coding the most salient event contours

3.2.1 *Clause initial **ma** with ongoing events/states*
The normal position of the free aspectual particle *ma* (for present events/states) is clause initial. Here *ma* points to the event-initiating boundary that has already been crossed at Speech Time, while the event is still ongoing or the state is still in force, cf. Examples (11)–(13) and Figure 3.

> (11)   ***ma*** *ne ana'i behté pa*
>   now 1sg here live   Junct
>   'I live here *now*.'

> 12.   ***ma***   *ne gará bosá pa*!
>   Perfective I   well full   Junct
>   'I'm full!'

> 13.   *a'riko binó **ma***   *ku-simi-am*   *pa...*
>   soon   he   starts to again-go-Nomz Junct...
>   'Pretty soon he *starts to* leave ...' (historical present)

$$\text{🖙} \quad ST = ET$$
$$\texttt{-----------|-----------> '\textbf{now}'}$$
(Speech Time = Event Time)

Figure 3. *The interpretation of **ma** with ongoing states and events*

3.2.2 *Clause initial **ma** in completed past events*
For events and states narrated in past time, the free form *ma* **points to** the boundary of completion prior to the reference time (default = Speech Time). The sense is similar to that of English 'already'. The free form *ma* (for completed past events/states) likewise occurs in clause initial position. Examples 14 and 15 illustrate this perfective function of the free particle *ma*, cf. also Figure 4.

> (14)   *ma*   *ne batari newa-am*   *pa*
>   Perfect 1sg teswino make-Nomz Junct
>   'I have *(already)* made the beer.'

> (15)   ***ma***   *suwí pa*
>   Perfect finish Junct
>   '(S/he) has di*ed*.'

ET 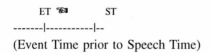   ST
-------|-----------|--
(Event Time prior to Speech Time)

Figure 4. *The interpretation of **ma** with completed past events*

3.2.3 *Verb suffix -**ma** in coding unrealized events*

Events and states with an EVENT TIME (ET) that is uninitiated (i.e. unrealized) at SPEECH TIME are normally coded with the verbal suffix -*ma* or -*méa* when stressed (showing breaking). Since the verb *mae-ma*, 'believe', suggests a source for irealis and/or future, it is possible that the grammaticalizing lexical parent of the bound suffix -*ma* is distinct from that of the free form *ma*. But it is quite possible that the source of the seeming homonyms is ultimately the same, with different paths of grammaticalization. It is clear that the -*ma* suffix, coding non-initiated events/states is a relatively late innovation, i.e. within Southern Uto-Aztecan. Under the assumption that the suffix -*ma* has developed from the same source as the free aspectual particle *ma* (from 'hand' via the deictic function), the suffixing -*ma* can be seen as **pointing to** the initial boundary of the mentioned event/state that is as yet unrealized at Speech Time, cf. Example 16 and Figure 5.

(16)   *re'pari mana-**ma** pa ra'ne-ra-ka*   *ba*
        up   put-Fut   rifle   (thunder Nomz) Junct
        He *is going to* put the rifle up there now.

ST   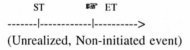 ET
-------|------------|---------->
(Unrealized, Non-initiated event)

Figure 5. *The interpretation of **ma** with unrealized events*

3.3 *Grammatical pointing to discourse boundaries: conjunctions, relatives, endpoint markers, and particles*

A further development is seen in the progressive grammaticalization of *ma* for pointing to discourse boundaries: conjunctions, relatives, endpoint markers, and other discourse particles.

3.3.1 *Conjunctive functions of ma*

The path of metonymic extension goes from 'now' to 'and now' to 'and/also' (coding sequentiality or linking propositions and other conjoinable discourse segments, and leading to increasing generalization within ever broader contexts (cf. Examples (17)–(27), below).

First, consider some examples of the additive conjunction *ma*, 'and now', 'and' (items (17)–(20)).

(17) *nahtetera ba* **ma** *ne ku-isá ma ré pa*
      thanks Junct and now I again-rest now Mod Junct
      'Thank you. *And now* perhaps I'm going to go back to resting again.'

(18) *...kin si'á* **ma** *sinéuma ná ma-pu-ikí hu pa e'témara*
      my father-in-law Conj all Rel-33 Vcop Junc family
      ba...
      Junct...
      '...my father-in-law, *and then* everyone who is part of the family...'

(19) *Pasiko ma Sahwani.*
      Fransisco and Juan.
      'Fransisco *and* Juan.'

(20) *...ma simi-a pa noke-am pa...*
      ...and go-Pres Junct move-Nomz Junct...
      '...*and* he's leaving, moving away...'

Similarly, the form *ma* has colexicalized with other grammatical forms, to express spatial and temporal conjunction in spoken discourse (cf. Copeland 1991). Example (21) contains relevant occurrences of Tarahumara *mapu-goná*, 'where', a spatial conjunction, and *ma*, 'then after that', a temporal conjunction.

(21) **ma** *me'a-re mi ga'ó mapu-goná behte-re*
      Conj kill-Past over there Conj-Loc live-Past
      wa'ru-be-ra...
      big-Intens-Nomz
      '*Then after that* they killed the giant over there (up in front of the cave) *where* he lived.'

Examples (23)–(25) illustrate additional forms containing reflexes of *ma* that code more specialized temporal linkages of propositions: *mapu-a'rí* 'when' (same time), **mapu-sí**, 'until, when', and *ma*, 'since'.

(23)   ...*ke   na'awa-ga*   **ma**pu-a'ri   *tum bahí*
       ...Neg quarrel-Cont Conj-Simul you drink
       (...said,) not to fight, *when* you drink...

(24)   *pacá   'nina   ahtí*   **ma**pu-sí *másimi ko ba*
       inside prefer sit   (T₁) Conj-T₂ leave
       (The spirit) had better stay inside (grave), *until* he goes away.

(25)   ...**ma**-tam   go ocer-am   ba   ne
       ...since-we- Tp grow-Nomz Junct Part
       ...*since* we are so old.

A further development is seen in the progression from temporal to causal
conjunction. It is of course well known that forms used to signal a temporal
association of events/states may become reanalyzed to code a causal association,
e.g. Tarahumara **ma**pu-gita, 'in order that', 'because', (cf. Examples (26)–(27)).

(26)   *sepi   waki-gá irí pa   we'é* **ma**pu-gita *sinéoma napai-bo*
       Intens dry-Stat be Junct soil Conj-Inst all   gather-Fut
       pagótuame
       people
       'The earth is very dry, *so* all of people (we) come together...'

(27)   *tam 'nina   ci   'á kiri awa-ra   ba   **ma**pu-gita*
       me preferably me   give horn-Poss Junct Conj-Inst
       nehé o'rú kam   pa
       I   big   Vcop Junct
       'You'd better give me your antlers, *because* I'm big.'

3.3.2 *Relative particle*

One grammaticalized form of *ma* functions as a relative particle, which, either
alone or in construction with a post-clitic pronominal form coding person and
number agreement with the antecedent, introduces relative clauses in Tarahumara. In this case, *ma* points to the antecedent of the relative construction, cf.
Table 7 (the separate plural/distributive forms for first and second person are not
given here).

Table 7. *Relative particles containing the particle **ma***

***ma**-ne*	(I) who	(Rel Pn 1sg)
***ma**-tam*	(we) who	(Rel Pn 1pl)
***ma**-mu*	(you) who	(Rel Pn 2sg)
***ma**-tum*	(you-pl) who	(Rel Pn 2pl)
***ma**-pu*	(s/he/they) who, that	(Rel Pn 3sg/pl)

Examples (28)–(30) illustrate the use of the particle *ma* in Tarahumara for introducing relative clauses.

(28) *neko hu   aré pa **ma**-ne civa me'á-re ba*
      I   Vcop Mod   Rel-I goat kill-Past Junct
      'Maybe I am the one *who* killed the goat.'

(29) *... muhé, **ma**-mu ma suwi-reke éera   ba   ...*
      ... you, Rel-Pn Perf die-Past   mother Junct ...
      '...you, *whose* mother died ...'

(30) *miná mukí   huku **ma-pu** uwa ra'íca-re rehoi ko ba*
      that woman be   Rel-she with talk-Perf man   Junct
      'That is the woman *whom* the man talked to.'

It is important to note again that in some cases the relative particle alone introduces the relative clause without an accompanying person and number specifying stem.

3.3.3 *Discourse particle functions*

A still more advanced development is seen in the frequent occurrence of *ma* as a general discourse particle in Tarahumara, punctuating the discourse and at times merely providing a hesitation filler that also simultaneously echoes the more propositionally oriented functions associated with *ma* introduced above. Example 31 illustrates the use of *ma* as a discourse particle similar in function to the English discourse particle/hesitation forms, 'well', 'well-then'.

(31)   ... *cihóonsago hipi 'wir' awe-a   regá ena koáci- go*
        ... hence   now long antler-Cont Mod walk headgear -Tp
        '... (the deer) now walk around contentedly with long antlers on
        their'

        *gan'rea **ma** berá we   ku-moia   pa*
        content well truely intens again-climb junct
        'heads. *Well*, it's true. After this, they climbed back up (went
        home).'

4.   Summary

Tarahumara presents an intriguing linguistic landscape for understanding the
synchronic distribution and functions of apparent homonyms like the various
forms of *ma*, i.e. the suspected reflexes of the Uto-Aztecan word for hand. Of
course not all of the occurrences of the phonological sequence *ma* are related to
this etymon. The path of development proceeds initially from an association of
manual gesture (pointing), signifying 'here!', with the word for the focal body
part itself. The result of the association is a lexicalization of the physical gesture,
metonymically employing the word for the EXECUTOR of the gesture, i.e. *ma,*
'hand'. Once the first step is taken and a new lexical form is created, e.g. *ma,*
'here', the new form is then subject to all of the grammaticalizing forces that
normally assault such lexical items in the languages of the world. In the case of
Tarahumara *ma*, the continuing lexicalization process has extended the spatial
reference to a temporal one, and subsequently the process of grammaticalization
has further extended the form to code aspectual and conjunctive distinctions as
well as other discourse functions. The overarching commonality of the grammaticalized functions is the notion of *pointing* — initially *physical* pointing *with the
hand. Subsequently the notion of pointing surfaced in the language as lexical*
pointing, coded by linguistic forms containing traces of the word for hand.
Further along, the notion of pointing shows up again as more clearly *metaphorical* — pointing to a whole array of *grammatical* topographies, including temporal
and aspectual boundaries as well as various types of discourse junctures, cf.
Figure 6.
     Methodologically it is first necessary to reconstruct the proto form for
'hand' by the comparative method in order to establish the source form, which
no longer exists in Tarahumara. Accordingly **ma* is reconstructed for 'hand'.

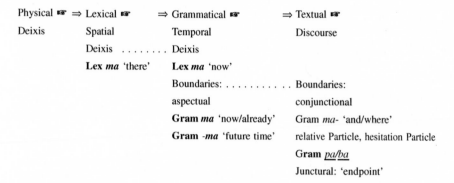

Figure 6. *Summary of the development of **ma** in Tarahumara*

Subsequently it becomes apparent that the multilayered traces of the etymon are evident only from internal reconstruction. The method allows the identification of those *ma* phonological sequences that are likely reflexes of the proto word for hand. The method naturally excludes the larger number of *ma* sequences in the language as fortuitous.

Further, we have seen from a limited set of data from actual Tarahumara spoken discourses that by internal reconstruction we can trace many of the developments that have resulted in a chain of layered reanalyses of the Uto-Aztecan word for hand. The form *ma* has been incorporated by metonymy into many lexemes that show a natural relationship with the body part. In other cases, by reason of its association with MANUAL GESTURE, the form has been recruited further to perform specific grammatical tasks, including spatial/temporal deixis, tense/aspect distinctions, conjunction, and relativization. The lexical and grammatical traces of the source lexeme that remain in the language continue to cooexist and document a layered network of developments. Understanding the source and the multiple paths of grammaticalization of this form enables a fuller appreciation of the synchronic structure of the language, and contributes to our growing understanding — of language change and of the evolution and functions of grammar.

References

Copeland, James E. 1988. Comparisons of similarity in Tarahumara. *The Four-teenth LACUS Forum 1987.* ed. by Sheila Embleton, 248–260. Columbia, South Carolina: Hornbeam Press.

Copeland, James E. 1990. Intensification, contrast, and metaphor in Tarahumara comparisons of dissimilarity. *The Sixteenth LACUS Forum 1989.* ed. by Michael P. Jordan, 335–345. Lake Bluff, Illinois: The Linguistic Association of Canada and the United States.

Copeland, James E. 1991. The relativizing complementizer **mapu** in Tarahumara discourse. *The Seventeenth LACUS Forum 1990.* ed. by Angela Dela Volpe, 195–205. Lake Bluff, Illinois: The Linguistic Association of Canada and the United States.

Copeland, James E. 1993. Unmotivated free alternation in Tarahumara: the principle of emergence in phonology. *Language Sciences* 16.1:213–227.

Copeland, James E. 1994. Tarahumara reduplication: the grammaticalization of iconic intensification. *The Nineteenth LACUS Forum. 1992.* ed. by Peter Reich, 313–335. Lake Bluff, Illinois: Linguistic Association of Canada and the United States.

Copeland, James E. 1994. Variation in language and culture: the case of Tara-humara. *The Twentieth LACUS Forum 1993.* ed. by Valerie Makkai, 5–30. Chapel Hill, North Carolina: Linguistic Association of Canada and the United States.

Copeland, James E. 1996. the copula in Tarahumara: paths of grammatica-lization. *The Twenty-Second LACUS Forum. 1995.* ed. by Bates Hoffer, 157–166. Chapel Hill, North Carolina: Linguistic Association of Canada and the United States.

Copeland, James E. 1997. On the Tarahumara particle pa: an optional mode of delimiting information segments. *The Twenty-Third LACUS Forum 1996.* ed. by Alan Melby, 313–324. Chapel Hill, North Carolina: Linguistic Associa-tion of Canada and the United States.

Givón, T. 1996. La gramaticalizaci ón de verbos a posposiciones en ute. *Tercer Encuentro de Lingu'stica en el Noroeste, Tomo I. Lenguas Ind'genas,* 2: 359. Hermosillo: Universidad de Sonora.

Greenberg, Joseph H. 1991. The last stages of grammatical elements: contractive and expansive desemanticization. *Approaches to Grammaticalization.*

Volume I. ed by Traugott, 301. Elizabeth and Bernd Heine. Amsterdam: John Benjamins.

Hopper, Paul. 1990. *Where do words come from? Studies in Typology and Diachrony for Joseph H. Greenberg.* ed. by Croft, William, et al., 151–160. Amsterdam: J. Benjamins.

Lamb, Sydney. 1959. Some proposals for linguistic taxonomy. *Anthropological Linguistics.* 1: 33–49.

About the author

James E. Copeland is Professor of Linguistics and German at Rice University, where he has chaired the Department of Linguistics since 1988. He had previously taught at the University of California, Davis. His work has centered principally on Germanic and Uto-Aztecan (Tarahumara). As a graduate student at Cornell, Copeland was influenced as a result of hearing Lamb in a series of guest lectures in 1963. Then in 1966, Copeland attended Lamb's stratificational course at the UCLA summer Linguistic Institute. Contact continued, and in 1980, Copeland was able to bring Lamb to Rice University to help in establishing the Department of Linguistics.

CHAPTER 26

Investigating Syntactic Change through Synchronic Textual Comparison

A Case Study

David C. Bennett

SOAS, University of London

1.   Introduction

Since syntactic change takes place gradually rather than suddenly, there is always a period of time during which the old and the new structures exist side by side, with the old structure gradually becoming less common and the new structure becoming more common. Such a change in the proportion of the two structures over time can be demonstrated by comparing texts from different points in time. Ideally, the texts compared should be parallel stylistically and in subject matter, but it is not always easy to find appropriate texts. In some cases, however, another method is available, namely if a group of languages within some family — or a group of dialects of some language — are all changing in the same direction and represent different stages of development. In such cases, comparison of material from different languages/dialects at the same point of time may be treated as equivalent to comparing material from the same language/dialect at different points in time. And if the texts for comparison are taken from the present time, it is quite straightforward to ensure comparability in style and subject matter; for instance, it may be possible to use translations of a text from another language into the various languages/dialects in question. The present article is intended to demonstrate the usefulness of this method in relation to ongoing changes in the word order of the South Slavic languages/dialects Slovenian, Serbian and Croatian. (Serbian and Croatian are dialects of Serbo-Croatian. Slovenian is a separate but closely related language.)

The remainder of this article is organized into six sections. Section 2 indicates the aspects of word order to be discussed and the kind of evidence suggesting that Slovenian, Serbian and Croatian represent different stages of development. Section 3 lists a number of general issues on which the Slavic data might be expected to throw light and Section 4 summarizes the findings of earlier work (both by other writers and by the present writer) in relation to these issues. Section 5 then states two hypotheses of the present work and Section 6, in reporting the results of the textual comparison, indicates the extent to which the hypotheses are supported. Section 7, finally, is devoted to a number of concluding remarks.

2.   Preliminary Observations

Earlier textual comparison of Slovenian and Serbo-Croatian, on the basis of a Slovenian short story called *Bela krizantema* by Ivan Cankar and a Serbian translation of it, revealed that by far the commonest word order difference between Slovenian and Serbo-Croatian involves the position of a category of clitics comprising short forms of object pronouns, auxiliary verbs and a small number of sentence particles such as the Serbo-Croatian interrogative particle *li* (Bennett 1986: 3–5, 1987:270–77). Unlike the Romance languages, whose clitics are attached to the verb, Slovenian and Serbo-Croatian are both at the stage of having second position (P2) clitics. As is apparent from the frequently-invoked diachronic development in (1) — see, for instance, Jakobson (1971), Steele (1976), (1977), Renzi (1986), Benacchio and Renzi (1987) — the P2–clitic stage is an earlier stage than the verb-clitic stage.

(1)   independent words – 2nd position clitics – verb clitics – verb affixes
         (A)   (B)   (C)   (D)

The difference in clitic placement between Slovenian and Serbo-Croatian involves a distinction, within the P2–clitic stage, between word-based and constituent-based P2 clitics. This distinction is illustrated by the Serbo-Croatian examples in (2) and (3), both of which have a complex clause-initial constituent:

(2)   *Prošle **ste** **mi**   godine napisali nekoliko riječi*
last   (aux) to-me year   written some   words
o   vašim dečkima
about your boys
'Last year you wrote me a few words about your boys.'

(3)   *O'Brajenov sluga **ih** **je**   oboje pustio unutra*
O'Brien's   servant them (aux) both let   inside
ne   trepnuvši   okom
not having-blinked with-eye
'O'Brien's servant let them both in without batting an eyelid.'

The first syntactic constituent of (2) is the temporal adverbial *prošle godine* 'last year'. The (bolded) clitics *ste mi*, whose meaning in this example is 'you-have to-me', are attached as enclitics to the first word (*prošle* 'last'), thereby interrupting the constituent. In (3), on the other hand, the clitics follow the first constituent as a whole (*O'Brajenov sluga* 'O'Brien's servant'). In a discussion of Latin, Benacchio and Renzi (1987:5) claim that positioning clitics after the first word must be older than positioning them after the first constituent. Trávníček (1956:146–7) — reported in Ard (1975:107–8) — makes a similar observation in relation to Czech. As regards Serbo-Croatian, too, it is clear that word-based P2 is older than constituent-based P2 (Brabec 1964–5:144, Browne 1975:114). Stage B in (1) therefore needs to be broken down into two separate stages B1 and B2. A B1–language would be a language in which P2 clitics attached to a clause-initial complex constituent necessarily follow the first accented word of the constituent. A B2–language, by contrast, would be a language in which P2 clitics cannot interrupt such a constituent but need, instead, to follow the constituent as a whole. Modern Slovenian is a B2–language in this sense; placing clitics in the same position that they occupy in the Serbo-Croatian example (2) yields an ungrammatical sentence in Slovenian — see (4a), by comparison with the corresponding grammatical sentence (4b).

(4)   a. **Lansko **ste**   **mi**   leto napisali nekaj besed o   vaših fantih*
last   (aux) to-me year written some words about your boys
b.   *Lansko leto **ste mi** napisali nekaj besed o vaših fantih*

Serbo-Croatian, on the other hand, is in transition between B1 and B2. As a measure of the extent to which a particular variety of Serbo-Croatian has progressed from B1 towards B2, one could calculate, in relevant texts, the proportion of B1–sentences, such as (2), and of B2–sentences, such as (3). More literary varieties would presumably exhibit a higher proportion of B1–sentences than more colloquial varieties, since literary varieties are in general more conservative (Browne 1975:114). As Slovenian is already a B2–language whereas Serbo-Croatian is transitional between stages B1 and B2, it is clear that Slovenian has developed further than Serbo-Croatian in relation to clitic placement.

Since the textual comparison using *Bela krizantema* involved only one Serbo-Croatian version (specifically, a Serbian version), it could not disclose any differences between Serbian and Croatian. More recent comparison, on the other hand, has made use of separate translations of George Orwell's novel *Nineteen Eighty-Four* into Slovenian, Serbian and Croatian, and on the basis of these texts it soon became clear that the proportion of complex constituents interrupted by clitics is higher in the Croatian translation than in the Serbian translation (for precise details, see Section 6). In this respect, then, it would seem that Croatian is more conservative than Serbian. As regards (2), for instance, whereas Serbian speakers that I have consulted consider the word order of the example somewhat old-fashioned (and therefore more literary than colloquial), it in fact represents a Croatian written style that can reasonably be classified as intermediate in terms of the literary/colloquial distinction — namely it was part of a message added to a Christmas card by a Croatian former neighbor.

Elaborating stage (B) of (1) into stages (B1) and (B2) in accordance with the above discussion, it would seem, then, that the facts of clitic placement in the three varieties with which we are concerned can be shown as in (5).

(5)   (B1) ——————————————————▶ (B2)
                          ↑   ↑   ↑
                     Croatian   Serbian   Slovenian

A second important difference between Slovenian and Serbo-Croatian revealed by the textual comparison based on *Bela krizantema* involved the position of the main verb. Where there was a discrepancy between the two languages in the position of the finite main verb, in the overwhelming majority of cases (52 out of 54) the finite main verb was in second position in Slovenian and in a later position in Serbo-Croatian (Bennett 1987:277–79).[1] Berneker's (1900:1–59) account of word order in the Slavic languages classifies finite main verbs

---

1. There was one further example in which the verb was second in Slovenian and in first position in Serbo-Croatian.

according to whether they occur at the beginning, in the middle or at the end of clauses, and claims that within the family as a whole the middle position has gradually been gaining ground (1900:58–9). In the light of this observation, the recorded difference in finite main verb position between Slovenian and Serbo-Croatian, as in the case of the difference in clitic position, depends again on Slovenian having developed further than Serbo-Croatian. Of course, the *Bela krizantema* texts permitted no conclusion concerning Serbian and Croatian. This matter is taken up below on the basis of the *Nineteen Eighty-Four* texts.

3.   Some Questions

Among the general questions raised by the kind of data with which we are concerned are the following:

(i)   What is the phonological status of the clitics in terms of the distinction between enclitics and proclitics?

(ii)   What is the syntactic status of the clitics?

(iii)   What is the relationship between the position occupied by clitics (including clitic auxiliary verbs) and that of finite main verbs?

(iv)   What is the relationship between the position occupied by finite main verbs and that of infinitives and participles?

4.   Some Answers

4.1 *Phonological status*

Grammars of Serbo-Croatian treat the clitics with which we are concerned as being strictly enclitic and incapable of following a pause (Brabec, Hraste & Živković 1965:221–22, Pešikan 1958–9:308). The corresponding Slovenian items, on the other hand, frequently follow a pause when the immediately preceding constituent is complex, and in such cases are proclitic to the following constituent. In his grammar of present-day Slovenian Toporišič (1976:58, 535) therefore describes them as being either enclitic or proclitic. Evidently the change from word-based P2 to constituent-based P2 placement is accompanied by a shift from strict enclitic status to dual enclitic/proclitic status. One discussion of Serbo-Croatian with which I am familiar (Brabec 1964–5:144) claims that proclitic uses of the Serbo-Croatian clitics are gradually becoming more acceptable, for example in sentences such as (6), where speakers are likely to pause after the complex subject *vjetar i šum valova*.

(6)   *Vjetar i   šum   valova   **su   se**   jasno   čuli*
        wind   and noise of-waves (aux) self clearly heard
        'The wind and the noise of the waves were clearly heard.'

Many writers, however, would prefer to place the clitics in this sentence after the word *jasno* rather than before it, thereby accommodating them in a position where they are enclitic.

4.2 *Syntactic status*

Delbrück (1900: 49–51) distinguishes two classes of enclitics: those that follow the word with which they are semantically most closely associated, e.g. verb-clitics, and those that follow the first word of the clause. (He does not discuss constituent-based P2 clitics.) He regards P2 clitics (in his sense) as being positioned on a "rhythmic-musical basis" (in other words, on a phonological basis) as opposed to a syntactic basis. Certainly it seems reasonable to argue that the clitics in Serbo-Croatian example (2), which interrupt the constituent *prošle godine* 'last year', do not occupy a syntactic position — interrupting the first syntactic constituent is not itself a syntactic position.

    In Slovenian, on the other hand, as we saw in relation to (4), clitics do not interrupt complex syntactic constituents. The position that they fill (in declarative sentences) is immediately after the first constituent, irrespective of how complex this is (Bennett 1987: 271). They thus occupy P2 within the syntactic structure. Since they are unstressed, however, the term *clitic* is still appropriate.

    In present-day Serbo-Croatian, clitics occur not just after the first accented word of a clause or after the first syntactic constituent but in a variety of other positions, such as after the second constituent, interrupting the second constituent, or after the third constituent. To see something of the variety of positions possible in Serbo-Croatian, we may consider the examples in (7), which represent the

English (En), Slovenian (Sl), Serbian (Se) and Croatian (Cr) versions of a
sentence from *Nineteen Eighty-Four*.[2]

(7)   Although he had a good pretext for coming here, he was haunted at
       every step by the fear that...   En.

       [čeprav je imel dobro pretvezo za prihod sem],   [ga je]
       although-he-had-a-good-pretext-for-coming-here   him (aux)
       [pri vsakem koraku] [preganjal] [strah [da...]]
       at   every   step   haunted   fear   that   Sl.

       [Iako je imao dobar razlog što je ovamo došao],   [ipak] [ga je]
       although-he-had-a-good-pretext-for-coming-here still   him (aux)
       [na svakom koraku] [proganjao] [strah [da...]]
       at   every   step   haunted   fear   that   Se.

       [Premda je imao valjanu izliku što ovamo dolazi],
       although-he-had-a-good-pretext-for-coming-here
       [na svakom koraku]
       at   every   step   Cr.
       [progonio] [ga je]   [strah [da...]]
       haunted   him (aux) fear   that

Looking, first of all, at the Slovenian version, the sentence-initial constituent is
the concessive clause [*čeprav* ...], functioning adverbially within the sentence as
a whole, and this is followed immediately by the clitics [*ga je*], which therefore
occupy second position within the syntactic structure of the sentence as a whole.
Because of the complexity of the initial clause, speakers are likely to pause after
it, with the result that the clitics *ga je* are attached (along with the preposition
pri) to the first following accented word, *vsakem* 'every', and are thus proclitic
rather than enclitic. The corresponding position is not possible in Serbo-Croatian,
owing to its strong preference for accommodating clitic pronouns and auxiliary
verbs as enclitics. Interrupting the first constituent of the sentence is also not
possible in this case, since main clause clitics are never inserted into a subordinate clause. With [*na svakom koraku*] 'at every step' as the constituent after the
subordinate clause, the clitics could be attached to the first accented word of this

---

2. In comparing the four versions, one should note that the English passive of *He was haunted at
every step by the fear that* ... is represented in the three translations by an active clause meaning 'the
fear that ... haunted him at every step.'

constituent, *svakom* 'every', giving: ...*na svakom ga je koraku*... (The preposition *na* is itself proclitic to *svakom*.) In fact, however, neither the Serbian nor the Croatian translator took this option. The position after [*na svakom koraku*] is, again, a position where a speaker might pause, owing to the relative complexity of the constituent, though a pause is rather less likely here than after the sentence-initial subordinate clause. In any case, neither Serbo-Croatian translator opted to place the clitics after *na svakom koraku*. The Croatian translator opted for attaching them to the participle *progonio* 'haunted', which is the third constituent of the sentence as a whole in this version. The Serbian translator, on the other hand, inserted a word immediately after the subordinate clause which has no equivalent in any of the other three versions — *ipak* 'still, nevertheless' — and attached the clitics to this (short) second constituent. A further possibility, again adopted by neither Serbo-Croatian translator, would be to allow the participle *proganjao/progonio* to occur immediately after the subordinate clause and to attach the clitics to this. As regards future changes to Serbo-Croatian clitics, it seems likely that if the clitics develop to the point of allowing either enclitic or proclitic use, as the Slovenian clitics have done, they may also come to occupy second position within the syntactic structure, since there would then be no need for delaying the clitics to a convenient point where they can be accommodated as enclitics.[3]

4.3 *Clitics and finite main verbs*

As was noted in Section 2, Slovenian is ahead of Serbo-Croatian not only in relation to its placement of clitics but also with regard to the order of its finite main verbs. Bennett (1987: 279) related these two facts by hypothesizing that after Slovenian clitics — including auxiliary verbs — became positioned on a syntactic (as opposed to phonological) basis, the position occupied by the clitics could begin to be generalized also to finite main verbs. (This hypothesis parallels Wackernagel's (1892: 427–28) account of the adoption of verb-second order in main clauses in Germanic.) Since the textual statistics available at the time of Bennett (1987), based on *Bela krizantema*, did not distinguish between Serbian and Croatian, it will be of interest to determine whether Serbian is intermediate

---

3. Bennett (1987:272–77) was concerned to demonstrate that the variation in clitic position exhibited by present-day Serbo-Croatian is consistent with the hypothesis that the language is in transition between word-based and constituent-based P2 positioning of its clitics.

between Slovenian and Croatian in relation to the position of finite main verbs as well as with regard to clitic placement.

4.4   Finite and non-finite main verbs

In German, finite main verbs occupy second position in declarative main clauses. On the other hand, when the verb is complex, it is only the finite auxiliary verb which occupies second position, while the remainder of the verb occurs at the end of the clause. Thus the position occupied by non-finite main verbs can be quite independent of the position of finite main verbs. It will be of interest, therefore, to determine whether there is the same degree of independence in the case of Slovenian, Serbian and Croatian.

5.   Two Hypotheses

A prediction was made in 4.3 to be tested on the basis of the *Nineteen Eighty-Four* textual comparison. It was hypothesized, namely, that Serbian might be intermediate between Slovenian and Croatian not only in relation to clitic placement but also with regard to the position of its finite main verbs.

A further hypothesis — stated but not tested in Bennett (1990: 1311) — concerns the transition from P2–clitics to verb-clitics. Namely, it was predicted that the transition from the word-based P2 stage to the constituent-based P2 stage, coupled with the partly observed (*Bela krizantema*: Slovenian vs. Serbian) and partly hypothesized (*Nineteen Eighty-Four*: Serbian vs. Croatian) progressive favoring of P2 for finite main verbs, involves at the same time a greater approximation to the verb-clitic stage. This hypothesis was suggested by discussions of the transition from P2 clitics to verb clitics in Uto-Aztecan (Steele 1977: 555–6) and the Romance languages (Renzi 1986: 9–10), where it was pointed out that in a language with SVO word order the transition in question involves no reordering of constituents — merely a restructuring, as the clitics cease to be enclitic to what precedes them and become proclitic to what follows them. The case of Slovenian seemed similar: on the one hand, its clitics, which regularly follow the first constituent of a sentence, may be proclitic to a following accented word; and, on the other hand, as was revealed by the *Bela krizantema* comparison, there is a stronger tendency in Slovenian for finite main verbs to occupy second position.[4] By way of making a prediction about the three dialects/languages, it was hypothesized, then, that the extent to which they have proceeded from B1 to B2, as shown in (5), would be matched by the extent to which they have proceeded towards the verb-clitic stage. Specifically, it was predicted that the Slovenian text would yield the largest proportion of adjacent clitics and finite main verbs; and that, within Serbo-Croatian, Serbian would yield a greater proportion than Croatian.

In addition to these two hypotheses, it will be of interest (as indicated in 4.4) to investigate the word order relationship between finite and non-finite main verbs.

6.   The Textual Comparison

Since the different versions of *Nineteen Eighty-Four* are available in machine-readable form and have already been used with a concordance program in another connection (Bennett 1989), it was originally hoped that relevant textual comparison might be carried out by computer and that statistical information might be assembled on the basis of the entire novel. Recognizing clitics in the texts is no problem, since we are dealing with a relatively small number of items, which can be listed. Recognizing finite and non-finite main verbs on the basis of their inflections is more problematic owing to overlaps between verb inflections and endings of non-verbs; nevertheless, machine-assisted analysis would be feasible. The main problem would be trying to identify complex clause constituents, including discontinuous constituents. As there was no prospect of an early solution to this problem, it was decided to carry out the textual comparison manually on only part of the texts in question.

Textual analysis was begun from the beginning of the book (Part 1, Chapter 1). Since this chapter involves predominantly past-tense narrative, the Slovenian and Croatian versions contain mainly compound past tenses, consisting of (clitic) finite forms of the verb 'to be' (used as an auxiliary) together with the past participle of the main verb. (This is not true to the same extent of the Serbian text since it also uses simple past tenses — imperfect and aorist.) After

---

4. It should be noted here that since Slovenian clitics regularly follow the first constituent, whereas finite main verbs still occupy a variety of positions, it is the main verbs which are gravitating to the position of the clitics — including auxiliaries — rather than the reverse.)

4 pages of Part 1, Chapter 1, it was decided, therefore, to continue the analysis in another chapter (Part 2, Chapter 8), which contains a higher proportion of dialogue and consequently a higher proportion of (simple) present tenses as opposed to compound tenses. This decision reflects the fact that we were interested more in the position of finite main verbs and accompanying clitics than in that of non-finite verbs — see Sections 4.4 and 5. Approximately 6 pages of Part 2, Chapter 8, were analyzed, bringing the number of words analyzed altogether to between 5000 and 6000.

If the textual analysis were to support the hypotheses of Section 5, it would be appropriate to demonstrate statistically the extent to which the analyzed text is likely to be representative of the languages as a whole. In fact, however, the main hypothesis — that the order of advancement towards the verb-clitic stage would be: Slovenian – Serbian – Croatian — was not supported. The remainder of this section will therefore be devoted mainly to: (a) indicating the details of the data derived from the texts; and (b) attempting to explain why the main prediction was not upheld. In addition, there will be a brief discussion of the relationship between the positions of occurrence of finite and non-finite main verbs.

The account in (5) of the stages reached by Slovenian, Serbian and Croatian in relation to clitic placement was based on our early observation that the Croatian version of *Nineteen Eighty-Four* contains rather more examples of clitics interrupting complex constituents than the Serbian version, and that the Slovenian version — like the *Bela krizantema* text — contains no such examples. Table 1 gives a more detailed account of clitic placement in the three versions. The percentages listed in the table are based on approximately 400 occurrences of clitics or strings of clitics. It has been suggested above that the Slovenian clitics regularly occupy the second position within the syntactic structure of declarative sentences. However, from the point of view of comparability in Table 1, the position of clitics in all three versions is specified in relation to that

Table 1. *Positions occupied by clitics in Slovenian, Serbian and Croatian (based on approximately 400 occurrences of clitics or clitic strings)*

	initially	inside P1	after P1	inside P2	after P2	after P3
Slovenian	6%	0%	94%	0%	0%	0%
Serbian	1%	2%	84%	0%	12%	1%
Croatian	2%	3%	76%	1%	16%	2%

of other clause-constituents. Moreover, in arriving at the figures for main verbs shown in Tables 2 and 3, no numbered position was assigned to clitics in Slovenian any more than in Serbian and Croatian. The "initial" occurrences of clitics involve coordinate clauses; since conjunctions meaning 'and', 'but' and 'or' are treated as clause-linkers rather than as belonging to the second clause, any clitics following such items are initial within their clause. In Slovenian, clitics may immediately follow any such coordinate conjunction, including *in* 'and'. In the Serbo-Croatian versions, on the other hand, there are no examples of clitics following *i* 'and'. However, there are several occurrences of clitics immediately following the conjunction *ili* 'or'. A relevant example from the Croatian version is the following:

(8) *ili ću   postati druga osoba, s   drugačijim licem*
     or (aux) become other person with different   face   Cr.
     'or I shall become another person, with a different face'

This difference between *i* and *ili* presumably depends on the fact that *ili* 'or' may be accented whereas *i* 'and' is unlikely to be accented; thus clitics following *ili* are attached to it as enclitics. The only other position occupied by clitics in Slovenian, accounting for 94% of occurrences, is the position following the first constituent of a clause. In Serbo-Croatian, on the other hand, clitics may also follow the second or third constituents, examples of which were given in (7.Se) and (7.Cr), respectively. Such examples account, jointly, for 13% (12% + 1%) of Serbian occurrences and 18% (16% + 2%) of Croatian occurrences. As regards clitics which interrupt a clause-constituent, there were 7 such examples in the Serbian text, accounting for 2% of occurrences, and 16 examples in the Croatian text, accounting for 4% of occurrences (3% interrupting the first clause-constituent and 1% interrupting the second constituent). An example of a clitic interrupting the second constituent of a clause is provided by the Croatian version of (9):

(9) In the far distance a helicopter skimmed down between the roofs
                                                                      En.

     [Daleč zadaj] je   [zdrsnil] [med   strehe] [helikopter]
     far   behind (aux) slipped between roofs   helicopter   Sl.

     [U daljini] se   [jedan helikopter] [obruši] [među   krovove]
     in distance self one   helicopter dived   between roofs   Se.

[U daljini] [jedan je   helikopter] [skliznuo dolje]
in distance one   (aux) helicopter slipped   down
[među   krovove]
between roofs   Cr.

As has already been pointed out, Serbian is intermediate between Slovenian and Croatian in relation to the interruption of clause-constituents by clitics. On percentages of clitics following the first constituent, which represent the majority of occurrences in all three versions, Serbian also occupies the middle position. By way of further investigating the possibility that Serbian represents an intermediate stage, the Serbian and Croatian texts were examined from the point of view of the relative complexity of the constituent preceding the clitics, to determine whether there might be a difference in the likelihood of proclitic uses of the clitics. A relevant example is given in (10).[5]

    (10)   The instrument (the telescreen, it was called) could be dimmed.En.

        Instrument (zvao se   telekran) se   mogao utišati...
        instrument called self-(aux) telescreen self-(aux) could   quieten Se.

        Aparat   se   (zvali su   ga telekran) mogao zatamniti...
        apparatus self-(aux) called (aux) it telescreen could darken   Cr.

In view of the likelihood of a pause after the parenthetical remark in (10), the second *se* in the Serbian version would presumably have to be attached as a proclitic to the word *mogao*. In the Croatian version, by contrast, the corresponding clitic precedes the parenthetical remark and is attached as an enclitic to the word *aparat*. This is the clearest such example, though there are several other examples where clitics follow a rather more complex constituent in the Serbian than in the Croatian version. Thus there is some evidence that Serbian may be intermediate between Slovenian and Croatian in relation to the possibility of proclitic uses. However, the situation is by no means clear-cut since in one instance it is the Croatian version which exhibits clitics following a complex constituent — see (11), where the Serbian auxiliary *beše* (an imperfect form of the verb *biti* 'to be') is not a clitic.

---

5. With regard to the gloss on Serbo-Croatian *se*, it should be noted that the combination of the reflexive pronoun *se* and the third person singular auxiliary *je* is realized simply as *se*.

(11)   Sure enough, the little yellow-faced servant had come in without
        knocking.   En.

    [Odista], [sitni sluga   žutog   lica]   [beše ušao]
    Indeed   tiny   servant of-yellow of-face (aux) entered
    [bez   kucanja]
    without   knocking   Se.

    [Doista], [mali žutoliki   sluga] je   [ušao]
    Indeed   small yellow-faced servant (aux) entered
    [bez   kucanja]
    without   knocking   Cr.

Table 2. *Positions occupied by finite main verbs in Slovenian, Serbian and Croatian (based on approximately 200 occurrences)*

	P1	P2	P3	P4
Slovenian	17%	67%	12%	4%
Serbian	15%	63%	18%	4%
Croatian	13%	61%	20%	6%

Turning now to finite main verbs, Table 2 shows the positions that they occupy. The percentages are based on approximately 200 occurrences. As regards our first hypothesis in Section 5, admittedly the Serbian figure for P2 occurrences is intermediate between that of Slovenian and that of Croatian. However, the percentage differences are quite small and may not be statistically significant. With regard to P1 occurrences, there are three possibilities: verb-initial declarative sentences (both Slovenian and Serbo-Croatian are "pro-drop" languages); imperatives; and yes-no interrogatives. In the latter case, the initial verb in Serbo-Croatian is followed by the enclitic question particle *li*. The corresponding question particle in Slovenian, *ali*, occurs sentence-initially and verbs following this particle are regarded as occupying P2. However, the particle is sometimes omitted and in such cases the verb, of course, occupies P1.

Table 3. *Positions occupied by non-finite main verbs in Slovenian, Serbian and Croatian (based on approximately 330 occurrences)*

	P1	P2	P3	P4	P5
Slovenian	15%	55%	22%	7%	1%
Serbian	11%	52%	29%	7%	1%
Croatian	20%	46%	27%	6%	1%

For comparison with Table 2, Table 3 gives the corresponding figures for participles and infinitives, based on approximately 330 occurrences. P1 occurrences in this case represent only declarative sentences; there are no interrogatives or imperatives beginning with a participle or infinitive. Relevant examples are seen in the Slovenian and Croatian versions of (12).

(12)　He was a small dark-haired man...　　　　　　　　　　　　En.

　　　[Bil] je　*[majhen, temnolas　moški...]*
　　　been (aux) small　dark-haired man　　　　　　　　　　Sl.

　　　[To] je　　*[bio] [sitan, crnomanjast čovek...]*
　　　that (aux) been tiny　swarthy　　　person　　　　　　Se.

　　　[Bio] je　　*[to] [mali crnokosi　　čovjek...]*
　　　been (aux) that small black-haired person　　　　　　Cr.

Setting aside P1 occurrences, it is clear from the figures in the two tables that non-finite main verbs occur somewhat later in sentences than finite main verbs. For instance, the number of P2 occurrences is somewhat lower in Table 3 than in Table 2. However, neither Slovenian nor Serbo-Croatian is like German in requiring the non-finite part of compound verb-forms to occur at the end of a clause.

Table 4. *Proportion of clitics adjacent to their main verb (based on approximately 50 examples in the case of finite verbs and 300 in the case of non-finite verbs)*

	finite main verbs	non-finite main verbs
Slovenian	70%	72%
Serbian	74%	69%
Croatian	70%	74%

Turning now to the main hypothesis of Section 5, Table 4 indicates the proportion of clitics that were adjacent to their main verb (as opposed to separated from it). The percentages given for finite main verbs are based on approximately 50 occurrences; in this case the clitics consist of object pronouns and/or sentence particles but exclude auxiliary verbs. The percentages given for non-finite main verbs are based on approximately 300 occurrences. The figures may be interpreted as indicating the extent to which the three dialects/languages have progressed towards the stage of having verb-clitics. It is clear that the figures do not support the main hypothesis of Section 5, which was that the order of advancement towards the verb-clitic stage would be: Slovenian – Serbian – Croatian. In the light of our subsequent textual analysis we are now in a position to point out why the hypothesis was ill-conceived. Admittedly, where clitics follow the first constituent in all three varieties, the likelihood of the clitics and main verb being adjacent is proportional to the extent to which the varieties favor P2 for their main verbs and therefore highest in Slovenian. What was overlooked was that when clitics occur later in a clause, which is frequently the case in Serbian and Croatian, this may result in the main verbs and clitics being adjacent in these two dialects but separated in the corresponding Slovenian clause. The effect on the overall figures for adjacent main verbs and clitics is that these two separate tendencies cancel each other out. If the Serbo-Croatian clitics develop in the way that the Slovenian clitics have developed and stabilize in syntactic P2, it is still possible that Slovenian and Serbo-Croatian may reach the verb-clitic stage in the order Slovenian – Serbian – Croatian. However, textual evidence at the present time does not support the view that any one of the three is closer to the verb-clitic stage.

7.   Concluding Remarks

In addition to the conclusion reached at the end of the previous section in relation to the main hypothesis of Section 5, there are two other issues on which our textual comparison throws light.

First, it encourages us to reconsider the hypothesis of Bennett (1987: 279), summarized in Section 4.3 above, to the effect that after the Slovenian clitics became positioned on a syntactic — as opposed to phonological — basis, the place that they occupied could begin to be generalized to finite main verbs (a hypothesis which parallels Wackernagel's account of the adoption of V2 order in main clauses in Germanic). The situation with regard to present-day Serbo-Croatian now seems problematic for this hypothesis: on the one hand, Serbo-

Croatian has not yet regularized its clitic placement to syntactic P2; on the other hand, it exhibits some favoring of P2 for its finite main verbs, even if this is not as strong as in the case of Slovenian. Thus it seems likely that Serbo-Croatian has been affected by a shift towards what Berneker (1900: 58–9) calls a middle position for its main verbs even before its clitic placement has become stabilized. Thus one is forced to consider other factors, at least in addition to the earlier hypothesis. One such factor is language contact. Another is the possibility that main verbs moved from the end of sentences towards the middle as constituents representing new information became placed at the end.

Secondly, the data derived from the textual comparison encourage us to examine more closely the assumption that the Serbo-Croatian clitics are P2 clitics. The fact that they are not attached to any particular syntactic category does suggest that they are associated with a particular position. However, while the position in question is sometimes after the first word or constituent, examples such as (7.Cr) demonstrate that they may sometimes occur as late as after the third constituent. A possible way of preserving the appropriateness of the label 'P2 clitic' is by postulating that early constituents of some sentences may be detached from the rest of the sentence and said as a separate intonation unit, with the result that the clitics are then in second position in what remains of the sentence. From one point of view, this is a reasonable way of describing the facts: it emphasizes that the units within which the Serbo-Croatian clitics are accommodated are not syntactic units of the same type as in Slovenian. Where the textual comparison approach of the present study is particularly useful is in protecting us from one possible interpretation of such an analysis. Confronted with (7.Cr) on its own, one might argue that the constituent *na svakom koraku* 'at every step' is a (secondary) topic (following the primary topic represented by the initial subordinate clause). The clitics would then be in second position in the remainder of the sentence, after its two topics have been introduced as separate information units (Halliday 1970: 162–4). Such an interpretation carries the implication that the speaker/writer has chosen to present *na svakom koraku* as one unit of information. However, like (7.Sl) and (7.Se), (7.Cr) is a translation of the English version (7.En) in the discourse context in which the latter appears. Moreover, translators aim to preserve not only the meaning of individual sentences but also their information structure. In view of this, it would be unwise to argue that the speaker/writer of (7.Cr) is placing a different emphasis on the sentence than, say, the speaker/writer of (7.Se). It seems preferable to argue that

(7.Cr) and (7.Se) merely employ different strategies for accommodating the clitics as enclitics.

In the present study we have been able to confront a number of important issues relating to the historical development of clitics. To that extent, the usefulness of the method of comparing parallel translations of the same text seems to have been demonstrated.

References

Ard, W. Josh. 1975. Raisings and word order in diachronic syntax. UCLA Ph.D. dissertation.

Benacchio, Rosanna, and Lorenzo Renzi. 1987. *Clitici slavi e romanzi*. Quaderni Patavini di Linguistica, Monograph 1. Padova: University of Padova Department of Linguistics.

Bennett, David C. 1986. Towards an explanation of word-order differences between Slovene and Serbo-Croat. *Slavonic and East European Review* 64: 1–24.

Bennett, David C. 1987. Word order change in progress: the case of Slovene and Serbo-Croat and its relevance for Germanic. *Journal of Linguistics* 23: 269–87.

Bennett, David C. 1989. Ablative-locative transfers: evidence from Slovene and Serbo-Croat. *Oxford Slavonic Papers* 22: 133–54.

Bennett, David C. 1990. On the progress of clitics: evidence from Slovene and Serbo-Croat. *Proceedings of the Fourteenth International Congress of Linguists,* ed. by W. Bahner et al., 1309–12. Berlin: Akademie-Verlag.

Berneker, Erich K. 1900. *Die Wortfolge in den slavischen Sprachen*. Berlin: Behr.

Brabec, Ivan. 1964–5. Enklitika — šta je to? *Jezik* 12: 143–51.

Brabec, Ivan, Mate Hraste and Sreten Živković. 1965. *Gramatika hrvatskosrpskoga jezika*. Zagreb: školska Knjiga.

Browne, E. Wales. 1975. Serbo-Croatian enclitics for English-speaking learners. *Contrastive Analysis of English and Serbo-Croatian*, ed. by Rudolf Filipović, 105–34. Zagreb: Institute of Linguistics, University of Zagreb.

Delbrück, Berthold. 1900. *Vergleichende Syntax der indogermanischen Sprachen* (Part III). Vol. 5 of Brugmann, Karl. and Berthold Delbrück, *Grundriss der vergleichenden Grammatik der indogermanischen Sprachen*. Strassburg: Trübner.

Halliday, M. A. K. 1970. Language structure and language function. *New Horizons in Linguistics*, ed. by John Lyons, 140–65. Harmondsworth, Middlesex: Penguin.

Jakobson, Roman. 1971. Les enclitiques slaves. *Word and Language* (Selected writings, Vol. II), 16–22. The Hague: Mouton.

Pešikan, Mitar. 1958–9. O mestu enklitike u rečenici. *Naš jezik* 9: 305–11.

Renzi, Lorenzo. 1986. Essor, transformation et mort d'une loi: la loi de Wackernagel. Paper presented at the 19th annual meeting of the Societas Linguistica Europea, Ohrid, Yugoslavia, August-September 1986.

Renzi, Lorenzo. 1989. Two types of clitics in natural languages. *Rivista di Linguistica* 1.2: 355–372.

Steele, Susan. 1976. On the count of one. *Linguistic Studies Offered to Joseph Greenberg, Vol. 3: Syntax*, ed. by Alfonse Juilland, 591–613. Saratoga, Calif.: Anma Libri.

Steele, Susan. 1977. Clisis and diachrony. *Mechanisms of Syntactic Change*, ed. by Charles N. Li, 539–79. Austin: University of Texas Press.

Trávníček, Franíšek. 1956. *Historická mluvnice česká, Vol. III: Skladba*. Prague: Státní Pedagogické Nakl.

Toporišič, Jože. 1976. *Slovenska slovnica*. Maribor: Založba Obzorja.

Wackernagel, Jacob. 1892. Über ein Gesetz der indogermanischen Wortstellung. *Indogermanische Forschungen* 1.333–434.

About the author

*David Bennett is currently Senior Lecturer in Linguistics at the School of Oriental and African Studies of the University of London. He completed his Ph.D. in Linguistics at Yale in 1969 under Syd Lamb's direction. He had earlier studied linguistics at the University of London and first became interested in studying stratificational grammar when he heard a series of lectures given by Lamb at London in 1964. His 1975 book **Spatial and Temporal Uses of English Prepositions** is a revision of his dissertation. In addition to stratificational grammar, his main research interests are lexical semantics, syntactic change, and speech perception.*

CHAPTER 27

The Ablauts of l

Carleton T. Hodge
Indiana University

The comparison of the Afroasiatic (AAs) languages began in earnest with Erman's article on Egypto-Semitic in 1892.[1] His approach was conservative. There were many queries, and a number of the similarities noted were considered to be due to loans. There were nevertheless quite a few sets with multiple correspondences, some involving *l, r* and *n*. Observations of variant forms involving these sounds have frequently been made. We may cite as typical the alternations of *l-r-n* (as well as *l-d, l-t,* etc.) given by Fürst and Ryssel, primarily for Hebrew and related Semitic but with some other examples (1876: 644–46). More recently Leslau describes such variants as "alternation of liquids" (e.g., Ar.[2] *batala* 'separate', Geez *batana* 'disperse'; and in Cushitic, Oromo *belbel* 'flame', Bilin *birbir,* 1987: 112, 95). In Egyptian *3* [l] and *r* have been seen to alternate in *ǧ-3̣-t* 'hand', usually *ǧ-r-t* (Co. *tōre*) (Edel 1955: 57). *3* and *n* vary in *m-3–3/m-3–n* 'see' (Gardiner 1957: 364) and in *ʔ-3–f-w* 'discharge (from eyes)' (not in Wb.) and *ʔ-n-f-w* of the same meaning (Meeks 1981: 16, who

---

1. This paper is a rewriting of one presented to the joint session of the American Oriental Society and the North American Conference on Afroasiatic Linguistics in 1989. The pattern *l-r-n* has been used in more recent publications (e.g., Hodge 1991b), but it seemed advisable for the fuller treatment to be made available.

2. The following abbreviations for languages will be used in this paper:

Akk	Akkadian	Co	Coptic	Heb	Hebrew
Ar	Arabic	Cu	Cushitic	Or	Oromo
Aram	Aramaic	Eg	Egyptian	Sem	Semitic
Bil	Bilin	G	Geez		
Ch	Chadic	Ha	Hausa		

treats the variation as "graphic"). In Hausa one may have *l* in the dialect of Sokoto (S), where Kano (K, standard) has *r* : *halšèè* (S) 'tongue', *haršèè* (K). All three, *l-r-n*, are found in the *N-n-N* construction 'Nominal A pertaining to Nominal B', as in *màatal Audù* (S) 'Audu's wife', *màatar Audù* (K) and *dookìn Audù* 'Audu's horse'. For the feminine *l* or *r* the corresponding long form is *ta* (*màataa ta Audù*) for the masculine (or plural) *n* it is *na (dookìi na Audù)*. As we have in the short forms the *l-r-n* variants found elsewhere, the derivation of *r/l* from *ta* is to be rejected. In Indo-European (IE) we not only have the familiar *r/n* stems (see, e.g., Burrow 1965: 126, Sturtevant and Hahn 1951: 82), but other *l-r-n* alternations occur (for an older summary see Hirt 1927: 199–208). There have been a few attempts to define such variants as phonologically conditioned, but none has proved useful. The existence of the unexplained IE variation may well have led to the tacit acceptance of the irregular correspondences in AAs.

All three phonemes (*l, r, n*) occur in all branches of the phylum, and one would therefore expect all to be reconstructable for Lislakh (LL). Vycichl derived Eg. *3, r* and *n* all from **l* (1934: 59), but there was no explanation as to how the diversity was arrived at. The phonetic qualities of the sounds involved are, of course, uncertain before recorded observation, but some inferences may be made from other evidence. We assume that the writing systems used for Egyptian and for the older Semitic languages included symbols which represented three different phonemes (*l, r, n*), and, apart from Egyptian, such usage has been generally recognized.

In Egyptian the hieroglyph EGYPTIAN VULTURE (Gardiner Sign List Gl, 1957: 467; further references to the Sign List will give letter and number only), transcribed as *3,* is the Old Egyptian monoconsonantal spelling of *l* (cf. Edel 1955: 58, Hodge 1977, 1990). This had two allophones, [l] and [lʸ], the former being later replaced by *ʔ* or zero, the latter by *y* (Hodge 1988a). There were also dialect survivals of *l* in Coptic (Vycichl 1983: 93).

With regard to *l-r-n* alternations, some languages show more variation than others, and there are languages or dialects which favor one sound over another. For example, the Fayumic dialect of Coptic greatly favors *l* (Vycichl 1983: 93). On the IE side Burrow points out that 1) Iranian has mostly *r*, as does Western Indic, 2) Classical Sanskrit has *l* in a number of words where Vedic has *r*, and 3) Eastern Indic has "original *l*" where the word was transmitted with no literary influence (1965: 83). His "original *l*" is based upon the occurrence of the words with *l* elsewhere in IE.

Since Erman's 1892 paper scholars have accepted etymologies which have Egyptian *3* (Gl) corresponding to Semitic *l*, *r* (D21) to *r*, and *n* (N35) to *n*. Table 1 presents representative examples of these correspondences. Such regular correspondences need no discussion unless it can be demonstrated that they are loans. This is not the case with any of the items in Table 1.

Table 1. *Example correspondences involving Egyptian 3, r, and n.*

Egyptian			Semitic			
3	*ğ- 3–w*	'night'	*l*	**ẓill-*	'shade'	(Hodge 1969: 108, 1990: 644)
r	*p-r-t*	'fruit'	*r*	Heb. *pərī*	'fruit'	(Erman 1892: 110)
n	*ʔ-d-n*	'ear'	*n*	Ar. *ʔuðnun*	'ear'	(Erman 1892: 108)

There are also accepted what may be termed mixed sets. Examples of mixed sets are given in Table 2.

Table 2. *Representative Examples of Mixed Sets of Correspondences Involving Egyptian 3, r, l, and n.*

Egyptian			Semitic			
3	*q-3–b*		'insides'	*r* Akk. *qirbu*	'insides'	(Vycichl 1958: 371)
r, l	*ᶜ-r,*	Co. *ale*	'go up'	*l* Ar. *ᶜaliyun*	'high'	(Vycichl 1958: 378)
n, l	*n-s,*	Co. *las*	'tongue'	*l* Ar. *lisa:nun*	'tongue'	(Vycichl 1958: 377)

Calice also had Eg. *ᶜ3* 'big' equated with Sem. **ᶜ-l-y* 'be high', considering *ᶜ-3* and *ᶜ-r* to be doublets (1936: 25, 26).

In 1911 Ember introduced another correlation, Eg. *n* Sem. *r* : Examples are provided in Table 3.

Table 3. *Examples of Correspondence Between Egyptian n and Semitic r Taken from Ember (1911: 90).*

Egyptian			Semitic			
n	k-n-k-n	'to dance'	*r*	Heb.	*kirkēr*	'to dance'
	p-n-w	'mouse'		Ar.	*faːratun*	'mouse'
	k-n-s	'pubic region (?)'		Akk.	*karšu*	'belly'

There had been no examples in Erman (1892). This was included in later literature, but sporadically and with some hesitation.

Several aspects of the situation call for comment. One is that our presentation of the matter is colored by hindsight. When Ember began publishing, the two sets *3–l* and *3–r* were still unexpected and puzzling. Due to an endemic Egyptological misunderstanding, *3* (Gl) was then considered to be a glottal stop — and still is by some scholars (for discussion see Hodge 1977, 1990: 648, 1991a: 383). Ember therefore thought that its use as a "substitution for Sem. *r* and *l*" was the "*most striking phonetic peculiarity* of Egyptian" (1912: 86; italics his). Actually, the Egyptian hieroglyph for *ʔ* was REEDLEAF (M17). Sethe recognized that this was used to write prothetic alif (1892), but it was also erroneously recognized as a writing for *y* (Steindorff 1892). This misconception has survived to the present day (Edel 1955: 60) and has led to even greater confusion (as in Callender 1975: 8). For comparative purposes *3* must be consistently recognized as *l* and single REEDLEAF as *ʔ*.

These infelicities, along with a failure to recognize prothetic alif in a large number of spellings, contributed to the problem of multiple correspondences as found not only in Erman's comparisons but those of later scholars. Re-examination of prothetic alif and its role in Egyptian has not only strengthened the case for REEDLEAF as *ʔ* but has also led to better understanding in the reading of numerous Egyptian words (cf. Hodge 1988c, 1987a).

It is appropriate to note here that at all times, since the early nineteenth century, there has been a tendency on the part of some scholars to broaden the comparison to other language families. Ember, for example, on comparing Eg. *p-3* 'to fly', Ar. *farra* 'to flee', Tigre *farra* 'to fly', adds in a footnote, "English 'fly' and 'flee', as well as German 'Fliegen' and 'fliehen' are ultimately identical" (1912: 897). It has taken over seventy years to put this into perspecive and to accept such statements, along with more details, as a matter of course. What has been needed has been an overall frame of reference, a large segment of which is now in place.

Calice's 1936 collection of Egypto-Semitic etymologies has the items graded as to probability. He puts the above *n-r* set into his List B, i.e., not of top credibility but higher than many. He says, "If we assume with Ember and Sethe that Egyptian *n* may represent not only a Semitic *l* but also Semitic *r*, we have a number of further comparisons" (1936: 91, tr.). Among those he lists are the examples in Table 4. He also gives Eg. *m-n* and *m-r*, both meaning 'to be sick' and suggests that this is an inner Egyptian example of this alternation.

Table 4. *Representative Correspondences Between Egyptian **n** and Semitic **r** from Calice* *(1936: 92)*

Egyptian			Semitic		
n	*n-b*		'all'	r	Ar. *rubba*	'many a',
					Heb. *r-b-b*	'be many'
	n-b	Co. *nēb*	'lord'		Ar. *rabbun*	'lord'
					Aram. *r-b*	'lord'

Vergote gives no examples of Eg. *n* Sem. *r* in his history of Egyptian consonants (1945). Cohen does in his Hamito-Semitic but says, "*n* for *r* is not without difficulty" (1947: 115, tr.). In 1958 Vycichl made a valiant attempt to stem the tide of multiple correspondences in a major reassessment. In this he accepts Eg. *n* Sem. *r*, his example being Eg. *q-n-d* APE (E32, the meaning being taken from the shape of the hieroglyph), Ar. *qirdun* 'ape' (1958: 377, see also 1983: 342).

We have, then six well accepted Egypto-Semitic sets and one other worthy of mention. These correspondences are given in Table 5. The intra Egyptian alternations of *3–n* and *r-n* reflect the same kinds of variation as do the inter-language correspondences. We expect further comparisons will give us such examples on an inter-language basis and so fill out the pattern. We have omitted, along with Calice, Ember's *3–n* example: Eg. *ʔ-b-3* 'playing piece', Heb. *ʔeben* 'stone' (see Calice 1936: 16)

Table 5. *List of Egypto-Semitic correspondences*

3 — l	*3 — r*	
r — r	*r — l*	
n — n	*n — l*	*n — r*

These seven sets sit somewhat precariously in an overall picture of unresolved multiple correspondences. Considered from the point of view of comparative linguistics, this is an unacceptable situation. Regularity seems either lost sight of or considered to be unattainable. If one has proto **l*, **r* and **n*, why is it assumed that proto **l* becomes *l* in Co. *las* and *Ar . lisa:nun* but *n* in older Egyptian *n-s* ? And so on. It is not an acceptable answer to label these dialect variants, as the dialect forms themselves must be accounted for. (Reconstructions by the present writer are preceded by **.)

It is a basic principle of comparative linguistics that we must reconstruct sufficient forms (phonemes or clusters of phonemes) in the proto-language to account for the variants found in the extant languages. If we have seven sets, as above, and the differences cannot be reasonably explained as secondary phonological developments, we must reconstruct seven elements to account for them.

This situation is similar to that of the variation of *b*, *m* and *mb* in AAs. Greenberg posited three proto phonemes to account for these — **b*, **m* and **mb* (1965). The **mb* was to account for those forms which showed alternation between *b* and *m* . This did not resolve the difficulty, as Semitic and Egyptian show both *b* and *m*, as Sem. *bi-* 'in' but *min* 'from', Eg. *b-w* 'place', Co. *ma* . This lack of predictability has led to a certain amount of scepticism regarding it. Vycichl, for example, denies any connection between Eg. *b-w* 'place' and Co. *ma* (1983: 103).

A solution to this problem was proposed by the present writer and called "consonant ablaut" (Hodge 1988b and other). It involved not only *b*, *m* and *mb* but also *bʔ* (from Chadic, etc.) and *bh* (from Egyptian and IE). The same root, or base, could in the proto-language be modified by the addition of an affix, a pharyngeal (*H*, covering ʔ, h and pharyngealization) or a nasal (*N*), or both. Some examples of the resulting forms are given in Table 6. This system works with the stops *p t k b d g*, and the data supporting it are voluminous (Hodge 1986, 1987ab, 1988b, 1989, 1990, 1991ab, 1992).

Table 6: Correspondences involving Consonantal Ablaut with b, m, mb and bʔ

	Plain *b* - **b	*b* plus pharyngeal – **bH	Nasal plus b – **Nb
Eg.	*b*	*f* [ph]	*m*
Hausa	*b*	*bʔ*	*m, mb*
IE	*w* (rarely *b*)	*bh*	*m, mb*

As the consonant ablaut hypothesis developed, it became apparent that the alternation of *l*, *r* and *n* paralleled that of the stops. One therefore hypothesizes that the alternants *l*, *r* and *n* derive respectively from ***l*, ***lH* and ***Nl* . The first and third of these appear reasonable, but one looks for some evidence that the *r* involved had a back quality. On the AAs side we note that Ladefoged has described one of the Hausa *r*'s as a "retroflex flap", as opposed to an alveolar tap or trill (1964: 30).

There is considerable IE evidence for the back quality of *r* . In Sanskrit the dental sibilant *s* is replaced by retroflex *ṣ* after *r* (among other sounds), e.g., *várṣman* — 'summit'. In Lithuanian *s* is replaced by *š* after *r* . In Sanskrit dental *n* becomes retroflex *ṇ* when preceded in the same word by *ṣ, r or ṛ* (unless blocked by a palatal or dental), e.g., *kāraṇa* — 'cause'. In Middle Indic a retroflex stop may result from *r* or *ṛ* plus a stop: *vikaṭá* — 'enormous' from *vikṛta* — (Burrow 1965: 79, 96).

The Sanskrit evidence is particularly significant, as it shows a well attested early *r* of back quality. As AAs and IE are related, the evidence is relevant to the phylum as a whole.

The distribution, both inter-lingually and intra-lingually, also suggests that *l* is the more basic sound and *r* a modification of it. Such a direction of change fits the IE situation (as described by Burrow above) better than the assumption that *r* becomes *l*. Eastern Indic appears to be a marginal area, relatively unaffected by the spread of the *l* to *r* shift in the west. In the Iranian *r* region *r* predominates, but *l* is observed to survive in some words even in Modern Persian, e.g. *lištǽn* 'to lick' (Burrow 1965: 82). This is comparable to the survival of Co. *las* 'tongue' as against older Eg. *n-s* .

Another evidence is morphological. Eg. *m-3* 'see' usually occurs reduplicated, *m-3–3* There is also, as noted above, the form *m-3-n,* which has reduplication with *N* modification (**Nl*). Similarly, we have the word *ᶜ-3* 'big, great, senior (in age)' and the reduplicated form *ᶜ -3–r-w* (also *ʔ-ᶜ-3–r-w*) '(deceased) elders'. The latter was previously read *ʔ-3–r-w* and translated 'field of reeds'. The spelling with *ᶜ* has only recently been observed Meeks 1981: 16). The *ʔ-* is prothetic before the cluster *-ᶜ3–*. The meaning '(deceased) elders' was proposed for *ʔ-3–r-w* before its connection with *ᶜ3* was known (Hodge 1971, to be modified as to the connection with Semitic; Eg. *ʔ- 3–w* 'old man' is probably to be read *ʔ [-c]-3–w*). The implication of the spelling *ʔ-c-3–r-w* is that the *-r-* is a modified reduplication of *-3-*. The reduplicative morpheme is *-CH-*.

We may now assign the examples of *l-r-n* alternation given above to columns reflecting the origin of the attested phoneme as in Table 7, which assumes that the extant shapes all go back to alternants which existed in the proto language. This is probably the case with these and most other examples. It would, however, be an oversimplification to attribute all like alternants to an origin at this period. We know that the addition of pharyngealization has continued up to the present day in Arabic (Lehn 1963), and many of the nasal infixes of IE appear to be later formations.

Table 7. *Examples of l-r-n alternations assigned to proto phonemes*

**l	**lH	**Nl
Ar. *batala*		G *batana*
Or. *belbel*	Bil. *birbir*	
Eg. *ǧ-3–t*	Eg. *ǧ-r-t,* Co. *tōre*	
Eg. *m-3–3*		Eg. *m-3–n*
Eg. *ʔ-3–f-w*		Eg. *ʔ-n-f-w*
Ha. *halšèè*	Ha. *haršèè*	
Ha. *-l -*	Ha. *-r -*	Ha. *-n -*
Eg *ǧ-3–w,* Sem. *ʒill-*		
	Eg. *p-r-t,* Heb. *pərī*	
		Eg. *ʔ -d-n,* Ar. *ʔuðnun*
Eg. *q-3–b*	Akk. *qirbu*	
Eg. *ᶜ-3,* Ar, *ᶜaliyun,*		
Co. *ale*	Eg. *ᶜ-r*	
Co. *las,* Ar. *lisa:nun*		Eg. *n-s*
	Heb. *kirkēr*	Eg. *k-n-k-n*
	Ar. *fa:ratun*	Eg. *p-n-w*
	Akk. *karšu*	Eg. *k-n-s*
Eg. *p -3*	Ar. *farra*	
	Sem. *r-b-b*	Eg. *n-b*
	Ar. *rabbun*	Eg. *n-b*
	Ar. *qirdun*	Eg. *q-n-d*

While *H* (*ʔ, h* and pharyngealization) and *N* are considered to be morphemes, affixes changing the meaning of the forms to which they were added, it is not yet possible to determine their semantic content. This must await the examination of hundreds of bases, their ablauts and their historic meanings.

It remains to give some more detailed examples involving the *l-r-n* set of alternants. They are selected from the large number of proto LL bases so far identified. Certain conventions are followed. The shape of the reconstructed form precedes the examples, with presumed stem formative affixes given in parentheses. (Endings such as *-t* and-*w* are not noted.) The references are given by abbreviations, for which see the bibliography. *Y* indicates proto palatalization, probably phonologically conditioned.

**k-l* 'call out'. Eg. *k-3* 'say' (Wb 5.85, Fa 283). Ch. **k-l* 'call (summon)' (J-S 59). IE **kel -(ə -)* 'shout' (W28, P 548). **k-lH* : IE **kar-* 'praise loudly' (W27, P530). **(ð-)k-lH*: Sem. **ð-k-r* 'call to mind, remember' (Les 87.636).

Akk. *zakāru* is 'to speak, declare'. Heb. *zākar* 'mention, remember' is used of the recitation of praise poetry, i.e., the calling to mind what someone has done. An example is found in 1 Chron. 16.4. This is usually mistranslated, but the Geneva version (1560) has "to rehearse (To wit, Gods benefites towarde his people)" and the Douay (1609) has "should remember his workes". ****kY-lH* : Eg. *č-r-y-t* 'complaint' aut sim. (Fa 306). IE **ker* -'croak, shriek' etc. (W29, P567 with *k̂*). ****k-Nl* : Eg. *k-n-ʔ* 'to call' aut sim. (Wb 5.132). ****(ʔH-)k-Nl* : Eg. *ḥ-k-n* 'to acclaim' (Fa 179). ****kY-Nl(-s:)*: IE **kens-* 'to proclaim, speak solemnly' (W29, p 566 with *k̂*). ****k-l* 'to burn'. Ch. **k-l* 'burn' (J-S 57). Cu. **kal* — 'burn' (Eh 87.29). IE **kel-(ə)* 'warm' (W 28, P551). ****(t-)k-l*: Eg. *t-k-3* 'torch, flame' (Fa 301). ****k-lH* : Ch. **k-r* 'burn' (J-S 57). IE **ker-ə-)* 'burn, heat, fire' (W30, P571). ****k-Nl:* Ch. **k-n* Ch. 'burn' (J-S 57). IE **ken-(i-)* 'ashes' (W29, P.559). Note that both Chadic and IE have *k-l*, *k-r* and *k-n*.

****g-l* 'round'. Sem. **g-l-l* 'be round', **gull(-at)* -'bowl' (Fr 2.43). Ch. **g-l* ('calabash' (J-S 58). Om. Dizi *geli* 'round' (Bender p.c.). IE **gel-* 'form into a ball' (W18, p 357). ****g-lH:* Ch. Mafa-Mada **gar* 'head' (Rossing #355). Om. Sheko *gari* 'head' (Bender p.c.). IE **ger-* 'curving' (W19, P 385). ****g-Nl:* WCh. **gun-* 'to bend' (St 218). IE **gen-* 'compress-into a ball' (W 19, P370). ****gY-Nl(-C_2*): Eg. *ǧ-n-n-t* 'skull' (Fa 322).

Our final example calls for more extended discussion but illustrates how this approach opens up new possibilities for the interpretation of known data.

****l(-C)* (negative). Ember listed Eg. *n* 'not', Heb. *lō* 'not' (1911: 90). Since that time an Egyptian negative *3* has been identified (Edel 1964: 411). Gardiner credits Gunn with the idea that Egyptian had a negative 1 (1948: 13nl). In examining the occurrences of negative *3*, we need to remind ourselves of the initial pattern of the hieroglyphic writing system, that of core plus margin. The core writing is ideographic; the margin gives some or all of the consonants. The core hieroglyph for negative is ARMS IN GESTURE OF NEGATION (D34, hereinafter ARMS). To this there were at least two margins, *n* and *3*. Egyptian also has reflexes of the proto base ****b(-C)* (negative). *B-w* (negative) occurs unambiguously in Late Egyptian (Erman 1933: 389, Černý and Groll 1978: 204), and some believe that not only did it occur in older Egyptian but was at times spelled with ARMS, which was ideographic and therefore phonetically ambiguous (see the discussion in Davis 1973: 168–202).

Edel distinguishes, quite rightly, between an enclitic particle *3* and a negative *3* (1964: 411), but some of the examples need re-examination. In the particle paragraph he cites *n 3 ǧ-d-k n-[ʔ]* 'you would not say to me'. The *n 3* is

written ARMS *3*. It is more likely that the *3* is the phonetic margin to the ideographic ARMS, that is, that it is the negative *3* which corresponds directly to
Semitic *l-* . We should therefore read *3 ğ-d-k n-ʔ*. There are spellings which can
be so interpreted reaching into the New Kingdom. Gardiner has a Middle
Egyptian example: *s-ğ-m-w n 3 s-ğ-m-n-k* 'thou hearer, indeed thou hearest not'
(1957: 184), where he takes *3* to be a particle having "a vague exclamatory or
interjectional force". Here also ARMS *3* is to be read simply *3* 'not': "O hearer,
you do not hear", i.e., "you're not paying attention". Another spelling for
negative is ARMS-*n-3* (New Kingdom, Urk. 4.158.9, qu. Lefebvre 1955: 269).
ARMS-*n* is a common spelling for negative and indicates that it is the n-form
rather than the *3*–form. ARMS-*n-3* is probably this *n* spelling used by a scribe
who used *3*, so he added *3* to the spelling.

Semitic furnishes graphic evidence of a consonant after *l*, as Hebrew *l-ʔ* for
lō, Arabic *l-ʔ* for *la:*. The -*ʔ* is usually assimilated or lost, but we reconstruct the
LL base as **l-ʔ*.

**l-ʔ* (negative). Eg. *3* (negative). Sem. *l-ʔ* (negative), IE Hitt *lē* (strong
negative) (G-H 55). ***(w-)l-ʔ:* Ber. *wəla* 'there isn't' (Pr 1.245, who considers it
a loan). ***(w-)lH- ʔ* : Ber. *war* (negative) (Pr 1.244). ***Nl-ʔ* : Eg. *n* (Negative).
IE *ne* 'not' (W 43, P756). ***Nl-ʔ(-t)*: Ch. Fyer *nàát* (negative) (J 1970: 77).

Consonant ablaut, applied to the *l-r-n* alternation, has been shown to reduce
the problem to manageable size and to give us a way of describing the data with
greater regularity in correspondences and in phonological development. Secondary developments may have obscured many of the lines of descent, and much is
still tentative, but it is imperative to recognize that even a relatively correct set
of LL correspondences cannot be achieved unless something like consonant
ablaut is taken into consideration.

References

Burrow, T. 1965. *The Sanskrit Language*. 2nd ed. (*The Great Languages*)
London: Faber and Faber.

Calice, Franz Graf. 1936. *Grundlagen der ägyptisch-semitischen Wortvergleichung*. (Wiener Zeitschrift für die Kunde des Morgenlandes, Beiheft
1) Vienna: Orientalisches Institut der Universität.

Callender, John B. 1975. *Middle Egyptian*. (= *Afroasiatic Dialects,* 2) Malibu:
Undena.

Černý, Jaroslav and Sarah Israelit Groll. 1978. *A Late Egyptian Grammar.* 2nd ed. (= *Studia Pohl*, SM, 4) Rome: Biblical Institute Press.

Cohen, Marcel. 1947. *Essai comparatif sur le vocabulaire et la phonétique du chamito-sémitique.* (Bibliothèque de l'École des Hautes Études, 291) Paris: Honoré Champion.

Davis, Virginia Lee. 1973. *Syntax of the negative particles bw and bn in Late Egyptian.* (Münchner Ägyptologische Studien, 29) Munich: Deutscher Kunstverlag.

Edel, Elmar. 1955, 1964. *Altägyptische Grammatik.* (= Analecta Orientalia, 34, 39) Rome: Pontifical Biblical Institute.

Ehret, Christopher. 1987. Proto-Cushitic reconstruction. *Geschichte in Afrika* 8: 7–180. (Eh 87)

Ember, Aaron. 1911. Semito-Egyptian sound-changes. *Zeitschrift für die Ägyptische Sprache und Altertumskunde* 49: 87.92.

Ember, Aaron. 1912. Notes on the relation of Egyptian and Semitic. *Zeitschrift für die Ägyptische Sprache und Altertumskunde* 50: 896.90.

Erman, Adolf. 1892. Das Verhältniss des Ägyptischen zu den semitischen Sprachen. *Zeitschrift der Deutschen Morgenländischen Gesellschaft* 46: 93–129.

Erman, Adolf. 1933. *Neuaegyptische Grammatik.* 2nd ed. Leipzig: W. Engelmann.

Erman, Adolf, and Hermann Grapow. 1957 [1926–]. *Wörterbuch der ägyptischen Sprache.* 6 vols. Berlin: Akademie-Verlag. (Wb)

Faulkner, Raymond O. 1962. *A Concise Dictionary of Middle Egyptian.* Oxford: Clarendon Press. (Fa)

Fonzaroli, Pelio. 1964–1971. *Studi sul lessico comune semitico.* I-VII. *Rendiconti dell'Accademia Nazionale dei Lincei, Classe di Scienze morali, storiche e filologiche*, Series VIII, 19: 155–72, 243–80; 20: 135–50, 246–69; 23: 267–303; 24: 285–320; 26: 603–42. (Fr plus list number)

Fürst, Julius and Victor Ryssel. 1986. *Hebräisches and Chaldäisches Handwörterbuch über das Alte Testament.* Leipzig: Bernhard Tauchnitz.

Gardiner, Alan H. 1948. The first two pages of the Wörterbuch. *Journal of Egyptian Archaeology* 34: 12–18.

Gardiner, Alan H. 1957. *Egyptian Grammar.* 3rd ed. London: Oxford University Press.

Greenberg, Joseph H. 1965. The evidence for */ᵐb/ as a proto-Afroasiatic phoneme. *Symbolae linguisticae in honorem Georgii Kuryłowicz* 88–92. Warsaw: Polska Akademia Nauk.

Güterbock, Hans G. and Harry A. Hoffner. 1980. *The Hittite Dictionary.* Vol. 3.1. Chicago: The Oriental Institute. (G-H)

Hirt, Hermann. 1927. *Indogermanische Grammatik.* Teil 1. *Einleitung.* I. *Etymologie* II. *Konsonantismus. Indogermanische Bibliothek*, 13.1 Heidelberg: Carl Winter.

Hodge, Carleton T. 1969. Egyptian ǧ amid Afroasiatic. *American Oriental Society Middle West Branch, Semi-centennial Volume*, ed. by Denis Sinor, 104–10. Bloomington: Indiana University Press.

Hodge, Carleton T. 1971. Is Elohim dead? *Anthropological Linguistics* 13: 311–19.

Hodge, Carleton T. 1977. Review of John B. Callender, Middle Egyptian. *Language.* 53: 930–40.

Hodge, Carleton T. 1986. Indo-European consonant ablaut. *Diachronica* 3: 143–62.

Hodge, Carleton T. 1987a. Lislakh cluster resolution. *Anthropological Linguistics* 29: 91–104

Hodge, Carleton T. 1987b. Review of Allan R. Bomhard, *Toward Proto-Nostratic. Journal of African Languages and Linguistics* 9.63–65.

Hodge, Carleton T. 1988a. Lateral drift. *The Fourteenth LACUS Forum 1987*, ed. by Sheila Embleton, 373–77. Lake Bluff: LACUS.

Hodge, Carleton T. 1988b. Consonant ablaut in Lislakh. *FUCUS, a Semitic/ Afrasian gathering in remembrance of Albert Ehrman*, ed. by Yoël Arbeitman, 267–76. (Current Issues in Linguistic Theory, 58) Amsterdam: John Benjamins.

Hodge, Carleton T. 1988c. Prothetic alif and canonical form in Egyptian. *On Language: Rhetorica, Phonologica, Syntactica, a Festschrift for Robert Stockwell*, ed. by C. Duncan-Rose and T. Vennemann, 195–202. London: Routledge.

Hodge, Carleton T. 1989. Touching the bases. *The Fifteenth LACUS Forum 1988*, ed. by Ruth M. Brend and David G. Lockwood, 5–21. Lake Bluff: LACUS.

Hodge, Carleton T. 1990. The role of Egyptian within Afroasiatic (/Lislakh). *Linguistic Change and Reconstruction Methodology*, ed. by Philip Baldi, 639–59. Berlin: Mouton/deGruyter.

Hodge, Carleton T. 1991a. Review of Karel Petráček, *Altägyptisch, Hamito-semitisch, und ihre Beziehungen zu einigen Sprachfamilien in Afrika und Asien. Journal of the American Oriental Society* 222: 382–84

Hodge, Carleton T. 1991b. Indo-European and Afroasiatic. *Sprung from Some Common Source*, ed. by Sydney M. Lamb and E. Douglas Mitchell, 141–65. Stanford: Stanford University Press.

Hodge, Carleton T. 1992. Consonant ablaut in Egyptian. *Discussions in Egyptology* 23: 15–22.

Jungraithmayr, Herrmann. 1970. *Die Ron-Sprachen. Afrikanistische Forschungen*, 3 Glüuckstadt: J. J. Augustin

Jungraithmayr, Herrmann, and Kiyoshi Shimizu. 1981. *Chadic Lexical Roots. II.* Marburger Studien, Serie A. Afrika, 26. Berlin: Dietrich Reimer. (J-S)

Ladefoged, Peter. 1964. *A Phonetic Study of West African Languages*. West African Language Monograph Series, 11. Cambridge: Cambridge University Press.

Lefebvre, Gustave. 1955. *Grammaire de l'égyptien classique.* 2nd ed. Bibliothèque d'étude de l'Institut Français d'Archéologie Orientale, 12) Cairo: Institut Français d'Archéologie Orientale.

Lehn, Walter. 1963. Emphasis in Cairo Arabic. *Language.* 39: 29–39.

Leslau, Wolf. 1987. *Comparative Dictionary of Ge͑ez (Classical Ethiopic).* Wiesbaden: Otto Harrassowitz (Les 87)

Meeks, Dimitri. 1981. *Année Lexicographique.* Vol. 2 (1978). Paris: D. Meeks.

Pokorny, Julius. 1959. *Indogermanisches etymologisches Wörterbuch.* Vol. 1. Bern: A. Francke. (P)

Prasse, Karl-G. 1972, 1974, 1973. *Manuel de grammaire touarègue.* 3 vols. Copenhagen: Akademisk Forlag. (Pr)

Rossing, Melvin Olaf. 1978. Mafa-Mada: A Comparative Study of Chadic Languages in North Cameroun. University of Wisconsin Dissertation. Ann Arbor: University Microfilms.

Sethe, Kurt F. [1892]. *De aleph prosthetico in lingua Aegyptiaca verbi formis praeposito.* (Inaugural dissertation, Berlin) Berlin: Gustav Schade (Otto Francke).

Steindorff, Georg. 1892. Das altägyptische Alphabet and seine Umschreibung. *Zeitschrift der Deutschen Morgenländischen Gesellschaft* 46: 709–30.

Stolbova, O. V. 1987. Sravnitel'no-istoričeskaja fonetika i slovar' zapadnočadskix jazykov. *Afrikanskoe istoričeskoe jazykoznanie*, ed. by V. Ja. Porxomovskij, 30–267. Moscow: Nauka. (St)

Sturtevant, Edgar H., and E. Adelaide Hahn. 1951. *A Comparative Grammar of the Hittite Language*. Vol. 1. Rev. ed. (William Dwight Whitney Linguistic Series) New Haven: Yale University Press.

Vycichl, Werner. 1934. Hausa und Ägyptisch. *Mitteilungen des Seminars für Orientalischen Sprachen zu Berlin* 37. 3: 36–116.

Vycichl, Werner. 1958. Grundlagen der ägyptisch-semitischen Wortvergleichung. *Mitteilungen des Deutschen Archäologischen Instituts (Abteilung Kairo)* 16: 367–405.

Vycichl, Werner. 1983. *Dictionnaire étymologique de la langue copte*. Leuven: Peeters.

Watkins, Calvert (ed.). 1985. *The American Heritage Dictionary of Indo-European Roots*. Rev. ed. Boston: Houghton Mifflin.

About the author

Carleton T. Hodge died September 8, 1998. He was Professor Emeritus at Indiana University, where he taught from 1943 to 1944 and again from 1964 to 1983. From 1946 to 1964 he taught at the Foreign Service Institute. He received his doctorate from the University of Pennsylvania in 1943, writing a dissertation on Hausa, though his studies there had concentrated on ancient Near Eastern Languages. He became acquainted with Syd Lamb at LACUS, of which both were founding members. He was President in 1987–1988. In his later years, his research concentrated on Lislakh, the language ancestral to Afroasiatic and Indo-European.

PART II

B. Language Change: Lexicon and Culture

CHAPTER 28

Notes on Hispanisms: California

William Bright
University of Colorado

The Survey of California Indian languages — initiated at the University of California, Berkeley, in 1953 — is notable for having sponsored extensive field research and for producing a whole bookcase full of dissertations (not to mention many published articles) on the structure and history of the native Californian languages. A valuable by-product has been a substantial group of studies on HISPANISMS, or Spanish loanwords, in the native languages which came under Hispanic influence, namely those of central and southern California. The encouragement of Professor Yakov Malkiel, founding editor of the journal *Romance Philology,* was especially important; and that periodical published numerous articles on the topic, beginning with Bright and Bright 1959 on hispanisms in Patwin. Papers which have surveyed general features of the topic have included Bright (1960), on terms for domestic animals throughout California; Shipley (1962), examining characteristics of hispanisms in central California; and Bright (1979), focusing on Spanish loans in Cahuilla and other languages of southern California. Publications on the Hispanic element in particular languages have included Sawyer (1964a,b) for Wappo, McLendon (1969) for Eastern Pomo, Crawford (1979) for Cocopa, Schlichter (1980) for Wintu, Hill (1984) for Serrano, Kroskrity and Reinhart (1984) for Western Mono, and Gamble (1989) for Wikchamni Yokuts.

The accumulated file of Californian hispanisms which I have compiled from these works, and from works on the lexicons of particular languages, contains several thousand items. This body of data is significant in several ways: e.g., it sheds light on the processes of language contact in the context of Native California, and it accounts for important features in the recent history of individual Californian languages. In addition, it tells us something about characteristics of

the Spanish which was spoken in California from the 18th century to the early
20th century. The 'Californio' dialect of Spanish existed for over a century in
relative isolation from Mexico, and borrowed Native Californian words such as
islay 'choke-cherry' and *aulón* (whence Eng. 'abalone') which are still known in
California. However, this dialect has been little studied; the few relevant
publications include the article of Harrington 1944, which refers to Indian words
in the local Spanish of both California and the southwestern U.S., and the book
of Blanco (1971). (For etymologies of Spanish vocabulary in general, see
Corominas and Pascual 1980–88.)

The present paper is an attempt to fill in some details on Californian
hispanisms, from the viewpoints both of the native languages and of the Spanish
dialect from which they borrowed. In effect, I am ignoring the thousands of
cases of obvious, straightforward borrowing, and focusing on a small number of
cases where etymologies are difficult or disputed. It is frequently possible to shed
light on such cases if one consults, not dictionaries of Standard Spanish, but
more specialized data on Mexican Spanish such as that contained in the dictionary of Santamaría (1959). Thus the mini-lexicon which follows, alphabetized in
terms of Spanish etyma, represents an attempt to clarify issues which have arisen
in the literature on Californian languages up to the present.

The list refers to the languages and dialects named below, with abbreviations as shown.[1] Examples are from the sources indicated unless specified
otherwise.

---

1. Other abbreviations: Amer[ican], Cal[ifornia], dia[lect], Eng[lish], Mex[ico], Sant[amaría],
Sp[anish], St[andard]. Spanish etyma are given in boldface; those not found in standard dictionaries
are marked with an asterisk.

NC: N[orthern] C[alifornia]

Mai[duan]	Chico	Shipley (1962)
	Mt. [Mountain]	Shipley (1963)
	Nis[enan]	Uldall & Shipley (1966)
Miw[ok]	Bod[ega]	Callaghan (1970)
	Lake	Callaghan (1965)
	Pla[ins]	Callaghan (1984)
	Sie[rra] N[orth]	Callaghan (1987)
	Sie[rra] S[outh]	Broadbent (1964)
Num[ic]	Kaw[aiisu]	Zigmund et al. (1991)
	Pan[amint]	Dayley (1989)
	Mo[no]W[estern]	Kroskrity & Reinhart (1984)
Pom[oan]	C[entral]	Mithun (1991)
	E[astern]	McLendon (1969)
	S[outhern]	McLendon (1969)
	S[outh]W[est]	Oswalt (1975)
Sal[inan]	Ant[oniano]	Turner MS
Tüb[atulabal]		Mace & Munro MS
Win[tu]	Pat[win]	McLendon (1969)
Yok[uts]	Chuk[ohansi]	Gamble (1989)
	Tachi	Turner MS
	Wik[chamni]	Gamble (1989)
	Yaw[elmani]	Gamble (1989)
Yuk[ian]	Wap[po]	Sawyer (1964a)
	Yuki	Sawyer & Schlichter (1984)

SC: S[outhern] C[alifornia]

Chu[mash]	Bar[bareño]	Whistler (1980)
	Obis[peño]	Bright (1960)
Num[ic]	Chem[ehuevi]	Press (1979)
Tak[ic]	Cah[uilla]	Bright (1979)
	Cup[eño]	Hill & Nolasquez (1973)
	Gab[rielino]	Hill (1971)
	Kit[anemuk]	Anderton (1988)
	Ser[rano]	Hill (1984)
Yum[an]	Coc[opa]	Crawford (1979)
	Die[gueño]	Couro & Hutcheson (1973)
	Moj[ave]	Munro & Brown (1976)

Lexicon

a tiro (Mex.) 'very close' (Sant.): SC Tak. Cup. *ətírə* 'real, very, just a'.

acemita 'bran bread', (Mex.) **semita** 'a type of biscuit' (Sant.): NC Miw. Bod. *semíita* 'biscuit sp.', Miw. Lake *semíita* 'biscuit', Pom. S. *simíita* 'mixture of seed flour & wheat flour' (Callaghan 1970: 64); SC Num. Che. *samita ʔap(i)* 'bread'. This etymology for the Pom. S. form seems preferable to *semillita* 'little seed'.

aguja 'needle': the non-standard pronunciation *abuja* is found in all Calif. forms, e.g. NC Miw. Bod. *abúuha, ahúuba* (with metathesis);[2] Miw. Lake *áwha*; SC Chu. Bar. *awuxa*. Documents from the period of Spanish California show the spellings *abuja, ahuja, hauja* (Blanco 1971).

ahorcar 'to kill by hanging', (Mex.) **horcar** (Sant.): NC Miw. Lake *orkáar* 'to strangle someone'.

albérchigo 'clingstone peach', SC Sp. 'apricot':[3] SC Chu. Barb. *alwechiwu*, Tak. Cah. *elvéerčgu*, Cup. *əlvéerču*, Kit. *alvertigo*, Ser. *alveerču ʔ*.[4] The St. term **albaricoque** is attested in Cal. only from the southeast corner: Yum. Moj. *virkok*. The alternative Mex. Sp. *chabacano* is not attested in Cal. Ind. languages.

alcalde 'mayor': in several NC languages, used for 'law officer; boss', thus Mai. Nis. *kaalte* 'officer, constable, official', Miw. Pla. *kalte-* 'police(man)', Sie.N. *kalte-* 'cop, officer, sheriff', Pom. C. *káltee* 'boss', Pom. E. *kálte ʔ* 'boss, sheriff, police'. In the southern Sierra region, the sense of 'boss' is conveyed instead by **amo** 'master': Miw. Sie.S *aamo-*, Num. Mon.W *aamu ʔ*.

alcanfor 'camphor', (Mex.) 'eucalyptus' (Sant.): attested in SC Tak. Cup. *alkanfóor*. The alternative term **goma**, perhaps from local Eng. 'gum (tree)', is reflected in SC Chu. Bar. *woma* 'eucalyptus' (Beeler 1976).

---

2. Sporadic metathesis in Hispanisms is reflected in many Cal. languages (Shipley 1962:15); cf. also Sp. (Mex.) *guajolote* 'turkey', NC Miw. Lake *wolohote*.

3. Occasional references here to Cal. Sp. are based on personal acquaintance with it from the period (1930's and 40's) when I was growing up in a largely Spanish-speaking community of Southern California

4. Final glottal stop, as seen in examples here and below, is sporadic in Hispanisms found throughout California, the southwestern U.S., and Mexico. Attempts at explanation made to date (cf. McLendon 1969) do not seem to account for the wide distribution of the feature.

amo 'master, boss': see **alcalde**.

asar 'to roast': see **guisar**.

atole (Mex.) 'corn gruel' (Sant., < Aztec *atolli*): NC Miw. Lake *átol* 'a type of mush', Num. Kaw. *atɨɨniʔi* 'gravy', Yuk. Wap. *átooleʔ* 'mush' (Sawyer 1965); SC Tak. Kit. *atoliʔ* 'mush'. Two other words glossed as 'mush', namely Chu. Bar. *moš* '(acorn) mush' and Yum. Moj. *maš* 'mush', are probably from Eng., since Sp. *mosh* '(oatmeal) mush' is not recorded for Mex. Sp. by Santamaría (it is attested elsewhere in Latin America, e.g. in Guatemala).

bagazo 'bagasse, sugar cane waste', (Mex.) **gabazo** (with metathesis, Sant.): provides a word for 'sugar' in NC languages of the Clear Lake area, namely Miw. Bod. *kaw(w)ačču,* Lake *kawáaču,* Pom. S. *kawaaču* (Sawyer 1964a).

balde 'bucket': see **jarrilla**.

bandeja 'tray', (Mex.) 'basin' (Sant.) is used in many Cal. languages to mean 'dishpan, cooking pan', perhaps reflecting a Cal. Sp. usage: NC Miw. Bod. *wandéeha* 'pan', SC Tak. Cah. *vendéexaʔ* 'dishpan'. Probably NC Mai. Nis. *watteeya* 'pan' belongs in this group, rather than being derived from *batea* 'trough, wooden bowl'.

barrilla 'little bar': perhaps reflected in NC Pom. E. *waarí* 'fence' (rather than Sp. *barrera* 'barrier'). More widely distributed words for 'fence' reflect **cerca** (NC Miw. Bod. *sérku,* Miw. Lake *sérka, sélka,* SC Tak. Cah. *séerkaʔ*;[5] and **corral** 'pen, corral' (NC Miw. Sie.N *kunaana-, kuraana-* 'corral, fence, cage', SC Num. Che. *kurar(i)* 'fence, corral'). Also related may be NC Miw. Sie.S *punaana-* 'fence', with a change of *k* to *p* which is found elsewhere (cf. Sp. *borrego* 'sheep', NC Yok. Wik. *kuulika, puliikaʔ*).

*biscuita (Cal. Sp.) 'biscuit', from Eng.: not attested in Sp. dictionaries, but apparently reflected in NC Miw. Bod. *biskwíita.*

blanquillo(s) (Mex.) 'egg(s)' (Sant.), a euphemism to avoid the use of Sp. *huevos* 'eggs, testicles': reflected in SC Yum. Die. *blankíiyas* (Bright Ms).

---

5. The Miw. Bod. form with final *u* might reflect Sp. *cerco* ; however, variation in final unaccented short vowels is characteristic of Hispanisms from all parts of California. In many languages it seems to be independent of native phonological processes (but cf. Shipley 1962:15–16). Further examples will be seen below.

Elsewhere, however, the word **huevo(s)** is widely reflected, e.g. in NC Miw. Pla. *weewo-* 'egg, penis', SC Yum. Die. *wéevas* (Bright MS).[6]

bola 'ball': reflected in languages of both NC (Miw. Sie.S *woola-* 'ball, bullet') and SC (Tak. Cup. *vóola* 'ball'). The alternative term **pelota** is reflected only in SC (Cup. *pəlóotə*).

borrego/a(s) 'lamb(s)', (Mex.) 'sheep in general' (Sant.) is reflected in most Cal. words for 'sheep' (cf. Bright 1960), e.g. NC Mai. Nis. *woteeka*, SC Chu. Barb. *wulewu*. The alternative Sp. terms *oveja* and *carnero* are not reflected in Cal. languages, although the latter is common in languages of the southwestern U.S.

bote 'canister': see **jarra**.

burro 'donkey': see **mula**.

Cahuilla (Calif.) 'unbaptized Indian' (cf. Blanco 1971): originating in Baja California, this term was used in SC during Mission times, and then came to be applied to a well-known tribe on the fringe of the missionized area, in Riverside County. The word was eventually borrowed into the Cahuilla language itself as the self-designation *kawíiya*, but in modern times has been given a folk etymology from Cah. *qáwiʔa* 'master' (Bright 1977).

cajón 'box, coffin': widely reflected in Cal. languages, e.g. NC Mai. Nis. *kahoni* 'coffin', SC Tak. Cah. *qaxóon* 'box'. The alternative **caja** is a common borrowing in the southwestern U.S. and Mexico, but not in California. Gamble 1989 proposes *caja* as the origin of NC Yok. Chuk. *k'eexaʔ*, Wik. *k'axa*, Yaw. *k'eexaʔ* 'box'; but both the glottalized initial and the mid vowel are hard to explain.

calzón(es) 'breeches': used both for 'trousers' and 'underpants' in many Cal. languages, e.g. NC Miw. Sie.S *kalso-* 'pants, underpants', SC Yum. Die. *kalsoon* 'pants'. This is perhaps the preferred etymology for NC Yok. Wik. *khalšuwaš*, rather than Sp. *calza* 'breeches' (cf. Gamble 1989).

campana 'bell': see **tilín**.

campo 'field', Cal. Sp. 'camp' (from Eng.): reflected in several Cal. languages, e.g. NC Miw. Lake *ká(a)mpu-*, SC Yum. Die. *kaamp* 'camp'.

capote 'coat': see **chaquetón**.

---

6. In these and other examples, particularly to designate objects which are usually found in groups, borrowings are often based on Sp. plural forms (cf. Shipley 1962:17); most Cal. Indian languages do not distinguish singular/plural in nouns.

carreta 'wagon': reflected in many Cal. languages, e.g. NC Mai. Nis. *kaleeta,* SC Yum. Die. *karreet* 'wagon, car'. This is perhaps the preferred etymology for NC Yok. Wik. *kaaletha,* rather than Sp. *galera* 'wagon'. Several SC languages also reflect Sp. **carro** 'cart, wagon', e.g. Yum. Die. *kaar.*

catota (Mex.) 'marble (game)' (Sant. says 'in the State of Sonora'): attested in NC Pom. SW *katóote* and in SC Yum. Coc. *katóot,* instead of St. Sp. *bolita,* attested elsewhere (e.g. NC Tüb. *boliida²*).

centavo 'cent': see **jola**.

cerca 'fence': see **barrilla**.

coche, cochi (Mex.) 'pig' (Sant.): this word is reflected in most Cal. languages (cf. Bright 1960), e.g. Miw. Bod. *kóoči,* SC Tak. Cah. *kóoči².* A few NC languages reflect the alternative term **cochino,** namely Miw. Bod. *kocíina* 'to be piggish', Num. Kaw. *kičina,* Sal. Ant. *košén, kočén.* Alternative Sp. terms such as *cerdo* and *marrano* are not reflected in Cal. languages.

col(es) 'cabbage(s): see **repollo**.

corral 'pen, fence': see **barrilla**.

costal 'sack, bag': reflected in most NC languages, e.g. Mai. Nis. *kostal.* But in a few, and in all SC languages, we find reflexes of **saco** 'sack', e.g. NC Miw. Bod. *sáaku,* SC Tak. Cah. *sáaku²* (Bright 1979).

cha 'tea', a loan from Chinese: said to be used in the Philippines and in some parts of Latin America (but not listed in Sant.); reflected in NC Miw. Lake *čá-,* Sie.N *čaahɨ-,* Yuk. Wap. *čá²* (Sawyer 1965); SC Tak. Cah. (Desert dialect) *čá, čáh,* Kit. *ca².* (NC Pom. SW *caayu* is not from Spanish, but from Russian; cf. Oswalt 1958.) Elsewhere we find reflexes of **té**, e.g. in NC Miw. Bod. *tée,* SC Tak. Cah. (Mountain dia.) *tée.*

*chaquetón 'big jacket': reflected with the meaning 'coat, overcoat' in SC Tak. Cah. *čaketóon,* Cup. *čəkətóon,* Yum. Die. *čaketoon.* In many NC languages, 'coat' is expressed by **capote** 'cloak', e.g. Mai. Nis. *kapoota.*

cherife (Cal. Sp.) 'sheriff' (fr. Eng.): reflected, with the meaning 'police(man)', in several NC languages of the Clear Lake region, namely Miw. Lake *čiríife,* Pom. S. *čiríife* (Sawyer 1964a), Yuk. Wap. *číriifa²* .

chicote (Mex.) 'thong, rope' (Sant.): provides the usual term for 'rope' in most Cal. languages, e.g. NC Miw. Lake *čikóote,* SC Tak. Cah. *čikóoti².*

chícharo(s) 'pea(s)': provides the usual word used in Cal. languages, e.g. NC Miw. Lake *číičaru,* SC Tak. Cup. *číičara.* This contrasts with **arveja, alverjón** 'vetch', which frequently provide terms for 'pea(s)' in Indian languages of the southwestern U.S. and of Mexico.

chichigua (Mex.) 'wet nurse, milk cow' (< Aztec *chichihua* 'having teats', < *chichi* 'teat'): provides a word for 'milk cow' in two NC Miw. languages, Pla. *čiččiwa-* and Sie.N *čiččiwa-*. This derivation seems preferable to that proposed from Sp. *chiva* 'female goat' (Shipley 1962).

chivato 'young male goat', (Amer.) 'goat in general': reflected in several languages of inland central and southern California: NC Num. Kaw. *čivaʔatoʔo*, Num. Pan. *tsipaattu(ttsi)*, Tüb. *čibaadu*, Yok. Tachi *tsiwatuʔ* (Turner Ms); SC Tak. Kit. *civatoʔ*, Ser. *čivaatuʔ*, Yum. Coc. *siiváč*, Yum. Moj. *θqivat*. The term is also reflected in Indian languages of the southwestern U.S. and northwestern Mexico — but only rarely in central Mexico, where we usually find *cabra* and *chivo/a*. Of these terms, *cabra* is not reflected in Cal. languages, but **chivo/a** provides the usual terms for 'goat' (cf. Bright 1960), e.g. NC Miw. Lake *číiwa*, *číiwo*, SC Tak. Cup. *číiva*.

chucho, an exclamation used to call a dog, (Mex.) 'dog' (Sant.): provides the usual word for 'dog' in many NC languages (cf. Bright 1960), e.g. Miw. Pla. *čuuču-*. However, many American Indian languages, in Cal. and elsewhere, have similar words of native origin — e.g. Karuk (NW Cal.) *čišii*, Yana (central Cal.) *suusu*, Aztec *chichi* — and some mixture is possible (cf. Shipley 1962:19, fn. 16).

dos reales 'two bits, 25¢': reflected straightforwardly in SC Yum. Coc. *δoryáal* '25 cents' (cf. also **real**, below). A more complex case is that of SC Tak. Gab., where we find *doreales, toriyaliʔ, toraareʔ, turaariʔ, tulaari* 'peso' in the notes of J. P. Harrington (Hill 1971). This may seem a simple combination of phonological changes with a semantic change; however, *toraareʔ, turaariʔ* is also explained as meaning 'round', cf. *toraarkeweʔ* 'they are round'. In addition, *toraanat, turaanat* is given as meaning 'money'. It seems likely that Gab. *doreales* 'peso' was created by popular etymology from a native stem meaning 'round'.

español 'Spanish': see **Méjico**.

*esteche (Cal. Sp.) 'stagecoach' (< Eng. *stage*): reflected in NC Miw. Sie.S. *esteeči-*.

frazada, (non-St.) **frezada** 'blanket' (Sant.; cf. Blanco 1971): NC Sal. Ant. *pelsáataʔ*, SC Chu. Bar. *pilisala*, Yum. Die. *frisáada* (Bright Ms).

gabazo (Mex.) 'sugar-cane waste': see **bagazo**.

gamuza 'chamois', (Cal.) 'buckskin' (Blanco 1971): reflected, with the meaning 'buckskin', in NC Sal. Ant. *kamóosaʔ*, SC Tak. Cah. *gamúusaʔ*.

gato 'cat': see **tonchi**.

goma 'gum (tree), eucalyptus': see **alcanfor**.

güiro (Mex.) 'a type of gourd, used as a musical instrument' (Sant.): evidently reflected as a verb stem in SC Tak. Cah. *wíiru* 'to play the flute' (derived *wíiru-piš* 'flute'), Tak. Kit. *wiroʔi* 'to play an instrument'.

guisar 'to cook': reflected, with the meaning 'to fry', in NC Miw. Lake *ísar* 'to fry', *íisal* 'to fry quickly', Pla. *hisalte-,* Num. Kaw. *išaydɨ-,* Pom. E. *ísarʔ,* Yuk. Wap. *ísalʔ* 'fried' (Sawyer 1965); SC Tak. Cah. *gisáar* 'to fry' (Bright MS), Tak. Cup. *gisáar-* (Bright Ms). Mixture with **asar** 'to roast' may be reflected in NC Miw. Bod. *ašálit* 'to fry'.

hilo 'thread': see **pita**.

horcar 'to hang': see **ahorcar**.

huevo(s) 'egg(s), testicle(s)': see **blanquillo(s)**.

indianilla 'calico' (Blanco 1971): reflected in NC Yuk. Wap. *iiyániiyaʔ* 'calico', SC Tak. Cup. *əndəníiyə* 'cloth' (Bright MS).

jarra 'jug, jar, pitcher', **jarro** 'jug, pot': reflected as a usual word either for 'tin can' or for 'cup' in many languages, e.g. NC Miw. Sie.S. *haano-* 'cup, can', Pom. E. *háaroʔ, háaruʔ* 'cup, dipper, can', SC Tak. Ser. *xaaruʔ* 'cup'. (This etymology may be preferable, for NC Mai. Nis. *haatom* 'tin', instead of that from Sp. *latón* 'brass'.) However, in the meaning 'tin can', many NC languages use reflexes of **tarro** 'earthen jar': Miw. Bod. *táara*, Lake *táara* 'can', *táaru* 'tin', Pom. C. *táaru* 'tub, five-gallon can', Yuk. Wap. *táaroʔ* 'tin can'. This etymology seems preferable to the suggestions of Sp. *tara* 'tare (weight)' or *lata* 'tin can'. In the meaning 'tin can', SC languages tend to reflect **bote** 'canister': thus Tak. Cah. *vóotiʔ.* In the meaning 'cup', NC languages of the Clear Lake region, as well as SC languages, more often reflect **taza** 'cup': Miw. Lake *táasa* 'teacup', SC Tak. Cah. *táasaʔ.*

jarrilla 'small jar': often reflected in Cal. languages in the meaning 'bucket, (small) pail', e.g. NC Miw. Lake *haríiya,* SC Tak. Cah. *xaríiyuʔ.* Other words glossed as 'bucket, (large) pail' derive from **balde** 'bucket', e.g. NC Miw. Bod. *wáalde,* SC Tak. Cah. *váldiʔ.* Two NC terms, Yok. Tachi *lawuʔ* (Turner Ms) and Yuk. Yuki *laawe* 'bucket, bowl, big basket', are perhaps from **lawe,* a methesized derivative of Sp. *balde.*

jola (Mex.) 'a small coin' (Sant.): SC Tak. Cup. *xóola* 'penny, cent' (Bright Ms). Corresponding terms in other languages are from Sp. **centavo**, or nonstandard *centado,* e.g. NC Miw. Lake *sentáado,* Sal. Ant. *sɛntááðoʔ;* SC Chu. Bar. *sentawu,* Tak. Cup. *səndáadu.*

lepe (Mex.) 'orphan calf, dogie' (Sant.), is reflected, with the meaning 'orphan', in two SC languages: Tak. Cah. *lépi,* Cup. *léepe.*

leva (Mex.) 'coat' (Sant.), corresponding to St. Sp. *levita* 'frock coat', is reflected in SC languages: Tak. Cah. *léevaʔ* 'coat', Cup. *léevə* 'blouse', Ser. *leevaʔ* 'coat'. But **levita,** perhaps formed anew as a diminutive of *leva,* is reflected, with the meaning 'blouse', in two NC languages: Pom. C. *léwiita,* Yuk. Wap. *léwiitaʔ.*

ligar 'to tie (a knot)', (Mex.) 'to be successful at cards' (Sant.): reflected, with the meaning 'to exchange or draw a card', in two NC languages of the Clear Lake area: Pom. S. *likáryo* (Sawyer 1964a), Yuk. Wap. *líikaʔ* (Sawyer 1964a).

mascada (Mex.) 'silk neckerchief' (Sant.): NC Miw. Lake *maskáala,* Yuk. Wap. *máskaalaʔ*; SC Tak. Cah. *maskáada.* This etymology seems preferable to those which have been proposed from Sp. *máscara* 'mask' or *mascada* 'chewing'.

Méjico 'Mexico': evidently reflected, with the meaning 'European, non-Indian', in some languages at the southern end of California — Yum. Die. *haaykuu* 'Mexican', Moj. *hayiko* 'white man, Anglo' — as well as in the adjacent southwestern U.S.[7] Some languages elsewhere in Cal. reflect **mejicano** 'Mexican', e.g. NC Miw. Pla. *mehikaanu-, meykaanu-,* SC Chu. Bar. *mexikanu.* More common in NC, however, are reflexes of **español** 'Spaniard', used to mean 'Mexican' as well, e.g. NC Mai. Nis. *panyol* 'Mexican'.

mesa 'table': reflected in most Cal. languages, and always borrowed as *la mesa,* with the Sp. definite article, e.g. NC Miw. Bod. *laméesa,* SC Chu. Bar. *lamesa.* It is noteworthy that most Indian languages of Mexico also reflect the form with the article.[8] Such incorporation of articles occurs sporadically in other Hispanisms, both of Mexico and of California; thus, from Sp. *pipa* 'pipe', we find NC Miw. Lake *piipaʔ,* but Mi. Pla. *lapíipa-* (cf. Shipley 1962: 17).

mis, a word for calling cats: see **tonchi.**

---

7. I have this etymology from Pamela Munro, who attributes it to Judy Crawford.

8. It also occurs in Philippine languages; thus Tagalog has *mesa* or *lamesa* 'table'.

molino 'mill': reflected in NC Miw. Sie.S. *moliina-*, Pom. E. *múliinaʔ*. This is probably a preferable etymology for NC Miw. Sie.N *muliina-* 'mine', rather than Sp. *mina*.

montón 'a pile': NC Miw. Lake *mónton* 'to stack', Pla. *monoot-u-*, *moloot-u-* 'to pile up, to gather'. This is probably a preferable etymology for Miw. Lake *móonto-* 'mound, pile', rather than Sp. *monto* 'amount'.

moro (Mex.) 'dappled' (of horses, Sant.): reflected in NC as Num. Kaw. *mooroʔo* 'dark brown color'. This is probably a preferable etymology for Miw. Sie. S *mooro-* 'gray, spotted', rather than Sp. *moreno* 'dark-skinned'.

mula 'mule': reflected in most Cal. languages (cf. Bright 1960), e.g. in NC Mai. Nis. *muula*, Miw. Lake *múula*; SC Chu. Bar. *mula*. In NC Miw. Lake, 'mule' can also be *wúulu*; but this, like Miw. Lake *wúuru* 'donkey', is probably from **burro**.

naranja 'orange': widespread in, e.g., NC Miw. Lake *naráaha*, Num. Kaw. *naranka*; SC Tak. Cah. *naráaŋxaʔ*. Forms with initial *l-* do not necessarily reflect *la naranja*, but may arise by simple assimilation to the following liquid: NC Miw. Pla. *laraŋha-*, Sal. Ant. *laráaŋxaʔ*; SC Chu. Bar. *lalanxa*. The form of NC Miw. Sie.N. *aalīmča-* may reflect not the Sp. word, but rather Eng. *orange*.

navajero 'razor-case': NC Yuk. Wap. *nawahéeraʔ* 'single-edged razor' (Sawyer 1964a).

*navajuela 'small knife': NC Miw. Sie.N. *nawheela-* 'pocket knife'.

palo blanco (Mex.) 'hackberry tree' (Sant., Blanco 1971): NC Yuk. Wap. *páaloʔ blánkuʔ* 'pimp' (Sawyer 1964a). The semantic shift is also documented in New Mexican Spanish (Cobos 1983).

pañito 'small cloth', (Mex.) 'handkerchief' (Sant.): reflected in several NC languages as a word for 'handkerchief', e.g. Mai. Nis. *panitu*, Miw. Bod. *paníitu*. However, **paño** 'cloth' is even more widely reflected in the meaning 'handkerchief', e.g. NC Miw. Lake *pánnu*, *páanu*, Num. Pan. *paiyuʔyu(ppɨh)*; SC Tak. Cah. *páañu*, Yum. Coc. *paañ*.

pasear 'to take a walk': reflected in several areas in the meaning 'to visit, go visiting': NC Miw. Sie.S. *pasyal-ni-*, Pom. E. *pášalʔ*; SC Tak. Cah. *pasyáar.* This is perhaps also the etymology of NC Miw. Lake *pásal* 'to visit', *pasálṭi* 'to go and visit', Pla. *paslaay-i-* (with metathesis from **pasyal-*) 'to walk around; to visit', Win. Pat. (Hill dia.) *pásalʔaʔ* 'to visit' (Callaghan 1965: 106), Yuk. Wap. *pása?l* 'to go to town for a while' (Callaghan ibid.)

— as compared to a derivation from **pasar** 'to pass', which is not independently attested in the meaning 'visit'.

peine 'a comb': Cal. forms seem usually to reflect a form *peina,* e.g. NC Miw. Pla. *peena-,* Miw. Sie.S. *peena-,* Pom. C. *péena,* Pom. E. *péeno*ʔ, *péyno*ʔ, *péyna*ʔ, Pom. S. *péyiina* (McLendon 1969), Yuk. Wap. *péyiina*ʔ; SC Tak. Cah. *péyna.* A derivation from the Sp. verb form *peina* 's/he combs' seems unlikely; an alternative is from a non-standard noun **peina* 'a comb', though this is not attested in Santamaría.

pelota 'ball': see **bola**.

peón(es) (Cal.) 'an Indian gambling game, played with short sticks' (Blanco 1971). Reflected in Tak. Cah. *pyóon,* Cup. *pyóonis,* Yum. Coc. *pyuun.*

pimienta '(black) pepper': many Cal. forms seem to reflect a pronunciation **pimiente,* although this is not recorded by Sant.: NC Miw. Lake *pimiyénte,* Sie.S. *pimyente-,* Num. Mon.W. *paniyenta*ʔ, Pom. C. *pimyénte,* Sal. Ant. *pɛnyéɛntɛ*ʔ, Yuk. Wap. *pimiyénte*ʔ; SC Chu. Bar. *pimyentu,* Tak. Cah. *pimyéente,* Cup. *pəmyéentə,* Kit. *pimyente,* Yum. Coc. *pimyént,* Die. *pimyéenta* (Bright Ms.).

pita 'agave, agave thread', (Mex.) 'string': reflected as the usual word for 'string' in SC, as in Tak. Cah. *píita*ʔ. The word **hilo** 'thread', and the non-St. pronunciation *jilo,* are widely used in NC for both 'thread' and 'string', e.g. Miw. Pla. *hiila-* 'string', *hiilo-* 'thread, string', Pom. C. *íilo,* Yok. Wik. *iilu, hiilu.* In SC, however, reflexes of *hilo* are found only in the meaning 'thread', e.g. Tak. Cah. *íilu*ʔ.

pizcar (Mex.) 'to gather, harvest': SC Chu. Bar. *piskal.* The Mex. Sp. word, and the related noun *pizca* 'a harvest', are apparently not from St. Sp. *pizcar* 'to pinch' (or from *pescar* 'to fish'!), but rather from Aztec *pixca* 'to harvest', *pixquitl* 'a harvest'.

platito 'little plate': used in Cal. languages for 'saucer' (instead of St. Sp. *platillo*), e.g. NC Miw. Bod. *platíitu,* SC Tak. Cup. *platíita.*

potro 'colt; bubo, inguinal tumor', (Mex.) 'stallion' (Sant.): reflected in NC mainly with reference to venereal disease, e.g. Miw. Bod. *póotro* 'unbroken young horse', Pom. C. *pótli* 'gonorrhea', Pom. E. *póthle, póthile* 'gonorrhea, syphilis', *póthooro*ʔ 'colt, wild horse', Pom. S. *bóotolo* 'venereal disease', Yuk. Wap. *pótlo*ʔ 'syphilis'. More usual terms for 'colt' throughout Cal. reflect Mex. Sp. **potrillo**, e.g. NC Miw. Bod. *potríiyu,* Yok. Chuk. *potiṭniija*ʔ (Shipley 1962); SC Tak. Cah. *putríiyu.*

preso 'prisoner': reflected in NC terms such as Mai. Nis. *peleesu* 'arrest', Miw. Lake *pélees-weji* 'jail' (*-weji* 'house'), Pom. C. *péleesu* 'jail', Pom. E. *pélesuk* 'prisoner', Pom. SW *peleesu* 'prisoner, convict'. This etymology seems preferable to proposed connections with Sp. *pelear* 'to fight', with Sp. *policía* or Eng. *police*, and with Sp. *prisión* or Eng. *prison*.

real(es) 'Spanish bit(s), 12 1/2 cents'; (U.S. Sp.) 'ten cents': widely reflected in several senses, e.g. NC Mai. Chico *líyani* 'silver (money)', Nis. *peel-lali* '25¢' (with *peel-* 'two'), *čiy-lal* 'four bits' (with *čiy-* 'four'), Miw. Lake *reyáal* '12 1/2 cents', Num. Mon.W. *-niya⁊* 'dime', Pom. E. *k'áli-ràl⁊* '10¢' (with *k'áli* 'one'), Sal. Ant. *liáales*; SC Yum. Coc. *šyaal* 'money', *šyaal xwak* '25 cents' etc. (with *xwak* 'two').

rentar 'to yield (profit)', U.S. Sp. 'to rent' (based on Eng.; cf. Galván & Teschner 1977, Cobos 1983): SC Chu. Bar. *lental.*

repollo 'cabbage': this usual S. Cal. Sp. term is reflected in, e.g., NC Sal. Ant. *repóoyo⁊*; SC Tak. Cah. *rapóoyu*, Kit. *repoyo⁊*, Yum. Coc. *ripúy.* Elsewhere, the alternative **col(es)** 'cabbage(s)' is reflected in, e.g., NC Miw. Lake *kóleš,* Pom. C. *kóoles*; Tak. Ser. *koolis.*

rosillo 'clear red', (Mex.) 'roan (horse)' (Sant.): attested from NC as referring to a type of horse: Miw. Sie.S. *losiiyo-.*

saco 'sack': see **costal**.

semita (Mex.) 'a type of biscuit': see **acemita**.

serrucho 'handsaw', widely reflected in Cal. languages to designate any kind of saw, instead of St. Sp. *sierra*: NC Miw. Bod. *serúuču,* Sal. Ant. *sarúuča⁊*; SC Tak. Cah. *seróoči⁊.*

silla 'chair, saddle': reflected in Cal. languages only by terms meaning 'saddle', e.g. NC Mai. Nis. *siiya,* Num. Pan. *siiya*; SC Tak. Cah. *síiya⁊.* Words meaning 'chair' are generally of native derivation, but **sillita** 'little chair' may be reflected in SC Tak. Cah. *siyíitu⁊* 'chair'. Sp. *silleta* 'chair', which has been borrowed into many Indian languages of the southwestern U.S. and Mexico, is not attested in California.

tápalo (Mex.) 'shawl' (Sant., Blanco 1971): reflected in several NC languages, e.g. NC Miw. Bod. *táapalo*, Pom. E. *táapaalu⁊, táapaalo⁊.* This is probably a preferable etymology for Num. Mon.W *tapoono⁊,* instead of Sp. *trapo* 'rag'.

*tapeza (Mex.) 'shelf': not listed in Sant., but evidently from Az. *tlapixcan* 'place where something is kept'. Reconstructable from NC Pom. SW *tapéesa* 'shelf', Yuk. Wap. *tápeesa⁊* 'bench, shelf', and SC Yum. Die.

taapées 'bed' (Bright MS). There may be some mixture with Mex. Sp. *tapestle, tapesco* 'platform' (< Aztec *tlapechtli,* locative *tlapechco*; cf. Blanco 1971).

taza 'cup': see **jarra**.

té 'tea': see **cha**.

tendero, (Mex.) **tiendero** 'store clerk' (Sant.): both pronunciations may be reflected in NC Miw. Pla. *tenteeru-* 'clerk', Miw. Sie.S. *tyenteeno, čenteeno-* 'store', Num. Mon.W *tendeeno?* 'store, town'.

tilín 'sound of a bell': several NC languages of the Clear Lake area contain onomatopoetic terms which seem to show a mixture of Spanish and native origins, as NC Miw. Lake *ṭílle* 'noon; dinner bell, dinner' (Callaghan 1965), Pom. E *tílli?* 'church bell, bell', Pom. S. *ḍílle* 'dinnertime' (Callaghan 1965: 149), Pom. SE *ṭílle* 'noon' (Callaghan ibid.), Yuk. Wap. *ṭílle?* 'church bells, ringing sound, sound of a bell'. The alveolar *ṭ* in some of these words, as contrasted with Sp. dental *t,* reflects a native Pomoan type *ṭil* 'tinkle' (p.c. from R. L. Oswalt, who also cites Pom. S. *deele ~ ṭ'le* 'middle, midday.) In other areas, the word for bell is generally derived from **campana**, e.g. NC Miw. Pla. *kampaana-,* Num. Mon.W. *qanipaana?*; SC Tak. Cah. *kampáan.*

tonchi (Mex.) 'cat' (Sant.), is attested in several NC languages, e.g. Miw. Pla. *tonči-.* A few other languages use adapatations of Sp. **mis**, a word for calling cats, e.g. SC Chu. Obis. *misina.* Many others have borrowed **gato** 'cat', e.g. NC Miw. Lake *káatu.* Finally, many have borrowed Eng. *kitty* or *pussy,* e.g. Washo *kíidi, búuši.* (On all the above, cf. Bright 1960: 227–8.)

tuétano, non-St. **tútano** 'marrow' (Sant.): the latter pronunciation is reflected in two SC languages: Chu. Bar. *tutanu* (Whistler 1980) and Tak. Lui. *túutana* 'marrow' (Kroeber 1909).

túnica 'tunic, gown', (Mex.) **túnico** 'woman's one-piece dress' (Sant.): reflected, with the meaning 'dress', in several Cal. languages, e.g. NC Miw. Lake *túuniku, túuniko* 'dress', Miw. Sie.N. *tuuni(i)ka-*; SC Chu. Bar. *tuniku,* Tak. Cup. *túunəka* (cf. Blanco 1971).

vaca(s) 'cow(s)': reflected in most Cal. languages (cf. Bright 1960), e.g. NC Mai. Nis. *paaka* 'beef, cattle', Miw. Bod. *báaka, wáaka* 'cow', Num. Kaw. *vaaka?a*; SC Chu. Bar. *waka,* Num. Che. *wankasi(i).* However, several NC forms of the type Mai. Mt. *wóha* 'cow, calf, bull, cattle' are perhaps not from Sp., but rather from regional Eng. *wo-haw* 'beef, cattle'. This is said to be from the call 'Whoa! haw!' used by cattle drovers (cf. Bright 1960: 221–2). In SC, Tak. Gab. *paaka?* is glossed not only as 'cattle' but also as 'a real, 12 1/2¢'. Could this reflect the early use of cowhides as a medium of exchange?

vuelta 'a turn, an excursion', (Mex.) 'a short walk' (Sant.): NC Miw. Sie.N. *welta-* 'to march'. This etymology seems preferable to Sp. *avanzar* 'to advance'.

yerba buena 'mint', lit. 'good herb', also applied to several other species of medicinal plants: reflected in NC Miw. Bod. *yérba béenu*, Miw. Lake *yérwa wéenu*, Yuk. Wap. *yerwaawénuʔ*. There are intriguing resemblances here to what seem to be two sets of words which have diffused among several NC linguistic stocks. The first is Miw. Sie.S. *yenwa-* 'poison', Num. Mon.W. *enipaʔ, yenipaʔ* 'poison' (cf. **yerba** 'herb'); the second is Miw. Lake *wéne* 'medicine, herb', Pom. C. *wéno* 'medicine', Pom. E. *wénoʔ, wínoʔ* 'medicine', Win. Pat. *wene* 'medicine' (McLendon 1969), Yuk. Wap. *wénuʔ* 'medicine' (Sawyer 1965; cf. **bueno/a** 'good').

Acknowledgments

Thanks for helpful suggestions go to Jerry Craddock, Lise Menn, and Robert L. Oswalt.

References

Anderton, Alice. 1988. The language of the Kitanemuks of California. UCLA dissertation.

Beeler, Madison. 1976. Barbareño Chumash grammar. *Hokan Studies*, ed. by Margaret Langdon & Shirley Silver, 251–70. The Hague: Mouton.

Blanco S., Antonio. 1971. *La lengua española en la historia de California*. Madrid: Cultura Hispánica.

Bright, William. 1960. *Animals of Acculturation in the California Indian Languages*. (University of California publications in linguistics, 4:4.) Berkeley. [Reprinted in Bright 1976:121–52.]

Bright, William. 1976. *Variation and Change in Language*. Stanford: Stanford University Press.

Bright, William. 1977. The origin of the name 'Cahuilla'. *Journal of California Anthropology* 4.116–18.

Bright, William. 1979. Hispanisms in Cahuilla. *Journal of California and Great Basin Anthropology, Papers in Linguistics*, 1.101–16.

Bright, William. Ms. Field notes on Southern California languages (1959–61).

Bright, William, & Elizabeth Bright. 1959. Spanish words in Patwin. *Romance Philology* 13.161–164. [Reprinted in Bright 1976:116–120.]

Broadbent, Sylvia M. 1964. *Southern Sierra Miwok Language.* (University of California publications in linguistics, 38.) Berkeley.

Callaghan, Catherine A. 1965. *Lake Miwok Dictionary.* (University of California publications in linguistics, 39.) Berkeley.

Callaghan, Catherine A. 1970. *Bodega Miwok Dictionary.* (University of California publications in linguistics, 60.) Berkeley.

Callaghan, Catherine A. 1984. *Plains Miwok Dictionary.* (University of California publications in linguistics, 105.) Berkeley.

Callaghan, Catherine A. 1987. *Northern Sierra Miwok Dictionary.* (University of California publications in linguistics, 110.) Berkeley.

Cobos, Rubén. 1983. *A Dictionary of New Mexico and Southern Colorado Spanish.* Santa Fe: Museum of New Mexico Press.

Corominas, Juan, & José A. Pascual. 1980–88. *Diccionario crítico etimológico castellano e hispánico.* 5 vols. Madrid: Gredos.

Couro, Ted, & Christina Hutcheson. 1973. *Dictionary of Mesa Grande Diegueño.* Banning, California: Malki Museum Press.

Crawford, James M. 1979. Spanish loan words in Cocopa. *Journal of California and Great Basin Anthropology, Papers in Linguistics,* 1.117–32.

Dayley, Jon P. 1989. *Tümpisa (Panamint) Shoshone Dictionary.* (University of California publications in linguistics, 116.) Berkeley.

Galván, Robert A., and Richard V. Teschner. 1977. *El diccionario del español chicano.* 2nd edn. Silver Spring, Maryland: Institute of Modern Languages.

Gamble, Geoffrey. 1989. Spanish loans in Wikchamni. *General and Amerindian Ethnolinguistics in Remembrance of Stanley Newman,* ed. by Mary Ritchie Key & Henry M. Hoenigswald, 123–28. Berlin: Mouton de Gruyter.

Harrington, John P. 1944. Indian words in Southwest Spanish, exclusive of proper names. *Plateau* 17:2.27–40.

Hill, Jane, & Rosinda Nolasquez. 1973. *Mulu'wetam: The First People. Cupeño Oral History and Language.* Banning, California: Malki Museum Press.

Hill, Kenneth C. 1971. Gabrielino data from J. P. Harrington's field notes. [Computer printout.]

Hill, Kenneth C. 1984. Hispanisms and other loanwords in Serrano. *Journal of California and Great Basin Anthropology, Papers in Linguistics,* 4.91–106.

Kroeber, Alfred L. 1909. *Notes on Shoshonean Dialects of California.* (University of California Publications in American Archaeology and Ethnography, 8:5.) Berkeley.

Kroskrity, Paul V., & Gregory A. Reinhardt. 1984. Spanish and English loanwords in Western Mono. *Journal of California and Great Basin Anthropology, Papers in Linguistics,* 4.107–38.

Mace, William E., & Pamela Munro. Ms. A new Tübatulabal dictionary. [Los Angeles.]

McLendon, Sally. 1969. Spanish words in Eastern Pomo. *Romance Philology* 23.39–53.

Mithun, Marianne. 1991. Spanish loans in Central Pomo. Ms.

Munro, Pamela, and Nellie Brown. 1976. *A Mojave Dictionary.* [Los Angeles: Pamela Munro.]

Oswalt, Robert L. 1958. Russian loanwords in Southwestern Pomo. *International Journal of American Linguistics* 24.245–47.

Oswalt, Robert L. 1975. A Kashaya vocabulary. (Kashaya Pomo Language in Culture Project, working paper no. 32.) Rohner Park, California: Dept. of Anthropology, California State College, Sonoma.

Press, Margaret L. 1979. *Chemehuevi: A Grammar and Lexicon.* (University of California publications in linguistics, 92.) Berkeley.

Santamaría, Francisco J. 1959. *Diccionario de mejicanismos.* México: Porrúa.

Sawyer, Jesse O. 1964a. Wappo words from Spanish. *Studies in Californian Linguistics,* ed. by William Bright (University of California publications in linguistics, 34), 163–69. Berkeley.

Sawyer, Jesse O. 1964b. Sp. /r/ and /rr/ in Wappo history. *Romance Philology* 13.165–77.

Sawyer, Jesse O. 1965. *English-Wappo Vocabulary.* (University of California publications in linguistics, 43.) Berkeley.

Sawyer, Jesse O., and Alice Schlichter. 1984. *Yuki Vocabulary.* (University of California publications in linguistics, 101.) Berkeley.

Schlichter, Alice. 1980. English and Spanish loanwords in Wintu. *American Indian and Indoeuropean Studies: Papers in Honor of Madison S. Beeler,* ed. by Kathryn Klar et al. (Trends in linguistics: Studies and monographs, 16), 221–27. The Hague: Mouton.

Shipley, William. 1962. Hispanisms in indigenous California. *Romance Philology* 16.1–21.

Shipley, William. 1963. *Maidu Texts and Dictionary*. (University of California publications in linguistics, 33.) Berkeley.

Turner, Katherine. Ms. Spanish loans in Salinan. [Based on Ms. materials, mainly of William H. Jacobsen Jr. Also includes a few forms from Chumashan and Yokuts.]

Uldall, Hans Jørgen, & William F. Shipley. 1966. *Nisenan Texts and Dictionary*. (University of California publications in linguistics, 46.) Berkeley.

Whistler, Kenneth W. 1980. *An Interim Barbareño Chumash Dictionary*. [Washington, D.C.]

Zigmund, Maurice L., et al. 1991. *Kawaiisu: A Grammar and Dictionary with Texts*. (University of California publications in linguistics, 119.) Berkeley.

About the author

William Bright is currently Professor Adjoint in Linguistics at the University of Colorado, Boulder. He taught linguistics and anthropology at UCLA from 1959 to 1988. He was a fellow student of Syd Lamb at the University of California, Berkeley, where he completed his doctorate in 1955. He has made particular contributions as an editor: of **Language** *(1966–1988), of the* **International Encyclopedia of Linguistics** *(1988–1992) and currently of* **Language in Society**. *He has done field work in native California, Mexico, Guatemala, and India. His principal interests are ehtnolinguistics, sociolinguistics, and oral tradition.*

CHAPTER 29

Slang and Lexicography

Connie Eble

University of North Carolina at Chapel Hill

In recent years, Sydney Lamb has emphasized the role of lexicalization in language, a theoretical position that diminishes the importance of syntactic operations in the production of sentences and makes the lexeme the important unit in the cognitive system of language users. In this view, a lexeme is a combination of previously learned units which itself has become a unit. It need not be constructed anew after its first use or after it has been identified as a unit by users. A lexeme can consist of a single word, like *computer* for 'electronic data processing device', or a string of words, like *where you're coming from*. Semantically, the units that compose the lexeme as well as the combination can have varying degrees of transparency; an idiom is the extreme instance in which the lexeme lacks transparency. Take, for example, the transparent *beer-opener* 'something to open a beer' and its idiomatic synonym *church key*. Compared with explanations of language based on syntactic operations, Lamb's view puts a greater burden on human memory and the processes of analogy and substitution.

Working out a theory which gives increased importance to prefabricated combinations that can be remembered and listed eventually leads to the intersection of linguistics and lexicography, two analytic approaches to language which have not always taken advantage of the insights of each other. Because lexicography has a product as its goal — a dictionary — it is necessarily a practical activity. In the United States, in particular, lexicography has been viewed as a commercial enterprise and linguistics as an academic one. Nonetheless, the practical decisions that dictionary-makers make are guided by general and abstract notions about the nature of language. Within the past decade two books have explored the two sides of lexicography. As their titles imply, Sidney I.

Landau's *Dictionaries: the Art and Craft of Lexicography* gives greater attention to the practice of lexicography, whereas *Lexicography: Principles and Practice*, a collection of essays edited by R. R. K. Hartmann, explores the relationship between linguistic theory and lexicographic practice.

In an introductory essay "On Theory and Practice", Hartmann singles out five general postulates that underlie lexicography. The first two pertain here.

1. Lexicography is concerned with the description and explanation of the vocabulary of a language or language variety.

2. The basic unit in dictionary-making is the "lexeme", the close combination of form and meaning. (4)

Subsequent essays elaborate on the consequences of these postulates, discussing what is required and desirable in order to describe and explain lexemes in a dictionary format.

This essay explores the demands that one ordinary kind of lexeme, slang, puts on lexicography.

The kind of lexeme now labeled slang is documented early in the history of English lexicography, beginning with a glossary of 114 *cant* terms in Thomas Herman's *Caveat or Warening, for Commen Cursetors vulgarely called Vagabones*, of 1566 or 1567 (Starnes and Noyes 1946: 214). CANT is the secret vocabulary of vagabonds, thieves, and various categories of rogues and for English is the earliest kind of ephemeral, group-identifying vocabulary collected for publication. Cant enjoyed a certain vogue at least through the seventeenth century, as attested in many publications of the period. Somewhere between 1690 and 1700, the first dictionary of cant was published, authored by "B. E., Gent". *A New Dictionary of the Terms Ancient and Modern of the Canting Crew* contains, in addition to cant, other kinds of fashionable or group-related vocabulary that today might be classified as *slang* or *jargon* (Starnes and Noyes 1946: 222) and allows B. E.'s work to be characterized as the first dictionary of English slang. Two centuries of interest in cant and in the vocabulary of rather unsavory groups like common seamen, gamblers, and pick-pockets culminates in 1785 with publication of Francis Grose's *Classical Dictionary of the Vulgar Tongue*, now the standard source of Early Modern English colloquial vocabulary (Starnes and Noyes 1946: 227).

The early general dictionaries of English, from Cawdry of 1604 through Phillips of 1658, do not include cant or other types of colloquial or obviously ephemeral or specialized vocabulary (Starnes and Noyes 1946: 213). The first occurrence of cant in a general dictionary of English comes in Elisha Coles's *English Dictionary* of 1676. In the preface Coles justifies the inclusion of cant by practical motives: "'Tis no Disparagement to understand the Canting Terms: It may chance to save your Throat from being cut, or (at least) your Pocket from being pick'd" (Starnes and Noyes 1946: 220). Dictionaries after Coles's include slang to varying degrees. But the usual pre-twentieth century attitude towards slang in dictionaries follows that of Samuel Johnson's influential *Dictionary of the English Language* of 1755, which, seeking to protect English from corruption, admits little slang (Starnes and Noyes 1946: 221).

Twentieth century lexicographers are no longer constrained by prescriptive motives with regard to slang. Yet the complexity of this type of vocabulary has resulted in a tradition of slang lexicography, both in specialized and general dictionaries, that has only incompletely realized the lexicographer's aim to 'describe' and 'explain' this segment of vocabulary.

The current descriptive philosophy of lexicography assumes the inclusion of lexemes based on use. Once slang is admitted on that basis, the first difficulty is judging whether a given lexeme is slang or not. In his overview article "Lexicology 1942–1973" James B. McMillan pinpoints the source of the dilemma as a faulty definition of the term *slang*: "Until slang can be objectively identified and segregated or until more precise subcategories replace the catchall label *slang*, little can be done to analyze linguistically this kind of lexis, or to study its historical change, or to account for it in sociolinguistic and psycholinguistic contexts" (1978: 146). Since McMillan's assessment, advances have been made in defining slang, namely the seminal article by Bethany Dumas and Jonathan Lighter, "Is Slang a Word for Linguists?", in which four criteria are proposed for identifying slang. None of these criteria is formal, and only one is loosely semantic. All concern the social relationships of the participants, and the "ultimate identifying characteristic" is the consciousness of shared knowledge between speaker and hearer (Dumas and Lighter 1978).

Nevertheless, labeling problems persist. My 1984 study of fifty items in *Webster's Third*, five desk dictionaries, and three collections of new words (Eble 1985) confirms the difficulty of categorizing by a system of labels lexemes like *beat it* 'leave'; *bummer* 'bad experience'; *chow down* 'eat'; *haul ass* 'leave'; and *zap* 'kill, defeat'. Of the fifty items surveyed, only six are labeled *slang* in all sources in which they appear: *boss* 'excellent'; *bread* 'money'; *ice* 'diamonds'; *ralph* 'vomit'; *schmo* 'oaf'; and *toke* 'drag on a marijuana cigarette'.

Landau offers an explanation of the situation.

> [Slang] is sometimes grouped with the style labels ("formal/informal") and sometimes with the status labels ("standard/nonstandard"), but it does not comfortably fit with either. Slang does not represent a vocabulary that one can adopt to suit a social situation, as one can with terms on the "formal/informal" index ... Slang is deliberately nonstandard. (1984: 189)

The dictionaries of Merriam-Webster, Inc. use the label *slang* most sparingly, leaving entirely unlabeled lexemes like *guts* 'courage'; *mooch* 'beg, cadge'; *put down* 'criticize'; and *rap* 'converse'. The absence of a label implies that the lexeme belongs to the general unremarkable vocabulary of English, whose use conveys no social implications. This is clearly not so for these lexemes.

The three editions of *The American Heritage Dictionary* (Morris 1969; 1982; Soukhanov, 1992. Henceforth AHD) and in particular the second unabridged *Random House Dictionary* (Flexner 1987. Henceforth RHD2) do better at explaining the nature of slang in the prefatory matter and in applying the label. For instance, *floozy* 'a gaudily dressed, usually immoral woman'; *fuzz* 'police'; *gold brick* 'loaf'; *jerk* 'fatuous or foolish person'; *scarf* 'eat voraciously'; *schlep* 'lug, move slowly'; *stud* 'virile male'; and *suds* 'beer' are all designated *slang* in both *AHD* and *RHD2* but carry no label in *Merriam Webster's Collegiate Dictionary* (Mish 1993).

The heart of the matter is that the definition of slang used by both linguists and lexicographers must incorporate the social, contextual, and rhetorical dimensions inherent in this type of vocabulary — and that if grammars and dictionaries are to explain language accurately they must find ways to describe slang lexemes. Although he mentions slang only briefly, in his essay "On Specifying Context: How to Label Contexts and Varieties of Usage" Hartmann calls for the lexicographical treatment of precisely the dimensions that are salient in slang. He suggests that a pragmatic approach to context can provide a unified way to classify the covariance of linguistic form with style, register, regional dialect, sociolect, and the like (1983: 118). Regardless of the exact shape that such a pragmatic approach would take, or the methodology that it would entail, it could then accommodate slang as akin to other linguistic phenomena.

The remainder of this essay illustrates three inter-related characteristics of slang vocabulary that a more sophisticated kind of lexicography would consistently incorporate: 1) group-identifying functions; 2) ephemerality; 3) systematic relationships with other lexemes. All examples of college slang, unless otherwise indicated, were submitted as good, current campus slang by undergraduates at the University of North Carolina at Chapel Hill during the academic years 1990–91 and 1991–92.

1.   Group Identifying Functions

Slang is in essence socially sensitive. The use of a slang lexeme always makes a claim about the speaker's identification either with a particular marginal subculture (e.g. drug dealers) or with an ill-defined group who, at least in a specific situation, feel superior in awareness, knowledge, or taste to those outside the group (e.g. the audience of the television show *Saturday Night Live*). The groups recognized earliest for their special vocabulary were of the first type. Operating on the fringes of respectable society and depending for their survival on various kinds of shared knowledge, they found it to their advantage to create and maintain a vocabulary that identified insiders and excluded outsiders. Although many groups that use slang today, e.g. musicians, surfers, and computer users, are not excluded from the dominant culture, the insider/outsider function of their vocabulary is still important.

Sometimes groups develop lexemes for the interest or activity that unites them. College students, for example, use *Dr. Slide* 'an easy professor'; *McPaper* 'a hastily written paper'; and *flag* 'the grade F'. Such lexemes ·are hard to distinguish from jargon. But most of the ever-changing vocabulary of college students pertains to succeeding or failing and to their precarious place in the social order among their peers. Most obvious in separating the *ins* from the *outs* is a set of words to designate directly 'someone who is socially inept or who does not fit in': *butthead, cheeseball, dork, dorkus pretentious, dweeb, geek, goob, goober, loser, moe, nerd, wally, yuck-a-buck.* Other terms poke fun in a good-natured way at those who are behind the times but are otherwise not objectionable. Current synonyms for 'someone whose appearance suggests the back-to-nature values of the 1960s and 1970s' include *earthmuffin, granola, tree-hugger,* and *Woodstock wannabe.*

But, for the most part, slang promotes a feeling of belonging more subtly. For instance, college students know the word *vomit*, and when they need to describe their symptoms to a doctor, they use it. However, if their solidarity with other students is an element of the communication, they will more likely use *ralph, barf,* or another slang equivalent to describe the same illness. If the vomiting is the result of excessive drinking, the use of slang is an even more important forger of solidarity, as it identifies the indisposed person as a participant in the favorite student pastime of overindulging in alcohol. Clever and humorous expressions like *blow grits, bow to the porcelain god,* and *ride the porcelain pony* are often used to convey an attitude that the situation is funny rather than serious and that drinking too much is just a lark and a part of being a good sport at college.

Not all college students drink excessively or approve of it, yet even the most unregenerate geek among them can reel off a dozen terms for 'drunk': *blasted, buttcranus, choked, fubar, gone, hammered, heinous, tore up, ripskated, sloshed, wasted, zooted*. And a college student needs no direct experience of 'cocaine' to refer to it off-handedly as *booger sugar, dummy dust*, or *snow*.

The early recognition of slang as the peculiar vocabulary of less than respectable subcultures brought with it the recognition of the power of offensive vocabulary for such groups. Groups with no social status to lose have the freedom to violate the linguistic taboos of the general culture. For English, the flouting of social norms shows up in the proliferation of slang terms for such referents as intimate body parts, bodily elimination, and sex. Because all groups that use slang picture themselves to some degree alienated from or in opposition to established authority, it is not surprising that numerous offensive terms are characteristic of slang.

Current college students enjoy defying proscriptions concerning the buttocks, for example, by making up or appropriating from other groups lexemes built on *ass* and *butt*. *Asshole* and *butthead* are the most common nouns for 'an obnoxious person'. The phrase *up the butt* means 'in great quantity' in sentences like *I have math problems up the butt this weekend*. It also occurs in descriptive expressions indicating 'extreme anxiety', e.g. *pole up your butt* or *corncob up your butt*. *Butt* alone conveys the meaning of 'extreme' as a qualifier, e.g. in *That party was butt wild*, or as the first member of a compound, e.g. *I have buttloads of chemistry this weekend*. *Butt-kisser* now rivals *ass-kisser* for 'someone who curries favor'. A *smartbutt* is 'someone who is cocky or flippant', and a *poopbutt* doubly defies taboo by combining a word for 'excrement' with *butt* to mean 'an undesirable person'.

Words that originally referred to the penis are frequent in slang, often with transferred and ameliorated senses. For instance, a *dork* on college campuses is 'someone who does not fit in', and most current users are not aware of the original reference to the male anatomy. *Dick,* on the other hand, retains clear associations with maleness, as in the expression *a dick thing*, meaning 'characteristically associated with males'. As a verb, however, *dick* means 'treat unfairly' — a sense also associated with words that refer to sexual intercourse, e.g. *fuck, hose,* and *screw*.

The appropriation of the slang of one subculture by another subculture or by the dominant culture is a pattern of long standing. General American slang, for example, has borrowed vocabulary from the military. *Chew out* 'reprimand'; *shack up* 'live together while unmarried'; and *snafu* 'very confusing' (from *situation normal, all fucked up*) all became popular in vernacular forms of English during World War II. Musicians have transmitted vocabulary from African-Americans into more widespread colloquial usage: *bad* 'good'; *burn* 'perform well'; *get down* 'attend to a task'; *jive* 'banter'.

The two groups that are currently providing trendy vocabulary to the youth of the United States are African-Americans and gays. Borrowings from African-Americans fashionable on college campuses are *dap* 'respect'; *dope* 'good'; *gaffle* 'have sex'; *illin'* 'in a bad mood'; and *perpetrate* 'pretend'. Gays are being imitated with expressions like *breeder* 'a heterosexual'; *chickenhawk* 'an older gay male who pursues young men'; *read* 'to verbally insult'; and *queeny* 'effeminate'.

Borrowing of African-American vocabulary and communicative styles is widespread among middle-class white adolescents. Anne C. Roark of the *Los Angeles Times* quotes one white, Amherst-College-bound male as saying, "There is a lot of yearning to be black. Everyone calls each other *bro* [for brother]. They say, *What's up, G*? [gangster]. And you hear all the time, *Are you dissin' me*? [Are you being disrespectful?]" (1992: E1)

Borrowing from groups of lower prestige is a type of role playing or performance, a temporary identification with the exciting elements of being different and in opposition to the establishment without the drawbacks of actual membership in such groups. My 1993 study of the lexemes associated with African-Americans in Robert Chapman's *New Dictionary of American Slang* shows that, taken as a group, the image conveyed by borrowings from African-Americans is a pleasant one: African-Americans like to get all dressed up and to get together having a good time greeting each other and laughing and dancing and making music and love. On the surface, the vocabulary items seem to depict a group of lower status as appealing and worthy of imitation. Yet a closer look shows that they are filtered by the stereotypes of mainstream society (Eble 1993).

Groups as closed and secretive as drug pushers and incarcerated criminals and as open-ended and diverse as middle-class adult Americans cultivate slang. Because forming and maintaining group identity is such an important function of slang, to describe a slang lexeme adequately it is important for dictionaries to specify the group that originates a slang term and to trace the route by which it spreads.

2.   Ephemerality

Almost every discussion of the nature of slang points to its ephemerality. It is true that some slang terms persist for centuries, e.g. *mooch* 'to beg' from the fifteenth century; *prick* 'penis' from the sixteenth century; *flush* 'having plenty of money' from the seventeenth century; *pop off* 'to die' from the eighteenth century; and *pull* 'influence' from the nineteenth century. However, most slang comes and goes within a matter of months or years rather than decades or centuries. The use of *red*, a shortening of *redneck*, to mean 'conservative' enjoyed a brief vogue among North Carolina students in 1974 but failed to compete with *redneck*, which persists to the present. Americans of middle-age who still say *See you later, alligator* show themselves to be stuck in the adolescent slang of the 1950s. The cool teenager of the early 1990s said *peace up* or *word* as a farewell.

Because of the element of fashion associated with slang, the date of the earliest attestation of a slang term is often not so instructive as is the date of its peak of popularity. *Bad* for 'good, excellent' is attested among African-Americans from the period of slavery, but it did not achieve recognition and use beyond that group until the 1950s. Among college students it has remained in constant favor since at least the early 1970s. Another example is *bun(s)* 'buttocks'. *Bun* is attested in Northern and Scots dialects for 'tail of a rabbit' as early as the fourteenth century, showing up in various vernacular expressions meaning 'human posterior' by the time of Captain Grose's dictionary at the end of the eighteenth century. In 1974 it showed up among North Carolina college students first in the expression *bun this j*, meaning 'to leave', and not until the early 1980s did *buns* become widespread for 'buttocks'. In the 1990s with the emphasis on exercise and physical fitness, *buns* is the term of choice of thousands of aerobics instructors who daily urge their clients, *Squeeze those buns*.

The fact that so many slang terms arise by semantic change rather than by alteration of form further complicates the dating of slang. Semantic change always results in polysemy, at least for a short while. During the Middle English period the word *quick* 'alive' acquired the related meaning 'rapid', and for a while *quick* evoked both senses. Now the earlier sense of 'alive' is known mainly in the phrase *the quick and the dead* in the old version of The Apostles' Creed. Of course, polysemy always presents challenges to lexicographers, and the dating of 'new' senses is just one of them. The most common practice in general dictionaries that do not claim to be historical is to give one date per main entry. Thus the entry for *bitch* typically indicates that the etymon *bicce* is attested from the Old English period, or before 1000, when it meant 'female canine'. Although later slang senses like 'ill-tempered female' and 'to complain' may be included and labeled, there is ordinarily no indication when they developed.

Even the *Random House Dictionary* (Flexner 1987), which is superior to other contemporary, general dictionaries of American English in the treatment of slang lexemes, is inadequate in dating them. The slang senses of *creep* 'obnoxious person' and *moon* 'to exhibit one's posterior' are recorded, but the etymological information indicates only that the forms date to 'before 900'. *To go ape over* is included in the entry for *ape* but is not separately dated; although *ape* dates to the Old English period, the combination *go ape over* with its meaning 'act crazy' arose in the twentieth century. The entry for *crash* is better. It lists 25 senses and three dates: 'break', 1350–1400; 'gain admission though not invited', 1920–25; 'sudden general collapse of a business enterprise', 1870–75.

Compounds pose problems in dating also. *Belly* has been in the language since Old English, entering into the compound *belly-ache* around 1545–55, but the slang sense 'to complain' is not dated. *Blockhead* is similar. It arose from *block* + *head* to indicate 'a wooden stand for a wig'. But just how long did it take for the figurative sense of 'stupid person' to come about? The citations in the *Oxford English Dictionary* suggest that the transfer took place almost immediately. The original sense of the compound is now obsolete.

Sometimes a lexeme bursts into popularity and gets used in a much wider variety of contexts without really developing a new sense. Thus *awesome* became the all-purpose positive evaluation of the 1980s — from an *awesome dunk* to an *awesome haircut* to an *awesome shade of blue*. The very overuse of the term in this way becomes part of its meaning, and the time span of its popularity is essential to its history.

Lexicographers seldom have the data, space, or format to record more than an approximate date for a slang lexeme or to give multiple dates to trace the semantic changes a form undergoes. To supplement the brief, formulaic etymologies, the third edition of the *American Heritage Dictionary* inserts for selected lexemes a paragraph entitled *word history*, which discusses in prose important features of their semantic and chronological development. An example is at the entry *nerd*, which is attributed to Dr. Seuss in 1950. Regrettably, very few slang lexemes are accompanied by a *word history* box.

3.   Systematic Relationships with Other Lexemes

Perhaps for lexicographers the most challenging characteristic of slang lexemes is their tendency to occur in systematic relationships with other lexemes. Dictionaries have long included formal relationships among words, e.g. *block-head, blockheadedness, blockheadish, blockheadishness,* and *blockheadism.* But slang usually occurs in sets that are not simply formal variants among words.

Groups that use slang deliberately create synonymy and at any given time can summon numerous words and expressions for the same meaning. College students, for example, currently refer to a 'beer' as a *brew, brewdog, brewski, barley pop, ice pop,* and *cornflakes in a can.* The choice of one synonym rather than another is conditioned by such factors as the vogue of the term, the intention of the speaker, and the familiarity of the hearer. Although some of the lexemes in the set are related by form, the links that any speaker of English will make are metonymic and pragmatic. *Brew* is the process by which beer is made; beer is made from grains, like *barley*; and *cornflakes* are a common processed cereal made from the grain corn and packaged in a box.

Because slang is so attuned to culture, sometimes the knowledge a speaker must have to appreciate a lexeme is quite specific. Among the current slang synonyms for 'to leave' are *bolt, cruise,* and *jet* — all of which refer to movement and are fairly transparent. But *do the Heisman* requires that the hearer know about the Heisman trophy in football, and *Audi 5000* — made popular by the lyrics of rap music — calls to mind a model of automobile which began to move on its own. Three mock-honorifics achieved popularity because of the television program *Saturday Night Live*: *the X-meister, -san,* and *-ster*. These attach to a personal name to convey some air of pretended importance: *Here comes the Michael-meister /Michaelster/ Michaelsan.*

Often a set of synonymous slang lexemes develops from a controlling image or metaphor. One current set elaborates on cheese as a negative evaluation. 'A person who does not act appropriately' can be a *cheese, cheeseball, velveeta, cheese covered cornchip, captain cheddar, large cheddar,* or *fromage.* 'To act inappropriately' is to *cheese out*; and 'to belittle' is to *cheese on*. A comment that assigns someone to the cheese category is *gouda, gouda, gouda*! Form and function vary within the set; the link is a cognitive one.

Other synonymous lexemes are linked in part by form. The pattern *get an X* means 'become aware, take control': *get a clue, get a life, get a real life, get a job,* and *get a real job. Get a clue*, in turn, is linked with a set of lexemes for 'awareness' built around *clue*: *clueless* 'unaware'; *catch the clue bus* 'become aware'; and *a clue* 'someone who lacks awareness', perhaps a clipping of *a clueless person.*

Different members of a set can be motivated in different ways. A current slang term for 'sandals' is *Jesus gliders*, because of contemporary notions about the kind of shoes worn in the Middle East at the time of Christ. A variation based on the association of Jesus with the city of Jerusalem is *Jerusalem cruisers*. The most recent synonyms, *Air Jesus* and *Air Hebrews*, acquire their form by analogy with the widely-advertised and high-priced *Air Jordans*, which, by inference, help the famous basketball player Michael Jordan jump so high in the air. The *air* in *Air Jesus* and *Air Hebrews* evokes another association with air, that of ventilation because sandals are open.

Sometimes sound provides the link in a set. With the popularity of African-American comedians came the form *ho*, a dialect pronunciation of *whore*, for 'a promiscuous woman'. The same sequence of sounds, spelled *hoe*, refers to 'an implement for tilling the earth', i.e. a *garden tool*. Thus *ho* and *garden tool* are current slang synonyms for 'a promiscuous woman'.

Perhaps most akin to the kinds of constructions that Lamb sees as lexicalized are the highly productive fixed phrases in slang that attach to large classes of words. A current widespread example is the phrase *X from hell*, which can occur after almost any noun phrase to signal 'the best or worst example of': *My aerobics instructor has legs from hell. Last semester I had the history TA from hell.* Another is *go on an X run*, meaning 'leave for X or for the purpose of acquiring X': *I need to go on a post office run. Joe's going on a pizza run.* In each of these instances, hearers must use contextual and situational knowledge to interpret the phrase as intended by the speaker: the aerobics instructor is likely to have highly developed leg muscles; and the post office is certainly a destination rather than something to be acquired.

Because the type of lexeme commonly called slang relies heavily on social experience and on cognitive links, this ordinary kind of vocabulary presents challenges to grammarians and lexicographers alike.

References

The American Heritage Dictionary of the English Language. Second edition. 1982. Boston: Houghton-Mifflin Co.

Dumas, Bethany K. and Johnathan Lighter. 1978. Is slang a word for linguists? *American Speech* 53:5–17.

Eble, Connie C. 1985. Slang: Variations in dictionary labeling practices. *The Eleventh LACUS Forum 1984*, ed. by Robert A. Hall, Jr., 294–302. Columbia, South Carolina: Hornbeam Press.

Eble, Connie C. 1993. African-American contributions to American slang. *The Nineteenth LACUS Forum 1992*, ed. by Peter A. Reich, 371–378. Lake Bluff, Illinois: LACUS.

Flexner, Stuart Berg. (ed.) 1987. *Random House Dictionary of the English Language.* Second edition, unabridged. New York: Random House.

Hartmann, R. R. K. (ed.) 1983. *Lexicography: Principles and Practice.* London: Academic Press.

Landau, Sidney I. 1984. *Dictionaries: The Art and Craft of Lexicography.* New York: Charles Scribner's Sons.

McMillan, James B. 1978. American lexicology 1942–1973. *American Speech* 53:141–163.

Mish, Frederick (ed.). 1993. *Merriam Webster's Collegiate Dictionary.* Tenth edition. Springfield, Massachusetts: Merriam-Webster Inc.

Morris, William. (ed.) 1969. *The American Heritage Dictionary of the English Language.* First edition. Boston: Houghton-Mifflin Co.

Roark, Anne C. 1992. It's dope, so chill. *Los Angeles Times.* Aug. 18: E1, E5.

Soukhanov, Anne H. (ed.) 1992. *The American Heritage Dictionary of the English Language.* Third edition. Boston: Houghton-Mifflin Co.

Starnes, DeWitt, and Gertrude E. Noyes. 1946. *The English Dictionary from Cawdry to Johnson 1604–1755.* Chapel Hill: University of North Carolina Press.

About the author

Connie Eble has taught in the English Department of the University of North Carolina at Chapel Hill since 1971. She received her Ph.D. from that university in 1970, with a dissertation treating Old English noun inflections. From her teaching of morphology to prospective language arts teachers, she became interested in slang and in 1989 published **College Slang 101** *and in 1996* **Slang and Sociability: In-Group Language Among College Students**. *She has been President of the Southeastern Conference on Linguistics, and in 1996 became editor of* **American Speech**. *Her work on slang and vernacular English was encouraged by Syd Lamb, whom she met through the Linguistic Association of Canada and the United States, which she served as Secretary-Treasurer, 1993–1998.*

CHAPTER 30

On Sugar, Sumac and Sewers

F. W. Householder
Indiana University

In Householder 1992 I remarked on the fact that true phonetic change (Neogrammarian sound change) is possible only for basically oral words (in literate societies mainly learned in childhood), which I call type 1, while type 2 words, basically written (in languages like English) are the domain of many kinds of random change, especially spelling-pronunciation. We noted then the change which produced initial [š] in *sugar* and *sure*, commenting on the existence of another such word in eighteenth century English, *sewer* (regularly pronounced like *shore*, as we are told by both Sheridan (1780) and Walker (1791)), which must have been type 1 in London at that time. There is also a word *sumac*, for which both [š] and [sy] or [s] pronunciations are now attested, but which was not included in Johnson's dictionary (1785), and hence is not assigned a pronunciation by either Walker or Sheridan. But the examples in the Oxford English Dictionary (Simpson and Weiner 1989 — henceforth OED) show that initial [š] appears already in the sixteenth century, and that it dominates into the nineteenth. As for *sewer*, the OED editors doubt that '*shore*' is really a pronunciation of the same word and try to find another etymology for it. However, since sy > š is otherwise well attested (even for *suet*, and, dialectally at least, for *sue* and *suit*), and the vowel change also occurs by the eighteenth century in *sure*, there seems to be no need of a new etymology. Both Walker and Sheridan certainly believe *sewer* is the correct spelling, though *shore* represents the universal, if "corrupt" pronunciation of the word.

All this leads to the hypothesis of a regular sy > š change, in initial position as well as medially (in words like *tissue, fissure, noxious, censure*, for instance), limited basically to type 1 words, but also extended by some speakers to spelling pronunciations of type 2 words. Type 1 words, of, course, cannot "change back", but type 2 words, since they have no phonetic basis to change, are readily subject to new spelling pronunciations, which may or may not resemble earlier pronunciations. It is true, of course, that words may shift type, belonging to the illiterate vocabulary at one period and later to the learned vocabulary, or vice versa, and also that, at any time, certain words may belong to a boundary zone, being type 1 (often heard), for some speakers — e.g. U speakers — and type 2 (usually only read), for others — e.g. non-U, but these facts do not alter the basic proposition. An examination of the pronunciations (including those in the prefaces) in Walker 1791 and Sheridan 1780 will surprise many people both by the number of variant pronunciations which were the same then as now and by the number of cases where the preferred variant now (in either England or America) was then assigned to "affected", "fashionable" or "pedantic" pronunciation. Though some spelling pronunciations are reinvented repeatedly, others are, of course, sometimes transmitted.

What are the words, current in the sixteenth and seventeenth centuries, which might have been subject to a sound change sy > š in initial, pre-stress position? And is there evidence that such a change actually took place in words other than *sure, sugar, sumac* and *sewer*? First we must separate out two classes of words: (1) pure Latin expressions like *sui generis, suum cuique,* and the like; (2) Latin derivatives, changed only at the end, like *suicide, supreme, sudorific*. A third special type, words belonging to particular trades and crafts, is not represented in this group, but *boatswain, ensign* and *steelyard* in Walker are examples. Their peculiarity is that the speakers who have them as type 1 pronounce them in a more reduced manner than ordinary people (for whom they are type 2) are allowed (by Walker) to do.

The Latin derivatives beginning with *su-* (and *pseudo-*; there are none with *seu-* or *sew-*) are "sweat" words in *sud-, suicide,* words beginning in *super-* or *supra-, supine, supreme, susurr-, suture* and the compounds of *-sume* (with prefixes *as-* and *con-*; after *pre-* and *re-* the s becomes [z] or [ž]. They form a special class because OED lists no early pronunciations, and no misspellings or variant spellings (perhaps there were none), so that all our evidence must come from lexicographers. Walker gives [sy] for all of these, without exception; Sheridan, however, gives [š] for all except *assume* and *consume,* though he assigns [š] to *reassume,* a fact which Walker notes to Sheridan's discredit. (This difference between *assume* and *reassume* matches other differences which clearly indicate a lapse of time between Sheridan's vol. I (A-K) and II (L-Z), a time during which he evidently decided to generalize the palatal to fricative changes (sy > š, ty > č, zy > ž and dy > ǰ), though he still leaves some exceptions. This story, and our general lack of other evidence, leads us to ask the Bloomfieldian question, "are lexicographers prescriptive or descriptive?" (and perhaps the related Webster-III (Gove et al, 1961) question, "Which should they be?") The relevant remarks are found in the two prefaces, and in dozens of Walker's comments on individual words. On Sheridan's opening page (1780: 3) we find: "it became a work of immense time and labour, even to the best educated natives, to give a right pronunciation to words in reading" and "to enable all ... to acquire a just pronunciation of our tongue, is one of the main objects proposed in the following work". After the preface, Sheridan has an appendix which starts with a section dealing with the special errors made by speakers of Irish, Scottish and Welsh origin (and, in a kind of postscript, those from Somersetshire). In general this appendix is intended to "solve all difficulties in dubious cases". Here he says "In all disputable cases, preference has been given to that pronunciation which is most conformable to rule", and devotes the rest of the appendix to such rules. As one might guess, he very seldom allows two possible pronunciations for any word.

Neither does Walker, but he frequently mentions pronunciations which he rejects, and makes comments about the particular defect of each rejected pronunciation. Some of these are "vulgar", others "affected", "irregular", "solemn", "pedantic", "improper", "coarse", "corrupt", "incorrect", "too refined for the general ear", "contrary to custom and analogy", "quaint". He also objects to changing the spelling: under *skeptick* "I think conforming our spelling to a prevailing pronunciation, when this pronunciation is contrary to analogy, is pregnant with the greatest evils that can happen to a language". A similar remark occurs under *victuals*, although, under *hyssop* he says "therefore, if the mode I have adopted [sc. hísəp] be not the best, the orthography ought ... to be changed". I think he merely means that his pronunciation **is** the best. Quite clearly, then, both Sheridan and Walker are prescriptive about pronunciation (and also spelling, which both have taken, along with the word list, from Dr. Johnson), and believe in the primary argument from analogy (i.e. rules of pronunciation), though both also pay heed to what is "current", "firmly fixed", "universal", "frequent", "polite", "fashionable", "general", "learned", used by "every good speaker", by "people of refinement", by "polite speakers" in "the fashionable world". Walker is quite willing to disagree with famous men: with Swift under *wind* and *victuals* and Johnson (e.g.) under *skeptick* and *sinister*. So, while Walker's main criterion is conformity to (his) rules, he also takes into account the majority practice of educated Londoners, e.g. for *Rome* [ruwm] and *yes* [yɪs] (in both cases spelling pronunciation has won the day now, though *yes* might seem a reliable type 1 word).

So neither lexicon can support an argument *ex silentio*; the failure to mention some pronunciation of any given word is no proof that it was not in use. Returning now to the possible sy > š words listed above; Walker allows [š] only in *sure, sugar* and their derivatives; Sheridan keeps *sy* only in *sue, suit* and *assume* (but not *reassume*). Walker gives evidence for the existence of [š] pronunciations in the case of *insuperable*. This seems to suggest that Sheridan's preferred pronunciations are not entirely personal whims.

For some of these words, though not the barely altered Latin derivatives, the OED provides evidence, in the shape of *sh* spellings, as follows: (1) for *sudary* (not in Walker or Sheridan), a kind of kerchief, *shouldarie* is attested from 1500; (2) for *suet* there are at least three *sh-* spellings (*showitt, shewet* and *shuet*) from 1563, 1615, 1634; for *sue, shue* is attested; for *suit* five different spellings (*shute, shutte, shuite, shuett*) from 1552, 1579 and 1688 (plus *shoot* in dialog from 1862); for *sure* we have *shure* from 1602, for *sugar*, *sh-* spellings from 1682, and for *sumac* several from 1586, 1600, 1612, 1634, 1655. The evidence suggests that the change *sy* to *š* in all such words took place in the sixteenth century, that *š*-forms continued to be used in the seventeenth and eighteenth, but that *sy* spelling-pronunciations continually arose in the seventeenth and eighteenth, and were victorious in the cases of *sue, suit* and most of the Latin derivatives in the early eighteenth century. I think it is fair to say that *sue, suit* and the Latin words were all type 2 at that time. (In my childhood, because of the expression 'union suit', *suit* was probably type 1.) It is also fair to say that *sure* and *sugar* have always been type 1, but *sewer* (where OED lists the *shore* examples as etymologically different) and *sumac* are not so clear. In London, at least, *sewer* must have been type 1, and *sumac* must have been type 1 for country people. But, at any rate, it was not either Latin or French, so [š] was not quite eliminated. The word is the only one for which competition between [š] and [sy] (and, in some places, [s]) still exists. Of the seven dictionaries cited in Webster II (Neilson et al. 1960: lxxvi) only Hempl shows a single pronunciation [sy], and Jones shows three ([šuː], [syuː], and [suː]), as does Wentworth 1944 (though he rejects the [sy] version for American dialects). The most similar case in Walker is *duke*, for which he rejects both [džuːk] and [duːk].

We might briefly now sum up the situation in Walker and Sheridan (1) for unstressed *su* and (2) for stressed and unstressed *tu, du* and voiced *su* (*zu* occurs only in *azure*, which is [æžr] or [æžuːr] for almost everyone, though Jones allows [æzyĕr] also).

(1) Walker's rule (1791: 54) for [sy] vs. [š] is simple: if the following vowel is stressed, [sy] remains unchanged except for *sure*, *sugar* and their derivatives; if unstressed, it goes to [š]. Sheridan agrees with the unstressed rule in general, but disagrees by preferring [sy] in *insular*, *alliciency*, *antonomasia*, *capsular* etc., *commensurate* etc., and *exudation*; Walker does so only in *exudation*. All these words are in Sheridan's first volume. But Sheridan also prefers [š] before stressed vowel, except in *sue*, *ensue*, *pursue*, *suit*, *pursuit*, *assume*, *consume*, *caesura*, *hirsute*, (accented on ultima), *cynosure*, *insuperable* (etc.), *exuperable* (etc.), of which only *sue*, *suit* and their derivatives are in volume II.

The voiced examples agree: *luxurious* etc. (where accent is on the second syllable) have [ž] in Sheridan, [zy] in Walker, though luxury has [š] in both. Similarly with *presume*, *resume*, etc. and *zeugma*, Walker has [zy]. Sheridan [ž], though both have [zy] in *exuberant* etc. and *exuviae* (Vol. I for Sheridan). Unstressed, they agree on [ž].

The choice between [č] and [ty] is not quite as well determined, though Walker flatly excludes [č] from stressed position, where Sheridan prefers it, at least in volume II (with the exception of *mature*, *premature* and *serrature*). In volume I he generally follows Walker's rule (1791: 55) that, in -*ture*, [č] occurs immediately after the accent, as in *creature*, but not after an unstressed syllable, as in *furniture*. Walker holds Sheridan's rendering of *tune* (etc.) as [čuwn] in contempt, but seems to like [tuwn] even less, and probably felt the same way about *Tuesday*.

For [dy] vs. [ǰ] Sheridan agrees almost perfectly with Walker: no stressed [ǰ] (except in *produce* and its derivatives — but not in *reduce* or *seduce* or *traduce*) but in post-stress position [ǰ] occurs in both. However, there are several words where Walker has [ǰ], while Sheridan favors [dy]: *assiduous* etc., *educate* etc., *audience*; and a longer list where Walker allows both [dy] and [ǰ], but Sheridan only [ǰ]: *audience*, *medium*, *module* etc., *radiant* etc., and a few more. On *Indian* both are agreed on [dy], but we know of the [ǰ] pronunciation from other sources; clearly the current variation in the eighteenth century is not perfectly captured by either Walker or Sheridan.

This kind of variation ([ty] vs. [č], [sy] vs. [š], [dy] vs. [ǰ]) is always a mark of type 2 words, or else of words in transition from type 1 to type 2 (so perhaps *sumac*, and most of the *sh*- spellings cited above from OED).

In the end, only *sugar, sure* and their derivatives or compounds have been continuously type 1 from the sixteenth century on, and Walker recognizes their unique status, though without assigning an explanation. In a sense, these words are exceptions to his rules, whereas, from a historical linguistics perspective, they are regular and all the rest are exceptions. But they are not really dialect borrowings, as Bloomfield thought; there is no spelling pronunciation "dialect". And there is no phonological change of [š] to [sy], [č] to [ty], or [ǰ] to [dy]; in a sense you can speak of "rule addition" but it is concerned only with rules for spelling-pronunciation, not phonological rules. And since only *sure, sugar* and ten or twelve of their derivatives remain unaffected, only they are truly type 1, as against about 120 or so words in Walker with stressed initial *su-, sew-* or *pseu-* pronounced even today [syuw-] or [suw-], which are type 2, we may ask whether this ten-to-one ratio holds throughout the vocabulary?

Appendices

Appendix: Type Ratios in Spoken English

Many guesses have been made about the relative frequency in English of type 1 (basically oral) and type 2 (basically written) vocabularies, or about the number of words in a pre-school child's vocabulary (which is a closely related matter), but I have spent a good bit of time this year in producing another estimate. Out of several available collections of spoken English, I chose Dahl 1979, which analyzed the vocabulary in transcripts of recordings of 15 psychoanalyitic cases (each involving a number of interviews), consisting of dialogs between the patients (seven female and eight male) and psychoanalysts (one female, 13 male) in eight cities of the United states. The complete corpus was not analyzed, but only 15 randomly selected sessions from each patient-psychoanalyst pair. For linguistic purposes some choices made by Dahl must be allowed for: (1) each inflected form is counted as a different word, including possessives; (2) references to an individual person are represented by code letters (e.g. "NLR") and count as instances of an English word; (3) false starts, unfinished words, are represented with a final dash (e.g. "wou — ") and count as distinct words; (4) homographs, on the other hand, count as one word — e.g. *lead* [liyd] or [led]. Making allowances for all these things involves reducing the total number of types (i.e. lexemes) by five or ten percent, though not so much for tokens, since few of these items occur more than two or three times, and many only once. All of these things combined with the uncertainty of some classifications ("Is word *x* basically oral or written?" and human fallibility make the following figures only a little less unsatisfactory than previous guesses. Incidentally, there are clearly two distinct kinds of oral words, those learned in early childhood and those which are slang or obscene. The latter are usually obvious, while for the former I considered whether my young granddaughter used the word and whether I remembered using it as a child. The increase of television-watching in recent years makes some of these choices even more difficult.

Dahl gives the total number of tokens as 1,058,888, which I would reduce to a round million by throwing out inflected forms, individuals and false starts; The number of word-types (lexemes), given as 17,871, which I would reduce to 17,000. The partition between my type 1 and type 2 is given in Table 1 (based on marking every item in the list as one or the other or as an item to be rejected).

Table 1: Estimate of Numbers of Type 1 and Type 2 Lexemes

	Lexemes	Tokens
Type 1	5,000	927,000
Type 2	12,000	73,000

The 20 words with the highest number of tokens per type, ranging from 8,300 up to 65,000, are these: *I, and, the, to, that, you, it, of, a, know, was, uh, in, but, is, this, me, about, just, don't*. These twenty account for over 400,000 occurrences. There are no type 2 words in the 350 most frequent words except perhaps *father* and *mother*, which are surely known by most 3– year old kids, but hardly ever used by them.

References

Dahl, Hartwig. 1979. Word Frequencies of Spoken American English. *Verbatim*. (Distributed by Gale Research Co., Detroit, Michigan)

Gove, Philip Babcock, et al. 1961. *Webster's Third New International Dictionary*, Third edition. (*Webster III*). Springfield, Mass., G. and C. Merriam Company.

Householder, F. W. 1992. Pronunciation rules and improper sound change. *Who Climbs the Grammar Tree?* ed. by Rosemarie Tracy, 77–91. Tübingen: Niemeyer.

Johnson, Samuel. 1785. *A Dictionary of the English Language* — 6th edition. London, J. F. and C. Rivington, L. Davis (etc.)

Neilson, W. A., T. A. Knott and P. W. Carhart, (eds.). 1932. *Webster's New International Dictionary*, Second Edition, (*Webster II*) Springfield, Mass., G. & C. Merriam Publishers.

Simpson, J. A., and E. S. C. Weiner (preparers). 1989. *The Oxford English Dictionary*, Second Edition. Oxford: Clarendon Press.

Sheridan, Thomas. 1780. *A General Dictionary of the English Language*. London, J. Dodsley, C. Dilly, and J. Wilkie. (Reprint by the Scolar Press Limited, Menston, England, 1967)

Walker, John. 1791. *A Critical Pronouncing Dictionary*. London, G.G.J. and J. Robinson, and T. Cadell. (Reprint by the Scolar Press Limited, Menston, England, 1968)

Wentworth, Harold. 1944. *American Dialect Dictionary*. New York: Thomas Y. Crowell Co.

About the author

Fred W. Householder, Jr. died on January 4, 1994. He was Research Professor Emeritus of Linguistics and Classics and Professor of Central Eurasian Studies at Indiana University, where he taught from 1948 until his retirement in 1983. He received his doctorate from Columbia in 1941, and held teaching positions there and at Allegheny College before going to Indiana. Accomplishments over his distinguished career included the presidency of the Linguistic Society of America in 1981 and several visiting appointments at other universities. His acquaintance with Syd Lamb, beginning in the 1960s, involved primarily exchanges of information about funding for computer-based linguistic research.

CHAPTER 31

Why *Kaka* and *Aya*?

Merritt Ruhlen
Stanford University

It has long been known that the nursery words *mama* and *papa* are widely distributed around the world and the general consensus has been that such similarities are due to convergence rather than common origin. Convergence, however, is not generally characteristic of linguistic evolution — since the sound/meaning relationship is arbitrary — unlike biological evolution where the convergent similarity of bats and birds (or fish and dolphins) is motivated by the environment. How then can we explain the linguistic convergence of terms such as *mama* and *papa*? In 1959 Roman Jakobson (1960) suggested an answer based on the order of development of consonants in child language. Jakobson argued that since *m-* and *p-* are among the earliest consonants produced by children learning language, they would quite naturally come to be associated with the mother and father regardless of the specific language being learned. This putative explanation has won general favor in the linguistic community, but I would like to suggest in this short essay that Jakobson's explanation is subject to doubt.

The problem with Jakobson's explanation is that there are other nursery words, of comparable distribution, that do not seem susceptible to the same explanation. For example, there is a widespread root based on velar consonants, *kaka* or the like, that is found at least in Eurasia, Oceania, and the Americas (and perhaps elsewhere since I have not made an exhaustive search); its most usual meaning is 'older male relative, older brother, uncle'. The following data are taken from Ruhlen (1994b).

KAKA 'older brother, uncle'

Uralic-Yukaghir: Yukaghir *aka* 'older brother', Proto-Uralic **ekä* 'older male relative, uncle'.

Altaic: Proto-Altaic *āka* 'older brother', Proto-Turkic *āka* 'older brother', Mongolian *aqa* 'older brother', Tungus *akā* 'brother'.

Ryukyuan *aka* 'older brother'.

Ainu *ak/aki* 'younger brother'.

Gilyak *ikin* 'older brother'.

Sino-Tibetan: Proto-Tibeto-Burman *ik* 'older brother'.

Maio-Yao: Proto-Yao *kɔ* 'older brother'.

Austronesian: Proto-Austronesian *kaka* 'older brother'.

Amerind: Almosan: Nisqualli *kukh* 'older brother', Okanagan *kīka* 'older sister', Shuswap *kix* 'older sister', Kalispel *qax̄e* 'maternal aunt', Kutenai *kokt* 'maternal aunt'; **Keresiouan:** Seneca *-hak* 'aunt', Tuscarora *gus-xahg* 'paternal aunt', Adai *ahhi* 'aunt', Hidatsa *ika* 'aunt'; **Penutian:** Alsea *hāʔt* 'older brother', Bodega Miwok *kaaka* 'uncle', Southern Sierra Miwok *kaka* 'uncle', Yuki *kīk-an* 'maternal uncle', Tfalatik *kaka* 'aunt', Zuni *kaka* 'maternal uncle', Natchez *kāka* 'older brother', Mixe *ahč* 'older brother', Sayula *axč* 'older brother, uncle', Kekchí *as'* 'older brother', Zoque *ʔatˢi* 'older brother', Totonac *kuku* 'uncle'; **Hokan:** Achomawi *kex* 'uncle', East Pomo *kēq* 'uncle', North Pomo *-ki-* 'older brother', Kashaya *-ki-* 'older brother', Salinan *kaai* 'older brother', Karok *xukam* 'uncle', Jicaque *kokam* 'uncle'; **Central Amerind:** Tewa *koʔō* 'aunt', Varohio *kukuri* 'paternal uncle', *ka'ká* 'maternal aunt', Ixcatec *kwaʔa* 'aunt'; **Chibchan:** Tirub *kega* 'uncle', *kak* 'aunt', Matagalpa *kuku-ke* 'uncle', Paya *uku* 'uncle', Kagaba *kukui* 'aunt, niece'; **Andean:** Ona *kakan* 'paternal aunt'; **Macro-Tucanoan:** Yeba *kako* 'uncle', Masaca *kokomai* 'uncle'; **Equatorial:** Waraicu *ghuk* 'uncle', Manao *ghooko* 'maternal uncle', Sanamaika *koko* 'uncle', Mashco *kokoa* 'uncle', Kushichineri *koko* 'uncle', Cuniba *kuku* 'uncle', Bare *koko* 'aunt', Canamari *ghughu* 'uncle', Piro *koko* 'uncle'; **Macro-Carib:** Apiaca *koko* 'uncle', Bakairi *kxuɣu* 'uncle', Pimenteira *kuckú* 'uncle'; **Macro-Panoan:** Cavinena *ekoko* 'uncle', Panobo *kuka* 'uncle', Pacawara *kuko* 'uncle'; **Macro-Ge:** Palmas *kēke-* 'older sibling', Apucarana *kanki* 'older brother', Oti *koaka* 'brother'.

There is another nursery word with the general shape *aya* and the general meaning 'older female relative, older sister, aunt, grandmother' that is even more widespread than the *kaka* root. The following data are adapted from Bengtson and Ruhlen (1994).

AYA 'older sister, aunt, grandmother, mother'

Khoisan: ≠ Au.//ei *ai* 'female, mother', !Kung *ʔai* 'mother'; Naron *ai* 'mother', Hadza *aiya* ~ *aiyako* 'mother, grandmother, aunt'; /ˈAuni *aiya* 'mother'.

Niger-Congo: Yoruba *iya* 'mother'; **Bantu:** Proto-Bantu *yíyà* ~ *yíyò* 'mother'.

Nilo-Saharan: Saharan: Daza *aya* 'mother', Kanembu *yia* ~ *ya*, Kanuri *ya*; Fur *iya*; **Maban:** Runga *ya*; **Koman:** Gumuz *iyo*; **Central Sudanic:** Mangbetu *aya*, Madi *ia*, Lombi *yaiya*; **East Sudanic:** Gulfan *aya*, Midob *iya*, Suk *iyu*, Nyangiya *yoiyao* 'thy mother'.

Afro-Asiatic: Omotic: Wolamo *ayē* 'mother'; **Cushitic:** Oromo *ayo*, Somali *hooyo*; **Chadic:** Kotoko *īya* ~ *iya* ~ *ya*, Mubi *íyà*.

Dravidian: Tamil *āy* ~ *āyi* ~ *yay* 'mother', *āyāḷ* 'mother, grandmother', Kannada *āyi*, Kolami *ay*, Parji *ayal* 'woman, wife', *iya* 'mother', Gadba *aya* 'mother', *ayal* 'woman, wife', Gondi *ayal* 'mother', Konda *aya*, Pengo *aya* ~ *iya*, Manda *aya*, Kui *aia* ~ *aya* ~ *iya*, Kuwi *īya* 'mother', *aya* 'woman', Kurux *ayaŋg* ~ *ayo*, Malto *aȳa* 'my mother'.

Burushaski *-ʌi* 'daughter, girl'.

? **Indo-Pacific:** Isabi *aiyo* 'mother', Korafe *aya* 'mother'.

Nahali *ayi* 'husband's younger sister'.

Austroasiatic: Munda: Sora *ayaŋ-tsɔr* 'bitch' (= female-dog, cf. *kin-tsɔr* 'male dog'); **Mon-Khmer:** Proto-Mon-Khmer *yaʔ* 'grandmother'.

Miao-Yao: Proto-Yao *ya* 'father's sister'.

Daic: Tai: Proto-Tai *ya* 'father's mother'; Sek *ya* 'father's mother'; **Kam-Sui:** Proto-Kam-Sui *ya* 'grandmother', Sui *ya* 'grand-mother, old woman'; **Li:** Proto-Li *ya* 'mother, grandmother', Small Cloth Loi *ya* 'mother'; Lakkia *yə* 'grandmother'.

Austronesian: Proto-Austronesian *ˈayah* 'father', Atayal *yayaʔ* 'mother', Pazeh *yah* 'older sister', Malay *ˈayah* 'father', Javanese *(y)ayah* 'father'.

Amerind: Penutian: North Sahaptin *áyaD* 'woman', Nez Perce *ʔayat* 'woman', Tzotzil *yaya* 'grandmother'; **Hokan:** Washo *-ya* 'paternal aunt', Quinigua *ʔyaak* 'paternal aunt', Tonkawa *ʔeyan* 'woman's sister'; **Central Amerind:** Tewa *yia* 'mother', Proto-Oto-Manguean *ya* 'female', Proto-Uto-Aztecan *ye* 'mother', Tarahumara *iye* 'mother', Yaqui *ʔaiye* 'mother', Nahua *-yeʔ* 'mother'; **Chibchan-Paezan:** Xinca *aya* 'woman', Matagalpa *yoaya* 'woman', Cuna *yaa-kwa* 'young woman', Colorado *aya* 'mother'; **Andean:** Ona *yoy* 'grandmother', Auca *-yæ̃yæ̃* 'grandmother'; **Macro-Tucanoan:** Amaguaje *ayo* 'old woman', Masaka *yaya* 'older sister', Ticuna *yake* 'old woman'; **Equatorial:** Mapidiana *aya* 'aunt', Tora *iye* 'paternal grand-mother', Arikem *haya* 'aunt'; **Macro-Panoan:** Mayoruna *yaya* 'aunt',

Shipibo *yaya* 'paternal aunt', Moseten *eye* 'grandmother', *yaya* 'mother-in-law'; **Macro-Carib:** Accawai *aya* 'mother'; **Macro-Ge:** Coropo *ayan* 'mother', Coroado *ayan* 'mother', Palmas *yā* 'mother'.

In both of these roots there are cases where the gender seems to have switched polarity, e.g. Bare *koko* 'aunt' and Proto-Austronesian **'ayah* 'father'. Such polarity switching is not unusual in kinship terms (for additional examples, see Ruhlen 1994a). Even with *mama* and *papa* polarity switching is not unknown, e.g. Proto-Kartvelian **mama* 'father'.

If we are to extend Jakobson's explanation to take care of these examples, we must hypothesize that older male relatives somehow appear on the scene at the moment the child is learning velar consonants, which are not particularly early in their development, while older female relatives somehow come to be associated with *aya*. It does not seem to me plausible that human society could be organized so neatly — or could follow the child's phonological development so strictly — as to account for these regularities. Furthermore, there are other well known examples that have to be accounted for, e.g. *tata* ~ *dada* 'father', *nana* 'older female relative'. That all of these specific sound/meaning relationships are due to the order of development of consonants in child language seems to me unlikely. Rather I believe we must recognize that similarities among such forms have a much higher genetic component than has previously been recognized. There may well be a germ of truth in Jakobson's explanation of *mama* and *papa*, but this explanation cannot reasonably be extended to *kaka* and *aya*, and because of this even its appropriateness for *mama* and *papa* is suspect.

References

Bengtson, John D., and Merritt Ruhlen. 1994. Global etymologies. Ruhlen 1994c: 277–336.

Jakobson, Roman. 1960. Why *mama* and *papa*. *Perspectives in Psychological Theory, Essays in Honor of Heinz Werner,* ed. by Bernard Kaplan and Seymour Wapner, 124–134. New York; International Universities. Reprinted in Roman Jakobson. 1960. *Studies on Child Language and Aphasia*, 21–29 (Janua Linguarum Series Minor 1/4) The Hague: Mouton.

Ruhlen, Merritt. 1994a. Amerind T'A?NA 'child, sibling'. Ruhlen 1994c. 183–206.

Ruhlen, Merritt. 1994b. Linguistic origins of Native Americans. Ruhlen 1994c. 207–241.

Ruhlen, Merritt, (ed.). 1994c. *On the Origin of Languages: Studies in Linguistic Taxonomy*. Stanford: Stanford University Press.

About the author

Merritt Ruhlen is currently a lecturer in Human Biology at Stanford University. He received his Ph.D. in linguistics from Stanford in 1973, working under Charles Ferguson, Joseph Greenberg, and Alphonse Juilland. His connections to Syd Lamb relate to their common interests in language classification. They first met at the Rice Symposium treating this topic in 1986. Ruhlen is best known as an outspoken supporter of Greenberg's approach to distant relationship, as reflected in three recent books: A Guide to the World's Languages (1987), The Origin of Language (1994), and On the Origin of Languages (1994)

PART II

C. History of Linguistics and Culture

CHAPTER 32

Medieval Views on the World and Nature

Edgar C. Polomé
University of Texas at Austin

How did medieval man see nature? What were his cosmological concepts? A whole encyclopedic literature shows us what the average intelligent, educated layman wanted to know, and a fourteenth century moralist describes it in the following terms: "the course of the stars, the foundation of the earth, the power of herbs, the complexions of men, and a knowledge of whatever there is in the heavens, on earth and in hell..."

Where did this wisdom come from? After the collapse of the ancient world, the heritage of Rome and Greece only survived fragmentarily in the west, first in its reflexes in the early Christian literature, later through the writings of the Syrians, the Jews and the Arabs, and like the latter, the scholars of Western Europe became disciples of Plato through the Church Fathers and the *Timaeus* of Chalcidius, and of Aristotle through his Islamic commentators. The success of Aristotle was tremendous and his views on the structure of the universe and the theory of the elements were accepted as God's truth, preventing any further investigation in this field. Like Pythagoras, he conceived the movement of the heavenly bodies as the rotation of homocentric spheres around a central motionless Earth. The four elements of Empedocles — earth, water, air, and fire — combined with the four "properties" of matter — heat, cold, dryness, and moisture — were the key to all nature. Moreover, fire was supposed to **tend** to go **spontaneously** "upwards", towards the periphery of the cosmos, water and air to the intermediate regions, and "earth" downwards, to the center — a belief which contradicted the Aristotelian notion of the **total passivity of matter** which could only be moved by an **outside** motor. It was thought that whatever was above the circle of the moon was part of divine immutability and eternity: only the sublunar world was affected by change.

The *Physics* of Aristotle — erroneous as it might have been both in principle and in detail — struck the medieval mind with its neat pseudo-explanations which put everything in order with dialectic virtuosity in a majestic universal synthesis: they could be meshed perfectly well with the teachings of the Bible in the west as they had been coordinated with the Quran in the Islamic world by Averroës and others.

The prototypes of the books which would tell medieval man about the system of the universe, the "properties" of things and the marvels of nature are the works of Pliny the Elder, Solinus (third century A.D.) and Martianus Capella (end of the fifth century A.D.). The first compilations of ancient lore produced in the Germanic kingdoms after the collapse of the Roman Empire are the celebrated *Etymologies* of Isidorus of Sevilla, dedicated to the king of the Visigoths in Spain in the early seventh century A.D.; the *De natura rerum* of the Venerable Bede, a monk of Wearmouth in England (died 735), and the *De universo* of Hrabanus Maurus, the abbot of Fulda in Germany (died 856).

With the twelfth century Renaissance, there was a blossoming of similar works, some mediocre like the *Liber Floridus* of Lambert of Saint-Omer (died 1120), some very important by the influence they exerted, like the *Imago mundi* of a certain recluse called Honorius, and the *Philosophia mundi* of Guillaume de Conches (died 1153). At the turn of the thirteenth century, two Englishmen produced important works: Gervase of Tilbury, *Otia Imperialia* (he was chancellor of emperor Otto IV), and Alexander Neckam, *De naturis rerum* (he was abbot of Circencester, died 1217). Then came the monumental medieval encyclopedia of Bartholomaeus Anglicus, *De proprietatibus rerum*; Thomas de Cantimpré, *De rerum natura*; Vincent de Beauvais, *Speculum naturale*, leading up to the great scholastic *Summae* of Albertus Magnus, Thomas Aquinas, etc.

Most of these works are sheer compilations, of attentive and painstaking authors who display no originality nor personality in their writing, but occasionally direct observations and personal remarks are inserted, e.g., by Bede and Guillaume de Conches. Others try to gather materials to please or astonish the reader; their work is essentially didactic and edifying, e.g., Isidorus, Gervase of Tilbury, Alexander Neckam. More specifically: some writers point out the correspondences between natural phenomena and religious and moral "truths" in order to guide man in his earthly life and to help him interpret the symbols of the Scripture (e.g., Bartholomaeus Anglicus, Thomas de Cantimpré).

Since direct observation of the phenomena and description of factual evidence was out of the question when it came to talk about nature, translations from the works inherited from classical Antiquity were the basic sources, but those bestiaries, lapidaries, and herbariums were glossed with symbolic interpretations: as early as the first quarter of the twelfth century, Philippe de Thaon was reciting (with hurdy-gurdy accompaniment) "natural histories" in the shape of poems based on late Latin models. Rhyming natural history became a common activity for the clerics attached to princely houses: thus, Simon of Boulogne, working for the count Baudouin of Guines (died 1206), translated Solinus in verse for him. The work is lost, but we have other samples such as the *Philosophie la petite* by a minstrel called Pierre de Beauvais who was in the pay of the princes of Dreux before 1218. Very celebrated is the translation of the apocryphal letter of Priest John on the marvels of his State, due to recent events involving emperor Frederick Barbarossa (Redbeard) and the "East Roman" emperor Manuel Comnenus, and including the current fantasies about the lands beyond the *orbis romanus*. Also very popular was the pseudo-Aristotelian *Secreta Secretorum*, a Syrian fake, composed of fragments of ancient lore, almost unrecognizable through their alteration, but presented as the quintessence of ancient wisdom. There are also translations of such works as Bartholomaeus Anglicus's *De Proprietatis Rerum* by Jehan Corbechon or Thomas de Cantimpré's *Speculum naturale* by Conrad von Megenberg *(Das Puch der Nature)*; the only more original compilation in a western language is Brunetto Latini's *Li Livres dou Tresor*, a work that directly influenced Dante. Different again are the works in dialogue form: *Sidrac* and *Placides et Timeo*. Though unsystematic and sometimes difficult to follow, they differ from the other works by their freer style, their relative harshness to the verge of cynicism, their basic neglect of important facts, all of this foreboding changes in views and trends.

Altogether there are three types of works relevant to our topic:

(a) writings of the philosophers and "technicians" of cosmology and natural science;

(b) works for clerics involving the tenets of the Christian doctrine;

(c) literature for laymen, translations and presentations in a style accessible to the reader.

It is however, this last category which best reflects the views on the world current in the medieval society of the twelfth till the fourteenth centuries: they were the books written for and read by those who shaped that society, and if we had any doubt as to the validity of this statement, we would simply have to remember how these concepts permeated the writings of the great authors, from Chaucer to Milton: was it not usual in Elizabethan times to be

> Talking of stones, stars, plants, of fishes, flies:
> Playing with words and idle similes...?

And is this not the very topic Bartholomaeus Anglicus devotes his *Liber de Proprietatibus Rerum* to? When King Lear asks: "Why the seven stars are no more than seven? What is the cause of thunder? How an oyster makes his shell", his questions seem to come straight out of the *Book of Sidrac*. And in *Paradise Lost* II. 898, Milton tells us how

> Hot, Cold, Moist and Dry, four champions fierce,
> Strive here for Maistrie...

* * * * *

In order to fully appreciate the views of medieval man, it might be useful to examine somewhat more closely the contents of some of the texts mentioned. Let us start with a very simple type, the so-called *Bestiaire moralisé* of Philippe de Thaon, actually a French adaptation of the anonymous *Physiologus* ('The Naturalist') and the accompanying alphabetically ordered *Lapidaire*, based on the work of Damigeron (a first century A.D. Greek author). The influence of Isidorus of Sevilla is clearly visible in various parts, and Philippe de Thaon reports the most fantastic stories without even wincing, e.g., on the **ant**, whose zeal Solomon praised: it gathers wheat for the winter — **not** barley, which it does not care for. This brings about a comparison with the story of the wise virgins: *put away for winter* is reserve for **Doomsday**; *wheat* is the word of **God**; *barley* is heresy! He then goes on to say:

> Isidorus adds that ants carry heavier loads in proportion to their size than camels and dromedaries. They can also screen healthy grain which they store, from spoiled grain which they reject. In Ethiopia there are ants as big as dogs; they collect gold powder in a river there, but no one can approach their hoard without being bitten and dying from it. The people of the land have devised a trick: they send to these ants mares which have just foaled, loaded with open trunks; the ants fill these trunks with gold; then, they make the colts whinny and the mares come to them in a gallop...

Another example is his entry for **ibex** (actually, a wild mountain goat with long curved horns) which he confuses with **ibis** (a large wading bird of the heron family):

Stork of the Nile, lives of carrion, cannot swim, collects dead fish on the shores. When necessary, gives itself an enema with its beak.

To which the allegorical explanation is added:

the man who cannot swim in the spiritual waters and refuses the food of the Scripture, also lives of carrion! — Men, spread your wings! Lift your hands to the sky to worship God!

As for the reference to enemas, it alludes to "flatterers who speak well in front of you and lie behind your back!"

The description of stones is in the same vein: **Chelidonium** (a fictitious stone, assumed to be found in the gizzard of swallows — Gk. *khelidôn* means 'swallow') comes in two varieties, black and reddish-brown. The latter, tied to the left arm with a piece of cloth will heal "languor", lunacy and deliriousness; it makes one eloquent and amorous. The black one makes you succeed in the world, and wrapped up in a red cloth, it is a fever remedy; in powder in water, it is used as eyewash; it also helps pregnant women's delivery. But the swallows that supply the chelidonium have to be caught in their flight, without touching the soil! As for the **Magnet**, iron-colored, it attracts iron; it is found in the waters of the Jordan. "It is used to test the faithfulness of wives. Put this stone on the head of your wife while she sleeps. If she is virtuous, she will turn on her stomach; otherwise, on her back. It also cures dropsy, but makes whoever 'drinks' it three times (man or woman) impotent or sterile. Thieves use it to scare and make the people living in a house they intend to break into, flee", because this stone put on burning coal will give to whoever breathes its fumes the impression that everything is going to collapse.

The *Letter of Priest John*, a document allegedly sent to the emperor Manuel Comnemus, was based on the rumor spread in the West that there was a very powerful Christian king-priest in Asia. The oldest information relevant to this legend is the mention of a "patriarch of India" brought to Rome in 1122 by agents of the Pope who met him in Byzantium, where he had come to study the ceremony for the installation of patriarchs. The data he provided about his country amazed the Church authorities in Rome, and an anonymous record of his alleged address to Pope Calliste II has been preserved. Twenty-three years later, Pope Eugene III was in Viterbo, when a Syrian bishop paid him a visit and talked to bishop Otto von Freisingen, uncle of the German emperor Frederick Barbarossa, about a certain John, a Nestorian Christian, a priest-king whose territory was situated beyond Persia and Armenia *in extremo Oriente*, where he had defeated the Persians and tried to come and rescue the Holy Land, without success, however. From then on, the legend grew and spread: in 1165, chronicles mention letters sent by priest John to Manuel, emperor of Constantinople, and to emperor Frederick Barbarossa; in 1177, Pope Alexander III had the Pontifical Chancery write a letter to "our very dear son John, illustrious and magnificent king of India". Of course, no answer ever came... But faith in the existence of the mythical kingdom persisted and the Crusaders, while in the Holy Land, tried again to contact it and to obtain its support. And Marco Polo looked all over Asia for it...

The *Letter of Priest John* contains descriptions of the most curious people and beasts:

> there are birds strong enough to carry a whole ox to their brood, and eagles whose wings are fire-colored and sharp like razors. ... We have horned men; others with only one eye; others with eyes in front and behind their head. ... But the river Physon which flows from Paradise cannot be waded by live people who have only the size of 6 year old children; their horses are only as big as sheep; they are Christians and their enemies are birds which attack them every year when the crops are ripe, and they fight bloody battles with each other...

One of the favorite myths about this kingdom was the "fountain of youth":

> At the foot of Mount Olympus there is a spring whose water tastes like all the spices of the world, one after the other; it comes from Paradise. If you drink three times from it on an empty stomach, you will no longer be ill, and whatever your age may be, you will be again as you were when you were 30.

It was an idyllic society: no poor people; everybody was cozy; foreigners were welcome guests; no thieves, no scoundrels, no deceivers, no misers, because all property was shared by the community. They claimed they had only few horses, but, then, they pretended they could line up 10,000 knights and 200,000 infantry, plus all the helpers, to fight the pagans...

Of a different character is the compilation ascribed to Ibn Yahya Al-Batrik (died 815) and assigned to Aristotle, which became known in the West via a Latin translation made by a Spanish Jew in Sevilla in the early twelfth century Another version of the Arabic text was acquired by a cleric, called Philip, who was in the service of an English priest (Guy de Vere) in the Middle East in the first half of the thirteenth century, and directly channeled to Roger Bacon, who used it for his comment on the *Secreta secretorum* written in about 1243.

Nobody ever doubted that the text was Aristotle's; whatever appeared wrong or improbable was ascribed to translators. The success of the work was tremendous: it was translated into French, English, Welsh, Dutch, German, Italian, Castilian, Catalan, Provençal, etc.

The basic idea of the book is to provide a guide to "princes and kings on the art of governing", allegedly compiled by Aristotle for his pupil, Alexander of Macedonia. It contains a lot of wise saws and anecdotal knowledge: "to govern is to see ahead" — avoid fickleness and sudden change of mood; admit your mistakes when necessary; don't act too fast, nor too late — Alexander, do prefer incorruptible treasures over perishable goods. Avoid the fierceness of the lion, and especially the filth of the pig. Speak well, but little...

Interesting is the position of the author versus **astrology**:

> Galenus and Isidorus point out that a good doctor needs to be an astronomer. Do not believe the fools who say that no man can attain the knowledge of the stars and the planets because of their distance. The continuous research of Antiquity has accounted for the movements of the heavenly bodies. On the other hand, do not believe the fools who claim that God has foreseen and regulated everything that will happen. The elements are governed by the stars and the planets: the action of the moon on the ebb and flow of the tides shows and proves it; the mussel which is of the nature of water among all animals, waxes and wanes with the moon. This is the reason why it is advisable to know the movements of the heavenly bodies to foresee the phenomena in this lower world. If the planets indicate that the winter will be cold, one should get supplies to be prepared for it. It is therefore absurd to pretend that the knowledge of the stars is not profitable to man. But man's intelligence would not suffice without the help of God, and one has to pray anyway because the virtue of the stars does not hamper the almightiness of God...

(and this is then illustrated by histories from the Bible showing the **efficacy of prayer**). The book deals with every aspect of human knowledge — *de omni re scibili* — e.g., **anatomy**: The four main body parts are the heart, the brain, the liver and the genitals; the first three concern the individual; the fourth, the human species.

> The arteries through which the "spirits" move, come from the heart and cover the whole body; that is why wise doctors, feeling the pulse, can know the state of the heart. From the brain come the nerves which give life and movement to the whole body — to wit: if you cut a nerve or drink too much! From the liver come the veins through which the blood flows. The lungs are used to cool the

heart. The spleen between the heart and liver, close to the stomach, also moderates the heat of all these organs. The stomach serves as a cauldron, common to the whole household, for the whole body. Gall comforts the stomach and the bowels...

(and it goes on like this for the teeth, the eyes, the ears, etc.).

Sometimes, tales illustrate the text, e.g., when it states: "Don't trust anyone who does not share your religion". As an example a story found in *Ikhwan as-safa*, an Arabic encyclopedia of the tenth century, is given, showing a Jew and a philosopher from the East discussing their respective beliefs:

the Jew claims his creed forbids him to trust a "goy" and damns him if he helps a non-Jew; the Philosopher proclaims his sympathy with all suffering mankind and willingness to share with anyone in need, whereupon the Jew, who travels without luggage or food, challenges the Philosopher to put his principles into practice and to share with him. The Philosopher feeds the Jew and lets him ride his mule, but the Jew speeds away with the animal. The Philosopher protests, but finally accepts his fate. However, somewhat later, he finds the Jew with a broken hip under the mule which kicked him out of the saddle. The animal comes to the Philosopher who mounts it, but the Jew cries for mercy, claiming he only obeyed his own law. Upon this, the Philosopher takes pity on him and brings him to his destination. When the king of the land hears of this, he makes the Philosopher his councilor.

Just as fascinating are the works dealing with geography. They tell us the same stories as the fantastic *Letter of Priest John*. Thus, the *Mappemonde* of Peter of Beauvais, dedicated to Robert de Dreux (died 1218), talks about the parts of the world, after describing the egg-shaped universe, consisting of the starry sky (= white), the atmosphere (= yolk) and the earth (= the "germ"), with the four elements and their specific "qualities". In India, there are people who are only two cubits high (about 3 1/2 feet), the Pygmies, who fight against the cranes which attack their lands; they bear children at 3, and are among the elderly at 7. There are also people with one eye in their forehead, or with only one foot — but, using a pole, they run as fast as horses. Moreover, there are hairy humanoids without heads; others have a dog's head; others merely bark instead of talking. All kinds of fantastic animals are also referred to, e.g., the **manticore**, resembling man, with three pairs of teeth, the body of a lion and the tail of a scorpion; it whistles like a snake and runs as fast as a bird flies. The **santicora** is a big and strong animal with the body of a donkey, lion paws, a horn on the head and the voice of a man. The proud and cruel **eale** has a horse's body, an elephant's tail, and two big horns in the middle of the forehead (it can, however, move one of these horns behind its back and hit with the other one); it gets black when enraged. Finally, there is also the **unicorn**, with the head of a deer, the body of a horse, the legs of an elephant and the tail of a pig; its horn, in the middle of the forehead, is 4 feet long, sharp and shining like a burning fire.

Similar statements are found in the *Image du Monde*, composed in the abbey of St. Arnoul of Metz in the first quarter of the thirteenth century. It often supplies further details, describing the "Cyclopes" — faster than the wind — with only one foot whose sole is so big they use it as a shield and as an umbrella; men with one clear red eye in the middle of the forehead; men with their face and their mouth in the middle of their chest, an eye on each shoulder, their nose falling into their mouth, with bristles on their muzzle like on a pig's back. Here, the **manticore** has a man's face and the eyes of a goat, but is lighter than a bird, attracting people by its songs to devour them. We also get additional data on the **unicorn**: it charges, destroying everything with its sharp, cutting horn; when captured it lets itself die, but it can only be caught with **a virgin as bait**: the beast falls asleep in the beauty's lap, and they tie it up in its sleep...

The author is well informed about the mythical lands: he quotes Plato as his source for the presence, in the neighborhood of the island of the Cyclopes, of a bigger island than Europe and Africa, which sank into the frozen sea beyond Ireland. Besides the lost continent of Atlantis, he has also heard of the Lost Island "one can neither see nor get to", which was discovered by Saint Brendan. More than any other medieval writer, he devotes a lot of time to **astronomy**, telling how the use of geometry has made it possible to measure the moon, the sun, the stars versus the earth. Only three are smaller than the earth: the moon, Mercury and Venus, as *king Tolomeus* has shown (the author ascribes to the Ptolemaic dynasty of Egypt the work of the astronomer Ptolemy, known through its Arabic version entitled *Almagest* — a confusion already made by Isidorus of Sevilla!). "This king of Egypt had a passion for books and instruments with which one proves the size of the earth and the height of the sky". The same is alleged to have made several discoveries, such as that of the clock. The clocks indicate time, night and day,

> which is very useful for the churches to establish the time of prayers whose regularity pleases God. It would be better anyhow to perform all the functions of life like eating at fixed times: one would live longer. But the eagerness to hunt for money prevents most men from living as they should — with order and method... Too many people go to church early or late, these days, as it

> suits them; besides, they do not go so much to pray as to be praised by people;
> if they pray, it is merely to ask for their business to prosper...

After these personal notes, the author reverts to *Tolomeus* and adds: " We owe him the calendar, revised by Caesar of Rome; he is the man, who after Adam (who knew everything), has known most about astronomy".

Of a different character is the *Book of Sidrac*, an anonymous work already quoted in 1140, which was extremely popular in the Middle Ages and is found in French, Provençal, Italian, Dutch, Low German and other versions; the Middle Dutch was repeatedly printed in *incunabula*. The origin of the work is disputed; it seems, however, that the French version is the oldest, and there is no trace of a Latin or other model, although dependence on the work of Honoré d'Autun or better the *Imago Mundi* of the recluse Honorius is obvious. Historical allusions in the prologue point to the first half of the thirteenth century and specific mention of *Todre le philosophe* refers to the Greek Jew, mentioned as *Theodorus, philosophus noster* in the correspondence of emperor Frederick II, who was in epistolary contact with Muslim courts and surrounded himself with scholars versed in Arabic science and philosophy (Theodorus was his secretary for Arabic, his astrologer and ... confectioner!). It also appears that the anonymous author used a well-known anonymous catechism called *Elucidarium*, the *Philosophia mundi* of Guillaume de Conches (especially Book IV, which is the direct source of most gynecological questions), and the classical astrological treatise of Albumazar known in the Latin world as *Introductorium in astronomiam*. The author must have been a cleric using a manuscript containing all these works (such manuscripts are extant) — a man of limited intellect, who was, nevertheless, able to cater to the needs of his public with his blindly conservative approach and his promotion of a strong government, although he is also an egoistic, cynical, sometimes very gross Sybarite, who does not bother to tone down his strong misogyny.

The pattern of the work is a conversation between king Boctus of Bactriana and the philosopher Sidrac. It starts with theological questions to which the answers are the standard medieval views and therefore lack real interest. King Boctus then asks a lot of details about obstetrics, after which he switches to geography where we get a set of fantastic stories about the "eastern islands". Among the weird humanoids populating these strange places, there are those who

> have but one eye in the middle of the forehead: they are afraid of us; they eat
> meat and cover themselves with hides. Elsewhere, the natives have a tail like
> sheep; on another island, they have a skewer, long as a hand, screwed in their

buttocks, so that they can not sit down unless they have some space to lodge that caudal appendage in; They are hairy and eat crows — their only game!

Sometimes, however, one hears a distant echo of real habits such as *suttee* when Sidrac talks about natives building pyres and women sacrificing themselves upon them. But the message is garbled: it is ascribed to a planetary cult inspired by the devil (they make relics out of their ashes), and men also participate in such *auto-da-fés*! The book also alludes to the practices of hunters' societies, still common in subsaharan Africa: women raise male children until they are 5; then, they are taken over by men and trained for fighting. But once more, the report is mixed up with the description of some *potlach*-type practice and vague remembrances of the story of the Amazons: four times a year they gather for a week to eat and celebrate together, after which all return to their lair; the women who bear daughters keep them with them (we know what happens to sons); between these four love seasons, big battles are waged between men, armed with iron, and women, armed with silver, the latter often get the better of the former...

As regards the author's views on women, a couple of examples may suffice:

Boctus: Should one beat one's wife?

Sidrac: You should not beat a good wife: warnings are sufficient. As for a bad woman, it is useless. They will not improve! There is only one solution: "The mind of a bad woman is the will of the devil", and "one should not deal with whoever is possessed by demons; if you can not abandon her completely, get away from her and her whims!"

Boctus: What is better, the love or the hatred of woman?

Sidrac: A good woman is excellent, but a bad one is the worst thing there is; she is like the crocodile, so unthankful for the little bird that cleans its teeth!

Typically naive are statements like

—   Which are the parts of the body most necessary to man?
—   The tongue and the teeth.

—   Who made the first musical instrument?
—   Japhet, when he listened to water running over stones and the wind blowing in the trees.

—   Which language does a deaf-mute hear in his heart?
—   The language of Adam, i.e. Hebrew. Any child who would be raised without being taught any of our modern languages would

> spontaneously speak Hebrew, just as the fruit of a tree grafted
> with a wild stock reproduces the wilding.

Sometimes Sidrac's response or advice is rather unexpected:

— What is the most enjoyable thing there is?
— Sleeping.
— What should a man do if he catches his unfaithful wife in the act?
— Castigate her courteously and let the man go. Then, do not worry
   too much about it. You are not the only one in the world in this
   predicament, and whatever happened, the rivers will not dry up,
   nor the trees stop carrying fruit. Nobody has died of it, and
   nobody will!

The dialogue of *Placides and Timeo*, or *Book of the Secrets of the Philosophers*, as it is also called, was written at the end of the thirteenth century by an Averroist and disciple of Siger de Brabant. It is definitely of a higher intellectual level than the *Book of Sidrac* and occasionally displays a genuine scientific spirit, although the ideas presented are hardly original and can mostly be traced to the *Philosophia mundi* of Guillaume de Conches. The properties of things are described according to the Aristotelian pattern of SUBSTANCE and ACCIDENCE in agreement with the famous tree of *Porphyros* model, dividing "corporeal things" into those endowed with a soul and those without a soul. Corporeal is anything that takes up space, e.g., the four elements, even the **air** since it supports the birds in their flight, and the **water** since it sustains the fish. **Fire** is also corpore-al because it makes noise! They have no soul, but the trees and plants do because they are alive.

Timeo makes a strange apology for human dignity: man is a microcosm; he is round as the world; when he stretches his arms he must be as high as his full span. His head is comparable to fire, his chest to air, his stomach to the sea, and his feet, "on which he rests", to the earth. When Placides asks how man is "made", Timeo answers: "Moses the Jew told the story of the first man in Genesis", and he gives *ad hoc* etymologies of the names of Adam and Eve — the latter from *Extra Vadens* (EVA) "because, as the philosopher says, woman is apt to **go outside** the path of wisdom or reason". Since the Fall, mankind reproduces like animals...

Meteorology seems to interest the author very keenly, but he often skips from one subject to another, telling us how the Seven Liberal Arts survived the flood and how **chivalry** was invented by the great hunter *Nemrod* (or *Nimrod*), who also was the first to introduce **toll taxes**. The book actually contains a kind of appendix ascribed to a certain Albert of Trebizond: it deals with the "complexions" of man, gynecology, the art of government, and such topics, but another version focuses on astronomy and the relation between the microcosm (man) and the macrocosm (the Universe); it insists on the influence of the stars and planets, and switches over without transition to medieval medicine, listing appropriate remedies for old ailments.

We will end this brief survey with a few words about the best medieval encyclopedic work in a western language — the *Livres dou Tresor* or *La Naissance de toutes choses*, written in France (in exile) by Brunetto Latini about 1266. An important Florentine statesman, he was well-educated, well-read and shrewd. His work scored an immediate success: all the princes of the fourteenth and fifteenth centuries had it in their library, and John Gower used it when he wrote his *Confessio amantis*. Nevertheless, the work is not very original: he borrows abundantly from the usual sources: Pliny, Solinus, St. Ambrosius, Isidorus, Paladius (about rural economy) and others. The mistakes are numerous, and he added a few to those taken over uncritically from his models, but as it is, the book reflects medieval lore as it will appear in Dante in three areas: cosmography, ethics and politics.

The first part dealing with the world and the nature of things follows the pattern of previous works: history is covered with zest and expediency from the creation of the world to the present day. After the fall of Adam, mankind was prone to evil, and laws had to be invented for the safety of the community. World history is divided into six ages: from Adam to Noah, from Noah to Abraham, from Abraham to David, from David to Nebuchadnezzar, from the capture of Jerusalem by Nebuchadnezzar to the birth of Christ, and from this momentous event to the end of the world. Then comes the usual analysis of the structure of the cosmos, from the original matter, called *yle* (formless and shapeless), which God used for his Creation, to all the creatures, with the **elements** and their "properties". After computing the size of the planets, the author surveys the geography of this world, from the "columns of Hercules" to the land of the "Seres" (= Chinese), who are supposed to use bark and leaves as garments. There are still some statements about weird beings, but they are fewer. However, India is still the home of the headless and canine-head people, and horrible stories about people killing their parents so that they would not grow old are calmly repeated with the comment: "to them, eating their father is an act of piety". In general, however, the information is more adequate. To a degree, this also true of the data Brunetto Latini supplies on natural history, although he faithfully repeats the fantastic stories of other encyclopedias, e.g., the legend of the Ethiopian gold-gathering ants. He also describes the **manticore** and advises one to use the same trick to capture a **unicorn**! The *Livres dou Tresor* thus remains a typical medieval work in its content and its essence.

It will take generations to come to a sounder approach to the study of the world and nature, and medieval ideas will linger after the Renaissance, e.g., in Elizabethan England where an English translation of Bartholomaeus Anglicus's *De proprietatibus rerum* enjoyed considerable popularity. Although the publisher of the book adds comments to the statements of its medieval author, *Batman vppon Bartolome* (1582) faithfully reproduces their contents, to wit the following passage about **sirens**:

> Isidorus (lib. 12) says that in Arabia there are serpents with wings, called *sirene*, [that] run more swiftly than horses,... and it is also said that they do fly with their wings, and their venom is so strong that death is felt sooner than ache or sore.

The same goes for the entry on the **onocentaurus**:

> a beast of strange form... between a bull and an ass, for an ass is called *onos* in Greek, and so it is a beast lecherous as an ass and strong-necked as a bull. But *Physiologus*... says that **Onocentaurus** is composed of the shape of a man and of an ass: he has the shape of a beast from the navel downward

— and the text goes on quoting Pliny on the occurrence of the **onocentaurus** in India and telling about the centaurs in ancient Greece, to which the Elizabethan translator comments:

> As ancient men spent their time in writing of "follies" to make the common people wonder at what they did not know themselves, so in the last discovered Indies, the barbarous people seeing from afar the Spaniards on horseback, having never seen such a sight before, supposed they had been monstrous devourers...

About the author

Edgar C. Polomé is Christie and Hanley Adams Jr. Centennial Professor of Liberal Arts at the University of Texas at Austin. A native of Belgium, he received his Ph.D. in Germanic Languages from the University of Brussels in 1949. From 1956 to

1961, he taught at the University of the Belgian Congo at Elisabethville (now Lumumbashi, Democratic Republic of Congo), where he founded a linguistics Department. He has done research on African languages as well as Germanic and other Indo-European materials, writing books on Old Scandinavian myth and literature, Indo-European topics, and a guide to research for linguists. He has taught diachronic Germanic and other subjects.

CHAPTER 33

Linguistics in India

Past and Future

M. B. Emeneau

University of California, Berkeley

This slight paper on some aspects of linguistics in India — past and future — is based on my 'keynote' address to the twelfth session of SALA ('South Asian Linguistics Analysis') held at the University of California, Berkeley, June 8–10, 1990. It may fittingly, I think, be included in a volume of papers presented to Sydney M. Lamb on 70th birthday (in India it would have been on his ṣaṣṭipūrti, his 60th birthday). His distinguished linguistic career included beginnings at Berkeley. Most recently he was one of the editors and prime movers of a noteworthy volume, *Sprung from Some Common Source* (Lamb and Mitchell, 1991). The title is quoted from that prime event in the linguistics of India and the Indo-European linguistic world, Sir William Jones's 1786 address to the Asiatick Society in Calcutta. This paper I now present to Sydney Lamb in this congratulatory and honoring volume. His linguistic interests have been notably synchronic and theoretical, but the 1991 volume springs from his other, diachronic interests, and a few remarks especially directed to diachronic studies of the languages of India may not be unwelcome.

India's synchronic linguistic achievements — in the record for well over 2000 years, Pāṇini's grammar and phonetic texts on the Vedas — spring to mind at once as India's greatest linguistic accomplishment. On the other hand, in the Western linguistics of the last two centuries, whatever one's theoretical linguistic base may be, it is to be accepted, I think, that morphological and derivational analysis such as Pāṇini's involves some process statements which can be regarded as non-historical only if one postulates that "time" is to be rigorously eschewed as an element in the analysis. However, fixed within a cultural and religious dogma (e.g., "Sanskrit is the language of the gods", which we find it impossible to base our thinking on), the Hindu linguistic thinkers were unable to achieve anything which we would regard as an acceptable historical view of language. The statement of the dissimilation of aspirates ("Grassmann's law") is part of Pāṇini's synchronic analysis (8.4.54); for us it is hard to regard it as entirely free of historical implications.

The failure to achieve a firm diachronic stance becomes evident when we glance at the statements of Hindu grammarians when they were confronted with India's linguistic diversity. The relationship between Sanskrit and the languages of North India which they knew, in literary and colloquial forms, in the period of perhaps half a millennium immediately following Pāṇini, was such that an awareness of historical development could hardly be avoided. The similarities between Sanskrit and some at least of the Prakrits leaped to the eye, and a tradition developed which remained in some of the treatments of the Prakrits for many centuries (and in fact down to the most recent times). It is exemplified in Hemacandra's first statement in his Prakrit grammar (twelfth century A.D.): prakṛtih saṃskṛtam. tatrabhavaṃ tata āgataṃ vā prākṛtam. 'Sanskrit is the original (or, primary) form. Prakrit has its origin in that or has come from that.' But there were other, and more unsettling, factors in the situation. Beside some Prakrits whose relationship with Sanskrit was very evident, there were others which by locality or by temporal development showed much more diversity from Sanskrit, as well as languages of other families, such as Dravidian, which, though not derivable (in our historical sense) from Sanskrit, yet over time acquired many Sanskritic lexical items, both in literary use and in the colloquial. The Hindu grammarians made varying attempts to solve the (for them) insoluble problems presented by this complex situation. Varying statements were made, frequently attempting to find a solution in the opposition literary vs. non-literary, which often failed because the dramatists were prone to record any colloquial variety as it might be used by some low character. It ended with the term Apabhraṃśa, which originally denoted the latest phase of Prakritic language, being used by the seventeenth century Mārkaṇḍeya to denote 26 identified speech varieties, including Kāliṅgya, Kārṇāṭaka, and Drāviḍa, i.e. Telugu, Kannaḍa, and Tamil. This is, of course, to ignore the distinction between Indo-Aryan and Dravidian, and is another way of putting the doctrine that the Dravidian languages are "Prakrit" descendants related to Sanskrit in the same way that Hindi, Bengali, and Marathi are.

A much earlier manifestation of this mistaken view is to be seen in the famous passage in Kumārila Bhaṭṭa's mīmāṁsā text (Tantravārttika, about seventh century) in which he gives two or three examples of the way in which his contemporaries derived Tamil words from Sanskrit (e.g., pāp, which probably represents the attributive form pāppu of pāmpu [pāmbu] 'snake' is derived from Sanskrit pāpa- 'sin, sinful'). This kind of etymologizing was the orthodox way of treating Dravidian material as "Prakritic" right down to modern times. Whatever Kumārila's use of this material was (we may neglect the controversy involved), it is clear that he represents the common type of ahistorical Hindu thinking that we have referred to and that is represented by Mārkaṇḍeya's seventeenth century classification. This is indeed the Hindu version of India as a "linguistic area". For them the Dravidian languages were related to Indo-Aryan Sanskrit — and presumably the Munda languages too would have been if they had had literary forms. We, to be sure, also hold that India is a linguistic area — but their and our views have little in common but the term as we have just applied it.

For the history of the change of scholarly view, one would refer to the first recognition of Dravidian as a separate family of languages. It was first published by Francis Whyte Ellis of the Madras Civil Service in 1816. He dropped out of sight as the discoverer until his publication in a "Note to the introduction" of A.D. Campbell's *A Grammar of the Teloogoo Language* was brought to modern attention again by N. Venkata Rao (1954–55) followed by Burrow and Emeneau, (1961: v; 1984: vii). and Krishnamurti, (1969: 311–12). (Bishop) Robert Caldwell's *Comparative Grammar of the Dravidian or South Indian Family of Languages*, which established the presently-used name of the family and was "a real breakthrough" and incentive to Dravidian comparative studies, was first published in 1856 (40 years after Ellis, 70 after Jones) and much revised in 1875. Caldwell was a Church of England clergyman serving the English congregations in South India. Later as bishop, he was domiciled in the Tamil area. It is to be noted that he studied and wrote long (20 years) before the neogrammarians had established the comparative method in its full rigor in the 1870s.

On the Indo-Aryan side — it was German (and marginally Danish and other) scholars who developed so fruitfully, and finally rigorously, Jones's suggestion of an Indo-European family. They had used Sanskrit, especially Vedic, data to the full — at first in what came later to be recognized as a wrongheaded way. When this was corrected, Indo-European studies began to reach their full nineteenth century flowering. It must be noted that Indo-Aryan studies,

i.e. on the development from Sanskrit through Middle Indo-Aryan to Modern
Indo-Aryan (the languages of North India plus Sinhalese), came remarkably later
and were conducted until this century in what was really a very desultory way —
apart, of course, from the provision of grammars as teaching materials for the
use of administrators and missionaries. It was, in fact, not until the 1870s
(roughly a century after Jones, and 20 years after Caldwell) that the first real
effort was made to trace this development.

This was the work of John Beames, of the Bengal Civil Service; the book
was entitled *A Comparative Grammar of the Modern Aryan Languages of India:
to wit, Hindi, Panjabi, Sindhi, Gujarati, Marathi, Oriya and Bangali*, and was
published in London in three volumes in 1872, 1875, and 1879. Beames
(1837–1902) was a prodigious reader from the age of three (so his mother is said
to have said); he was educated in the manner of his time by studying Latin and
Greek (intensively, writing Latin and Greek verse, etc.), and added, to one degree
of competence or another, French, Hebrew, German, Italian, and Spanish, having,
as he said, a real interest in languages. He left after his death a manuscript
account of his life up to 1878, which was published in 1961 by a grandson,
Christopher Cooke, as *Memoirs of a Bengal Civilian*. His account of his higher
education preparatory to service in India gives us a picture of the last years of
the East India Company's "college" at Haileybury. For the required two years
(the calendar years 1856–57) he studied (rather hard, we gather) among other
subjects, more classics, and Persian, Hindustani, and Sanskrit, in which last his
teacher was Monier-Williams. In India, during the year 1858 he was at Calcutta,
nominally acquiring more knowledge of Persian and Hindustani with native
speakers. Thereafter, his long periods of field service gave him the opportunity
to learn much also of Panjabi, Hindi, and Oriya.

His *Memoirs* and the *Grammar* tell us something about why he undertook
his *Comparative Grammar* and how he worked. A revealing statement is in the
Memoirs where he says (p. 184): "I generally managed to screw out an hour or
two every day for a plunge into Sanskrit and Prakrit, which refreshed my weary
soul in the midst of all the official trouble and worry." He needed relaxation,
and, as we shall see in a moment, his idea of R and R was not that of his official
colleagues: he reverted to his early language interests. And of course for a
Dravidianist and areal linguist the most significant of all is the statement in the
preface to the *Comparative Grammar* (pp. vii-viii): "to a hardworked brain
change of labour is often a greater relaxation than absolute idleness, and ...
having always been a student of languages from my childhood, I had adopted

this form of amusement [this word puts us in our place!] in preference to any other, and had collected and grouped together many examples of the most salient peculiarities in the languages which I heard spoken round me long before any idea of writing a book entered my head. It was, I think, in 1865 that I first saw Dr. Caldwell's *Grammar of the Dravidian Languages* [published 1856], and it immediately occurred to me that a similar book was much wanted for the Aryan group." Then he writes much about the defective and often wrong statements in books on the various vernaculars, and on the need for an aspirant author to live among native speakers. He knew of no one who planned such a work. Then to resume quotation: "... I thought that it would be well for me to try ... so that, while waiting for some Bopp or Grimm to arise, students might have a handbook of some sort to guide them, and might no longer be misled by the astoundingly false etymologies which occur in the ordinary grammars and dictionaries." His concern with "etymologies" seems to betray that his primary linguistic interest was diachronic — but he is only following his European, German teachers in this. He mentions in one place notebooks in which he recorded language details. There are occasional important statements, such as that his knowledge of Sindhi was derived entirely from published sources (he only heard Sindhi spoken once).

He mentions having to work hard at reading the early Indo-Europeanists, Pott, Grimm, and Bopp. The only reference that I can find in the *Grammar* (apart from that quoted from the preface) is (vol. I, p. 269): "It will be observed that Grimm's law of positional changes holds good to a great extent in the case of these aspirates [i.e. the Sanskrit aspirated stops, whether voiceless or voiced, which he says "almost regularly" become h in the middle of a word but are retained as initials]..., one of those landmarks which are so cheering to the student, pointing as it does... to the existence of deep underlying laws, which a longer research and more intimate acquaintance with these languages will enable us eventually to unearth." One wonders whether he really understood Grimm.

Gordon H. Fairbanks in his sketch of "Comparative Indo-Aryan" (1969: 36f) says of Beames's work: "it is remarkable that so much of the discussion is still valid at present. It is well worth perusing by modern students of Indo-Aryan." This is a fair judgment indeed, perhaps more so than is really deserved.

Beames is the earliest work of note on the Indo-Aryan side. There is no need to review later works; Fairbanks has done so, as has also Ashok R. Kelkar (1969). One may mention A. F. Rudolf Hoernle (1880; based on Beames); R. G. Bhandarkar; the magnificent fiasco, *Linguistic Survey of India* (11 volumes, 1903–27), "compiled and edited" by George A. Grierson, though the work on at least one volume (vol. 4, *Muṇḍā and Dravidian Languages*, 1906) was done by Sten Konow; Jules Bloch, who provided the first modern general and detailed works in *La formation de la langue marathe* (1919) and *L'indo-aryen du veda aux temps modernes* (1934). But Suniti Kumar Chatterji's *The Origin and Development of the Bengali Language* (1926) was a real landmark work in that, though concentrating on the one language, it used in a previously unparalleled sweep most, if not all, of the other languages in great detail in its comparisons. All earlier studies have now been utilized in a great summing-up by Colin Masica, *The Indo-Aryan Languages* (1991). If much detailed work still remains to be done, we are now in a position that is respectably comparable with that of the languages of Europe. This slight survey cannot be ended without mentioning Sir Ralph Turner's *A Comparative Dictionary of the Indo-Aryan Languages* (1966). No historical and comparative work on Indo-Aryan henceforth can fail to start from this work, since (as written elsewhere, Burrow and Emeneau 1961: v, 1984: vii) "the first step in comparative grammar is to find the etymologies"; Sir Ralph has done this magnificently and (within the usual scholarly limits) definitively.

This is not the place to detail the history of Dravidian studies, since I am too intimately involved, and it has been done elsewhere. But I should at least mention (very selectively) Sir Denys Bray, W. W. Winfield, L. V. Ramaswami Aiyar, my late colleague Thomas Burrow, Bhadriraju Krishnamurti, and P. S. Subrahmanyam. All of these have, in their different ways, added immensely to our knowledge of the field.

Since my title mentions the future, what do I see as some of the tasks before students in Indian linguistics? It goes without saying that many languages in the area remain undescribed or sketchily described, many of the topics of modern linguistics study (typological, etc. etc.) remain unexplored, much detailed historical-comparative work remains undone.

On this last topic I would remark that, in spite of Masica's work, there is still no really good, usable, detailed treatment of the Middle Indo-Aryan languages (the Prakrits and Pali), either synchronic or diachronic. Pischel (1900) still remains our basic collection of data, but is in many ways antiquated and incomplete; I can only agree with Fairbanks who made this judgment in 1969 (40–41). Turner's dictionary makes us realize, I think, that much of the older work must be done all over again in detail, since we now have so much more, and reliable, data that must be fitted into the neogrammarian kind of statement of phonetic laws, analogic situations, borrowing, etc. I cannot think that his entry of so much material under a "defective" rubric is anything more or less than a failure to achieve analysis. It is a pity indeed that Turner's devotion for so many of his productive years to the building and development of the London School of Oriental and African Studies took him away from the *Comparative Grammar of the Indo-Aryan Languages* which he was so well equipped to produce. We must be content with what we have in his *Dictionary* and in the 1975 volume of *Collected Papers 1912–1973*. I may be allowed to add the acid remark that no etymological dictionary like Turner's, nor in fact any descriptive grammar with vocabulary, should be published without an index of meanings (in this instance in English). Without that, no one, Westerner or Indian, can use the work with any ease. Modern methods of handling masses of data should make the preparation of such an index not too difficult. I regard it as a desideratum of the utmost urgency. I would note that Burrow and I (it was my idea) provided such an index in our *A Dravidian Etymological Dictionary* (1961, 1984). It has made my own and others' subsequent studies so much easier than it would have been otherwise.

Burrow and I had expected that the collection of data, as complete as we could make it, in our Dravidian etymological dictionary would enable concerned scholars to reach, much more easily and more exactly, statements of phonetic development; in fact, that result has been seen in such fine work as P. S. Subrahmanyam's on Dravidian phonology. Burrow's papers on Dravidian "phonetic laws" in the period 1938–48 had, in fact, attempted such statements in greater detail than had been done by previous scholars, but his statements had of course been premature, since they were based on still very incomplete collections of data. Our dictionary has allowed great advances in Dravidian historical-comparative phonology. But there has been a somewhat unexpected tendency to leave Burrow's early results unexamined, as if they could be the last word. My recent paper on Proto-Dravidian initial *c- (1988) has, I think, shown that the DED/DEDR data do allow advances, and that similar studies on the Tamil-Malayalam-Telugu palatalization rule, the alternation of *a and *e after palatals, Tamil-Malayalam initial y-, etc., will yield results. And I have no doubt that study of Turner's collections will yield equally interesting results for Indo-Aryan.

Statements can be made about obvious gaps in our scholarly performance, such as that, excellent as is our basic Kui grammar and vocabulary by Winfield, we still have no body of texts that can be studied to cast light on the morphology and syntax of this language. My own voluminous text collections in Kota and Toda have already proved to be of great use in P. S. Subrahmanyam's researches into the comparative grammar of South Dravidian and even Proto-Dravidian. For detailed work both in Dravidian and in Indo-Aryan we need many more text collections.

Finally, for semantic and sociolinguistic studies, we need a "Buck", or perhaps even several "Bucks". I refer of course to Carl Darling Buck, *A Dictionary of Selected Synonyms in the Principal Indo-European Languages; a Contribution to the History of Ideas* (1949), data and philological and historical linguistic notes arranged by semantic categories. This we need, not only for Indo-Aryan or Dravidian, but for all the languages of the sub-continent together, no matter of what family. How else will we be able to know of and evaluate such facts as that old Tamil literature has Dravidian words for 'sun' and 'moon', but the colloquial uses Sanskrit borrowings, and that Toda retains an old Dravidian word for 'sun' only in archaic song and story language and otherwise uses a word that in the other languages means only 'heat of sun, sunlight', while Kota uses a Dravidian word which is quite different from either of those used in Toda? To provide a "Buck" would of course be a tremendous labor, to be done by a consortium of scholars, including research assistants (as was the first "Buck").

This is enough to suggest some of the research that is needed in the Indic field, and to hope that students inspired by the twentieth century teachers, including Sydney Lamb, will continue the work in the next century.

References

Beames, John. 1872–79. *A Comparative Grammar of the Modern Aryan Languages of India: To Wit, Hindi, Panjabi, Sindhi, Gujarati, Marathi, Oriya and Bangali.* (3 volumes, Volume I 1872, Volume II 1875, Volume III 1879.) London: Trübner and Co.

Beames, John. 1961. *Memoirs of a Bengal Civilian.* London: Chatto and Windus.

Bloch, Jules. 1919. *La formation de la langue marathe.* Paris: Champion.

Bloch, Jules. 1934. *L'indo-aryen du veda aux temps modernes.* Paris: Adrien-Maisonneuve.

Buck, Carl Darling. 1949. *A Dictionary of Selected Synonyms in the Principal Indo-European Languages.* Chicago: University of Chicago Press.

Burrow, Thomas and M. B. Emeneau. 1961. *A Dravidian Etymological Dictionary.* Oxford: Clarendon Press.

Burrow, Thomas and M. B. Emeneau. 1984. *A Dravidian Etymological Dictionary,* Revised edition. Oxford: Clarendon Press and New York: Oxford University Press.

Caldwell, Robert. 1856. *A Comparative Grammar of the Dravidian or South-Indian Family of Languages*. London: Harrison.

Chatterji, Suniti Kumar. 1926. *The Origin and Development of the Bengali Language*. Calcutta: Calcutta University Press.

Emeneau, M. B. 1988. Proto-Dravidian *c- and its developments. *Journal of the American Oriental Society* 108.239–68.

Fairbanks, Gordon H. 1969. Comparative Indo-Aryan. Sebeok 1969: 36–45.

Grierson, Sir George A. 1903–27. *Linguistic Survey of India*. Calcutta: Office of the Superintendent of Government Printing.

Hoernle, A. F. Rudolf. 1880. *A Comparative Grammar of the Gaudian Languages with Special Reference to Eastern Hindi*. London: Trubner and Co.

Kelkar, Ashok R. 1969. General linguistics in South Asia. Sebeok 1969: 532–38.

Krishnamurti, Bhadriraju. 1969. Comparative Dravidian studies. Sebeok 1969: 311–12.

Lamb, Sydney M. and E. Douglas Mitchell (eds.). 1991. *Sprung from some Common Source: Investigations into the Prehistory of Languages*. Stanford: Stanford University Press.

Masica, Colin. 1991. *The Indo-Aryan Languages*. (Cambridge Language Surveys.) Cambridge: Cambridge University Press.

Pischel, Richard. 1900. *Grammatik der Prakrit Sprachen: Grundriss der Indoarischen Philologie und Altertumskunde*. Strassburg: Trübner. [English translation by Subhadra Jha. *A Grammar of the Prakrit Languages*. Delhi: Motilal Banarsidass, 1981.]

Rao, N. Venkata. 1954–55. Dissertation on the Telugu Language by Ellis (1816). *Annals of Oriental Research*, University of Madras. 12.1–35.

Sebeok, Thomas (ed.). 1969. *Current Trends in Linguistics 5: Linguistics in South Asia*. The Hague: Mouton,

Turner, Sir Ralph L. 1966. *A Comparative Dictionary of the Indo-Aryan Languages*. London: Oxford University Press.

Turner, Sir Ralph L 1975. *Collected Papers 1912–1973*. London: Oxford University Press.

About the author

Murray B. Emeneau is Professor Emeritus of Sanskrit and General Linguistics at the University of California, Berkeley, where he taught from 1940 to 1971. After a

B.A. in classics, he received a Yale Ph.D. in classics and Sanskrit in 1931, remaining until 1935 to attend Edward Sapir's linguistics classes. He then did fieldwork and research on Dravidian tribal languages of South and Central India from 1935 to 1938. His intensive descriptive and comparative research in Dravidian and other languages of the Indian subcontinent has continued to the present. He served as Sydney Lamb's adviser during Lamb's graduate career at Berkeley, and was later his faculty colleague.

CHAPTER 34

Some Reflections of Vico in Semiotics

Thomas A. Sebeok
Indiana University

In preparation for this article, now dedicated to my friend Sydney Lamb, I reread some of the principal works of Vico which I had no opportunity to consult closely since my formal and informal studies and conversations in the early 1940s at the University of Chicago with my teacher, the Italian classicist Giuseppe Borgese. My over-all interests have recently refocused on the Continental roots of semiotics in the United States. My contribution reflects this current preoccupation and concern (as do, more extensively, several recent works of mine: Sebeok 1990,1991a: 21–93, 1991c; Sebeok and Petrilli 1998).

In making the claim that "Peirce was the heir of the whole philosophical analysis of signs....", we know that Charles Morris (1971: 337) was surely exaggerating. Peirce neglected to mine, for one source, the foundational semiotic of the seventeenth century's John Poinsot (Deely 1988). He also seems to have been unaware, among his own American predecessors or contemporaries, of the likes of Alexander Bryan Johnson (Fann 1990), Frederick A. Rauch (Sebeok 1991c: 8–11), and Garrick Mallery (Sebeok and Umiker-Sebeok, 1978), who, each in his own way, clearly made substantive and noteworthy contributions to semiotics, including the philosophy of language.

Had Peirce read Vico? Fisch tells us that Peirce nowhere mentions Vico (although, in 1905, he did refer once to Robert Flint's 1884 book, *Vico*; see Tagliacozzo and Verene 1976: 430, n1). Fisch himself, following hints by Feibleman, attempted "the outline of a tentative approach to a more comprehensive and more historical comparison which goes back to the origins of pragmatism and therefore compares Vico primarily with Peirce...." (1986: 201). John Michael Krois has essayed to confront Vico's and Peirce's *sensus communis*. He also brings Victoria Lady Welby into the picture, claiming that it was a consequence

of his correspondence with her that Peirce came to connect his "semeiotic" with
Vico's theory of the *sensus communis* (Tagliacozzo 1981: 58–71). Many years
earlier, Feibleman (1956: 69f.) found it "interesting to observe the similarities in
the reactions of Vico and Peirce toward the Cartesian innovations".

While Vico endeavored to reconcile scholastic philosophy with the new
empiricism of the 18th century, efforts at refuting Descartes overshadowed such
attempts at an accommodation in Peirce's own development. Peirce's insistence
that for claims to be true they must have practical consequences is certainly in
line with Vico's condensed formula, *verum factum convertuntur*, that the truth is
in the deed. Yet, well beyond such amorphous and uncredited resemblances,
Peirce obviously, if implicitly, built on the heritage of Giambattista Vico. As
Masani justly remarks (1990: 62), the pragmatism, viz., pragmaticism, of Peirce
— whom he calls "America's first Leibniz" — was in essence Vico's, in that
"the understanding of theory is deepened by its use in concrete construction".
Discussing the achievements of Norbert Wiener — whom Masani calls
"America's second Leibniz" — he also points out that the cybernetic attitude of
studying the inaccessible internal structure of organisms by observing their
responses to different stimuli (the so-called "black box" approach), namely, their
behavior, and by fabricating a model organism exhibiting the same behavior, was
also emphasized by Vico, and then "it was reiterated by C. S. Peirce" (1990:
255). Too, it is provocative that Bertrand Russell (1959: 206) likewise perceived
Vico — especially with respect to his radical criticism of the rationalist line of
thought and in setting up his new principle of epistemology — as having been
an inheritor and enhancer of Leibniz's suggestion that only God had perfect
science.

Eco (1984: 107f.) reminds us that Vico, in the context of the production and
interpretation of metaphors, "seems to put into question the existence...of a
preestablished process of semiosis" (as, by the way, did Locke in his *Essay*).
Blumenberg's rehabilitation of metaphor — especially of the pivotal metaphor of
the Book of Nature (1986) — parallels other modern returns to rhetoric. This too
received its impetus from Vico: "der Anfang der Weisheit sei Dichtung gewesen
und die Erfinder der Sprache hätten *in poetischen Character* gesprochen"[1]
(1986: 171 emphasis in source). Blumenberg's further observation, that the
central problem posed by Vico — concerning the ability of men to form law-

---

1. "The beginning of knowledge was supposedly poetry, and the inventors of language presumably
spoke *in a poetic character*". [Editors' note.]

governed communities and to exercise altruism — was, *mutatis mutandis*, solved by Kant, is well taken (1986: 176). Accordingly, it is hardly surprising that Ernst Cassirer and his neo-Kantian semiotic, or philosophy of the symbol — being itself an enlargement on Kant's necessary doctrine of schemata — is closest to "metaphorology", the label Blumenberg coined to account for the operations of figurative thinking in changing historical conditions; (see further Blumenberg's over-all 1974 evaluation of Cassirer).

Herzfeld's book, with its epigraphic citations from Vico, pursues, as it were, while it perhaps overvalues, the pseudo-philological uses to which Vico put etymology (1987: 22), as for instance his obeisance to the doctrine of divine nomathesia — that the names for all objects Adam signified mirrored their "essence", or their "nature" (Bedani 1989: 47). The Cartesian expectation that ordinary language shall forge ever sharper tools for the purposes of scientific discovery, and its concomitant demand for clear and distinct ideas, was not understood by Vico, who "therefore missed the significance of rationalist philosophy for science" (Russell 1959: 209). In any event, however, the Vichian project as such has not had much directly traceable effect on modern semiotic inquiry or methodology. This is so despite the fact that Vico was interested, at the very least programmatically, in the most diverse applications of signs; he states, in his *De constantia jurisprudentis* (Mooney 1985: v), that humanity is "the affection of one man helping another. This is done most effectively through speech — by counseling, warning, exhorting, consoling, reproving — and this is the reason…that studies of language are called 'humanities' [*studia humanitatis*], the more so since it is through language that humanity is most strongly bound together". For the purposes of this essay — more about Cassirer and Langer, less, in truth, about Vico — it is sufficient to understand that the several versions of Vico's "New Science" — "a mixture of various ingredients that are not properly distinguished", as Russell excoriated (1959: 207) — are wide open and therefore subject to any number of interpretations. The opacity of Vico's style, and what Russell also called "the obscurity of his message" (1959: 206), invite more or less dubious allegations or claims of his having been a precursor of the most disparate intellectual movements, including anthropology and social sciences in general; historiography (from Trotsky to Toynbee) and a kind of romantic historicism (rediscovered and reinforced by Jules Michelet and Thomas Carlyle); literary criticism, theory, and practice (Yates and Joyce); and philosophy (Comte and Collingwood) (White 1968: 316). Croce (1913), in particular, projected onto Vico notions which characterized his own rather than his subject's extreme idealistic position, and thus managed to misdirect, to a degree, two generations of his readership.

For Vico, as is well known, art, myth, and poetry were important genres, or means for understanding the spirit of culture. As Bedani put it (1989: 35), "'Poetry' and 'myth' in the *Scienza Nuova* are concepts which describe *necessary* forms of primitive linguistic and mental processes", but these terms are "anthropological/historical rather than 'aesthetic' categories", which is to say, "they describe forms of language and thought characteristic of early historical epochs". In other words, in Vico's frame of reference, "poetry" was, as a part of the world of nature, a more rudimentary form of language than narrative, particularly scientific, prose or any other language tending toward context-freedom. Poetry was not by any means, for Vico, a "higher" form of aesthetic expression: to the contrary, he compared the mental processes of the early poets with those of feeble-minded idiots and, more particularly, of women (*Scienza Nuova* 456f.)!

Comparably, as Dorfles came to testify (1968), Cassirer was later to insist on the precedence of figurative over utilitarian language, and to maintain that such Vichian concepts determine the way we experience the natural world for every manifestation of culture — that, for example, shapes of mythical thought can be unearthed by examining the forms of language. In this way, as in other aspects of his methodological strategy, Vico inverted traditional conceptions of natural and conventional signification.

It was this diachronic view of signification, according to which poetry was early man's natural form of expression, that Vico regarded as the "master key" to his new science. Iconicity, or what Peirce later elaborated as the category of Firstness, is inherent in such passages as this one: "Mutes make themselves understood by gestures or objects that have natural relations with the ideas they wish to signify" (quoted ibid. 42, from the *Scienza Nuova* 225).

The consonance of Vico's view in this respect with that of Francis Bacon's semiotic (cf. Sebeok 1987: 22f.) is especially conspicuous. Bacon, in his *De dignitate et augmentis scientiarum*, remarked that it is evident "that hieroglyphs and gestures carry a certain likeness to the signified object", and further that: "Signification of objects, which is either without aid or by means of words, is of two kinds; of which the first relies on congruity or likeness. The other signifies by convention. Hieroglyphs and gestures belong to the first whilst the others are what we call letters or words" (Bacon 1815, Ch. 1, 281).

It is not at all surprising nowadays to find Vico's name linked with Cassirer's as his forerunner in this or that respect, although Vico scarcely figured in Schilpp's collection (1949) of some 23 descriptive and critical essays (by various hands) about his philosophy. In Schilpp's massive tome, Vico was accorded a mere handful of inconsequential entries, once as the founder of the "new philosophy" of language and mythology (1949: 368). We owe it to Verene, I think, who first elaborated on the fact that Cassirer looked upon Vico "as the founder of a theory of knowledge based on a philosophy of the humanities and cultural ideals" (Cassirer 1979: 43). Although Cassirer seldom cites Vico directly, he had nonetheless been familiar with his writings since 1922. Verene also made accessible to a wide Anglophone readership Cassirer's short but illuminating Yale seminar lecture (ca. 1941) on "Descartes, Leibniz, and Vico" (1979: 95–107). In this presentation, Cassirer interpreted Vico's philosophy of civilization as unified and progressive, and as being at root of romantic fascination with the myth of origins of culture. All the same, one is compelled to agree with Paci's over-all observation (1969) that Vico's presence in Cassirer's writings is like that of "a ghost, which acts without revealing its human story or its name".

As Domenico Vircillo (1970) had observed, Cassirer "closed his life" with a lecture on "Structuralism in Modern Linguistics", reverting to the theme of —   .
and, as it were, coming to full circle from — his classic trilogy of the 1920's on symbolic forms. As I relate more fully in my book on *Semiotics in the United States* (Sebeok 1991c), I was privileged to attend that lecture (Cassirer 1946b) in the Fall of 1944. Since I must surely be one among the vanishing handful of survivors — I am unaware of any others — who spent that evening with Cassirer, I now offer some of my personal impressions of him. These I propose to follow, and thus conclude, with some notes about Suzanne K. Langer.

In 1981, on Friday, April 10th, having barely landed in Hamburg where I had flown to take part in the Third German Colloquium of the Deutsche Gesellschaft für Semiotik, I received a phone call from Klaus Oehler, the organizer, my friend and my host, asking me to accompany him immediately to a wreathe-laying observance beneath a bust erected in memory of Ernst Cassirer. This piece of sculpture stands in the foyer of the University of Hamburg's *Philosophenturm* (the same building where my own office was located during my visiting professorship in 1966). Cassirer had been Professor of Philosophy (that is, he had occupied the same Chair that a foremost German specialist on Peirce, Oehler, later occupied) at the University of Hamburg from 1919 until his dismissal and departure for Oxford and then to Göteborg in 1933. Those standing around at this ceremony included members of the Board of the Deutsche

Gesellschaft für Semiotik, plus a scattering of senior American semioticians. I was taken aback when I was unexpectedly called upon to make some commemorative remarks, but then it turned out that, fragile as this link may have been, I was the only one present who had ever come face to face with Cassirer. This affair spurred impromptu recollections along lines much like the following.

I recounted, off the cuff, that I had attended Cassirer's lecture, in the Fall of 1944, on "Structuralism in Modern Linguistics". He delivered this, at Jakobson's invitation, before the Linguistic Circle of New York, at the New School for Social Research, some weeks before his sudden death, on April 13, 1945, near the campus of Columbia University.

Cassirer and Roman Jakobson chanced to cross from Göteborg to New York on the same freighter, "Remmaren", May 20–June 4, 1941. What I remember vividly even to this day is that these words, adapted from *Genesis* XXVII,22, pressed on my mind throughout Cassirer's lengthy lecture: "The voice is Cassirer's voice, but the hands are the hands of Jakobson".

After his lecture, in the course of which Cassirer stressed the word and concept "semiotics", Jakobson and I dined with him, in the company of a few others. Both the linguist and the philosopher gave an animated account of their daily conversations aboard ship, and I concur that "these talks no doubt influenced Cassirer's interest and work on structuralism..." (Krois 1987: 30, 222fn.86). On the other hand, I never could find any trace of Cassirer's reciprocal influence on Jakobson's thinking, to whom Vico was also totally alien. Between this odd couple, Jakobson, then at his cerebral pinnacle, was doubtless the dominant personality, although Cassirer, in his younger days, could be quite self-assured in public.

Not long after Hitler had come to power, Cassirer's senior colleague, Jakob von Uexküll, read a paper tinged with the classic semiotic flavor of his *Umwelt-Forschung*. He reported, at a Hamburg Congress of Psychology, on a piece of research he had recently concluded on the cognitive maps of dogs. As these are constructed of and demarcated by scent-signs, he asserted that a dog takes everything located within its olfactory field for its property. Cassirer opened the discussion by recalling that Rousseau had said that the first man who erected a fence and declared "This is mine" should have been beaten to death. "After the lecture of Professor von Uexküll we know", he then expanded, "that wouldn't have sufficed. It was the first dog which should have been beaten to death". This bandying about territoriality was attacked in next morning's "Völkische Beobachter" by Herr Göbbels himself, under the punning headline: "Kötereien eines deutschen Professors!"[2]

Cassirer, whom von Uexküll, a profoundly original idealist yet empirical semiotician, deemed the greatest living German philosopher, one who shaped an entire generation of students in neo-Kantian ways of thinking, left for Vienna at the beginning of May, in 1933. In his *Essay on Man*, a condensed American reworking of his *Philosophy of Symbolic Forms*, Cassirer's argument is avowedly, although metaphorically, based on von Uexküll's biosemiotic principles (Sebeok and Umiker-Sebeok 1992) extended into the human world: man's acquisition of the "symbolic system", he contended, transforms the whole of our existence; accordingly, Cassirer designated man *animal symbolicum* (1944: 26).

The neo-Kantian von Uexküll's impact on the neo-Kantian Cassirer (1944: 23f.) cannot be overestimated, even though a careful study of the writings of the senior scholar will, I am convinced, show that Cassirer (and generations of **his** followers) failed to grasp the fundamental idea of the former's "functional circle" (briefly, a construct made up of signs arrayed in a negative feedback circuit), or his independently innovative fashioning of a new pragmatic, sensory semiotics; (he also, more mysteriously, re-christened Jakob von Uexküll "Johannes"). Readers can verify this adverse judgment for themselves by reading von Uexküll's works (whose own extensive writings, by the way, evince no awareness of Vico). While I concur with Verene (1976: 311) that it is mistaken to think of Cassirer's philosophy as merely a form of Kantianism, it is equally erroneous to leave unmentioned, as it has thus far generally remained, the powerful, if to a degree muddled, impact of von Uexküll's thought and personality on the junior (by a decade) Cassirer.[3]

Susanne Langer, like Sydney Lamb (Regan et al. 1992), a follower of Kant and Whitehead (Huntley 1971: 115), has also long been regarded as the American "philosopher most influenced by Cassirer" (Krois 1987: 12), although his

---

2. The phrase can be approximately translated as "mongrelisms of a German professor". The punning reference is between *köter* 'cur, mongrel' the base of the first word, and *kot* 'dirt, manure, excrement'. [Editors' note.]

3. For further particulars on Cassirer, who is currently undergoing a kind of mini-revival in this country as well as in Western Europe, see Krois's recent splendid book (1987); and as to Cassirer's brand of semiotics, see Verene's authoritative lemma (1986). The secondary sources about Cassirer are staggering in quantity, as the nearly 500–page annotated bibliography by Eggers and Mayer (1988) testifies. An edition of Cassirer's complete works, including his many unpublished remarks on semiotic topics, is in preparation under Krois's direction.

conception of the symbol seems to have eluded her, as did its derivation reaching back to Vico. If Vico was a ghost for Cassirer, he evanesced into a sheer shade of a wraith for Langer. "This symbol concept, as it emerges in use, in the course of work", she wrote (1962: 56), "cannot be defined in terms of denotation, signification, formal assignment, or reference. The proof of the pudding is in the eating, and I submit that Cassirer's pudding is good; but the recipe is not on the box".

Morris put Langer down too, together with Wilbur M. Urban (cf. Schilpp 1949: 403–441), as a "follower" of Cassirer (1946: 189). And she herself has told us as much: "In many years of work on the fundamental problems of art", she wrote, she found Cassirer's philosophy of symbolic forms, however slippery, "indispensable; it served as a key to the most involved questions" (1962: 58). In 1946, she translated Cassirer's little book *Language and Myth*, characterizing it in her Preface as imbued "by a final flash of interpretive genius" (p. x). And her appraisal of his theory of language and myth (Langer 1949) is both sympathetic and insightful. "Symbols are the indispensable instruments of conception", she reaffirms in connection with Cassirer's "greatest epistemological contribution", which lay in "his approach to the problem of mind through the study of the primitive forms of conception". If she was aware of Vico's seminal role in Cassirer's formulation of this central problem, that is, "the diversity of symbolic forms and their interrelation in the edifice of human culture" (1949: 386–387), she passes over it in silence.

After World War II, because of the easy accessibility of her attractive paperback, *Philosophy in a New Key*, Langer became something of a campus celebrity, but her work, while never regarded as trivial, seldom seems to have been taken for more than "a point of departure" by such professionals as Morris (1946: 50). Thus Charles S. Stevenson (in Henle 1958, Ch. 8) dissected her arguments ascribing "a symbolic function to the arts", viz., music, "that other writers have often denied to them" (1958: 202), and judged them implausible. Stevenson (1958) tried to show, more generally (as Abraham Kaplan did earlier, in 1943), "that the importance of the theory of signs to all the arts, rather than merely to those commonly classified as representational, is seriously open to question" (Henle 1958: 210). Similar difficulties, he stated, "arise in **any** theory of signs" (Henle 1958: 219), yet he concentrated his specific criticisms on Langer's views alone. Years later, Morris, while completely ignoring Langer's thesis, found Stevenson's arguments not to be compelling (1964: 67).

In mid-May, 1969, Langer was a featured speaker at a symposium held at the Smithsonian Institution, where I was also a guest. She read a paper titled "The Great Shift: Instinct to Intuition" (Eisenberg and Dillon 1971, Ch. 10), the indicant concept of which turned out to be how she thought language began — "with symbolic utterance" (Eisenberg and Dillon 1971: 325), she asserted. She held that "Speech is not derived from animal communication; its communicative and directive functions, though all-important today, are secondary; its primary function is the symbolic expression of intuitive cognition" (Eisenberg and Dillon 1971: 326; she had made the same point in 1962, Ch. 2).

In other words, language evolved, in her view (though the terminology here is mine; cf. Sebeok 1986: 10–16, and 1991b, Ch. 5) as a uniquely human modeling system. In spite of its unfortunate oral delivery — Ms. Langer was tiny, dwarfed behind the lectern, and practically inaudible because of the placement of the microphone — I was enthusiastic about her talk (some participating biologists, I gathered, were, by and large, not) and told her so at one of the social functions we attended afterwards.

It is fascinating to note a clue *in nuce* lurking in this very quotation to Langer's equivocal position in American semiotics. Her frame of reference was sharply at variance with views promoted by simplistic physicalist technicians (some of whom are mentioned in Demers 1988, but there are others, especially Lieberman 1988), who strove to pursue an illusory comparison of language and animal communication systems. On the other hand, it is in line with critical doubts expressed by thinkers as different as Popper (1972: 121), Chomsky (e.g., 1980: 229f.), and many others (e.g., Sebeok 1991b: 81n5). This kinship is not at all surprising, considering Ms. Langer's proximal intellectual lineage, including the pervasive (although riven) impact of the neo-Kantians, via Wilhelm von Humboldt and Peirce or, as the case may be, von Uexküll and Cassirer, on the parties involved.

The only comments known to me specific to Langer's "properly" semiotic project, which is said to focus "on the foundations of the theory of signs from within a highly differentiated philosophical matrix", are Innis's (1985: 87–89). Clearly, however, her work merits detailed reconsideration in the near future, especially in its implications for aesthetics. But Innis's allusion to Nelson Goodman's ideas of notationability and similarity, to which, he alleges, "Langer's position...bears remarkable similarities" (1985: 89), was stated with quite a different emphasis by Goodman himself (1968: xii): "I am by no means unaware of contributions to symbol theory by such philosophers as Peirce,

Cassirer, Morris, and Langer.... I reject one after another ... the views common to much of the literature of aesthetics..." Goodman acknowledged congruences between his different ways of "worldmaking" and Cassirer's effort to distinguish various "symbolic forms", but added: "Cassirer undertakes the search through a cross-cultural study of the development of myth, religion, language, art, and science. My approach is rather through an analytic study of types and functions of symbols and symbol systems" (1968: 6).

Clearly, Langer's semiotic work merits detailed reconsideration in the near future, especially in its implications for music and the whole range of the fine arts — the creation of symbols of value, of apparent forms expressive of human feelings — in short, aesthetics, the vast estate where she perhaps unknowingly caught up with Vico (see now Sebeok and Petrilli 1998, and Berthoff 1999).

References

Bacon, Francis. 1815 [1623]. *The Works of Francis Bacon*, Vols. 6–7. London: M. Jones.

Bedani, Gino. 1989. *Vico Revisited: Orthodoxy, Naturalism and Science in the Scienza Nuova*. Oxford: Berg.

Berthoff, Ann. 1999. Susanne K. Langer and "the odyssey of mind." *Semiotica* (forthcoming).

Blumenberg, Hans. 1974. Ernst Cassirers gedenkend bei Entgegennahme des Kuno Fischer-Prizes der Universität Heidelberg im Juli 1974. *Revue Internationale de Philosophie* 28: 456–463.

Blumenberg, Hans. 1986. *Die Lesbarkeit der Welt*. Frankfurt am Main: Suhrkamp.

Cassirer, Ernst. 1923. *Philosophie der Symbolischen Formen: I. Die Sprache*. Berlin: Bruno Cassirer.

Cassirer, Ernst. 1944. *An Essay on Man*. New Haven: Yale University Press.

Cassirer, Ernst. 1946a. *Language and Myth*. New York: Harper & Brothers.

Cassirer, Ernst. 1946b. Structuralism in modern linguistics. *Word* 1: 99–120.

Cassirer, Ernst. 1961 [1942]. *The Logic of the Humanities*. New Haven: Yale University Press.

Cassirer, Ernst. 1969 [1956]. *Wesen und Wirkung des Symbolbegriffs*. Darmstadt: Wissenschaftliche Buchgesellschaft.

Cassirer, Ernst. 1979. *Symbol, Myth, and Culture: Essays and Lectures of Ernst Cassirer 1935–1945*, ed. by Donald Philip Verene. New Haven: Yale University Press.

Chomsky, Noam. 1980. *Rules and Representations*. New York: Columbia University Press.

Croce, Benedetto. 1913. *The Philosophy of Giambattista Vico*, trans. R. G. Collingwood. London: Howard Latimer.

Deely, John. 1988. The semiotic of John Poinsot: Yesterday and tomorrow. *Semiotica* 69: 31–127.

Demers, Richard A. 1988. Linguistics and animal communication. *Linguistics: The Cambridge Survey*, Volume III, *Language: Psychological and Biological Aspects*, ed. by Frederick J. Newmeyer. Cambridge: Cambridge University Press.

Dorfles, Gillo. 1968. Mito e metafora in Cassirer e Vico. *Il Pensiero* 13: 147–158.

Eco, Umberto. 1984. *Semiotics and the Philosophy of Language*. Bloomington: Indiana University Press.

Eggers, Walter and Sigrid Mayer. 1988. *Ernst Cassirer: An Annotated Bibliography*. New York: Garland Publishing.

Eisenberg, John F. and Wilton S. Dillon (eds.). 1971. *Man and Beast: Comparative Social Behavior.* Washington: Smithsonian Institution Press.

Fann, K. T. 1990. Alexander Bryan Johnson: The first linguistic philosopher (1786–1867). *The Semiotic Web 1989*, co-ed. by Thomas A. Sebeok and Jean Umiker-Sebeok, 31–60. Berlin: Mouton de Gruyter.

Feibleman, James K. 1956. *An Introduction to Peirce's Philosophy Interpreted as a System*. New Orleans: The Hauser Press.

Fisch, Max. 1986. *Peirce, Semeiotic, and Pragmatism*. Bloomington: Indiana University Press.

Gadol, Eugene T. 1969. Der Begriff des Schöpferischen bei Vico, Kant, und Cassirer, II. *Wissenschaft und Weltbild* 2: 8–19.

Goodman, Nelson. 1968. *Languages of Art: An Approach to a Theory of Symbols*. Indianapolis: Bobbs-Merrill.

Goodman, Nelson. 1978. *Ways of Worldmaking*. Indianapolis: Hackett.

Hardison, O. B., Jr., ed. 1971. *The Quest for Imagination: Essays in Twentieth-Century Aesthetic Criticism*. Cleveland: The Press of Case Western Reserve University.

Henle, Paul, ed. 1958. *Language, Thought, & Culture*. Ann Arbor: The University of Michigan Press.

Herzfeld, Michael. 1987. *Anthropology Through the Looking Glass: Critical Ethnography in the Margins of Europe*. Cambridge: Cambridge University Press.

Innis, Robert E. 1985. *Semiotics: An Introductory Anthology*. Bloomington: Indiana University Press.

Kaelin, Eugene F. 1970. *Art and Existence: A Phenomenological Aesthetics*. Lewisburg: Bucknell University Press.

Kaplan, Abraham. 1943. Content analysis and the theory of signs. *Philosophy of Science* 10: 230–247.

Krois, John Michael. 1987. *Cassirer: Symbolic Forms and History*. New Haven: Yale University Press.

Langer, Suzanne K. 1948. *Philosophy in a New Key*. New York: Penguin Books.

Langer, Suzanne K. 1949. On Cassirer's theory of language and myth. Schilpp, 1949: 381 — 400.

Langer, Suzanne K. 1962. *Philosophical Sketches*. Baltimore: The Johns Hopkins Press.

Lieberman, Phillip. 1988. Voice in the wilderness: How humans acquired the power of speech. *The Sciences* 28.4 (July-August): 22–29.

Masani, Pesi Rustom. 1990. *Norbert Wiener 1894–1964*. Basel: Birkhäuser Verlag.

Mooney, Michael. 1985. *Vico in the Tradition of Rhetoric*. Princeton: Princeton University Press.

Morris, Charles. 1964. *Signification and Significance: A Study of the Relations of Signs and Values*. Cambridge: M.I.T. Press.

Morris, Charles. 1971. *Writings on the General Theory of Signs*, ed. by Thomas A. Sebeok. The Hague: Mouton.

Paci, Enzo. 1969. Vico and Cassirer. In: *Giambattista Vico: An International Symposium*, ed. by Giorgio Tagliacozzo and Hayden V. White, 457–473. Baltimore: The Johns Hopkins University Press.

Popper, Karl K. 1972. *Objective Knowledge: An Evolutionary Approach*. Oxford: Clarendon Press.

Regan, John, et al., eds. 1992. *Whitehead and Lamb: A New Network of Connection*. Claremont: College Press.

Russell, Bertrand. 1959. *Wisdom of the West*. London: Macdonald.

Schilpp, Paul Arthur, ed. 1949. *The Philosophy of Ernst Cassirer*. Evanston: The Library of Living Philosophers.

Sebeok, Thomas A. 1986. *I Think I am a Verb: More Contributions to the Doctrine of Signs*. New York: Plenum Press.

Sebeok, Thomas A. 1987. Messages in the marketplace. *Marketing and Semiotics: New Directions in the Study of Signs for Sale*, ed. by Jean Umiker-Sebeok, 21–30. Berlin: Mouton de Gruyter.

Sebeok, Thomas A. 1990. Semiotics in the United States. *The Semiotic Web 1989*, ed. by Thomas A. Sebeok and Jean Umiker Sebeok, 275–395. Berlin: Mouton de Gruyter.

Sebeok, Thomas A. 1991a. *American Signatures: Semiotic Inquiry and Method*. Oklahoma Project for Discourse and Theory. Norman: University of Oklahoma Press.

Sebeok, Thomas A. 1991b. *A Sign is just a Sign*. Bloomington: Indiana University Press.

Sebeok, Thomas A. 1991c. *Semiotics in the United States*. Bloomington: Indiana University Press.

Sebeok, Thomas A. and Susan Petrilli. 1998. Women in semiotics. In: *Interdigitations: Essays for Irmengard Rauch*, ed. by Gerald F. Carr, Wayne Herbert, and Lihua Zhang, pp. 469–478. New York: Peter Lang.

Sebeok, Thomas A. and D. Jean Umiker-Sebeok, eds. 1978. *Aboriginal Sign Languages of the Americas and Australia*, Vol. 1. New York: Plenum Press.

Sebeok, Thomas A. and D. Jean Umiker-Sebeok, eds. 1992. *Biosemiotics: The Semiotic Web 1991*. Berlin: Mouton de Gruyter.

Stevenson, Charles S. 1958. Symbolism in the nonrepresentative arts. Henle 1958: 196–225.

Tagliacozzo, Giorgio ed. 1981. *Vico: Past and Present*. Atlantic Highlands: Humanities Press.

Tagliacozzo, Giorgio and Donald Philip Verene, eds. 1976. *Giambattista Vico's Science of Humanity*. Baltimore: The Johns Hopkins University Press.

Verene, Donald Philip. 1976. Vico's science of imaginative universals and the philosophy of symbolic forms. Tagliacozzo and Verene 1976: 295–317.

Verene, Donald Philip. 1986. Ernst Cassirer (1874–1945). *Encyclopedic Dictionary of Semiotics*, ed. by Thomas A. Sebeok, 103–105. Berlin: Mouton de Gruyter.

Vircillo, Domenico. 1970. La fenomenologia del linguaggio nel pensiero de E. Cassirer. *Revista Rosminiana di Filosofia e di Cultura* 44: 187–202.

White, Hayden V. 1968. Giovanni Battista Vico. *International Encyclopedia of the Social Sciences* 16: 313–316. New York: The Macmillan Company & The Free Press.

About the author

*Thomas A. Sebeok is Distinguished Professor Emeritus of Linguistics and Semiotics at Indiana University. He also retains affiliations with the Universities of Helsinki and Toronto. A native of Hungary, he completed his Princeton doctorate at Indiana in 1945, after emigrating to the United States. His connections to Syd Lamb arise out of their common interests in semiotics. They have, in particular, collaborated in seminars at the Claremont Graduate School as well as at international conferences at Burg Wartenstein, in Austria. Sebeok has been President of both the Linguistic Society of America (1975), and the Semiotic Society of America (1984). He has served as editor of many publications, and has edited the journal **Semiotica** since 1969.*

CHAPTER 35

The Forerunners of Scientific Phonology
Diacritical Marks and Other Reforms in Orthography

Saul Levin

State University of New York at Binghamton

.

In honor of Syd Lamb, my colleague in the Linguistic Association of Canada and the United States (LACUS), whom I admire and who has taught me a great deal, I now offer my thoughts on a subject that will doubtless interest him — his curiosity being so broad — and may benefit others sharing our concern for accurate notation. Many of my previous writings have touched upon this theme, and several of them have gone into detail regarding certain aspects of it (Levin 1979, 1982, 1983, 1984a, 1984b); but this is the first time for me to focus upon what, if anything, differentiates the modern linguist's understanding of phonology from that of previous ages, and how our predecessors have prepared the way for us.

It could be argued that there is only a difference of degree, though not a small difference, between the most scientific phonology of the twentieth century and the crude beginnings of phonetic or semi-phonetic writing, when some primarily pictorial characters were made to serve also for words of identical or similar sound. For instance, the Egyptian hieroglyph ⌒ (a simple drawing of a mouth) stood not only for 'mouth' but for the preposition 'to', which shared with it the consonant [r].[1] I, however, believe in an **essential** difference between makeshift adaptation and systematic reconsideration. The latter is eminently scientific; the former, although intelligent, does only enough to overcome a particular shortcoming in a defective script.

---

1. Vowel-sounds were not shown at all in this early script.

To be sure, the very idea of letting something drawn by hand represent an invisible sound was truly original and immeasurably clever; it bridged the total gap between the senses of hearing and sight. In comparison with that, all subsequent progress in the direction of a perfect phonological script was just a series of step-by-step advances. And yet I would draw attention to certain noteworthy advances that extended beyond an *ad hoc* remedy for an evident defect in the existing script.

1.   Ancient Precedents Governing the International Phonetic Alphabet

The IPA, now about a hundred years old, illustrates the conditions under which even the most scientific study of language must labor. It was prompted not just by the general spirit of science, calling for research into any and every field, but by a particular sense that (a) serious linguistic discussion, and effective instruction of foreigners in larger and larger numbers, could no longer be based upon the received spelling of certain European languages, especially French and English; nor could scientifically minded scholars and teachers limit themselves to minor tinkering with those deeply flawed adaptations of the Latin alphabet; and (b) that all the languages of the world deserve equally a notation that will do justice to their full apparatus of sounds.

Nevertheless, even the IPA is not a radically new script but a revision of the Latin alphabet in minuscule lettering, with supplementary characters that include several of the familiar letters as small capitals; e.g. [ɪ]. It uses, on a larger scale, devices similar — or in some cases identical — to the ones introduced over the centuries by previous reformers, who coped with the inadequacy of the Latin or a related alphabet for the sounds of some particular language. To be scientific, and at the same time not impractical, the authors of the IPA availed themselves of many good precedents, and thus reduced the need to invent new characters, arbitrary in shape, not reminiscent of any known letters, and therefore harder to learn. Such new characters might, conceivably, have had the countervailing advantage of freedom from any confusing association — e.g., some beginners mistake [j] in the IPA for an affricate (like the English *j*) rather than a semivowel. Each character, to be sure, and each supplementary mark in the IPA is precisely defined, which ought in principle to obviate any misinterpretation.

The basic strategy of the IPA — employing the traditional letters insofar as they can be made to serve an unambiguous, scientific purpose — has a weighty consequence: The IPA implicitly sets aside any challenge, or any alternative, to the model of alphabetic segmentation for pinpointing the distinctions of sound whereby each language expresses differences in meaning. So the IPA reinforces the concept of the PHONEME, which Baudouin de Courtenay formulated previously. The phonemes of a language are scarcely inherent in the phenomena of sound; rather they emerge from an **alphabetic** analysis of its phonetic features, an analysis inherently committed to a succession of vowels and consonants, with supplementary symbols for sounds of any other kind.

Being rooted in the Latin alphabet, the IPA cannot encourage us to treat any unit other than the vowel or consonant phoneme as fundamental. Thus the syllable is bound to be secondary. It was discovered and defined by the ancient Greek grammarians as a combination of a vowel with another vowel and/or one or more consonants. Although they found it more natural for the voice to analyze a word into syllables than to go further — analyzing it into vowels and consonants — yet for the purpose of writing they had no choice but to keep the vowel- and consonant-letters as their units. For they were pre-committed to the Greek alphabet, which antedated by centuries any other analysis of the language. The prominence of vowels in Greek, their almost absolute independence from any perceptible influence of the neighboring consonants, had prompted the Greeks early in the first millennium B.C. to change basically the consonantal alphabet which they learned from the Phoenicians.[2] The Greeks revalued certain letters to be vowels instead of consonants — beginning with the first letter, which for them represented no longer the glottal stop [?], as in Phoenician, but the vowel-sound [a] (unrepresentable within the restrictive principles of the Phoenician script).

That huge step forward was a reformation; to call it just a reform would appear insufficient, since no specimens remain (if indeed there ever were any) of Greek written in the unreformed, consonantal Phoenician alphabet, neglecting the vowel-sounds. It was a fateful move, decisive for the writing of the other ancient languages of Europe — Latin above all — and through Latin, the languages that emerged in the middle ages, and even (as I have said) the modern IPA. Notwithstanding the indisputable gain from the vowel-letters, I must put on record one demurrer against their looks: Since they are the same size as consonant-letters

---

2. Greeks of the "golden age" (e.g., Herodotus 5.58–59) credited the mythical hero, Cadmus the Phoenician, with the introduction of letters into their country. See Bernal, 1990: 3–4.

and are made of similar strokes, in effect they mask the phonological difference between vowel- and consonant-sounds.

By way of contrast, in the Nāgarī script for Sanskrit and Prakrit the unit is the syllable. As exemplified by the word स वे ल्ो के [s(ʌ)-rv(ʌ)-lo-ke] 'in the entire world', vowels are indicated by adding a stroke to the consonant (or consonant-group) that begins the syllable. But the most frequent vowel [ʌ] is left unwritten, being taken for granted in the absence of a mark for any other vowel — a nice economy indeed, but it imposes a major complication upon the Nāgarī script: Two consonants (or three) with no vowel-sound separating them have to be combined into one character, such as वे; for र व would stand for [r(ʌ)-v(ʌ)]. Furthermore, some of the combined characters do not lend themselves to an easy visual analysis into their components; so, on balance, this script is intrinsically more difficult to learn than any form of the alphabet that includes vowel-letters. It also forces a demarcation of many words into graphic syllables that come out contrary to the phonology: [s(ʌ)-rv(ʌ)] instead of the real [sʌr-vʌ].

Accordingly we need not regret the triumph of the vowel-and-consonant alphabet throughout Europe, nor its recent spread to non-European languages, nor the persistence of this principle in the scientific IPA. It is, to be sure, "Euro-centric" (so is all modern science throughout the world), and it could therefore be a target for dissident intellectuals in many Occidental countries, manifesting their allegiance to a faddish counter-culture while writing, of course, in the only languages that they know. Until the nineteenth or even the twentieth century, certain writing systems — the Arabic alphabet (essentially consonantal), the Indian syllabary, and the Chinese characters — were able to spread beyond their home ground, without effective competition from the vowel-and-consonant alphabet; but they are not destined for adoption by any more language-communities. Experience has proved that a vowel-and-consonant alphabet is more readily adaptable to the phonological peculiarities of nearly any language. However, a good adaptation does not come about automatically; and a bad adaptation, as in English, may through adverse circumstances become practically irremediable.

Yet in the writing of many other languages quite a few devices have been successfully developed and have served as helpful precedents beyond their place of origin. For the most part I shall not treat the original adaptation, whether skillful or inept, of the alphabet to a given language, but rather **the subsequent improvements**, insofar as these reflect an awareness of phonological inadequacies that needed to be remedied in the script.

2. The Origin of Diacritics as Supplementary Marks

The first diacritical marks were added by Greek scribes in the Ptolemaic period
(third to first century B.C.). Some of them made it a habit to write a diaeresis
(consisting of two dots) for a syllable boundary above the vowel I or Y if
preceded by another vowel; thus AΪ, AΫ, not to be pronounced as a diphthong
— e.g. OΪΣTOI 'arrows' *(Iliad* 1.46). Also when either I or Y began a word,
they would write the diaeresis above it. For the Greeks had long ago abandoned
the early Phoenician practice of showing the boundary between words; but the
new device, while properly signaling the beginning of a syllable (after a syllable
that ended in a vowel), served just as well to separate its letter from a consonant
at the end of the previous word, as in AYTIΣΪONTA 'coming again' (1.27).

Around the same time they also took to writing an apostrophe at the end of
a word whose final vowel was elided before the initial vowel of the next word:
ΔHΘYNONT'H 'loitering or' (1.27), where the participle (accusative singular
masculine) would have been ΔHΘYNONTA at the end of a verse or before a
consonant. For a strictly phonetic purpose the apostrophe may well have been
irrelevant, like the diaeresis in AYTIΣΪONTA: at this point in the text the
syllable was pronounced [tɛ:] or [si] regardless of these little marks. But serving
as devices for analytical phonology, they drew attention to the word as it would
be in some other phonetic environment.

While the ordinary scribes limited themselves to the diaeresis and the
apostrophe, the expert readers who corrected new copies of classical poetry
introduced other diacritical marks for the benefit of less educated persons. They
would write a long horizontal line above certain vowel-letters, and occasionally
a short curve to signal the opposite treatment of the vowel- sound; e.g., in the
papyrus of Bacchylides's odes, NĀON 'temple' (15.12) but MYPĬAΣ 'countless'
(10.126).[3] Never in ancient times was this done uniformly or consistently to the
vowels of a text; instead the marking was sporadic, mainly (though not always)
when it occurred to the corrector that a word was liable to be misread and
misunderstood because of the ambiguous quantity of a vowel. His chief concern
was to correct out-and-out misspellings by the scribe, or inadvertent omissions,

---

3. The neat visual symbolism of a long horizontal line suggested to a reader *Hold this vowel-sound,*
whereas the short curve suggested (not quite so directly) *Let go of this vowel-sound.* But since the
invention of printing, or rather the use of it in Latin and Greek texts marked with macrons and
breves, too often a macron comes out no wider than a breve.

repetitions, etc.; but in passing he might also disambiguate a long or short vowel, as the Greek alphabet itself failed to do so.

Likewise the corrector would mark an accent — acute, grave, or circumflex — upon a vowel, when he felt it necessary or helpful to bring out the proper pitch contour, as OÍKOI 'at home' differed from OÎKOI 'houses' (nominative; *Iliad*. 1.113, 17.738, etc.).

He would also remedy the most untoward development in the spread of one form of the alphabet throughout Greece — i.e., the lack of a letter to represent the consonant-sound [h] (mostly but not exclusively at the beginning of a word). The Ionians of Asia Minor and the neighboring islands were the intellectual leaders of Greece in the sixth century B.C. and part of the fifth; among other things, they excelled in the tradition of epic poetry, reaching back to Homer. Now one characteristic of their current dialect (though not of Homer's) was the loss of [h]; accordingly, on the acrophonic principle, they reinterpreted the letter H: as they called the name of the letter [êːta] instead of [hêːta], they made it stand for their long open front-vowel. For the Ionic dialect this change in the function of one letter was definitely an improvement.

But when the Ionic version of the alphabet was adopted in the fifth and fourth centuries by other parts of Greece that wished to share in the flourishing culture of the Ionians, the gain in representing the vowel-sounds more precisely was counterbalanced by a loss: In abandoning the former consonantal function of the letter H, the non-Ionians left one sound in their repertory unwritten. Around 200 B.C., however, the scholars of Alexandria reintroduced the letter H as a reduced superscript ᚻ above a vowel;[4] thereafter a corrector would write it whenever he sensed that without it someone might misread or misunderstand a word — e.g., ἙN 'one' (nominative/accusative singular neuter; *Iliad* 13.260, etc.). Occasionally he would also write the opposite sign ᚼ for a negative purpose — to stand for no [h]: the preposition ἘN 'in' (1.14, etc.).

The shape ⊦ existed previously as a full-size letter in the local alphabet of certain Greek cities of southern Italy, notably Tarentum and Heraclea; it was their version of H. Before they switched to the Ionic alphabet, the people of the latter city spelled it ⊦ΕΡΑΚΛΕΙΑ. Even after switching, they were understandably reluctant to spell it ΗΡΑΚΛΕΙΑ, as other Greeks did, indicating the long

---

4. According to one influential tradition, it was Aristophanes, formerly of Byzantium (not the more famous Aristophanes, the Athenian comic poet).

vowel of the first syllable but ignoring the initial consonant. They found an easy way out, clinging to the local ⊦ as a consonant while embracing the Ionic H as a vowel: thus ⊦HPAKΛEIA.[5] Afterwards the scholars of Alexandria seized upon this device. In the midst of a movement away from local variation and towards uniformity, they were the ones who cherished the old literary classics — products of the diverse culture of the city-states, now on the wane; and they reached out also for something worth salvaging from a local alphabet.

Papyri marked with sporadic macrons and breves (¯ ˘), accents, and "breathings" (⊦ or ˥) have come to light from sites as early as the first century B.C., though the dating is uncertain.[6] Little by little, these diacritics gained in usage; but only in the sixth century of the Christian era did it become a rule to add the accents and "breathings" above all the appropriate letters, so that the scribes were trained to treat these simply as a part of orthography. By that time, however, it was too late for macrons and breves; the stark opposition in classical Greek between long and short vowels had virtually disappeared from even the most conservative pronunciation, and whatever theoretical knowledge of it may have lingered within a small residue of scholars, they were not moved to mark the texts with ¯ and ˘.

The Greeks who devised the diacritics toward the end of the pre-Christian era were worthy successors of those who, many centuries earlier, had adapted the Phoenician alphabet to the Greek language in the first place. Just as the addition of vowel-letters to that originally consonantal alphabet had been a giant step toward practical literacy for the population at large, enabling anyone with a tolerably keen ear to segment an utterance into its sequential graphemes, so now the added diacritics — if used to the full — would serve to obviate any uncertainty which the letters themselves left unresolved. It is, however, a significant fact that for centuries in the early Christian era the Greek diacritics were treated as an optional supplement, rather scantily used. One could almost call them a

---

5. ΤΩN⊦HPAKΛEIΩN (Inscriptiones Graecae 14.645.I.10, II.9) furnishes not the name of the city but the inhabitants, 'the Heracleans' (genitive).

6. Ancient copies of literary texts did not carry a date, but in many cases their penmanship matches in detail that of officially dated documents from the same site. In the middle ages it was common for a scribe, after he finished copying a literary text, to add at the end a colophon with his name as well as the time and place.

The term *macron* is just the Greek adjective μακρόν 'long' (nom./acc. sing. neuter), while *breve* is the Latin translation of βραχύ 'short'.

hobby of the scholars, although inherently suited to assist a broader circle that read the classics from the "golden age" of Greek literature.

When at last the accents and "breathings" became a requirement (in the sixth century and thereafter), it was to assure that the Biblical text should be read correctly in church; that evidently mattered to the ecclesiastical authorities. In the ensuing centuries, a sort of dark age, very few new copies were made of any books except the Bible; an occasional reader of the pagan authors could avail himself of codices left over from the fifth century or earlier. Thus it turned out that when a taste for the pagan classics revived among the Byzantines in the ninth and especially the tenth century, they took for granted the model of the Bible codex, with accents and "breathings" written meticulously, even though by that time no one still pronounced the [h], and the pitch-accents — acute, grave, and circumflex — had been leveled to a simple, undifferentiated stress. From then on, paradoxically, the language of Homer, Plato, and the other classics was written with more thorough and exact representation of its ancient sounds than had ever been shown by the pagans themselves, before the Christians took over their heritage.

3.   The Influence of the Greek Diacritics upon Other Ancient Languages

The vowel-and-consonant alphabet of Greece was modified, not in principle but in substantial details, to suit Latin, Coptic, Slavic, and several other languages of less enduring cultural import. The Greek diacritics also exercised some influence upon them, although minor and mostly indirect. However, it was the Semitic languages, written in a consonantal alphabet, that profited the most from the Greek precedent of adding small marks above the letters.

Since the Latin adaptation was well established at least two centuries before any diacritics began to be employed in Greek, it is no wonder that when, in the first century B.C., the Latins confronted the chief inadequacy of their form of the alphabet — namely, the lack of a graphic distinction between long and short vowels — they did not embrace the Greek solution. Whether or not they had any awareness of the Greek macron and breve (which, as I have said, were beginning to be used by scholars but not by the literate Greek public at large), the Latins most often chose simply to extend the letter I to show length; less often they placed above the other vowel-letters an apex ⌃ rather similar in shape to the

Greek circumflex accent ^ and possibly influenced by it;[7] e.g., LOCÍ 'of the place', PARATV̂ 'equipment'.[8] The need to mark the length of a vowel was much greater in Latin, where on the average a fourth to a third of the vowels in any utterance are long. So the movement to use the I *longa* and the apex made headway until the second century of the Christian era; then it died out, probably because people then lost the vocal habit of prolonging certain vowels.[9] Knowledge of the two Latin devices did not altogether disappear; ultimately, in the sixteenth century, the I *longa* was made to serve as a consonant — our familiar J.

The Copts — i.e., Egyptian Christians who in the second or third century translated the Greek Bible into dialects of their ancestral language — seem to have taken over the macron, placing it not over a vowel-letter (as in Greek) but over a consonant to show that it is pronounced syllabically, or with a weak, blurred vowel-sound; e.g., TB̄T [təbt] 'fish' (Steindorff 1953: 1–2, 34–36). Since the only Greek texts from that time which have come to light exhibiting macrons are pagan poetry, I cannot be sure that the Coptic mark, graphically identical with the Greek macron, was indeed a deliberate, intelligent adaptation of it to represent a phonological peculiarity of Coptic, somewhat analogous to the prolongation of certain vowels in Greek. After all, a horizontal superscript is so simple a device that the Copts might have hit upon it quite independently, even if there had not been in their country a sprinkling of Greeks who wrote that mark in texts of Homer, Bacchylides, etc. But even so, the very idea of a superscript diacritic, for a text of exceptional import, bespeaks the influence of Greek culture. For it was, above all, the Christian scriptures, needing to be translated from the Greek language, that motivated the Copts to cut loose from the cumbersome Demotic Egyptian script and to fashion in its place an alphabet based upon the Greek. The supple inventiveness of the Greek mind furnished a model to satisfy not only the practical but even more the ritual requirements of another nation.

Similarly, but more drastically, the translation of the Bible into Syriac motivated the Nestorian sect, and later the Jacobites, to remedy the deficiencies

---

7. While the circumflex accent is restricted to a long vowel or a diphthong, the apex can occur on an unstressed as well as a stressed vowel, and sometimes looks more like an acute accent.

8. Steffens 1929: 3 (Carmen Actiacum). The long vowel in the middle syllable of *paratu* was left unmarked, like many other occurrences in this text.

9. See Levin 1991.

of the twenty-two-letter consonantal alphabet. In the first place, cursive penmanship had neutralized the narrow graphic difference between ‏ד‎ and ‏ר‎ ({d} and {r}
respectively). Instead of reverting to an earlier style of lettering (as the humanists
of Italy in the fifteenth century revived the "roman" minuscule script of Charle-
magne's time and abandoned the crabbed, confusing minuscule that they
stigmatized as "gothic"), the Syrians as early as the fourth century got the idea
of putting a dot above their ‏ܪ‎ to stand for {r} and below it for {d}. This
diacritic, in a contrasting position either above or below, was a graphic remedy
— rather like a crutch — for a graphic failure. Doubtless it strikes the eye more
vividly than the small distinctive notch in the corner of the letter ‏ר‎ as mandated
by the "square", non-cursive script.

So the Syrians did well to introduce the dot; but they went on to write a
pair of dots above any plural noun or adjective, and the eastern or Nestorian
Syrians furthermore elaborated a system of finer dots — single or paired — to
show the vowel-sounds, as well as the precise articulation, plosive or fricative,
of certain ambiguous consonants; e.g.

ܘܓܒܪ̈ܝܗܘܢ {wg^{a}br^{a}yhẇn} 'and their men' (II Kings 25: 23, etc.).

The second letter {g} is marked with a pair of fine dots — one above and one
below — to symbolize the wide-open vowel [a]. The next letter {b} gets only
one dot below to show that it is fricative. After it, {r} has a pair of fine dots
(one above and one below) for [a], and two full dots to show that the noun is
plural; one of the full dots does double duty, distinguishing {r} from {d}.
Perhaps the dot under {g} is also serving doubly, as part of a vowel-sign and as
a mark of fricativation, for which we have some indirect evidence. The next-to-
last letter {w} gets a fine dot above to show that instead of its consonantal
function it stands here for the vowel [o]; a dot below would make it [u].

Now, each function of the contrasting dots ought in itself to work simply
enough. But when it is juxtaposed — as happens so often — to some other
function, the reader's mind must then operate at a high level of expertise, in
order to disambiguate the diacritical dots themselves. The Syrian commentators
recognized how this system is liable to bewilder a reader, and the scribes often
copied the dots wrong.[10] Still other dots, sometimes made very large, at the

---

10. See Segal, 1953: 1–2; 34–36.

beginning or the end of a word served for punctuation, in nearly the modern Occidental sense of that term.

Over several centuries (from the seventh to the thirteenth) the western or Jacobite Syrians used their heads, took another lesson from Greece, and for their five vowel-sounds (which agree only in part with those of the Nestorians) they settled upon writing small Greek letters above the Semitic consonants: ܘܓܐܒܪܐܝܗܘܢ {wg^abr^ayhẅn}. At least in principle, this constitutes an improvement over the earlier scripts, insofar as the vowels are visually, no less than phonetically, of a different order from the consonants, and from any other features of language. But many disadvantages, whether inherent or due merely to external circumstances, have combined to keep the Jacobite system from being adopted beyond the religious community where it originated.

The earlier Syriac notation, however, exercised a strong influence upon the writing of Arabic. The Arabic letters all go back to the twenty-two-letter alphabet of Phoenician-Hebrew-Aramaic, minus the ܣ {s}; but the Arabic language, at any rate in its classical form, had twenty-eight consonantal phonemes. So a dot was needed, for instance, to distinguish the velar fricative غ {ġ} (nearly identical in sound with the modern Greek γ) from the pharyngeal ع {ʕ} (غ and ع respectively in an initial position).[11] Moreover the cursive penmanship, with its elegant arabesques, neutralized the graphic difference between several other letters, such as the Aramaic ܦ {p} and ܩ {q} both coming out ڢ and needing to be distinguished as ف and ق respectively. One, two, or three dots above a given letter, and one or two below were introduced to create a semblance of a twenty-eight-letter alphabet.

Wisely the Arabs refrained from the use of dots for any purpose but to distinguish consonant-phonemes from one another. In classical Arabic, ا (the first letter of the alphabet) was written, more often in not, in words where no glottal stop [ʔ] was pronounced. The occurrences where it was pronounced were marked with a reduced ء above or below: thus أ or إ .

In many other non-initial occurrences of ا no consonant-sound was pronounced in classical Arabic, but the letter could be understood to stand for the long vowel /ā/, as in لا {lʔ} 'not' (2.2 et passim).[12] However, when a word

---

11. ء is clearly derived from the Aramaic � {ʕ}.

12. The ligature لا , of ل {l} followed by ا {ʔ}, tilts the second letter from lower right to upper left.

with that vowel-sound was written in the Qur?ān without this letter, as in the second syllable of كَتبك {ktbk} 'your (masc. sing.) book' (accusative case, 17.14[15]), a small vertical ' was added above: كَتْبك ; /k-tāb-k-/ Furthermore a sign for the short vowel /a/ was devised by laying the reduced ' nearly sideways: كَتَبَك ; /k-tābaka/.

The slant of this vowel-sign ˘ was probably suggested by that of the short back-vowel ' /u/, as in the plural كُتُب /kutubun/ 'books' (nominative, 98.2[3]).[13] The ' is just a reduction of the letter و {w}, which slopes essentially from upper right to lower left. That letter, when non-initial, serves often for the long back-vowel /ū/, as in ذو /ðū/ 'able, endowed' (3.3[4], etc.).

Likewise the letter ى {y} (whose initial shape is ﻳ) serves often for the long front-vowel /ī/; e.g. فى /fī/ 'in' (2.10 et passim). Perhaps the subscript for the short front-vowel /i/ originated also as a simplification of the shape of that letter ى ; in any case, it is written just like the superscript ˘ /a/: كِتَبَك /kitābaka/. In most manuscripts and editions of the Qur?ān the long vowels are shown redundantly, the letter being preceded (or accompanied) by the superscript or subscript stroke: ﻻ {l^a?} = /lā/, فى {f$_i$y} = /fī/, ذو {ð^{u}w} = /ðū/.

The Arabic vowel-notation is phonemic; for there are only the three **contrasting** vowel-qualities, although they are actualized over much of the spectrum, depending upon the consonantal environment — the /a/ often verges upon [ε], and the /u/ upon [o] or [ö]. Such sub-phonemic variants did not need to be shown graphically, because the notation was intended for readers to whom the sounds came naturally.

For readers of the Hebrew Bible, however, a meticulously phonetic notation was more necessary, since the language had long ceased to be vernacular but was perpetuated orally, with more or less accuracy, by school traditions. The Jews were very slow to learn from the Greek and Syriac Christians; but they did begin, rather soon after the Muslim conquest of much of the Byzantine empire, to try out notations for supplementing the consonantal text. The fullest of these, the one destined for eventual adoption by all synagogues, was devised in Tiberias

---

13. The double ˘ (a simplification of the double ʾʾ) above the final letter stands for /-un/, the nominative case-ending followed by the indefinite article, since this consonant-sound of classical Arabic was not written as a regular letter. Presumably, in the Arabic dialect for which the Aramaic alphabet was adapted, no consonant [n] was pronounced, but at most a nasalization of the vowel.

(by the Sea of Galilee);[14] it distinguishes seven vowel-qualities. It owes the most to the Nestorian system, but with a simple and at the same time an enormous improvement: besides the dot, it employs the dash (a short line, mainly horizontal but for certain secondary purposes vertical or diagonal); the idea may have come from the Arabic ´ and . .

In some ways the Tiberias notation is actually more logical than the IPA could afford to be, more than a thousand years later; for the IPA was practically bound to adhere to the Latin alphabet, as far as the existing letters would suffice. Accordingly, it used one dot . for the least open front-vowel [i], as in מִן {mᵢn} 'from'; two dots side by side .. for the next degree of aperture [e]; and three ∴ for the widest of the front-vowels [ɛ]. Now the shape of the IPA character [ɛ] does aptly suggest a more open sound than [e],[15] whereas our association of the character [i] with its phonetic value depends upon our prior familiarity with this letter in various European languages. In the Hebrew notation the one dot for [i] and the two dots for [e] go back to the Nestorian punctators; but in Hebrew they are used exclusively to stand for these vowels.

The one innovation that eventually had the most influence beyond the bounds of Hebrew is what the punctators called [šəwɔ]. They were not actually the first to devise a sign for the slight quasi-vocalic sound that makes the consonant or consonants of a syllable audible in the absence of a distinct vowel. The Copts had done that already, with a horizontal superscript line, as we have seen (above, p. 575) in T̄B̄T. A Hebrew notation somewhat earlier than the Tiberias, and attributed to the Jewish community of Babylonia, apparently took that over from the Coptic, but gave it a slight tilt: בֿנֿי {bᵊnⁱy} 'my son' (Pr. 1: 8, etc.).[16] The Tiberias punctators, however, had to devise something else for [ə], because they used the horizontal superscript instead for the weaker sound of certain consonantal letters: fricative in the case of ת פ כ ד ג ב {b̄ ḡ d̄ k̄ p̄ t̄}, and silent א and ה. For [ə] they resorted to a pair of dots arranged vertically: בְּנֵי; but that involved a troublesome ambiguity, because of a lesson they learned from the Arabs. In Arabic it was judged worthwhile to write a negative sign, shaped like a tiny zero, above a consonant-letter — showing that no vowel is

---

14. The earliest dated specimens are from the 9th century of the Christian era. (Of course they did not use any Christian chronology.)

15. On the source of the character ɛ in the IPA, see below, p. 585.

16. This "Babylonian" notation is entirely superscript.

pronounced with it.[17] The "Babylonian" vocalizers of Hebrew did nothing of the sort; but those in Tiberias chose to follow the Arabic example, in principle.[18] However, they used the two dots ֗ for both purposes — to show [ə], and to show no vowel-sound; for in Hebrew there are many border-line cases, where it is unclear whether or not a barely perceptible vocalic transition occurs between two consonants.

The seven full vowels, along with [ə], are involved in such morphological complications as to make Arabic seem easy at times, next to Hebrew. For 'hand' in Arabic is always vocalized يَد /yad-/ throughout the singular and dual,

whereas in Hebrew	'a hand' is	יָד	{yₒd̄},
but the construct	'(so-and-so's) hand' is	יַד	{yₐd̄},
	'my hand'	יָדִי	{yₒd̄ᵢy},
	'his hand'	יָדוֹ	{yₒd̄⁶w},
	'our hand'	יָדֵנוּ	{yₒd̄ₑynᵤw}, etc.,
but	'your (pl.) hand'	יֶדְכֶם	{yₑd̄₍ₒ₎k̄ₑm},
	'hands'	יָדַיִם	{yₒd̄ₐyᵢm},
but	'(so-and-so's) hands'	יְדֵי	{yₒd̄ₑy}, etc.

The main difference is between the accented and the basically unaccented words, but other factors enter; e.g., [ɔ] cannot be separated from the accented vowel by more than one consonant. It could be argued that the underlying vowel in the root of all the Hebrew forms is /a/, as in Arabic; but that would not avail to guide the reader of Scripture as to the actual vowel-sound [ɔ], [a], [ɛ], or [ə].

Accent plays an indispensable role in Hebrew, far more than in Arabic; and the Hebrew accentual notation, consisting of some two dozen distinct signs, is supremely elaborate and supple.[19] Although the transmission of the texts, on the oral side, was by chanting, not by reading in a flat voice, the notation for guiding it is essentially elocutionary rather than melodic; it shows the varying

---

17. The graphic resemblance of the Arabic sign, called /suqūn/ (literally 'rest'), to the Hindu numeral may have been deliberate; for the Arabs were exposed to that cultural influence from India around the same time as they became concerned to supplement their consonantal alphabet.

18. Most Hebrew words, unlike most words in classical Arabic, end in a consonant-sound. So the Hebrew punctators of Tiberias found it economical to dispense with ֗ under the final letter, except for a few — notably ךְ {-k̄} — because they do often come with an accompanying vowel-sound; ךָ {-k̄ₒ} is the suffix 'you' or 'your' (masc. sing.).

19. See Levin 1968.

degrees of conjuncture or disjuncture between the words and phrases of each verse. A given sign does not stand for one musical note or trill; instead it receives a different melodic value, depending on whether the text is from the Pentateuch or the Prophets, or on which occasion in the liturgical calendar the text is read.

In its way the Hebrew accentual system is more than a precursor of the modern scientific analysis of junctural phenomena. I wish it could serve, in other languages too, as a practical model for a good elocutionary notation: how to mark a text so as to evoke, without ambiguity, one semantically valid reading — somewhat as the IPA evokes one normal pronunciation of the sequential segments in a text, even if not necessarily the same pronunciation, in all details, that an individual speaker of the language would produce spontaneously. But we do not seem to be at all close, in any modern language, to arriving at a success- ful notation that surpasses the meager traditional apparatus of commas, colons, etc. These marks go back to the Greeks of the early Christian era, with minor changes and additions later on. No effective motivation has arisen to produce something substantially more accurate than that, and at the same time not forbiddingly hard to learn.

The Scripture readers of medieval Tiberias had a strong enough religious motive to devise such a notation; future experience will tell whether linguistic science can equal — and even surpass — that accomplishment.

4.   Orthographic Improvements in Modern European Languages

The immersion of Anglophone and especially of American linguists in the English language, while quite natural, has had untoward consequences, including a degree of indifference to some practical applications of linguistic science. Their lack of interest in spelling reform is understandable, since every movement aiming at that in Anglophone countries has failed. To be sure, the lexicographers, teachers, and printers of the late seventeenth and the eighteenth century did succeed in standardizing a single spelling for most English words, which has endured with only the most minor changes since then. But they had no consistent principles, apart for making *j* and *v* rank as separate letters, distinct from *i* and *u,* and reserved for a voiced affricate and a voiced fricative respectively.[20] Otherwise the English people, or the only ones among them able to exercise any sort of real authority over the language, have been dead-set against changing the way it is written. Even the spelling reformers, aside from the most radical ones, have eschewed the introduction of diacritics or of additional letters. So an unbiased linguistic observer might well conclude that written English is not amenable to improvements that would better represent the actual English sounds. **Why** is it not amenable — unlike most other European languages? The cause or causes ought to be of great theoretical interest to scientifically minded linguists, even after the negative fact is well established from five hundred years or more of history. My present purpose, however, is only to argue that the relative backwardness and ineptitude of English orthography should not mislead the linguistic profession into supposing that in other languages phonology has likewise been to little or no avail. On the contrary, these languages have benefited more or less extensively from the actions of a few respected experts.

Of these the first that I would single out, and the greatest, was Jan Hus, the Czech reformer of both religion and orthography (1370?-1415). A treatise in Latin is attributed to him,[21] in which the most serious deficiencies of the alphabet, as it had been applied to his vernacular, are remedied. Like his English predecessor Wyclif, he was determined to have his people read the Bible in their own language, and to circulate copies of his sermons. But whereas Wyclif did not make an issue of the obstacles to rational literacy that had resulted from the past influence of French scribes upon English spelling, Hus — like many other Czechs — hated the Germans and was alert to the clumsy devices of Czech spelling modeled upon German. Fundamentally he kept the Latin alphabet, but supplemented it with better devices that he picked up from diverse prior sources. For palatalized consonants he introduced a superscript dot, which presently gave

---

20. For centuries *j* and *v* had been merely variant shapes; but Petrus Ramus (Pierre de la Ramée), a French Latinist around 1550, proposed to differentiate them phonetically. Within a hundred years or so, his reform was generally adopted, not only for Latin (where he had no inkling of how grossly it was at odds with the true ancient pronunciation) but for the modern languages written in the Latin alphabet; there it certainly was a change for the better.

21. See the excellent edition of John Schröpfer 1968. Schröpfer's book has been particularly useful to me because of his expertise in Czech; Russian is the only Slavic language of which I can claim to have a reading knowledge.

way to the more distinctive *háček*. For long vowels he added the acute accent ´.[22]

He made no move, however, to put aside the Latin alphabet for the Cyrillic or Glagolitic, in which several eastern and southern Slavic languages were written. The missionaries of the Orthodox Church had perceived the utter inadequacy of the Greek alphabet for many Slavic sounds, and therefore altered it extensively. For them, furthermore, the Orthodox faith was not bound up with the Greek language, to anything like the same extent as the Catholic faith was with Latin. Some Slavic scholars in Orthodox monasteries indeed kept up the study of the Greek texts, but their people heard the Bible and the liturgy only in Church Slavic. So far as I know, Hus was not at all inclined to unite with the Orthodox Slavs, either in script or in liturgy; it would have amounted to a secession from Latin culture as well as Latin Christendom. Rather he worked for a rational reordering **within** the tradition that he had inherited.

We as linguists can rightly esteem the reforms of centuries past as scientific, but only insofar as a given diacritic, like a given letter, was used consistently. A dot is just a makeshift if it serves merely to warn that a letter has some sound or other unlike what it would be without the dot — e.g. in Arabic it differentiates the fricative ذ /ð/ from the plosive د /d/, but also ز . /z/ from ر /r/, where nothing but careless penmanship had neutralized the clear graphic distinction between ו and ר in the Aramaic source (see above, p. 576); the **sound** of ز . is by no means a modification of /r/. The Czech diacritics have indeed been used consistently and have eliminated the confusing array of digraphs that the earlier scribes had resorted to. Only the digraph *ch* for the velar fricative was retained in Czech, the same as in German.[23]

---

22. At that time the macron ‾ would scarcely have served. The medieval scribes had long since preempted the horizontal superscript stroke as an abbreviating sign, most often to dispense with writing the letter *m* or *n*. Hus favored economy in penmanship, unless it entailed ambiguity. The simple diagonal above a vowel, to show length, may have been based upon a by-form of the ancient Latin apex, ´ instead of ˆ (see above, pp. 574–575).

23. In medieval Europe the *h* had become a sort of miscellaneous diacritic; in combination with the previous letter, it indicated various sounds. Originally, in ancient Latin, it formed the digraphs CH TH PH to transliterate the Greek letters X /k^h/, Θ /t^h/, Φ /p^h/ quite accurately. But over time these ancient aspirates changed: in Greek they became fricative; in Latin only the *ph* came to be pronounced like *f*, while *th* and *ch* simply lost their aspiration and became ordinary plosives. So the medieval scribes no longer regarded the letter *h* as standing simply for the sound [h], and instead they manipulated it variously: *sh* in English for /š/, *lh* in Portuguese and Provençal for /l^y/ and *nh* in Portuguese for /n^y/, etc.

The spelling reformers of other European languages were, on the whole, more successful in eliminating sheer futilities inherited from preceding generations, than in introducing any positive improvement. The Accademia della Crusca, in Florence, through its *Vocabolario della lingua toscana* (1608 with subsequent revisions) got rid of the "silent letter" *h-* in all but a few words.[24] The grave accent of ancient Greek, where it is restricted to the last syllable, was adapted in Italian to mark the small but important minority of words stressed in that position — thus *amò* 'he/she loved' in contrast to *amo* 'I love' (where the actual stress upon the penult ['amo] is not shown in writing). But the ambiguities in accentuation between the penult and the antepenult remain: in spite of many proposals to write an accent — whether grave or acute — upon the antepenult, the old practice of indifference persists.

In Spanish the *h-,* based in large part upon Latin etymology, continues to complicate an otherwise well-reformed orthography. The Real Academia Española, in the eighteenth and nineteenth centuries, through successive editions of its *Diccionario de la lengua castellana,* enacted several sensible changes. Two of them are exemplified in *santísimo* 'most holy': the simplification of the double letter *-ss-,* inherited from the Latin *sanctissimus* although only a single [-s-] has been pronounced in Spanish for many centuries, and the acute accent on the antepenult. Using only that accent, the Academia gradually worked out the most economical system, so as to mark the stress upon words only if they deviate from these elementary rules:

(a)   stress upon the penult if the word ends in a vowel or in *-s* or *-n;* e.g., *termino* /term'ino/ 'I end' but *terminó* 'he/she ended' and the noun *término,* 'end'.

The Cyrillic x for the velar fricative carried over the medieval Greek phonetic value of χ. But if introduced into Czech, it would have made for confusion, because in the Latin alphabet the single letter *x* served — unfortunately — for a consonant-group /ks/. In Spanish, to be sure, the Latin /ks/ has ultimately come out a velar fricative, after passing through /ss/ and /š/; thus, Latin *dīxī* 'I said' Old Spanish *dixe* [-š-], spelled *dije* in modern Spanish orthography but [dixe] in the International Phonetic Alphabet.

24. Migliorini 1958: 450–53, 463–64. The silent letter lingers down to the present in *ho* 'I have', *hai* 'you have', *ha* 'he/she/it has', *hanno* 'they have', to avoid homography with *o* 'or', *ai* 'to the' (masc. pl.), *a* 'to', *anno* 'year'. A few purists prefer to differentiate the four verb-forms by means of a grave accent: *ò, ài, à, ànno.*

(b)   stress upon the ultima otherwise; e.g., *animal* /anim'al/ but *árbol* 'tree'.

Thus the great majority of Spanish words do not need to be marked, while all the rest are attended to easily.

One unsuccessful reformer of Italian spelling, Giangiorgio Trissino (1478–1550), deserves mention because the IPA, nearly four hundred years later, profited from his initiative. He was a native of Vicenza, where the courtiers wished to speak in conformity — more or less — to the standard of the prestigious Tuscan dialect, far though it was from their native pronunciation. He perceived the need, among other things, to distinguish graphically between the two Tuscan vowel-sounds (phonemes in modern terminology) that were written indifferently with the letter *e*, and the two written indifferently with the letter *o*. For the more open front-vowel he introduced the Greek letter ε.[25] and for the more open back-vowel ω. His choices were somewhat arbitrary; later he changed his mind about ω and made it serve instead for the closed back-vowel.[26] No Italians of his age followed his lead, nor did they afterwards, with the isolated exception of Girolamo Gigli of Siena (in Tuscany) about two hundred years later (Migliorini 1958: 345–349, 368–369, 516). But the ε was inherently a good idea; for the shape of the letter symbolizes well the openness of the mouth, in contrast to the shape of *e*. And so, much later still, when the IPA adopted [ɛ] as a phonetic character, the counterpart [ɔ] was modeled upon it to symbolize a back-vowel more open than [o].

In Italian, /v'enti/ 'winds' and /v'enti/ 'twenty' are still spelled alike *(venti),* and so are /v'ɔlto/ 'turned' and /v'olto/ 'face' *(volto);* but foreign students of the language enjoy the benefit of this phonetic notation, if their textbooks introduce them to it. The distinction is pertinent to many other languages besides; and far beyond Italy, modern linguistics owes something to an intelligent, if untimely, innovator who wrote quite in the spirit of the Renaissance. He had a secular rather than a religious motive: to enhance the elegance of courtly life, not on the

---

25. ε and ϵ are merely variant shapes of the same Greek minuscule letter. By the time the study of the Greek language was revived in Italy, the Greeks were undoubtedly pronouncing a more open sound than the Tuscan [e], for example in the pronoun *me*. In classical Attic, however (around 400 B.C.), ME was pronounced [me] rather than [mɛ].

26. In the Greek of his time (and for many centuries before then) the letters ω and o were pronounced the same. Recent research has proved that Ω in classical Attic stood for a more open vowel-sound than O; but Trissino could hardly have been aware of this. If he had been, why would he have changed over to *o* for the open sound?

visual side by teaching the painters to make subtler tints on their murals, but on the auditory side, enabling his readers to master the more complex and gracious articulation of sounds.

5.   Phonological Markedness

More generally, scientific phonology has been influenced, and indeed enlightened, by the struggles of our predecessors to determine what **needed marking** beyond the inherited practices of the scribes or printers. In the abstract, one might well argue that in Spanish the stress upon the penultimate syllable of /term'ino/ 'I end' is, to the ear, no less noticeable a feature than the stress on the ultima of /termin'o/ 'he/she ended', and that the spelling *termino* for 'I end' lacks something essential — as though none of the three syllables were more prominent than the others. It is a curious historical fact that a committee of the Real Academia at first proposed, in 1713, to mark with an acute accent such words, characterized by stress on the penult; as examples they gave *famóso, caballéro, apercebído*.[27] They were somehow under the impression that their language needed written accents nearly to the same extent as classical Greek (where the accents — acute, grave, or circumflex — are indeed indispensable in all but a few short words); but they scaled it down sharply, before their dictionary ever went to press.

Had they stuck to their original idea, it would have been impractical pedantry. But moreover, their common-sense decision was in line with the theoretical conclusion they would have reached in the twentieth century, by studying N. S. Trubetzkoy's *Grundzüge der Phonologie* (1939.) His principles, advancing beyond his predecessors' in the analysis of phonemes, require not only the identification of the one minimal feature that differentiates the crucial phonetic segment in a pair of semantically opposed words — e.g., the voicing in *zeal* /zil/ : *seal* /sil/. We must also state that voicing is the mark, or additional feature, of one — absent from the other (Trubetzkoy 1931). Furthermore, the difference in frequency becomes an important criterion; for in general, if not universally, what is marked occurs less often, and so the hearer notices it as something positive, while taking the unmarked for granted.

---

27. Their pamphlet was entitled "Planta, y methodo, qve . . . deben observar los Academicos en la composicion del nuevo Diccionario ... ", copied by Conde de la Viñaya, 1893: 749–53.

Now the penultimate stress in /term'ino/ 'I end' is phonologically unmarked, because that is by far the prevailing pattern in such trisyllabic words, and the Hispanophones take it for granted, unless counteracted by the unusual stress upon the ultima in /termin'o/ 'he/she ended' or upon the antepenult in the noun /t'ermino/. Their language (unlike French) has no trisyllabic words in which the syllables are inherently of equal prominence; so the orthographic rule that calls for *termino,* rather than *termíno* (with a redundant accent), is phonologically sound.

To be sure, this official orthography has from the outset presupposed the graphic separation of words, each of which may — in the actual stream of speech — be just a part of a rather long polysyllabic chain.[28] If scientific phonology were to "start from scratch", purposely disregarding all the experience with written notation from before the modern age, we might come up with a very different set of symbols. Instead of spacing between words, we might adopt the juncture mark # and certain contour-lines for intonation, and several other marks for the degrees of stress, etc. Without discarding the Latin alphabet altogether, we would conceivably symbolize the initial consonant of *zeal* as /s^v-/, marking it thus for VOICE, and likewise *veal* as /f^v-/. But to go on this way becomes more and more bizarre.

Experience has shown, however, how the traditional resources can — at least in some cases — be applied quite rationally as well as practically. The Germans in the eighteenth century, beginning with J. S. V. Popowitsch,[29] found a better way to show the Umlaut vowels than by the digraphs *ue, oe, ae,* which by that time were usually written with a small superscript letter: *ú, ó, á* . This ungainly expedient was eliminated by resorting to the two dots as they had been used in German during the middle ages: *ü, ö, ä.* That did not follow the remote Greek model of the diaeresis above the second of two vowel-letters to mark a new syllable (instead of the two constituting a diphthong; see above, p. @000). The two dots were arbitrarily revalued to serve the phonological structure of the German language.

---

28. In the last, unfinished chapter (see the posthumous preface), "Die Abgrenzungslehre: Die delimitative oder abgrenzende Schallfunktion" (Trubetzkoy 1939), he broached the difficult problem of analyzing the oral clues to the morphological structure of an utterance.

29. His magnum opus, *Die nothwendigsten Anfangsgründe der Teutschen Sprachkunst zum Gebrauche der Österreichischen Schulen* (1754), appears to be inaccessible in America, but see Jellinek 1913–14: I, 254–55; II, 26.

These Umlaut vowels are fronted modifications of the three back-vowels. Phoneticians nowadays describe *ü* and *ö* customarily as rounded front-vowels; but they originated in the Germanic languages as **back-vowels diphthongized** to anticipate the front-vowel *i* or its homorganic semi-vowel in the ensuing syllable. Furthermore, the Umlaut vowels in modern German words have a morpho-phonemic relation to the back-vowels, not to the front-vowels *i* and *e*. So it makes good sense to write — for example — *Töchter* 'daughters', the plural of *Tochter;* for this spelling marks the vowel-sound in the plural as an offshoot of the plain vowel *o*. The two dots do not, in themselves, define what kind of offshoot; but the German language has only the fronted kind, and so the device works well enough.[30]

Whereas a **theoretical understanding** demands the most exact statement of all the pertinent facts, a **communicative notation** makes compromises with the existing and familiar graphic resources. Being literate Occidentals before we became professional linguists, we have inherited a powerful tradition for the analysis of languages. In the course of applying it, we learn more and more; but all the while we remain constrained, to a degree, by its framework. We can broaden our understanding through the difficult study of an independent analytical tradition, such as that of the Sanskrit grammarians. But most of our terminology will continue to be from Greek and Latin sources, however redefined. So, while aiming at universal validity, we should take care not to claim prematurely that we have arrived at that distant goal.[31]

---

30. When the Turks under Kemal Atatürk, around 1928, revolutionized the written form of Turkish by replacing the Arabic script with a modified Latin alphabet, the phonology of their language appeared to call for four plain vowels *u o a ı* (written without dots) and the fronted counterparts *ü ö ä i* (cf. Trubetzkoy, 1939: 95, 98–99). But *ä* promptly gave way to *e*, following the model of all European languages, which use *e* for the main front-vowel of intermediate aperture before they resort to any other letter plus diacritic to stand for a different front-vowel. In the abstract scheme of scientific phonology, *ü ö e i* may look grossly unsymmetrical next to *u o a ı*; but *e* has a weighty **cultural** advantage over *ä*.

In German of the eighteenth century, when Popowitsch proposed *ä* instead of *å* or *ae*, this fronted vowel was pronounced [æ] rather than [ɛ]. So upon settling in England, the composer Haendel (whose name meant "Little Hand") changed the spelling to Handel. But now the would-be purists (including some musicologists), who are unaware of the subsequent change within German eliminating the [æ], imagine that it is a mistake to pronounce this name like the English word *handle*.

31. I thank the graphic artist Stanleu Kaufmann for drawing the characters not available in electronic fonts.

References

Bernal, Martin. 1990. *Cadmean Letters*. Winona Lake, Indiana: Eisenbrauns.

Jellinek, M. H. 1913–14. *Geschichte der neuhochdeutschen Grammatik von den Anfangen bis auf Adelung*. Heidelberg: Carl Winter. (2 volumes)

Levin, Saul. 1968. The traditional chironomy of the Hebrew Scriptures. *Journal of Biblical Literature* 87: 59–70.

Levin, Saul. 1979. The מֵתֶג according to the practice of the early vocalizers. *Hebrew Annual Review* 3: 129–139.

Levin, Saul. 1982. Defects, alleged or real, in the Tiberias pointing. *Hebrew Studies* 23: 67–84.

Levin, Saul. 1983. Syllabic writing and the discovery of verb roots. *The Ninth LACUS Forum, 1982*, ed. by John Morreal, 505–514. Columbia, South Carolina: Hornbeam.

Levin, Saul. 1984a. The Greek diacritical marks and their application to other languages in the Renaissance. *General Linguistics* 24: 21–37.

Levin, Saul. 1984b. Dē prōductīs ā correptīs uōcālibus sēdulō distinguendīs. *Hermes Americanus* 2: 166–172.

Levin, Saul. 1991. Review of Pulgram 1986. *General Linguistics* 31: 57–58.

Migliorini, Bruno. 1958. *Storia della lingua italiana*. Firenze: Sansoni.

Pulgram, Ernst. 1986. *Practicing Linguist: Essays on Language and Languages 1950 — 1985*. Heidelberg: Carl Winter.

Schropfer, John. 1968. *Hussens Traktat 'Orthographia Bohemica': Die Herkunft des diakritischen Systems in der Schreibung slavischer Sprachen und die älteste zusammenhängende Beschreibung slavischer Laute*. (= Slavische Studienbucher IV). Wiesbaden: Otto Harrasowitz.

Segal, J. B. 1953. *The Diacritical Point and the Accents in Syriac*. (= London Oriental Series, 2) Oxford: Oxford University Press.

Steffens, Franz. 1929. *Lateinische Paläographie*. Second edition. Berlin: Walter de Gruyter.

Steindorff, Georg. 1951. *Lehrbuch der koptischen Grammatik*. Chicago: University of Chicago Press.

Trubetzkoy, N. S. 1931. Die phonologischen Systeme. *Travaux du Cercle Linguistique de Prague* 4: 96–116.

Trubetzkoy, N. S. 1939. *Grundzüge der Phonologie*. (= *Travaux du Cercle Linguistique de Prague* 7.)

Viñaya, Conde de la. 1893. *Biblioteca histórica de la filología castellana*. Madrid: M. Tello.

About the author

Saul Levin is Distinguished Professor of Ancient Languages at the State University of New York at Binghamton. He received his doctorate from the University of Chicago in 1949. He became acquainted with Syd Lamb at the 1974 inaugural LACUS Forum. He was President of LACUS in 1980–1981. He also participated in the 1986 Rice Symposium on the Prehistory of Languages. His major works include **The Indo-European and Semitic Languages: An Exploration of Structural Similarities Related to Accent, Chiefly in Greek, Sanskrit, and Hebrew,** *and the recent book* **Semitic and Indo-European: The Principal Etymologies.**

CHAPTER 36

Early MT Research at M.I.T.

The Search for Context

Victor H. Yngve
University of Chicago

Because of Sydney Lamb's early and distinguished research on machine translation (MT), and his continuing interest in linguistic problems, some of which
came out of that effort, it seems appropriate to relate here a few of the highlights
of the MT research at the Massachusetts Institute of Technology. Perhaps that
era can be seen a bit more clearly now with the advantage of several decades of
hindsight. Both Syd and I took an approach to MT that, more than most others,
insisted on making use of the best insights from linguistics.

In retrospect, much of the M.I.T. work centered around the problem of how
to take context into account. In this paper I intend to focus mainly on research
up to the early 1960s, but will also say a few things about what has happened
since. I will concentrate on the more important technical papers during this
period, leaving aside a number of general and popular discussions, which,
however, should be consulted by anyone writing a history of the period.

1. MT and the Promise of Linguistics

As was the case with Syd Lamb, my interest in MT was kindled in graduate
school. I am often asked how I ever happened to move into linguistics from
physics. The reader will see that the shift was a gradual and quite natural move
from physics through MT to linguistics. I perceived my early full-time commit-
ment to MT and its renewal every year or so in the beginning as exciting and
adventuresome, but entailing considerable career risks. I realized acutely that

each year away from physics would make it that much harder to return to the forefront of research there. I have never regretted the move.

1.1 *The promise of the machine*

As part of my research assistantship at Chicago under Marcel Schein, the distinguished cosmic ray physicist, I was involved in preparing instrumentation and running experiments for detecting the incoming cosmic radiation in the stratosphere using high-altitude balloon flights and airplane flights. (Gill, Schein and Yngve 1947, Schein, Yngve and Kraybill 1948, Schein and Yngve 1952, Yngve 1954b). The instrumentation was designed to detect and record high-energy particles capable of triggering several Geiger counters in a row simultaneously while penetrating up to 22 cm. of lead. The means for detecting and recording the coincident electrical pulses from the counters were similar to techniques found in the literature on the new automatic electronic computers, the so-called giant brains of the late 1940s.

It seemed to me that these new machines might be useful for other purposes besides computing — perhaps for playing chess, searching a library file, or translating languages. Of these, translating seemed potentially the most important, for it might help to eliminate some of the barriers between countries in a post-war world.

Other early influences were the law of E. U. Condon, further developed by George K. Zipf, that the product of the frequency of different words in text by their frequency rank was approximately constant, and Claude Shannon's work on the entropy of printed English. I remember that people were amazed that one could have that kind of predictability in something like linguistic behavior, which seemed to be directly under the control of the will. This apparently lawful behavior of language reinforced the idea that it might be possible to mechanize translation.

1.2 *Word-for-word translation*

Around 1948 we had been experimenting with recording our cosmic ray data on the new tape recorders. At one point I toyed with the idea of building a word-for-word translation machine in which a dictionary in digital form would be magnetically recorded. Such a machine would be comparatively simple to design and build. I realized that its translations would be very imperfect, but they might go a long way toward being useful.

Even this early scheme illustrates an important design feature: The translation algorithm (input, dictionary look-up, and output), which was to be realized in the hardware and useful for any language pair, was conceptually separate from the linguistic information or dictionary (here to be stored on the magnetic medium and to be specific for a particular language pair)

1.3   *Problems with word-for-word translation*

The linguistic difficulties involved in word-for-word translation even then loomed larger than the mechanical difficulties. It seemed evident that adjectives in French would have to be moved in front of the nouns in an English translation, and in the case of German even more complex changes in word order would be required. In addition, there was the suspicion that for many words it would be difficult or impossible to find a single word to serve everywhere as its translation. I did not actually try to build such a machine, postponing such work for after I had finished my dissertation. In the meantime I consulted with some University of Chicago linguistic faculty members and entered on an extracurricular program of reading in the field of linguistics.

While still a graduate student, I was privileged to attend the first international conference on machine translation, organized by Yehoshua Bar-Hillel, which took place at M.I.T. on June 17–20, 1952. Through the organizing activities surrounding that conference I became acquainted with the early research of others on MT.

Yehoshua Bar-Hillel had visited most of the few people who had done any MT work and had written a report on results achieved up to the end of 1951 which was distributed in mimeograph form (1951).

The work of Oswald and Fletcher (1951) on the mechanical resolution of German word-order problems was particularly impressive. They proposed a scheme of scanning back and forth in the German sentence searching for the words, phrases, and clauses in a prescribed English word order. A scheme like this runs into problems with homonyms. For example, how could the machine in its searches distinguish between *der* as an article or as a relative pronoun, or *sein* as a verb or as a possessive adjective? Their paper did discuss some of these problems, but there remained many that were unresolved.

There was then the growing realization of the full dimensions of the multiple meaning problem in translation. A look at any bilingual dictionary is sufficient to convince one that many of the most frequently occurring words are paired with many different words in another language, and one could not easily choose one that could serve everywhere.

Some threw up their hands in despair. If a machine were to present lists of all the meanings for each word so as not to eliminate arbitrarily any important information from the translation, the reader or a post-editor would have a hopeless task threading his way through the maze, choosing the correct meaning from each list. Even for an average sentence of twenty words there would easily be billions of paths through the maze, only one of which presumably would be the correct path.

Word-for-word translation did, however, promise to the most optimistic to be a good first step toward an adequate translation. On that hope, some researchers did work hard on automatic dictionaries on the basis that a dictionary would be needed eventually in any case. I concluded that we should take a word-for-word translation as a first approximation, and concentrate on trying to improve it (Yngve 1955b: 208).

1.4 *The focus on syntax*

It seemed clear that the information necessary for the resolution of the multiple meaning problem resides in the context (Yngve 1955b: 209). But it was not initially clear how actually in practice to take the context into account. Erwin Reifler had suggested in a series of reports he circulated that a pre-editor be used to add tags to the input words to make their parts of speech explicit and to indicate the fields of knowledge to which they belonged. He later became convinced that the machine could in principle select and add these tags mechanically.

Oswald suggested the use of a microglossary, a glossary of the words found in publications in the special field of the material being translated, for example brain surgery, in which would be listed only brain surgery meanings (Oswald 1952, Oswald and Lawson 1953). This suggestion would also help solve the storage problem, for computers in those early days had very small memories and the vocabulary used in articles from a single field would be smaller than the vocabulary used in articles not restricted to a single special field.

It seemed to me and to others that a solution for many of the multiple meaning problems could be achieved if the machine could work out a syntactic analysis for each sentence (Yngve 1955b: 213ff.). This would immediately help with the translation of grammatical words, for the machine could then distinguish the article *der* from the relative pronoun *der*, the verb *sein* from the adjective *sein* and translate them accordingly. This would go a long way toward solving the multiple meaning problem, for not only are grammatical words among the most frequently occurring words in running text, they also average more meanings per word than do other words such as nouns and verbs. It was also felt that a syntactic analysis of the sentence would help with the multiple meaning problem of certain content words. Particularly in a language like English there are systematic homonyms between nouns, verbs, and adjectives, as *the walk* and *to walk*, and *a good person* and *the greater good*. These would often have to be translated differently in another language. The information from a syntactic analysis would also be valuable in adjusting the word order of the translation.

Bar-Hillel enunciated the necessity of having what he called an operational syntax, that is, an inherently mechanizable scheme for the syntactic analysis of sentences (1951). He later suggested a scheme following the work of Casimir Adjukiewicz, the Polish logician, a scheme that now goes under the name of categorial grammar. I was not convinced that this scheme was optimal. In the case of longer sentences it became quite cumbersome, and it seemed to me that the syntactic distinctions it made did not do sufficient justice even to the traditional part-of-speech distinctions.

I did, however, agree on the importance of syntax, and bent every effort in that direction. It did seem that the inherent limitation of syntax to phenomena within a sentence would not cause us much of a problem, for it seemed that the constraints and clues needed for resolving word-order problems resided within a sentence length, and most multiple-meaning problems could be resolved with clues found within a sentence, and special field glossaries could cope with most of the rest (Yngve 1955b: 212).

1.5 *The linguistic background*

The University of Chicago faculty had been very helpful, and directed me to the current literature in structural-descriptive linguistics.

I was greatly impressed by Bloomfield's *Language* (1933), which gave me a good introduction to the best linguistic thinking of that era. I remember being impressed with his statement that "The single cells in the many-celled animal co-operate by means of such arrangements as the nervous system; the individuals in a human society co-operate by means of sound waves" (1933: 28). As a physicist I knew something about sound waves, so this didn't sound too difficult or daunting to study. Fries (1952) had used the methods of structural linguistics to work out from scratch the structure of English by analyzing some fifty hours of mechanically recorded telephone conversations. This appealed to my experimental nature. The use of diagnostic frames in working out the parts of speech was particularly intriguing. I was also most impressed with Zellig Harris's *Methods in Structural Linguistics* (1951). Here was something worked out with as much care and attention to the details of observation and experiment as the physics that I had been studying.

I became convinced that linguistics studied stable and repeatable phenomena like the phenomena found in cosmic-ray physics, and that the phenomena were every bit as complex and interesting, and even more important. I was convinced that under the methods of the structuralists the study of linguistic phenomena could be eminently scientific. Furthermore, the possibility of a linguistics methodology following strict structural procedures not relying on knowledge of the meaning suggested the possibility of a mechanizable translation methodology that did not rely on the machine understanding the meaning of what it was translating, for it was clear (wasn't it?) that a machine could never understand meaning, something that even the linguists were hard-pressed to deal with.

2.   Early Research

On completion of my dissertation in cosmic-ray physics at Chicago (Yngve 1953b), I moved to M.I.T. in July of 1953 to take over the position in the Research Laboratory of Electronics vacated by Yehoshua Bar-Hillel when he moved back to Israel. Bar-Hillel had been the first person ever to be employed full-time on mechanical translation research, and I became the second.

2.1   *The partial translation experiment*

One of the first things I turned to at M.I.T. was to test the proposition that a solution of grammatical and syntactic problems would also be a solution for considerably more than half of all the multiple-meaning problems and that a specialized field glossary could cope with most of the rest (Yngve 1953a, 1955b: 210–213).

For this purpose a German book review of an American book on mathematics was secured. A secretary was asked to prepare vocabulary cards for the review, one card for each different word appearing in the review. Different inflected forms of the same stem were to count as different words.

I then took these cards and, not having read the book review or the book being reviewed, chose one correspondent for each German word and wrote it on the card for that word. For those words that had a special sense in mathematics, the mathematical sense was chosen so as to simulate the effect of a specialized field glossary. But for many of the grammatical words such as *der* and *sein*, no one translation would be adequate. For these, the original German word was retained as the "translation" Furthermore, the grammatically significant endings for many words were also retained untranslated and added to the translated stems. Words and portions of words translated into English were rendered in all caps; the untranslated words and endings were rendered in lower case. German compounds were hyphenated in the translation.

A "translation" of the book review was then prepared using these cards so as to simulate the output of a machine doing a word-for-word translation. The original German word order was, of course, retained. One sentence from the resulting "partial translation" follows as an example: Die CONVINCINGe CRITIQUE des CLASSICALen IDEA-OF-PROBABILITY IS eine der RE-MARKABLEen WORKS des AUTHORs.

Readers of the partial translation who knew no German could grasp the subject matter from the translated stems but were generally unable to get much of an idea of what was being said about that subject matter. However, readers who knew a little German grammar were able to understand quite well and fairly rapidly what was being said. This was thought to simulate the result of the machine having solved the grammatical and word-order problems. From the great difference between these two types of readers in their ability to understand the translation, it was concluded that a solution to the grammatical problems was well worth the trouble. Furthermore, the experiment seemed to confirm that if specialized field glossaries were used, very few multiple meaning problems would remain.

Some consideration was given to the possibility that partial machine translations would be useful in themselves if readers were prepared with a short course in German grammar. I estimated that the historic Whirlwind computer, designed and built at M.I.T., could be programmed to translate 20,000 words per hour using a 10,000 word dictionary (Yngve 1953a). However, with the importance of the grammatical problems for MT underscored, research at M.I.T. proceeded to focus on the grammatical problems.

2.2 *Structural ideas*

An important tenet of structural linguistics was the distinction between form and function. The form *walk* in English can function as a noun in *the walk* or as a verb in *to walk*. Since nouns and verbs would generally be translated differently in another language, part of the problem for MT was to determine for each word its grammatical function in context. How could the computer take the context into account?

I proposed to attack this problem in a straightforward way using structuralist principles (Yngve 1955b: 213 ff.). The words in the dictionary were to be assigned to *mutually exclusive* word classes in such a way that each word in one of these word classes would bring the same grammatical information to the sentence as any of the other words in that word class. Thus for English there would be a word class for words that could function only as nouns, a word class for words that could function only as verbs, and a word class of words each of which could function either as a noun or a verb. For purposes of solving grammatical multiple-meaning and word-order problems in translation, however, it was expected that we would have to go beyond the usual simple parts of speech and distinguish perhaps hundreds of mutually exclusive word classes.

A modification of the structuralist procedures using substitution frames was applied to the task of setting up mutually exclusive word classes and assigning words to them (Yngve 1955b: 216). Consider that a corpus of *n* words defines *n* contexts in the sense that any word position in the corpus could be used as a substitution frame. Finding *The walk was good* in the corpus, the second word position would define the substitution frame or context *The — was good*.

Now take a corpus and number the word positions or contexts sequentially for convenience. Then take a vocabulary of words, perhaps the words found in the corpus. A matrix of squares in rows and columns is then set up. The columns are numbered across the top for the different contexts or word positions in the corpus; the rows are marked down the left side with the words of the vocabulary. Then, by using the contexts as substitution frames, all the words are tried in turn in each frame, and a square in the matrix is marked for each word that is accepted in the frame. The strictness of the criteria of acceptance in each frame depends on how fine a distinction is desired in solving grammatical multiple-meaning and word-order problems in translation

Now all words with identical rows are words that substitute in all the same contexts. They constitute a word class. Similarly, all contexts with identical columns are contexts that accept the same list of words. They constitute a context class. Thus the word-context matrix can be reduced to a much smaller word-class-context-class matrix, a great simplification that recognizes the considerable amount of the grammatical structure of the language uncovered by the substitution-in-frames tests.

We now note that just as all the words in a word class bring the same grammatical information to a sentence, similarly, all the contexts in a context class bring the same contextual information to bear at that word position because they all accept exactly the same list of words at that position.

Much of the syntactic research of the M.I.T. MT group made use of these techniques. Chomsky became quite interested in the matrix representation of form and context, but it did not fit with his own agenda.

2.3 *The sample translation algorithm*

A translating machine would be able to determine the word class of each word in a sentence by a dictionary look-up. The sentence sequence of these word classes would contain just the information needed for working out the context class at each word position in the sentence and thus the grammatical function of the word at that position.

In fact, because of the way in which the word-classes and context-classes were set up, each sentence sequence of word-classes would uniquely determine a sentence sequence of context classes. Therefore, we could in principle simply look up a sentence sequence of word classes in a syntactic dictionary and retrieve the corresponding sentence sequence of context classes. However, this is entirely impractical because of the huge number of possible sentence sequences of word-classes.

The means for getting around this difficulty was again suggested by structuralist principles; the insight that a sentence is structured in layers in terms of phrases and clauses. It might be possible to list just the phrase sequences of word classes and the short sequences of phrase classes, etc. in a dictionary.

Perhaps the machine could then somehow look up a phrase at a time, then phrases of phrases and so on.

The proposed algorithm searched left-to-right through the sentence a layer at a time looking for a longest match to a sequence of word-classes and phrase-classes in the syntactic dictionary. Each match then retrieved codes from the dictionary to aid in choosing among the multiple meanings of a word, codes to indicate word-order change under translation, and a code for the phrase-type to be used in scanning through the sentence at the next higher layer.

The complete algorithm was published, together with small sample word and syntactic dictionaries and some sample German sentences illustrative of those that the system could translate into English, making appropriate choices in cases of multiple meaning and changing the word order appropriately. I believe this was the first table-driven syntactic analyzer to appear in the literature (Yngve 1955b: 221–225).

Efforts were made to try to expand this scheme to a larger number of words in the dictionary and more phrase types in the syntactic dictionary. Some difficulties were experienced, however, in assigning codes in the syntactic dictionary for resolving the multiple meanings of the words in a recognized phrase or clause type and codes for their proper order in the translation. It was not immediately clear where the source of these difficulties was to be found.

Table-driven routines have the merit that they can be applied unchanged to any language pair simply by installing the appropriate word and syntactic dictionaries. This was seen as a separation of the translating problem into a machine part and a linguistic part. It opened the way for a division of labor between computer people and linguists unfamiliar with computer programming. Consequently, with support from the National Science Foundation, several trained linguists were gradually brought to M.I.T. to work on the linguistic problems connected with MT. This separation of descriptive linguistic from algorithmic considerations may have inadvertently fostered and promoted the traditional distinction between language and language use, of generation and production in our terms (Yngve 1957: 63), and of competence and performance in Chomsky's later conception (1965).

2.4 *Gap analysis*

Work was going on in the M.I.T. Research Laboratory of Electronics on coding and switching theory, on Shannon's information theory, and on error-correcting codes. Some of this work dealt with encoding telephone, radio, or TV messages to be sent through a noisy channel using special error-correcting codes and then being able to decode the messages correctly on the other end in the presence of noise in the channel. There seemed to be a rough parallel between this and the encoding of a message by a speaker into a language and the decoding of the message by a hearer (Yngve 1954a).

In our MT work we were faced with the task of discovering the code, the word classes and phrase classes of the language, so as to build usefully complete word and syntactic dictionaries. This was a large task because of the great complexity of language. It was simply a very large job to try each word in each substitution frame or context position in a text and make a judgment as to whether the word was accepted by the frame to the degree desired for the purpose of translation.

Information theory understood that order and disorder are in a sense complementary. A code (or a grammar) specifies the order or constraints of structure in the encoded messages, the way in which they deviate from random sequences of elements; a random sequence of letters or words would have no order, no structure. This suggested that testing a text for deviations from randomness would help to reveal its structure (Yngve 1954c). For our purposes, one would want to see the effect of substitution frames on the probability of occurrence of a given word. A first step in this direction would be to locate all the occurrences of a given frequent word in a text and determine its effect on the probability of occurrence of particular other frequent words nearby in the text by comparing their frequency of occurrence with what would be expected if they occurred at random.

To try this out, a text of 9490 words was selected. The six most frequent words in it were determined to be: *the*, 599; *to*, 252; *of*, 241; *a*, 221; *and*, 207; and *in*, 162. The text was then transcribed onto punched cards using single-character codes for each text word. Taking each of the six words in turn as a context word, data-processing and computer techniques were used to determine the frequency of occurrence of each of the other five at text positions up to thirty-two word positions before and after the context word.

For comparison with what would be expected if the words occurred at random, the observed frequencies were displayed as histograms plotting the frequency of occurrence of a word against the number of word positions (gap length) before or after the context word. For example, the estimated probability of *of* occurring at any position in this text is just its frequency in the text (241) divided by the length of the text (9490), or 2.54%. Then if we use *the* as a context word, we will have 599 contexts (the frequency of *the*). The expected frequency of *of* in any context defined by *the* is 2.54% of 599 or 15.2. This turned out to be the approximate value at gaps of five or more word positions. But with a preceding gap of zero (text *of the*) the frequency was 69, and with following gaps of zero through three (text *the of*, *the — of*, *the — — of*, and *the — — — of*) the frequencies were 0, 72, 31, and 6 respectively. It is easy to see that these results point to major syntactic constraints due to constructions with *of* and *the*.

A glance at the complete results (Yngve 1955a, 1956b) shows that reduplication is absent with these words; structures with *the* can be expected to have two or three words; and constructions with *and* frequently involve at least fifteen words. Furthermore, even with this small corpus, the results clearly group together *a* and *the*; *of*, *in*, and *to*; and leave *and* as different from these. Then *the* is shown to be different from *a* in that it is preferred after *of*. Also *of* is different from *to* and *in* in that it frequently follows *a* or *the* with a gap of one or two. *To* is different from *of* and *in* in that it has a relatively low broad peak before *the* caused by the competition of the use of *to* before an infinitive.

The results were very encouraging, but we did not develop the method further because of the unavailability of large enough corpora in machinable form. It would take at least a hundred thousand and perhaps a million or more words to do the method justice. Today, with such long corpora easily available and with much more powerful computers and software tools, the method could become quite powerful, and its further development is to be recommended. The publication (Yngve 1956b) gives a number of suggestions for this, such as using as contexts also the frequent constructions that emerge like *of the* and *the — of*.

2.5 *The two-step approach*

The parallel between coding theory and linguistics had led to seeing linguistic communication as a speaker encoding a message into a language and sending it through a channel and a hearer then decoding it at the other end. This conception suggested that translating by a machine should proceed in two steps instead of one. It should first, like a hearer or reader, decode messages expressed in the input language and then, like a speaker or writer, encode the messages again in the output language. The "message", of course, would be that which was to be preserved under translation, presumably some representation of the meaning.

Under structuralist principles in linguistics, and coding theory conceptions as well, this would simply be a compact representation of the choices that the languages provided within the constraints of their grammars. There thus developed the idea of a special transition language in which the "messages" would be represented.

The decoding algorithm was to be similar to the bottom-up scheme used in the one-step algorithm above, but instead of trying to decode the input text directly into the output language, it would decode it into an explicit representation of the message in the transition language. As in the one-step scheme, the grammar of the input language was to be written with a view toward what output language one was translating into so as to take advantage of simplifications stemming from similar structurings of the input and output languages. The separation of the problem into separate decoding and encoding steps obviated some of the difficulties in assigning codes in the one-step scheme, which were now seen as caused by confusing and conflating input-language problems and output-language problems, which were now neatly separated.

The encoding algorithm was to use the selections provided by the transition-language representation of the messages to guide it in constructing output sentences from the top down through the layers of clauses and phrases to word classes and words. The idea of having a separate encoding step for the output language brought with it the realization that there was a multiple-meaning problem for the output language as well as for the input language: It wasn't just a question of choosing among the multiple output-language correspondents for each input-language word, as everybody had been assuming; it was also important that the words in the output language be embedded in the appropriate output-language context so that their multiple meanings would be resolved by the reader seeing them in a normal context. For example, a word-for-word translation from German retaining the German word order might read, *The man had his house painted*, whereas the correct translation providing the proper English context to resolve a serious multiple-meaning problem in English should be, *The man had painted his house*.

These ideas were put forth in a paper at the Third London Symposium on Information Theory, September 12–17, 1955. This was published (Yngve 1955c) in the journal *Mechanical Translation* which Bill Locke, the chairman of the Modern Language Department, and I had started in March of 1954. A shortened version was published in the conference proceedings (Yngve 1956a).

A state-transition network representation of the grammars, augmented to take into account the layer structure of the sentence, was presented in these papers for the purpose of explaining the decoding and encoding steps to information-theory people. Similar augmented transition-network schemes figured in the MT and AI literature in later years.

3.   An Expanded Program

By August of 1956 it had become clear that most if not all of the problems associated with word-for-word translation could be solved by the proper manipulation or utilization of the context, where context was to be understood in its broadest interpretation. Six types of contextual clues were identified as used by a person for resolving the considerable ambiguity of words taken out of context (Yngve 1956c). The first type of clue was the field of discourse of the terms being translated, which could shift even within a sentence. For this the machine could make use of certain diagnostic terms appearing in the text. The second type of clue had to do with idioms and certain compound technical terms like *red lead*, and *white lead*, which are chemical compounds, and word complexes like *pocket lighter*, which is not for lighting pockets and *burning glass*, which is not a glass that is burning. These could be listed in full in the dictionary. The third type of clue was the grammatical or syntactic category of the word, which could distinguish the case of *der* in *der Mann* 'the man (nominative)' and *der Frau* 'of the woman (genitive)', and thus aid in its translation, or the senses of *sound* as an adjective, noun, transitive verb, or intransitive verb. The fourth type of clue was meaning categories or selectional restrictions between words in open classes. The fifth was the determination of antecedents, which was necessary not only for correctly translating pronouns, but also nouns and other words referring in different terms to things previously mentioned. The sixth encompassed all other clues, particularly the common-sense ability of the person to understand what was being translated, which posed the greatest challenge. For all of these clues, a syntactic analysis of the sentence was seen to be essential, and this continued to be the focus of the group.

We distinguished between ad-hoc rules and rules based on a correct analysis of sentence structure (Yngve 1956d). For example, *der* in German can be translated as "the", "of the", "who", "that", "which", "he", or "it". The ad hoc rule that if *der* follows a word that is capitalized without an intervening comma, it should be translated "of the" will be correct perhaps 95% of the time. On the other hand, if the machine can provide a proper syntactic analysis of the sentence, there is the possibility that the translation would be right 100% of the time. Although an ad hoc approach could lead to early and superficially impressive results on a computer, we saw our task as trying to move as many problems as possible out of the realm where only an ad hoc solution was possible, if at all, into the realm where a 100% solution would be possible. This underlined the earlier conclusion that if the machine is to recognize the structure of the input sentence, we must have an adequate description of sentence structure to serve as a basis for the recognition routine.

3.1 A framework for mechanical translation

The two-step translation scheme had separated conceptually the tasks of recognizing the structure of the input sentences and of producing to order their translations in the output language. This focused our attention on the transition language in which the message or meaning to be translated would be expressed.

Further consideration led to doubt that the idea of a transition language made much sense here: the natural output of a recognition routine was the choices representing the input text within the constraints of the input-language grammar, and the natural input to a sentence-construction routine would be the choices representing the desired output text within the constraints of the output-language grammar. In general, the choices provided by the two languages would not be the same. We thus saw the need to conceive of translation as a three-step process (Yngve 1957).

The first step would be a syntactic analysis of the input sentences in terms of the constraints of the input-language grammar producing what we called a *specifier* of the input-language sentence. This specifier would contain explicitly all the information implicit in the input sentence (tense, voice, verb class, selection of the verb, sentence structure, and so forth). Specifiers would be of the nature of values of the natural coordinates of the sentence in that language.

Since the structures of the input language and the output language were not in general identical, the second step would use a statement of equivalences under translation and a structure-transfer routine to produce a specifier for the translationally equivalent sentence in the output language.

The third step, then, like the second step in the two-step scheme, would produce an output sentence under the guidance of the output-language specifier.

In each of these steps there was, of course, still a conceptual separation between the algorithms or routines that carried out the translation steps and the stored linguistic information they used to direct their operations.

This three-step scheme remained as the framework for all our subsequent research on MT and a three-step conception is still very much alive in the literature and practice of MT today.

Consideration was given to conceiving specifiers in a narrow sense and also in a broad sense (Yngve 1957). In the narrow sense, the English verb *can* has two forms, present and past, but it cannot be made future or perfect as most other verbs can. One does not say *He has can come*, but says, instead, *He has been able to come*, which is structurally very different. Again the auxiliary *must* has no past tense and again one uses a circumlocution *had to*. If we want to indicate the connection in meaning (parallelling a similarity in distribution), we would have to use coordinates that are not structural in the narrow sense. Another example is the use of the present tense in English for past time (in narratives), for future time (*He is coming soon*), and with other meanings.

These considerations raised the question of whether translation ought actually to be considered as a five-step process: input sentence to narrow input specifier, narrow specifier to broad input specifier, structural transfer to broad output specifier, broad specifier to narrow output specifier, and narrow specifier to output sentence.

3.2 *The COMIT programming effort*

The question of what was the proper form of a grammar to be used in a translation machine remained a central concern of the growing M.I.T MT group. In November, 1956 we had Robert B. Lees from Chicago, and Noam Chomsky, Joseph R. Applegate, and G. H. Matthews, from Penn (Yngve 1956d). Traditional materials on German and English grammar were useful, but did not lend themselves to easy mechanization. The English grammar of Eugene Nida (1960), in an earlier version, was particularly valuable in laying out the grammar of English in immediate-constituent form. The notations of Zellig Harris (1946) were suggestive, as was the paper on immediate constituents by Rulon Wells (1947). Bob Lees had become impressed with Chomsky's large opus, which he had made available to us in ditto form. His phrase-structure and transformational notations seemed to resemble a computer program.

We were also faced with the practical problem of how linguists without computer experience could actually become productive in MT research. We needed an automatic programming system that would allow the computer to accept notations of a sort familiar to linguists in analogy to FORTRAN and COBOL which were being designed for use by mathematicians and business people who were not programmers. To this end, the linguists were encouraged to think about what sorts of general linguistic notations they would be comfortable with. We wanted to free the linguist to do linguistics (Yngve 1958, 1961a). But because MT was an unsolved problem, we wanted to preserve the general-purpose nature of the computer. After much discussion, and several preliminary internal memos and drafts, we came up with a complete programming-language design (Yngve & Matthews 1958; Yngve 1958).

We took our ideas to the M.I.T. Computation Center where we found Sheldon Best, Arnold Segal, and Frank Helwig, who were interested in working on an automatic programming system. They agreed to help us out. Their considerable expertise and efforts in developing the program were crucial to the success of our research.

COMIT, as it came to be called, was originally programmed for the IBM 704, a computer with a magnetic core memory of 32K 36–bit words and magnetic tape for large-capacity storage and off-line input from punched cards. It was programmed in assembly language before the days of macro-assemblers, debugging being done with assembler listings, check points, and octal memory dumps. Turn-around for checkout runs was often one to two days. By 1960 about twelve people had contributed to the COMIT system and had devoted perhaps eight man-years to it, the work being divided about equally between the two groups (Yngve 1961a: 440). When the programming was nearly finished, IBM 709 upgraded the machine to a 709. We did have a first successful grammar run on the 704 over the Fourth-of-July weekend of 1960, just before the machine was shut down. Converting the program to the 709 set us back six months.

Programming manuals were published (Yngve 1962c, 1962d), and translations appeared in French and Italian. We continued our efforts to improve COMIT and eventually COMIT II came out (Yngve 1972). COMIT found many uses besides linguistic research. For a bibliography see Yngve (1972). The system was subsequently converted also to the IBM 7094 and IBM 7044. It ran on the pioneering Project MAC time-sharing system at M.I.T. With the help of Washington State University, it was later converted to the IBM 360. Bell Telephone Laboratories developed their own version of COMIT, which they called SNOBOL, and there were several other languages that exhibited features that had originally appeared in COMIT.

3.3 *The COMIT language*

We built on a notation from Harris[1]. It had been adapted by Chomsky, but we further reinterpreted it for purposes of the computer. We would write a rule $A + B = C + D$ to indicate that a constituent A followed by a constituent B was to be replaced by the constituent C followed by the constituent D. A rule could have any number of constituents indicated on the left and on the right. The derivation in which these constituents were to be found was reinterpreted as a portion of the computer memory called the workspace, which could contain an indefinitely long string of constituents, each consisting of an arbitrarily long string of characters (for example words or phrase types). The left side of the rule was interpreted to mean that the computer would search from left to right through the workspace for the indicated adjacent constituents, and when it found them, it would replace them in the workspace by the constituents indicated on the right side of the rule. If one wrote $A + B = 2 + 1$ the order of the found constituents would be reversed in the workspace.

We introduced means to direct the flow of control of the computer from one rule to another. Each rule started with a name section for its name (or an asterisk if it had no name) and ended with a go-to section for the name of the rule to be executed next (or an asterisk meaning to go to the rule next below). If the search by the left side of the rule failed to find the indicated constituents in the workspace, the rest of the rule would not be executed, control going instead to the rule next below. This gave us a conditional branch in the program.

A rule (having one left side) could optionally have up to 36 different named subrules with possibly different right sides and go-tos. The choice of subrule to be executed could be controlled by the program. This could be used to choose among different options as to what a found constituent was to be replaced by in the workspace. Or the choice could be made at random, a feature that was used for random generation, as explained below.

---

1. "Equations will be used to indicate substitutability. $BC = A$ will mean that the sequence consisting of a morpheme of class B followed by a morpheme of class C can be substituted for a single morpheme of class A. In cases where unclarity may arise, we shall write $B + C$ for the sequence BC." (Harris 1946: 166).

Constituents in the workspace could carry any number of *subscripts*, each with up to 36 values, as */PERSON FIRST THIRD, NUMBER PLURAL*, and these subscripts could figure in convenient ways in specifying a left-side search operation. Subscripts could be placed on workspace constituents by writing them on the right side of rules. Subscripts on found workspace constituents could be carried over onto specified constituents in the right-side of the rule in controlled ways. For example, a singular or plural subscript could be placed on an *S* and automatically carried over to the *NP* and *VP* to ensure number agreement. We were particularly proud of this notational innovation as a method for handling selectional restrictions. They solved a problem of subject-verb agreement that Chomsky had raised (1957: 28–29; n. 3), but he would not accept the notation. It was only much later that he adopted related methods. The scheme was also adapted by others under other names.

A flexible feature was the introduction of what are now called "wild cards" for specifying search operations as found in modern editors and word processors, and even in DOS. This was possibly the first published use of wild cards (this was in the punched-card and batch-processing era, long before people started using consoles for editing and even before operating systems were developed). In our notation, $1 written as a constituent in the left side of a rule would find a single constituent in the workspace, $2 would find two consecutive constituents, and so on. A single $ would find any number of constituents between two definitely determined positions. The use of COMIT for information retrieval was explored in Yngve (1962a).

There was a built-in facility for entering a dictionary into a program. It provided for fast look-up in the dictionary of items in the workspace, substituting dictionary equivalents, and tagging them appropriately for initiating arbitrary processing.

Each rule could also optionally specify an input or output operation, and material could be moved between the workspace and specified storage areas called "shelves". There were a number of other facilities. The best general discussion of COMIT and its history is Yngve 1976. The original publications on COMIT include Yngve 1958, 1962c, 1962d, and 1972.

3.4 *The simple sentence-producing algorithm*

For the three-step translating scheme we needed an output algorithm and a scheme for stating the rules of grammar that it used in producing sentences.

Chomsky's book (1957), which he had written while he was employed on the MT grant, had just come out and it seemed that his generative grammar scheme would be just the thing. Matthews and I spent considerable time trying to adapt it to this purpose, but the effort ended in failure. Chomsky's vision of generating (simultaneously in the mathematical sense) all the grammatical sentences of a language simply did not lend itself to the task of producing particular specified sentences one at a time to order as a native speaker does. His scheme, if one were to be true to it, would require, for example, that the machine generate all possible relative clauses and then select the one that would fit in the sentence being produced. And since the number of possible relative clauses was unlimited, no computer memory could contain them all. There was also the problem of how to assign a phrase structure to the result of a transformation and several other technical difficulties.

The failure of Chomsky's scheme in this first test of it was a disappointment to us and it was not for lack of trying or any ineptitude on our part. The question of how competence, in his theory, could direct performance has remained, in his own words, not just a problem but a real mystery. Our early discovery of this quirk or flaw in generative theory was due entirely to the heuristic advantage of trying to program an actual computer model (Yngve 1957: 63, 1960).

Since there was no grammatical limit to the length of a sentence, and since people often start long sentences before they have much idea of how they are going to finish them, it seemed reasonable that a sentence-producing routine should operate from left to right, producing output words in their correct temporal order. This was a departure from the recognition routine of the sample translation algorithm of §2.3 above, which scanned a whole sentence a multiple number of times.

The sentence-producing routine proposed was simplicity itself. It operated with three types of rules: choice rules, expansion rules, and discontinuous expansion rules (Yngve 1960, 1962b), each of which could be represented easily in COMIT.

Choice rules were of the type

SUBJECT	= NOUN-PHRASE	or	NOUN	= MAN
	= NOUN-CLAUSE			= BOY
	= PRONOUN			= WOMAN
				= GIRL

where a constituent *SUBJECT* or *NOUN,* whenever it is the first constituent in the workspace, would be replaced by one of the constituents on the right under the control of a specifier (or at random). If this were a word, it would be printed out and deleted from the workspace, bringing the next constituent in the workspace into first position.

Expansion rules were of the type

SENTENCE = SUBJECT + PREDICATE

where the constituent *SENTENCE,* again when it is the first constituent in the workspace, would be replaced by the two constituents *SUBJECT* and *PREDI-CATE* in such a way as to leave *SUBJECT* in first position ready for the next operation and *PREDICATE* in second position out of the way (technically on a push-down) until *SUBJECT* had been fully expanded to words and printed out. At that time, *PREDICATE* would find itself in first position and it would then in turn be expanded. In this way the phrase structure and words of the sentence would be produced from top down and from left to right, with the output words printed in their normal temporal order.

Discontinuous expansion rules were of the type

VERB-PHRASE = VERB + ... + VC

as in *called ... up* in "He called her up". This rule would replace *VERB-PHRASE* by *VERB* in first position as in a regular expansion rule, but *VC* would be inserted in the workspace in third position rather than second, jumping it over the constituent in the second position.

3.5 *Grammar testing by random generation of sentences*

We had a need to develop relatively complete grammars. As rules were proposed, they would have to be tested for accuracy and consistency with the rest of the grammar. But since a grammar generates an infinite set of sentences, it would be impossible to test them all against the grammaticality judgments of native speakers. We would be forced to fall back on a sampling procedure, for which COMIT had been equipped with a random choice feature.

To test a version of a grammar, each choice rule would be set to choose at random from among its subrules. The program would then produce a random set of sentences conforming to the grammar that could be examined by native speakers for grammaticality. To test this idea, I wrote during the spring and summer of 1959 a grammar based on the first ten sentences of a children's book selected for its simple prose. The grammar had a 38 word vocabulary, 24 expansion rules, 5 discontinuous expansion rules, and 22 choice rules with from 2 to 11 subrules each. Subscripts were not used in this first grammar, but it was equipped to accept their later addition.

When COMIT was finished in 1961 this program was run and the results presented in September of that year in London and published in the conference proceedings (Yngve 1962b), but with typos in the output, program, and grammar listings introduced by the publisher. An accurate version of the grammar and output appeared later in *Scientific American* (June 1962).

This program validated the random generation scheme, the simple sentence-producing algorithm, and the workability of the discontinuous expansion rules even with nested discontinuous constructions. We also found that coordination must be restricted so as not to repeat an item (as *A, A, and B*), and that many of the longer and more complicated sentences, particularly those involving coordination, were either awkward or confusingly ambiguous. It was interesting that some of the words changed their meanings drastically when embedded in different, though similar contexts. For example, the children's book had the engineer of the little train keep his engine oiled and polished. The program produced *He is oiled and polished*. We concluded, though, that fixing this with subscripts for animate and inanimate would not be correct, for the restriction is semantic, not grammatical (of the type that would rule out *He are oiled and polished*).

One cannot overemphasize the importance of the general method of random generation, developed at M.I.T., for validating grammars. It shows up errors very rapidly. Linguists sometimes fail to appreciate the extent of interaction of rules and the consequent impossibility of validating any but a tiny grammar without computer assistance in this way. Once COMIT became available, all our grammars were validated by this method.

4.   Results from Computer Grammars

Having the COMIT notation available greatly improved our productivity even before COMIT was up and running. It helped us to formulate our ideas in exact terms and share them with each other. In fact, while we were developing the simple-sentence-constructing algorithm of §3.4 above in the spring and summer of 1959, some surprising insights emerged.

One of these was the discovery that a pushdown is very convenient for producing sentences through immediate-constituent expansions from top down and left to right.

Another was the curious discontinuous expansion rule, the easy way in which it could handle discontinuities associated with inversions as *could ... go* in *Could he go?*, that it jumped in the forward direction only, that it jumped over just one constituent, not two or three or more, and that it worked properly in sentences like *Could there have been a cup of tea on the table into which the jewels had been dropped?*, which involves the following five interleaving discontinuous constructions:

1. *Could ... have been* a cup of tea etc.
2. *there ... a cup of tea* on the table etc.
3. *have been ... on the table* into which etc.
4. *a cup of tea ... into which* the jewels etc.
5. *into which ... had been dropped*

The discontinuous expansion rule was interesting in that it easily handled in a left-to-right phrase-structure grammar many of the things that were thought to require a transformational approach, which we had already rejected for other good reasons.

4.1 *The depth hypothesis*

Another curious discovery during development of the simple-sentence-constructing algorithm was the depth hypothesis. We had already considered memory storage problems in rejecting a transformational approach. We now had to ask how much temporary memory would be needed to hold the extra unexpanded constituents introduced by each application of a regular or discontinuous expansion rule. Since sentences could be arbitrarily long, it might be that they would involve an arbitrarily large number of unexpanded constituents during their production.

In the early summer of 1959 I diagrammed and analyzed sentences from texts to see what was the maximum extra temporary memory required to produce each sentence (its depth). That is, what was the maximum number of unexpanded constituents at any one time during its production? It turned out that even very long sentences seldom had a depth of more than two or three! I tried to construct sentences with depths of more than six or eight. They invariably were stylistically awkward, nearly unintelligible, or downright ungrammatical, and would never in practice be used. Furthermore, there was always another fully acceptable way of lesser depth of saying the same thing. These typically involved grammatical complexities for which one could find no other motivation than to keep the depth of sentences less than six or eight by replacing regressive constructions (those that increased depth) with progressive constructions (those that did not increase depth).

In light of this evidence, I proposed a hypothesis concerning depth and presented it to the American Philosophical Society in November of 1959 (1960: 452):

a. Although all languages have a grammar based on constituent structure,

b. the sentences actually used in the spoken language have a depth that does not exceed a certain number

c. equal or nearly equal to the span of immediate memory (presently assumed to be 7±2).

d. The grammars of all languages will include methods for restricting regressive constructions so that most sentences will not exceed this depth,

e. and they will include alternative constructions of lesser depth that would maintain the power of expression of the language.

f. For all languages, much of the grammatical complexity over and above the minimum needed for the signaling function can be accounted for on this basis.

g. When languages change, depth phenomena will frequently be involved, and will often play an important role.

On the basis of structural arguments, seven grammatical and syntactic devices were identified that would be expected to occur if depth considerations played a role in language design. These are listed below together with examples showing that these devices do actually occur and appear to have the postulated functions:

1. An ungrammatical first step to prevent the potential recursive regressive reapplication of an expansion rule. Example: the progressive *the dog that worried the cat that killed the rat that ate the malt* vs. the regressive **the malt that the rat that the cat that the dog worried killed ate*.

2. Restricted relabeling to tick off each increase in depth and impose a limit. Example: the English hierarchy of sentence, subordinate clause, noun

phrase, primary attribute (adjectival), secondary attribute (adverbial), and tertiary attribute (adverbial) as in *When very clearly projected pictures appeared, they applauded*, which is a regressive construction with a controlled depth of five. The grammar supplies rules for this but lacks rules to go much deeper.

3. A preference for binary constructions to conserve depth. Example: ((*He*) ((*sees*)(*her*))), which has a depth of one, instead of the ternary construction ((*He*) (*sees*) (*her*)), which has a depth of two,

4. Changed pattern of modification to conserve depth. Example: the progressive ((*the boy*) ((*loves*)(*the girl*))), but not the regressive though logically similar (((*the girl*)(*is loved*)) (*by the boy*)); instead, the progressive but logically changed ((*the girl*) ((*is loved*)(*by the boy*))).

5. Word building to eliminate depth-increasing syntactic expansions. Example: progressive *to construct again*, but *reconstructing*, instead of regressive **re construct ing*. Also agglutinative suffixes and postpositions in verb-final languages.

6. Structure reversal to postpone potentially deep constituents to start at a point of one less depth. Example: *He gave her the candy he liked best* vs. the potentially deeper type ?*He gave the candy he liked best to her*. Also *He gave it to the girl he liked best* vs. the potentially deeper type **He gave the girl he liked best it*. Also *It is operated by a pitman that is oscillated by a crank stud which extends eccentrically from a shaft*, where a passive provides structure reversal motivated by depth considerations, instead of the potentially deeper active type **It is operated by a pitman that a crank stud which extends eccentrically from a shaft oscillates*.

7. Discontinuous constructions to postpone potentially deep constituents to start at a point of one less depth. Example: *a good man for the job* vs. the potentially deeper type **a good for the job man*. Also *Results were presented on a controlled experiment to determine the health effects of second-hand smoke on children under the age of five in households where the parents smoke one or more packs of cigarettes a day* vs. the potentially deeper type ?*Results on a controlled experiment to determine the health effects of second-hand smoke on children under the age of five in households where the parents smoke one or more packs of cigarettes a day were presented*. Also, all five of the discontinuous constructions in the above cup-of-tea example serve this function.

For further details the reader is referred to the original articles on depth (Yngve 1960, 1961b).

The depth hypothesis came out of actually trying to write grammars that could be used with computer algorithms. I should like to emphasize the great advantage of computer modeling to fix one's understanding and to suggest questions for exploration.

4.2 *Testing the depth hypothesis*

Although the depth hypothesis did predict and motivate a number of the features of the syntax and morphology of English, and it did seem to correspond to what I knew about some other language families, it had come out of MT research and I considered it not as a finished linguistic theory to be defended, but a scientific hypothesis about language structure to be tested by other linguists working on other languages. Confirmation did soon come from other linguists, particularly those who were comfortable with the widely-held immediate-constituent view of grammar. Japanese was sometimes cited as an example of a language that favored regressive rather than progressive structures, a view encouraged by earlier work on Japanese by Bernard Bloch, but not by the Ph.D. dissertation of his student Eleanor Harz Jorden. My own work with Japanese informants seemed to confirm the hypothesis in that language. Attempts to elicit very deep sentences often resulted in the informant insisting on substituting two sentences for one.

According to the hypothesis, depth phenomena in a language would come about through historical change (Yngve 1960: 466). If a person tried to produce a sentence that required more than the available seven or eight units of temporary memory, he would experience some kind of processing failure. If this happened often enough, he would try to avoid the sorts of constructions that got him into trouble by seeing them as awkward and substituting alternative constructions. If he then tended to avoid awkward constructions, they would not be passed on to succeeding generations, thus becoming ungrammatical. The depth phenomena we observe today in a language would then be the result of many such historical changes. Awkwardness and ungrammaticality were observed, but I wanted to test this idea further by trying to find both a processing problem and an attested language change clearly attributable to this mechanism (1960: 452).

It was not until a dozen years later that I found a way to search for the postulated processing failure, which would be expected to be a rare event. It seemed possible that the temporary memory used to hold unexpanded constituents might be used for other nonlinguistic purposes as well. Perhaps if a person in the process of speaking were suddenly confronted with an unrelated task that also made memory demands, we might be able to cause him to forget what he was about to say. An experiment was carried out whereby speakers were occasionally interrupted during a normal conversation by one of two small lights coming on in the periphery of their vision. The task was to report immediately whether the light was yellow or white and then return to the conversation.

The predicted induced forgetting was observed after many of the interruptions. Furthermore, the speakers reported subjective feelings of groping and having forgotten what they were going to say. This may be an important link in associating the postulated feeling of awkwardness with particular constructions. But we were not able from the data to correlate the induced forgetting with the apparent depth of the sentence the speaker had embarked on. The experiment did, however, reveal a number of other unsuspected and curious phenomena. Subjects would stop, often in the middle of a word or phoneme, with a glottal closure in the manner of a self-interruption to correct a speech error. On returning to the conversation, they would backtrack, repeat, and finish the phrase that had been interrupted, but then they could not remember what they were going to say, although they did remember the general topic under discussion. There were other interesting results on intonational matters and results bearing on phrase structure. The reader will find a more complete account in the original publication (Yngve 1973).

In regard to finding depth-related historical change, there is one construction in English that seems to allow an indefinite regressive expansion, the inflected genitive as in *John's father's father's father's father's father's father came over from England* (Yngve 1960: 463). Although acceptable, it does seem marginal in that one might count on one's fingers or break it up into intonation groups as *John's father's-father's-father's, father's-father's-father's, father*, which would have less depth, Perhaps the English genitive represents a change still in progress. So I had been asking people about the history of the English genitive. Joseph Williams suggested I look at work done by Charles C. Fries and his students in the late 1930s. They counted occurrences of inflected genitives and genitives with *of*, among other things, in texts dating from 900 to 1300 A.D., the period when English was losing many of its inflections. Their resulting picture of the ongoing historical change in the genitive, and in the other constructions they looked at, corresponded in remarkable detail to the predictions of the depth hypothesis (Yngve 1975). My conclusion is that there is more that a grain of truth to the hypothesis

Psychologists and psycholinguists were from the beginning interested in the depth hypothesis, and a number of studies were published. There is truly a large literature on depth. It needs a thorough and careful review from the point of view of my latest thinking on linguistic theory.

4.3   *The depth hypothesis and linguistic theory*

The significance for linguistic theory of the depth hypothesis was understood from the beginning (Yngve 1960: 495). Human speech is produced by a finite state device (a brain) by an essentially left-to-right process (forward in time). There is a temporary or working memory that can contain about seven items, which is used to make possible a factoring of the state into several unexpanded constituents held in the temporary memory. This factoring of the state results in great economies in the use of the permanent memory. In our model this follows from the constituent-structure organization of the grammar, which allows sentences to be produced by expanding one constituent at a time by applying rules from the top down. This process, if unconstrained, would lead to sentences requiring more than the available temporary memory. For this reason, grammars develop various restrictions and complications to nearly eliminate problems caused by running out of memory and to provide alternative constructions to retain as much as possible of the expressive power of the language brought by the immediate-constituent architecture. Thus the grammar is effectively brought back within the capabilities of the finite state device.

This view turned Chomsky's research program on its head. Chomsky had been seeking to *prove* that transformations were necessary. He tried first to show that in a hierarchy of grammars arranged by their generative power, a finite-state grammar (of a restricted kind) was not powerful enough in that it could not generate sentences illustrating phenomena for which he thought phrase-structure rules were necessary. Then he tried to show that a phrase-structure grammar (of a restricted kind) in turn was not powerful enough in that it could not generate sentences for which he thought transformational rules were required. He hoped to show that a transformational grammar was the least powerful grammar that could do the job. But this program, based on logical arguments and *a priori* assumptions about requirements on the generative power of an abstract grammar, ignored the fact that sentences are produced and understood by people using a finite processor. An unrestricted phrase-structure grammar is already too powerful. The very complications which he thought required the extra power of a transformational grammar are found in language just to keep it within the bounds of a finite state device, while allowing maximum use of the innately given limited temporary memory to optimize the use of the available innately given permanent memory. The way in which Chomsky was able to admit most of the essential principles of the depth hypothesis while appearing to reject it altogether is a revealing study in linguistic polemics, and more relevant to defending a previously taken position than to finding out the essential truth in the matter.

4.4 *What kind of grammar?*

I showed the depth results to Chomsky while they were still in preliminary draft form, thinking he would be most interested in the insights they provided about language and that he might want to take them into account in his theory. After all, he had championed "the method of rigorously stating a proposed theory and applying it strictly to linguistic material with no attempt to avoid unacceptable conclusions by *ad hoc* adjustments or loose formulation" (1957: 5), and had said that, "By pushing a precise, but inadequate formulation to an unacceptable conclusion, we can often expose the exact source of this inadequacy and, consequently, gain a deeper understanding of the linguistic data" (1957: 5). This seemed to me to be a scientific attitude.

But he apparently took the depth hypothesis not as a scientific hypothesis to be tested but as a rival linguistic theory to be opposed. He attacked it by claiming that my way of drawing phrase-structure trees was wrong in not conforming to his views of how to draw them. For example, I had analyzed a string of coordinated nouns like *John, Bill, Frank, ... and Carl* as a progressive construction which, like a speaker, would produce the nouns one at a time, and at each step choose between continuing with the coordination or ending it with *and* in construction with the final element. But Chomsky insisted that coordination should be diagrammed as multiply branching since by the very definition of coordination the elements coordinated were all equal. It wasn't clear, however, how he could accommodate the infinite number of rules implied by the unlimited nature of coordination, nor how the multiply branching phrase structure was to be assigned if the elements were added transformationally.

Chomsky also objected to the depth hypothesis on the basis that if there were an effect of a memory limitation it would be to rule out "center embedding" rather than regressive structures ("left branching", as he insisted on calling it). I found the analysis on which he based this claim not to be really cogent. Since his grammars were supposed to be generative in the mathematical sense, they did not actually construct sentences one at a time to order in real time. Consequently his theory of grammar did not involve time in any way and therefore it did not provide a principled way of distinguishing past from future (left from right in his phrase-structure diagrams). Consequently, the best he could do was to predict a constraint with left-right (past-future) symmetry. But there was abundant evidence that a temporal asymmetry was an observational fact about the architectures of all the languages we examined.

In the summer of 1962, Gilbert H. Harman, a student of philosophy at Harvard, joined the MT group for a few months. He had become interested in COMIT and the arguments over the form of grammar. Starting with grammars written and published by Chomsky, Harman was able to rewrite them in our notation to produce grammars every bit as compact and revealing as the original transformational versions. He was then able to test them on the computer and find errors in them. Furthermore, he was able to demolish Chomsky's complex arguments that phrase-structure grammars were inadequate and therefore transformations were required (Harman & Yngve 1963). His report in *Language* should be read by everyone interested in formal grammatical theory and argumentation (Harman 1963).

As I write this three decades later, it is rumored that Chomsky is finally about to abandon transformations.

4.5 *Results using COMIT*

With the availability of COMIT, our collaborative grammars of German and English progressed rapidly using the technique of random generation. Some students and visitors also developed computer grammars of various sizes for French, Russian, Arabic, Finnish, and Chinese. Some work was done on logic in an attempt to analyze what was to be preserved under translation. Jared Darlington wrote a number of COMIT programs for translating English into logic notation and for proving theorems in logic. Studies also progressed on recognition routines. I can only mention a few highlights here of all the work made possible by COMIT during this productive period.

Robert Fabry did an M.S. thesis (1963) in Electrical Engineering, the department where the nascent work in computer science, communication research, and artificial intelligence found a home. He developed a COMIT program that would accept a grammar in a very simple notation and translate it into two other COMIT programs, one to generate sentences at random, the other to parse sentences according to the grammar.

Kenneth C. Knowlton did a Ph.D. dissertation (1962), also in Electrical Engineering, on a self-organizing heuristic program written in COMIT. The machine attempted to parse input sentences on the basis of experience gained from all previous attempts and their hand-parsed correct answers. The results demonstrate that a statistically guided program can produce correct parsings even with a grammar involving extreme overgeneralization, and that strategies can be developed automatically from a training sequence of sentences and their correct parsings.

As Chomsky and Halle launched the new linguistics graduate program at M.I.T., they were content to let the MT program's NSF grant employ some of their students and visitors, and we welcomed them. But in their thesis work, the students were constrained to do research within Chomsky's transformational framework. Students from Harvard, on the other hand, were not so constrained, and by 1962 two Harvard Ph.D. dissertations had been completed using COMIT.

Arnold Satterthwait's dissertation (1962) involved parallel computer grammars of Arabic and English and a complete, though small-scale, translation program designed for research purposes. He investigated some translation problems that shed light on the question of specifiers, statements of translational equivalence, and the step of structural transfer.

David A. Dinneen's dissertation (1962) involved a rather intricate grammar of French that solved a number of descriptive problems. His work featured an especially interesting development, a grammar of specifiers that added subscripts at a high level in the phrase structure to properly constrain lower levels during sentence construction.

Further details of the work during this productive period may be found in the final report to the NSF as the project moved to the University of Chicago in July of 1965. This report, later published (Yngve 1967) contains a bibliography of all the publications of the M.I.T. MT group. There are 101 items representing 28 authors.

At Chicago, COMIT and our rather extensive computer grammars of English and German were further developed by a group of students including

Robert Binnick, Georgia Greene, Robert Fabry, Holly Huber, Beverly Klassen, Ellie Reed Lewis, Jerry Morgan, Alan Perlman, Stuart-Morgan Vance, and others. Building on the latest version, English Grammar Six, D. Kathryn Weintraub developed a dissertation (1970) covering the English relative clause in great detail. COMIT continued to prove itself an excellent language for teaching computer programming, and a number of interesting, sometimes even spectacular, term projects and theses were done using it.

5.   Whither Linguistics?

For many years doubts had been growing in my mind concerning the health of linguistics as a science. Most disturbing was the unscientific conduct of discourse in linguistics. Instead of reliance on scientific criteria, too often one found *ex-cathedra* pronouncements, polemics, intellectual bullying, bowing to authority or tradition, trading on charisma and personal reputation, adherence to the orthodox views of a school or ism, and other sorts of appeals irrelevant to deciding scientific questions. Such tactics raised the suspicion that scientific criteria were lacking.

MT research had highlighted a number of specific fundamental questions that linguistics did not seem able to answer satisfactorily. What is the nature of meaning? How can we handle metaphor and other figurative language? How can we handle implications and allusions? How can we understand pronominal reference and other constraints extending across sentence boundaries? How can we understand reference in general? How can we take pragmatic considerations into account? How can we take into account the subject-matter knowledge of readers? Most of all, how can we take the context into account?

Most worrisome for me as a scientist were questions raised by the depth hypothesis. How could it be definitively tested? It had been put forward as a scientific hypothesis concerning restrictions on the types of phrase structures to be found in the languages of the world. But linguists were not in agreement on how to analyze sentences in terms of phrase structure. Some even rejected the phrase-structure concept entirely. How could I choose scientifically between my own current theory and those of Chomsky, Gleason, Harris, Hockett, Lamb, McCawley, or any of the many others? Criteria seemed lacking.

Could the answers to some of these questions be found at the University of Chicago, a true university strong in the humanities and the social sciences as well as the biological and physical sciences?

In approaching these problems and questions, should we seek the future of linguistics in philosophy, from which it has emerged, or in science, to which it has aspired? I have tried to work for its future in science. But that is a whole other story that would take us from the 1960s up to the present. I hope some day to relate it elsewhere. Those wishing to anticipate what I might say about what I have found out will find clues in my 1986 book; in a series of articles starting with the *First LACUS Forum 1974* and continuing in the *Sixth*, the *Ninth* through *Fifteenth*, and the *Seventeenth* on; and in other articles cited there. Another source since 1991 is nearly every issue of the workshop-by-mail *Communications of the Workshop for Scientific Linguistics*. Now see also Yngve 1996.

References

Bar-Hillel, Yehoshua. 1951. The present state of research on mechanical translation. *American Documentation* 2.229–237.

Bloomfield, Leonard. 1933. *Language*. New York: Holt.

Chomsky, Noam. 1957. *Syntactic Structures*. The Hague: Mouton.

Chomsky, Noam. 1965. *Aspects of the Theory of Syntax*. Cambridge, Massachusetts: M.I.T. Press.

Dinneen, David A. 1962 (Dec). A left-to-right grammar of French. Ph.D. Dissertation. Harvard University.

Fabry, Robert S. 1963. Sentence generation and parsing with a single grammar. M.S. Thesis. M.I.T. Department of Electrical Engineering

Fries, Charles C. 1952. *The Structure of English*. New York: Harcourt, Brace & Co.

Gill, Piara Singh, Marcel Schein, and Victor H. Yngve. 1947. The latitude effect of the hard component as a function of altitude. *Physical Review* 72: 733.

Harman, Gilbert H. 1963. Generative grammars without transformation rules: a defense of phrase structure. *Language* 39.597–616.

Harman, Gilbert H. and Victor H. Yngve. 1963. Generative grammars without transformation rules. *Quarterly Progress Report of the Research Laboratory of Electronics, M.I.T.* Jan. 1963, 171–173

Harris, Zellig S. 1946. From morpheme to utterance. *Language* 22: 161–183.

Harris, Zellig S. 1951. *Methods in Structural Linguistics*. Chicago: University of Chicago Press.

Knowlton, Kenneth G. 1962.(Aug.) Sentence parsing with a self-organizing heuristic program. Ph.D. Dissertation, M.I.T. Department of Electrical Engineering.

Nida, Eugene A. 1960. *A Synopsis of English Syntax*. Norman, Oklahoma: Summer Institute of Linguistics.

Oswald, Victor A., Jr. 1952 Microsemantics. Mimeographed, 10 pp.

Oswald, Victor A., Jr. and Stuart L. Fletcher, Jr. 1951. Proposals for the mechanical resolution of German syntax patterns. *Modern Language Forum* 36, 3–4: 1–24.

Oswald, Victor A., Jr. and Richard H. Lawson. 1953. An ideoglossary for mechanical translation. *Modern Language Forum* 38, 3–4: 1–11.

Satterthwait, Arnold C. 1962 (June). Parallel sentence-construction grammars of Arabic and English. Ph.D. Dissertation, Harvard University, The Department of Linguistics.

Schein, Marcel, and Victor H. Yngve. 1952 (February 15). The absorption curve of the cosmic radiation. Physical Review 85: 607–608.

Schein, Marcel, Victor H. Yngve, and Henry L. Kraybill. 1948 (April 15). The east-west asymmetry of the hard component of the cosmic radiation. Physical Review 73: 928–929.

Weintraub, D. Kathryn, 1970 (March). The syntax of some English relative clauses, Ph.D. Dissertation, The University of Chicago, The Graduate Library School.

Wells, Rulon S. 1947. Immediate constituents. *Language* 23: 81–117.

Yngve, Victor H. 1953a. Mechanical Translation. *Quarterly Progress Report of the Research Laboratory of Electronics, M.I.T.* Oct. 1953, 35–36.

Yngve, Victor H. 1953b (October 15). The time variation of cosmic-ray heavy nuclei. *Physical Review* 92: 428–435.

Yngve, Victor H. 1954a. Language as an error correcting code. *Quarterly Progress Report of the Research Laboratory of Electronics, M.I.T.* Apr. 1954, 73–74.

Yngve, Victor H. 1954b. A logarithmic barometer. *Review of Scientific Instruments* 25: 43–45. (Jan).

Yngve, Victor H. 1954c. Mechanical Translation. *Quarterly Progress Report of the Research Laboratory of Electronics, M.I.T.* July, 1954, 74.

Yngve, Victor H. 1955a. Syntactic Categories. *Quarterly Progress Report of the Research Laboratory of Electronics, M.I.T.* Jan. 1955, 93–95.

Yngve, Victor H. 1955b. Syntax and the problem of multiple meaning. *Machine Translation of Languages*, ed. by William N. Locke and A. Donald Booth, 208–226, New York: Technology Press and Wiley.

Yngve, Victor H. 1955c. Sentence-for-sentence translation. *Mechanical Translation* 2: 29–37.

Yngve, Victor H. 1956a. The translation of languages by machine. *Information Theory.* ed. by Colin Cherry, 196–205. London: Butterworths; New York: Academic Press.

Yngve, Victor H. 1956b. Gap analysis and syntax. *IRE Transactions on Information Theory* IT-2 Number 3, (Sept. 1956), 106–112.

Yngve, Victor H. 1956c. Terminology in the light of research on mechanical translation. *Babel* 2 Number 3 (Oct. 1956), 128–132.

Yngve, Victor H. 1956d. Mechanical translation research at M.I.T. *Mechanical Translation* 3 Number 2 (Nov. 1956), 44–45.

Yngve, Victor H. 1957. A Framework for syntactic translation. *Mechanical Translation* 4 Number 3. (Dec. 1957), 59–65.

Yngve, Victor H. 1958. A programming language for mechanical translation. *Mechanical Translation* 5 Number 1 (July, 1958), 25–41.

Yngve, Victor H. 1960. A model and an hypothesis for language structure. *Proceedings of the American Philosophical Society* 104: 444–466.

Yngve, Victor H. 1961a. The COMIT system. *Proceedings of the National Symposium on Machine Translation, UCLA, Feb. 2–5, 1960*, ed. by H. P. Edmundson, 439–443. Englewood Cliffs, New Jersey: Prentice Hall.

Yngve, Victor H. 1961b. The depth hypothesis. *Structure of language and its Mathematical Aspects*, 130–138. Proceedings of Symposia in Applied Mathematics, XII. Providence, Rhode Island: American Mathematical Society.

Yngve, Victor H. 1962a. COMIT as an IR language. *Communications of the Association for Computing Machinery* 5, 1: 19–28.

Yngve, Victor H. 1962b. Random generation of English sentences. *1961 International Conference on Machine Translation of Languages and Applied Language Analysis*, Vol. I., 65–80.

Yngve, Victor H. 1962c. *An Introduction to COMIT Programming*. Cambridge, Massachusetts: M.I.T. Press.

Yngve, Victor H. 1962d. *COMIT Programmers' Reference Manual*. Cambridge, Massachusetts: M.I.T. Press.

Yngve, Victor H. 1967. MT at M.I.T. 1965. *Machine Translation*, ed. by A. D. Booth, 451–523. Amsterdam: North-Holland

Yngve, Victor H. 1972. *Computer Programming with COMIT II*. Cambridge, Massachusetts & London: M.I.T Press.

Yngve, Victor H. 1973. I forget what I was going to say. *Papers from the Ninth Regional Meeting, Chicago Linguistic Society*. ed. by Claudia Corum T. Cedric Smith-Stark and Ann Weiser, 688–699. Chicago: Chicago Linguistic Society

Yngve, Victor H. 1975. Depth and the historical change of the English genitive. *Journal of English linguistics* 9: 47–57.

Yngve, Victor H. 1976. COMIT. *Encyclopedia of Computer Science and Technology*, Vol. 5. ed. by Jack Belzer, Albert G. Holzman and Allen Kent, 146–174. New York: & Basel: Marcel Dekker.

Yngve, Victor H. 1986. *Linguistics as a Science*. Bloomington & Indianapolis: Indiana University Press.

Yngve, Victor H. 1996. *From Grammar to Sience: New Foundations for General Linguistics*. Amsterdam/Philadelphia: John Benjamins.

Yngve, Victor H. and G. H. Matthews. 1958. A Compiler-Interpreter for Mechanical Translation. *Quarterly Progress Report of the Research Laboratory of Electronics, M.I.T. July 1958,* 176.

About the author

Victor H. Yngve is Professor Emeritus of Linguistics and Psychology at the University of Chicago, where he received his Ph.D. (in Physics) in 1953. From 1953 to 1965 he worked on machine translation at the Massachusetts Institute of Technology, and he met Syd Lamb who was doing related work at Berkeley. The M.I.T. work led to the COMIT computer programming language and the "depth hypothesis" of 1960. Since 1965, he has taught at Chicago where his 1970 analysis of videotaped conversation recognized "backchannel signals". His recent book **From Grammar to Science: New Foundations for General Linguistics** *summarizes his major research of several decades.*

Index

CURRENT ISSUES IN LINGUISTIC THEORY

E. F. K. Koerner, Editor
Department of Linguistics, University of Ottawa
OTTAWA, Canada K1N 6N5
koerner@uottawa.ca

The *Current Issues in Linguistic Theory* (CILT) series is a theory-oriented series which welcomes contributions from scholars who have significant proposals to make towards the advancement of our understanding of language, its structure, functioning and development. CILT has been established in order to provide a forum for the presentation and discussion of linguistic opinions of scholars who do not necessarily accept the prevailing mode of thought in linguistic science. It offers an alternative outlet for meaningful contributions to the current linguistic debate, and furnishes the diversity of opinion which a healthy discipline must have. In this series the following volumes have been published thus far or are scheduled for publication:

1. KOERNER, Konrad (ed.): *The Transformational-Generative Paradigm and Modern Linguistic Theory.* 1975.
2. WEIDERT, Alfons: *Componential Analysis of Lushai Phonology.* 1975.
3. MAHER, J. Peter: *Papers on Language Theory and History I: Creation and Tradition in Language. Foreword by Raimo Anttila.* 1979.
4. HOPPER, Paul J. (ed.): *Studies in Descriptive and Historical Linguistics. Festschrift for Winfred P. Lehmann.* 1977.
5. ITKONEN, Esa: *Grammatical Theory and Metascience: A critical investigation into the methodological and philosophical foundations of 'autonomous' linguistics.* 1978.
6. ANTTILA, Raimo: *Historical and Comparative Linguistics.* 1989.
7. MEISEL, Jürgen M. & Martin D. PAM (eds): *Linear Order and Generative Theory.* 1979.
8. WILBUR, Terence H.: *Prolegomena to a Grammar of Basque.* 1979.
9. HOLLIEN, Harry & Patricia (eds): *Current Issues in the Phonetic Sciences. Proceedings of the IPS-77 Congress, Miami Beach, Florida, 17-19 December 1977.* 1979.
10. PRIDEAUX, Gary D. (ed.): *Perspectives in Experimental Linguistics. Papers from the University of Alberta Conference on Experimental Linguistics, Edmonton, 13-14 Oct. 1978.* 1979.
11. BROGYANYI, Bela (ed.): *Studies in Diachronic, Synchronic, and Typological Linguistics: Festschrift for Oswald Szemérenyi on the Occasion of his 65th Birthday.* 1979.
12. FISIAK, Jacek (ed.): *Theoretical Issues in Contrastive Linguistics.* 1981. Out of print
13. MAHER, J. Peter, Allan R. BOMHARD & Konrad KOERNER (eds): *Papers from the Third International Conference on Historical Linguistics, Hamburg, August 22-26 1977.* 1982.
14. TRAUGOTT, Elizabeth C., Rebecca LaBRUM & Susan SHEPHERD (eds): *Papers from the Fourth International Conference on Historical Linguistics, Stanford, March 26-30 1979.* 1980.
15. ANDERSON, John (ed.): *Language Form and Linguistic Variation. Papers dedicated to Angus McIntosh.* 1982.
16. ARBEITMAN, Yoël L. & Allan R. BOMHARD (eds): *Bono Homini Donum: Essays in Historical Linguistics, in Memory of J.Alexander Kerns.* 1981.
17. LIEB, Hans-Heinrich: *Integrational Linguistics. 6 volumes. Vol. II-VI n.y.p.* 1984/93.
18. IZZO, Herbert J. (ed.): *Italic and Romance. Linguistic Studies in Honor of Ernst Pulgram.* 1980.
19. RAMAT, Paolo et al. (eds): *Linguistic Reconstruction and Indo-European Syntax. Proceedings of the Colloquium of the 'Indogermanischhe Gesellschaft'. University of Pavia, 6-7 September 1979.* 1980.
20. NORRICK, Neal R.: *Semiotic Principles in Semantic Theory.* 1981.
21. AHLQVIST, Anders (ed.): *Papers from the Fifth International Conference on Historical Linguistics, Galway, April 6-10 1981.* 1982.

22. UNTERMANN, Jürgen & Bela BROGYANYI (eds): *Das Germanische und die Rekonstruktion der Indogermanischen Grundsprache. Akten des Freiburger Kolloquiums der Indogermanischen Gesellschaft, Freiburg, 26-27 Februar 1981.* 1984.

23. DANIELSEN, Niels: *Papers in Theoretical Linguistics. Edited by Per Baerentzen.* 1992.

24. LEHMANN, Winfred P. & Yakov MALKIEL (eds): *Perspectives on Historical Linguistics. Papers from a conference held at the meeting of the Language Theory Division, Modern Language Assn., San Francisco, 27-30 December 1979.* 1982.

25. ANDERSEN, Paul Kent: *Word Order Typology and Comparative Constructions.* 1983.

26. BALDI, Philip (ed.): *Papers from the XIIth Linguistic Symposium on Romance Languages, Univ. Park, April 1-3, 1982.* 1984.

27. BOMHARD, Alan R.: *Toward Proto-Nostratic. A New Approach to the Comparison of Proto-Indo-European and Proto-Afroasiatic. Foreword by Paul J. Hopper.* 1984.

28. BYNON, James (ed.): *Current Progress in Afro-Asiatic Linguistics: Papers of the Third International Hamito-Semitic Congress, London, 1978.* 1984.

29. PAPROTTÉ, Wolf & René DIRVEN (eds): *The Ubiquity of Metaphor: Metaphor in language and thought.* 1985 (publ. 1986).

30. HALL, Robert A. Jr.: *Proto-Romance Morphology. = Comparative Romance Grammar, vol. III.* 1984.

31. GUILLAUME, Gustave: *Foundations for a Science of Language.*

32. COPELAND, James E. (ed.): *New Directions in Linguistics and Semiotics.* Co-edition with Rice University Press who hold exclusive rights for US and Canada. 1984.

33. VERSTEEGH, Kees: *Pidginization and Creolization. The Case of Arabic.* 1984.

34. FISIAK, Jacek (ed.): *Papers from the VIth International Conference on Historical Linguistics, Poznan, 22-26 August. 1983.* 1985.

35. COLLINGE, N.E.: *The Laws of Indo-European.* 1985.

36. KING, Larry D. & Catherine A. MALEY (eds): *Selected papers from the XIIIth Linguistic Symposium on Romance Languages, Chapel Hill, N.C., 24-26 March 1983.* 1985.

37. GRIFFEN, T.D.: *Aspects of Dynamic Phonology.* 1985.

38. BROGYANYI, Bela & Thomas KRÖMMELBEIN (eds): *Germanic Dialects:Linguistic and Philological Investigations.* 1986.

39. BENSON, James D., Michael J. CUMMINGS, & William S. GREAVES (eds): *Linguistics in a Systemic Perspective.* 1988.

40. FRIES, Peter Howard (ed.) in collaboration with Nancy M. Fries: *Toward an Understanding of Language: Charles C. Fries in Perspective.* 1985.

41. EATON, Roger, et al. (eds): *Papers from the 4th International Conference on English Historical Linguistics, April 10-13, 1985.* 1985.

42. MAKKAI, Adam & Alan K. MELBY (eds): *Linguistics and Philosophy. Festschrift for Rulon S. Wells.* 1985 (publ. 1986).

43. AKAMATSU, Tsutomu: *The Theory of Neutralization and the Archiphoneme in Functional Phonology.* 1988.

44. JUNGRAITHMAYR, Herrmann & Walter W. MUELLER (eds): *Proceedings of the Fourth International Hamito-Semitic Congress.* 1987.

45. KOOPMAN, W.F., F.C. Van der LEEK , O. FISCHER & R. EATON (eds): *Explanation and Linguistic Change.* 1986

46. PRIDEAUX, Gary D. & William J. BAKER: *Strategies and Structures: The processing of relative clauses.* 1987.

47. LEHMANN, Winfred P. (ed.): *Language Typology 1985. Papers from the Linguistic Typology Symposium, Moscow, 9-13 Dec. 1985.* 1986.

48. RAMAT, Anna G., Onofrio CARRUBA and Giuliano BERNINI (eds): *Papers from the 7th International Conference on Historical Linguistics.* 1987.

49. WAUGH, Linda R. and Stephen RUDY (eds): *New Vistas in Grammar: Invariance and*

Variation. *Proceedings of the Second International Roman Jakobson Conference, New York University, Nov.5-8, 1985.* 1991.

50. RUDZKA-OSTYN, Brygida (ed.): *Topics in Cognitive Linguistics.* 1988.

51. CHATTERJEE, Ranjit: *Aspect and Meaning in Slavic and Indic. With a foreword by Paul Friedrich.* 1989.

52. FASOLD, Ralph W. & Deborah SCHIFFRIN (eds): *Language Change and Variation.* 1989.

53. SANKOFF, David: *Diversity and Diachrony.* 1986.

54. WEIDERT, Alfons: *Tibeto-Burman Tonology. A comparative analysis.* 1987

55. HALL, Robert A. Jr.: *Linguistics and Pseudo-Linguistics.* 1987.

56. HOCKETT, Charles F.: *Refurbishing our Foundations. Elementary linguistics from an advanced point of view.* 1987.

57. BUBENIK, Vít: *Hellenistic and Roman Greece as a Sociolinguistic Area.* 1989.

58. ARBEITMAN, Yoël. L. (ed.): *Fucus: A Semitic/Afrasian Gathering in Remembrance of Albert Ehrman.* 1988.

59. VAN VOORST, Jan: *Event Structure.* 1988.

60. KIRSCHNER, Carl & Janet DECESARIS (eds): *Studies in Romance Linguistics. Selected Proceedings from the XVII Linguistic Symposium on Romance Languages.* 1989.

61. CORRIGAN, Roberta L., Fred ECKMAN & Michael NOONAN (eds): *Linguistic Categorization. Proceedings of an International Symposium in Milwaukee, Wisconsin, April 10-11, 1987.* 1989.

62. FRAJZYNGIER, Zygmunt (ed.): *Current Progress in Chadic Linguistics. Proceedings of the International Symposium on Chadic Linguistics, Boulder, Colorado, 1-2 May 1987.* 1989.

63. EID, Mushira (ed.): *Perspectives on Arabic Linguistics I. Papers from the First Annual Symposium on Arabic Linguistics.* 1990.

64. BROGYANYI, Bela (ed.): *Prehistory, History and Historiography of Language, Speech, and Linguistic Theory. Papers in honor of Oswald Szemérenyi I.* 1992.

65. ADAMSON, Sylvia, Vivien A. LAW, Nigel VINCENT and Susan WRIGHT (eds): *Papers from the 5th International Conference on English Historical Linguistics.* 1990.

66. ANDERSEN, Henning and Konrad KOERNER (eds): *Historical Linguistics 1987.Papers from the 8th International Conference on Historical Linguistics,Lille, August 30-Sept., 1987.* 1990.

67. LEHMANN, Winfred P. (ed.): *Language Typology 1987. Systematic Balance in Language. · Papers from the Linguistic Typology Symposium, Berkeley, 1-3 Dec 1987.* 1990.

68. BALL, Martin, James FIFE, Erich POPPE &Jenny ROWLAND (eds): *Celtic Linguistics/ Ieithyddiaeth Geltaidd. Readings in the Brythonic Languages. Festschrift for T. Arwyn Watkins.* 1990.

69. WANNER, Dieter and Douglas A. KIBBEE (eds): *New Analyses in Romance Linguistics. Selected papers from the Linguistic Symposium on Romance Languages XVIIII, Urbana-Champaign, April 7-9, 1988.* 1991.

70. JENSEN, John T.: *Morphology. Word structure in generative grammar.* 1990.

71. O'GRADY, William: *Categories and Case. The sentence structure of Korean.* 1991.

72. EID, Mushira and John MCCARTHY (eds): *Perspectives on Arabic Linguistics II. Papers from the Second Annual Symposium on Arabic Linguistics.* 1990.

73. STAMENOV, Maxim (ed.): *Current Advances in Semantic Theory.* 1991.

74. LAEUFER, Christiane and Terrell A. MORGAN (eds): *Theoretical Analyses in Romance Linguistics.* 1991.

75. DROSTE, Flip G. and John E. JOSEPH (eds): *Linguistic Theory and Grammatical Description. Nine Current Approaches.* 1991.

76. WICKENS, Mark A.: *Grammatical Number in English Nouns. An empirical and theoretical account.* 1992.

77. BOLTZ, William G. and Michael C. SHAPIRO (eds): *Studies in the Historical Phonology of Asian Languages.* 1991.

78. KAC, Michael: *Grammars and Grammaticality.* 1992.
79. ANTONSEN, Elmer H. and Hans Henrich HOCK (eds): *STAEF-CRAEFT: Studies in Germanic Linguistics. Select papers from the First and Second Symposium on Germanic Linguistics, University of Chicago, 24 April 1985, and Univ. of Illinois at Urbana-Champaign, 3-4 Oct. 1986.* 1991.
80. COMRIE, Bernard and Mushira EID (eds): *Perspectives on Arabic Linguistics III. Papers from the Third Annual Symposium on Arabic Linguistics.* 1991.
81. LEHMANN, Winfred P. and H.J. HEWITT (eds): *Language Typology 1988. Typological Models in the Service of Reconstruction.* 1991.
82. VAN VALIN, Robert D. (ed.): *Advances in Role and Reference Grammar.* 1992.
83. FIFE, James and Erich POPPE (eds): *Studies in Brythonic Word Order.* 1991.
84. DAVIS, Garry W. and Gregory K. IVERSON (eds): *Explanation in Historical Linguistics.* 1992.
85. BROSELOW, Ellen, Mushira EID and John McCARTHY (eds): *Perspectives on Arabic Linguistics IV. Papers from the Annual Symposium on Arabic Linguistics.* 1992.
86. KESS, Joseph F.: *Psycholinguistics. Psychology, linguistics, and the study of natural language.* 1992.
87. BROGYANYI, Bela and Reiner LIPP (eds): *Historical Philology: Greek, Latin, and Romance. Papers in honor of Oswald Szemerényi II.* 1992.
88. SHIELDS, Kenneth: *A History of Indo-European Verb Morphology.* 1992.
89. BURRIDGE, Kate: *Syntactic Change in Germanic. A study of some aspects of language change in Germanic with particular reference to Middle Dutch.* 1992.
90. KING, Larry D.: *The Semantic Structure of Spanish. Meaning and grammatical form.* 1992.
91. HIRSCHBÜHLER, Paul and Konrad KOERNER (eds): *Romance Languages and Modern Linguistic Theory. Selected papers from the XX Linguistic Symposium on Romance Languages, University of Ottawa, April 10-14, 1990.* 1992.
92. POYATOS, Fernando: *Paralanguage: A linguistic and interdisciplinary approach to interactive speech and sounds.* 1992.
93. LIPPI-GREEN, Rosina (ed.): *Recent Developments in Germanic Linguistics.* 1992.
94. HAGÈGE, Claude: *The Language Builder. An essay on the human signature in linguistic morphogenesis.* 1992.
95. MILLER, D. Gary: *Complex Verb Formation.* 1992.
96. LIEB, Hans-Heinrich (ed.): *Prospects for a New Structuralism.* 1992.
97. BROGYANYI, Bela & Reiner LIPP (eds): *Comparative-Historical Linguistics: Indo-European and Finno-Ugric. Papers in honor of Oswald Szemerényi III.* 1992.
98. EID, Mushira & Gregory K. IVERSON: *Principles and Prediction: The analysis of natural language.* 1993.
99. JENSEN, John T.: *English Phonology.* 1993.
100. MUFWENE, Salikoko S. and Lioba MOSHI (eds): *Topics in African Linguistics. Papers from the XXI Annual Conference on African Linguistics, University of Georgia, April 1990.* 1993.
101. EID, Mushira & Clive HOLES (eds): *Perspectives on Arabic Linguistics V. Papers from the Fifth Annual Symposium on Arabic Linguistics.* 1993.
102. DAVIS, Philip W. (ed.): *Alternative Linguistics. Descriptive and theoretical Modes.* 1995.
103. ASHBY, William J., Marianne MITHUN, Giorgio PERISSINOTTO and Eduardo RAPOSO: *Linguistic Perspectives on Romance Languages. Selected papers from the XXI Linguistic Symposium on Romance Languages, Santa Barbara, February 21-24, 1991.* 1993.
104. KURZOVÁ, Helena: *From Indo-European to Latin. The evolution of a morphosyntactic type.* 1993.
105. HUALDE, José Ignacio and Jon ORTIZ DE URBANA (eds): *Generative Studies in Basque Linguistics.* 1993.
106. AERTSEN, Henk and Robert J. JEFFERS (eds): *Historical Linguistics 1989. Papers from the 9th International Conference on Historical Linguistics, New Brunswick, 14-18 August 1989.* 1993.

107. MARLE, Jaap van (ed.): *Historical Linguistics 1991. Papers from the 10th International Conference on Historical Linguistics, Amsterdam, August 12-16, 1991.* 1993.

108. LIEB, Hans-Heinrich: *Linguistic Variables. Towards a unified theory of linguistic variation.* 1993.

109. PAGLIUCA, William (ed.): *Perspectives on Grammaticalization.* 1994.

110. SIMONE, Raffaele (ed.): *Iconicity in Language.* 1995.

111. TOBIN, Yishai: *Invariance, Markedness and Distinctive Feature Analysis. A contrastive study of sign systems in English and Hebrew.* 1994.

112. CULIOLI, Antoine: *Cognition and Representation in Linguistic Theory. Translated, edited and introduced by Michel Liddle.* 1995.

113. FERNÁNDEZ, Francisco, Miguel FUSTER and Juan Jose CALVO (eds): *English Historical Linguistics 1992. Papers from the 7th International Conference on English Historical Linguistics, Valencia, 22-26 September 1992.*1994.

114. EGLI, U., P. PAUSE, Chr. SCHWARZE, A. von STECHOW, G. WIENOLD (eds): *Lexical Knowledge in the Organisation of Language.* 1995.

115. EID, Mushira, Vincente CANTARINO and Keith WALTERS (eds): *Perspectives on Arabic Linguistics. Vol. VI. Papers from the Sixth Annual Symposium on Arabic Linguistics.* 1994.

116. MILLER, D. Gary: *Ancient Scripts and Phonological Knowledge.* 1994.

117. PHILIPPAKI-WARBURTON, I., K. NICOLAIDIS and M. SIFIANOU (eds): *Themes in Greek Linguistics. Papers from the first International Conference on Greek Linguistics, Reading, September 1993.*1994.

118. HASAN, Ruqaiya and Peter H. FRIES (eds): *On Subject and Theme. A discourse functional perspective.* 1995.

119. LIPPI-GREEN, Rosina: *Language Ideology and Language Change in Early Modern German. A sociolinguistic study of the consonantal system of Nuremberg.* 1994.

120. STONHAM, John T. : *Combinatorial Morphology.* 1994.

121. HASAN, Ruqaiya, Carmel CLORAN and David BUTT (eds): *Functional Descriptions. Theorie in practice.* 1996.

122. SMITH, John Charles and Martin MAIDEN (eds): *Linguistic Theory and the Romance Languages.* 1995.

123. AMASTAE, Jon, Grant GOODALL, Mario MONTALBETTI and Marianne PHINNEY: *Contemporary Research in Romance Linguistics. Papers from the XXII Linguistic Symposium on Romance Languages, El Paso//Juárez, February 22-24, 1994.* 1995.

124. ANDERSEN, Henning: *Historical Linguistics 1993. Selected papers from the 11th International Conference on Historical Linguistics, Los Angeles, 16-20 August 1993.* 1995.

125. SINGH, Rajendra (ed.): *Towards a Critical Sociolinguistics.* 1996.

126. MATRAS, Yaron (ed.): *Romani in Contact. The history, structure and sociology of a language.* 1995.

127. GUY, Gregory R., Crawford FEAGIN, Deborah SCHIFFRIN and John BAUGH (eds): *Towards a Social Science of Language. Papers in honor of William Labov. Volume 1: Variation and change in language and society.* 1996.

128. GUY, Gregory R., Crawford FEAGIN, Deborah SCHIFFRIN and John BAUGH (eds): *Towards a Social Science of Language. Papers in honor of William Labov. Volume 2: Social interaction and discourse structures.* 1997.

129. LEVIN, Saul: *Semitic and Indo-European: The Principal Etymologies. With observations on Afro-Asiatic.* 1995.

130. EID, Mushira (ed.) *Perspectives on Arabic Linguistics. Vol. VII. Papers from the Seventh Annual Symposium on Arabic Linguistics.* 1995.

131. HUALDE, Jose Ignacio, Joseba A. LAKARRA and R.L. Trask (eds): *Towards a History of the Basque Language.* 1995.

132. HERSCHENSOHN, Julia: *Case Suspension and Binary Complement Structure in French.* 1996.
133. ZAGONA, Karen (ed.): *Grammatical Theory and Romance Languages. Selected papers from the 25th Linguistic Symposium on Romance Languages (LSRL XXV) Seattle, 2-4 March 1995.* 1996.
134. EID, Mushira (ed.): *Perspectives on Arabic Linguistics Vol. VIII. Papers from the Eighth Annual Symposium on Arabic Linguistics.* 1996.
135. BRITTON Derek (ed.): *Papers from the 8th International Conference on English Historical Linguistics.* 1996.
136. MITKOV, Ruslan and Nicolas NICOLOV (eds): *Recent Advances in Natural Language Processing.* 1997.
137. LIPPI-GREEN, Rosina and Joseph C. SALMONS (eds): *Germanic Linguistics. Syntactic and diachronic.* 1996.
138. SACKMANN, Robin (ed.): *Theoretical Linguistics and Grammatical Description.* 1996.
139. BLACK, James R. and Virginia MOTAPANYANE (eds): *Microparametric Syntax and Dialect Variation.* 1996.
140. BLACK, James R. and Virginia MOTAPANYANE (eds): *Clitics, Pronouns and Movement.* 1997.
141. EID, Mushira and Dilworth PARKINSON (eds): *Perspectives on Arabic Linguistics Vol. IX. Papers from the Ninth Annual Symposium on Arabic Linguistics, Georgetown University, Washington D.C., 1995.* 1996.
142. JOSEPH, Brian D. and Joseph C. SALMONS (eds): *Nostratic. Sifting the evidence.* 1998.
143. ATHANASIADOU, Angeliki and René DIRVEN (eds): *On Conditionals Again.* 1997.
144. SINGH, Rajendra (ed): *Trubetzkoy's Orphan. Proceedings of the Montréal Roundtable "Morphophonology: contemporary responses (Montréal, October 1994).* 1996.
145. HEWSON, John and Vit BUBENIK: *Tense and Aspect in Indo-European Languages. Theory, typology, diachrony.* 1997.
146. HINSKENS, Frans, Roeland VAN HOUT and W. Leo WETZELS (eds): *Variation, Change, and Phonological Theory.* 1997.
147. HEWSON, John: *The Cognitive System of the French Verb.* 1997.
148. WOLF, George and Nigel LOVE (eds): *Linguistics Inside Out. Roy Harris and his critics.* 1997.
149. HALL, T. Alan: *The Phonology of Coronals.* 1997.
150. VERSPOOR, Marjolijn, Kee Dong LEE and Eve SWEETSER (eds): *Lexical and Syntactical Constructions and the Construction of Meaning. Proceedings of the Bi-annual ICLA meeting in Albuquerque, July 1995.* 1997.
151. LIEBERT, Wolf-Andreas, Gisela REDEKER and Linda WAUGH (eds): *Discourse and Perspectives in Cognitive Linguistics.* 1997.
152. HIRAGA, Masako, Chris SINHA and Sherman WILCOX (eds): *Cultural, Psychological and Typological Issues in Cognitive Linguistics.* 1999.
153. EID, Mushira and Robert R. RATCLIFFE (eds): *Perspectives on Arabic Linguistics Vol. X. Papers from the Tenth Annual Symposium on Arabic Linguistics, Salt Lake City, 1996.* 1997.
154. SIMON-VANDENBERGEN, Anne-Marie, Kristin DAVIDSE and Dirk NOËL (eds): *Reconnecting Language. Morphology and Syntax in Functional Perspectives.* 1997.
155. FORGET, Danielle, Paul HIRSCHBÜHLER, France MARTINEAU and María-Luisa RIVERO (eds): *Negation and Polarity. Syntax and semantics. Selected papers from the Colloquium Negation: Syntax and Semantics. Ottawa, 11-13 May 1995.* 1997.
156. MATRAS, Yaron, Peter BAKKER and Hristo KYUCHUKOV (eds): *The Typology and Dialectology of Romani.* 1997.
157. LEMA, José and Esthela TREVIÑO (eds): *Theoretical Analyses on Romance Languages. Selected papers from the 26th Linguistic Symposium on Romance Languages (LSRL XXVI), Mexico City, 28-30 March, 1996.* 1998.
158. SÁNCHEZ MACARRO, Antonia and Ronald CARTER (eds): *Linguistic Choice across Genres. Variation in spoken and written English.* 1998.

159. JOSEPH, Brian D., Geoffrey C. HORROCKS and Irene PHILIPPAKI-WARBURTON (eds): *Themes in Greek Linguistics II.* 1998.

160. SCHWEGLER, Armin, Bernard TRANEL and Myriam URIBE-ETXEBARRIA (eds): *Romance Linguistics: Theoretical Perspectives. Selected papers from the 27th Linguistic Symposium on Romance Languages (LSRL XXVII), Irvine, 20-22 February, 1997.* 1998.

161. SMITH, John Charles and Delia BENTLEY (eds): *Historical Linguistics 1995. Volume 1: Romance and general linguistics.* 2000.

162. HOGG, Richard M. and Linda van BERGEN (eds): *Historical Linguistics 1995. Volume 2: Germanic linguistics.Selected papers from the 12th International Conference on Historical Linguistics, Manchester, August 1995.* 1998.

163. LOCKWOOD, David G., Peter H. FRIES and James E. COPELAND (eds): *Functional Approaches to Language, Culture and Cognition.* 2000.

164. SCHMID, Monika, Jennifer R. AUSTIN and Dieter STEIN (eds): *Historical Linguistics 1997. Selected papers from the 13th International Conference on Historical Linguistics, Düsseldorf, 10-17 August 1997.* 1998.

165. BUBENÍK, Vit: *A Historical Syntax of Late Middle Indo-Aryan (Apabhramśa).* 1998.

166. LEMMENS, Maarten: *Lexical Perspectives on Transitivity and Ergativity. Causative constructions in English.* 1998.

167. BENMAMOUN, Elabbas, Mushira EID and Niloofar HAERI (eds): *Perspectives on Arabic Linguistics Vol. XI. Papers from the Eleventh Annual Symposium on Arabic Linguistics, Atlanta, 1997.* 1998.

168. RATCLIFFE, Robert R.: *The "Broken" Plural Problem in Arabic and Comparative Semitic. Allomorphy and analogy in non-concatenative morphology.* 1998.

169. GHADESSY, Mohsen (ed.): *Text and Context in Functional Linguistics.* 1999.

170. LAMB, Sydney M.: *Pathways of the Brain. The neurocognitive basis of language.* 1999.

171. WEIGAND, Edda (ed.): *Contrastive Lexical Semantics.* 1998.

172. DIMITROVA-VULCHANOVA, Mila and Lars HELLAN (eds): *Topics in South Slavic Syntax and Semantics.* 1999.

173. TREVIÑO, Esthela and José LEMA (eds): *Semantic Issues in Romance Syntax.* 1999.

174. HALL, T. Alan and Ursula KLEINHENZ (eds): *Studies on the Phonological Word.* 1999.

175. GIBBS, Ray W. and Gerard J. STEEN (eds): *Metaphor in Cognitive Linguistics. Selected papers from the 5th International Cognitive Linguistics Conference, Amsterdam, 1997.* 2001.

176. VAN HOEK, Karen, Andrej KIBRIK and Leo NOORDMAN (eds): *Discourse in Cognitive Linguistics. Selected papers from the International Cognitive Linguistics Conference, Amsterdam, July 1997.* 1999.

177. CUYCKENS, Hubert and Britta ZAWADA (eds): *Polysemy in Cognitive Linguistics. Selected papers from the International Cognitive Linguistics Conference, Amsterdam, 1997.* 2001.

178. FOOLEN, Ad and Frederike van der LEEK (eds): *Constructions in Cognitive Linguistics. Selected papers from the Fifth International Cognitive Linguistic Conference, Amsterdam, 1997.* 2000.

179. RINI, Joel: *Exploring the Role of Morphology in the Evolution of Spanish.* 1999.

180. MEREU, Lunella (ed.): *Boundaries of Morphology and Syntax.* 1999.

181. MOHAMMAD, Mohammad A.: *Word Order, Agreement and Pronominalization in Standard and Palestinian Arabic.* 2000.

182. KENESEI, István (ed.): *Theoretical Issues in Eastern European Languages. Selected papers from the Conference on Linguistic Theory in Eastern European Languages (CLITE), Szeged, April 1998.* 1999.

183. CONTINI-MORAVA, Ellen and Yishai TOBIN (eds): *Between Grammar and Lexicon.* 2000.

184. SAGART, Laurent: *The Roots of Old Chinese.* 1999.

185. AUTHIER, J.-Marc, Barbara E. BULLOCK, Lisa A. REED (eds): *Formal Perspectives on Romance Linguistics. Selected papers from the 28th Linguistic Symposium on Romance Languages (LSRL XXVIII), University Park, 16-19 April 1998.* 1999.

186. MIŠESKA TOMIĆ, Olga and Milorad RADOVANOVIĆ (eds): *History and Perspectives of Language Study.* 2000.
187. FRANCO, Jon, Alazne LANDA and Juan MARTÍN (eds): *Grammatical Analyses in Basque and Romance Linguistics.* 1999.
188. VanNESS SIMMONS, Richard: *Chinese Dialect Classification. A comparative approach to Harngjou, Old Jintarn, and Common Northern Wu.* 1999.
189. NICHOLOV, Nicolas and Ruslan MITKOV (eds): *Recent Advances in Natural Language Processing II. Selected papers from RANLP '97.* 2000.
190. BENMAMOUN, Elabbas (ed.): *Perspectives on Arabic Linguistics Vol. XII. Papers from the Twelfth Annual Symposium on Arabic Linguistics.* 1999.
191. SIHLER, Andrew L.: *Language Change. An introduction.* 2000.
192. ALEXANDROVA, Galina M. and Olga ARNAUDOVA (eds.): *The Minimalist Parameter. Selected papers from the Open Linguistics Forum, Ottawa, 21-23 March 1997.* 2001.
193. KLAUSENBURGER, Jurgen: *Grammaticalization. Studies in Latin and Romance morphosyntax.* 2000.
194. COLEMAN, Julie and Christian J. KAY (eds): *Lexicology, Semantics and Lexicography. Selected papers from the Fourth G. L. Brook Symposium, Manchester, August 1998.* 2000.
195. HERRING, Susan C., Pieter van REENEN and Lene SCHØSLER (eds): *Textual Parameters in Older Languages.* 2000.
196. HANNAHS, S. J. and Mike DAVENPORT (eds): *Issues in Phonological Structure. Papers from an International Workshop.* 1999.
197. COOPMANS, Peter, Martin EVERAERT and Jane GRIMSHAW (eds): *Lexical Specification and Insertion.* 2000.
198. NIEMEIER, Susanne and René DIRVEN (eds): *Evidence for Linguistic Relativity.* 2000.
199. VERSPOOR, Marjolijn H. and Martin PÜTZ (eds): *Explorations in Linguistic Relativity.* 2000.
200. ANTTILA, Raimo: *Greek and Indo-European Etymology in Action. Proto-Indo-European *aǵ-.* 2000.
201. DRESSLER, Wolfgang U., Oskar E. PFEIFFER, Markus PÖCHTRAGER and John R. RENNISON (eds.): *Morphological Analysis in Comparison.* 2000.
202. LECARME, Jacqueline, Jean LOWENSTAMM and Ur SHLONSKY (eds.): *Research in Afroasiatic Grammar. Papers from the Third conference on Afroasiatic Languages, Sophia Antipolis, 1996.* 2000.
203. NORRICK, Neal R.: *Conversational Narrative. Storytelling in everyday talk.* 2000.
204. DIRVEN, René, Bruce HAWKINS and Esra SANDIKCIOGLU (eds.): *Language and Ideology. Volume 1: cognitive theoretical approaches.* 2001.
205. DIRVEN, René, Roslyn FRANK and Cornelia ILIE (eds.): *Language and Ideology. Volume 2: cognitive descriptive approaches.* 2001.
206. FAWCETT, Robin: *A Theory of Syntax for Systemic-Functional Linguistics.* 2000.
207. SANZ, Montserrat: *Events and Predication. A new approach to syntactic processing in English and Spanish.* 2000.
208. ROBINSON, Orrin W.: *Whose German? The ach/ich alternation and related phenomena in 'standard' and 'colloquial'.* 2001.
209. KING, Ruth: *The Lexical Basis of Grammatical Borrowing. A Prince Edward Island French case study.* 2000.
210. DWORKIN, Steven N. and Dieter WANNER (eds.): *New Approaches to Old Problems. Issues in Romance historical linguistics.* 2000.
211. ELŠÍK, Viktor and Yaron MATRAS (eds.): *Grammatical Relations in Romani. The Noun Phrase.* 2000.
212. REPETTI, Lori (ed.): *Phonological Theory and the Dialects of Italy.* 2000.
213. SORNICOLA, Rosanna, Erich POPPE and Ariel SHISHA-HALEVY (eds.): *Stability, Variation and Change of Word-Order Patterns over Time.* 2000.
214. WEIGAND, Edda and Marcelo DASCAL (eds.): *Negotiation and Power in Dialogic Interaction.* 2001.

215. BRINTON, Laurel J.: *Historical Linguistics 1999. Selected papers from the 14th International Conference on Historical Linguistics, Vancouver, 9-13 August 1999.* 2001.

216. CAMPS, Joaquim and Caroline R. WILTSHIRE (eds.): *Romance Syntax, Semantics and L2 Acquisition. Selected papers from the 30th Linguistic Symposium on Romance Languages, Gainesville, Florida, February 2000.* 2001.

217. WILTSHIRE, Caroline R. and Joaquim CAMPS (eds.): *Romance Phonology and Variation. Selected papers from the 30th Linguistic Symposium on Romance Languages, Gainesville, Florida, February 2000.* n.y.p.

218. BENDJABALLAH, S., W.U. DRESSLER, O. PFEIFFER and M. VOEIKOVA (eds.): *Morphology 2000. Selected papers from the 9th Morphology Meeting, Vienna, 25-27 February 2000.* n.y.p.

219. ANDERSEN, Henning (ed.): *Actualization. Linguistic Change in Progress.* 2001.

220. CRESTI, Diana, Christina TORTORA and Teresa SATTERFIELD (eds.): *Current Issues in Romance Languages. Selected papers from the 29th Linguistic Symposium on Romance Languages (LSRL), Ann Arbor, 8-11 April 1999.* n.y.p.

221. D'HULST, Yves, Johan ROORYCK and Jan SCHROTEN (eds.): *Romance Languages and Linguistic Theory 1999. Selected papers from 'Going Romance' 1999, Leiden, 9-11 December.* 2001.

222. HERSCHENSOHN, Julia, Enrique MALLÉN and Karen ZAGONA (eds.): *Features and Interfaces in Romance. Essays in honor of Heles Contreras.* 2001.

223. FANEGO, Teresa, María José LÓPEZ-COUSO and Javier PÉREZ-GUERRA (eds.): *English Historical Syntax and Morphology. Selected papers from 11 ICEHL, Santiago de Compostela, 7-11 September 2000.* n.y.p.

224. FANEGO, Teresa, Belén MÉNDEZ-NAYA and Elena SEOANE (eds.): *Sounds, Words, Texts and Change. Selected papers from 11 ICEHL, Santiago de Compostela, 7-11 September 2000.* n.y.p.

Printed in the United Kingdom
by Lightning Source UK Ltd.
442